Saskatchewan Premiers
of the Twentieth Century

Saskatchewan Premiers of the Twentieth Century

edited by Gordon L. Barnhart

2004

Copyright © 2004 Canadian Plains Research Center, University of Regina
Copyright Notice
All rights reserved. No part of this work covered by the copyrights hereon may be reproduced or used in any form or by any means — graphic, electronic, or mechanical — without the prior written permission of the publisher. Any request for photocopying, recording, taping or placement in information storage and retrieval systems of any sort shall be directed in writing to the Canadian Reprography Collective.

Canadian Plains Research Center
University of Regina
Regina, Saskatchewan S4S 0A2
Canada
Tel: (306) 585-4758
Fax: (306) 585-4699
e-mail: canadian.plains@uregina.ca
http://www.cprc.uregina.ca

National Library of Canada Cataloguing in Publication
Saskatchewan premiers of the twentieth century / Gordon L. Barhart, editor.
(TBS ; 8)
Includes bibliographical references and index.
ISBN 0-88977-164-2
1. Prime ministers--Saskatchewan--Biography. I. Barnhart, Gordon Leslie II. Series.
FC3505.S28 2003   971.24'009'9   C2003-906096-9

Cover and interior layout and design by Brian Danchuk Design, Regina, Saskatchewan
Printed and bound in Canada by Houghton Boston, Saskatoon
Index prepared by Patricia Furdek (www.userfriendlyindexes.com)

We acknowledge the financial support of the Government of Canada through the Book Publishing Industry Development Program (BPIDP) for our publishing activities.

Many of the photographs which appear in this volume originally belonged to the former Saskatchewan Government Photographic Services, and now are part of the holdings of the Saskatchewan Archives Board.

Contents

Introduction
    Gordon L. Barnhart vii

Fredrick Haultain
    Gordon L. Barnhart xi

Walter Scott
    Gordon L. Barnhart 1

William Martin
    Ted Regehr 39

Charles Dunning
    J. William Brennan 69

James G. Gardiner
    David Smith 89

J.T.M. Anderson
    Patrick Kyba 109

William Patterson
    Beth Bilson 139

T.C. Douglas
    Thomas McLeod & Ian McLeod 161

Woodrow S. Lloyd
    Dianne Norton 213

Ross Thatcher
    Dale Eisler 237

Allan Blakeney
    Dennis Gruending 271

Grant Devine
    James M. Pitsula 317

Roy Romanow
    Gregory J. Marchildon 353

Index 395

Contributors 416

To Elaine, my late wife, partner and best friend. The idea of a collection of biographies of Saskatchewan's Premiers of the twentieth century was hers. Thank you.

— Gordon

Introduction

The Making of a Premier

Within the British parliamentary tradition a Premier (sometimes also referred to as a Prime Minister or First Minister, depending on the jurisdiction) is the elected leader of the majority party in a Legislature and is the head of the government. In Canada, provincial Premiers are first chosen as leaders by the members of their respective political parties. The method of choosing a leader has changed. In the twentieth century, political leaders were chosen at a leadership convention, where representative delegates were chosen to attend a provincial meeting to vote for a new leader. More recently, taking advantage of new technologies, political parties have attempted to expand the selection process. Many (but not all) political parties now allow for a one-member/one-vote procedure whereby party members across the province may vote for their candidate by mail-in or electronic ballots, in addition to the traditional ballots cast by members at the convention itself.

Once a leader has been chosen, he (or she) leads the party into a general election. If the party wins a majority of the seats in the legislative body, the leader will then become Premier. It is by convention (although not by law) that the Premier must also be an elected member of the Legislative Assembly (MLA). There are also occasions (because of the death or retirement of the incumbent) when a governing party must choose a new leader, who thus becomes Premier without having won a general election. Although there have been cases where a leader chosen in this manner has been Premier for a period of two to three years without calling an election, such instances are rare.

Due to the anomalies of our "first past the post" electoral system, in which the candidate with the most votes wins a constituency, most governments, and thus Premiers, are elected without having gained 50% or more of the popular vote. In other words, a Premier can be chosen and lead a government for up to five years without having the support of the majority of the people. In Saskatchewan, for example, there have been 13 provincial elections since 1952, with the winning party taking more than 50% of the total vote in only four cases. Furthermore, on two occasions (in 1986 and in 1999), the party winning the most seats actually garnered fewer votes than its closest rival.[1]

A party leader who has been elected as Premier henceforth fills two distinct and separate roles. As leader of the party, he (or she) must attend party functions, listen to the party membership, and be accountable to the members for the policies and actions of the government. The Premier, as president of the Executive Council (the Cabinet), fulfills a very separate role from that of party leader. In this role, the Premier is responsible for the overall direction of the government, is its chief spokesperson, and must take responsibility for its actions. Through recommendations to the lieutenant-governor, the Premier appoints—and sometimes dismisses—the members of Cabinet, members of the senior public service, and individuals in many of the more important public positions within the province. As Jeffrey Simpson has argued in his book, *The Friendly Dictatorship*, First Ministers in Canada wield considerable power because of their control of patronage appointments.[2] Those lobbying for Cabinet portfolios or important public service positions must court the favour of the Premier.

The Premier is held accountable for his (or her) actions at a variety of levels. At the most basic level, the Premier must address the concerns first of the caucus, and then of the party membership. Beyond this, the Premier is often the focus of Question Period in the Legislative Assembly, and through the media must answer questions from the opposition and the general public. Premiers often have the pleasant task of announcing good news, but conversely must also defend the government's position and actions when things have not gone well. The Premier and the Cabinet must defend government policy in the Assembly when legislation is being considered or government financial estimates are being debated. Nevertheless, even with these various levels of accountability, as long as the Premier has the support of the majority of the elected MLAs, he (or she) is not obliged to resign until the next election. Under our system of government, Premiers, and the political parties which they lead, can only be removed in a general election, which does not have to be called for up to five years.

It is a great responsibility to be Premier of a province, especially with the increasing role of government within our society. As the old adage has it, the "buck stops" on the Premier's desk. The success or failure of a political party in a general election often rests singly with the Premier. Although it is usually not just the Premier who is to blame when a government is defeated, people often tend to look first to the Premier when things go badly.

Although the role of the Premier is not mentioned in the Constitution of Canada, the powers of the office, through evolution and parliamentary precedent, have steadily increased over the past century. The size and role of government have grown dramatically over the twentieth century. When Saskatchewan was formed in 1905, the provincial level of government was considered to be of limited significance, responsible only for issues of local concern; the federal government retained most of the financial resources and political power in the Canadian federation. Indeed, Canada's first Prime Minister, Sir John A. Macdonald, only reluctantly accepted the federal model—as opposed to a unitary system—as a compromise, and he believed that the provincial governments would eventually wither and disappear. The reverse has actually been the case. When the provinces were awarded responsibility for specific roles in the British North America Act, such as education and health care, those areas were small and relatively unimportant. As the century progressed, however, increasing emphasis and financial resources were devoted to schools and universities, hospitals and health care. This led to a substantial increase in the size of the provincial government, with a larger civil service and budget. The provincial governments across the country grew in influence, size and power, with a corresponding increase in the powers and responsibilities of the provincial Premiers. Their roles will continue to evolve, with the evolution of Canada itself, as the nation moves further into the twenty-first century.

The Saskatchewan Experience

For Saskatchewan, the twentieth century was a period of tremendous upheaval and change: from the optimism associated with the creation of the province in 1905, the trials of Depression and war, the boom times of the post-war period, to the economic vagaries of the 1980s and 1990s. Through it all, the ebb and flow of this province's fortunes have been guided by a series of men from a variety of political parties and from very different backgrounds. One, Sir Frederick Haultain, who is sometimes referred to as "the best Premier we never had," was never the Premier of Saskatchewan per se. Haultain is included here because he was the first, and only, Premier of the Northwest Territories, which included the area that is now known as Saskatchewan, but failed to become Premier of the new province because he did not support the policies of the federal government of the day.

In the twentieth century, only three political parties ever formed the government in Saskatchewan. To begin with, there was a long string of Liberal governments from 1905 to 1944, with the brief interruption of a Conservative coalition government from 1929 to 1934. The province then experimented with democratic socialism: the Co-operative Commonwealth Federation (CCF) drew worldwide attention when it first formed a government in 1944. The CCF stayed in power until 1964, when the province returned to a Liberal government for seven years. In 1971, the New Democratic Party (NDP), the successor to the CCF, was elected. The NDP remained in power for the remainder of the century with the exception of a Progressive Conservative government from 1982 to 1991.

As Saskatchewan's first century draws to a close, it is appropriate that we reflect upon our collective past, and the individuals who were so instrumental in the shaping this province. The purpose of this book, then, is to help increase awareness of Saskatchewan's Premiers. When the book project was first conceived, it was not certain who would be Premier at the time of publication, and for that reason it was decided to end the biographies with that of Roy Romanow, the last Premier of the twentieth century. Thus, a total of thirteen profiles are included here. The names of some of the men—like T.C. Douglas and Grant Devine—are still household words, while others—like Charles Dunning and William Patterson—have been all but forgotten. Yet each in his unique way, for better or for worse, helped to mould and steer the destiny of the province he governed. These are their stories.

Gordon L. Barnhart
October 2003

Notes

1. For more information on voting patterns in Saskatchewan, see Howard Leeson (ed.), *Saskatchewan Politics: Into the Twenty-first Century* (Regina: Canadian Plains Research Center, 2001), Appendix A.
2. Jeffrey Simpson, *The Friendly Dictatorship* (Toronto: McClelland and Stewart Ltd., 2001).

Acknowledgments

I want to thank the Canadian Plains Research Center and in particular Brian Mlazgar (publications coordinator), Donna Achtzehner (layout), Anne Pennylegion (publicity) and David McLennan (photo selection). This is a hard-working and inspired team who believe in Saskatchewan and its history, as I do. I also want to express my thanks to the authors who contributed their time and skills to the chapters of this book. Each author brought a new dimension to the collection of biographies. Thanks should also go to the Saskatchewan Archives Board, particularly all those involved within the photograph section.

The final word of thanks goes to the Premiers of this fine province who served over the 20th century through harsh times and happy times. Their dedication to this province shines through in each of these stories. They came from different backgrounds and political beliefs but they shared one thing in common—they all wanted to make this province a better place in which to live and work.

Frederick Haultain

Gordon L. Barnhart

Attorney-General Haultain with staff, 1905 (SAB RB 3874).

Haultain, as Premier of the North-West Territories, c. 1904 (SAB RB 3200).

Haultain campaigning for the 1912 election (SAB RA 12114 (1)).

SASKATCHEWAN PREMIERS OF THE 20TH CENTURY

Frederick Haultain, 1897–1905

Frederick William Alpin George Haultain was born on November 25, 1857, in England. He came to Ontario, Canada, with his family at the age of three. As a boy, he was active in sports and joined the militia as a young man. After receiving his Bachelor of Arts from the University of Toronto in 1879, he went on to study law, and was called to the Ontario Bar in 1882.[1] He initially practiced law in Kingston, but in 1884 he, like many of his contemporaries, decided to try his fortune in the Canadian West, which was beginning to open up to settlement. After a long voyage by train and stage coach, Frederick Haultain arrived in Fort Macleod, North-West Territories (in what is now Alberta), where he joined a law practice.

Within three years, Haultain was so much a part of his community and the western way of life that he was elected to the Legislative Council of the North-West Territories.[2] He quickly gained experience in territorial politics and assumed the position of chair of the Executive Committee.[2] By the time of the amendment to the North-West Territories Act in 1897, which granted responsible government to the Territories, Haultain was the most influential figure in the government, and was appointed Premier.[3] In addition to his duties as Premier, he was also the attorney general and the commissioner of Education. Haultain was thus the first, and only, Premier of the North-West Territories, and was also unique in that he was the first Premier of the area that now constitutes both Saskatchewan and Alberta, although he was never a provincial Premier per se.

By 1900, as the population of the Territories increased, there was growing agitation for the government in Ottawa to grant the region provincial status. Under the existing system, the federal government exercised nearly total financial control, and most local initiatives required Ottawa's approval before they would be funded. It was argued that provincial status would give the local government a broader tax base, which in turn would provide it with the resources and independence necessary to best respond to the needs of its citizens.

Haultain was a forceful proponent of provincial status, but unfortunately for his long-term political prospects, his position on several key points brought him into direct opposition with Sir Wilfrid Laurier, the Liberal Prime Minister.

To begin with, Haultain advocated the creation of a single province in the area lying between Manitoba and British Columbia (for which he proposed the name "Buffalo"). This idea had considerable support in the West, but did not meet with Laurier's approval. Laurier and his government worried that the proposed single new province would exceed the provinces of Quebec and Ontario in both size and, one day, in population—and hence would disturb the balance of power which had been carefully crafted at the time of Confederation.

Haultain also argued that when provincial status was attained, the new province(s) should have control over natural resources, as was the case for the other provinces. The

SAB RB 3770

Frederick Haultain (front row, centre) as Premier of the North-West Territories, with a group of civil servants, August 31, 1905, the day before the inauguration of Saskatchewan as a province.

Laurier government, on the other hand, believed that federal control over resources would ensure that federal settlement programs in the West would continue uninterrupted.

The third contentious issue between Laurier and Haultain concerned separate schools. Laurier, a French-Canadian from Quebec, proposed to include provisions for separate schools in the legislation creating the new province(s). This, Laurier believed, would better protect the linguistic and religious interests of his fellow French-Canadians in the West. Haultain disagreed, arguing that education was a provincial responsibility, and that any decisions in this respect should be left to the new province(s).

As the deadline for provincial status approached, Walter Scott, the Liberal member of the House of Commons for Assiniboia West, played an increasingly important role as mediator between the two conflicting camps. In the end, two new provinces—Saskatchewan and Alberta—were created on September 1, 1905. They did not receive control over their natural resources, but education, and the ultimate decision on the contentious separate school question, was left under provincial control.

Although Haultain had carefully maintained an image of nonpartisanship in territorial politics, he supported the Conservatives on the federal level. This, and more particularly his opposition to Laurier during the autonomy debate, made him unacceptable to the federal Liberals, and likely cost him the premiership of the new province of Saskatchewan.

On September 4, 1905, A.E. Forget was sworn in as lieutenant-governor. His first task was to choose an acting Premier, who would form a provisional government until elections could be held. It was widely anticipated that the task would fall to Haultain, who was, after all, the outgoing territorial Premier. Nevertheless, the next day, Forget chose Walter Scott over Haultain. It was believed, with justification, that whoever became the first Premier would have a distinct advantage in fighting the subsequent general election. This indeed proved to be the case, and Scott won the election held on December 13, 1905. Haultain, as leader of the Provincial Rights Party, had to content himself with being leader of the opposition.

Haultain contested two further provincial elections, in 1908 and 1912, but in both cases he was defeated by Scott, and he resigned from the Legislative Assembly in 1912 to assume the post of chief justice of the Superior Court of Saskatchewan. In 1917, he was appointed chief justice of the Saskatchewan Court of Appeal and was elected chancellor of the University of Saskatchewan. In 1939, he retired from public life.

Frederick Haultain is sometimes viewed as a sad historical figure, who worked hard as a territorial leader but was overlooked for political reasons when the province was formed. Yet he was not a failure. He was recognized as a formidable debater, provided sound leadership through the territorial days, and offered alternatives during the discussions leading to provincial status. Even though his ideas were not all accepted by the federal government, he represented a large body of opinion in the West as to how its government should be organized. Nevertheless, despite Haultain's many strengths, by the time that Saskatchewan became a province, the march of events had passed him by. As will be argued in the following chapter, on Walter Scott, Haultain was consistently outmaneuvred by Scott, and forced to defend unpopular positions. As a result, for a variety of reasons, the people of Saskatchewan chose not to reward Haultain with the office of the Premier, for which he had fought so long.

Notwithstanding his disappointments in the provincial political scene, Frederick Haultain devoted over 50 years of his life to the service of the people of the North-West Territories and later Saskatchewan. This was truly a remarkable achievement, and his role in the development of western Canada should not be overlooked.

Frederick Haultain was married twice, in 1906 to Marian St. Clair Castellain, and following her death, in 1938 to Mrs. W.B. Gilmour of Montreal. He died on January 30, 1942, at Montreal, Quebec. His ashes were buried near the Memorial Gates at the University of Saskatchewan, in Saskatoon.

Notes

1. Grant MacEwan, *Frontier Statesman of the Canadian Northwest, Frederick Haultain* (Saskatoon: Western Producer Prairie Books, 1985), 12.
2. The Legislative Council was renamed the Legislative Assembly once the Territories attained responsible government in 1897. Similarly, the Executive Committee was renamed the Executive Council.
3. MacEwan, *Frontier Statesman*, 105.

Walter Scott

GORDON L. BARNHART

Scott asked women to "speak" clearly for their right to vote
(SAB B 6493).

Scott, formal portrait
(SAB RA 2470).

Constitutional difficulties
abounded (Scott is on the left)
(SAB RB 1872(1)).

SASKATCHEWAN PREMIERS OF THE 20TH CENTURY

Walter Scott, 1905–1916

"I make the promise that so far as lies in my power, if the people of Saskatchewan support the policy we present to them, good government, clean government, honest government and, so far as I have the energy and ability for it, progressive government shall be given the people of this province." [1]

The Early Years

There was a hint of frost in the air in rural Ontario when Thomas Walter Scott was born on October 27, 1867, the birth year of the new nation called Canada. That, surely, was an auspicious beginning for this infant who, according to Scott's autobiography, written just before he entered politics and subsequently included in newspaper reports, was the son of George Scott and Isabella Telfer.[2] It was also reported that George died before Walter was born. However, the official census records for 1871 show that Isabella Telfer was not married when Walter was born. According to family oral history and some interfamily correspondence, Walter's natural father was Adam Scott, son of George. It appears that Walter made up the story about his father being George Scott and married to his mother to cover up the embarrassing fact that he was "illegitimate" or born out of wedlock. This fact, if known by the people of Saskatchewan, could have been damaging to Walter's political career. Walter was able to hide the truth about his background throughout his life but he lived with the fear that someday, someone would find out about his secret.

Walter Scott was born in his grandmother's house at lot 29, concession 9, township of London, County of Middlesex, approximately halfway between Strathroy and London. This section of rural Ontario was agricultural with 100-acre plots of rich land carved out of the forest. The farm houses were located near the main roads and less than a quarter of mile apart. It was a closely knit, staunchly Presbyterian community.

Walter Scott attended Telfer school, which was approximately one quarter of a mile up the road from home. Telfer Corner was the site of the school, the United Presbyterian Church, the post office, the "antiburger" Presbyterian Church, and a cemetery, and became the focus for Walter Scott in his first formative years with regular attendance at school and the United Presbyterian Church. According to his reminiscences later in life, Scott had a strict upbringing within the church. Sunday was reserved for going to church and Sunday school; no pleasurable activities were allowed.

Scott's favourite schoolteacher, a woman by the name of Miss Langford, prepared him for his high-school entrance exams. Scott passed these exams but quit school after he had completed his eighth grade, a decision he was always to regret. Even though he succeeded in his subsequent careers as a journalist and politician, he felt that he had to work harder than most in order to compensate for his lack of formal education. Scott suffered from asthma and missed many days of school. He left home on July 2, 1883, at the age of 15 to work for neighbouring farmers.

On March 17, 1885, Scott left his family, boarded a train and headed for Portage la Prairie, Manitoba. Several members of Scott's community had already moved West, and reports they sent home described a rugged land, but a land of opportunity. Those willing to work hard could make their fortune in the West, and Walter was able to convince his mother that the move would be financially beneficial. Furthermore, he assured her that the fresh, western air would be sure to improve his asthmatic condition. His move could have also been an attempt to leave his embarrassment of birth behind and make a new start in the West, where no one would know his past.

Scott's original plan was to go to Portage la Prairie, where he would live and work on a farm with his mother's twin brother, James Telfer. However, by the time he arrived there, the North-West Resistance had broken out and Scott's uncle had left to help suppress Riel and the Métis insurgents. Because there was now no position on the farm with his uncle, a change of plans was necessary, and Scott took a job at Strome Henderson General Store as a delivery boy for $20 per month.

After five months at the general store, C.J. Atkinson, owner and editor of the *Manitoba Liberal*, offered Walter Scott a job as a "printer's devil." This meant doing miscellaneous jobs around the print shop, including lighting the fires in the morning and sweeping the floor. Scott soon moved from printer's devil to try his hand at typesetting and printing jobs, and evidently he impressed his employer. In the summer of 1886 Atkinson left Portage la Prairie to start a new newspaper, the *Journal*, in Regina. By December, Scott was also in Regina, working for Atkinson at the *Journal*.

In addition to his move to Regina that year, 1886 was influential for Scott because he met J.H. (Jim) Ross, a prominent Liberal organizer in the Regina and Moose Jaw communities. Ross later went on to become a member of the Legislative Assembly (MLA) of the North-West Territories, a member of the House of Commons (more commonly referred to today as a member of Parliament, although, strictly speaking, Senators are also members of Parliament) for the Yukon, and ultimately a Senator. Like Atkinson, Ross would be influential in Scott's decision to make a career in the Liberal Party.

Up to this point, Scott had not taken a high political profile, but during the 1887 election campaign, which he covered for the *Journal*, he referred to Ross, the Liberal nominee, as "our candidate." Even though Ross was defeated in the Assiniboia West constituency by the Conservative, Nicholas Flood Davin—a journalist and owner of the Regina *Leader*—it was apparent that Scott had developed a taste for politics.

But life was not all newspapers and politics for the young Walter Scott. He attended picnics and summer events where the local young men and women could meet. It was at one of these picnics in the summer of 1887 that Walter met Jessie Florence Read, daughter of E.B. Read, of Regina. They dated through that winter. He escorted her to "several assemblies" and went skating and tobogganing. Scott had been increasing his earning power as he became a typesetter and later a reporter at the newspaper, but according to his own admission, he had increased his spending even more due to high living and found that he was continually in debt. With his attraction to Miss Read, he decided to gain control of his finances. He had "learned a lesson" on indebtedness.

On May 14, 1890, Jessie and Walter were married by Reverend Leonard Dawson in a small ceremony at St. Paul's Church, Regina. Walter reminisced that it was the "most auspicious event of my life." The *Journal* extended its congratulations to the young couple on their marriage. The *Leader* noted that Walter Scott was receiving congratulations from "his many friends" on the joining "in the holy bonds with Miss Jessie Read."

In his first few years in Regina, Scott worked for the *Journal*, and then, in the hope of career advancement, he shifted to the *Leader*. By the fall of 1892, Scott decided it was time to stop working for others in the newspaper business and he struck off on his own. With the town of Regina expanding at a dizzying pace, the newspaper business along with general printing seemed to be the way to make a fortune.

On September 17, 1892, Walter Scott went into equal partnership with J.K. McInnis to buy the *Standard*. The paper's revenue came from sales, advertising, and printing contracts. Business was so good that in less than two years Scott was able to buy the Moose Jaw *Times* at a discounted price of $600, a decision prompted by Jim Ross and A. Hitchcock, a Moose Jaw banker. Scott noted that the purchase was a "good bargain," and he remained the owner of the *Times* for the rest of his life. It was a money-maker for him over the years, and a vehicle to spread his own political philosophy. Scott initially announced in the paper that he would not be taking sides in political battles but would be giving readers balanced reports with plenty of local news. In an editorial dated August 31, 1894, Scott surprised many by supporting the Conservative MP, N.F. Davin. Scott noted, though, that Davin was "off colour"—apparently from alcohol—but hoped that he was "not losing his power of eloquence, for if facility of expression left him he would not be Mr. Davin at all."

Thus by 1894, nine years after leaving Ontario, Walter Scott was the owner of one newspaper and half-owner of another, becoming a prominent citizen in the community. Scott and McInnis had agreed that Scott would move to Moose Jaw to operate the *Times*, while McInnis would stay in Regina to look after their interests at the *Standard*. It was not long before Scott expanded his newspaper holdings even further.

On August 22, 1895, Scott bought the Regina *Leader* from Davin.[3] This was a sign of the arrival of a new generation and the changing of the guard. By this point, Davin was interested in lightening his load as newspaper owner and as a member of Parliament. As part of the deal in buying the newspaper, Scott agreed that Davin would write or at least control the contents of the first two editorials each week. Davin seemed to have won the best part of the bargain, as he had lightened his load and at the same time knew he had the support of the largest newspaper in the area. For his part, Scott increased his hold over the newspaper industry in Regina and district.

Two years later, on January 10, Scott's ties to the Liberal Party were strengthened when he was unanimously chosen by the party "to dispense the patronage of this [Moose Jaw] district." As well, with Jim Ross and L.B. Cochran, Scott was appointed to a committee to arrange speakers for political meetings in the area. The combination of newspaper ownership and influence over the patronage levers for Moose Jaw and district meant that Scott had much political and financial control over the events in the community.

As the new century approached, Scott owned two newspapers and had equal partnership in a third. He covered elections and moved in political circles. He had some patronage influence for the Moose Jaw area and he associated with people such as Atkinson and

Ross, two of the Liberal leaders in the North-West. The combination of newspapers and politics was a comfortable fit. As well, his roots in a rural, Presbyterian, English-speaking and Liberal Ontario community had strongly influenced his beliefs and values. Scott had worked on several farms as a young man, and he had gained knowledge of agriculture and its importance to the economy and the lifestyle of the people. Scott was raised to believe that the secret to success on the farm was hard work. Honest labour could overcome even poor soil and weather conditions. The combination of Scott's rural roots and Saskatchewan's big skies and open spaces led him to believe that the future for his adopted province was unlimited. Now, 15 years after arriving in the North-West, he was ready to launch his political career.

Entry into Politics

Walter Scott was involved in politics as a journalist, newspaper owner and Liberal Party activist soon after he arrived in Regina in 1886. In 1900, however, he became a candidate for elected office when he accepted the Liberal nomination for the federal constituency of Assiniboia West. In the ensuing election, Scott defeated N.F. Davin, and thus began a five-year political apprenticeship during which he learned much from old political masters in Ottawa. He was subsequently re-elected in the federal general election of 1904.

After the 1904 election the stage was set for discussions on the autonomy of Western Canada. The first point of contention was whether to divide the territories into one or two provinces. Frederick Haultain, territorial leader, argued for one big province, while supporters of the "two-province" concept believed that one large province, due to its size, would "result in jealousies and frictions detrimental to Canadian unity."

The second point of debate was the transfer of Crown land to the new provinces. The federal government retained administration of the public lands in Saskatchewan and Alberta, not just for railway construction but also to ensure continuity of the federal government's homestead policy. In lieu of control of the land, the provinces were granted financial compensation.

The final and most contentious issue in the autonomy debate pertained to separate schools. The issue of separate schools was important for the Liberals because they relied on Roman Catholic support in Quebec and in the Territories. The initial provisions in the Autonomy Bills were too pro-Catholic, according to Clifford Sifton, minister of the Interior, and Walter Scott. Sifton resigned from Cabinet over the issue but a compromise was struck where the school system was left as it was in 1905 before autonomy, thus avoiding private religious schools. Scott argued, "We have separate schools but not a separate system, which makes all the difference in the world." Even though a compromise was found, Sifton never returned to Cabinet.

Formation of Saskatchewan

One of the first decisions to be made for the new province of Saskatchewan was the location for the seat of government. In 1883, the federal government moved the territorial capital from Battleford to Regina to be on the main line of the Canadian Pacific Railway (CPR). It seemed logical to many that the capital would remain in Regina with the formation of the province. However, there were other centres in Saskatchewan which dreamed of becoming the capital city. The Saskatchewan Act, as passed by the Parliament of Canada, named Regina as the provisional capital subject to a final decision by the province's Executive Council.

Another important decision for the federal and provincial Liberals was who should be the provincial leader. On July 6, when Scott met Laurier in his office, Laurier knew that the Saskatchewan provincial Liberals had decided to field candidates in the first election and that he needed a strong person to carry the Liberal flag in the fledgling province.

There is no record of what was said at the meeting, but it became known that Scott left his resignation in abeyance after the defeat of the railway tax exemption amendments and he continued sitting as a member of the House of Commons. It seems clear that Laurier asked Scott not to embarrass the government by resigning, and almost certainly asked Scott to let his name stand as Liberal leader in the new province of Saskatchewan.

What was Scott's relationship with Laurier? Scott was not a "pushover" in caucus or in the House of Commons. He was a loyal Liberal but he also defended his principles to the point of standing up to the Prime Minister on the school clauses and the railway tax exemption provisions in the Autonomy Bills. However, it does not seem as if Scott was on the fringe of the party. Laurier consulted Scott from time to time to seek his opinion. Scott was not a party rebel, but in order to remain credible in his constituency, he had to represent western interests. Even though Scott defended territorial concerns, he accepted compromise and won federal compensation for CPR tax-exempt land. Scott also won on the establishment of the school system as it existed in 1905. He balanced territorial interests with federal Liberal policy. The compromise permitted him to stay in the party and to remain popular with his electors.

On the other hand, Laurier did not choose Scott as the new minister of the Interior when Sifton resigned. Perhaps Laurier could not replace Sifton with Scott since the two had worked too closely together. Was Scott considered for the Cabinet post? To P.M. Bredt of Regina, Scott hinted that he was supporting Greenway, or Oliver, or Turriff, for the post of minister of the Interior rather than taking on this responsibility himself. He revealed: "I am perhaps myself to some extent responsible for the selection [of Oliver]." Yet to G.W. Brown, Scott confided: "I have no intimation as to Laurier's intention but of course will not be greatly surprised to be sent for myself." Even though he did not want to admit it, Scott was secretly hoping that he would get the call to enter the Laurier Cabinet, but this call did not come. To his half-brother John, Walter admitted, "I am not looking for it [the Cabinet post]. I see very clearly that there is more work and worry than compensation or satisfaction in such a position, but of course some victim will have to be found and I would not say absolutely that I would refuse it under certain conditions." Had Scott gone into Cabinet, the necessary by-election,[4] in his estimation, would have been an easy victory for him but such was not to be. Scott claimed that he had no regrets in not being chosen for Cabinet. Laurier's biographer and friend, O.D. Skelton, described Walter Scott as having "much promise" and that Laurier held him in warm affection.[5] From all outward appearances, Scott and Laurier had a close working relationship, even though they disagreed on several key policies. In the end, they were able to find compromise they both could live with. This friendship would last their lifetimes.

When was Scott first approached about becoming the Saskatchewan Liberal leader? On November 13, 1904, Scott wrote to the Liberal secretary in Moose Jaw, W.E. Seaborn, acknowledging that he (Scott) had been approached to run for leader. Scott felt that G.H.V. Bulyea would be the strongest candidate for the job, observing that while Bulyea was not "spectacular," he was "straight and sound." By February 1905, Scott was still considering the Liberal leadership. However, he doubted his own capacity to do the job. With all the work and worries involved, why would a person seek to become Premier? By August 18, after the Saskatchewan Liberal convention that chose Scott as leader, he wrote to a colleague that he would find it hard to leave Ottawa, but "the finger of duty seemed to point very clearly in the local direction."

On June 30, Scott wrote that the "Chief" (Laurier) still favoured Haultain but was meeting opposition from some of his own supporters. The concern was that Haultain appeared, to many Liberals, to be a Conservative. As well, Haultain had to decide in which province to seek election. His territorial constituency of Macleod, where he had his own electoral base, was in the new province of Alberta, yet his residence and law practice were in Regina. Haultain finally chose to maintain his roots in Regina and sought election in Saskatchewan. This meant that the Liberals had to choose someone who could compete against him. Some Liberal insiders considered James Calder for leader, but George Brown, for one, doubted that Calder could beat Haultain. Calder, the former deputy commissioner of Education in the Haultain administration, and later a Regina lawyer, was a great detail person but lacked the public flourish to capture the imaginations of the people. By June 1905, Scott seemed assured of taking on the leadership of the provincial Liberal Party. Yet he had to reassure his local colleagues that he had not campaigned for the position: "The truth is that I had absolutely no idea in the world of going into local politics." Scott had experience and leadership qualities that Brown admired. And so Brown, in July 1905, urged Scott to give up Ottawa because there were not many opportunities for him there. If Scott were to become leader, he could always return to federal politics at a later time. Scott replied that even if he was asked to be leader, he was not sure he would accept the invitation.

Liberals considered Bulyea for the leader's post. Scott believed that Bulyea could do a good job, and he had been faithful to the Liberal Party during the difficult nonpartisan years in the territorial Legislative Assembly. However, Scott had doubts about Bulyea's ability to rally the people of Saskatchewan to defeat Haultain, who was clearly the competition. A sound, energetic and popular leader had to be found to defeat him.

Scott had to be careful how he managed the convention and his leadership bid. Five days before the convention, he wrote: "It seems to be much better that no statement on the subject [of leadership of the party] should emanate from myself." The background work would have to come from others. Within a week of the convention, Scott began to show some optimism that the leader's post was his. He wrote: "I am sorry to have to say that it begins to look as if I might be obliged to leave Ottawa for a time at least." Scott kept denying that he was a possible candidate for the position but did nothing to stop others who were promoting his leadership. Scott knew that he lacked the education that Haultain and others had, but he was honoured to be considered by his party.

On August 5, 11 days before the convention, Scott wrote to Laurier: "From what I have been able to learn since arriving here [Regina], I fancy that the proceedings may result in harmony with the suggestions which were discussed with you a couple of weeks ago." The suggestions Scott refers to must have been Laurier's offer on July 6 that Scott become Liberal leader. The wheels were in motion for a successful convention and the beginning of a new chapter in Scott's political career.

August 1905 was a crucial month for the formation of provincial political parties in Saskatchewan and Alberta, with both Liberals and Conservatives holding their conventions in Alberta and Saskatchewan that month. The Liberals, at their conventions, "declared their determination to contest the provincial elections on federal party lines."[6] The Liberals claimed that this step was in response to the provincial Conservatives' decision in Moose Jaw in 1903 to organize along party lines and accused the Conservatives of being the first to practice partisan politics. The Alberta Conservatives declared their intention to follow the Liberal lead and to run Conservative candidates in the next provincial election. At the Saskatchewan Conservative convention, Haultain declared his support for nonpartisan candidates.

When Scott entered the House of Commons in 1900, he had been shy and reluctant to engage in debate, but after nearly five years, he had become more comfortable with parliamentary give-and-take. He had been a representative of the southern and western segment of the new province and was well known, certainly in Liberal circles. Scott had proven that he was sound in judgement, able to raise points of principle but willing to accept compromise and party policies. Judging by the reception he received from the 300 enthusiastic Liberals at their convention in Regina, he was a popular leader. The motion to name Scott leader was unanimous and greeted by a round of cheers and applause. The Regina *Leader*, a paper still owned by Scott, reported enthusiastically: "Round after round of cheers, accompanied by the waving of hats, prevented Mr. Scott from speaking for some little time, and his first attempt at utterance only provoked another round of cheers." The farm boy from Strathroy had arrived.

Scott later indicated to a colleague that he had been approached by many within the party, including the Prime Minister, to be the leader, and when the convention was unanimous in choosing him, he could not refuse. However, he was careful not to appear to be campaigning for it. Instead, he was in a better position to lead if it looked as if he had been persuaded by the cheering throng to take on the challenge—Scott was leading because he had been asked to lead. In his correspondence, he was quick to point out that there were many responsibilities in being provincial leader, but with "the assistance of the energetic aid of all the good friends throughout the Province," victory could be achieved.

Saskatchewan's First Government

The new provinces of Alberta and Saskatchewan came into being on September 1, 1905. However, Saskatchewan had to wait until September 4 for the official party of Governor General Grey to arrive in Regina for the inaugural ceremonies, when A.E. Forget was sworn in as the lieutenant-governor. Forget, former clerk of the territorial Legislative Assembly and territorial lieutenant-governor, became Saskatchewan's first representative of the Crown and of the federal government. Under the authority of sections 8 and 10 of the Saskatchewan Act, Forget had the responsibility to choose an interim Premier who would form a government and recommend the date for the first provincial election. The Canadian Parliament had established the provincial electoral boundaries, subject to alteration in subsequent years by the provincial Legislative Assembly.

There had been much speculation preceding the selection of the first Premier. One school of thought argued that the position of lieutenant-governor, as representative of the sovereign, must be nonpartisan. As such, since Frederick Haultain had been the government leader in the North-West Territories and was a popular figure in the new province, he should be chosen Premier. The other school of thought contended that the Liberal leader was the obvious choice because the lieutenant-governor was the servant of the federal government. Like Haultain, Scott had parliamentary experience. Wanting to maintain his public image of not interfering with provincial matters, Prime Minister Laurier stated that it was up to the lieutenant-governor to choose a desirable candidate to be Premier. On the day following the inaugural ceremony, Forget called on Scott to form the first provincial government, later arguing that he had chosen the leader of the party that had a majority of members sitting in the former Legislative Assembly of the North-West Territories. However, it is also clear that Scott was Laurier's choice. Haultain would have to wait for the first election to offer himself to the people and win the Premier's chair.

In the four months after Scott became Premier, he had much to do to organize the province for a general election. The Autonomy Acts divided a portion of the old North-West Territories into two new provinces and the division of the two provinces was smooth. The governmental infrastructure stayed in Regina but one commissioner and two deputy commissioners moved to Alberta to establish that province's new government.[7] Scott's first task was to continue the established territorial government and mould it for the new province of Saskatchewan.

The Legislative Assembly, the Cabinet, and the public service met and worked in two territorial buildings on Dewdney Avenue near the North-West Mounted Police barracks. All territorial sessional papers and official documents remained in Regina.

The first task for the new Premier in September 1905 was to pick a strong and representative cabinet that would carry the party through the first election. Jim Calder was one of the first candidates on Scott's list. Even though Calder had been the deputy commissioner of Education in Haultain's administration, he and Scott had known each other since the federal election of 1900. In 1905, Calder resigned his post in the Education Department in order to practice law in Regina. Shortly thereafter, Scott invited Calder to his office with the offer of a Cabinet post. After several meetings and some persuasion, Calder finally agreed. He later reminisced that it was "a decision that profoundly affected all my future activities." Calder would go on to be one of Scott's strongest and most loyal Cabinet ministers, serving as acting Premier during Scott's many absences. Calder was, during his political career in Saskatchewan, minister of Education, Highways, Railways, Telephones and provincial treasurer.

The other cornerstone of the Scott cabinet was W.R. Motherwell, one of the founders of the Territorial Grain Growers Association. Motherwell was a farmer near Abernethy and an influential leader in the farm community. The choice of Motherwell is an example of Scott's ability to attract farm leaders to serve in his government, which allowed the farmers to be central to government policy in the province and also kept the Liberal Party in power in Saskatchewan. Motherwell became the minister of Agriculture and was the first of many farm leaders to be invited into Cabinet.

John Lamont, as attorney general, was the fourth member of the Scott Cabinet. Lamont originally joined Scott as a fellow member of the House of Commons for the constituency of Saskatchewan, North-West Territories, in November 1904. A graduate from Osgoode Hall, Lamont practised law in Prince Albert before entering politics. Evidently the professional and personal relationship between Lamont and Scott was positive because they left federal politics together in September 1905 to form the first Saskatchewan cabinet. With the four ministers in place, the Scott government was ready to set policy that would attract popular support for the forthcoming election.

During the first four months that Scott was Liberal leader and then Premier, he prepared his party and constituents for the upcoming election. On August 21, 1905, he sent a "manifesto" to his former constituents in the federal riding of Assiniboia West, giving his reasons for leaving federal politics and outlining the Liberal platform for the pending provincial election. A month later, he sent another manifesto to the citizens in the new provincial riding of Lumsden, the constituency that he intended to contest in the first provincial election. Then in October, Scott embarked on a whirlwind speaking tour of the province. Scott kept a similar pace for November and December, culminating in a joint rally with Haultain in Regina on December 11, two days before the election. Scott travelled by train and buggy to visit all of these centres.

Scott waged a low key campaign and offered a low profile for the Provincial Rights Party. He urged his party workers to make "no noise" and to work quietly amongst the German settlers. The campaigners were not to have too many meetings: "Incessant quiet work will be the best." Flashy and high-profile patronage appointments would raise the Liberal profile, which was not the attention Scott wanted.

Scott formulated the broad policies and the issuance of the party manifesto while Calder attended to the finer details of the campaign, such as the organization of the nominating conventions. Surprisingly, Scott did not even attend his own nominating convention in Lumsden. He sent his regrets and advised his party workers in Lumsden that Calder would attend in his place: "I am more than sorry to be prevented from attending the Convention but trust that Mr. Calder filled the bill. He can deal with the school question better than I can."

Rather than having his Cabinet ministers run in safe ridings, Scott insisted that they pick difficult ones: "Lamont, Motherwell and Calder have every one of them won districts which in each case nobody else could have held. It was a risky looking think [sic] to put the three ministers in such risky places, but it is the bold play that usually wins in politics." This was the first of many bold plays that kept Scott at least one step ahead of his political opponents.

The Liberal platform, as adopted by the August convention, promised to "promote the welfare of the common people and to safeguard their interests." The party pledged provincial rights, common schools supported by provincial taxes and supervised by a provincial Department of Education. The Liberals promised, if elected to government, to build roads and bridges, to promote agriculture, and to lobby the federal government for construction of the Grand Trunk Pacific and Canadian Northern branch lines as well as a line to Hudson Bay. A Liberal government would push the federal government for the removal of the CPR land-tax exemption and public control of utilities. While the Liberals were promising government control of public utilities, the Conservatives favoured government ownership of those utilities. In all, the government would be "progressive and economical." Scott claimed that he was in league with "no railway monopoly, but free and determined to work for more roads and better service." Liberals owed allegiance to no one, just the common people of Saskatchewan.

Scott's campaign was forward-looking, and the slogan was "Peace, Progress and Prosperity." According to the Liberals, to vote Conservative would be to look to the past and to court challenges over the Saskatchewan Act, resulting in "agitation and strife." Scott, on the other hand, pledged to the people of Saskatchewan that the Liberals would provide "clean government, honest government, and ... progressive government." Frederick Haultain, the leader of the Provincial Rights Party (the Conservative Party in everything but name), promised that if he gained power, he would continue to "fight for Provincial freedom." Even though the Liberals wanted to talk only about the future of the province in the election campaign, they were obliged to respond to the Provincial Rights Party's concerns over the past negotiations for provincehood. Scott defended the terms of the Saskatchewan Act as passed by the Parliament of Canada.

On December 13, 1905, the Scott government was elected with 16 of the 25 seats in the Assembly. Liberal support was evenly divided between the northern and southern parts of the province, and they won eight seats in each area. The Opposition's support was concentrated in the south, winning only one seat in the northern area. Even though the province was primarily rural with as yet no major cities to boast of, the Liberals did win six constituencies with larger towns, while the Provincial Rights Party won two urban ridings.

In 1905, Scott could look back on the last five eventful years with three electoral victories—two federal and one provincial—under his belt. Proud of his adopted province, and confident of his ability to lead it into the future, Scott became one of Saskatchewan's biggest "boosters," stating:

> Very few people are ever content in the East after once having lived West, no matter how much they disliked the prairies at first nor how much they longed to get back East. In my own case I longed for Ontario the whole nine years from the time I went out in 1885 until I got back home the first time in 1894. Since then I have never felt the faintest inclination to return to live in Ontario.

Scott seemed to be describing himself when he wrote: "a young man of fair intelligence and industrious habits can scarcely fail to reach an independent position before he has passed middle life." Not only did he love the West, Scott was filled with optimism about the future: "This province has as yet less than half a million souls and there is plenty of

SAB R-B12-2

The first Saskatchewan government. Clockwise from left: Walter Scott, James Calder, W.R. Motherwell, and John Lamont. In the centre is Lieutenant-Governor Amédée Forget.

room for at least ten million." In another letter, he wrote: "Just as sure as the sun shines there will be within this Province alone some day a population running into the tens of millions." It was with this optimistic attitude that Scott and his government set off in January 1906 to create an infrastructure that would serve the people of the province for generations to come.

One of the first choices to be made by the new government was the location of the provincial capital. On May 23, 1906, W.C. Sutherland, MLA for Saskatoon, introduced a motion to locate the capital city in his constituency. Speaking in the debate in the Legislative Assembly, Scott clearly favoured Regina, and the members defeated the motion 21–2.[8] The result of the vote showed that the northern members had voted in favour of Regina, leading historian Jean Murray to speculate that, of the 16 members in the Liberal caucus, 11 were in favour of Saskatoon. Yet Walter Scott had been able to win over the northern members and convince them to vote against Saskatoon without causing a major split in the caucus. The Saskatoon "boosters" were disappointed but they were confident that they would win future battles.

How then did Scott win over his members to support Regina? There is speculation that he promised the northern members that if they supported Regina this time, he would commit the government to granting other large institutions, such as the proposed university, to the northern centres (as had been done in many American states).[9] Scott believed that if the Regina people lost something already located in their city, their disappointment would be far greater than if they failed to get something new.[10] Scott knew that his government had to give some rewards to the south or the Liberal Party would be weakened in that part of the province.

Although it was suggested that Scott favoured Regina because he owned land both in and around the city, there is no evidence that he supported Regina in order to boost his financial investments. Rather, political considerations seem to have been the main reason Scott supported Regina's bid to remain the capital city of the new province.

Construction of a New Legislative Building

With the heavy legislative load and the influx of new immigrants to the province, it was clear that the government had to increase the size of the Legislative Assembly in order to give appropriate representation to the people. As a result, a larger legislative chamber was needed. Similarly, a public service would have to be hired and housed to serve this expanding province for generations to come. When Scott took on the role of minister(commissioner) of Public Works in the first Cabinet, one of his initial tasks was to begin the process of building a new Legislative Building. The Territorial administrative and legislative buildings, located on Dewdney Avenue, near Government House and the NWMP barracks, were too small. A new site would have to be chosen and a building constructed to match the grand future of the province.

Under Jim Calder's scrutiny and with the approval of the Premier, the government bought the old Sinton property from McCallum Hill and Company for $96,250. This property, just south of Wascana Creek, was well away from the centre of town. Critics argued that the site was too far from town but it did offer 162 acres of land which could accommodate a sizeable building with land left for an impressive park.

As minister of Public Works, Scott began the search for an architect who would design this building and oversee its construction. Initially inclined to use his patronage power to choose a well-connected Liberal, on June 26, 1906, Scott wrote to Calder that he was tempted to hire F.M. Rattenbury, a friend and well-known architect. However, Scott resisted the temptation, later writing to Rattenbury:

> While my personal view is pretty strongly in favor of putting the work directly in the hands of an architect if [sic] acknowledged standing, I found the competitive method, especially with regard to a public building, appealed to some of my colleagues with force. We have decided in favor of holding a competition.

Obviously, there had been division in the Cabinet and Scott bowed to the consensus of his colleagues. Cabinet decided to enlist the "best talent in architect which exists in the English-speaking world." The government did not want the importance of such a public building tarnished by charges of patronage or corruption.

Cabinet chose Professor Percy Nobbs of McGill University to lead an independent selection committee with the mandate of conducting a competition for architect. The three adjudicators chosen were Nobbs, Frank Miles of Philadelphia and Bertram Goodhue of New York, all three being recognized experts in the architectural field. Cabinet set the initial estimate for the cost of the construction at between $750,000 and $1 million. The design was to take into account that Saskatchewan was part of the British Empire.

Scott's absence from the province due to pneumonia delayed the start of the architectural competition. Nobbs was ready to solicit designs but F.J. Robinson, deputy commissioner of Public Works, asked him to wait until Scott's return. The government had hoped to have the architect and design chosen in time for construction to begin by the spring of 1907, but since the competition did not commence until Scott's return in June, the construction of the Legislative Building was postponed by a year.

Nobbs recommended that seven architects from Britain, the United States and Canada be invited to submit designs for the new Legislative Building. This would be the beginning of many public projects for the Scott government where key choices were made based on recommendations by outside experts. Robinson was in charge of assessing the needs of the public service and the Legislative Assembly for "all time to come."

Early in the design phase, the government made several key decisions concerning the exterior of the building. Since the Legislative Building was to be located on the bald prairie, Scott felt it needed a dome that would be visible for miles around. Second, the government commissioned a landscape architect, Frederick Todd, to design the layout of the land surrounding the building. Thus, the building would not only be visible, it would also harmonize with the planned park that would surround it.

The competing architectural firms viewed the competition as fair, the firm of Darling and Pearson writing that: "we know of no competition that has been framed during recent years that has met with so much universal approbation among the profession." F.J. Robinson received all designs, replaced the names on the designs with codes, and forwarded the copies to the three adjudicators. On December 7, 1907, the selection committee chose the design from the Montreal architectural firm of Edward and W.S. Maxwell. Clearly not wanting to be seen as having any part in the final decision, Scott stayed out of the province when Robinson received the choice of design and announced the decision to the public. Scott had consciously decided to eliminate any political interference in the choice and wanted everyone to see that he was not involved.

By June 1908, the government chose the firm of P. Lyall and Sons of Montreal as the general contractors. By the close of the competition and the awarding of the general construction contract, the projected price for the building had risen to $1,750,000. The government instructed the architects to avoid waste and extravagance yet have the building "worthy" of the province. For every decision made on the project, the attitude of Robinson and Scott was that this was going to be built only once, so it had to be done correctly the first time. An example of this philosophy of "doing it right the first time" was when Scott noted in the original design drawings that the exterior of the Legislative Building was to be red brick. Scott wrote to Robinson seeking a price on Tyndal stone. Even though this cost an additional $50,000, they decided to proceed. This meant a delay in the construction because the stone quarry in Manitoba had to be opened and a rail line built. In all, Cabinet — or in most cases Scott and Robinson — approved 91 changes to the specifications of the building. The overall quality of the finished product improved but the costs also went up.

On October 4, 1909, the governor general, Earl Grey, laid the cornerstone for the Legislative Building. In addressing the assembled crowd, Premier Scott said that the building represented the character and ambitions of the people:

> [L]aws originating in and emanating from the tens of thousands of happy fire-sides within the borders of the Province, will be framed, revised and perfected and put into statute form in the committee rooms and legislative chamber of this building.
>
> How many thousands of feet may climb these stairs in this entrance in the years to come—carrying a burden of responsibility as legislators, one long continuous line of them, year after year, generation after generation, century after century,—the trusted, invaluable administrative officials and experts and staffs, contemporaneous lines of them, generation succeeding generation,—studious or merely curious processions of spectators and visitors, week after week, year after year!

Three years later, the new governor general, the Duke of Connaught, officially opened the Legislative Building on October 12, 1912. Thus, just seven years after the formation of the province, the government and the Legislative Assembly had a new building in which to perform their functions. It was a building of which the people could be proud. Unfortunately, Walter Scott himself—the driving force behind the design and construction of this building—missed the opening of the building due to illness.

The total cost of the Legislative Building was $1.8 million, double the original estimates. Even though it was a landmark that became a showpiece for the province, not

SAB R-B170(2)
The new Legislative Building in 1913, shortly after its completion.

everything worked as initially expected. Just after the official opening, the deputy minister of Municipal Affairs wrote to the acting deputy minister of Public Works: "We will make no comment on the wonderful clocks which ornament certain portions of the Department but which were evidently never intended to give any reliable information regarding time." When the government made the final payment to P. Lyall and Sons for the construction of the building on March 12, 1914, the Saskatchewan Legislative Building was finally complete.

Even though the building was a centrepiece for representative and responsible government, there was some criticism about its overall cost. In defence, Scott wrote:

> The policy adopted is to put up a Chamber and set up offices adequate for at least twenty-five years without additions and which may for a century yet be creditable enough to form the main building on the Capital grounds. Disraeli said that nothing more completely represents a nation than a public building.

The University of Saskatchewan

Scott was keenly aware that in order for the British parliamentary institutions to be able to function in the new province, an educated and well-informed population was essential. Even though Scott had only a grade eight education himself, he believed that the province needed a university—in his mind, parliamentary democracy and education were the twin pillars of society. To this end his government introduced the University of Saskatchewan Act, which provided for the positions of registrar and president. Jim Calder appointed his deputy minister, D.P. McColl, as the first university registrar.[11] McColl's first task was to establish convocation composed of graduates of any university who had lived in Saskatchewan for more than three months. It was the duty of convocation to elect a chancellor and a senate. Chief Justice Edward L. Wetmore was chosen as the chancellor.[12] By September 1907, elections were underway for members of the senate.

The urban centres which were vying to become the site for the university tried to have as many of their citizens as possible on convocation, the senate, and the board of governors in order to affect the choice of site—a decision that was to be made by the board of governors. The nine-member board consisted of three persons appointed by the Cabinet, five chosen from the university senate, and the president of the university. In the University Act, the board of governors was made responsible for the "management, administration and control of the property, revenues, business and affairs of the university." As historian Michael Hayden wrote, the university was to be "state supported but not state controlled." The Scott government purposefully created an institution that was a "comprehensive state-financed, self-governing university." Scott withstood the temptation to use political interference or patronage in the operation of the university.

The first major decision facing the board of governors was the choice of a site for the university. As in the selection of the provincial capital, aspiring centres sought the site of the university in the belief that this institution would bring more business, economic activity, and prestige to their community. The Premier's absence due to illness delayed this decision, but when he called the second general election for August 14, 1908, choosing the location of the university became one of the issues in the campaign.[13] A.P. McNab, a Saskatoon Liberal candidate, raised the stakes by promising that, if elected, he would work to get the university for Saskatoon. He further promised that if Saskatoon did not get the university, he would resign. Ever the careful diplomat, Scott stated that the decision on the site for the university would be made by the board of governors, but would be subject to ratification by the Cabinet. Scott promised that this would not be a political decision.[14]

On August 20, 1908, the board of governors offered Walter Murray, a philosophy professor at Dalhousie University, the position of president of the as-yet-unbuilt university. Scott told Murray, when they met for the first time: "This is a great country. It needs big men with large ideas."[15] Murray, for his part, was insistent that partisan politics should not interfere with the operation of the university, as he stated forcefully: "I would rather see a minister rob the charity boxes than see a university pollute the springs of education. To me education is a religion and the university as sacred as the Church."

The new board of governors held hearings around the province before meeting in Regina on April 7 to make its decision about the university site. Murray made known his preference for Regina, believing that the university would gain influence if it was close to the seat of government. On the other hand, Scott favoured Saskatoon, so as to spread the public institutions around the province. Before deciding on the site, the board first agreed that there would be a College of Agriculture and that it would be located on the main campus of the university. This marked the first time in Canada that an agricultural college would be associated directly with academic and professional colleges. The second item on the board's agenda was to decide on a site for the campus. The vote was conducted by secret ballot, with the alleged result being six to three in favour of Saskatoon.[16]

UNIVERSITY OF SASKATCHEWAN ARCHIVES A-32
The newly completed College of Agriculture, University of Saskatchewan, c. 1913.

The official ceremony to lay the cornerstone of the university was on July 29, 1910. The following day, the Regina *Morning Leader* reported on Scott's speech, which praised the pioneers of the prairies for always setting a priority on education for their children. At the same time, Scott reaffirmed his belief that agriculture was not only a noble profession and vocation but the centre of the world economy:

> Saskatchewan is essentially an agricultural province, which is no misfortune. Agriculture is the basis of the business of the world. Farming is the foundation of civilization. It is in keeping with the character of our province that the main part of the highest institution of learning in the province shall be an agricultural college.

Walter Murray was proud that the university would be the meeting ground of agriculture with other academic pursuits: "All are greatly benefitted by the intercourse and better prepared for service in the state, where the farmer, the doctor, the lawyer, the teacher and the engineer must work together for the public good." Scott had a high regard for universities but relied on President Murray to advise him on what the University of Saskatchewan required to become a top-level educational institution. Scott believed in a well-rounded liberal arts education and knew that the university would be more than a technical school. Murray and Scott both believed that the university should fulfil three other important functions: to train the men to farm scientifically; to train women to be good mothers and homemakers; and, through theological colleges, to train ministers to look after the spiritual needs of prairie families.

Scott's Second Term

When Scott called an election for August 14, 1908, less than three years since the last election, the opposition cried foul. The Provincial Rights Party claimed that Scott had called a snap election to catch the opposition off guard. The Liberals were re-elected with a 2% decrease in popular vote but a 2% increase in the number of seats. Scott wrote that this majority was large enough to be "sufficient to support a progressive policy while not so large as to be a menace to good government."

For Saskatchewan, the first 10 years of the twentieth century were at a time of remarkable growth and expansion, particularly in agriculture.[17] The population of the province increased fivefold and there was rapid expansion in the agricultural industry. Wheat was the primary crop. In 1900, Saskatchewan accounted for 7.8% of the total production of wheat grown in the nation; by 1910, the total was 50.7%. The rapid increase in tilled acreage proved a boon for the provincial economy, with revenue from wheat production growing from $4.5 million to nearly $80 million per year.[18]

Even if he did not have much power or jurisdiction in agriculture, Scott was masterful at sensing public sentiment and the needs of the province. Although his own profession was not directly related to agriculture when he entered politics, Scott soon learned that to be a successful Saskatchewan politician, one had to have rural roots and close ties with the land. His first inclination in government policy was not to have government directly involved in economic ventures. Yet, as he faced pressures from the Saskatchewan Grain Growers' Association (SGGA) and demands that the government deal with the many problems that were confronting his constituents, he became more inclined to experiment with limited government involvement in the economy.

One of the key elements in Scott's successful leadership style was his ability to consult with experts in assessing needs and formulating new policies. In this respect, he made every effort to cultivate the SGGA. The importance of this organization was tremendous, as the *Canadian Annual Review* noted in 1913: "No single organization in the West had so great an influence in directing legislation as the Grain Growers' Association of Saskatchewan." Historian Evelyn Eager noted the close connection between the SGGA and the provincial government, arguing that these close ties were not a coincidence but were "carefully guarded and cultivated" by the Scott government.[19] The SGGA was a pipeline of information and opinion from the farmers to the government. Scott was also able to reverse the flow from time to time, using the SGGA as a means of persuading the farmers to follow the government's lead. In any case, wheat was king and if the government hoped to stay in power, the interests of the farmers had to be paramount.

One means by which Scott stayed in touch with Saskatchewan farmers was to bring farm leadership into his government,[20] and W.R. Motherwell and George Langley are two of the more important examples of Scott's success in this regard. As historian W.L. Morton noted, in Saskatchewan, unlike other jurisdictions, the agricultural reform movement was incorporated into the government.[21] The Scott Cabinet, it seems, had its fingers firmly on the pulse of the farmer.

An important challenge facing the Scott government was how to encourage people to stay on the land. In a speech to members of the Legislative Assembly, Scott said that people would be less inclined to move away from the farms if they had proper services such as roads and telephones. Transportation and communication would shorten the miles between farm families and make life more convenient for everyone. It was the role of government to provide these amenities in order to support not only an agricultural economy, but an entire way of life.

With the invention of the telephone, the distances between farm families could be reduced. In an effort to keep people on the farm and to limit the feeling of isolation, the Scott government sought to meet the challenge of providing the telephone to every farm family. Scott was committed to the principle of public ownership of telephones for the long-distance lines and the links to other provinces. On the other hand, he felt that it would be "suicidal" for the government to try to provide a telephone to every rural resident.

By mid-summer of 1909, the provincial government took over the existing telephone system from Bell Telephones and encouraged the rural areas to form their own telephone companies composed of local shareholders, which charged rental for the services and looked after their own line construction and repair. The provincial government provided the telephone poles and a coordinating service to the rural telephone companies. Farm families had to show an interest by signing up, and they had to be prepared to invest a small amount of money in the telephone service. By forming a company, the rural residents took on the responsibility of owning and operating their own service. This spirit of cooperation made it possible for the people of Saskatchewan to establish a provincewide telephone service without having the government assume all of the responsibility.

The Saskatchewan Cooperative Grain Elevator Company

Communication was not the only problem facing the farmers. Even though railways were built to transport the grain, and branch lines were spreading across the province, the weakest point in the system involved the storage, loading and selling of the grain. Most elevators were owned by a few large companies, creating an impression that they had a monopoly. When the SGGA pressured the government to find a solution to the eastern companies that were stifling the western grain industry, Scott decided that a commission should be appointed to recommend solutions and began the difficult task of finding the correct experts to serve. When searching for qualified commissioners, Scott often consulted with Walter Murray, president of the University of Saskatchewan. The political stripe of the potential commissioner was not necessarily an important factor. In writing to Murray, Scott said: "Where you procure him [the potential commissioner] matters not,—from either side of the line,—granted that he carries the qualifications and what these are you will understand much better than I do."

Scott was careful to portray the outward image of an independent commission, but, since every commission needed some "guidance," the government appointed people who were sympathetic to its philosophy. Scott wrote to Murray that "it will be a mistake to assume that no care is needed towards properly guiding the enquiry which is underway." However, the government allowed the commission latitude to search for all possible solutions: "Unless a condition is radically unsound and wrong a complete ventilation can do no ultimate harm and any condition which is unsound and wrong ought to be ventilated and reformed."

The SGGA put considerable pressure on the Scott government by passing resolutions calling for it to purchase existing elevators and become involved in the grain-handling system. Notwithstanding this pressure and a general trend toward public ownership, Scott announced that a commission would be established to examine all avenues for a solution to the grain elevator problem. In most cases where Scott established a commission, he had a preferred general course of action and chose commissioners with similar preferences. It was then up to the commission to examine the matter carefully, to explore other options and to recommend a practical and detailed course of action. In the case of the grain elevators, Scott believed that having the government directly involved in the ownership and operation of the elevators would "be attended by grave economic and political dangers." Instead, he favoured a system somewhat similar to the telephone system that his government had just established, whereby there would be "the granting of a measure of Government aid sufficient to make a locally owned system financially possible and leaving the responsibility of the maintenance and operation upon the local communities." Scott hoped a way could be found to avoid government ownership of the elevators, writing to his old friend and political ally, Jim Ross: "Probably some scheme will be worked out for a system of elevators free from public control but without the Government directly having to do with the operation." Even though no easy solution seemed apparent, Scott hoped that "the application of good common sense to such a question will remove the seeming difficulties." From the beginning of the commission, Scott believed a cooperative program could be a possible outcome.

Thus on February 26, 1910, the government established the Magill commission, chaired by Professor Robert Magill, an economics expert from Dalhousie University, who was one of the candidates proposed by President Murray. The other two commission members were F.W. Green, the secretary treasurer of the SGGA, and George Langley, a director of the SGGA and a Liberal MLA. Since the SGGA had favoured a government-owned elevator company as one way of breaking the perceived eastern monopoly, one would assume that the commission would have recommended such a system. However, the SGGA historically had supported cooperative ventures. In the end, the commissioners favoured a system somewhat similar to the one Scott had outlined privately in his correspondence with Green and Langley—a system of cooperative ownership and operation with government financial backing.[22]

On October 28, 1910, Scott wrote to Magill saying that he was happy with the report and noting its unanimity. Representatives of the SGGA received advance copies of the report so that, Scott hoped, the association would react before he publicized his response. He intimated to the SGGA that he favoured the report but was careful not to commit himself publicly before knowing the reaction of the association. Scott also had to balance the business interests of the province. He urged Magill to handle the matter carefully so that the provincial business sector would not resent having the elevator company receive support from the province while the business community did not.

It was Scott himself and not W.R. Motherwell, the minister of Agriculture, who introduced the bill in the Legislature to establish the Cooperative Elevator Company. Bill 25, entitled "An Act to Incorporate the Saskatchewan Cooperative Elevator Company," received third reading and Royal Assent on March 14, 1911. As time would show, the elevator company provided a successful service to the farming industry and was profitable as well. The company's board of directors came from the executive of the SGGA. Charles Dunning, a member of the executive of SGGA and a future Premier of Saskatchewan, became the first general manager of the elevator company.

Through an independent but carefully chosen and guided commission, Scott came up with a solution that won the farmers over to his point of view. Once he had convinced the SGGA to share his point of view, this organization became the means of bringing the farming population on side. The Scott government applied the same principles of cooperation and limited government involvement in the provision of crop insurance and farm credit.

Prohibition

Agriculture and farm issues were not the only problems facing the government. With the outbreak of World War I in 1914, prohibition increasingly became both a social and a political issue. Even though the prohibition movement had been pressuring the government for some time to limit, and finally eliminate, the sale of alcoholic beverages in the province, the war brought a coalescing of the public will and new pressure on the government to bring change. Scott had long been a supporter of prohibition, writing as early as 1905:

> I cannot say that I look with favour upon the licensing system at all. I should very much like to bring about the adoption of a system which would eradicate the bar… while I am not a pledged abstainer I do not use intoxicating liquor in any form.

Scott knew that the government had to be very careful not to get too far ahead of the public will on the sale and consumption of alcohol or it would create the danger of a backlash against methods of liquor control. Scott planned to have the prohibition or "ban the bar" lobby push the government to implement legislation. He was clearly aware of the counter pressure coming from the "Licensed Victuallers" to keep the bars open. Without a surge of popular support to close the bars, Scott was not prepared to go out on a limb.

Scott knew the anti-alcohol lobby would not provide stable support for the government, and that if the bars were closed, bar owners, liquor interests and many immigrants would vote against the government. Likewise, Scott knew that he could not count on the prohibitionists for their support after the bars were closed: "Putting law on the statute book is only the beginning. Unless the moral reform forces are ready to take their clothes off and do something more practical than frame resolutions and have sermons given to help enforce the law, it would have been better not to pass the law." To a colleague he wrote: "the political party which depends on the so-called temperance people for support is sitting on a very shaky stool."

Scott was determined to wait with liquor legislation until he was certain that the majority of the people wanted controls on the sale of alcohol. He knew, as well, that to close the bars would wreak havoc on the local hotel and bar owners. Any measure to close the bars would have to be done in the spring or summer and not in the winter, in order to cushion the impact of laying off employees. Scott withstood the criticism for not taking

Walter Scott leading the charge for Prohibition, c. 1915.

action until he felt the "time was right," but on March 18, 1915, at a meeting in the town of Oxbow, Scott announced that the government would introduce legislation to close the bars as of July 1, 1915. He was able to keep the plan secret until the announcement, thus dropping a bombshell on both sides of the debate: "I rather think the opposing element had its breath so completely taken away at first that the proposal got the advantage of a seemingly almost universal endorsation [sic], which is always a most valuable advantage for any political proposal."

In the Speech from the Throne on May 10, 1915, the lieutenant-governor announced that the major initiative for the Session would be to terminate the bar licences as of June 30. The sale of "intoxicating liquors in bars and clubs" was harming the country's "strength in prosecuting the war." Instead of total prohibition, however, the government had decided to open a system of publicly controlled liquor dispensaries, based on local option. Districts could vote on whether they wanted these dispensaries. In the same speech, the government announced that there would be a referendum no earlier than December 1916 on the question of closing or reopening the bars. The government did not opt for prohibition because the province did not have the authority to enforce it. The Speech from the Throne outlined one further measure. No earlier than 1919, the people of Saskatchewan could decide whether they wanted the dispensaries to continue. Scott made a bold announcement to close the bars and provided several opportunities for the people to decide to close the dispensaries at a future time. Yet by May 1915, the government had not shown a commitment to go for full prohibition.

Female Suffrage

World War I brought another social change to the prairie landscape: female suffrage. Women in Britain had led the way in pushing for the vote, but it had been a long uphill battle. Pressure for granting the franchise to women in Saskatchewan was evident before the war. In February 1912 and 1913, the SGGA, at its annual meetings, passed resolutions in favour of giving the vote to women. In December 1912, J.E. Bradshaw, Conservative MLA for Prince Albert, moved a resolution in favour of female suffrage without creating the firestorm he had expected.[23] Members of the government spoke in favour of the motion and the resolution passed unanimously. Even though the Legislature adopted the motion, Premier Scott did not take action on this measure, waiting instead for a groundswell of public support.

Scott's support of female suffrage was clear in his correspondence long before the war, as indicated in a letter of August 1910: "Personally I have always held the view that just as soon as a majority of women desire to exercise the franchise they should be granted the right by law. I have never given the subject serious study and I should at present prefer not to commit myself publicly on the question." As in the closing of the bars, however, even though Scott personally favoured a measure, he was reluctant to move on the issue until he was convinced that the majority of the people were in favour.

When the Legislature again passed a resolution in favour of female suffrage in December 1913, Scott said that he favoured the measure but did not think the time was "ripe" yet for women's suffrage. However, he openly encouraged women to take action, advising Mrs. Lawton, President of the Equal Suffrage Association, to keep pushing its campaign for suffrage. Scott offered advice to women on how to organize politically and how to collect the petitions needed to convince the government to move on extending the franchise, but he refused to introduce the necessary legislation unless they organized a strong public lobby.

On January 18, 1916, in the Speech from the Throne, there was a hint that the government was prepared to make a move on the franchise question. On February 14, with the galleries full of women who had come to Regina to present thousands of petitions, Scott rose in his place in the Chamber to announce that his government would introduce legislation to extend the vote to women.[24] To the president of the Women's Grain Growers' of Saskatchewan, he wrote:

> I was very pleased indeed to be in position to give a favorable reply to the delegation who presented the petition. The women of Saskatchewan have helped and are helping to build up this Province of which we are so justly proud and I am very glad indeed that it is my good fortune to occupy the position of Premier in a Legislature which is extending to our women, through the franchise, further and fuller powers of assistance and service in the development of Saskatchewan.

The Act to grant the franchise received Royal Assent on March 14, 1916. For several reasons, the women of Saskatchewan gained the vote after a relatively short battle. To homestead on the prairie and to make a success of farming required work by both men and women, and their cooperative efforts built prairie society. Because the men generally recognized the importance of this joint service to the land and the province, they supported the concept that women deserved the vote as well.[25] Scott was also aware that, by the end of 1915, the neighbouring prairie provinces were preparing to introduce legislation to grant the vote to women, and his pride in Saskatchewan as a socially progressive province prompted him to take action before they did. When Scott finally acted, he knew that "the time was ripe and the demand was broad."[26]

"A Whiff of Scandal"

February 1916 was not only a positive time for the announcement on the extension of the vote to women, but also the beginning of a firestorm for the Scott government.

SAB B6493

A February 26, 1913, cartoon from the Grain Growers' Guide, *satirizing Scott's approach to female suffrage.*

Three days before Scott made his February 14 address to the women of the province, J.E. Bradshaw, Conservative MLA for Prince Albert, rose in the Chamber to announce that there was corruption in the government, and that he had evidence to show that members of the government had accepted bribes. He refused to name names or give any details, however, until the government agreed to establish a Royal Commission. If the government would not do this, the Opposition threatened to go to Lieutenant-Governor Richard S. Lake, a federal Conservative appointee, to ask him to establish a Royal Commission.

On February 23, 1916, Jim Calder charged that Bradshaw was part of a plot hatched by Robert Rogers, a federal Conservative Cabinet minister from Manitoba, who was intent on embarrassing the government. Since the government was afraid that the Conservative opposition would convince the lieutenant-governor to establish a commission on his own accord, Scott met with Lake on several occasions and received his assurance that the government would be consulted before any action was taken.

An editorial in the *Evening Province* accused the government of playing for time, charging that the delay in setting up a commission was a sign of the government's guilt. However, Scott argued that a legislative committee was the proper route whereas a commission would weaken the authority of the Legislative Assembly.

Astonishingly, in the midst of the crisis, Scott left for Montreal en route to Nassau, in the Bahamas. From Montreal, Scott wrote to Jim Ross explaining why he left when he did: having expected the session to be over by that time, he had booked a ship to Nassau and he felt that he could not cancel his vacation. He was sure that matters of state in Saskatchewan could be handled by Jim Calder. As reckless as his actions may have seemed,

Scott felt that it was a good tactic, one that would actually ease the pressure on the government when he was away.

Scott had hitherto acted cautiously but progressively in introducing policy that had broad public support in the province. However, his behaviour in the Bradshaw affair was the first, unmistakable sign that illness was beginning to affect his judgement. In these, the final months of his premiership, Scott began to take political chances and alienated many of the people whom he had taken great pains to accommodate in the past.

From a distance and by means of a series of telegrams, Scott and Calder planned a strategy to meet the Bradshaw charges. Scott advised Calder that they should establish a Royal Commission to "lay bear [sic] the whole unthinkably treacherous game." Scott had another motive in sending the telegrams. On March 1, 1916, he sent a copy of a telegram to Calder to Stewart Lyon of the *Globe*, emphasizing that they were establishing a commission to get to the bottom of the affair. That he sent a copy of his telegram to the press indicates that Scott wanted to appear clean and untouched by the scandal and that he was doing everything in his power to clean it up.

Once the government announced that it would create a Royal Commission, Bradshaw revealed the information he had on the scandals. In the end, the government appointed not one, but three commissions. The first was chaired by Sir Frederick Haultain, former Leader of the Opposition, and comprised Judge Newlands and Judge Lamont. The government charged this commission with investigating allegations of graft in the construction of the Battleford asylum, the Regina jail and the Department of Telephones.

Judge Wetmore chaired a second commission to examine all road construction contracts from 1913 to 1916 and the construction of a bridge in Saskatoon. And finally, the government established the Brown Elwood commission to examine the charges made by Bradshaw concerning the acceptance of bribes by certain MLAs over liquor legislation. Since Scott was out of the province, he was not directly involved with the commission hearings. Even though the final reports of the three commissions cleared him and his Cabinet of any wrongdoing, several public servants and MLAs were found guilty of fraud and the acceptance of bribes.[27]

The political effect of having scandal among the Liberal MLAs and the civil service could have been disastrous for Scott's government. Yet Scott and his Cabinet survived because they were seen by the public as having had the Bradshaw charges investigated fully, albeit unwillingly. The three independent Royal Commissions erased any hint of cover-up and when those who were implicated were charged and tried, the government could argue that the charges were in the past and that it was time to move on to other issues. However, there was no time for Scott to breathe easily. The culmination of another storm that had been brewing for the past three years came in 1916.

The School Question

The question of separate schools had been controversial since the creation of the province. In 1905, Scott had been satisfied with the autonomy bills that created Saskatchewan and Alberta, giving some protection to separate schools, which were administered like the public schools, under one governmental system. Religious minorities had the right to have religious education for half an hour at the end of the school day, but the curriculum and the general administration of the school system were handled by the Department of Education. The school boards were very much involved in the day-to-day administration of the schools in their systems. The separate school supporters paid their taxes to help finance the separate schools, as did the public school supporters for the public schools.[28] Believing that this system was "essentially a national school system," Scott fought the 1905 provincial general election on the autonomy bill issue and the people elected him. Even though the schools issue was not prominent for the next eight years, it was always in the background. Neither side was totally happy with the solution.

On September 14, 1911, Judge McLorg issued a court decision concerning the Vonda school district which reopened the school debate. McLorg wrote: "the option of supporting the public or the separate school system rested with each individual ratepayer."[29] Taxpayers who were supporting the separate school system could switch their taxes over to the public system or vice versa. Afraid that ratepayers would exercise this choice and jeopardize the financial stability of some school boards, the government claimed that the ruling was against the constitution and the School Act.

On November 18, 1912, Scott, in his role as minister of Education, introduced amendments to the School Act to restore the tax system as he believed it had been under the 1905 Act. Separate and public ratepayers would dedicate their taxes to their respective school boards. Even though both political parties supported passage of the amendments, a political storm began to brew shortly thereafter. The Orange Order argued that religious minorities, particularly the Roman Catholics, were given special treatment. The *Daily Standard* charged that Scott gave in to the Roman Catholics to repay them for their support in 1905, suggesting that he was paying allegiance to the Roman Catholic Church. In late December 1912, the Reverend Murdock MacKinnon, minister of Knox Presbyterian Church in Regina, protested to Scott that the amendments gave too much power to the Roman Catholics. He argued that the amendments promoted the separate schools by forcing separate school ratepayers to dedicate their taxes to the separate school board. Given a choice, perhaps the separate school system supporters would direct their taxes toward the public system, thereby weakening the separate system. The Scott amendments brought greater financial security and thus new life to separate schools.

In the case of businesses, the government divided the taxes between the two systems even though there might not be any separate supporters associated with the business. MacKinnon argued in favour of free choice but in one direction only: Catholics should be free to direct their taxes to the public system, but Protestants should not be allowed to support separate schools. MacKinnon and his followers believed that it was their mission to bring assimilation to the prairies so that one day everyone would be English-speaking and Protestant.

Scott was liberal in his views, believing that assimilation would come over time as part of an evolutionary process. In the meantime, he felt it was his duty to protect the rights of the minority. The provincial Conservatives took up MacKinnon's point, arguing that Scott was harbouring foreigners and was an agent of the Catholic Church.

In writing to his old friend, J.W. Dafoe, Scott noted that "anything involving the term 'separate schools' is very easily used to stir people up because it is a subject which so easily arouses a latent prejudice." Scott continued to argue that the School Act amendments reaffirmed the law as it had been in 1905. Again the Liberal government was performing a balancing act. Relying on the support of the new immigrants, many of whom were Roman Catholic, the government had to protect the rights of this minority.

Most French Canadians in Saskatchewan and many Germans were Roman Catholics. As a result, the separate schools often had children who spoke a language other than English, so the question of schools involved not only religion but language as well. W.R. Motherwell, who favoured English in the schools but was critical of any plan to force people to speak English, reflected Scott's liberal views on this issue:

> English, by all means, should be the language of our schools but just whether you can make British subjects quicker out of non-English by the lionizing process of squeezing their mother tongue out of them all at once is, to me, a very open and doubtful question. Make our schools, our laws and institutions generally so attractive to them that they will gladly drop the past, is, to me, a more preferable ... method.

The entire school question heated up for Scott when Reverend MacKinnon waded into the issue. The debate began with an exchange of letters between the two men, each letter becoming longer and more vitriolic than the last. The two men extended their written debate to the public forum through open letters to editors of the local newspapers. On December 26, 1915, with Premier Scott present in the congregation, Reverend MacKinnon delivered a 100-minute sermon criticizing Scott and his government for being soft on Catholics with the amendments to the School Act. MacKinnon charged that Scott was accepting direction from the Catholic Church and making it easier for Roman Catholics to establish separate schools. At first, Scott gave the impression to one of the key German Liberals in the province that there was nothing to worry about concerning MacKinnon's charges:

> My friend and pastor, Reverend Mr. MacKinnon, Sunday evening opened up with vigor against the little amendment which we adopted three years ago with regard to separate schools. The sword which Mr. MacKinnon wields is a double edged one, and I am not losing any sleep over the matter.

Scott's early bravado changed to action when in January 1916, he wrote to a friend in Victoria that MacKinnon "broke loose again." It troubled him that MacKinnon delivered this critical sermon in Scott's own church: "Anyway controversies with clergymen are very delicate business for politicians." Scott was determined, though, to speak his mind: "Ecclesiastical fur will be flying in this neighbourhood the next few weeks." Scott was convinced that he was right and that he had the public on his side.

On February 25, 1916, with Reverend MacKinnon in the galleries of the Legislative Chamber, Scott sought his revenge, announcing in debate that the government intended to repeal the Education Act amendments because they were no longer needed. He informed the Legislative Assembly that in correspondence with Judge McLorg, the justice had admitted that in the Vonda decision, he had not been aware of "earlier and contrary decisions of two higher court judges." Because of this retraction by Judge McLorg, Scott believed that the previous amendments to the School Act were redundant. The day after Scott's speech, McLorg publicly denied that he had reconsidered his decision.

Nonetheless, the *Leader* reported that Scott was in "excellent form and his presentation of facts was a masterly effort." He gave a detailed account of the history of the School Act and the McLorg judgement. It was only near the conclusion of his speech that he went beyond his usual cautious path, explaining to the MLAs and the public why he had written so many public letters about the school question. Calling Reverend MacKinnon a "moral leper," he felt it was his duty to reveal to the public this threat to society: "The intellectual and spiritual leper is very much more dangerous, especially when he is found in the most sacred position in our civilization." Scott had crossed the line in his attack on his rival. His controversial remarks, although brief, were caustic, and in attacking the Presbyterian minister, he made Presbyterians the enemy. Scott had devoted his political career to cultivating the support of diverse groups, including the Presbyterians. He had taken pains not to alienate any segment of society and he was proud of his ability to unite disparate groups into the Liberal Party. In his agitated state over MacKinnon, however, he caused more damage than he realized.

By August 10, 1916, the Scott Cabinet was cleared of any wrongdoing by the Brown Elwood Commission, and the time was right for Scott to bow out gracefully. Calder, having felt the strain as acting Premier whenever Scott was away, finally decided to consult with J.H. Ross and a few "close friends." "In the end we [Ross and Calder] decided that in his own best interest he [Scott] should resign. When we broached this matter to him a day or so later he fully agreed without hesitation. That same evening he handed his resignation to Senator Ross on the understanding that it would be handed to the Lieutenant Governor as soon as his colleagues and supporters agreed on his successor."

Calder wrote to W.S. Fielding, a federal Liberal, that Scott's resignation had required very careful handling out of respect for the Premier and for the good of the party: "Now that it is accomplished I am convinced that taken all in all we have improved our position in the province."

Scott signed his letter of resignation while he was in hospital in Philadelphia and it became effective October 20, 1916. According to Calder, he and Ross had consulted before the latter went to Philadelphia to meet with the Premier. This must have been difficult for Ross, for he and Scott were old friends, but the party had become convinced that Scott was no longer an asset and it was time for him to resign. After several days of reflection and advice from his physicians, Scott agreed to sign the letter, bringing to an end a career of more than eleven years in service to his province.

Scott's Declining Health

Throughout Scott's political career, he was often reported to be away from the office and seemed to be in frail health. From early childhood, Scott had suffered from chronic illnesses. Asthma was a continual complaint as he attended school and was one of the reasons given for his move west at age 17. Pneumonia struck him in 1906–07, followed by a nervous breakdown. The year 1911 was a watershed in Scott's deteriorating health. For five years following this breakdown, Scott was able to cover his symptoms and, with winter holidays, continue his political career. However, during 1912, Scott missed the annual Session of the Legislature and the official opening of the Legislative Building. He returned to Saskatchewan only for the election campaign but left again shortly after polling day. From this point onward, Scott was not able to regain his health, and this ultimately led to his retirement four years later.

Notwithstanding that Scott was away from his office so much, he was proud of the talent in his Cabinet and felt reassured that he had a "splendid team" supporting him. J.H. Lamont was acting Premier on Scott's first medical absence, but after Lamont was appointed to the Bench, Jim Calder filled in for Scott for any absences during the remainder of Scott's term as Premier. Scott rationalized his absences to his caucus by writing that it might be good for the people of the province to see that, when he was away, the government continued to function well without him. Scott knew that he had to be away for part of the year, especially during the short winter days, when he sought the warm sunshine of the Caribbean, the southern United States or the Mediterranean. However, even though Scott had a good team "stoking the home fires" while he was away, he felt guilty because he was not able to put in a full year's work. His need to rest and to have a break from the stress was in conflict with his Victorian work ethic.

Scott's illnesses created delays in the government's programs. For example, the government delayed the commencement of the architectural competition for the Legislative Building several months because of Scott's voyage to the south. Cabinet postponed the 1908 Session and a decision on the site of the new university for the same reason. The allocation of the judicial districts in 1907, and the introduction of Direct Legislation in 1912, were all decisions that the government put on hold, pending Scott's return.

Rather than being critical of Scott for his absences, the public viewed his illnesses with sympathy and understanding. Scott's many friends sent letters of support, wishing him a restful recovery. J.W. Dafoe and Clifford Sifton, of the *Manitoba Free Press*, sent a letter of support during Scott's bout of pneumonia in 1907. Dafoe resorted to an old newspaper custom of writing a eulogistic obituary notice for his friend Scott—newspaper custom had it that if an obituary notice was prepared, the men "for whom this is done, invariably recover." Scott indeed did regain his health, much to the relief of his friends at the *Manitoba Free Press* and Liberals across Saskatchewan.

By early April 1912, as his condition deteriorated, Scott decided to consult Dr. Silas Weir Mitchell, a well-known therapist in the treatment of depression, who prescribed rest, excessive feeding, massage, seclusion, and electricity. Mitchell intended this therapy to build up the patient's fat and blood as a way of restoring mental health. Scott, desperate to try any solution in order to bring an end to his depression, underwent treatment for four months at Mitchell's clinic in Philadelphia. Scott also tried the sea air, horseback riding, and golf. He showed some signs of improvement during the summer months and wrote: "I am very well, and for the fact golf and the horse I am sure are largely responsible. These are the medicines I now recommend."

Scott wrote that Dr. Mitchell had told him that if he wanted to recover his "share of nervous energy," he would have to rest and avoid nervous strain for several years. His doctors advised Scott that he should have only light political duties for two or three years in order to achieve a complete recovery. Scott wrote to Laurier that "nervous breakdown is a condition much easier to get into than to get away from." He described Mitchell as the "most noted nerve specialist in America… To him [Mitchell] and an assistant Mr. A.S. Pennington I owe my recovery."

Despite Mitchell's opposition, Scott decided to leave the clinic and return to Saskatchewan just in time to launch his third provincial election campaign as Premier. Scott wrote to a friend that "I am by no means as well as I should like to be but feel that I am quite well enough to give my friend Haultain just one more defeat." He hoped that, by the end of 1912, he would be fully recovered.

Scott returned for the election campaign but made fewer appearances on the campaign trail than had been his practice in previous elections. He was home to wave the flag for his party and his record, but his health did not allow him to give his usual energetic, campaign-style tour of the province.

SAB R-A12113

Walter Scott with William M. Martin (left) standing in front of the Empress Hotel at the end of a day's campaigning during the 1912 election. Despite assurances to friends that his health was stable, Scott is looking gaunt and tired. Martin would succeed Scott as Premier in 1916.

In his manifesto to the Saskatchewan voters before the election, Scott declared that his health had been poor due to "overwork" and that he had been "temporarily absent." But he promised that, if the people renewed their faith in him and if his government were re-elected, he would continue to devote his "best energies to the cause of good government for Saskatchewan." The Scott Liberals scored the largest electoral victory on record, winning 44 out of the 52 constituencies.

The extensive trips that Scott took in search of good health meant, however, that during his premiership he was out of the office and the province for more than half the time. An analysis of his extensive correspondence with friends while he travelled provides an estimate of the accumulated time away from home. By his own admission, from December 1905 to August 1908, during his first term as Premier, he was away 18 months, including a six-month Caribbean cruise and a tour of southern United States in 1906 and a three-month Mediterranean cruise in 1907–08. During his second term, he went to Jamaica in

February 1909, made another visit to Europe and took a Mediterranean cruise of 10 weeks in March 1910, was away for six months in 1911 in Victoria, London and Norway, and visited Florida, Nassau, and the Bahamas in January 1912. He spent four months at Dr. Mitchell's clinic in Philadelphia in the spring of 1912, until the provincial election campaign, but left for Europe immediately after the election. In his final term, he made a nine-month world tour in 1913, writing that from February to November he had travelled 50,000 miles. January 1914 saw him leave on a five-month voyage to Australia and Hawaii. To stave off depression, he travelled from country to country and from city to city at a frenetic pace. It is true that at many of his stopovers he met with government officials, but for the most part his travels were a desperate effort to avoid depression.

Retirement for Walter Scott at age 49 was very difficult, after 11 years as Premier of Saskatchewan, with a full schedule of meetings, responsibilities and travel. At the time of his resignation, he was in the Mitchell clinic, Philadelphia, where instead of finding a cure, his spirits plunged further into the depths of despair for nearly two years. He moved to Los Angeles and stayed there in a hotel. According to Scott, his daily mood was as if he was going to his own hanging. Finding that, when he was depressed, he could neither write letters nor meet with people, he became a recluse. After having been a journalist and prolific letter writer all of his professional life, he did not write for a period of two years, with the exception of an occasional letter to W.R. Motherwell. Scott described to Motherwell his inability to go out of the house and to meet people. Occasionally he would make the effort to go out, which often led to greater fatigue and more depression. Scott found that the easiest route was just to stay home: "for 18 months I was incapable of consecutive thinking and altogether lost touch with current literature and progress of thought on these and all other questions."

Life After Politics

By the spring of 1918, the depression lifted and Scott began to feel somewhat better. He returned to Regina for a brief visit before travelling to Victoria to take up residence in the Empress Hotel. The Scotts were able to live comfortably in retirement on an income from their real estate holdings and the Moose Jaw *Times*.

In November 1918, Walter Scott began to write editorials for the *Times*, which many thought marked the beginning of a return to normal life for the former Premier. In the first article, which appeared on November 23, 1918, Scott gave his background and an outline of his political career, and announced that he was returning to journalism.

After producing on average two articles or editorials per week from November 23, 1918, to March 20, 1919, Scott found that he could not continue to write coherently. The title he adopted for his column was "Silly Squibs by that 'Sick Slacker' Scott." His return to sound mental health had been short-lived.

One of the most tragic events for Walter Scott was the death of his wife of 42 years in 1932. There is nothing in Scott's correspondence files about Jessie's death but judging from his correspondence about her while she was alive, this loss must have been devastating. With his bouts of depression and lengthy absences, Scott had not been an easy person to live with, yet Jessie was always at his side. We know little about Jessie Read Scott. She disliked the spotlight of politics and was not relaxed with sea travel, yet she went with Walter by sea, moved to Ottawa, back to Regina, and finally to Victoria without obvious complaint. Together, they raised an adopted daughter, Dorothy, who stayed near them throughout their lives. Even though Walter idolized his daughter, child care was Jessie's responsibility. Scott always referred to his wife in his correspondence as "Mrs. Scott," yet appeared to love her and counted her as his best friend. Her death must have been a cruel blow to a man who had had his own share of personal grief.

Walter Scott's last years in Victoria were ones of isolation and depression. It was only by June 1935 that he began to feel somewhat better. On June 22, he wrote to his old friend, Reverend Inkster, a minister at Knox Church in Toronto. Scott had just had a day trip to downtown Victoria and he was feeling euphoric. He felt physically handicapped with a lame left leg, one eye was "totally blind," and he was unable to read with the other, yet his spirits were good enough to leave the house to visit the dentist and to get his hair cut; during his years of depression, both the doctor and barber had visited him at his home. He noted that over the past years he had even lost his ability to speak in public. He reminisced about a farewell party in 1920 for Reverend Inkster when the latter was leaving Victoria. When Scott rose to speak, his mind went blank. He did say a few words, but it was then that he knew his political days were over: "So an old political war horse, get him on his feet and prop him up, will always be able to say something, no matter how little intellect he has left."

Walter Scott died in a psychiatric institution with no family or loved ones present, yet he had been a popular Premier of Saskatchewan. He and his government enjoyed larger majorities after each general election. The people generally knew that he was ill and away a great deal but they still supported him. The opposition press and the Conservatives publicly criticized Scott's absences but the majority of the people continued to support Scott and his vision for the future of the province. They accepted him for who and what he was, believing that it was common for people, especially hard-working, talented people, to overwork and be away for lengthy periods of time. It was a common belief that with a bit of rest and relaxation, a person would return refreshed and ready to continue the battle. Even after Scott's resignation, he received letters from friends and supporters urging him to return to the political field.

Even though Scott was absent from the province for up to six months of every year, he was more than just a popular figurehead. As has been shown, his Cabinet delayed many key decisions until he returned to the province. Scott led his government on a broad philosophical plain and was content to rely on Calder and Motherwell for the implementation of the new programs. Calder seemed content to continue as the "second in command." Both he and the Liberal Party knew that they needed Scott to rally public support, particularly during election campaigns. Jim Ross and Jim Calder travelled with Scott when he was ill and Calder particularly kept the government functioning in his absence. They were quick, however, to spirit him out of town when a breakdown was imminent. Scott's colleagues in Saskatchewan were influential in his committal to Homewood, an Ontario psychiatric centre, which was out of the Saskatchewan eye. Even on his death, there was a cover-up as to the circumstances so that the people of Saskatchewan could remember him as the popular leader of old.

Conclusion

What kind of leader was Walter Scott? His style was pragmatic rather than dogmatic. He certainly had principles that he would defend, such as the need to eliminate the CPR tax exemption. Yet he was able to adjust his principles to follow the Liberal Party line on the retention of the Crown lands with the federal government. During his time in Ottawa, Scott learned the art of compromise and merits of delay. He lobbied hard for the interests of his constituency and the West and was able to follow the party line in exchange for larger compensation grants from the federal government. Scott had strong beliefs and far-reaching goals but was cautious not to implement a new program until he was convinced that the majority of the public was ready to support him. He did not throw out his point of view to the people and hope that they would follow. First, he carefully educated and guided the public. Having learned patience and sense of timing, he did not want to be too far ahead of popular support. Notwithstanding the delays, and compromises, Scott's long-term principles and goals remained intact.

Scott assumed portfolios within his own Cabinet that were the pressure points at the time. He was minister of Public Works during the crucial construction phase of the Legislative Building and minister of Education during the establishment of the University of Saskatchewan. At Oxbow, Scott announced the closing of the bars and on Valentine's Day, 1916, he announced that his government would grant the vote to women. He announced agricultural programs such as the cooperative grain elevator system even though he had a capable minister of Agriculture. Scott was in the centre of decision making and was clearly visible as the leader of the government.

Scott's guiding principles were that government could support society by regulation or by independent boards but he preferred not to have government directly involved in public ventures. Instead, he supported the cooperative principle. Government became involved with the sale of alcohol after the government closed the bars but this was done at arm's length through an independent board.

Even though Scott had been raised in a strong Presbyterian home, religion was not a determining factor in his adult life. He was married in a church but his funeral was in a private home. Scott defended the rights of Roman Catholics to practice their religion and to have religious instruction after school because he believed in these rights. However, it was also a fact that the Liberals depended on the largely Catholic immigrant vote. Scott's public policy was based on his search for a politically acceptable stance rather than religious dogma.

Another important principle in Scott's life was education. He did not have much formal education and he regretted having quit school after grade eight. Thus, he saw the importance of education for others and he continued to increase his knowledge and education even if it was not through formal schooling. Scott believed in the common school supported by a Department of Education with the rights of the minorities protected. He was rightfully very proud of the new university in Saskatoon.

As a member of Parliament for five years and then Premier of Saskatchewan for 11 years, Walter Scott represented the ideas and defended the interests of his constituents and his province. He had a keen sense of the ever-changing public mood. He was a supporter of

Liberal policy such as freer trade, the rights of minorities and public education. He believed that the role of the state was to protect the interests of the minorities and to build a public infrastructure that would serve all the citizens of the province. Scott's government presided over an era of unprecedented population growth and development in Saskatchewan. The government built roads, bridges, schools, court houses and a university and supported the expansion of the railway system within the province.

Behind all of these principles, programs and policies, who was Walter Scott? He was an effective public speaker but not as flamboyant as Frederick Haultain. Able to use bombast in debate and interrupt with interjections, Scott was a fiery speaker who could quickly arouse his audience to anger or laughter. He understood the Saskatchewan people and knew how to outmanoeuvre Haultain, who was often forced to abandon his original position and look indecisive, or defend a position that was unacceptable to the people of the province.

Scott's legacy was in line with his first election slogan: "Peace, Progress and Prosperity." Perhaps he was fortunate in being Premier during the expansion years, but he also led his province and he brought domestic peace to it as he had promised. Immigrants flooded into the province from all parts of Europe to settle the land and put it into production. Under Scott's leadership, Saskatchewan grew to be the third most populous province in Canada, prosperous with an expanding economy.

Scott was one of Saskatchewan's strongest Premiers, comparable to T.C. Douglas. The two men were Premiers in different times, but both were prepared to set a new course for the province. Scott had the challenge of leading a new province with a rapidly growing population, which needed governmental infrastructure. He supported the formation of cooperatives as a mechanism to deliver programs which he did not think the government alone could support financially. The Scott government's program was dedicated to strengthening the rural way of life. Much of the governmental infrastructure that is still in place today—from rural municipalities to liquor boards—was begun during Scott's time as Premier.

In 1916, Scott left office, unhappy and feeling like a man who had been defeated from within. He died alone in an Ontario psychiatric sanitarium. The Saskatchewan Legislature gave little notice to his passing, and the Saskatchewan newspapers reported his death but did not mention his illness or that he had died in a psychiatric hospital. Reverend Inkster, a longtime friend, performed the funeral service in London on March 26, 1938. Scott's body was then taken by train to Victoria for interment in Royal Oak Bay Burial Park beside his wife, Jessie. Thus, his final resting place is in neither his province of birth nor his adopted province, the one that he had helped to create. The tombstone inscription for Walter and Jessie shows the usual information of their birth and death dates, and contains the inscription: "Peace Perfect Peace." In the 1905 election campaign, Walter Scott had promised "Peace, Progress and Prosperity," and ever a proponent of consensus rather than confrontation, the concept of "peace" was a constant throughout his life.

More than 60 years after the interment, Scott's tombstone is covered with moss, grass clippings, and soil, ignored and almost forgotten—not unlike Scott himself. This is a sad irony, for Scott's legacy—the system of government and the civil service, the Legislative

GORDON BARNHART

The tombstone of Walter and Jessie Scott, Royal Oak Burial Park, Victoria, British Columbia.

Building, the University of Saskatchewan, and the many agricultural programs started by his government—still remains in the service of the people of the province. Yet few Saskatchewan citizens today recognize Scott's name. The Liberal Party hid from public view his years of inner turmoil and pain both during and after his premiership, to the point that the man and his accomplishments are not remembered by the generations who continue to benefit from his vision and leadership. Under Scott, Saskatchewan enjoyed peace, progress, and prosperity. Sadly, Scott himself never did.

Notes

1. For a more detailed account of Walter Scott's life and career, and in particular, full references for the quotations from the Scott correspondence, see Gordon L. Barnhart, "Peace, Progress and Prosperity: A Biography of the Hon. Walter Scott" (PhD dissertation, University of Saskatchewan, 1998). See also Gordon L. Barnhart, *Peace, Progress and Prosperity: A Biography of Saskatchewan's First Premier, T. Walter Scott* (Regina: Canadian Plains Research Center, 2000).

2. The official description of the events in Walter Scott's early life is from Scott's autobiography, the parliamentary guide, and from newspapers of the day.
3. *Historical Directory of Saskatchewan Newspapers, 1878–1983*. Prepared by Christine MacDonald. Published by the Saskatchewan Archives Board, Regina and Saskatoon 1984, 61. The title of this newspaper varies. It was the Regina *Leader*, March 1883 to November 1905, and became the *Morning Leader*, November 10, 1905, to April 1930.
4. Under election law at this time, any member of Parliament who was appointed to the Cabinet was required to resign his seat in the House of Commons and run in a by-election. In many cases, the by-election was not contested by the opposing party.
5. O.D. Skelton, *Life and Letters of Sir Wilfrid Laurier*, Vol. II (New York: The Century Company, 1922), 243.
6. C. Cecil Lingard, *Territorial Government in Canada: The Autonomy Question in the Old North-West Territories* (Toronto: University of Toronto Press, 1946), 241.
7. G.H.V. Bulyea was the commissioner who became the lieutenant-governor of Alberta. The two deputy commissioners who moved to the new Alberta public service were D.S. MacKenzie and John Stocks.
8. J.E. Murray, "The Provincial Capital Controversy in Saskatchewan," *Saskatchewan History* 5, no. 3 (1952): 99.
9. David R. Murray and Robert A. Murray, *The Prairie Builder: Walter Murray of Saskatchewan* (Edmonton: NeWest Press, 1984), 43.
10. Ibid.
11. Michael Hayden, *Seeking a Balance: The University of Saskatchewan, 1907–1982* (Vancouver: University of British Columbia Press, 1983), 12.
12. Ibid., 14.
13. J.E. Murray, "The Contest for the University of Saskatchewan," *Saskatchewan History* 12, no. 1 (1959): 4.
14. Ibid., 9.
15. University of Saskatchewan Archives, J.E. Murray Papers, Walter Murray to W. S., December (no date given), 1937.
16. Murray, "Contest," 22. See also Hayden, *Seeking a Balance*, 43. Hayden argues that the vote was actually 5–3, with Dixon voting for Regina.
17. The population of Saskatchewan in 1901 was 91,279, had climbed to 257,763 by 1906, and 492,432 by 1911 (Source: Census of Canada, 1901, 1906 and 1911).
18. Acres of field crops in production in Saskatchewan in 1900 were 655,537 and 9,136,868 in 1911 (Source: Census of Canada, 1901 and 1911).
19. Evelyn Eager, *Saskatchewan Government: Politics and Pragmatism* (Saskatoon: Western Producer Prairie Books, 1980), 47.
20. David E. Smith, *Prairie Liberalism: The Liberal Party in Saskatchewan, 1905–1971* (Toronto: University of Toronto Press, 1975), 55.
21. W.L. Morton, *The Progressive Party in Canada* (Toronto: University of Toronto Press, 1967), 35.
22. D.S. Spafford, "The Elevator Issue, the Organized Farmers and the Government, 1908–11," *Saskatchewan History* 15, no. 3 (1962): 84.
23. June Menzies, "Votes for Saskatchewan's Women" in Norman Ward and Duff Spafford (eds.), *Politics in Saskatchewan* (Don Mills, ON: Longmans Canada Limited, 1968), 80–81. A resolution, also called

a motion, may be moved by any member of the Legislative Assembly in order to create debate and to measure the mood of the House. Even though resolutions are not binding on the government, they can apply pressure on Cabinet to change its policies.

24. Christine MacDonald, "How Saskatchewan Women Got the Vote," *Saskatchewan History* 1, no. 3 (1948): 7.
25. Catherine L. Cleverdon, *The Woman Suffrage Movement in Canada* (Toronto: University of Toronto Press, 1978), 46.
26. Menzies, "Votes," 90.
27. Of the 27 accusations raised by Bradshaw, 2 were dropped by counsel, 15 were dismissed by the Commissions. Of the remaining 10, 4 private members were charged in a court of law. E.H. Devline, MLA and H.C. Pierce pleaded guilty to charges of issuing forged documents and were sentenced to three years each in jail. C.H. Cawthorpe, MLA, was released due to a hung jury and Gerhard Ens, MLA, was cleared of the charges. J.P. Brown, chief clerk of the board of highway commissioners, was found guilty of issuing forged documents and sentenced to seven years in the Prince Albert penitentiary. See J. William Brennan, "A Political History of Saskatchewan, 1905–1929" (PhD dissertation, University of Alberta, 1976), 327.
28. Raymond Huel, "Pastor vs. Politician: The Reverend Murdock MacKinnon and Premier Walter Scott's Amendment to the School Act," *Saskatchewan History* 32, no. 2 (1979): 62.
29. Ibid.

William M. Martin

Ted Regehr

Martin with Prince of Wales, 1919 (SAB RB 3730).

Martin, formal portrait, c. 1917 (SAB RA 10 (1)).

Martin at the National Liberal Convention, 1919 (SAB RB 4545).

SASKATCHEWAN PREMIERS OF THE 20TH CENTURY

William M. Martin, 1916–1922

William Martin, politician and jurist, was born on August 23, 1876, in Norwich, Ontario, and died June 22, 1970, in Regina, Saskatchewan. He was a member of Parliament from 1908 until 1916, and served as Premier of Saskatchewan from 1916 until 1922, when he was appointed to the Saskatchewan Court of Appeal. He served as a judge on that court from 1922 until 1961, and was the chief justice from 1941 until his retirement in 1961.[1] He married Violette Florence Thompson of Mitchell, Ontario, in 1905. They had three sons: Walter Melville Martin who also studied law and later became a judge, Douglas Thompson Martin, and William Kenneth Martin, both medical doctors. Mrs. Martin predeceased her husband in 1946. Since this volume focusses on the biographies of Saskatchewan Premiers, this chapter will discuss in detail Martin's political career, but refer only briefly and in general terms to his work and influence as a judge.

Family Background and Early Career in Ontario

William Melville Martin was the son William Martin and Christina Jamieson. Both parents were of Scottish ancestry. The family moved, shortly after William's birth, from Norwich to Exeter, where his father served as minister of the Presbyterian church for 26 years. There young William was raised, in the words of one of his political successors, "on porridge, progress and predestination."[2]

Young William received his early education in the Exeter public school and the Clinton Collegiate in Huron County. In 1894 he entered the University of Toronto where he distinguished himself, both as a scholar and an athlete who earned awards in lacrosse and several other university sports. He graduated in 1898 with an honours degree in Classics, and then attended the Ontario School of Pedagogy in Hamilton where he obtained a teacher's certificate with a specialization in Classics. He taught for two years at the Harrison High School in Wellington County, during which time he became involved in a minor way in local Liberal politics.

Martin returned to Toronto in 1901 to take up the study of law at Osgoode Hall. That was followed by further study and practical experience with the law firm of T.C. Robinette in Toronto. Then, in 1903, he followed the call of the West. He later said young lawyers in Toronto at that time were only earning $50 a month.[3] The prospects in western Canada were much better. Martin's cousin, James Balfour, who had been active in Wellington County Reform and Liberal politics, had already moved West, and established a flourishing law practice in Regina. Contacts with prominent western Liberals brought Balfour clients and also made it possible for him to participate in a number of profitable land and development projects. In 1903, William Martin accepted Balfour's invitation to join him in Regina.

Much of the legal work of the firm at the time involved problems related to land and property issues. Homestead, pre-emption, abandonment, and succession or inheritance

SAB RA 3655

Men swimming at Regina Beach, c. 1909. William Martin is second from the right, while his cousin, James Balfour, is third from the right.

matters, and real-estate speculation in which lawyers as well as their clients participated, dominated court dockets. There were, however, also cases involving social problems. Neglected and dependent children, distressed wives or widows, drunken brawls, prostitution and numerous petty crimes were aspects of robust but sometimes uncouth pioneer life. Young William Martin handled a number of relatively routine cases, but he also became involved, very early in his legal career, in at least one quite unusual and controversial case. Edward Shoefelt, a notorious character variously described as a cattle rustler, horse thief, and common criminal, engaged Martin's services in a case to be heard at the small rural courthouse in Willow Bunch in what was then the District of Assiniboia. Shoefelt was despised in the rural and ranching communities, and Martin attracted considerable attention when he not only agreed to defend Shoefelt, but accompanied the accused, without escort or protection, from Regina to Willow Bunch for his preliminary hearing. Neither the local ranchers and homesteaders nor the presiding judge at Willow Bunch had much sympathy for the accused, but Martin's skill in defending him, and his courage in travelling with the accused without protection, enhanced the young lawyer's reputation.[4]

Introduction to Politics

James Balfour, Martin's cousin, was a friend, business partner and strong political supporter of Walter Scott. Scott, a newspaper man from Ontario, had been elected in 1900 as the Liberal member of Parliament (MP) for the vast constituency of Assiniboia West, and re-elected in the federal election of 1904. But when the two new provinces of Saskatchewan and Alberta were created in 1905, Walter Scott was invited by the lieutenant-governor to form Saskatchewan's first government.[5] Scott accepted the invitation and resigned his seat in the federal House of Commons, necessitating a by-election. Martin, as a member of a law firm with close Liberal ties, was encouraged to seek the nomination. He declined, and returned to Ontario shortly after the by-election to get married.

The constituency of Assiniboia West was divided in a 1906 redistribution, and as the federal election of 1908 approached, Martin was encouraged to accept the Liberal nomination in the newly created Regina constituency. He reluctantly agreed. He was still building his legal career and establishing his household in Regina. The rigours of a political campaign, followed by the necessary travel and prolonged absences from home as a western representative in distant Ottawa, were daunting.

The federal election, held on October 26, 1908, was preceded by a Saskatchewan provincial election on August 14. Promises of more railways, increased telephone service, road construction, readers for schools in the province, and the creation of rural municipalities were the major issues in the provincial campaign.[6] Some of these issues were matters under provincial jurisdiction, but chartering and providing financial support for more railways was primarily a federal responsibility and became the most important issue in the federal campaign.

The rigours of the campaign must have reinforced every candidate's enthusiasm for improved transportation facilities. The Regina constituency still extended from an area approximately 100 kilometres north of the city all the way to the American border. Campaigning in such a vast area with few good roads was an ordeal. More than 50 years later Martin recalled some of the horrors of that experience. He had engaged two men with a horse-drawn buckboard wagon to take him from farmstead to farmstead in the sprawling constituency. Since the two drivers each allegedly weighed more than 300 pounds, there was precious little space left between them on the seat of the buckboard for the tall, lean politician. The situation was even worse when political campaigners were obliged to stay overnight in the homes of supportive constituents. Sharing a bed with one, and sometimes both, of his overweight companions was not conducive to a restful respite for the neophyte politician. But the food served in those pioneer homes was much better, and after a hearty country breakfast, the tribulations of the night were soon forgotten.[7]

Martin later claimed that he did not directly canvass for the votes of those he met. He just told people who he was. Other accounts, however, indicate that he also included glowing accounts of what the federal Liberal Party was doing for western farmers in those introductions. These presentations, and whatever personal appeal the Ontario-trained and Regina-based lawyer was able to offer his agricultural constituents, were sufficient to carry the Regina constituency with a majority of 760 votes out of a total of 7,848 votes cast.

Martin's Federal Political Career

The Liberals won nine of the 10 Saskatchewan seats in the 1908 federal election. Only two of the nine members elected had previous experience in the federal Parliament, while two others had served in the provincial Legislature. William Martin, however, had strong political family connections in Ontario, and quickly established himself as a leading spokesperson for Saskatchewan. His first major speech in the House of Commons was made in support of federal financial assistance for the Grand Trunk Pacific Railway, but he included in it numerous other issues of interest and concern to western farmers. He apparently relied on Premier Walter Scott and other provincial politicians for appropriate information. A worried farmer had written to Scott in 1908, expressing concern that Martin's training in law and five years in a Regina law office might not fit him to understand the conditions affecting farmers. The farmer then outlined a number of problems faced by farmers.[8] Scott must have shared the letter with Martin since every problem identified in it was addressed in Martin's first major speech. The need for more branch lines, high freight rates, the federal tariff which increased the cost of machinery that farmers had to buy, and the shortage of railway cars to carry western grain to market in a timely manner, were all mentioned. In the speech, Martin blamed the spread between the track and street price for wheat on a shortage of railway cars.[9] That was, at best, a partial explanation and seemed to reflect an incomplete understanding of western grain handling and grain transportation problems.

Martin faced a trickier situation later in the session. The federal Liberals had created a three-member Board of Railway Commissioners which was to regulate a great variety of matters, including the freight rates charged by the railways. This required expert knowledge and understanding of the industry. The Conservatives sensed an opportunity to embarrass the government by moving an amendment which required that at least one of the commissioners must be a farmer. The potential for mischief if that amendment carried was enormous. Maritime, central Canadian and western farmers agreed on some aspects of Canadian rail polices, but sharply disagreed on others. It also seemed likely that any western farm member would demand sharply reduced freight rates without reference to the competitive conditions faced by the railways. Appointment of a farm member might then result in demands that other appointees represent the corporate interests of the railways, or of Canadian manufacturers or shippers. Special interest representation on a federal regulatory agency seemed a recipe for deadlock. The federal government therefore rejected the amendment, arguing that an adequate understanding of the issues was more important than the occupation of the appointees. William Martin rose to defend the government position with a motion which expressed "full confidence in the government to exercise wise discretion in appointments to the railway commission."[10]

A review of the *Debates* of the House of Commons during the years when Martin was a federal MP does not reveal any outstanding speeches. At various times, he raised issues of concern to western farmers and other constituents in Regina, and he made several speeches in support of new railway company incorporations. During the 1910–11 session, he worked hard to ensure the federal incorporation of the Grain Growers Grain Company, which had been granted a charter by the provincial government of Manitoba. Concerns and interests of the North-West Mounted Police, whose headquarters were located in his Regina constituency, were raised by Martin several times, and there were complaints about patronage appointments by the federal Conservatives after their 1911 election victory.

In the heated 1911 debates over a proposed reciprocity treaty with the United States, William Martin strongly supported the government position, but made no major speeches in the House of Commons on that topic until after the election. In Saskatchewan, federal tariffs were the overriding issue in the 1911 election, and the Liberals were again elected in nine of the 10 constituencies in the province. Martin's margin of victory was significantly larger in 1911 than it had been in 1908.

In the ensuing legislative session, Martin became increasingly active. He made a stirring speech attacking Conservative trade policies. He was particularly concerned when the federal government, in accordance with a recommendation from the Canadian Manufacturers' Association, created a tariff commission. That, it seemed to Martin and his constituents, was an attempt to shuffle off to a biased but allegedly independent agency the responsibility to recommend tariff increases which would be very unpopular in western Canada.

Martin also launched an aggressive campaign for the transfer of the natural resources of western Canada to provincial control when the Conservative government extended the boundaries of Manitoba northward to Hudson's Bay. It was a longstanding western grievance that the federal government had retained control Crown lands and natural resources in the prairie provinces when those resources in all the other provinces were under provincial jurisdiction. After the Conservative election victory in 1911, Martin also aggressively championed the construction of the moribund Hudson's Bay Railway. And, as a good MP, he raised various issues of local interest, ranging from the cost of the armoury buildings in Regina to the dismissal of a local postmaster and the distribution of seed grain.

A major review of western railway freight rates was begun by the Board of Railway Commissioners in 1912, following a formal appeal by the city of Regina. An agreement between the Manitoba provincial government and the Canadian Northern Railway had resulted in significant rate reductions of traffic moving from Manitoba to the Lakehead. Reginans demanded that comparable rate reductions be extended westward to their city. Railway and federal officials argued there was not yet sufficient traffic to justify such reductions.[11] Both sought to delay the hearings of the officially independent Board of Railway Commissioners. This drew a vigorous response from Martin, who argued that "all representatives from the western provinces know that there is scarcely a question in regard to which more time is devoted in the West or of which more is said than this question of freight rates."[12]

William Martin also took considerable interest in matters pertaining to the judicial system, and in 1914 he specifically addressed problems arising due to the low salaries earned by judges. He was critical of government efforts to economize in this aspect of public service. On May 12, 1914, he said in the House of Commons: "if the Government are [sic] going to practice economy, cutting down or keeping low, the salaries of judges would seem to me to be a very poor place to begin it. It would be better to begin in the Militia Department and cut down the construction of drill-halls, or perhaps in the Department of Public Works." He demanded that the federal minister of Justice appoint more district court judges in Saskatchewan, but warned that "Unless the salaries are made adequate to the position the minister will not be able to get the best men to occupy the position of District Court judges in the western provinces."[13]

Martin did not participate in the parliamentary debates regarding either the declaration (in August 1914) or the early conduct of World War I. His one war-related intervention in 1915 pertained to judges in the active militia. Some district and superior court judges, who were also members of the militia, received militia promotions. But they were not allowed to leave their judicial posts in which they were paid less. Martin suggested "that a man in that position ought either to be relieved of his position as a judge or be given the opportunity to go to the front and show what he is made of."[14]

SAB RB 4545
William Martin (third from left) with a group of other delegates at the National Liberal Convention in 1919.

It is never easy to assess the effectiveness of an MP, but William Martin evidently impressed his contemporaries. At the time of his death, the *Globe and Mail* mistakenly reported that Martin had been offered the leadership of the federal Liberal Party after Laurier's defeat in 1911.[15] He was, however, considered a serious potential leadership candidate after Laurier's death in 1919. He refused to become a candidate, choosing instead to support and nominate long-time Finance minister William Fielding (who lost to William Lyon Mackenzie King). But Emmet Hall, a judicial colleague and admirer, insisted that if Martin had been a candidate for the leadership of the federal Liberal Party in 1919 he would have won.[16] That is speculation, but it demonstrates that Martin was regarded as a bright and competent MP.

The Call of Saskatchewan

The Saskatchewan Liberal government led by Premier Walter Scott had followed cautiously progressive, farmer-friendly policies. While careful not to get ahead of public sentiment, Scott took pride in the passage of socially progressive but controversial legislation on issues such as temperance, votes for women, property rights of wives and widows, and improvements in the province's educational system. That approach had been endorsed by the voters in three successive elections in 1905, 1908 and 1912. Scott and his key ministers ran a competent and prudent but reform- and development-minded administration well suited to the sentiments of the electors.

Deputy Premier James A. Calder had created a strong and effective grassroots political organization, and the government seemed well entrenched. But in 1916, it faced several serious problems. Premier Scott suffered from ill health which resulted in frequent and prolonged absences from the province. In his absence, Calder ran the government, and generally did so effectively. But in February 1916, J.E. Bradshaw, the Conservative member of the Legislative Assembly (MLA), charged that there were serious irregularities in the government which included the acceptance of bribes by some of its members. He demanded that a royal commission be established to investigate the charges. Attempts by the Liberals to refer the matter to a legislative committee failed, and in March, Martin was invited to meet with key provincial Liberals. Calder, who knew most about party affairs, was confident that the charges could not be proven, and it was agreed that they should be referred to three separate royal commissions. The first, headed by Sir Frederick Haultain, the former leader of the opposition, was to investigate allegations of corruption in the construction of an asylum in Battleford, a jail in Regina, and in the Department of Telephones. The second, chaired by Judge Wetmore, was to examine road construction contracts, while the third, chaired by Brown Elwood, was to investigate charges that some MLAs had taken bribes to oppose proposed changes in the liquor legislation or in return for the awarding of liquor licenses.

The allegations of graft and corruption in government coincided with another unfortunate development. It involved an emotional dispute between Premier Scott and the Reverend Murdock MacKinnon, the minister of Knox Presbyterian Church in Regina where Scott attended. The dispute involved interpretations of the separate school provisions of the Autonomy Bills which had created the provinces of Saskatchewan and Alberta. That legislation provided for tax-supported public and separate schools. In 1912, a judge had ruled in favour of Roman Catholic taxpayers who wanted to opt out of the separate school system and instead dedicate their taxes to the public system. That, in Scott's opinion, violated the agreement reached in 1904 when he was a member of the federal government which passed the Autonomy Bills. There was also concern that if Roman Catholics could opt out of the separate system, there would be demands of a reciprocal right for non-Catholics who wished to support the separate system. As a result Scott introduced an amendment to the Saskatchewan School Act which required that school taxes paid by Roman Catholics be dedicated to the separate school system.

The legislation was unpopular with many Protestant leaders who were eager to strengthen what they described as a "national" school system. They demanded that Roman Catholic taxpayers have the right to dedicate their taxes to the public system, but that no non-Catholic taxpayers or businesses be allowed to dedicate their taxes to separate Roman Catholic schools. The Reverend Murdock MacKinnon of Regina was particularly outspoken in defense of this position. On December 26, 1915, with Scott in the congregation, MacKinnon preached a long sermon denouncing government educational policies.

Scott had his revenge on February 25, 1916. With MacKinnon in the visitor's gallery, Scott gave a detailed account of the history of provincial school legislation. It was, for the most part, a factual recitation, but Scott ended his speech on an emotional note. He described MacKinnon who, in his view, was demanding the breaking of the terms of the

Autonomy Bills, as a "moral leper," and went on to say that "the intellectual and spiritual leper is very much more dangerous, especially when he is found in the most sacred position in our civilization."[17] The speech was a political disaster, particularly, of course, among Presbyterian voters, but also among others who were opposed to separate schools for Roman Catholics.

Scott returned for the legislative session in June 1916, but evidence of his deteriorating health, his dispute with MacKinnon, and the allegations of graft and corruption, intensified talk of a reorganization of the government before the approaching election. James Calder, as deputy and frequently acting Premier, and one of the chief Liberal Party organizers, seemed the obvious heir apparent, but he was seriously tainted by the allegations of scandal. No other member of the Cabinet was regarded as a suitable successor. Nevertheless, close friends of Scott urged that, in view of his deteriorating health, he retire from politics. Scott reluctantly agreed to resign, effective October 20, 1916.

Upon receipt of Scott's letter of resignation, Lieutenant-Governor Lake called on James Calder to form a government. Calder declined, stating that he proposed to stand as a candidate in the next federal election. The lieutenant-governor then, on October 19, 1916, called on William Martin, who had a number of attributes which made him an attractive candidate for the premiership. His record as a federal MP was, if not brilliant, certainly honourable. He was not contaminated by the allegations of scandal, and he was a devout and committed Presbyterian. He shared Scott's interpretation of the Autonomy Bills, but also agreed with MacKinnon that the existence of a dual school system was unfortunate. Where Scott antagonized MacKinnon, the Presbyterians, and other Protestant leaders, Martin agreed with them and had their confidence.

Taking Control, 1916–17

Martin had been in close communication with the Saskatchewan ministers for months before Scott's resignation and moved quickly after his appointment to form his Cabinet. He took over the premiership and as minister of Education, Calder became president of the Executive Council, minister of Railways and minister of Highways, W.R. Motherwell continued as minister of Agriculture, W.F.A. Turgeon as attorney general and provincial secretary, and George Langley as minister of Municipal Affairs. The only new member of the Cabinet was Charles Avery Dunning (who would succeed Martin as Premier of Saskatchewan), who was appointed to the influential position of provincial treasurer.

The first Martin Cabinet did not suggest a radical change of government priorities or policies, but the appointment of Dunning as provincial treasurer strengthened the government's close links with agricultural organizations. Dunning had come from England to take up farming in Saskatchewan in the same year that Martin came to the province as a lawyer. He had provided leadership in the organization of the Saskatchewan Co-operative Elevator Company in 1911, and then served as its general manager. He was also a vice-president of the powerful Saskatchewan Grain Growers Association (SGGA), and a member of the Canadian Council of Agriculture. His appointment, and the continuing presence of Motherwell and Langley, both influential farm leaders, demonstrated the new administration's commitment to farm interests.

Martin also moved quickly and decisively to mend some political fences. As a devout Presbyterian, he made peace with the Reverend Murdock MacKinnon. An editorial in the Regina *Leader-Post* after his death noted that Martin was a "pillar of the church" in the most practical sense, and that he got great satisfaction out of his relationship with First Presbyterian Church.[18] He could explain to MacKinnon and other Protestant leaders that measures which undermined the financial support by Roman Catholics for the separate school system were fraught with serious constitutional, legal and political problems. It was more prudent to ensure that the separate schools adhered to the approved curriculum, and met other provincial standards, than to resort to measures which would result in both legal and political challenges.

Protestant leaders were also concerned about the allegedly poor quality of instruction provided in schools for children of eastern European immigrants, who were not learning English and becoming assimilated into Canadian society quickly enough to satisfy the wartime patriots. But Martin was able to buy time by appointing Harold W. Foght, a rural school specialist from Washington, D.C., to prepare a study of conditions in Saskatchewan's rural schools. The government needed accurate information before addressing alleged problems in the schools. The emotional heat of the school issue was thus lowered, and further action deferred until after the provincial election.

The three royal commissions investigating charges of graft and corruption in the government reported either late in 1916 or early in 1917. They cleared former Premier Scott and all Cabinet ministers, but found four Liberal MLAs guilty of using their influence to secure favours from liquor lobbyists or of accepting bribes. Martin demanded the resignations of all four. Two complied, although one then ran unsuccessfully in the by-election created by his resignation. A third was expelled from the Legislature and the fourth, who could not be expelled from the Legislature because he had not been found guilty of action justifying expulsion, was expelled from the Liberal Party. Thus purified, the party was better able to prepare for the next provincial election. It would be the first election in which women, who had been granted the franchise in 1916, would be able to vote.

In November 1916 Martin faced what provincial Liberals regarded as a dirty trick by their opponents. The Regina *Post*, a Conservative paper, published what were allegedly confidential Cabinet discussions and proceedings regarding changes in mortgage legislation. Martin moved quickly to quell any suggestion of impropriety by appointing a royal commission to investigate the source of the alleged disclosure of confidential information. At the hearings, the *Post* editor testified that he had obtained the information from the Premier himself, and gave a specific date. Four witnesses proved that the Premier could not have provided the information on the date indicated. The editor then changed the date. The Premier indicated that he had indeed met with the *Post* editor on the second indicated date, but there had been no discussion of the mortgage legislation; he admitted that a typewritten document on that subject had disappeared from his desk. That, the commissioners concluded, was the real source of the information. The quick and decisive action by the Premier in having the matter investigated, and his disciplining of errant members of the Liberal caucus, was praised as an indication that he would run a scandal-free government.[19]

Martin's First Legislation Session as Premier

The sixth session of the Legislature since the 1912 election opened on 25 January 1917. There was a general expectation that it would be followed almost immediately by a provincial election, and was marked by several important pre-election initiatives. The Legislature passed amendments to the Saskatchewan Temperance Act which further restricted the manufacture, storage, transportation and sale of alcoholic beverages. This earned it the gratitude and support of many reform-minded voters, and particularly of the Women's Section of the SGGA, the Women's Christian Temperance Movement, and the International Order of the Daughters of the Empire (IODE), in which Mrs. Martin was an active participant. The measure was also praised because grain used in the manufacture of alcohol would be used instead in support of the war effort. Reduced consumption would also avoid the debilitating effects of alcohol on the health and strength of the soldiers.

The farm vote was of great importance to the government. Pre-war financial scares and wartime exigencies had seriously restricted the amount and cost of credit available to farmers.[20] An international commission, to which Saskatchewan had named two members, had investigated the problem. The government responded by establishing a government mortgage lending organization for farmers. It provided for the establishment of a $5 million fund through the sale of government bonds. The fund, to be administered by a three-member, government-appointed board, would make loans to farmers at interest rates covering only the cost of raising the money.

The Martin government continued the Scott government's policy of providing financial and other support for farmer-organized cooperatives, incorporating several new ones. There were also reforms of the juvenile courts, and provision was made for direct soldier representation in the Legislative Assembly: two soldier members would represent the men in France and Belgium, and one would represent those in England. Another important legislative change in the 1917 session was an amendment to the School Act to make school attendance compulsory for all children between the ages of 7 and 14. That amendment was designed to meet criticism by those concerned about inadequate instruction, particularly in immigrant communities. It also responded to a genuine concern by government members that not enough was being done to ensure that all children received the instruction they needed to become productive and loyal Canadians. In general, the 1917 session demonstrated that Premier Martin would follow the progressive, pro-agrarian, but prudent course of his predecessor.

The 1917 Provincial Election

A large convention and rally of Liberals was held shortly after the legislative session and marked the real start of the election campaign. A new "Bill of Rights" for Saskatchewan was announced with great fanfare, promising vigorous defense of provincial rights, and demanding tariff reductions and the transfer to the province of Crown lands and natural resources. Changes designed to broaden and reform the organization of the Liberal Party were also announced.

The Legislature was dissolved on June 2, 1917, with the election date set for June 26. Canada was at war, but the conduct of the war itself was not a major issue in the election.

SAB RB 4621

Martin as Premier, c. 1917.

Both major political parties in the province strongly supported the war effort. Patriotic wartime passions nevertheless influenced the campaign. The Liberals had established close links with influential leaders in many immigrant communities. Anglo-Canadians, including many Protestant and organized farm leaders, had been concerned for many years about the large number of immigrants from eastern Europe. Serious doubts were expressed regarding the suitability of these people as prospective Canadian citizens, and their ability and willingness to become assimilated into Canadian society. Many of these immigrants, moreover, came from countries with which Canada was then at war. Hostilities toward these people were fanned by stories of gruesome atrocities committed by enemy soldiers overseas. The propaganda, moreover, sometimes tarred all Germans and Austro-Hungarians, whether they lived overseas or in Canada, with the same brush. Saskatchewan Liberals were accused of being soft and not taking adequate measures when dealing with these people.

Opposition critics, however, seriously overstated the case. There was little evidence of disloyalty in the immigrant communities—indeed, most of the immigrants had come to Canada because they were not happy with conditions and governments in their old homelands. These were people who, in spite of attachments to Old World customs, had already made important contributions to the economic growth and development of the province. There were a few unfortunate and ill-advised expressions of support for kinfolk in the old homeland, but these were quickly repudiated and retracted. There was also some resentment that Mennonites and Doukhobors relied on commitments made to them at the time of their immigration that they need not serve in the Canadian armed forces. But even people inclined to see every mishap as evidence of sabotage by enemy aliens could find little convincing evidence of disloyalty. Liberals argued that their education policies, and particularly compulsory school attendance legislation, would facilitate the integration of immigrants into Canadian society. Beyond that, the Liberals demanded fairness and tolerance in the treatment of immigrants, thus neutralizing the anti-immigrant sentiment. The legislative and administrative record of the government was good, and the Liberals won 50 of the 59 seats in the Legislature. It was the first provincial election in which women were allowed to vote, and they tended to support the government which had given them the franchise.

Union Government and the 1917 Federal Election

The political landscape of Canada changed dramatically shortly after the Saskatchewan provincial election. The allied overseas war effort was not going well: casualties were high, recruitments were lagging, and victory was not yet in sight. The resulting manpower crisis in the Canadian Expeditionary Force prompted the federal government to propose compulsory conscription for military service. This was strongly opposed by some nationalist French-Canadian leaders, who were convinced that the underlying causes of the war were rival imperialist aspirations which were of no immediate concern to them. In western Canada, by contrast, there was very strong support for the war effort and enlistments were much higher. Conscription for military service was interpreted by many as an attempt to force French Canadians to do their patriotic duty. It was consequently unpopular in Quebec, but popular in western Canada.

Attempting to diffuse these regional differences, Prime Minister Borden invited Liberals to join his Conservatives in a Union government in support of conscription policy. Sir Wilfrid Laurier, leader of the federal Liberals, declined the offer, but most Liberals from the Maritimes, Ontario and western Canada supported Borden. A new Union (Conservative/Liberal) coalition government, with 12 Conservative and 10 Liberal Cabinet ministers, was formed in October 1917. James A. Calder, Saskatchewan's former Deputy Premier and chief political organizer, became minister of the sensitive Immigration and Colonization Department in the new government. Partisan political battles were set aside for the duration of the war. Martin supported the conscription policy of the Union government, but he and other provincial Liberals remained opposed to tariff and other federal economic policies. The Premier also insisted that conscription should apply to all resources of the nation, including the profits of tariff-protected manufacturers and suppliers of war materials.

The Union government passed not only its conscription legislation, but also a draconian new Wartime Elections Act which disenfranchised all immigrants from countries with which Canada was at war, who had become Canadian citizens after March 1902, and all Mennonite and Doukhobor conscientious objectors. But it extended the franchise to close female relatives of men serving in the Canadian armed forces. These newly enfranchised women were sometimes called "the patriotic women of Canada," suggesting that those disenfranchised by the legislation were not patriotic. This contributed to increased hostility toward the "enemy" immigrants, and to demands that the provincial government do more to ensure their speedy assimilation or, failing that, deportation back to the countries from which they had come. Such demands undermined long-time Saskatchewan Liberal efforts to promote tolerance and acceptance of the immigrants who, in return, usually supported the Liberal Party.

A federal election was called for December 17, 1917. In Saskatchewan, Liberal and Conservative strategists worked together in support of Unionist candidates in many constituencies, and supporters of the Union government were elected in all 16 federal constituencies in the province. It nevertheless created a rift in Liberal ranks. Traditional party loyalties were disrupted, thereby facilitating the rise of protest movements, led by those who agreed with the Union government's military policies but not with its tariff and other economic policies.

The Conflict with "Old Colony" Mennonites

Wartime passions, fanned by the patriotic fervour of the 1917 federal election campaign, found some unusual victims in western Canada. School attendance, particularly in many non-Anglo-Saxon communities, increased significantly after the government passed its compulsory school attendance legislation in 1917. These schools were expected to teach children the English language and a patriotic pride in British and English-Canadian values, ideals and accomplishments. This was acceptable in most immigrant communities, but there were exceptions. The Doukhobors, while generally supportive of the public schools and of instruction in the English language, were offended by the glorification of war and Canadian military exploits, and the prescribed singing of the "God Save the King" and flag-raising ceremonies. Local school boards in those communities, however, tried to take advantage of curriculum choices to minimize the most blatant forms of English-Canadian chauvinism.

Some Mennonites offered much more determined resistance, and several thousand eventually left the province because of the school legislation.[21] The Mennonites living in Saskatchewan at that time were a mixed lot. Some had come from Russia to Manitoba in the 1870s and moved west after 1890. Others had moved north from the United States, while still others had come from Prussia or Russia after 1890. The migrants of the 1870s came mainly from the original Mennonite or "Old Colony" settlement in Russia, or from that settlement's "Bergthal" daughter colony. One of the main reasons for their migration was a desire to escape Russian military and educational reforms. In negotiations with the federal government, these prospective immigrants had been promised exemption from military service and "the fullest privilege of exercising their religious principles ... without any kind of molestation or restriction whatever, and the same privilege extends to the education of their children in schools." These assurances had been incorporated into a federal Order-in-Council, but with one significant modification. The words, "as provided by law" were added. Since education in Canada is primarily a provincial rather than a federal responsibility, the changed wording effectively destroyed the legal basis for the educational privileges the Mennonite immigrants of the 1870s thought they had been granted. That, however, only became evident after both the Manitoba and Saskatchewan governments passed compulsory school attendance legislation which the Mennonites rejected.

Premier Martin met with a number of "Old Colony" Mennonite leaders in an attempt to persuade them to send their children to the public schools, but his demands were rejected. Others, more familiar with Mennonite history and traditions, offered to mediate the dispute, but these overtures were rejected by the Premier. He believed the demand for compliance with provincial education laws was reasonable, and that any compromise was inappropriate. This was probably an accurate assessment of public opinion regarding the Mennonite problem. There was, during and immediately after the war, very little support for German-speaking immigrants who refused all forms of military service and insisted on German-language instruction in their schools.

When it became clear that the government would not agree to a compromise, the "Old Colony" Mennonite leaders began to explore emigration to other countries. Premier Martin initially thought this was an empty threat, but his response was clear: "If the price of retaining them is to tolerate their educational methods and abrogate the provisions of the compulsory School Attendance Act, it would be better for them to leave the Province as they threaten to do."[22]

As Mennonite emigration plans matured, they asked that the fines, which hit many of the parents very hard, be suspended. Specifically, one of the Mennonite leaders pleaded with the Premier: "I beg you, Honourable Sir, to be good enough to grant us two years time to leave this country if you consider us a bad class [of] people, we believe that we are worthy of such a privilege at least."[23] The Premier rejected the request. The result was a mass migration, at great financial cost, of several thousand "conservative" or "traditional" Mennonites from Saskatchewan to Mexico and Paraguay. Opposition critics at the time demanded even harsher measures and there were expressions of gratitude by the Saskatchewan Synod of the Presbyterian Church on the "success the government has attained in its firm dealing with the Mennonite problem." The Synod then went on to recommend that "the manual of Religious Exercises, now being prepared by a Committee of the Churches, should be brought into use in our Public Schools as soon as possible."[24] Tolerance of religious or educational dissent was in short supply in Saskatchewan during and immediately after the war and public schools were the front line in the domestic patriotic campaign. At the time of his retirement in 1922, Premier Martin was congratulated by both Conservative and Liberal editorialists on his success in dealing with the Mennonite problem.

The Language Issue in Saskatchewan Public Schools

The patriotic passions roused during the war, and exacerbated in the 1917 federal election, shifted in 1918. There was, with the exception of the "Old Colony" Mennonites, general compliance with the compulsory school attendance legislation. Patriotic vigilantes then pointed out that in some Roman Catholic separate schools in French-speaking communities, and in some public schools in non-Anglo-Saxon communities, English was not the sole language of instruction. Patriotic zealots argued that any use of other languages in the schools undermined their effectiveness as agents of assimilation. That concern, according to the *Canadian Annual Review of Public Affairs*, became "the chief issue of the year in Saskatchewan" in 1918."[25]

Under the educational provisions of the Autonomy Bills, some instruction in a language other than English was allowed during the last hour of the day. And, in some French-Canadian communities, the primary language of instruction during the first two grades could be French. In the higher grades, French could be taught as a subject if the local Board passed a resolution to that effect. Special religious and language instruction in other schools could be provided only during the last half-hour of the school day. In 1918, however, various school trustee, grain grower, religious and women's groups bombarded the government with demands that all instruction in any language other than English be prohibited. The tolerant and gradualist policies followed after 1905 by the Scott government no longer seemed acceptable, even though Premier Martin pointed out that in 1918 only 214 of the province's 4,200 schools availed themselves of the provisions which permitted them to supplement instruction in English with another language.

There was an exceptionally nasty and divisive meeting in Saskatoon of the provincial school trustees on February 20–21, 1918, which greatly inflamed the problem. P.M. Friesen, the president, was a "progressive" Mennonite from the Rush Lake district. He supported the compulsory school attendance legislation, but also allowed speakers who supported existing language rights to express their views at the convention. Those speakers, however, were booed, jeered and not allowed by other delegates to complete their speeches. Efforts by Friesen to maintain order and appropriate procedures were shouted down, and he was forced to vacate the chair. In the ensuing election, Friesen was replaced in office by J.F. Bryant, a fire-breathing, patriotic Protestant zealot and Conservative partisan. Bryant seemed determined to discredit the Martin government's efforts to promote a firm but also tolerant policy when dealing with educational matters in immigrant communities. Delegates to the annual meeting of the SGGA, and of its Women's Section, passed similar resolutions.

Three reports published in 1918 greatly influenced Martin's attitude and his resolve to bring in and enforce school reforms. The first, a commissioned report by Harold W. Foght,[26] was critical of the administration and of the instruction offered in many Saskatchewan schools, and specifically of the instruction in non-English-speaking communities.

The second study was published by E.H. Oliver, the principal of the Presbyterian Theological College in Saskatoon and vice-president of the Saskatchewan Public Education League. He visited or obtained information about 32 private Mennonite schools with 800 children. The language of instruction in these schools was German. Teachers, sometimes with only dubious qualifications, followed their own curriculum. Oliver's assessment of the quality of education provided for these children was scathing. He had not, in fact, visited most of the schools, but concluded that they provided what he said could not, by any stretch of the imagination, be considered as an adequate education. Oliver's ideal of what schools should offer is indicated in his statement that "the function of our schools must not be to make Mennonites, nor Protestants, nor Roman Catholics, but Canadian citizens."[27] He advocated creation of public schools in all the Mennonite communities, and rigid enforcement of compulsory attendance of all Mennonite children at such schools.

The third study was a book written by J.T.M. Anderson, a school inspector in the Yorkton district where there were a number of people who had come from various eastern European countries. Based on his experiences Anderson wrote *The Education of the New Canadian: A Treatise on Canada's Greatest Educational Problem*. The book focussed on "the great national task of assimilating the thousands who have come to settle in Canada from various lands across the seas."[28] Anderson was convinced that assimilation would be a great benefit not only to Canada, but also to the new Canadians. His attitude, however, was insensitive and his comments about non-Anglo-Saxon cultures can best be described as patronizing. He saw very little, if anything, in immigrant cultures and traditions worthy of preservation.[29]

The reports by Foght and Oliver, and the conclusions to be drawn from Anderson's work, all identified serious problems in Saskatchewan's educational system. Martin visited numerous schools in rural districts to examine personally the work done there. He was sincerely interested in school reforms and responded to the growing pressure in several ways. First, J.T.M. Anderson was appointed to the new position of Director of Education Among New Canadians. There, he preached one message: all immigrant children must be Canadianized by teaching them English, and instilling in them a love of Anglo-Saxon values and ideals. Achievement of these objectives required the appointment of properly qualified English-speaking teachers, and the government offered bonuses to qualified teachers who were willing to teach in immigrant schools.[30] These initiatives were followed by much more drastic action when the Premier proposed an amendment to the School Act, stating that "All schools shall be taught in the English language and no languages other than English shall be taught during school hours in any school in the Province." The only exception allowed for the teaching of French as a subject where a board passed a special resolution to that effect.[31]

The English-only requirements marked a departure from the more tolerant and gradualist educational policies of the Scott government and was therefore problematic for those members of Cabinet who had served under Scott and had to choose between Scott's and the new policy proposed by Martin. The removal of French language rights was particularly problematic. W.R. Motherwell, minister of Agriculture since 1905, found the provisions unacceptable and resigned from the Cabinet. The Premier immediately accepted the resignation, but the next day partially restored French language rights. Martin had apparently made the issue a test of loyalty for the older Cabinet ministers who had supported the educational policies of the Scott government which were no longer consistent with majority opinion in the province. He lost only one of the four ministers in his Cabinet who had also served under Scott, but Motherwell had deep roots in the agrarian movement, and was highly regarded by its leaders, even though most did not agree with his support of limited foreign-language instruction in the schools.

Settling a Dispute at the University of Saskatchewan

Martin faced another difficult educational situation in 1919. At the University of Saskatchewan Samuel Greenfield, the popular director of Extension, had reported what he regarded as serious financial irregularities at the university and was supported by three other professors. The university president, Walter Murray, and most other professors regarded the four as disloyal to the president and the university, and guilty of insubordination. As such, they were dismissed.

Appeals to the government left Premier Martin in a quandry. His predecessor, Walter Scott, had taken a keen personal interest in the establishment of the University of Saskatchewan in Saskatoon in 1907, and was a close friend and confidant of Walter Murray. The two agreed that the university, while dependent on government financial support, must not be subject to state control. If Martin intervened in the case of the four dismissed professors, he would undermine the supportive but arms-length relationship of the government with the university.[32] The Premier's office was, however,

> bombarded by protests from fourteen agricultural societies, six teachers' associations, three Homemaker Clubs, three church boards, two village

SAB RB 3730

Less divisive than the educational crises with which Martin was forced to deal during his second term was the official visit of the Prince of Wales in 1919. Nevertheless, Martin's diplomacy was still required. The Prince was self-conscious about his short stature, and Martin was very tall by the standards of the day. Note that Martin is standing on the step in front of the Prince, so that they appear to be the same height.

councils, two grain growers' associations, a ratepayers' association, a rural municipality, the Saskatoon Trades and Labour Council, and a number of other organizations and individuals. All asked for an investigation.[33]

Martin, Murray and others were convinced that a commission, appointed by and reporting to the government (which would then presumably be expected to take remedial action), would constitute undue interference in the internal affairs of the university. Efforts by Martin to calm the storm without direct government involvement resulted in an innovative procedure. The University Act named the lieutenant-governor as University Visitor. The role and responsibilities of this office were not clearly defined, but in 1919 it was suggested that an investigation of the problems at the university be carried out under the auspices of the lieutenant-governor acting in this capacity. To further expedite matters, the government passed a bill empowering the lieutenant-governor to ask the Court of King's Bench to handle the investigation for him. Three justices of the court served in that capacity, and their report upheld the dismissal of the four professors. The issue was thus resolved without the intervention of the government in the internal affairs of the university.

Premier Martin was described as "the man who kept the government out of the crisis of 1919."[34] The four dissident professors found work elsewhere, the university administrators were happy with the outcome, and the politicians escaped involvement.

Wheat Marketing and Better Farming Concerns

The most urgent concern of prairie grain farmers during the last two years of Premier Martin's administration was related to the marketing of wheat. During the war, farmers had been encouraged to grow as much wheat as possible, and prices had risen from an average price of 56¢ per bushel in 1912 to $2.32 in 1919. The federal government, in an effort to control rising costs and to ensure that available supplies would be allocated to wartime requirements, established first a Board of Grain Commissioners and then a Wheat Board. The Wheat Board, with a mandate to operate for the duration and one year after the end of the war, established the required wartime priorities, but also introduced a new feature. Instead of crediting individual farmers with the price of wheat on the date they delivered it, the Wheat Board paid an initial price, averaged the returns on all sales, and made additional payments to the farmers once all the wheat was sold. Under this system, all farmers got the same price for the same quality of wheat, irrespective of the market price on the day they delivered it.

During the war, when demand for Canadian wheat was high, the system worked well. But the mandate of the Wheat Board expired in November 1919, and the federal government was eager to return to market economics as quickly as possible. This turned out to be a disaster. Wartime inflation had increased farm costs by at least 45%. Wheat prices, until 1919, had increased even more, but after 1919 wheat prices fell from the 1919 high of $2.32 to a 1923 low of only 65¢ per bushel.[35]

Prairie farmers and their political representatives had always been suspicious of alleged market manipulations by private grain merchants operating on the Winnipeg Grain Exchange. Some of the merchants had been conscripted to operate the government Wheat Board during the war, but the collapse of grain prices was blamed by many on the abandonment of the government-sponsored Wheat Board and the return to the open marketing of grain. In fact, the situation was more complex. During the war, German naval blockades had seriously disrupted all grain shipments from Australia and Argentina. As a result, huge surpluses of grain were dumped on world markets after the war, seriously depressing prices. That, however, was not clearly understood by Saskatchewan grain farmers, or by their Premier. They had prospered under orderly wartime government marketing provisions, but faced disaster when private grain merchants regained control after the war. Demands that the federal government extend the mandate of the Wheat Board were rejected, resulting in much anger and a search for alternative solutions.

Premier Martin and members of his government were keenly aware of the anger in the farming communities. Martin apparently shared their view that the drastic post-war fall in wheat prices was due to market manipulation by private grain interests, and could have been prevented if the mandate of the Wheat Board had been extended. Historically, however, Saskatchewan Liberals had not been strong supporters of direct government involvement in the economy. They had instead supported the organization of cooperative organizations by farmers. The most successful organization of this kind was the Saskatchewan Co-operative Elevator Company, and in 1921 Martin contacted several of its key members, who had also been involved in the operation of the wartime Wheat Board. He asked them whether it would be possible to organize "any kind of pool comprising less than the whole of the Western wheat crop to market the crop to the same advantage from the producers' point of view as a system of national marketing of the whole crop by a Canadian Wheat Board."[36] This general question was supplemented by a number of more specific inquiries. What is clear, however, is that Martin sought the co-operation and insight of farm and grain industry leaders in his search for a solution to the problems facing grain farmers after the war. The response of the co-op leaders was cautious and noncommittal, but Martin tried to explore the concept of a Saskatchewan Wheat Pool before it was popularized in 1923 and 1924 by Aaron Sapiro, a charismatic farm and labour leader from the United States.

Crown Lands and Natural Resources Disputes

Premier Martin was also a strong advocate of provincial control over Crown lands and natural resources. On this issue he could provide leadership, particularly when the Conservatives were in power federally, without any negative repercussions at home. But more than partisan politics were involved. Martin could see no reason why the province should not have control over these resources, and that it should receive compensation for lands given away under the federal homestead policy or sold by the federal government. The province had received a subsidy in lieu of control of these natural resources, but this was not regarded as adequate compensation. Claims for compensation, however, complicated the negotiations for a transfer of the lands and resources to provincial jurisdiction. Premier Martin was, however, a persistent advocate of such a transfer and, at the time of his retirement in 1922, the Regina *Leader* noted:

> Another question which has engaged the close attention of the retiring premier in season and out of season is the matter of the return of the natural resources to the province. He has attended several inter-provincial conferences on this subject and at these conferences his voice was always heard in firm demand for the return of the resources with indemnification for the lands alienated by the Crown.[37]

This was a popular position to take in Saskatchewan, but little was accomplished to resolve the problem in the years of Martin's premiership.

The Response to Agrarian Protest

Prairie farmers had a long history of protest against key federal policies. These included federal tariffs which protected Canadian manufacturers but increased the cost of the machinery farmers needed for their operations, freight rates which western farmers thought were unfairly high, inadequate railway branch lines, federal control over Crown lands and natural resources in the prairie provinces, federal policies which admitted too many non-Anglo-Saxon immigrants whose education then became an expensive provincial responsibility, rural credit policies, wartime manpower and requisitioning policies which deprived farmers of the labour and supplies they needed for their operations, and federal wartime and post-war grain handling and marketing policies. On all these issues there was basic agreement between members of the Martin government and farm leaders in the province. Indeed, the government included two and sometimes three Cabinet ministers who held influential positions in the SGGA. Provincial grain growers' and farmers' organizations passed resolutions which soon found their way into government policies and legislation.

The federal election of 1917 left both Liberals and farm leaders in a quandary. They supported the Union government's conscription and war policies, but disagreed with its economic policies. Once the immediate wartime crisis was over, increased criticism of federal economic policies resulted in divergent responses. For the provincial Liberals, the question arose of when and how to return to partisan political strategies. Many farm leaders, however, had more fundamental concerns related to the organization and structure of both the Liberal and Conservative parties.

Efforts to ensure that their elected representatives would support the interests of the people who elected them, rather than the policies adopted by the caucus of a national political party, resulted in western demands for specific reforms. Such reforms included several specific measures which, collectively, were often referred to as direct democracy. The first of these involved local initiatives which required that if constituents drew up a proposed bill and obtained sufficient signatures, the issue in question must be debated and voted upon. Another direct democracy demand was that on controversial issues, again with sufficient supportive signatures, the matter must be referred back to the electors in a referendum. In this matter, a distinction must be made between a plebiscite, which is essentially advisory, and a referendum, the results of which are binding. A third demand of those advocating direct and more democratic government was that elected members represent and vote as the majority of their constituents wanted, and not necessarily along political party lines. To achieve this, voters in every constituency should be given the right to recall their elected representative at any time if that individual did not support the policies or vote in accordance with the wishes of the constituents. In practical terms, this involved a demand by agrarian reformers that their candidates sign an undated letter of resignation and deposit it with their constituency organization. If the member failed to provide the kind of representation approved by the constituency organization, they merely had to fill in the date and send it to the clerk of the House of Commons or of the Legislative Assembly, and the member was out of a job.

Taken together, these measures would reduce the power of party leaders and the discipline of caucus solidarity, forcing every member to represent the interests of those who elected him, rather than the interests of a political party. Critics insisted that such a system would create much confusion and instability. Every vote in the Legislature could become a battle, paralyzing the government's ability to enact balanced legislation which might provide a necessary compromise but which could be opposed for various and perhaps contradictory reasons by voters in different constituencies. These proposals, nevertheless, flourished in many parts of western Canada.

The economic policies of the Union government were unpopular in most western

Canadian constituencies, but after their disastrous defeat in 1911 and the party's schism in 1917, the federal Liberal caucus was dominated by members from Quebec whose economic interests differed markedly from those of prairie grain growers. The solution proposed was that western farmers support only independent candidates pledged to represent their constituents. In a closely contested election in which neither of the old-line parties obtained a majority, the independents would hold the balance of power and would thus be in a position to ensure government action on issues of concern to their constituents.

The discontent and anger of western farmers and several of their political representatives in Parliament, who had been elected as Unionists in 1917, resulted in these members breaking with the government in 1920 and formating an agrarian interest group which quickly evolved into what became known as the National Progressive Party. It was a western and farm protest movement, whose members sat as a separate group in Parliament as they prepared to contest the next federal election.[38]

The SGGA and the Canadian Federation of Agriculture supported the movement, but its likely impact on Saskatchewan provincial politics was uncertain. The Martin government had taken great care to bring influential farm leaders into the Cabinet. W.R. Motherwell, a practical farmer and one of the founders of the Territorial Grain Growers' Association, served as commissioner and later as minister of Agriculture in both the Scott and Martin governments until his resignation in December 1918. George Langley, a director of the SGGA and prominent farm organizer, became a Cabinet minister in Scott's government in 1912, and was appointed minister of Agriculture following Motherwell's resignation. Farm interests were further strengthened when Martin brought C.A. Dunning, another prominent farm leader and general manager of the Saskatchewan Co-operative Elevator Company, into his first Cabinet. Two other Cabinet ministers brought in later by Premier Martin—C.M Hamilton and S.J. Latta—had also been influential members of the SGGA before joining the Cabinet. The standing of the government in farm communities was further strengthened by the firm positions taken by the Premier on federal issues of interest to grain growers. There was consequently no immediate reason why farm leaders should nominate independent candidates to oppose the Liberals in a provincial election. Many farm leaders, however, were determined to nominate and support independent candidates in the next federal election, in which they expected the provincial Liberals to remain officially neutral but support candidates representing grain grower interests.

Relations between federal and Saskatchewan provincial Liberals after 1917 were often strained. Some Saskatchewan Liberals, most notably Motherwell, strongly advocated a return to partisan political action as soon as the wartime crisis was over. That, however, would antagonize farm leaders who supported the provincial government but did not trust the federal Liberals. Premier Martin approached the issue cautiously. The first test for him came in 1919.

J.G. Turriff, a long-time Liberal (and after 1917, Unionist) MP, was appointed to the Senate. A farmer candidate with strong local support was nominated to contest the by-election to be held on October 27, 1919. But W.R. Motherwell thought it important that a Liberal contest the seat. He was apparently encouraged by William Lyon Mackenzie King, the new leader of the federal Liberal Party, to seek the nomination, but there were grave apprehensions in the ranks of the provincial Liberals. They were unsure of federal Liberal economic policies under King's leadership, and reluctant to antagonize the organized farmers who had already nominated their candidate. Motherwell, however, was determined to launch a partisan Liberal campaign in the by-election.

The Conservatives decided not to contest the by-election. In light of the unsatisfactory record of the Union government, and serious doubts regarding the policies of the federal Liberals, someone supported by organized Saskatchewan farm groups would be by far the most popular candidate. Provincial Liberals tried to persuade Motherwell to withdraw and Premier Martin refused to do anything to assist him. As a result, Motherwell went down to a disastrous defeat. Martin's role in the by-election proved that he was determined to represent and defend the interests of his province. He clearly established the principle of a separation between provincial and federal Liberal politics.

The loss of Motherwell weakened the provincial government's links with the organized farmers, but Finance minister Dunning continued to represent those interests, and two other Cabinet ministers had also been involved in a more limited way with the grain growers. Then, on April 23, 1921, Martin made a Cabinet appointment which was clearly designed to strengthen grain grower representation. John A. Maharg, for 11 years president of the SGGA, was appointed first as minister of Telephones and a little later as minister of Agriculture.

Maharg was sharply critical of the policies, structure and organization of both the federal Liberal and Conservative parties. At the time of his appointment he explained that his objective was simply "the bettering of the conditions of those who are trying to secure a competence through following the pursuits of agriculture." He and other grain grower officials made special efforts to explain that "the Government of this Province has no connection with the Liberal party which is a Federal party."[39]

The Maharg appointment seriously undermined the efforts of other farm leaders who favoured the organization of a provincial farmers' or grain growers' party to contest the next election. And, having thus strengthened his standing with the farmers, Martin called a provincial election for June 8, 1921. It turned out to be a lopsided contest. Donald McLean, the Conservative leader, had resigned and had not been replaced. Farm leaders in some constituencies nominated independent candidates, but opposition to the government was not united. Martin and other government candidates emphasized their record of competent, farmer-friendly and scandal-free government. In a "Manifesto to the Electors," the Premier clearly distanced himself from any federal political party. Instead, in addition to his government's record on domestic issues such as school legislation, farm loans, co-operatives and highways, he pointed to efforts to gain lower freight rates, better wheat-handling and marketing facilities, and provincial control over Crown lands and natural resources. The Liberal identity of the government was scarcely mentioned. It was the Martin government which sought re-election. Most Conservative and Progressive candidates, in keeping with the anti-party mood, ran as Independents. The result of the election gave the government 46 of the 63 seats in the Legislature, with the Premier receiving a personal vote of 7,300—allegedly the highest in any provincial contest to that date.[40]

Premier Martin barely had time to savour the fruits of his great electoral victory before he became embroiled in two incidents which forced his resignation less than a year later. Both occurred on September 30, 1921. The first involved the forced resignation of George Langley, who had served in the Scott and Martin Cabinets since 1912 and had close links to the SGGA. Langley, who had been defeated in the 1921 election but elected in a subsequent by-election, wrote a letter to Thomas Murray, a special provincial magistrate who was conducting a judicial enquiry into the conduct of a man named William Sulaty. In his letter, dated September 23, 1921, Langley expressed support for Sulaty. It was a clear case of ministerial interference in the judical process, and on September 30, Premier Martin, in a harshly worded letter, demanded Langley's resignation. Langley complied, but complained about harsh and unfair treatment by the Premier and released confidential Cabinet information, which further angered Martin.

George Langley had provided important links between the government and the SGGA, but his forced resignation was supported by the entire Cabinet, including J.A. Maharg, who was still president of the SGGA and also the minister of Agriculture. Langley's controversial departure, nevertheless, strengthened the influence of those farmers who felt uneasy about the Liberal identity of the provincial government.

On the same day that Martin asked for Langley's resignation, he participated in a meeting in Regina where—this time—he supported W.R. Motherwell's bid for the Liberal nomination for the federal election which, it was widely expected, would be called later that year. Martin's government had won the 1921 provincial election with strong farm support, but in both Manitoba and Alberta the incumbent governments had either been reduced to a minority or been decisively defeated in provincial elections. The Progressives, with strong support from grain grower and other farm organizations, were preparing for vigorous contests in all rural and agricultural constituencies in the 1921 federal election. Premier Martin had clearly stated in the 1921 Saskatchewan provincial election that provincial governments should stay out of federal politics and tend to provincial matters. However, he insisted that this did not preclude participation in the federal campaign by individual members of the government. Agriculture minister Maharg's support of the Progressives was well known, but the Premier's support of the enthusiastically partisan former minister of Agriculture came as a surprise.

The divergent politics of the Premier and his minister of Agriculture suffered an irreparable rupture on December 1, 1921, when Premier Martin made a controversial and fateful speech in Regina. In it, he strongly endorsed Motherwell as the Liberal candidate in Regina, and then went on to declare his strong opposition to many of the most cherished policies of the Progressives. He was particularly critical of some direct democracy proposals. In denouncing the recall provisions, he said:

> No sensible man who has a proper appreciation of Parliament would agree to place his resignation in the hands of any group of men to be used under any condition during his term. It would create an undue interference with the independence of Parliament, and is unconstitutional under our system of government."[41]

Martin also sharply criticized Progressive support of class or group government. He believed that political parties should represent the broad interests of the electorate, not the narrower interests of only one group. Farmers and farm-related businesses still comprised a majority of Canadians in 1921, but that, in Premier Martin's publicly stated opinion, was no justification for an attempt to vote into office a party committed only to farm interests.

The speech placed Premier Martin, and by inference the government of which he was the head, in direct conflict with farm organizations which supported the policies of the Progressive Party but had previously given strong and vitally important support to the provincial government. It resulted in the resignation of John Maharg as minister of Agriculture and transformed him into one of the most effective critics of the provincial government. Old-time partisan Liberals such as W.R. Motherwell were delighted, but influential members of the provincial Cabinet and of the government knew that losing the support of the organized farmers could consign Saskatchewan Liberals to the same fate that had already overtaken their Manitoba and Alberta counterparts.

The available correspondence does not indicate clearly what Premier Martin's motives were when he made his December speech. He was an astute politician who must have recognized that the speech could result in Maharg's resignation and the alienation of the SGGA and of the Saskatchewan Section of the Canadian Council of Agriculture. He was, however, also convinced of the folly of some policies of the Progressive Party. He was a man of high personal integrity, and may have simply tired of the compromises he was being asked to make to keep all factions of the organized farmers satisfied.

The results of the 1921 federal election provided little comfort for the Premier. The Progressives captured 15 of Saskatchewan's 16 seats.[42] The only Liberal elected was W.R. Motherwell in Regina. Even more serious was the fact that the election returned Canada's first minority government. The Liberals were elected in 116 of 235 constituencies. They took all 65 seats in Quebec, but elected only two members in the three prairie provinces. If the Liberals were to regain their stature as a national political party, they had to broaden their base of support in western Canada. Fortunately, from a federal Liberal perspective, their policies were closer to those of the western Progressives than the high-tariff policies of the Conservatives. After the election, Progressive leader T.A. Crerar announced that his members would not serve as the official opposition in Parliament, even though they had more seats than the Conservatives. They would simply support what they regarded as good, and oppose what they or their constituents thought was bad, legislation.

When incoming Prime Minister Mackenzie King formed his first Cabinet, Martin and other Saskatchewan Liberals lobbied vigorously for the appointment of W.R. Motherwell as federal minister of Agriculture. However, the appointment of Motherwell, a fiercely partisan Liberal with little understanding of the need for compromise, was unacceptable to Crerar and most other Progressives. King therefore had little alternative but to leave Motherwell on the backbench. Martin might have gained some credibility with leaders of the organized farmers if he could have secured Motherwell's appointment as federal minister of Agriculture. Failure to do so, particularly after the speech criticizing many of the major Progressive proposals, effectively sealed his fate. Martin, in the words of a sympathetic political scientist, David Smith, "had cooked his goose."[43]

Martin's Resignation

The success and survival of Saskatchewan Liberal governments in the early decades of the twentieth century was based on their ability to deal effectively with the concerns of the province's farmers, and particularly of the organized farm groups. Both Scott and Martin initiated numerous progressive measures ranging from government financial support for the building of the province's economic infrastructure to temperance, school and electoral reforms, and a wide range of social policies. The government's support of farmer cooperatives and a rural credit program which eventually extended more than $15 million in low-interest loans, and its consistent advocacy of tariff reform, railway freight rate reductions, further railway branch line construction, and provincial control of Crown lands and natural resources, provided a basis for political success. The close links between provincial Liberals and prominent farm leaders, and an efficient political organization, also contributed to the longevity of the Saskatchewan Liberal Party. And, just when allegations of scandal threatened to tarnish the image of the government led by Walter Scott, Martin, who was untouched by those scandals and subsequently ran a scandal-free administration, became Premier. He won two provincial elections, in both cases by large majorities.

Martin met the Legislature on December 8, 1921, in the first session following the provincial election. The session was marked by the passage of a wide range of generally progressive, and mostly uncontentious, legislation and by Dunning's prudent but cautiously optimistic budget. The government still enjoyed broad public support, but in the Legislature, J.A. Maharg, who had been elected earlier that year as a member of the government, now became its harshest critic. The old alliance between the government and organized farmers had broken down, and Premier Martin seemed unable or unwilling to reach a reconciliation.

William Martin resigned as Premier of Saskatchewan on April 4, 1922, amidst speculation that he would be appointed as a fifth judge of the Saskatchewan Court of Appeal. His Cabinet colleagues and Liberal MLAs moved quickly, with Martin's support, to name Charles A. Dunning as his successor. The choice of Dunning, who had close links with organized farm groups, helped heal the breach between the Saskatchewan Liberal government and the SGGA.

Conclusion

Martin's resignation elicited a flood of laudatory public and newspaper statements. Civil servants in Regina arranged a large reception in the Legislative Building where the outgoing Premier was presented with a cabinet of silver tableware in token of their appreciation of his relations with them. The cost was covered by donations from more than 2,000 civil servants.[44] The Liberal caucus, as might be expected, passed laudatory resolutions expressing their appreciation of Martin's leadership. Newspapers across the province, whether Liberal, Progressive or Conservative, praised the premier for leading a government which was stable and clean. An editorial in the Regina *Leader* claimed that

> seldom has the first minister of a province in Canada so completely disarmed criticism or won the implicit confidence of all classes of citizens as

SAB RB 2592

Life after politics. Martin, third from left, administers the oath of office to the incoming lieutenant-governor, J.M. Uhrich (second from left), 1948. Premier Tommy Douglas stands on Martin's opposite side.

> Mr. Martin has done during the five and a half years that he has led the Saskatchewan Government. The bitterest of his political opponents have always been ready to pay tribute to the sterling personal qualities of the man and to the splendid standard of government he has set… The qualities that Mr. Martin, as Premier, displayed pre-eminently were progressiveness, cleanliness of administration, confidence in the people and an earnest desire to consult with them, obtain their point of view and grant every reasonable demand they made upon their Government.[45]

The praise was only slightly qualified in an editorial published by the Regina *Daily Post*:

> Mr. Martin had a very definite idea of what the majority of the people, the right-thinking people, of Saskatchewan, wanted, and he devoted himself with singular whole-heartedness to give the people the sort of government they wanted. But it was government from the top down; he never could realize, and none of the old-line politicians seem able to realize, that the people are demanding government by the people as well as for the people… That Premier Martin gave Saskatchewan honest and capable administration has never been seriously questioned; if he was a little weak in failing to see "the other side" of a question, he made up for this deficiency by clear thinking, quick action, sound judgment and absolute honesty of purpose."[46]

SAB RB 2904

William Martin as chief justice, c. 1960, shortly before his retirement.

W.M. Martin was not a leader who was comfortable with the direct democracy, government from the bottom-up style advocated by the Progressives and in the 1920s also by the Conservatives in Saskatchewan. Thus, at the relatively young age of 46, he left a distinguished political career.

Martin's appointment as a judge on the Saskatchewan Court of Appeal was announced on July 23, 1922. The court was headed at the time by Sir Frederick Haultain, the former territorial government and Provincial Rights Party leader. It had, until 1922, only four members, but Martin's appointment made it a five-member court, thus solving problems which had arisen when the court was evenly divided on some decisions.

Martin greatly admired Haultain as a judge, and at the time of Haultain's death in 1942 he wrote a eulogy for the *Saskatchewan Bar Review*. The editor described Martin as "one who had a very close and personal association with Sir Frederick." Haultain served as justice of the Superior Court of Saskatchewan from 1912 until 1917, and as chief justice of the Saskatchewan Court of Appeals and the Court of King's Bench from 1917 until his retirement in 1938. Martin was appointed to that position in 1941 and served until his retirement in 1961 at the age of 84.

Martin's judicial career is beyond the scope of this chapter, but at a retirement dinner in his honour he was described as an architect of Saskatchewan's greatness. The characteristics he brought to both politics and the judicial system were described as integrity, dependability and a great sense of confidence. He died on June 22, 1970, at the age of 93. At the time of his death an editorial in the *Leader* called him the "grand old man of the west... Never afraid to face an issue, unpleasant though it may have been, his sense of justice, tempered with mercy, characterized much of the daily pattern of his life."[47]

Notes

1. A lengthy obituary, appearing on the front page of the Regina *Leader-Post*, was published on June 23, 1970, under the title, "Saskatchewan's second premier dies at 93." It was followed the next day by an editorial entitled "Grand old man of the west."

2. Biographical information on William Martin's early life is taken mainly from the *Leader-Post* obituary, newspaper reports published at the time of Martin's appointment as Premier and at the time of his retirement from politics, the relevant issues of the *Canadian Parliamentary Guide*, and the several speeches recorded on SAB R-6052, tape cassette, W.M. Martin dinner, March 1961, which included a tribute by Premier T.C. Douglas.
3. Much of this information is drawn from the speech Martin made at his retirement dinner in 1961, SAB R-6052, tape cassette.
4. The Shoefelt case is discussed in the *Leader-Post* obituary and in W.H. McConnell, *Prairie Justice* (Calgary: Burroughs & Co., 1980), 185–86.
5. This controversial decision by Lieutenant-Governor Forget is discussed in C.C. Lingard, *Territorial Government in Canada: The Autonomy Question in the Old North-West Territories* (Toronto: University of Toronto Press, 1946), John T. Saywell, *The Office of the Lieutenant-Governor* (Toronto: University of Toronto Press, 1957), Lewis H. Thomas, *The Struggle for Responsible Government in the North-West Territories, 1870–1897* (University of Toronto Press, 1956). William Martin held Haultain in very high regard, and wrote a short biographical article and obituary entitled simply "Sir Frederick Haultain," which was published in *Saskatchewan Bar Review*, 1942.
6. Gordon L. Barnhart, *"Peace, Progress and Prosperity": A Biography of Saskatchewan's First Premier, T. Walter Scott* (Regina: Canadian Plains Research Center, 2000), 80–81.
7. Information on Martin's first political campaign is based on his own recollections, as recorded in SAB R-6053. Tape cassette, W.M. Martin dinner, March 1961, and, more generally, J. Castell Hopkins (ed.), *The Canadian Annual Review, 1908* (Toronto: Annual Review Publishing Company, n.d.).
8. There is a lengthy citation from this letter in David E. Smith, *Prairie Liberalism. The Liberal Party in Saskatchewan, 1905–71* (Toronto: University of Toronto Press, 1975), 71. Smith does not refer to the close parallel between this letter and Martin's speech in the House of Commons.
9. Canada, House of Commons, *Debates*, Session 1909, Vol. II, 3629–3635. The spread between track and street prices was also due to elevator and other handling charges.
10. Ibid., 2655–2659.
11. *Canadian Railway Cases*, Vol. XII, 203–16, Regina Tolls Case.
12. Canada, House of Commons, *Debates*, Session 1912–13, 8923.
13. Ibid., Session 1914, 3613.
14. Ibid., Session 1915.
15. *Globe and Mail*, June 24, 1970. Martin was encouraged by friends and supporters to seek the federal Liberal leadership in 1919, but it is incorrect that he was offered the leadership.
16. McConnell, *Prairie Justice*, 185–86.
17. As quoted in Barnhart, "Peace, Progress and Prosperity," 140.
18. "Grand old man of the west," Regina *Leader-Post*, June 24, 1970.
19. J. Castell Hopkins, *The Canadian Annual Review of Public Affairs, 1916* (Toronto: Annual Review Publishing Company, 1917), 721.
20. The rural farm credit crisis is discussed in greater detail in T.D. Regehr, "Bankers and Farmers in Western Canada," in John E. Foster (ed.), *The Developing West. Essays on Canadian History in Honour of Lewis H. Thomas* (Edmonton: University of Alberta Press, 1983), 303–36.
21. The response of Saskatchewan Mennonites to the compulsory school legislation is discussed in detail in William Janzen, *Limits on Liberty: The Experience of Mennonite, Hutterite, and Doukhobor Communities*

in Canada (Toronto: University of Toronto Press, 1990), Adolf Ens, *Subjects or Citizens? The Mennonite Experience in Canada, 1870–1925* (Ottawa: University of Ottawa Press, 1994), Harold Leonard Sawatzky, *They Sought a Country: Mennonite Colonization in Mexico* (Berkeley: University of California Press, 1971).

22. J. Castell Hopkins, *The Canadian Annual Review of Public Affairs, 1918* (Toronto: The Canadian Annual Review Limited, 1919), 687.
23. As cited in Janzen, *Limits on Liberty*, 108.
24. SAB, Martin Papers, 4127, Andrew Henderson, Clerk of Synod, to W.M. Martin, November 8, 1920.
25. Hopkins, *The Canadian Annual Review of Public Affairs, 1918*, 687.
26. Harold W. Foght, *A Survey of Education in the Province of Saskatchewan, Canada* (Regina: n.p., 1918).
27. As cited in Janzen, *Limits on Liberty*, 105.
28. J.T.M. Anderson, *The Education of the New Canadian: A Treatise on Canada's Greatest Educational Problem* (Toronto: Dent, 1918), 7.
29. *Prairie Liberalism*, 128.
30. Hopkins, *The Canadian Annual Review of Public Affairs, 1918*, 690.
31. As quoted in Smith, *Prairie Liberalism*, 119.
32. Michael Hayden, *Seeking a Balance: University of Saskatchewan, 1907–1982* (Vancouver: University of British Columbia Press, 1982), 78–116.
33. Ibid., 102.
34. Ibid., caption below the photo of William Martin opposite p. 108.
35. These figures are taken from Seymour Martin Lipset, *Agrarian Socialism: The Cooperative Commonwealth Federation in Saskatchewan. A Study in Political Sociology* (1950; New York: Doubleday Anchor, 1968), 46.
36. J. Castell Hopkins, *The Canadian Annual Review of Public Affairs, 1921* (Toronto: The Canadian Review Company, 1922), 798–99.
37. Regina *Leader*, April 4, 1922.
38. W.L. Morton, *The Progressive Party in Canada* (Toronto: University of Toronto Press, 1959).
39. As cited in Hopkins, *The Canadian Annual Review of Public Affairs, 1921*, 781.
40. Ibid., 812.
41. As cited in ibid., 779.
42. The number of Saskatchewan federal constituencies had been increased in a redistribution which took into account population increases in the province.
43. Smith, *Prairie Liberalism*, 92.
44. SAB, Martin Papers, 44407, Newspaper clipping from the *Leader*, April 29, 1922.
45. Ibid., newspaper clipping from the *Leader*, April 5, 1922.
46. Ibid., 44414, newspaper clipping from the Regina *Daily Post*, July 24, 1922.
47. "Grand old man of the west," Regina *Leader-Post*, June 24, 1970.

Charles A. Dunning

J. William Brennan

Visiting employees at Wright and Havelock Foundry in Leicester, England (SAB RB 29).

Dunning, c. 1925 (SAB RA 631 (1)).

Dunning at the signing of the Old Age Pension Bill (SAB RA 3288).

Saskatchewan Premiers of the 20th Century

Charles A. Dunning, 1922–1926

In Saskatchewan, where wheat was king and the Liberals held power for the first quarter century, a special relationship early developed between the ruling party and the Saskatchewan Grain Growers' Association (SGGA). Leaders of this powerful farmers' organization early found a place in Liberal Cabinets (W.R. Motherwell in 1905 and George Langley in 1912). This relationship proved to be a mutually beneficial one. The presence of prominent Grain Growers in the government assured Saskatchewan farmers of a sympathetic consideration of their wishes. Resolutions adopted at annual SGGA conventions quickly found their way into the province's statute books, and government policies generally followed the line advocated by the organized farmers. And for the Liberals, these close ties assured the continued support of rural voters at election time.[1]

The Early Years

The politician who best typified this special relationship was Charles Avery Dunning, who rose through the ranks of the farmers' movement to become Saskatchewan's third Premier in 1922. Born in Croft, Leicestershire, England on July 31, 1885, son of Samuel Dunning and Katherine Hall, Charles A. Dunning began his life on the Canadian Prairies as a transient farm labourer in 1902. He homesteaded near Yorkton in 1903, and experienced all of the hardships of early pioneer life. In 1913 he married Ada Rowlatt; they had two children: Avery Charles and Katherine Ada.

Dunning soon joined the SGGA, and it was through this farmers' organization that he rose to public prominence, first as a district director and then as its vice-president. A much more significant milestone in Dunning's career, however, was his appointment as general manager of the farmer-owned Saskatchewan Co-operative Elevator Company in 1911. Starting with only 46 elevators in 1911–12, the Saskatchewan Co-op grew rapidly under Dunning's direction. By 1916, it boasted 230 country elevators, and construction of its first terminal at the Lakehead was nearing completion. The last balance sheet he presented to its shareholders showed a record profit of more than $757,000 on its operations during the 1915–16 crop year.[2]

It was this business ability, as much as Dunning's connection with the SGGA, which made him so attractive to the Liberal government whose ranks he joined in October 1916. It had been rocked by a series of scandals. Liberal members of the Legislature had accepted bribes to vote against a 1913 bill to close Saskatchewan's bars. Another Liberal member had helped a senior civil servant embezzle a substantial sum of money from the government agency (the Board of Highway Commissioners) responsible for building highways in the province. There were also allegations of graft in the construction of the province's first mental hospital and two other government buildings. Premier Walter Scott, suffering from increasingly severe bouts of manic depression, was compelled to resign for health reasons.[3]

Saskatchewan Liberals turned to W.M. Martin, a Regina lawyer and the city's member of Parliament at the time, to lead the party and the government out of this crisis. Martin had not been implicated in the scandals, of course, sitting as he did in the House of Commons in Ottawa, and was therefore the obvious choice to succeed Scott.[4] Martin was sworn in as Premier on October 20. Joining him in the new Cabinet was Charles Dunning, who took the portfolio of provincial treasurer.

Dunning's popularity among the Grain Growers would certainly do the Liberals no harm, but there was another important reason why Martin would have wanted him in the cabinet. The ability he had demonstrated as general manager of the Saskatchewan Co-op well suited Dunning for the task of handling the province's finances and safeguarding the public treasury against any further looting by unscrupulous government officials or politicians. Never having been an active member of the Liberal or any other political party, he could not help but bolster the image of a government shaken by scandal. Dunning was certainly aware of the cloud of suspicion that still hung over the Legislative Building, yet this seems not to have deterred him from leaving the secure world of business for the much more uncertain world of politics. He was later to remark at a Grain Growers' convention in Moose Jaw that "I always found on the farm that if the pig pen needed cleaning out I had to get inside to do it."[5] As a Grain Grower, Dunning professed to find the Liberals more to his liking than the Conservatives, though his justification for such a preference—the attitude of the two on the tariff question—bore little if any relevance to provincial politics. Whatever his reasons for entering the political arena in 1916, the significant thing was that Dunning had chosen to cast his lot with Saskatchewan's governing party.

The Martin Government

Dunning held the portfolio of provincial treasurer for the next six years, and also served briefly as minister of Railways (1917–19), Telephones (1918–19), Agriculture (1919–20) and Municipal Affairs (1921–22). He proved to be a capable minister and an asset to the party at election time. This became especially evident after World War I, when Saskatchewan farmers (like their counterparts across much of Canada) began to show a new impatience with the established parties and a desire to strike out on their own. Saskatchewan Liberals early recognized that their political survival could only be assured by playing down all ties with the federal wing of the party and showing an even greater solicitude for the wishes of the organized farmers. It was Premier Martin who publicly severed the link with the federal Liberal party, in a speech at Preeceville in May 1920, but it was Dunning who made the rounds of farmers' picnics and the annual SGGA conventions, stressing his past involvement in the farmers' organization and urging that there was no need to upset a Liberal government of farmers simply to put in a "farmers' government."[6]

Martin was determined to leave nothing to chance, and in 1921 persuaded J.A. Maharg to join the Cabinet as minister of Agriculture. Maharg had served as president of the SGGA and the Saskatchewan Co-op since 1911, and had taken a leading role in the formation of the new Progressive party. It was a bold stroke, intended to demonstrate the Liberals' sympathy for the views of organized agriculture, and it enabled Martin to avoid defeat in the provincial election held in June 1921.

From this point on, Martin's political position steadily deteriorated. In December, he infuriated the farmers' political movement by urging Saskatchewan voters to elect a federal Liberal government and openly campaigning for W.R. Motherwell in Regina. This precipitated Maharg's resignation from the provincial Cabinet and drew the SGGA into provincial politics.[7] Martin realized himself that he had lost the support of the farmers, and the Liberals moved quickly to repair the damage resulting from his renewed embrace of the federal party. To replace Martin, who retired to the bench, the Liberals chose Charles Dunning, confident that he alone could stem the rising tide of agrarian unrest that threatened to sweep them away.

The Premiership

The actual transfer of leadership took place on April 4, 1922. The new Premier wasted little time in getting down to business. His first task was the selection of a Cabinet; it was sworn in two days later and differed little from its predecessor. Four had served under Martin: Dunning, of course, who retained the portfolio of provincial treasurer and took that of Railways as well; A.P. McNab, minister of Public Works and minister of Telephones and Telegraphs; S.J. Latta, minister of Education and C.M. Hamilton, minister of Agriculture and minister of Municipal Affairs. The others were newcomers. Col. J.A. Cross, a distinguished war veteran and the sole lawyer in the Legislature, was the logical, and indeed the only, choice for the post of Attorney General. J.G. Gardiner assumed the Highways portfolio and Dr. J.M. Uhrich was named Provincial Secretary.[viii] It was significant that although a farmer now led the government, his cabinet contained no other prominent Grain Growers, for political conditions in Saskatchewan had changed dramatically since J.A. Maharg had entered and quickly left the Martin government the year before.

In a short manifesto issued soon after he took office, Dunning pledged that his government would aid the province's farmers in solving the economic problems they then faced on account of falling commodity prices, and would continue to enforce the Saskatchewan Temperance Act (STA) "in accordance with the expressed will of the people." With the SGGA having recently decided at its annual convention to enter provincial politics, Dunning also took pains to insist that he was not out to fight the Grain Growers, and pointed yet again to his own record of service to Saskatchewan farmers.[9]

The survival of his Liberal government was not Dunning's most immediate priority; the economic plight of Saskatchewan farmers was. Canada's postwar inflationary boom had collapsed in the fall of 1920. Its impact had been aggravated on the prairies by a sharp decline in wheat prices which coincided with the federal government's decision to abolish the Canadian Wheat Board at the end of the 1919–20 crop year. In initial, interim and final payments the Wheat Board paid farmers as much as $2.63 per bushel for their wheat. Once the grain trade was returned to private hands, wheat prices began to fall, to under $2 per bushel for the top grade of wheat by November 1920 and to $1.08 by November 1921. Low prices continued through 1922, 1923 and 1924.

Farmers associated the Wheat Board with the highest prices in their memory, and began lobbying to have it reestablished. By the time Dunning became Premier, the prospects of success seemed brighter. Western farmers had elected 38 representatives of the new

Progressive party in the 1921 federal election, and it appeared that William Lyon Mackenzie King's Liberal government, without even a bare majority in the House of Commons, would be more receptive to the farmers' demands.[10] It was, and as a consequence, Premier Dunning became personally involved in two attempts to reestablish the Wheat Board as the marketing agency for Saskatchewan's and western Canada's staple crop.

The first step took place in Ottawa. After weeks of hearings, the House of Commons Committee on Agriculture recommended that a national wheat marketing agency be created to handle the 1922 crop, the legislation to take effect "as soon as two or more of the provinces have conferred upon this agency such powers possessed by the Wheat Board of 1919 as come within provincial jurisdiction." This provision was necessitated by the fact that Premier T.C. Norris had just called an election in Manitoba; there would therefore not be time for that province to enact the required legislation before the 1922 harvest got underway.[11]

SAB RB 631 1
Dunning as Premier, c. 1927.

Dunning was convinced that the federal government should move quickly to introduce a bill creating a new Wheat Board. Otherwise, he warned W.R. Motherwell, now minister of Agriculture in the King government, the Progressives would become the "Wheat Board Party" and use this "perpetual grievance" to garner support among western farmers, most of whom favoured the reestablishment of this compulsory marketing scheme. Thus when the Committee on Agriculture made its report public, Dunning was quick to announce that, if a Wheat Board similar to that of 1919 could be created, his government would call a special session of the Legislature to deal with the matter.[12]

Legislation was promptly introduced in Parliament and approved without much debate. In some respects, the new Wheat Board, if it came into operation, would differ significantly from its predecessor. The 1919 Wheat Board had controlled all of the wheat grown in Canada, it had controlled flour, and it had been backed financially by the credit of the federal government. The new Wheat Board would only function in those western provinces which passed the appropriate enabling legislation, it would sell only wheat, and the federal government would not be responsible for any deficit which the Board might incur. (Thus the risk involved in guaranteeing initial advances to farmers would rest with the participating provinces.[13])

Once Parliament approved the Canadian Wheat Board Act, Premier Dunning and his

Alberta counterpart, Herbert Greenfield, met in Regina to discuss possible action by their respective governments. They also consulted with James Stewart, president of the Maple Leaf Milling Company, and F.W. Riddell, general manager of the Saskatchewan Co-op—the men who had headed the 1919 Wheat Board. At the conclusion of the day-long conference Dunning announced that his government was prepared to call a special session, but would wait for Alberta's decision before deciding definitely to do so.

The Greenfield government agreed to cooperate and Dunning took the opportunity of writing Prime Minister King regarding the whole Wheat Board question. The Saskatchewan Premier confided that he did not like the principle of compulsion in matters of trade, but present economic conditions made some sort of mass selling desirable if the farmer was to receive a reasonable price for his wheat. Dunning was sure the enabling legislation would pass easily, since the members of the Legislature and Saskatchewan farmers were "practically a unit in favour of the scheme." He was not particularly troubled by the fact that the provinces would have to cover any deficit the new Wheat Board might incur, provided suitable men were found to head it. In this connection, he suggested the names of James Stewart and F.W. Riddell, and assured King that the Alberta and Saskatchewan governments would be perfectly satisfied with a Wheat Board headed by these two men.[14]

The special session of the Saskatchewan Legislature, which Dunning had promised, opened on July 20, 1922. It was the Premier himself who introduced the Wheat Board bill; as Dunning had predicted, it passed easily. The Alberta Legislature quickly followed suit, and the Premiers of the two participating provinces then set out to secure competent men to head the 1922 Wheat Board. Their first choices—Stewart and Riddell—declined to serve. Dunning and Greenfield then approached a number of others in the grain industry. (Some held senior positions in the farmer-owned United Grain Growers Limited, others in one or another of the private grain companies.) All declined as well, and the Premiers gave up their search.[15] The reasons for their failure they summarized in a public statement issued that evening:

> We feel now after spending over two weeks in the effort, that we have canvassed the field fully for suitable men and have to state that men having the necessary ability and experience are unwilling to assume the great responsibility involved.
>
> One of our greatest difficulties lay in the fact that most of the men best qualified for these positions belong to the ordinary grain trade and there is no doubt that the great majority of the men in the grain trade are opposed to the wheat board idea.
>
> Those who believe the board to be a necessity this year declined to take the positions because of the opposition of the grain trade in general. In this connection they repeatedly pointed out to us that the use of facilities controlled by the various branches of the trade was absolutely necessary, especially in view of the short time available for organization.

A few days later, the Winnipeg Grain Exchange issued a statement of its own expressing its continued opposition to any form of compulsory wheat marketing.[16]

The Wheat Board was dead, at least so far as the 1922 crop was concerned. But then early in 1923, it seemed that Manitoba would join the scheme. Premier John Bracken intimated as much to the United Farmers of Manitoba convention in January. In that speech, and in subsequent correspondence with his Alberta and Saskatchewan counterparts, Bracken made it clear that Manitoba's legislation would be for just one year, and would be brought down only if the governments and farmers' organizations in the three provinces declared their intention to develop a co-operative, non-profit, non-compulsory marketing scheme for the 1924 crop.[17] However, the Wheat Board bill which Bracken subsequently introduced as a non-party measure was narrowly defeated, and Saskatchewan and Alberta were left to go it alone. Dunning candidly admitted that this would make it more difficult for the two remaining provinces to form a Wheat Board, though he and Greenfield spent another two months trying to do so.[18] Finally, on June 22, the two Premiers issued a press statement announcing that they had again been unable "to secure a Board combining all necessary elements of experience ability and public confidence."[19]

In two successive years, Charles Dunning and his Alberta counterpart had taken an active part in efforts to secure a Wheat Board, and in two successive years these efforts had failed. The reaction of the *Grain Growers' Guide* could be considered typical of farm opinion on the Prairies:

> It will be a very difficult matter to apportion the blame for the downfall of the wheat board negotiations. Premier Greenfield and Premier Dunning have exhausted every effort in a sincere desire to carry out the wishes of the farmers of their provinces in the creation of a wheat board for the marketing of this year's crop. No blame can be laid at their door. They have done all that any person could have done.

Looking to the future, the Guide observed:

> In view of the efforts of the past two years to secure a wheat board and the complete failure that has been the result of these efforts, it may reasonably be assumed now that the wheat board idea is dead. ... Farmers in the prairie provinces will be wise now to turn their efforts toward the establishment of a voluntary pooling system under their own control.[20]

With all hope of securing a Wheat Board apparently gone, farmers did indeed turn to the organization of a voluntary pool to handle western grain. The work was undertaken by the farmers' organizations acting independently within each province. Aaron Sapiro, an American lawyer and pooling expert who had set up produce pools in the Mid-West and California, was invited to Alberta and Saskatchewan to popularize the concept. The short space of time remaining between the announced failure of Premiers Dunning and Greenfield to secure a Wheat Board and the onset of the harvest season hampered the activities of the pool organizers. Nevertheless by October, nearly half of Alberta's wheat acreage was signed up to five-year delivery contracts, and the Alberta Co-operative Wheat Producers' Limited was in business.[21]

In Saskatchewan, a much larger acreage was involved: there were 12.2 million acres seeded to wheat in that province as compared to 5.6 million in Alberta. The rivalry between the SGGA and the upstart Farmers' Union of Canada (founded 18 months earlier) also delayed the start of the organization campaign. The Farmers' Union was quick to endorse the pooling idea. It set about to organize a wheat pool based on five-year delivery contracts, invited the cooperation of the provincial government and the SGGA, and took the lead in bringing Aaron Sapiro to Saskatchewan. The SGGA was divided. Some of the executive favoured the pooling concept. Others, particularly those who had close ties with the Saskatchewan Co-op (like J.A. Maharg, who was still president of both) were lukewarm, if not openly hostile, to the scheme. Eventually the SGGA committed itself to organizing a rival pool that would operate without contracts.

As for the provincial government, it approached the idea of a pool cautiously at first. On July 10, Dunning felt obliged to deny rumours that his government was inviting Aaron Sapiro to come to Saskatchewan and organize a pool, although he did announce that such a scheme would receive his government's moral support. Dunning did act as chairman of the Sapiro meetings in Saskatoon and Regina, held early in August. He appealed to the two rival farm organizations to come together, arguing that the alternative was duplication and strife, and assured his audiences that any sound plan for the marketing of Saskatchewan's wheat would have the full support of the government. Dunning presented a resolution to the Regina meeting proposing the creation of a joint wheat pool organization consisting of representatives from farm and other interested groups, including the government. The resolution was adopted,[22] and the two farmers' organizations were soon persuaded to join in creating a single wheat pool in the province.

It was Aaron Sapiro who brought them together, and his speeches in Saskatoon, Regina and Moose Jaw spurred farmers to a frenzy of activity without parallel in the history of the province. Frank Underhill, who in 1923 was teaching history at the University of Saskatchewan, was one of those who attended Sapiro's first meeting. Forty-seven years later, the memory of that evening was still fresh:

> I can still recall vividly the evangelistic fervour of the great mass meeting in Third Avenue Methodist Church in Saskatoon at which Aaron Sapiro launched the Wheat Pool movement in that Province. His speech was the most magnificent to which I have ever listened. And as he led up to his climax about co-operation as a way of life and not merely a way of selling wheat or other commodities, he roused his audience as I fancy [William Jennings] Bryan must have roused the populist democracy of the American Mid-West by his famous Cross of Gold speech in 1896.[23]

Charles Dunning did not play the active part in this campaign that he had in connection with the attempts to reestablish the Wheat Board, but he did issue a public statement at the end of August urging those farmers who believed in the pooling scheme to sign up so that it could be given a fair trial.[24] He cautioned Saskatchewan farmers to read the contract carefully before signing it, and declared that it would do no good to get preachers in their pulpits to use emotional methods to get the necessary signatures.[25] As for himself, Dunning signed a pool contract.[26]

The wheat pool organizers failed to sign up half the province's wheat acreage before the 1923 crop began to move to market. And so the work was carried on over the winter, assisted by grants from the Saskatchewan Co-op, the United Grain Growers and the provincial government. That goal was finally reached in mid-June 1924, and the Saskatchewan Co-operative Wheat Producers Limited was formally established. It proved to be a great success, in part because the organization of the Wheat Pool (to use the name farmers used) coincided with the revival of the provincial and prairie economy. The 1925 crop was good, wheat prices were once more rising, and business was reviving across Saskatchewan and across the west.

The Prohibition Question

In 1922, Premier Dunning had also pledged his government to "continued vigorous enforcement of the Saskatchewan Temperance Act [STA] in accordance with the expressed will of the people." Of all the public issues with which Dunning became involved during his term of office, none proved to be more contentious than prohibition. No other issue so divided public opinion or brought so much criticism of him. A Presbyterian himself, Dunning had not expressed any strong views on this issue before 1922, but as Premier he found himself caught in the middle between those who wanted to see prohibition continue and those who did not.

The STA dated from 1917. The Legislature enacted this measure following a referendum held some months earlier in which Saskatchewan voters had decided to abandon the province's brief experiment with a system of government liquor stores (known as "dispensaries") in favour of complete provincial prohibition. The STA forbade the sale of liquor to anyone and by anyone except physicians and druggists who could buy and sell limited quantities under special permits for medicinal purposes. Public support for Saskatchewan's prohibition law was at first strong, but once the war ended, this began to change. National prohibition (introduced in 1918) ended in 1919, though Saskatchewan subsequently voted (in 1920) to again ban the importation of liquor into the province.[27]

However, that same year the United States adopted national prohibition, and this made the enforcement of the STA more difficult. "Export warehouses" suddenly sprang up in villages and towns close to the American border, the better to supply rumrunners smuggling liquor into the United States in defiance of the Volstead Act. Not all of the liquor in these export warehouses found its way south. A thriving local trade also developed, which gave rise to considerable disorder and lawlessness in Estevan and other border towns, and prompted the Legislature to urge the federal authorities to put an end to the export liquor business. The federal government eventually did so in December 1922.

This removed one source of beverage alcohol from the province, but another still remained to bedevil those charged with the enforcement of the STA: "home-brew." The illicit distillation of liquor was primarily a rural phenomenon. "Home-brew" was manufactured chiefly for local consumption, and usually consumed within a few days of distillation, but community "stills" built to supply the needs of city bootleggers and their thirsty customers were not unheard of. By one estimate, there were thought to be as many as 20,000 illicit stills operating in the province (or approximately one for every fifth farm).[28]

Such widespread flouting of the law contributed to growing public dissatisfaction with the STA by 1922. One sign of the change in public sentiment occurred at the annual convention of the Saskatchewan Association of Rural Municipalities (SARM). It had not formally discussed the prohibition issue in four years, but in 1922, SARM adopted a resolution calling for a referendum on the re-establishment of government dispensaries. A Temperance Reform League was launched in Regina in May "to assist temperance and oppose prohibition and other coercive measures." The meeting was attended by over 500 Regina citizens, including unofficial representatives from the Great War Veterans' Association, the Trades and Labour Council, the Retail Merchants' Association and the Roman Catholic and Anglican Churches.[29] Similar organizations soon began to appear in other communities in the province. To coordinate the efforts of these various anti-prohibition groups, the Moderation League of Saskatchewan was formed at a meeting in Regina in July. Modelled on an organization of the same name in Manitoba, and composed of "leading churchmen, professional and businessmen," its avowed purpose was to "bring pressure to bear on the Legislature to enact legislation that can be enforced to the moral and financial benefit of all."[30]

The Moderation League proceeded to circulate a petition asking for government control and sale of all liquor and the retail sale of beer, with the net revenue to be used for road building and for relief of taxation in school districts. This petition, bearing 65,075 names, was tabled in the Legislature in February 1923. Representatives of the League subsequently met with the Premier and other members of the Cabinet, and asked that the government test public opinion by means of a referendum if it was unwilling to introduce legislation giving effect to their wishes. In replying to the delegation, Dunning commented that this was the first intimation his government had received that the Moderation League would be content with a referendum. He made no definite commitment to the League beyond declaring, as Premier Martin had earlier done, that the government would not modify its liquor policy until convinced that the public desired such a change.[31]

The Moderation League's campaign for another vote on prohibition did not long go unchallenged. The Social Service Council (an organization composed of various religious and secular groups) urged rural municipal councils, churches, SGGA locals, Homemakers' Clubs and other organizations to make known to the government their "opposition to any move looking to a return of a legalized traffic in intoxicating liquor for beverage purposes." The Council also sponsored a prohibition convention in February 1923 to rally support for the STA. It concluded that there was no sufficient reason to believe that the people had changed their minds. The annual Grain Growers' and School Trustees' conventions, as well as the Presbyterian Synod of Saskatchewan, the Methodist Conference of Saskatchewan, the Baptist Church and the Women's Christian Temperance Union had all recently expressed themselves in favour of a continuation of prohibition. The government's duty was plain: it must continue to enforce the law with all possible vigour.[32]

The Premier himself shared this sentiment, and the government decided not to alter its liquor policy. While admitting in the Legislature that conditions were far from satisfactory and that there had been agitation in some quarters in favour of a change, Attorney General J.A. Cross declared that the government did not plan to introduce the legislation that the Moderation League had requested or submit the liquor question to a popular vote. It would continue, as in the past, to strictly enforce prohibition and attempt to foster greater respect for the law.[33]

Some members on both sides of the House were unhappy with this decision, but the harshest criticism came from the Regina *Morning Leader*. Ostensibly Liberalism's strongest voice in the province, it condemned the Dunning government for timidity in dealing with a situation it knew should be remedied. "With the Saskatchewan Liquor Commission openly discredited and the Saskatchewan Temperance Act either brazenly opposed or regarded with indifference by the vast majority of the people of the province," it argued, "something more might be expected of the government than an admission that it can do nothing but continue to 'enforce' the act and keep a propagandist on the road to lecture the people on respect for the law." The question should be put to a vote, the *Morning Leader* believed, as was being done in Alberta and Manitoba.[34]

The Moderation League spent the summer working to increase its membership and to secure a greater number of signatures for a second petition. The prohibitionists, meanwhile, fought a rearguard action, doing their utmost to postpone, as long as possible, any change in the liquor law or consultation of the voters. When Charles Dunning confidentially informed Rev. Charles Endicott, a leading prohibitionist and fellow Liberal, that "everything points to a exceedingly strong demand for a referendum at an early date, a demand which in all probability cannot properly be refused," the latter urged that the vote be held off as long as possible, and at least until the summer of 1924.[35] The Social Service Council was prepared to agree to another referendum, but not until the STA had been given a fair test. Three years from December 15, 1922, the date on which the export houses had been put out of business, was considered the minimum period of time before another vote should be held. The Prohibition League of Saskatchewan, formed in Regina later in the year to combat the efforts of the Moderation League, advocated a two year delay, as did the Grain Growers and the School Trustees. On the other hand, the Qu'Appelle Synod of the Anglican Church favoured an immediate referendum.[36]

The Moderation League presented a second petition to the government in November 1923. This one contained 79,003 names, and asked that immediate provision be made for a referendum on the liquor question. Dunning personally had no desire to see his government enter the "booze business," as he called it, but he now admitted that the people would have to be consulted. A plebiscite would be held on July 16, 1924. Saskatchewan voters would be asked to indicate whether they still supported prohibition and if not, whether in addition to the government sale of liquor they wished the sale of beer in licensed premises.[37]

Like the Wheat Pool drive that was just then winding up, the campaign leading up to the July vote stirred the emotions of the whole province. For weeks platforms, pulpits and editorial columns resounded with the arguments of the Prohibition and Moderation Leagues. The plebiscite resulted in the defeat of the first question, "Are you in favour of

SAB RB 29

During a trip to the Wembly Exhibition in Great Britain in 1924, Dunning visited the Wright and Havelock Foundry in Leicester, where he had worked as a boy before coming to Canada in 1902. Here, Dunning is shown shaking hands with "Old Bill" Briers, who was employed for over 50 years at the Foundry. Mr. Wright, the Premier's old employer, is standing behind Dunning.

Prohibition in Saskatchewan?" by 119,337 to 80,381, or a majority of 38,956. There was a smaller total vote on the second question, only 170,136. Of this number, 89,011 voted for the sale of liquor and beer in government stores, and 81,125 for the additional sale of beer in licensed premises. The vote was held on the provincial constituency boundaries: 45 constituencies voted "wet" and 15 voted to remain "dry." The vote for the sale of beer by the glass was almost evenly split, with 23 ridings voting in favour and 22 against. The strength of the moderationists lay in the cities, where a "dry" majority of 11,781 in 1916 was turned into a "wet" majority of 10,009 in 1924, but some rural areas, particularly those with a large concentration of European-born voters, also gave decisive majorities against prohibition. Nearly all the "dry" constituencies were in the central and southeastern portions of Saskatchewan, areas that were largely inhabited by people from the United States or eastern Canada.[38]

Legislation implementing the wishes of Saskatchewan's voters was introduced and adopted without much debate at the next session of the Legislature. The Liquor Act provided for the establishment of a Liquor Board which would have the general control, management and supervision of the government liquor stores. Voters were given the right to petition either for or against a store in any community, but no provision was made for the sale of beer in licensed premises.[39]

During the debate Dunning had made it quite clear that the purpose of the liquor stores was to provide alcohol rather than revenue, but Saskatchewan's towns and cities had other ideas. At its 1925 convention, the Union of Saskatchewan Municipalities (USM) passed a near-unanimous resolution (there were only three dissenters) urging him to distribute a substantial share of any profits from the sale of liquor among the province's urban centres, or alternatively, to reduce the Public Revenue Tax. When this resolution was presented to his government later in the year, Dunning informed the USM that any profits would be used to reduce Saskatchewan's public debt. If the money was used to finance existing services, or new ones, then any future change in liquor policy might leave these services without a source of revenue.[40]

Such a cautious approach was typical of Dunning's handling of the province's finances after 1922. (He retained the portfolio of Provincial Treasurer as long as he served as Premier.) Of course, hard times dictated caution. Slumping wheat prices and farm incomes had a negative impact on the entire provincial economy, and Dunning adopted a policy of retrenchment rather than impose new taxes. Capital expenditures were kept low and ordinary expenditures were curtailed. In this way, even though revenues increased only slightly, the budget was balanced in 1925 after three years of deficits. The estimates for 1925–26, including both capital and ordinary expenditures, were only 60% of what they had been four years previously. Grants to schools were not cut; indeed they rose with the increase in the number of schools and pupils in the province during these years, as did expenditures for public welfare. (The tripling of expenditures for mother's allowances was the most important single cause of this increase).[41]

As Saskatchewan recovered from the effects of the depression and returned to more prosperous times, Dunning sounded a note of caution for the future:

> There is every reason for confidence both in the future of our people in an economic sense and the future of this province as a governmental entity, but may I say in the same breath that in these times there is also every need for continued caution. I suppose most members of the House do read the Bible but if there ever was a country in the world with respect to which the experience of Joseph of old applied, this western province, surely, is the place. Take care in the fat years, waste not your substance in these years, but prepare for the days of leanness which may come.[42]

The 1925 Election

The Liberals' political prospects were on the rise too by 1925, with a provincial election looming. Here Dunning's former prominent association with the organized farmers served the Liberals well. Dunning could attack the farmers' political movement without appearing to criticize its foster parent, the SGGA. It was not simply fear of schism and a weakening of the farmers' organization which prompted Dunning to act as he did, of course, but also a desire, as a good party man, to keep the Liberal ship afloat in heavy seas. Political necessity dictated that the new Premier again put some distance between himself and the federal Liberals in order to mollify the Grain Growers, and by words and deeds Dunning sought to demonstrate after 1922 that his government had the farmers' best interests at heart. When Saskatchewan voters again went to the polls in 1925, the farmers failed to dislodge the Liberals from power: 52 Liberals were elected (three by acclamation), the provincial Progressives won only six seats and the Conservatives three.[43] It was not Dunning's adroit political manoeuvring alone which brought victory in 1925, however. Changes in the nature, leadership and philosophical underpinnings of the farmers' movement in Saskatchewan during the 1920s were also important.

It was no accident that the farmers' entrance into provincial politics was so hesitant in Saskatchewan. The close association between the government and the Grain Growers had served to enhance the reputations of a group of men who came to dominate the highest echelons of organized agriculture in Saskatchewan and they, no less than the Liberals, were determined to preserve it for their own benefit. These farm leaders—J.A. Maharg, J.B. Musselman, A.G. Hawkes, Thomas Sales, John Evans and H.C. Fleming—had found a power base in the Saskatchewan Co-op. Its phenomenal success (due in no small degree to the solid financial support provided by the Liberal government at Regina) ensured that their views would carry great weight within the ranks of the farmers' movement in Saskatchewan.

At first this small group, and particularly Maharg and Musselman, were able to thwart all efforts to commit the SGGA to provincial political action. Not until after the 1921 federal election, and Premier Martin's open endorsation of the federal Liberal party, was the entrenched leadership of the SGGA finally compelled to take the farmers' organization into provincial politics. After 1922, though, Maharg, Musselman and their cohorts found themselves increasingly on the defensive within their own organization. Maharg had already incurred the wrath of those rank and file members of the SGGA who objected to the close liaison in personnel and views between the Grain Growers' executive and the Liberals, and wished to see a true "farmers' government" at Regina. Antagonism toward the practice of multiple office-holding grew more widespread as time passed. One by one, the members of this group began to be replaced: A.G. Hawkes as vice-president by George F. Edwards, then J.B. Musselman as secretary by A.J. McPhail.

This internal struggle acquired a new dimension in 1923 with the inauguration of the wheat pool campaign, and its outcome was to sound the death knell of the farmers' political movement in Saskatchewan. George Edwards, A.J. McPhail and Violet McNaughton, the recognized leaders of the insurgent element within the SGGA, had initially favoured provincial political action, but they also became ardent champions of the wheat pool. This placed them in a dilemma. Their first goal—the creation of a provincial Progressive party—could only be realized by working with Maharg and the other Saskatchewan Co-op men who still remained on the Grain Growers' executive, most of whom were antagonistic toward the pooling concept. On the other hand, if Edwards, McPhail and the others placed their influence firmly behind the pool campaign, this would mean developing a close working relationship with the chief foe of the Grain Growers' political movement, Charles Dunning. Faced with such a choice, the insurgents (or

SAB RA 3288

Prime Minister William L.M. King, signing the Old Age Pension Bill in Ottawa, 1927. Charles Dunning, by then King's minister of Railways and Canals, is seated to the Prime Minister's left.

"Ginger Group" as they were popularly known) opted to devote their energies to dislodging Maharg from the SGGA executive and working with the provincial government to make the wheat pool a success. By 1924 the "Ginger Group" had triumphed on both counts. In January 1924, J.A. Maharg was defeated in his bid for reelection for a fourteenth term as president of the SGGA (and the Grain Growers decided to leave the provincial political field). Then in mid-June, the sign-up campaign reached its goal and the Wheat Pool began to sell farmers' wheat. With the "Ginger Group" firmly in control of the SGGA, Dunning and the Liberals no longer had anything to fear from that quarter.[44]

It is important as well to note that the farmers' movement was no longer a single monolithic organization after 1921, with the emergence of the Farmers' Union of Canada. Since the Farmers' Union considered political action futile and divisive, it offered no aid or comfort to the provincial Progressives, and instead directed all of its energies to the organization of the Wheat Pool.[45] The provincial Progressive party in Saskatchewan was clearly hampered by the unwillingness of either farmers' organization to support it at the critical time. Once the SGGA withdrew from politics, Dunning's appeal to an agrarian electorate ensured that the Liberals would carry the 1925 provincial election with ease.

With the Progressives no longer a threat, Charles Dunning could now accomplish what W.M. Martin had tried and failed to do in 1921: reunite the federal and provincial wings of the Liberal party. Dunning actively campaigned for William Lyon Mackenzie King in the 1925 federal election, and subsequently accepted a post in King's Cabinet (something Dunning had had his eye on as early as 1924). Charles Dunning was sworn in as minister of Railways and Canals on March 1, 1926. A seat was opened for him in Regina, where he was elected by acclamation.[46] In 1929 he brought down his first budget as minister of Finance.[47] Defeated in 1930, he entered the world of business in eastern Canada, returning to public life in the federal Cabinet as minister of Finance from 1935 until 1939. In 1940, he was named chancellor of Queen's University. The last 19 years of his life were spent in a third successful career in the financial world. He died in Montreal on October 2, 1958.

Conclusion

Charles Dunning was Premier for not quite four years, the second-shortest term of any of those who have held the province's highest elected office. What has been the legacy of this man who was so briefly the Premier of Saskatchewan? For the most part, Dunning continued the policies of the Martin government (of which he had been a key member) and was little inclined to chart a new path. In the case of liquor policy, Dunning was only respecting the wishes of the voters (as they could be ascertained in the 1924 plebiscite) when he introduced the system of government liquor stores that is with us still.

Dunning also deserves credit for his prudent management of the province's finances in difficult economic times. This helped to lay the basis for the prosperity which Saskatchewan would enjoy in the last half of the 1920s.

Reestablishing the Canadian Wheat Board might have been another of Dunning's legacies, but it was not to be. In pursuing this elusive goal, Dunning appears to have been motivated partly by a sense of duty as Premier—farmers in his province overwhelmingly favoured the compulsory marketing of wheat—and partly by political considerations. Making every possible effort to establish a new Wheat Board would steal the Progressive party's thunder. It had the added benefit of enhancing the Premier's own reputation. As one author has noted,

> The national coverage given the Wheat Board controversy thrust Dunning into national prominence and he became closely identified with the welfare of the wheat farmer and the search for a solution to the wheat marketing problem. Despite his lack of success ... he emerged unscathed, appearing as a champion of western interests through his tireless efforts to set up a Wheat Board.[48]

In politics, Dunning's crowning achievement was to save the Saskatchewan Liberal party from defeat at the hands of the farmers' political movement. The key to his success lay in his own popularity among the province's farmers. It was for this reason that the Liberals had turned to Dunning in 1922, and he proved equal to the task. During the relatively short time he held the office of Premier, Charles Dunning served his province and his party well.

Notes

1. E. Eager, *Saskatchewan Government: Politics and Pragmatism* (Saskatoon: Western Producer Prairie Books, 1980), 47–51; D.E. Smith, *Prairie Liberalism: The Liberal Party in Saskatchewan, 1905–71* (Toronto: University of Toronto Press, 1975), 54–56.
2. J.W. Brennan, "C.A. Dunning, 1916–1930: The Rise and Fall of a Western Agrarian Liberal," in J.E. Foster (ed.), *The Developing West* (Edmonton: University of Alberta Press, 1983), 246–47.
3. G.L. Barnhart, *"Peace, Progress and Prosperity": A Biography of Saskatchewan's First Premier, T. Walter Scott* (Regina: Canadian Plains Research Center, 2000), 136–43. For a more detailed account of these various scandals, and the outcome of the investigations into them, see J.W. Brennan, "A Political History of Saskatchewan, 1905–1929" (Ph.D. dissertation, University of Alberta, 1976), 292–328, 341–47, 375–76.
4. Brennan, "Political History," 330–32.
5. Regina *Morning Leader* (hereafter cited as *Leader*), February 15, 1917.
6. Ibid., May 6, 1920; *Grain Growers' Guide* (hereafter cited as *Guide*), August 4, 1920; Saskatchewan Archives Board (SAB), SGGA Papers, *Minutes of the Twentieth Annual Convention of the Saskatchewan Grain Growers' Association*, 56–57.
7. Smith, *Prairie Liberalism*, 84–95.
8. Uhrich also became minister of Public Health when that portfolio was created in 1923.
9. *Guide*, April 26, 1922.
10. The most detailed account of the establishment of the Canada Wheat Board, its discontinuance after a single year's operation, and farmers' lobbying efforts to persuade the federal government to resume the marketing of wheat is C.F. Wilson, *A Century of Canadian Grain: Government Policy to 1951* (Saskatoon: Western Producer Prairie Books, 1978), 130–75.
11. Canada, House of Commons, *Debates*, June 14, 1922, p. 2915; Wilson, *A Century of Canadian Grain*, 177–78.
12. SAB, C.A. Dunning Papers, Dunning to W.R. Motherwell, May 22, 1922, pp. 47064–66; *Leader*, June 15, 1922.
13. *Statutes of Canada*, 12–13 Geo. V, Chapter 14.
14. *Leader*, July 11, 1922; Library and Archives Canada (LAC), W.L.M. King Papers, C.A. Dunning to King, July 18, 1922, pp. 61651–54.
15. For a more detailed account of these negotiations see Brennan, "Political History," 544–46, and R.M.H. Dixon, "Charles Avery Dunning and the Western Wheat Marketing Problem" (M.A. thesis, Queen's University, 1974), 114–27.
16. SAB, C.A. Dunning Papers, press statement by C.A. Dunning and H. Greenfield, August 14, 1922, pp. 48261–62; *Guide*, August 23, 1922.
17. *Guide*, January 17, 1923; Provincial Archives of Alberta, Premier's Files, File 100–45(b), J. Bracken to H. Greenfield, January 23, 1923; SAB, C.A. Dunning Papers, J. Bracken to Dunning, January 23, 1923, p. 48273.
18. *Leader*, April 28, 1923. For a more detailed account of these negotiations see Brennan, "Political History," 556–58, and Dixon, "Charles Avery Dunning, "151–67.
19. SAB, C.A. Dunning Papers, press statement by H. Greenfield and C.A. Dunning, June 11, 1923, pp. 48409–10.

20. *Guide*, June 27, 1923.
21. L.D. Nesbitt, *Tides in the West* (Saskatoon: Modern Press, 1962), 34–59; G. Fairbairn, *From Prairie Roots: The Remarkable Story of Saskatchewan Wheat Pool* (Saskatoon: Western Producer Prairie Books, 1984), 15–43.
22. *Leader*, July 10, 1923, August 8, 1923, August 10, 1923.
23. F.H. Underhill, "What, then is the Manitoban, this New Man? Or This Almost Chosen People," *Canadian Historical Association Historical Papers* (1970): 41.
24. *Leader*, August 31, 1923.
25. Ibid., August 20, 1923, August 22, 1923. Dunning was referring to a request by the pool organizers that the clergy throughout the province discuss the wheat pool on August 26, the last Sunday before the deadline (ibid., August 14, 1923).
26. SAB, C.A. Dunning Papers, Dunning to S. Archer, March 25, 1924, p. 24508.
27. The most detailed account of Saskatchewan's experiment with a system of government sale (1915–16) and prohibition (1917–24) is E. Pinno, "Temperance and Prohibition in Saskatchewan" (M.A. thesis, University of Saskatchewan, Regina, 1971).
28. *Leader*, April 6, 1923.
29. Ibid., March 11, 1922, May 27, 1922.
30. Ibid., July 20, 1922; SAB, C.A. Dunning Papers, Moderation League to the barristers of Saskatchewan, December 27, 1922, p. 7142.
31. *Journals of the Legislative Assembly* (1923), 38; *Leader*, March 8, 1923.
32. SAB, C.A. Dunning Papers, memorial circulated by the Prohibition Committee of the Social Service Council (n.d.), p. 7623; "Memorandum for Presentation to the Government of Saskatchewan," February 28, 1923, pp. 7721–22.
33. *Leader*, March 15, 1923.
34. Ibid., March 17, 1923. The "propagandist" was Rev. John L. Nicol, who had been appointed Director of Temperance and Social Service in the Department of the Attorney General in 1921. Essentially a public relations officer, his function was to foster support for and obedience of the Saskatchewan Temperance Act.
35. SAB, C.A. Dunning Papers, Dunning to C. Endicott, July 9, 1922, p. 7821; Endicott to Dunning, September 8, 1922, pp. 7845–47.
36. Ibid., "Manifesto of the Prohibition Committee of the Social Service Council of Saskatchewan on the Present Temperance Situation," 1923, p. 7833; SAB, SGGA Papers, *Minutes of the Twenty-fourth Annual Convention of the Saskatchewan Grain Growers' Association*, 154; *Leader*, November 29, 1923; Saskatoon *Daily Star*, February 23, 1924.
37. SAB, C.A. Dunning Papers, Dunning to S. Metheral, February 9, 1924, pp. 6725–26; *Leader*, December 1, 1923, 8 March 1924; *Statutes of Saskatchewan*, 14 Geo. V, Chapter 50. Dunning consciously chose to consult the voters of Saskatchewan by means of a plebiscite rather than a referendum (which would be binding). It would be for the Legislature to interpret the wishes of the voters and enact appropriate legislation.
38. *Leader*, July 18, 1924, August 15, 1924.
39. *Statutes of Saskatchewan*, 15 Geo. V, Chapter 53.
40. *Leader*, June 26, 1925, November 15, 1925. The Public Revenue Tax (originally called the Patriotic Revenue Tax) had been introduced during World War I. It imposed a levy of two mills on the value of

all municipal property in Saskatchewan. Towns and cities resented having to share the property tax field with the province. [F. Colligan-Yano and M. Norton, *The Urban Age: Building a Place for Urban Government in Saskatchewan* (Regina: Saskatchewan Urban Municipalities Association, 1996), 31, 48–51.]

41. J.W. Brennan, "The Public Career of Charles Avery Dunning in Saskatchewan" (M.A. thesis, University of Saskatchewan, Regina, 1968), 106–12. For a more general discussion of public finance in Saskatchewan see D.B. Climenhaga, "Public Finance in Saskatchewan During the Settlement Process, 1905–1929" (M.A. thesis, University of Saskatchewan, 1949).
42. Budget Speech Delivered by The Honourable C.A. Dunning, Premier and Provincial Treasurer, on the Budget in the Legislative Assembly of Saskatchewan, January 12, 1926, p. 19.
43. J.W. Brennan, "C.A. Dunning and the Challenge of the Progressives, 1922–1925," *Saskatchewan History* 23, no. 1 (Winter 1969): 1–12. Two Independents were also elected in 1925.
44. Brennan, "C.A. Dunning, 1916–30," 251–53; L.D. Courville, "The Saskatchewan Progressives" (M.A. thesis, University of Saskatchewan, Regina, 1971), 107–42.
45. D.S. Spafford, "The Origin of the Farmers' Union of Canada," *Saskatchewan History* 18, no. 3 (Autumn 1965): 89–98.
46. Brennan, "C.A. Dunning, 1916–1930," 254–56; R.A. Wardhaugh, *Mackenzie King and the Prairie West* (Toronto: University of Toronto Press, 2000), 93–94, 102–14.
47. Dunning was the only federal minister of Finance to come from Saskatchewan until Ralph Goodale was appointed by Prime Minister Paul Martin in December 2003.
48. Dixon, "Charles Avery Dunning," 184.

James G. Gardiner
DAVID SMITH

Gardiner, February 26, 1926
(M. West, Regina. West's Studio Collection. SAB RA 632 (2)).

Gardiner at his desk in the Premier's office (SAB RA 6030).

Gen. McNaughton and Gardiner in England during World War II (SAB RB 9335).

Greeting Princess Elizabeth & Prince Philip, 1951 (SAB RB 8891).

Saskatchewan Premiers of the 20th Century

James G. Gardiner, 1926–1929, 1934–1935

Introduction

This is a book about Premiers of Saskatchewan, and as one of that number James G. (Jimmy) Gardiner meets the qualifications for inclusion. In fact, unlike the other twelve men who have held the position, Gardiner meets it twice, having been provincial Premier from 1926 to 1929, and, again, in 1934–1935. The point is worth making not just for the sake of factual accuracy but to underline an important feature of Gardiner's life in politics, whether one chooses to call it persistence, stubbornness or resilience. In one form or another—as backbencher, minister, Premier, leader of the opposition, federal Cabinet minister, or member of the federal opposition—Gardiner held uninterrupted elected office from 1914 to 1958.

Forty-three years may not be a Commonwealth or Canadian record (although 22 years in one portfolio, as federal minister of Agriculture, is), but compared to the other Premiers of Saskatchewan, Gardiner's immersion in politics was total, complete and all-absorbing. Scott left not only the premiership in 1916 but, because of illness, abandoned the political world; Martin did the same thing in 1922, only in his case to go to the Bench. When Dunning left Regina in 1926, he entered the federal government and became minister of Finance. Anderson and Patterson were single government Premiers with minimal legislative or cabinet experience; Grant Devine had no previous political experience, and left politics after the defeat of his two-term government; Lloyd, Blakeney and Romanow had longer experience of elected office, but because they were members of the Co-operative Commonwealth Federation or the later New Democratic Party, opportunities to move to federal politics were never sufficiently enticing. By contrast, Ross Thatcher spent 15 years as a member of Parliament (MP) before entering upon 11 years in Saskatchewan politics. T.C. Douglas is the Premier who most closely approximates Gardiner's longevity in politics —MP, Premier and (as leader of the federal NDP) MP again—with a total of 36 years of elected office.

This chronology provides context for Gardiner's career. While the majority of other Premiers entered and exited the Premier's office for a variety of reasons, the signal fact of the careers of Anderson and Patterson or, even, Scott, Martin and Devine is that they appeared and then departed. The same could not be said of Douglas, and, certainly, was never said of Gardiner. Indeed, a lingering feature of Saskatchewan politics long after Gardiner became federal minister of Agriculture in 1935 was the so-called Gardiner "Machine." Not only Liberal opponents but, in time, some Liberals came to rue Gardiner's unflagging interest and heavy hand in provincial affairs. In sum, to talk of Gardiner's four years as Premier, and to talk only of that, is to distort the man and his time as provincial first minister. Another reason for belabouring this point is that Gardiner himself never saw his years as Premier as the pinnacle of his political career. Nothing short of becoming the national spokesman for Liberalism in Canada and, with that, Prime Minister, would satisfy so consuming an ambition. His every action as Premier must be interpreted in light of this knowledge.

The premiership represented one, but not the top, rung of a ladder whose outward form was the Liberal Party organization. From 1922, when he entered Dunning's Cabinet as Highways minister—and Highways, with its inspectors, was the command centre of the much-abused organization—Gardiner dominated the party. Later Dunning was to say that under Gardiner, the organization became no longer the party's agent, but its master.[1] While Gardiner would have agreed with that comment, he would have been puzzled by it. In his eyes, the organization was indispensable to the party's electoral success as well as its survival. Those who did not share his order of priorities would, he believed, ultimately meet an unhappy fate.

From the perspective of a chapter on Gardiner as Premier, talk of party organization may seem peripheral, yet, once again, to compartmentalize his time as Premier would provide only a partial, and distorted, view of these crucial years in the long-term development of Liberalism in the province and on the prairies. It is important to recall that, extraordinary as it seems in retrospect, Gardiner sat as a backbencher in the ruling party of Saskatchewan for eight years before becoming a minister. None of the Premiers before 1926 had ever sat as a backbencher. The reason for the long probation is something of a mystery, although whatever the explanation, it clearly reflects the judgment of Scott and Martin that Gardiner's claims to promotion could be overlooked. Perhaps it had something to do with his combative political style; perhaps, relatedly, with his reluctance to cooperate with those who did not share his view of the central importance of party politics (including electoral competition) to the operation of what he liked to call "representative responsible government." On the last matter, Gardiner was a lifelong, passionate opponent of third parties; and it is only slightly theatrical to say that in his opposition he proved the nemesis of the Saskatchewan farmers when they flirted with entering provincial politics as an electoral organization.

In any case, Gardiner sat on the backbenches from the special session of the Saskatchewan Legislature called on the declaration of war in 1914, until Dunning brought him into Cabinet in 1922. He sat, but he was not idle. It is no exaggeration to say that in these years, Gardiner made himself indispensable to the party not through any acuteness as a legislator—his performance in that realm was undistinguished—but rather it was as a superlative organizer and campaigner in a period that saw war, the disintegration of the national parties, and the rise of powerful farmers' groups intent upon reforming the parliamentary system Gardiner so worshipped (the verb is not too strong) that Gardiner made his mark. And because the party in question was the national Liberal Party, whose organization was provincially based, Gardiner's influence grew. He became the pivot, the linchpin, through whose exertions and under whose direction the federal and provincial wings of the party operated. The touchstone of all policy was its effect upon the health of the party. Gardiner was first and foremost a politician in every sense of the term. The source of his drive, energy, and enthusiasm for the minutiae of politics lies in the years before he first ran for office. But that this background served to prepare and train him for the premiership and beyond, Gardiner was never in any doubt. As such, some biographical facts are in order.[2]

The Early Years

Gardiner was born in Farquhar, southwestern Ontario, on the boundary that divides Huron and Perth counties. Interestingly, this area was to produce several prominent politicians. William Aberhart, who was to electrify Alberta with Social Credit at the same time that Gardiner was moving from the Saskatchewan to the national scene, was born at Seaforth, a few miles from Farquhar. Arthur Meighen, John Diefenbaker and William Lyon Mackenzie King were born at different points about equidistant from Farquhar. Only slightly further away, to the south, were the early homes of Walter Scott (near Strathroy) and William Martin (Norwich). Not only were they born geographically close to one another, but they were also contemporaries. All were entering or already in young manhood when Canada entered its first great era of prosperity and expansion at the close of the 19th century. All had agrarian roots, although Gardiner alone of the group retained them. The farm at Lemberg, which he bought early in World War I and where he died in 1962, was never far from his thoughts. His voluminous correspondence with family and confidants, particularly once he had established a second home in Ottawa, is filled with advice about farming practices that should be carried out generally but, most especially, at Lemberg.

It was Gardiner's farming background and interests that brought him west in 1901. He joined a harvest excursion and then decided to stay at a paternal uncle's place at Clearwater, Manitoba. It was during the three years there that he attended high school. (His primary education had been disrupted when his father embarked on an unsuccessful quest to improve the family's fortunes by moving, first, to Nebraska and, later, to Michigan. Ultimately, Gardiner Senior returned to Ontario.) By 1904, he had completed a second-class teaching certificate and by 1911 a Bachelor of Arts from Manitoba College.

Although Gardiner proudly proclaimed his agrarian roots, teaching offered him escape from the confines they imposed. He was never so enamoured with agriculture as to consider limiting his career to it alone. On the contrary, as he said in his first nomination speech in 1914: "My ambition today is to be a farmer with education representing the farmers of this constituency in the Legislature."[3] This was not the only time that Gardiner was to refer to his education. As a college student, constitutional history and liberal economic theory appear to have made the most lasting impression on him. Throughout his correspondence, there is a recognizable pedagogical tone that reflects Gardiner's education (as well as his assessment of that training) and, also, his personality.

Gardiner taught for a decade before he was elected to the Legislature, and few young persons could have acquired such varied experience. At Alpha, where he taught in the fall term of 1904, he found a community of Dunkards.[4] At Hirsch, in 1905, he served in a solidly Jewish settlement, and for a time taught school in the synagogue. Sometimes, with the rabbi acting as translator, Gardiner served as an informal secretarial go-between in transactions involving Hirsch and outsiders. Warmley, where he taught in 1906, was predominantly an English settlement, and Vineberg (1907) had been settled with citizens from eastern Canada. West Weyburn (1909) was composed largely of Americans, and Lockwood (1910) included both Canadians and Americans, and a generous admixture of Austrians and Scandinavians. Lemberg, where he served as principal from 1911 to 1914, was a larger village with a Polish name but a typical mosaic of the prairies' population.

Gardiner's own grand design was what lay behind his choice of schools. It included covering vast parts of the southeastern prairie on bicycle or horseback, getting to know as many people as possible. His athletic skills were useful in giving him a quick rapport with his pupils everywhere he went, but they also meant travelling around from contest to contest, not only playing but learning the techniques of organization and management. In later years, Gardiner repeatedly reminded correspondents that his first political organization had been an athletic club.

What made Lemberg particularly attractive was that the provincial constituency of North Qu'Appelle, which contained it, had been lost by W.R. Motherwell in 1908, and he had moved to Humboldt; thus, there was a potential opening for another Liberal. Gardiner first sought nomination in a by-election in 1914; he won that contest and every other one in North Qu'Appelle until the constituency disappeared in a redistribution carried out during Gardiner's time as leader of the opposition.

It is a generalization (but with a large foundation in truth) that some leaders grow with their office while others come to power fully formed. As the previous paragraphs demonstrate, Gardiner falls into the latter category. Independent and resourceful, he was a champion of team play in a game in which he was the coach rather than a player: possessed of a liberal arts education that trained and befitted a debater (he won a gold prize for oratory at College), he dominated any political platform he mounted. Ambitious, and with no family advantage, Gardiner solitarily ascended the political slope. The tension between being a member of the team and the lone player remained throughout his political career. More than early personal characteristics endured, however. All of the great issues that were to confront him as Premier and later as federal minister of Agriculture were in play by the time Gardiner made his 1914 nomination speech. These included the pre-eminence of agriculture but the discontent of the organized farmers (Gardiner himself was a longtime member of the Saskatchewan Grain Growers Association); his exposure to and support of what today would be called multiculturalism; personal loyalty to leader and party which saw Gardiner, Motherwell and four other Saskatchewan Liberals remain true to Laurier in the campaign for Union government in 1917; and the separate school question which presaged the single (although not personal) defeat of his career—the 1929 election loss, in a campaign largely given over to anti-Catholic and anti-foreign feeling. Gardiner's positions on these issues, as on liquor (he was a teetotaler) and religion (a Presbyterian, he pressed for union of the major Protestant denominations leading to the creation of the United Church of Canada in 1925), formed early and thereafter were never subject to self-examination.

The Premiership

Gardiner succeeded Charles Dunning as Premier in February 1926. It needs to be said at the outset that, in Gardiner's mind, the prize was second best. After eight years as a backbencher and another four as minister, this response might seem perverse, especially since in becoming a First Minister he (unprecedently) continued to control the party organization. (Patterson, the new Highways minister and Gardiner's successor as leader in 1935, had only the maintenance of the roads with which to concern himself.) Nor did the prize

James G. Gardiner

© M. West, Regina. West's Studio Collection. SAB RA 632(2)

Formal portrait of Jame G. Gardiner, February 26, 1926, shortly after he became Premier of Saskatchewan.

come by tainted means; he was the unanimous choice of caucus as the name they would put before a subsequent Liberal convention. There were three other candidates—Charles Hamilton, Archibald McNab, and Samuel Latta—all of whom were Cabinet ministers.

What then was the source of Gardiner's ungenerous attitude toward his victory? The explanation lay partly in the knowledge that he was not Dunning's choice. It would have been surprising if he were, for behind the polite correctness of their political relationship, neither man trusted the other. Dunning believed that the best strategy for dealing with Progressives and farmer unrest generally was cooperation. This was a policy he carried with him when he went to Ottawa and which he continued to preach to Mackenzie King and his ministers as they fretted over what to do with the organized farmer governments in Manitoba and Alberta. Gardiner never shared Dunning's view; more than that, he believed such an approach positively dangerous to the future of prairie Liberalism. But there was another dimension to this matter that explained why the premiership came as a bittersweet victory.

By mid-decade Gardiner's was the not-so-hidden hand in federal and provincial party matters. King credited him with returning 15 of Saskatchewan's 21 federal seats in 1925, as well as 50 of the 63 seats at stake that year in the provincial election. Effusive in his expression of gratitude, the Prime Minister also spoke of "looking forward … to seeing you enter the larger sphere of politics and to your cooperation in the work of organization of adjoining Provinces."[5] Not unreasonably, Gardiner interpreted this statement to mean that an invitation to join the federal government would be forthcoming and, since the Progressive threat lingered, that the overture would be made sooner rather than later. On several occasions Gardiner declared that he could not manage the party on the prairies except as a federal Cabinet minister. Yet when King decided to bring a second Saskatchewan minister (after Motherwell) into Cabinet, he opted for the less abrasive and confrontational Charles Dunning. Thus, Gardiner's final ascent to the premiership was overshadowed in his mind by a sense of thwarted ambition. And in the circumstances—Dunning was 40 in 1925 and even Motherwell was only 65—Gardiner's call to Ottawa appeared indefinitely postponed. No one could predict then the economic and political whirlwind that would in five years change everyone's expectations.

A Non-political Police Force

It is important to a study Gardiner's period as Premier to understand how he saw the situation, at least at the beginning. The word that best describes what he saw (and how he felt) is "doldrums." It is common to talk of the years leading to the Depression as buoyant and, compared to the upheavals of boom and bust, war and post-war upheaval, they were indeed so. But they were also stable. For a brief few years, balance had been established, and when Gardiner entered the Premier's office, the task that confronted him was to maintain the status quo. It may be questioned whether any of Saskatchewan's Premiers excelled as maintenance politicians; it is beyond doubt that if any did, Gardiner was not one of them. He attracted controversy, it enveloped him. If the first half of Saskatchewan's third decade offered few provincial challenges, he made his own. Two in particular had long-term implications for the province's politics. To begin with, he took the police out of politics. High time and not soon enough, his critics said; but by the end of the decade, the RCMP had returned to local policing duties in Saskatchewan (they had been withdrawn as a wartime measure in 1917). Second, he set in motion (but did not secure during his premiership) the acquisition of the province's natural resources.

There is a certain irony in the disentangling of the police (more particularly, the Saskatchewan Provincial Police) and (provincial) politics under the auspices of Jimmy Gardiner. Gardiner, the boss of "the machine" that depended upon the labours of patronage-appointed inspectors, proved also to be Gardiner the reformer. His efforts began with working to free the public service of partisan influences.

He had been growing increasingly skeptical of the value of having party workers on the public payroll, as compared with those who were either paid by the party or worked voluntarily for love of the cause. In Saskatchewan's early history, the financing of party affairs through salaried public workers was always tempting, not just because they were paid but because, in days of poor communication and transportation, civil servants were among those who could get around the province most easily. It was no coincidence that the organization went with Highways, and until he became Premier, Gardiner not only accepted what he had inherited but improved on it, adding additional inspectors such as those who examined hotels, none of whom apparently even bothered to file departmental reports for the work they were ostensibly paid for.[6] Barely into his first premiership, however, he began to have serious doubts about party workers who were paid by the state.

Gardiner started by shifting hardened veterans out of their oldest haunt, the inspectorial forces in Highways. Their combined expense accounts for 1924–25 and 1925–26 consumed approximately 70% of the total payments allotted by the Legislature. At the same time, the number of inspectors paid out of capital dropped, in one year, from 22 in 1922–23 to nine, and it stayed there, or below, until Gardiner left office in 1929. Public accounts over half a century old are tricky to interpret, but the figures support Gardiner's contention that he was shifting the organization, and his explanation is clear. Writing in 1936 to one of his successors in Highways, Gardiner said forcefully:

> I think it would be an absolute mistake to place the organizers in Saskatchewan on Government pay, either in Saskatchewan or at Ottawa.

If the Liberal Party cannot finance these two men they had better close up shop. We have had one demonstration of the fact that the people of Saskatchewan will not stand for a party organization paid with Government funds. Our main difficulty at that time was that we did not make the change early enough.[7]

Like the highway inspectors themselves, the police had good reason to travel all over at public expense but, unlike the inspectors, they were endowed with some genuine power. The provincial police were a problem on another front: the laws they enforced included some not held in great affection by large segments of the public, such as the Liquor Act. So astute a politician as Gardiner was unlikely to overlook this, and he early concluded that Saskatchewan was over-policed. Two years before becoming Premier, he had told Motherwell that he thought Saskatchewan had three or four times the number of constables it needed (145 as against 45 in Manitoba).[8] A few months after becoming Premier, Gardiner told the federal minister of Justice that "the policing of this province is rapidly developing into a condition which is likely to bring the whole matter into the field of political controversy."[9] He proposed several alternatives that could either have seen the province take over the duties of the RCMP, which was briefly Gardiner's first preference, or the Mounties take over the duties of the provincial police, which was the preferred position of the federal minister of Justice, Ernest Lapointe. Gardiner, convinced that two separate police forces, both under Liberal governments, could lose the party more seats than any other single factor, did not oppose Lapointe's choice, and late in 1927 asked his own attorney general, James Cross, to negotiate the transfer of all provincial policing to the RCMP. Cross objected strongly, and Gardiner offered him the Education portfolio. Cross decided instead to retire, and T.C. Davis became attorney general, his first task being to "clean out the Saskatchewan Provincial Police"; the Provincial Police Act was repealed at the next session of the Legislature. About 50 of those rendered unemployed by the legislation joined the RCMP.

The record is clear that the police force, originally created to enforce prohibition at a time when World War I was cutting heavily into the manpower needed to staff the RCMP, was subjected to political influences at several levels. It was Gardiner's deathbed recollection that its first members were all selected by Liberals, and their unofficial duties included attending and reporting on opponents' meetings.[10] The royal commission appointed in 1929 to investigate charges of political interference in police activities and the administration of justice proved conclusively that Liberal organizers, as well as policemen, misused the force.[11] It should be emphasized that the charges affected a small number of people, and that the historical record of the whole force was not discredited, nor was it discreditable. Nevertheless, the inescapable result of the investigation was that Gardiner's opponents had little trouble attributing the charges, properly inflated with the passage of time, to the "Gardiner machine" so that one of the commission counsels, John G. Diefenbaker, would remember the report as one which "documents the whole sordid story of the early Gardiner machine."[12] The report actually had a narrow focus on certain specific allegations, and Gardiner's own papers make clear that from the first year of his premiership he was trying actively to do something about the police, and in 1927–28 he did so.

Natural Resources

Gardiner's second initiative concerned the transfer of the province's natural resources from the federal to the provincial government. The story of the Dominion's original retention of Manitoba's resources in 1870, and those of Alberta and Saskatchewan in 1905, and their subsequent return in 1930, is another of those chronicles that is interesting in itself, but provided only a series of incidents in Gardiner's life. From the start, Gardiner believed that jurisdiction over Saskatchewan's resources belonged in Regina and, almost without exception, so did every other provincial politician and party. Federal politicians from Sir Robert Borden on also favoured it, but Borden as Prime Minister was lukewarm to making deals of profit to provinces governed by non-Conservative parties, and the provinces concerned were all determined that any deal over resources would have to be profitable. All three prairie provinces had been receiving grants in lieu of the revenues they might have obtained from the resources, and all three believed that to obtain the resources and lose the grants would be to exchange a reliable asset for an unknown liability. In the meantime, the federal government was busily trading the resources off for its own purposes. In the Legislature in 1925, Gardiner had sounded a recurring theme in Saskatchewan politics, one on which he never changed his mind:

> To sum up, what is the price we have paid for our public domain to be a part of a Canada united from coast to coast? We have given:
>
> | | |
> |---|---:|
> | To Railway companies | 15,177,063 acres |
> | To Hudson's Bay Company | 3,183,600 acres |
> | To Colonization through homesteads | 27,616,100 acres |
> | To colonization through pre-emptions | 7,663,300 acres |
> | Total | 53,640,063 acres |
>
> If we were to receive settlement for these lands on the same basis as Prince Edward Island received consideration in 1873, we would be entitled to $2,482,000 per annum in perpetuity in addition to the return of those lands and resources not yet alienated.[13]

This observation posed many of the questions that Canada's politicians took two decades to answer and none of them involved the lands' original owners, the First Nations. Why were British Columbia and Prince Edward Island treated differently than Manitoba where their resources were concerned, when all three became part of Confederation in the 1870s? Why were Alberta and Saskatchewan treated like Manitoba? If the Maritimes received special compensation from Ottawa in the 1920s on the grounds of need, as recommended by two royal commissions, what did that imply for the prairie provinces, none of which was affluent? Did the prairies' resources belong to the provinces as a matter of constitutional right? With the lands alienated at differing rates in all three prairie provinces, and sometimes for differing purposes, what formula would treat all three fairly if the lands were transferred? The whole problem in due course produced a considerable literature, both journalistic and academic.

Some of the best of it was written by Chester Martin, Gardiner's professor of History at

Manitoba, and that helped give Gardiner a well-stocked armoury with which to approach Ottawa.[14] According to Bram Thompson, a Regina lawyer, Gardiner was the first Premier of Saskatchewan to accept the view that the lands and resources belonged by right to the provinces, and press on Ottawa that all unalienated lands in Saskatchewan should be handed over to the province, with adequate and continuous compensation for those already alienated.[15] King was at first reluctant to admit that the provinces could have both lands and subsidies, but by 1927, when Gardiner presented his case forcefully at the dominion-provincial conference, King was ready to yield, and all that remained was to work out the details. It was, Thompson noted, "truly a victory for Premier Gardiner."[16]

Paradoxically, it did Gardiner little good. The working out of the details, in King's deliberate fashion, required due consideration of how best to manipulate the return of the lands in the interests of Liberal-Progressive cooperation in Manitoba, and even after Manitoba's lands were returned to the province, a royal commission had to be appointed to devise a formula for compensation, which was to treat Manitoba as if it had had its resources since 1870.[17] A lesser commission might have found the task impossible, but its chairman was none other than W.F.A. Turgeon, a well-regarded former Saskatchewan attorney general, and an acceptable formula was forthcoming. Gardiner, meanwhile, was bargaining hard for Saskatchewan, urging that Saskatchewan's compensation should extend its boundaries northward to the Arctic Ocean, thus giving the province a saltwater port. He did not get that, nor did he get the resources. At a conference in Ottawa in February 1929, when negotiations were well advanced, Gardiner formally declined for Saskatchewan the terms offered Alberta,[18] and no settlement had been reached when he left office in September.

Public vs. Private Utilities

Another decision of long-term consequence, at least in light of confirming certain Saskatchewan values in the matter of public utilities, was the question whether power in the province should be developed by private interests or public enterprise, or by a combination of both. Gardiner's papers, usually a sensitive reflection of his views, do not reveal any long-standing convictions about electrical energy. But they do suggest that he looked on its manufacture and distribution as falling into the same category as the marketing of grain or the building of a telephone system: if it appeared that the best way to solve major problems was through a cooperative encouraged by the government, or by direct government takeover, the Liberal approach was to decide which way to move and then do it. He had inherited from Dunning a royal commission on power, and that put a constraint on his speeches until after the commission reported.

Gardiner may have nudged the commission along the route he wished it to take[19]—an intervention by no means unknown in Canada, and perhaps perceived in 1928 to be particularly advisable by a Premier who had not selected the commissioners. In any event, the commission's recommendations contained nothing to frighten a prairie Liberal. The core of its report, published in July 1928, urged public rather than private ownership, with provincewide coverage under one central administration as the ultimate goal, starting with the acquisition of the facilities of the three largest cities.[20] It meant a gradual approach to a large goal, and that was Gardiner's own approach. He embraced the commission's recommendations publicly, and was soon pointing out that they embodied the traditional Liberal and cooperative principles that had already been so strikingly applied to telephones, hail insurance, creameries, and grain elevators. Nonetheless he kept his options open. In announcing the negotiations with Saskatoon for acquisition of the plant there, he said:

> We are prepared to go a long way to retain public ownership but are not insistent that such ownership of necessity should be vested in the Provincial Government. It would appear, however, that the nature of this utility is such that even under public ownership it can give the maximum of service under central control.[21]

In due course the Legislature enacted the statutes required to set up the relevant department and the Saskatchewan Power Commission.

Electoral Defeat in 1929

Important as these foregoing policy decisions were to the future of the province, none can be considered as prologue to the defining issue of Gardiner's first government or, indeed, of his 43 years in public life. The issue, separate schools and the Ku Klux Klan, became a political *cause célèbre*, in the way that excesses of racial bigotry often do, where a long-dormant prejudice, ignited by an apparently inconsequential event, flares up, burns furiously and then dies. In this case, the spark was the Klan, with its anti-foreign, anti-Roman Catholic message; the tinder was a province whose population had burgeoned from 492,432 persons in 1911 to more than 921,000 by 1931, and which since provincehood had had the highest non-Anglo-Saxon component of any province.

To attribute the Gardiner government's defeat—actually, the loss of its majority, since the Liberals came out of the June 6, 1929, election with more seats than Conservatives—to the Klan's political astuteness or to extensive racial prejudice among the provincial population (both of which were factors) would fail to acknowledge that, after 24 years in power, the Liberals had acquired an accretion of public resentment in farm and business circles and among native-born Canadians as well as among some immigrants. The outcome of the 1929 election was neither foreordained nor the product of malign forces.

Gardiner believed otherwise when it came to malign forces. The Klan, most certainly—and the Conservatives, Orange Lodge, and Anglican Church as fellow travellers—indulged, in Gardiner's mind, in irrational and indefensible claims which 70 years later would without question be labelled incitement to race hatred. Gardiner preferred to call it intolerant, anti-liberal and anti-British propaganda directed generally at newcomers to Canada and at their church and clergy.

The details of the 1929 campaign and those who led the charge against the Gardiner government's school policy as it touched on language of instruction, religious exercises and symbols is recounted in the following chapter, devoted to Gardiner's successor as Premier, J.T.M. Anderson, a former civil servant (and thus, ironically, a product of the Liberal "machine") and author of the preeminent assimilationist treatise of the day, *The Education of the New Canadian*. As made clear already, Gardiner accepted, in the language of modern-day Canada, the country's bicultural origins and multicultural society. He disavowed throughout the 1929 campaign, and for the rest of his days, the monocultural ideal his opponents upheld. Nothing so became Gardiner's style of politics as his departure from office. The results of the 1929 election were ambiguous: the Liberals won 26 seats (with 46% of the popular vote), the Conservatives won 24 (with 36%); the Progressives and the Independents together had 11. Combative, aggressive, didactic, yet seldom overtly angry, Gardiner accepted the verdict of the electors as an honourable defeat, and on September 9, 1929, came Gardiner's first departure from the Premier's chair.

But only for the time being. Abandoning the convention of identifying the government of the day by the Premier's name, Anderson opted for the label "Co-operative government" to signify the coalition of forces now sitting to the Speaker's right. It is for others to reject the accuracy of the charge, but Gardiner believed Anderson and his supporters were united in only one matter—to dislodge the Liberals from power. For this reason, although Gardiner may have been willing to accept the electorate's decision, he did not go silently into opposition. In his mind, the outcome was far from being unambiguous. He had lost, but to whom, and on what issues? The non-sectarian schools on which Anderson had harped so much were not mentioned in the Conservatives' platform; that document cited only "thorough revision of the educational system of the province," assigning it equal weight with "furtherance of scientific research" and "eradication of bovine tuberculosis." Freeing the schools from sectarian influence was a specific clause in the Progressives' platform, as it was in the regular resolutions emanating from the "Klonvokations" of the Klan.[22]

If the school issue tied all three opposing groups together, as Gardiner believed it did, where did that leave the Independents, who were not so visibly organized? If the Liberals won the two deferred elections in the north they would then, with the support of any one of the other groups, have a majority in the assembly, whereas all three would have to coalesce against the Liberals to form a government. On the other hand, two Conservative victories in the north would mean that they, too, would need only the support of one other group to form a government. If there was some kind of anti-Liberal coalition, how was it that both Conservatives and Progressives had opposed Liberal candidates in eight constituencies? Could a coalition based on nothing more than a common opposition to the Liberals really survive in a post-election government that combined high-tariff Tories with low-tariff Progressives? Besides, were not the Progressives unequivocally on record against coalition, at least as far as elections were concerned?

Not for another 70 years (until the 1999 election) would similar questions be raised in Saskatchewan politics, although the innovation of what Canadians called minority government, and with it the potential for coalition, had occupied the attention of federal politicians ever since the Progressives burst upon the electoral scene in 1921. The answer to this confusing situation was quintessential Gardiner: he would force the opposition to defeat him in the Legislature. To abandon the field without any kind of commitment from his opponents was poor strategy: they had been elected on separate and in some ways conflicting platforms, opposing each other in several seats, and that could be used as a reason for deciding that they should take office only after some unequivocal further action. After a meeting with Liberal members and candidates, Gardiner announced that "responsible self-government calls for a decision by the Legislature itself, not by informal group caucuses held behind 'closed doors'."[23] Coincidentally, Gardiner consulted Winston Churchill, then in

Regina on a speaking tour, about his dilemma. What the great man advised (at this point in his career he had twice crossed the floor of the Commons at Westminster) cannot be verified. Still, it is reasonable to speculate that his counsel coincided with Gardiner's own assessment, which was to force the issue. The Legislature was summoned for early September, after the combined opposition groups had unsuccessfully sought to have the lieutenant-governor dismiss Gardiner and his ministers who (they were in no doubt) had lost the election. When the Legislature eventually did meet, the Liberals were defeated on an amendment to the Speech from the Throne moved by Anderson, which said that the confidence of the Assembly no longer "reposed in the present Ministers of the Crown." All non-Liberal MLAs supported the historic motion, an alignment that cheered Gardiner who thereafter depicted the Anderson government as just that—Anderson's, or, better still, a collection of Tories and their sympathizers.

Gardiner behaved in opposition as he had in government: he was relentlessly partisan. This despite the crisis of drought and depression that swept away any lingering emotion associated with the 1929 campaign. The economic upheaval presented the new Premier with problems whose substance let alone magnitude were unimaginable during the Gardiner years. The farm price of wheat fell from $1.03 per bushel in 1929 to 35¢ by 1932. The value of all products sold off Saskatchewan farms was $273.6 million in 1928, $179.7 million in 1929, and $66.2 million in 1931. The costs of direct relief rose from minuscule beginnings to average nearly $5 million in the years 1931–32 to 1934–35, and the total figures for all relief, including agricultural aid in feed and fodder, seed, and freight subsidies, averaged nearly three times that for direct relief.[24] The total for relief fell not far short of the province's budgetary expenditures on everything else.

Gardiner considered the Co-operative government counterfeit in its politics (as well as incompetent in its administration). By hammering this theme, he concentrated his attack on Anderson, with the side benefit of generalized damage to the new Conservative federal government led by R.B. Bennett. During Gardiner's last year as Premier, 116 questions were asked in the House; two years later that number had almost quadrupled. Returns ordered totalled nine in 1929, and 78 in 1931, and recorded formal divisions rose from five in 1929 to a peak of 28 in 1932.[25] While Anderson's supporters had questions to ask about the Gardiner administration, the Legislature from the first belonged to the Liberals. Their task was facilitated by mere numbers, for after 1929 they constituted the largest opposition the Legislature had ever seen. They also knew exactly what information to seek.

If, in time, the Co-operative government appeared a doomed enterprise deserving of pity, Gardiner's instinct for partisan combat could be sharpened on a new enemy, the Farmer-Labour Party (the predecessor to the CCF). Here was the realization, a decade after the Progressives emerged, of Gardiner's prophecy—the organized farmers, allied with a much smaller component of organized labour, entering politics. He treated the party with suspicion but also with derision. Citing the long list of Liberal achievements in the field of cooperatives and its role in state-provided medical services—for example free tuberculosis treatment—he proclaimed "the Liberal Party [as] the only socialistic party in Saskatchewan."[26] Here, at a crucial juncture in the political development of the province, with the electoral emergence of the social democrat forces for which the province was to become known internationally after 1944, Gardiner responded as he had a decade before in the face of the Progressive insurgents and as he would continue to do for the next three decades before any electoral threat to Liberal fortunes. The "socialists" (as he always called them) were ideologues, and the flaw of ideologues was pride. They always knew better than others. But Gardiner was an ideologue too: his belief may not have been as coherent as the new party's but its objective was as unassailable—in Gardiner's case, the maintenance of the Liberal Party. As a result, Gardiner lectured his opponents, and the public. With the emergence of the Farmer-Labour Party, which in the 1934 provincial election elected only five of its candidates but nevertheless monopolized the opposition, Saskatchewan entered upon a political war of words that was to last for decades. In the terrible early 1930s, with the Anderson government's defeat and Gardiner's return all but certain, Gardiner might be excused for his shortsightedness. Nonetheless, the fact remains that confronted by the foe that would vanquish Liberalism in Saskatchewan, Gardiner's political antennae failed him.

The Second Gardiner Government

The Conservatives won 26.75% of the popular vote but not a single seat in the election of June 19, 1934; with fewer votes (24%), Farmer-Labour candidates took five seats. The Liberals won the rest of the vote (48%) and 50 of the 55 seats. With an alignment of forces that included a minute and inexperienced opposition, Gardiner entered upon his second premiership a free agent, politically speaking. From an economic perspective, he may have been as much a hostage to fortune as his predecessor, but that did not prevent him from restoring, as far as he could, the administrative environment of pre-1929. This meant abolishing the Public Service Commission established by the Anderson government. For the purposes of this discussion, the feature of the commission that most commended it to reformers—its independence—offended Gardiner. The pros and cons of a merit-based public service must be debated elsewhere. The important point as far as this study of Gardiner's premiership is concerned is that he distrusted public bodies for which politicians ultimately were responsible but over which they had no control. To his mind, independence meant irresponsibility. The same motivation and reasoning lay behind his government's closure of the provincial Relief Commission and its replacement with a system of aid distributed under the authority of his ministers.

The second Gardiner government lasted from July 1934 until November 1935. The most dramatic event of those months was the Regina Riot. It was there that the famous "On-to-Ottawa" trek of unemployed single men, which had begun in Vancouver and was making its way by train across the country, was dispersed with violence and loss of life. Gardiner always blamed the federal government for the debacle. In fact, he did not see it as a bungled operation; on the contrary, he believed that the (Conservative) federal government had deliberately provoked the trekkers in the first Liberal jurisdiction east of British Columbia. Ironically, in light of Gardiner's earlier decision to abolish the Saskatchewan Provincial Police and return the RCMP to local policing, the central question at issue in the period before the riot was which level of government had control of the Mounties in a situation of escalating tension.

DICK AND ADA BIRD COLLECTION. SAB RA 27,613(2)
Gardiner in front of the Legislative Building, shortly after being re-elected as Premier in 1934.

The Riot, relief, and civil service reform ("unreform," theorists said) were part of the waiting game. Two months after the Riot, Parliament was dissolved and an election called for October 14. If depression and drought spelt doom for Anderson, the prognosis was no better for Bennett and his Tories. The Liberals swept back to power with King still the MP for Prince Albert, thanks to Gardiner.

Member of Parliament and Minister of Agriculture

Now Gardiner's move to Ottawa was a certainty—only the timing had to be settled. Among the issues to be decided was the seat in which he would run, since a by-election was necessary. It had been assumed that W.R. Motherwell would go gracefully into retirement and that Gardiner would take the Melville by-election that followed. He already held the Melville provincial seat, having been forced to move when the Co-operative government had carried out a redistribution which saw his long-held North Qu'Appelle seat vanish. However, Motherwell, ever unpredictable, refused to slip away (he stayed on until 1940). Gardiner campaigned and won in Assiniboia, where the resignation of an acquiescent Liberal opened a convenient seat, at least until 1940, when at last he shifted to Melville for good.

So long associated in Canadian political history with Agriculture, it is surprising to learn that Gardiner, initially, was reluctant to accept the portfolio. He entered negotiations with King as to Cabinet responsibilities with the prospect of Finance in mind; King countered with National Revenue; before Agriculture was agreed upon, Trade and Commerce and a new department, Mines and Resources, were also canvassed. Years later, Bruce Hutchison described Gardiner in his fiefdom of Agriculture as "a kind of semi-sovereign power."[27] If that description is true, and most students of Canadian politics of that era say

SAB RA 6054

Gardiner, as federal minister of Agriculture, surrounded by Young Liberals at their convention in Ottawa, 1954.

it is, then it was a form of sovereignty that he asserted against Liberal Cabinet opponents, who saw him—as electoral and party opponents had in Saskatchewan—as abrasive, combative and relentless.

His success in Agriculture—and it was a national success when tested by the upheavals in markets and production occasioned by war—redounded to Saskatchewan's credit. It was under Gardiner and through programs like the Prairie Farm Assistance Act (PFAA) that the federal government recognized for the first time a federal obligation to the region. In Gardiner's mind, the farmers had been encouraged, while Ottawa still controlled the West's natural resources, to settle on quarter- and half-sections, particularly in the semi-arid Palliser Triangle. These were the farmers who had opened the West and made the nation, and the Empire, prosper. A malign conjunction of events following the transfer of resources in 1930 did not absolve Ottawa of its responsibilities. Parts of the prairies were

SAB RB 7146(4)

An aging political warrior. When this photograph was taken in 1957, Gardiner had served as federal minister of Agriculture for twenty-two years. A year later, following the Diefenbaker "sweep," Gardiner retired from politics. He died in 1962.

overpopulated as a result of federal policies, while all farmers had "a claim of right" to assistance, even if it was only help in moving to better land and their old farms turned to dust. As well, Gardiner never tired of issuing warnings about the dismal consequences for the nation that would follow if young people refused to stay on the land, which he prophesied would happen without the kind of help the PFAA provided.[28]

Conclusion

Saskatchewan was Canada's agricultural heartland, and Gardiner its voice. But it was a voice that required amplification, and without torturing the metaphor too much, the party organization provided that amplification. Gardiner was an indefatigable advocate, a relentless politician, devoted to promoting the cause of Saskatchewan whether in Regina or Ottawa. It is ironic that "the machine" should be seen as his principal legacy. However, it is not his only legacy, for there is the South Saskatchewan River dam for which he fought in Cabinet for decades, a fight he ultimately lost as the Liberals, now under Louis St. Laurent, turned their economic attention to North America and away from the grain economy of the transcontinental Canadian state. (It took the Conservative government of John Diefenbaker to make the dam a reality.) Nevertheless, when the time came to name the mammoth engineering work, the Liberals were once more in power. They in true partisan spirit—and with some historical justification—called it the Gardiner Dam (the lake behind it was named after Diefenbaker). Tories frowned and Liberals smiled at this testimony to the persistence of politics in the Gardiner style.

Following the landslide victory of John Diefenbaker's Conservatives in 1958, Jimmy Gardiner retired from politics. He returned to his farm near Lemberg where, on January 12, 1962, he died.

Notes

Shortly after I joined the (then) Department of Economics and Political Science at the University of Saskatchewan in 1964, senior political scientist Norman Ward volunteered that if I were interested in a major research project, he had two suggestions: either a history of the Liberal Party in Saskatchewan, "since everyone else writes about the CCF," or a biography of James G. Gardiner, whose papers spanning a career of more than 40 years in elected office "equalled in richness," he said, the John A. Macdonald collection in the Public Archives of Canada. A couple of years later, he announced that he had simplified my choice by deciding to write the Gardiner biography himself. Later, however, when his health began to deteriorate, he asked me to complete the task. Roughly speaking, this division of labour saw Ward complete the chapters on Gardiner's Saskatchewan years, and I write those on his decades as a federal minister. In light of the Gardiner project's history, I wish to acknowledge Norman Ward's original scholarly contribution to public understanding of Saskatchewan's fourth Premier. The biography, *Jimmy Gardiner: Relentless Politician*, was published by the University of Toronto Press in 1990. It appeared a month after Norman Ward's death.

1. The comment was made to J.W. Dafoe of the *Manitoba Free Press*. Manitoba Archives, Dafoe Papers, Dafoe to Clifford Sifton, October 26, 1926.
2. Despite nearly half a century as one of Canada's most visible public figures, Gardiner remained an intensely private individual. He and his second wife Violet had four children: Florence, Edwin, Beth and Wilfrid. Edwin was an RCAF pilot who was killed in action in the fighting at Dieppe in 1942—a blow from which neither Jimmy nor his wife ever recovered, and which contributed to Mrs. Gardiner's early death two years later. Gardiner's younger son, Wilf, entered Saskatchewan provincial politics, and was minister of Public Works (1964–67) in the Liberal government of Ross Thatcher.
3. Saskatchewan Archives Board, Gardiner Papers. The plan of the nomination speech and three drafts (undated) are at 478–91; the quotation in this text is at 480–81.
4. According to the *Columbia Encyclopedia* (6th edition, 2001), the Dunkards are a religious group similar to the Mennonites. Dunkards received their name because they believe in dipping the person in

water during baptism. Dunkards originally lived in what is now Germany in the 18th century but moved to the United States due to persecution. They are pacifists, avoid alcohol and tobacco, and believe in living a simple life.

5. National Archives of Canada, King Papers, 97661, King to Gardiner, December 3, 1925.
6. David E. Smith, *Prairie Liberalism: The Liberal Party in Saskatchewan 1905–71* (Toronto: University of Toronto Press, 1975), 169, esp. n. 52.
7. SAB, Gardiner Papers, 42543, Gardiner to C.M. Dunn, February 4, 1936.
8. Ibid., 2423-4, Gardiner to Motherwell, February 28, 1924.
9. Ibid., 7625-8, Gardiner to E. Lapointe, undated copy of letter sent also to W.R. Motherwell, November 30, 1926; ibid., 5816-19, memorandum of interview with Commissioner Staines of RCMP and the Hon. Ernest Lapointe, March 22, 1927.
10. Glenbow Alberta Institute, interviews of Gardiner by Una Maclean Evans, December 29, 1961–January 6, 1962, tape 1.
11. *Report of the Royal Commission to Inquire into Statements made on Statutory Declarations and Other Matters* (Regina 1931), 68–69.
12. John G. Diefenbaker, *One Canada: Memoirs of the Right Honourable John G. Diefenbaker, The Crusading Years* (Toronto: Macmillan, 1975), 130. It was an academic study by Escott Reid that transmuted the party organization into a "machine" of mythic proportions. See "The Saskatchewan Liberal Machine Before 1929," *Canadian Journal of Economics and Political Science* 2, no. 1 (1936).
13. Saskatchewan, *Sessional Papers*, 1925, 151.
14. See, for example, Chester Martin, *"Dominion Lands" Policy* (Toronto: McClelland and Stewart, 1973).
15. Bram Thompson, "A Statement to the Electors on the National Resources Issue," Regina *Leader*, May 25, 1929, unnumbered clipping in Gardiner Papers.
16. Ibid.
17. Canada, *Report of the Royal Commission on the Transfer of Natural Resources of Manitoba* (Ottawa: King's Printer, 1929).
18. National Archives of Canada, C90400-18, King Papers, Conference with Saskatchewan re: Transfer of Natural Resources, February 19, 1929.
19. A critical history of power development is Clinton O. White, "Saskatchewan Builds an Electrical System" (PhD dissertation, University of Saskatchewan, 1968,) 118–19.
20. *Report of the Saskatchewan Power Resources Commission* (Regina: King's Printer, 1928).
21. SAB, Gardiner Papers, 11420-33, Speech at Craik, August 17, 1928; Regina *Leader*, August 15, 1928, unnumbered clipping.
22. See Peter Russell, "The Co-operative Government in Saskatchewan, 1929–1934: Response to the Depression" (MA thesis, University of Saskatchewan 1970), appendices A, B, D, where all three platforms are reproduced.
23. *Canadian Annual Review*, 1928–29, 469–70.
24. Russell, "The Co-operative Government in Saskatchewan," and "The Co-operative Government's Response to the Depression, 1930–1934," *Saskatchewan History* 24, no. 3 (Autumn 1971): 81–100. The files of *Saskatchewan History* contain numerous other relevant articles. See also George E. Britnell, "Saskatchewan, 1930–1935," *Canadian Journal of Economics and Political Science* 2, no. 2 (May 1936): 143–66; H. Blair Neatby, "The Saskatchewan Relief Commission," *Saskatchewan History* 3, no. 2 (Spring 1950): 41–56.

25. An Order for Return is a resolution passed by the Legislative Assembly that certain information be tabled in the Legislature by the government and, in doing so, the information is made public.
26. SAB, Gardiner Papers, 15528, Gardiner to E. Simington, January 30, 1933.
27. Bruce Hutchison, *The Incredible Canadian: A Candid Portrait of Mackenzie King, His Works, His Times, and His Nation* (Toronto: Longmans, Green, 1952), 431.
28. SAB, Gardiner Papers, 66781, Gardiner to Paul Martin, July 4, 1959; see also speech to the Canadian Club, Regina, September 16, 1936; Canada, House of Commons, *Debates*, June 5, 1941, 3586-7, and July 20, 1944, 5140-1; SAB, Gardiner Papers, Address to Kiwanis Club of Montreal, May 18, 1944, and September 30, 1954; address to annual meeting of the Lethbridge Board of Trade, January 15 1947; speech to the Kansas State Board of Agriculture, Topeka, January 13, 1955; address to the closing session of the Eighteenth Federal-Provincial Agricultural Conference, December 5, 1956.

J.T.M. Anderson

Patrick Kyba

Anderson, formal portrait
(SAB RA 629 (1)).

Dedication of the Albert Memorial Bridge,
November 11, 1930
(SAB RA 27549 (1)).

"Completing Confederation"—signing the agreement for the return of natural resources to Saskatchewan
(SAB RB 459 (4)).

SASKATCHEWAN PREMIERS OF THE 20ᵀᴴ CENTURY

J.T.M. Anderson, 1929–1934

Introduction

Early in 1924, at the urging of the federal party, some long-time Conservatives met in Saskatoon to discuss ways of rejuvenating the provincial party. Very quickly they agreed that it could not be done without a strong and capable leader and that none of the Conservative MLAs met the criteria. They then established a committee to seek out likely prospects and shortly thereafter William Dunlop, a three-time provincial candidate for Yorkton, suggested the name of James Thomas Milton Anderson, a schools inspector living in Saskatoon. Anderson was from Ontario, born in Fairbank—now part of Toronto—on July 23, 1878. He received his primary and secondary school education there and taught for six years until he migrated to Manitoba in 1906, where he taught for two years before moving to Saskatchewan. He taught first near Melville, then became principal at Grenfell where he met and married Edith Redgewick, with whom he had two children, Arthur and Edith. He moved to Yorkton as schools inspector in 1911 and remained there for seven years until the Martin government brought him to Regina as Director of Education among New Canadians. During this time he continued his own education, earning B.A., M.A., and law degrees from the University of Manitoba and a doctorate in Pedagogy from the University of Toronto. Anderson enjoyed his work in Regina, in large part because he regarded the teaching of English in ethnic areas of the province as a just cause as well as a responsibility. He wrote a book on the subject, entitled *The Education of the New Canadian: A Treatise on Canada's Greatest Education Problem*. Nevertheless, Anderson would have preferred to live in and work out of Saskatoon and eventually the Department of Education granted his wish, although not in the way Anderson expected. In 1922 he was transferred to Saskatoon, not as Director of Education among New Canadians, but as a school inspector and, of course, at the lower salary paid to inspectors. This did not please Anderson in the least. He regarded the transfer as a demotion and complained to both minister of Education S.J. Latta and Premier Dunning, but to no avail. His bitterness perhaps explains why he first listened to the overtures that led him to become head of the Conservative Party in Saskatchewan.

The prospect of Anderson as leader did not appeal to all Conservatives, especially those in Regina who preferred one of their own—J.F. Bryant, a local lawyer who had a province-wide reputation because of his work for the School Trustees Association and who was known to them as a long-time member of the party. They were suspicious of Anderson's new-found commitment to Conservatism. After all, he had spent more than a decade working for Liberal governments not known for keeping their opponents on the public payroll. In his defense, Anderson's supporters argued that he had resigned his position to protest Liberal education policies, that he was an outstanding public speaker and, further, that he possessed several qualities which made him suitable to the job. Anderson was a Mason, an Orangeman, a Kiwanian, and an Anglican. Ultimately, Anderson won

SAB RA 12057

J.T.M. Anderson (right) with friend and fellow teacher, Arthur T. McCulloch, c. 1908. The two men lived together for a time in Anderson's bachelor shack, which appears in the background.

the leadership by acclamation at the party's convention in Moose Jaw in March 1924 and, at the same time, became the federal party's paid organizer for Saskatchewan, an arrangement which gave new life to the provincial party.

Anderson approached his dual responsibilities with enthusiasm, although it did not take long for the enormity of the task to set in. Within months, he began to complain to federal leader Arthur Meighen about a lack of money, the fact that Saskatchewan possessed no Conservative newspaper in either Regina or Saskatoon, and that many constituency organizations had been moribund for so long that it was almost impossible to resuscitate them. All this also made it difficult for him to persuade people to run for the party, especially at the upcoming provincial election. The dearth of candidates troubled Anderson, but perhaps not as much as might have been expected because he soon resorted to a strategy that he would pursue unwaveringly to the end of his political career: he sought the cooperation of any person, group or party dedicated to the defeat of the Liberals. For the election of June 2, 1925, his most obvious target was the Progressive party. He tried to reach a formal agreement with the Progressives at the highest level to prevent Conservative and Progressive candidates running against each other in as many constituencies as possible. The strategy did not work flawlessly, however. Harris Turner, the Progressive leader, would have nothing to do with it and Conservatives were not allowed

SAB RA 3488

Dr. J.T.M. Anderson (prone, far right) with other teachers and a group of Ukrainian boys selected for an expedition to Lumsden Beach, Insinger District (n.d.). Throughout his professional and political career, Anderson was concerned with the quality of education in immigrant areas of the province, and promoted efforts to integrate immigrant children into the Anglo-Saxon mainstream.

to participate at some Progressive nominating conventions. However, the Liberals and their newspapers had no doubt as to the electoral potential of Anderson's tactic. Dunning and his candidates attacked the "unholy alliance" in every speech and the *Morning Leader* near the end of the campaign published a list of 30 Progressive candidates whom it called "rank Tories."[1] As it happened, Progressive candidates had to face Conservative opponents in only five constituencies and of the six Progressives who did win seats none had to run against a Conservative.

The Conservative Party was much better prepared for this election than it had been in previous campaigns. This time it had a leader, campaign committees in some constituencies, and a platform to put before the voters. This platform and indeed the entire Conservative campaign received scant publicity in the Liberal-dominated press. In the first week of the campaign, for example, the *Morning Leader* reported nothing at all on the Conservatives, although it attacked them a couple of times in editorials and, when referring to Dr. Anderson, preferred to call him the "Conservative organizer" rather than by name. Nevertheless, from the sparse accounts available it is clear that Anderson and his 19 candidates attacked the government for not obtaining control over the lands and resources of the province, for extravagance in the construction of public buildings, for using civil servants as campaign workers, and for dilatory action on the Hudson's Bay railway.

Two other important issues raised by the Conservatives during the 1925 election were education and immigration. In the case of education, it is perhaps surprising that Anderson did not raise the questions one might have expected from the former Director of Education for New Canadians. Instead, it appears that when he spoke on the subject he merely criticized the Liberals for their poor administration of some school districts and did not focus on either the quality of education in the immigrant areas of the province or the matter of sectarianism in the public school system. With respect to immigration, Anderson was more forceful. Near the end of the campaign he declared that "the immigration policy of the government is all wrong. The present government has done nothing to encourage a sane immigration policy," and promised that a Conservative government would begin a "constructive program of immigration."[2] The word "constructive" would be replaced by "selective" in a few short years, but in the 1925 campaign it was the Liberals not the Conservatives who made immigration a major issue. There is no doubt that anxiety had arisen recently over the growing numbers of immigrants to the province, many of whom were Catholic, and perhaps in an attempt to prevent the issue being used against the government, J.M. Uhrich, provincial secretary and a Catholic, characterized both the Conservatives and the Progressives as "anti-immigrant" and accused them of trying to use the issue for partisan advantage. The evidence does not support Uhrich's charge in this campaign. However, it would be more plausible in four years' time.

The Liberals swept to another overwhelming victory on June 2, 1925, winning 52 of the 63 seats in the Legislative Assembly. Their opposition would consist of the six Progressives mentioned previously; two Independents—one of whom, Salkeld of Moosomin, had sat in the last Legislature as a Conservative; and three Conservatives— W.C. Buckle, the mayor of Tisdale, M.A. MacPherson, a prominent Regina lawyer, and Dr. J.T.M. Anderson, in one of the two Saskatoon seats. Three seats, another crushing defeat perhaps, but in fact the Conservative Party emerged from this election far stronger than it had been for some time. The party had raised its share of the popular vote by four-and-a-half times, an indication that there were still many people in the province who would vote Conservative if given the chance. The party now had a solid platform on which to build towards the next election and it had its leader in the Legislative Assembly, supported by two very able MLAs and maybe more, since some of the Progressive MLAs had once been Conservatives. Nevertheless, Anderson needed determination, political skill, and the intervention of the Fates to take the next step to the premiership. He required a Conservative newspaper in either Regina or Saskatoon, the cooperation and support of all those opposed to the Liberal government, and a set of issues to split the coalition which had maintained the Liberals in power since 1905. All three occured over the next four years.

Sparks flew immediately after the Legislature reconvened, as the Liberals focused their attention on Dr. Anderson as the de facto leader of the opposition and attacked him for his overtures to the Progressives. For his part, Anderson reiterated that he was prepared to cooperate with anyone who wished to defeat the government and proceeded throughout the session to elaborate the important issues he thought confronted the province: immigration, education, and the return of the public domain. He maintained that there should be some restriction on immigration from central Europe. He attacked the government over the education system and he tried with some success to take back the lands and natural resources issue for the Conservative Party. In this way, Anderson showed the Liberals that they would not have the free run they had enjoyed during the previous four years, and that they would have to respond to opposition concerns. The next session of the Legislature proved that these were indeed "opposition" and not just Conservative issues. The new Progressive leader, Dr. Charles Tran, took up all of these questions and attacked the government and its new Premier, James G. Gardiner, with equal fervour. The Conservative and Progressive caucuses also reached the same size in 1927 when Howard McConnell won the other Saskatoon seat at a by-election and two Progressive MLAs defected to the Liberals. This made it easier for the two parties to work together, but agreement on issues and cooperation in the Legislature would not in themselves bring down the Liberals. Nor would the fact that Gardiner's Cabinet was the first in many years not to contain someone with direct and intimate links to the farm organizations. In addition, the province was prosperous, in the midst of an economic boom. Something else would be needed to shatter the coalition of Anglo-Protestant and European Catholic immigrants which had hitherto proven unbeatable. That catalyst proved to be the Ku Klux Klan.[3]

Klan spokesmen, calling themselves members of "the greatest Christian, benevolent fraternal organization in the world,"[4] spread across Saskatchewan in 1927, directing their attacks at everything non-Nordic, non-Protestant, and what they claimed to be non-Canadian. In a province populated by Protestants, Catholics and other religious groups, comprised of Anglo-Saxons and French Canadians, Scandinavians and Ukrainians, Germans and Poles, the effect of the Klan on religious and racial toleration was dramatic. It released prejudices submerged for years by the difficulties of a frontier existence and rapidly brought them into the open and eventually to the forefront of politics in the province. Premier Gardiner did not take the Klan very seriously at first. He regarded it as a group of outsiders dedicated to lining their own pockets and he appeared to be correct when the first two Klan organizers, Lewis A. Scott and Patrick Emmons, skipped the province late in the year with the proceeds of their venture. However, the Klan in Saskatchewan did not die. In fact, it kept growing, led now by men who had spent their adult lives in the province, some of whom were known Conservatives, but also some known to be Liberals and Progressives. Gardiner began to treat the Klan more seriously when both opposition parties began to direct the emotionalism stirred by the Klan into political channels.

The first evidence of this occurred during the legislative session of early 1928. Amidst attacks on the government for political favouritism when hiring for the public service, for the poor quality of roads in the province, and for not creating a utilities commission to develop electrical power in Saskatchewan, Anderson moved motions on two matters which were front and centre amongst Klan concerns—immigration and the public school system. The first proposed the appointment of an agent-general in London to promote immigration from Great Britain. As Anderson explained, he did not want to halt Slavic immigration but rather attract more people from the British Isles to keep the present balance amongst the various groups in the province. The second called for amendments to the School Act so that no teachers in religious garb could teach and no religious emblems could be displayed in public schools. These provoked a furious assault on the Klan by the Premier and, for the first time, Gardiner hinted publicly that there might be a link between the Klan and the Conservative Party.

Gardiner's suspicions were heightened by the number of known Klansmen who attended the Conservative convention in Saskatoon in mid-March and the resolutions passed there. The delegates debated and passed 26 motions ranging from balanced industrial development to the eradication of bovine tuberculosis, but those which attracted the most attention were the two which dealt with the same issues Anderson had raised in the Assembly a few weeks previously—immigration and the public school system. In Saskatoon, the delegates voted for an aggressive immigration policy based on the "selective" principle and committed the party to a public school system in which there would be no textbooks with denominational or unpatriotic biases, no religious emblems or garb, and no classes held in buildings devoted to religious purposes. No high-ranking Klan official spoke to the convention but, at the same time, no Roman Catholic was elected to any position on the Conservative executive. The prevailing sentiment seemed to be that while the Conservative Party should do everything possible to avoid the appearance of any direct link between itself and the Klan, if the Catholic vote was going to the Liberals anyway, then the party should do all it could to attract the Protestant vote.

The Protestant vote could be split between the Conservative and Progressive parties, however, and Anderson and Bryant wanted to ensure that this did not happen. Thus they met with representatives of the provincial Progressive association to work out an agreement not to oppose each other at the next election. The two sides decided that Conservative candidates should run in approximately 50% of the seats and Progressives in as many of the remaining constituencies as they believed they could win. In any seat where neither local association would step aside, an open convention of all those opposed to the Liberals would be held, and the candidate who won the nomination would run as an Independent. Both also agreed to form a cooperative government should the Liberals be defeated and, because of the Klan, this was becoming a more distinct possibility.

The Ku Klux Klan

The Klan reached its peak in 1928. Local Klans sprang up in towns all across the province and Klan speakers tapped a deep reservoir of anti-immigrant and anti-Catholic sentiment. More than 20,000 people immigrated to Saskatchewan in 1927, the majority of whom were from central and southeastern Europe and were either Roman or Greek Catholic. Furthermore, organized labour did not like the competition for jobs and wages posed by the steady influx of immigrants. War veterans complained that while they had fought for their country, immigrants had stayed home and prospered. The United Farmers of Canada (Saskatchewan Section) urged the government to limit immigration "until our own unemployed are cared for, and those brought out in former years have been assimilated and stabilized."[5] Protestant families in Catholic-dominated public school districts began to keep their children out of school because they were receiving instruction in the Roman Catholic faith, because they were forced to kiss the crucifix, or because certain subjects were being taught in French. The Orange Order complained that the Catholic Church was attempting to subvert the public school system and warned Protestants to guard against the menace which threatened them. The implications of such attacks were not lost upon the Catholic and immigrant communities in the province and, believing the separate school system to be in danger, they struck back bitterly in defense of themselves, their church, and the school system as it existed at the time. By the summer of 1928 it was clear that a racial and religious prairie fire had broken out in Saskatchewan, one which the Premier decided to douse as quickly as possible.

At first, Gardiner confined his attacks on the Klan to attempts to destroy its respectability and credibility. Gradually however, as he became convinced that the Klan was linked intimately to the Conservative Party, his tactics changed. In May he had Emmons brought back from the United States to stand trial for defrauding the public. Emmons, in sworn testimony, declared that Dr. Anderson and other Conservatives had approached him several times to interest the Klan in politics, and that he had been forced to leave Saskatchewan because they had finally secured control of the Klan and were using it for political purposes. The trial received widespread publicity but, unfortunately for the Premier, the case was dismissed and Emmons' testimony discredited. Undaunted, Gardiner and other members of his Cabinet toured the province during the summer to alert people to the "cabal" which threatened Saskatchewan's social harmony. Late in June Gardiner debated a prominent American Klansman, J.H. Hawkins, in the Premier's home town of Lemberg and then had him deported. Despite the protestations of Klan leaders that their organization was non-partisan and, in fact, had supporters of all parties as members, the Liberals never gave up their attempt to tie this "band of scoundrels" to the Conservatives.

Conservatives, for their part, were vehement in their denial of any collusion between themselves and the Klan. Anderson and his colleagues were convinced that the attempt to tie them to the Klan was simply a political ploy on the part of the Liberals to stem the pro-Conservative tide running in the province. Just the same, the Conservative approach to the question of the Klan's place in Saskatchewan was quite different from that of the Liberals. Anderson always maintained that he was never a member of the Klan, but also stated time and again that he wanted the support of all persons who were opposed to the Gardiner government. In his attempt to win them over he would have a powerful ally, because in July 1928 a new paper began publishing—the Regina *Daily Star*. Its first edition claimed that it would be independent in politics but, in fact, it was not. It was financed largely by the new leader of the federal Conservative Party, R.B. Bennett, and it gave Dr. Anderson and his party in Saskatchewan invaluable coverage and publicity. The war of words continued during the legislative session held between December 4, 1928, and February 2, 1929. Every major issue that would be raised during the 1929 election was debated: sectarianism in the public schools of the province; the problem of immigration; the return of lands and natural resources to Saskatchewan control; partisanship in the public service; political favouritism in the granting of government contracts; and the many scandal charges levelled against the government. Thus, it was almost anticlimactic when the Premier announced on May 11 that a general election would be held on June 6, 1929.

The 1929 Provincial Election

The campaign conducted by the Conservatives and their Progressive and Independent allies was far more aggressive than the Liberals', and the Liberals' insistence on appealing to their record in office left the opposition free to determine the major issues of the campaign, which they proceeded to do without hesitation. The one which probably brought them the most publicity rose out of the issue of sectarianism in the public schools of the province. In essence the problem was simple. Most of the schools in Saskatchewan were public schools run by boards of trustees who were predominantly Protestant, as was 75% of the population. However, in some areas, Catholicism was the dominant religion and the public schools in these districts were governed by boards composed of Catholics. In some instances, these trustees hired nuns as teachers and permitted crucifixes and other religious emblems to be placed in the schools. The Protestant minority in such districts had the right to establish a separate school, as did a Catholic minority in a Protestant area, but in some cases, there were not enough families to support a school of their own and Protestant children had no choice but to attend Catholic-run public schools. Inevitably, complaints were heard from the parents of these non-Catholic children.

Once the question of sectarianism in the public schools had arisen, the Conservative Party was able to create a political issue out of it which eventually became a potent weapon against the Liberals. Posing as defenders of the public school system, Conservatives promised to stop the animosity which had developed over the issue and, at the same time, insinuated that either the Gardiner government was unaware of the problem or that it favoured the Catholic minority. Unlike the "schools" questions which had disrupted the social and political concord of several provinces in the past, the issue in Saskatchewan in 1929 was not whether separate schools had a right to exist. The issue which the Conservatives brought to public attention was interference with the non-sectarian character of the public schools, which they promised to halt if elected. Premier Gardiner and the Liberal Party generally mishandled this issue. Instead of focusing their efforts on countering the claim that they were partial to Catholics, they spent most of their time attempting to prove that the charge of sectarianism in the public school system had little basis in fact. Liberals produced scores of statistics throughout the campaign to show that the problem was not sufficiently grave to cause alarm, and undeniably they were correct: in 1928 only 117 Protestant pupils had been taught by nuns. Nonetheless, the more important political problem facing the Liberals remained. What upset the majority in the province was the accusation that the government had shown favouritism towards Catholics, and statistics did not pacify the aroused Protestants.

The issue which went hand-in-glove with the religious question was that of immigration to Saskatchewan. The Conservative Party, which pressed the issue, was for the most part more temperate during the election than either the Klan or the Orange Order had been previously. Anderson maintained at all times that he was not opposed to the immigration of any particular ethnic groups to the province, but he expressed concern that so many immigrants were allowed to come to Saskatchewan before they had employment, and that little was being done by the Gardiner government to ensure their rapid assimilation. A Conservative government, he promised, would establish a provincial Department of Immigration that would work with the federal government to select the immigrants best suited to the economic and racial realities of the province. The reaction of the Liberals was simple and their approach to the question was similar to that used in meeting the sectarian issue—they condemned the Conservatives for injecting race into the election campaign and attempted to play down the issue as much as possible. Liberal speakers argued that the federal government controlled the admittance of immigrants to the country, that once in Canada, immigrants could not be turned away at the Saskatchewan border, and that the proportion of those in the province not born in Canada was extremely low and dropping every year. Once again, however, the truth in these arguments proved to be not as strong as either the Conservatives' concerns or the Klan's appeal to race.

One of the major issues raised by the combined opposition groups was that of obtaining from the Dominion full provincial control over the lands and natural resources which had been denied since 1905. The feeling that the Autonomy Bills had placed Saskatchewan in a position inferior to other provinces had never faded away and, in the late 1920s, two events occurred which brought the question back to the centre of the political stage. Bram Thompson, a Regina lawyer, found that when the Hudson's Bay Company relinquished control over its lands, they had reverted to the Crown. London had then transferred only "administrative" control to the Dominion, not ownership. In addition, by 1928 oil and minerals had been discovered on both borders of the province, giving rise to the expectation that Saskatchewan would be rich in these resources. The King government accepted Thompson's argument, and in February 1929, Gardiner went to Ottawa to settle this long-standing dispute. The federal government agreed to transfer the lands and resources to provincial control, but only if Saskatchewan would accept in perpetuity a subsidy $375,000 less than it could expect under the existing compensation arrangement. Gardiner refused the federal offer and the opposition parties were quick to attack him for not having enough faith in his own province to accept the lower figure in anticipation that revenues accruing from the lands and resources would exceed the amount the government at Ottawa refused to grant. The Premier found it difficult to counter this appeal to provincial pride. It is reasonable to assume that Gardiner hoped to return from the national capital to fight an election as the leader of the party which had brought back the public domain, but his failure forced him and his party to approach the issue in a different way. They were obliged to try to convince the electorate that the Premier was correct in his refusal to accept the federal offer, and that soon the government in Ottawa would accept the province's position, but this explanation could not be as effective as the opposition's promise to obtain the lands and resources immediately.

The last of the major issues raised by the opposition during the campaign was summed up in the slogan "Break the Machine." It was well known in Saskatchewan that the Liberal Party used a well-oiled political organization to help maintain itself in office, a widespread yet tightly knit group which watched constantly for grievances in the constituencies and advised Liberal governments as to the best means of handling them. In an era where a great many public works were needed throughout the province, the "Machine" did not hesitate to keep a constituency or important individuals in line by pork-barrel methods. No organization of this type can hide every occasion when it steps across the line separating legal and illegal means of obtaining support, and in 1929, the opposition parties found enough scandals to tar the Gardiner government with corruption. The fight against the "Machine" was long and vocal, opposition speakers presenting themselves as leaders of a movement growing within the electorate, an uprising which would overthrow a debased government. Charges were hurled at the Liberals with astonishing rapidity as the opposition used anything and everything of a scandalous nature to prove its point, regardless of how long ago or under whose administration the scandals had occurred. Conservatives especially condemned the government's practice of only hiring known Liberals for the civil service and for granting contracts to party supporters without public tender, promising to end both if elected. Other accusations exploited across the province were that the Gardiner government had little respect for the Legislature, the electorate, or the judicial system, and that the Liberals were in league with the liquor interests in Saskatchewan.

One should not conclude that the issues discussed thus far were the only ones raised during the campaign. Liberal insistence on appealing to the electorate on the government's record inevitably forced more mundane questions into the debate. Highways, long a political football in Saskatchewan politics, came up again in 1929. Provincial finances, the need for an independent audit, the administration of mental asylums and homes for the aged, and public ownership of power generation and distribution—all received some attention. Nevertheless, important though they might have been in previous elections, they were merely speech filler in 1929. The issues of greatest importance in the 1929 election were those that appealed, not to the pocketbook, but to the emotions—sectarianism in the public schools, the influx of foreigners, control of the province's lands and resources, and the scandal charges directed at the Liberal Party and the Gardiner government. The opposition forces, led by Dr. Anderson and the Conservative Party, built their campaign on these issues and the electorate's response to them would determine the outcome of the election.

The Co-operative Government

Election day produced the most remarkable turnaround in Saskatchewan political history since 1905. On June 6, enough voters abandoned their traditional allegiance to the Liberal Party to reduce Liberal representation in the Legislature by half—from 52 to 26 (2 more Liberal candidates would be elected at deferred contests). The Conservative Party increased its numbers from 4 to 24 and doubled its share of the popular vote. Progressive candidates won 5 seats, and 6 constituencies returned Independents opposed to the Liberals. The agreement between the Conservatives and Progressives not to oppose each other had paid dividends. So had Anderson's strategy of supporting Independents where agreements could not be reached between his party and the Progressives. However, the most important factor in the opposition's success was the campaign waged by the Conservatives from their convention in March 1928 right through to election day, for it directed into political channels the emotionalism which had arisen out of the ethnic and religious composition of the province and which had been brought to a boil by the Ku Klux Klan. None of the major issues raised by the Conservatives was in itself sufficient to defeat the Liberals, but each issue accentuated the growing belief that the Catholic and immigrant groups were subverting the traditional social system of the province, each increased the suspicion that the Liberals had sanctioned this in return for political support, and each attracted to the opposition camp enough former Liberal voters to account for much of its surge in support. The Liberal Party at the height of its power was a coalition of Catholic, new immigrant, and established Protestant, Anglo-Scandinavian farmers, and the continued support of all three, particularly the last, was necessary to retain power in 1929. The suspicion that the Gardiner government favoured the Catholic and the immigrant caused enough of the third group to defect from the Liberal party to bring about its defeat, and the constituencies won by the respective sides in the election bear this out. Generally speaking, the largest concentrations of Catholic and immigrant groups in the late 1920s were found in the southwest border region, the northern areas, and the region southeast of Saskatoon extending to the Manitoba border north of the CPR mainline. The constituencies in these areas contained the vast majority of those who bore the brunt of Klan attacks and who felt that the Conservative campaign was directed at them, and 22 of these 25 seats returned Liberals to the Legislative Assembly. It seems clear then that the reduction in Liberal representation on June 6 was due mainly to a voter realignment on religious and racial lines. That is to say, support for the Liberal Party was greatest in areas with a high percentage of Catholic and ethnic voters. As the concentration of these groups increased in the constituencies the Liberal vote tended to increase and, conversely, as the proportion of Protestant and Anglo-Saxon or Scandinavian people in constituencies increased, so did the percentage of votes for the opposition parties.[6]

As might be expected, reaction to the election outcome varied greatly across the province. Given past results the opposition forces had accomplished a truly remarkable feat and their supporters were elated with their success. The Conservative leadership, however, took no credit for itself. Dr. Anderson and his colleagues claimed that the result was the product of a popular revolt against a government that had outlived its usefulness. Just the same, people such as Anderson, MacPherson and Bryant must have felt a certain sense of accomplishment. They had brought the Conservative Party back from the brink of oblivion and they had done so in a very short time. Liberals, on the other hand, were both stunned and angered by the result. Although some had expected to lose a few seats, no one had predicted an outcome which might force the government from office. It appears that most Liberals, especially Premier Gardiner, underestimated the strength of their opponents' appeal. According to Gardiner's biographers, "He found it difficult to take seriously his opponents' nonsensical assertions about Catholic dominance of the Liberals and their government, about insidious ethnic and religious elements undermining the school system, and alien forces threatening Saskatchewan's clean British way of life."[7] Perhaps this is the reason why the Premier refused to accept Anderson's motions in the Assembly to make the public schools completely non-sectarian and to encourage British immigration, when to do so would have cost his government very little and would have deprived the Conservatives of the two issues which most harmed the Liberal cause on election day.

The fact that the election results left the Liberals as the largest party in the Legislature but without a majority gave rise to constitutional questions which were not settled until three months after the election. Conservatives, in eager anticipation of power, claimed that since the Progressives and Independents who had won seats had been elected in opposition to the government, Gardiner should resign immediately. In this they were joined by the Progressive and Independent members-elect, who met with their Conservative counterparts on June 11 and signed an agreement to support a new government headed by Dr.

Anderson should it come to power. The reason for the concerted action was to show Gardiner that his government could not be sustained at any future legislative session and thus convince him to resign, but the stubborn Premier would not give up so easily. Therefore, in early July the combined opposition petitioned the lieutenant-governor, H.W. Newlands, to dismiss Gardiner but he refused, declaring that the Liberals, as the largest group in the Legislature, had a constitutional right to meet the Assembly, where the matter would be resolved. Thus a special session convened on September 4, where the Liberals attempted to drive a wedge between the Conservatives and their allies, but to no avail. Representatives of both the Progressive and Independent members confirmed their decision to drive the Liberals from office and, after the Assembly adopted Anderson's want of confidence amendment to the Speech from the Throne, Gardiner tendered his resignation. Within a week, J.T.M. Anderson was sworn in as Premier at the

SAB RA 629(1)
Formal portrait of Premier J.T.M. Anderson (n.d.).

head of a "Co-operative" government, the culmination of a struggle which he had begun in the face of seemingly insurmountable odds over five years earlier. The Conservative Party would not be able to govern on its own, but at least and at long last it would taste power.

The new Co-operative government took office on September 9.[8] The cities of the province were well represented in the Cabinet, with two ministers from Saskatoon, one from Regina (Bryant was also from Regina, but he sat for Lumsden), one from Moose Jaw, and one each from Yorkton and Swift Current. Interestingly, Anderson included no farmers in his government, although Buckle had farmed prior to going into the farm implement business. Perhaps Anderson believed that since the concerns of agriculture so dominated the politics of the province, it was unnecessary to give farmers special representation. In total, while 4 ministers sat for rural constituencies, 9 of the 10 came from business or professional backgrounds. The average age of the Cabinet was 45, five years younger than its Liberal predecessor. The Anderson government apparently functioned in a collegial fashion, with few divisive battles, despite the fact that three different groups were represented within it and not one minister had any previous experience in government at the provincial level.

COURTESY THE SASKATCHEWAN ARCHIVES BOARD

"Saskatchewan's Newest Wild Animal." This cartoon, printed in the June 3, 1929, edition of the Leader, *which supported the Liberals, attempts to warn voters that the Anderson coalition would not be able to function effectively. Nevertheless, despite the diverse interests it represented, the Anderson "Co-operative" government had remarkably little internal discord.*

Much the same can be said about relations between the Cabinet and the diverse collection of men who supported it in the Legislature. It seems that the idea of cooperation struck a responsive chord. This might have been expected in the case of the Progressives, given their ideas on "group government," but less anticipated in the case of the Independents until one remembers that some of these men had come from Conservative backgrounds. As it happened, the government never lost a confidence vote in the Assembly during its years in office. Its supporters occasionally passed resolutions of which the government disapproved, and often took it to task for not doing enough to offset the worst effects of the Depression, but on any issue of major importance, they always rallied round. Nor should one underestimate the strength of anti-Liberal, anti-Gardiner, sentiment as an explanation for this solidarity. Even after two Progressive MLAs—Jacob Benson from Last Mountain and Samuel Whatley from Kindersley—joined the new Farmer-Labour party in 1932, both kept their seats on the government side and continued to uphold the Anderson Cabinet with their votes rather than make common cause with the Liberals. Finally, one must take note of the loyalty government supporters showed toward the Premier during the election of 1934. Only three Conservatives elected in 1929 did not run again; four of the six Independents ran as Conservatives, as did two of the five Progressives.

The idea of cooperation in politics, which had begun as one of Anderson's principal tactics to defeat the Liberals, took on added meaning as Saskatchewan plunged into the

SAB RB 8210

Premier J.T.M. Anderson (front row, fourth from right) and the Conservative, Progressive and Independent MLAs who supported him, taken at the first session of the Legislature, September 4–6, 1929.

depths of the Depression. Anderson was much impressed with John Bracken's "grand coalition" in Manitoba and, by the autumn of 1932, he began to sound out Gardiner as to the prospect of the Liberals joining his Co-operative government. In mid-November he wrote to Gardiner: "I wish to discuss with you the possibility of government and opposition forces uniting in the interests of our province in view of the difficulties facing our people as a result of the prolonged economic depression."[9] Negotiations continued for months, but by spring of the following year it was clear that Gardiner wanted no part of any formal coalition and talks ended in a public display of mutual recrimination. Nevertheless, the idea had one unexpected consequence. At an early stage in the process, the Liberal MLA for Kinistino, Charles McIntosh, declared himself in favour of cooperation with the government and, after negotiations failed, he crossed the floor of the Legislature to support the Premier. Shortly thereafter, Anderson appointed him to the Cabinet as minister of Natural Resources and, given the constitutional requirements of the time, McIntosh returned to his constituents to seek their approval of his actions at a by-election. Unlike in 1929, when the Liberals allowed every one of Anderson's Cabinet appointees to retain his seat by acclamation, this time Gardiner decided to run a candidate against McIntosh. McIntosh lost the by-election and thus holds the record for the shortest ministerial career in Saskatchewan politics—33 days (April 29–May 31, 1933). No other Liberal abandoned his party and, in fact, Gardiner and his Liberals provided a very strong opposition to the Anderson government throughout its term.

The government faced two additional sources of opposition in its five years of office, one potential, the other immediate. The trouble to come consisted of those individuals who founded the Co-operative Commonwealth Federation (CCF) and eventually brought it to power. The organized farmers of Saskatchewan had long been split between those who wanted their organization to enter provincial politics directly and those who preferred it to remain the very effective interest group that it was. Throughout the 1920s the moderates prevailed but, with the onset of the Depression, the United Farmers of Canada (Saskatchewan Section) finally decided to create its own political party in 1931. A year later it joined with the Independent Labour Party to form the Farmer-Labour group, with M.J. Coldwell as its first leader and Benson and Whatley its first MLAs. It became part of the new CCF in 1933, although it retained its original name for provincial purposes. Despite its eventual success, however, it did not pose any immediate threat to the Anderson government. It received scant attention from the Liberal and Conservative press in the province, spent most of its time in the constituencies trying to attract money and adherents and, as mentioned previously, its two MLAs continued to vote with the government.

The more immediate threat to Anderson came from within the ranks of his own party. Not all Conservatives shared the Premier's enthusiasm for cooperation with other political groups, in particular Dr. David Johnstone, party president from 1930 to 1932. Johnstone's principal complaints were that Anderson had abandoned Conservative principles in his pursuit of power, and that the government had not done enough for party workers since it came to power. After two uncomfortable years, the issue came to a head at the Conservative convention in June 1932 and Anderson won the battle. Party members replaced Johnstone as president and confirmed Anderson as leader, but Johnstone and his followers did not go quietly into political oblivion. Instead, calling themselves the "True Blues," they continued to attack the government at every turn, campaigned against McIntosh at the Kinistino by-election and, while they did not run any candidates themselves in 1934, worked hard to defeat those running as supporters of the Premier. In sum, they were another thorn in the side of the government when the Depression had already tossed it into the middle of the brier patch.

Issues Facing the Anderson Government

Despite the clouds on the economic horizon, Anderson and his colleagues approached the second session of the new Legislature with all the determination and confidence of any new government. They used the five months between taking office and the convening of the Assembly in February 1930 to get to know their portfolios and to prepare the legislation they would introduce. First amongst their priorities was action to fulfill the promises they had made in the election campaign. Thus, in the Speech from the Throne, the government announced that it would seek approval of legislation in the areas of education, natural resources, immigration, the public service, highways, health, and power generation in the province.

One of the first issues to be addressed was the question of sectarianism in the public school system. As Anderson explained when introducing amendments to the School Act:

> We have a tremendous human problem in this province caused by the [cosmopolitan] nature of our population. ... there are conditions existing in various parts of this province that, if they are allowed to continue, may cause only trouble and sorrow in the future. Now is the time when we must lay the foundation for that future period of peace, quiet, harmony, helpfulness, square dealing and cooperation which will not come if we allow our public schools to be affected by sectarian influence.[10]

Thus, from that time forward, no emblem of any religious faith, society or association was allowed on public school property during school hours, and no one was permitted to teach in the public school system if wearing the garb of any such faith or society.[11] Furthermore, all meetings of school boards were conducted in English. A year later, the Legislature passed additional government-sponsored amendments which did away with the right of local boards to teach Grade 1 in French and required candidates for school trustee positions to prove their ability to read and write English. In these ways, the Anderson government sought to create a public school system completely free of sectarian influence, one in which the English language would unite all the disparate elements in the province. The Klan in Saskatchewan approved of the changes, as did most of the public at large. Catholics and the Liberal Party opposed them bitterly but to no avail, and soon afterward the issue faded from the political arena, replaced by questions of how to maintain the integrity of the educational system in the face of the Depression.

During the legislative session of 1930 Anderson also rose in the Assembly to move acceptance of the agreement his government had reached with the King administration in Ottawa to turn over to the province control of the lands and natural resources of Saskatchewan retained by the federal government in 1905. Under the specific terms of the agreement more than half the total land area of Saskatchewan would shift from federal to provincial jurisdiction, with concomitant control of the resources on and under these lands, and Ottawa would continue to pay a subsidy to the province in perpetuity as compensation for revenues lost to Saskatchewan since 1905. In addition, administration of the School Lands Fund of approximately $16 million would become the responsibility of the province. Further negotiations would take place after the courts decided whether the province should be compensated for revenues lost between 1870 and 1905. The agreement did not give Saskatchewan everything it sought, but Anderson was pleased with it nonetheless. In his words:

> Now there are some ... who may say that it would have been better to have ... executed the agreement after a court decision had been handed down regarding the period prior to 1905. But we, as a province, are faced with this situation: We want control of our natural resources ... and we have to lay the foundation for the administration of these resources. Our future development depends on that foundation and that foundation might just as well be laid now as later; and we believe that this development should be undertaken without delay.[12]

SAB RB 459(4)

"Completing Confederation." Premier J.T.M. Anderson (front row, fifth from left) signs the official agreement turning over control of natural resources to Saskatchewan, 1930.

The Assembly approved the agreement shortly thereafter, ending a dispute between Regina and Ottawa which had gone on for more than 25 years, a nut that no Liberal Premier had been able to crack.

Another issue of importance to the Conservatives and their allies in the 1929 campaign was that of immigration to the province, and the Anderson government acted quickly to address it once in power. It appointed a royal commission to investigate all aspects of the matter, especially the impact on the rate of assimilation of the current practice of allowing immigrants to settle in ethnic and religious colonies, and the effect of mechanization on the need for additional settlers in the rural areas of the province. At the same time, the government sought and received assurances from the new Conservative government in Ottawa that no large groups of immigrants would be admitted to Saskatchewan without its prior approval. Despite these steps, however, events overtook the government before it could develop a comprehensive immigration policy. The Depression diverted the government's attention to other more pressing matters, and immigration to the province slowed to a trickle as the economy worsened. In fact, long before its term ended, emigration from rather than immigration to Saskatchewan became the more important problem.

The final issue of major concern to all groups opposed to the Liberals in 1929 involved corruption in the administrative and judicial systems of the province, and the new government wasted no time in its attempt to break "the Machine." It proceeded first to prove the campaign allegations of Liberal corruption, and then to ensure that it could not be tarred with the same brush. It hired a professional chartered accountant, Walter Weston, to audit the books of the Farm Loan Board, and his report gave credence to the charges of "political interference, maladministration of funds, huge losses and gross inefficiency."[13] However, neither the Public Accounts Committee nor the government itself made much of Weston's findings. Perhaps Anderson and his colleagues believed that they had bigger fish to fry since they had also created a royal commission to investigate allegations of political interference in the administration of justice by Liberal governments and their "Machine." The Royal Commission on Administrative Scandals consisted of J.F. Embury of the King's Bench and J. McKay and P.E. McKenzie of the Saskatchewan Court of Appeal. Their report, tabled in February 1931, showed that Liberal Cabinet ministers, MLAs, and political workers had interfered not only with the provincial police force but also the courts in both civil and criminal cases. For example, the commissioners found that former attorney general T.C. Davis had used the provincial police in an attempted prosecution of the Ku Klux Klan; that a member of the force had campaigned for W.J. Patterson, MLA for Pipestone; and that the MLA for Wynyard, W.H. Paulson, had used a police constable to drive him around his constituency at election time. They also found, amongst other crimes and misdemeanours, that Liberal organizers (whom they named) had improperly tried to persuade the police not to enforce the Liquor Act for political reasons, and they provided evidence later used against one of the province's most infamous bootleggers.[14] The commission's report provoked the expected outcry. Government supporters in the Legislature called on Davis, Patterson and Paulson to resign and the *Daily Star* gave the utmost publicity to each and every indiscretion revealed. Nevertheless, the scandals proved to be the "Sensation of the Session" only. The prominent Liberals denied every accusation and counterattacked with charges of their own. Gardiner was not implicated directly in any of the evidence given before the commission, the provincial police force had been disbanded in 1928, and Anderson chose to make the necessary reforms to civil service procedures quietly rather than prolong the distasteful affair. Furthermore, the government had already taken other steps to ensure the political neutrality of the public service. Within weeks of taking office Anderson appointed the Public Service Enquiry Commission, headed by M.J. Coldwell (then a member of the provincial Progressive executive), and when it reported a few months later the government accepted its recommendations to create a nonpartisan public service based on the merit principle and overseen by a strong and independent Public Service Commission. The new commission did not survive the return of the Liberals to power in 1934, but its creation fulfilled one of Anderson's major promises in the 1929 campaign. Furthermore, it would be resurrected by the CCF after its victory in 1944, and proved to be instrumental in providing Saskatchewan with a civil service envied by many other jurisdictions for many years to come.

Beyond action to deal with these particular election issues, the Anderson government began its term with ambitious plans in a host of different areas. Health care was one of these priorities and, over the years, Dr. Munroe, the minister of Health, made several improvements to the system. In 1930, for example, he created a cancer commission to oversee new diagnostic clinics designed to detect the disease early and treat it. Later he reorganized treatment of the mentally ill and took other steps to reduce the mortality rate of the population. Even as the Depression worsened, the government promised that "no service which is essentially a public health activity will be curtailed"[15] and, for the most part, it was able to keep that promise. Surprisingly perhaps, labour issues also received a good deal of attention from this government. John Merkley had been a trade unionist and, during his years as minister, he met often with the Saskatchewan Trades and Labour Council and introduced several labour-friendly bills: the One Days Rest in Seven Act in 1930, the Weekly Half-Day Holiday Act in 1931, a revised Mines Act in 1932 after the tragic events at Estevan, and amendments to the Workmen's Compensation and Minimum Wage Acts which extended benefits to thousands of workers. In addition, Anderson's presence as head of government guaranteed that education remained high on the Cabinet's list of priorities and, during his first years in office, he created a superannuation fund to provide pensions for retired teachers, established a provincial school for the deaf, altered the elementary school curriculum to improve the health of students as well as prepare them for their responsibilities as future citizens, cooperated with the federal government to enroll hundreds of students in vocational schools, and expanded the correspondence school concept so that thousands of rural children, hitherto deprived of a secondary education, could earn their high school diplomas. Other government initiatives during the first half of its mandate included: completion of the Saskatchewan section of the trans-Canada telephone system; negotiations to secure control of power-generating plants as part of its plan to develop a publicly owned power system; a scheme to encourage fruit growing in the province; and a program of highway construction to help both farmers and businessmen move their products to markets more quickly and cheaply. However, the highway program, and any others which cost large sums of money, had to be dropped or curtailed drastically as the Depression deepened. By 1931, all work on provincial roads was carried out as a form of relief to destitute farmers and by 1932, the attention of the Premier and his ministers had to be devoted almost exclusively to coping with the twin tragedies of drought and Depression.

Drought and Economic Depression

Much has been written about the effects of the Depression on the people of Saskatchewan.[16] For these purposes, it is sufficient to reiterate that within three years, from December 1928 through to the end of 1931, the province went from being one of the richest to one of the poorest grain-exporting areas in the world. Furthermore, in the last years of the Anderson government, "Impossible as it may seem, the net agricultural incomes for 1931 through 1934 ... were reported in minus figures, a reduction in income quite unmatched in any civilized country."[17] Saskatchewan farmers did not have the means to withstand the decline in prices, the loss of markets, and year after year of drought in some regions, and no other sector of the economy was large enough or strong enough to take up the slack. As farm incomes plummeted, so did government revenues, first at the municipal level as property taxes went unpaid, and then provincially as its sources of revenue began to wither.

The Depression did not strike everywhere with full force at the same time. Indeed, when the Anderson government took office the prevailing opinion across the province was that the economic downturn would be of short duration, that prices and markets would rebound quickly, and that drought-stricken areas would not have to wait long for crop-saving rains. The Speeches from the Throne in the early years reflect this belief and the opinion that the government would not have to do much out of the ordinary to meet the situation. In 1930, the Speech from the Throne opened as follows:

> Notwithstanding the fact that, owing to adverse climatic conditions in certain sections of the province the aggregate yield of grain during the past year fell short of the record achieved in the previous year, that ever-present spirit of optimism among our people that has played such a conspicuous and noble part in laying with solidity and care the foundation of our great province, still prevails.[18]

Thus, for most of its first two years in office, the government proceeded to treat problems on an ad hoc basis. Special grants were given to municipalities in financial difficulty to tide them over until conditions improved; bonds were issued to guarantee loans to the Wheat Pool, which saved it from bankruptcy; and repayable cash advances were made to farmers in need to enable them to plant their crops and feed their livestock. As late as the 1931 session, even the Liberals joined government backbenchers in voting overwhelmingly against a private member's motion which would have reduced the salaries of civil servants and the indemnities paid to Cabinet ministers and MLAs.

By 1932, the situation had changed dramatically for the worse and no one could pretend otherwise. Speeches from the Throne no longer spoke of "optimistic futures" but rather "widespread unemployment and distress," "human suffering," "adversity" and the need for the government "to provide state assistance on a scale never before experienced in the history of our Province."[19] In these circumstances, and in accordance with the prevailing economic wisdom of the day (espoused especially by the Conservative federal government of R.B. Bennett), the Anderson government cut expenditures where it could and attempted to raise money by both taxation and borrowing. It reduced the salaries of everyone on the public payroll, cut all but the most essential government programs and, as mentioned earlier, used the entire construction budget of the Department of Highways for relief purposes. It introduced Saskatchewan's first income tax in 1932, and raised gasoline taxes and the tax on corporations. It encouraged farmers in the drought-stricken southern areas to move north and paid the costs of resettlement. Anderson began his fruitless attempts to persuade Gardiner and the Liberals to join his coalition and settled eventually for an all-party Special Committee of the Legislature to study debt adjustment, tax consolidation, and other matters related to the Depression. The government also borrowed money from traditional lenders until its credit was exhausted.

None of this was sufficient to solve the many problems caused by the Depression, however, and eventually the government had to turn to other alternatives. The first problem was how to keep farm families alive and able to earn a living on their farms:

> So serious was the plight of many farmers that their initial problem was one of survival. Even such necessities as food, clothing and fuel were

beyond their income. Furthermore, the continuing depression soon made local credit arrangements impossible. Aid had to come from the government for these essentials. But the farmers also had to make financial arrangements for seeding and harvesting before they could become re-established. Here again the government proved to be the only available source of credit.[20]

Conditions were little, if any, better in the towns and cities of the province. In these circumstances, the government created the Saskatchewan Relief Commission in the late summer of 1931, a non-political body composed of four men and one woman who were to coordinate all relief measures in the rural areas of the province.[21] It remained in existence for three years, until disbanded by the Liberals on their return to power, and during that time it provided a host of goods and services it deemed essential to fulfill its mandate. The commission oversaw food, clothing and fuel relief; arranged fodder for livestock and poultry, and seed grain for planting; funded repairs to machinery, medical care, and advances on teachers' salaries; subsidized employment on farms which needed labour but could not afford to pay for it; and coordinated the distribution of aid from private-sector donors all across Canada through its Voluntary Relief Committee. It did not provide all this assistance as a form of charity. In fact, all applications for relief of any sort included a commitment to repay the Relief Commission when possible. Most of the money to finance the Relief Commission's operations and programs came from the federal government. Shrinking revenues at the municipal level and the ever-growing demands on local governments for relief soon surpassed their ability to provide the needed assistance and they turned naturally to Regina for help. However, it was not long before the provincial government found itself in exactly the same position and it had little choice but to "upload" the problem to its wealthier counterpart. The Relief Commission was undoubtedly the Anderson government's most important initiative to cope with the Depression. Despite its faults and Gardiner's charge that it was a partisan tool of the Conservative Party, the prevailing view is that it performed its main tasks well, that it succeeded in its principal objectives, and that it did so without "the slightest indication of political influence, profiteering or partiality … an enviable record."[22]

The Relief Commission may have solved the immediate problems of many farm families, but it did little to ensure that these families would retain title to their land. Many farmers had borrowed heavily to purchase land and machinery, as had entrepreneurs in the towns and cities to establish their businesses. So long as crop yields and prices remained high these debts were not an onerous burden. However, when both collapsed, many farmers could no longer meet their obligations and, as farm incomes declined, so did those of local businessmen. This was one part of the debt problem—mortgages and loans owed to banks and trust companies. The other part arose when landowners, both rural and urban, began to default on their property taxes and risked losing their livelihoods to government confiscation for tax arrears. Once the problems became acute, the Anderson government moved quickly to address them, first tackling the thornier issue of contracted debt. In 1931, it passed the Act to Facilitate the Adjustment of Agricultural Debts, which established a voluntary conciliation procedure through which farmers could appeal to a debt commissioner to have their payments on principal and interest postponed to a later date. A year later, the government extended the application of the act to the urban areas of the province and gave the debt commissioner the power to declare a moratorium on payments in some cases. This proved to be insufficient to meet the problem, however, and in 1933 the government introduced two bills—the Debt Adjustment Act and the Limitation of Civil Rights Act—which gave it and its agents new powers to intervene in cases where farms and businesses were threatened with foreclosure. The first act created the Debt Adjustment Board, from which creditors had to secure permission before they could take debtors to court. The board was also given the power to arbitrate cases on its own and to reduce both the principal and interest charged on debts if deemed unreasonable. The second act changed the law governing contracts so that creditors could not claim more than one-third of the revenues from the sale of grain in any year in payment of debts owed them, regardless of the terms of the original agreement.

Other bills passed in the same period dealt with the problem of tax arrears. One postponed for three years all sales of property because of non-payment of municipal taxes. A second established a schedule of dates by which defaulters, both rural and urban, could pay off their back taxes at a 5% interest rate by 1938. A later amendment cancelled all penalties levied by municipalities for non-payment of taxes. Neither the financial community nor all municipal governments regarded these actions with favour, but in the end, they did keep people on their farms and in their businesses for the short term, the expectation being that an eventual return to prosperity would take care of the long-term problems. It may have taken 20 years for the debt issue to be resolved finally and it may be argued that more could have been done, but in context, the actions of the Anderson government must be seen as appropriate to the circumstances of the time.

The length and severity of the Depression altered the course of the Anderson government completely and left it in a vulnerable position from which to wage its campaign for reelection. When it took office, it looked forward to an entire four- or five-year term in which to legislate its program. Instead, it had two years at the most and, inevitably, some initiatives were lost. During that time it did honour its major campaign promises in education, immigration, resources, and civil service reform, and began important new programs in areas such as power supply and health care. From mid-1931 onward, however, it found itself forced to devote almost all of its efforts toward alleviating the worst effects of the Depression. It may well be that no other government could have done more given the conditions in which it had to operate but, by 1934, the simple fact was that the province was in a sorry state and this did not bode well for Anderson and his Co-operative government in the upcoming election.

The 1934 Provincial Election

The Premier called the election for June 19, just as his mandate came to an end. The government had little choice but to run on its record, and this was apparent from the opening of the campaign. The Conservative Party prepared a 95-page pamphlet called "Something of the Achievements of the Anderson Government," which listed 35 specific accomplishments together with supporting statistics. It claimed that

> We Still Hold The Confidence Of Our People Because We Have: kept [the] promises of 1929; reformed public schools; provided work for thousands; aided land settlement; provided relief for one-third of our population; secured our Natural Resources; reformed the Civil Service; introduced far-reaching health measures; extended our provincial power system; secured provincial rights re immigration; given secondary education to thousands of our underprivileged rural boys and girls; helped save the wheat situation by getting behind the wheat pool at a critical time; provided a Debt Adjustment Commission; lightened the burden of tax arrears; established Teachers' Superannuation; [and] reduced costs of administration.[23]

The pamphlet listed numerous other achievements, and concluded with the statement that these were the reasons why the government deserved to be returned to power. Party speakers, especially Anderson, Bryant and Stewart, took the message to all corners of the province. In Saskatoon, where Anderson ran a joint campaign with Howard McConnell, their literature emphasized the point that "A Vote for Anderson and McConnell Is a Vote for Security and Stability," and warned voters "Don't Swap Horses When Crossing a Stream." Under the heading "They've Stood By You," people were reminded that:

> Premier Anderson, Mr. McConnell and their colleagues have faced conditions that have never before existed in the history of the Province… They have shown Courage and Leadership in times of Stress… They have saved your Homes from Tax Sale and made it possible to write down your Tax Debt… Their Relief Plans have enabled people to face the problem of Unemployment and Loss of Crops… They have maintained the Credit of the Province in the face of Liberal attacks… They have given us an Educational System that is a pattern for all Canada.

The advertisement ended by asking the electorate:

> Can this Province under the circumstances afford to change its Government and disturb the system which has been developed by the Provincial and Federal authorities? A system, under which, through mutual confidence, we are today enabled to finance ourselves in this last stage of the depression.[24]

Some Cabinet ministers and government candidates resurrected the scandals of the previous Liberal administration which had been revealed by the royal commissions three years earlier, and others predicted that a Gardiner government would repeal the amendments to the School Act intended to keep the public school system free from sectarianism, and abolish the Relief Commission which had saved so many from financial ruin. Others still pointed to the few new policies promised in the government's election manifesto: a commission to administer all aspects of education in the province; a minimum salary for teachers; additional provincial parks; new highway construction when finances permitted; a province-wide service of agricultural representatives to assist farmers; water conservation through government-sponsored irrigation projects; and support for national unemployment and health insurance schemes.[25] Overall, however, the government and its supporters ran a defensive campaign based on an appeal to their record in office and in response to the attacks of their opponents: J.G. Gardiner and his Liberals, M.J. Coldwell and the new Farmer-Labour (CCF) movement, and, as always, the "True Blues" led by the indefatigable Dr. Johnstone.

Throughout the campaign, Johnstone accused Anderson of subverting conservative principles and it is possible that he caused some Conservatives to abandon the government on election day. Be that as it may, the government faced far greater threats from both of its major opponents—the Liberals and Farmer-Labour. Gardiner's Liberals, as expected, ran a full slate of 55 candidates (the Legislature having been reduced by eight constituencies as a cost-cutting measure). Surprisingly perhaps, given that the party had been in existence for only two years, Farmer-Labour contested all but two seats. This meant that government candidates had to face two opponents almost everywhere they ran and, further, that the anti-Liberal vote had somewhere to go if it did not wish to support the government. Thus, Anderson's strategy of uniting all those opposed to the Liberals, which had helped him so much in 1929, did not work in 1934. Just the same, Gardiner accused Anderson and Coldwell of collusion to keep the Liberals out of office and the Premier found it difficult to disassociate himself from the charge. He denied it, as did Coldwell, and there was no truth to it, but it did lend credence to Johnstone's claim that Anderson was prepared to deal with anyone in order to retain power, and it is true that the two Farmer-Labour MLAs after 1932 had supported the government consistently. In addition, Anderson did not see Farmer-Labour as a serious challenge. He regarded the new party's socialist platform as too radical to be acceptable to most voters in the province and he gave the party little attention in his speeches. The Conservative organization did not match Farmer-Labour efforts in most constituencies, and the government paid a steep price for these mistakes on election day.

Another accusation that Anderson found difficult to counter was that he and his colleagues had allied themselves with the philosophy and policies of the federal Conservatives led by Prime Minister R.B. Bennett, not the most popular politician in the country at the time. In fact, Anderson had helped Bennett win eight seats in Saskatchewan in 1930 and had also tailored many of his government's Depression-fighting programs to meet federal requirements in order to save the province from bankruptcy. The Premier may have had little choice in the matter, but his association with the man who had brought the "Bennett buggy" to rural Saskatchewan did his cause absolutely no good at all.

Finally, and of greatest importance, neither Anderson nor any supporter of his government could deny the simple fact that most of the people of the province were worse off financially in 1934 than they had been when the Co-operative government came to power. They might claim correctly that the Premier should not be held responsible for the Depression and that his government had done everything possible to lessen its impact, but it was still a weak position to hold in a campaign for re-election.

Despite the unfavourable omens, the government approached election day with some confidence. In fact, workers at Conservative Party headquarters in Regina predicted that candidates supporting Dr. Anderson would win 35 seats—29 Conservatives and 6 Independents.[25] Even allowing for a certain amount of bluff and bravado, their predictions were totally incorrect. On June 19, the Liberals won 49 seats (and one more at the deferred election in Athabaska), while Farmer-Labour won 5. Neither Anderson nor a single government supporter won a seat. In Saskatoon, the Premier ran third behind the two successful Liberal candidates. This was a crushing defeat, total rejection by that most important of criteria in parliamentary electoral politics—the number of seats won. Government spokesmen could explain that although the Liberals had won 90% of the seats, they had done so with only 48% of the total vote. They could point out that government candidates had received more of the popular vote than Farmer-Labour (27% to 24%) and that they had come second in more seats (31 to 18). Nevertheless, no one could explain away the fact that not a single supporter of the government, from Premier to backbencher, had garnered enough votes from the electorate in any area of the province to win a seat. J.T.M. Anderson's experiment with cooperative government was over, rejected decisively by the people of Saskatchewan.

Anderson left the premiership a month to the day after the election, but he did not leave the political stage entirely. He stood as a Bennett Conservative at the federal election in 1935 and came a respectable second in Saskatoon City. He continued as leader of the provincial Conservative Party until its biennial convention in October 1936, when he stepped down in favour of John Diefenbaker. Nearly two years later, in the provincial election of June 8, 1938, he accepted Diefenbaker's call to run in Saskatoon, where he again came third behind the two victorious Liberals. Finally, he contested Rosetown-Biggar as a "National Government"[26] candidate in the 1940 federal election, losing badly to M.J. Coldwell (soon to become leader of the CCF). Neither the provincial nor the federal party provided Anderson with any sort of reward for his many years of service. A pension was probably beyond the means of the party in Saskatchewan at the time, but he might have expected something from the federal party, at least until it lost power in 1935. However, nothing came his way from Ottawa. It appears that Bennett and his federal colleagues did not share Anderson's belief in cooperation with other groups as being in the best interests of the party, and concluded that he was not a sufficiently reliable and committed Conservative to deserve such consideration. Thus, at the age of 58, Anderson found himself forced to find a job in a province and at a time when employment opportunities were scarce. With no position forthcoming from Ottawa and a return to the provincial public service out of the question, he had little choice but to look to the world of business. Eventually he became manager of the Crown Life Insurance Company's northern branch in Saskatoon, where he remained for eight years until the new CCF government made him superintendent of the school for the deaf in 1944. He served in that capacity in the school he had established as Premier until his death on December 29, 1946. He is buried in Woodlawn cemetery, Saskatoon, beside his wife Edith, who died the following year.

Conclusion

A one-term Premier of an impoverished province cannot compete favourably in any comparison of achievements in office or long-time legacy. Nevertheless, J.T.M. Anderson did have a significant impact on both the politics and government of Saskatchewan and he deserves to be remembered for this. Anderson was not an experienced politician when he accepted the leadership of the provincial Conservative Party in 1924. However, five years later he succeeded in driving the Liberals from office, a feat unmatched by any of his predecessors including the formidable Frederick Haultain. Nor was Anderson a committed Conservative partisan, which may explain why he achieved success in such a short span of time and in the face of such difficult odds. Anderson regarded the defeat of the Liberals as his principal objective and he was prepared to cooperate with anyone who shared this goal. This led first to an easy alliance with the Progressives and then to a more problematic relationship with the Ku Klux Klan. Anderson himself was never a member of the Klan, nor did he ever enter into any agreements with it. Nevertheless, he recognized that the Klan spoke for many people in Saskatchewan on at least two very important issues of the day and he was able to direct this sentiment against the Gardiner government. He also understood the electorate's growing distaste for "Machine" politics and promised to root out corruption in government. His strategy and tactics proved successful; they brought him to power in 1929, and they enabled him to hold together a disparate band of followers for his entire term of office. However, his short-term success did not lead to long-term benefits for the provincial Conservative Party. His emphasis on cooperative government led him to ignore and even discourage organization in the constituencies on behalf of his party. In addition, he seemed to regard the emergent CCF as little more than another anti-Liberal protest group that he could draw into his coalition. This proved not to be the case, but Anderson's success in 1929 seduced Saskatchewan Conservatives for the next two generations. Anderson may have ended the Liberal domination of the province, but he did nothing to ensure that his party would benefit from the new, competitive two-party system. Indeed, it would be 40 years before the Conservative Party reappeared as one of the principal contenders for power in Saskatchewan and, during that time, every leader of the party was either tempted by the prospect of cooperation or had to rebuff offers of coalition with one or other of its rivals: John Diefenbaker with the CCF; Rupert Ramsay, Alvin Hamilton, and Martin Pederson with the Liberals; and Ed Nasserden with Social Credit. Even today the Conservative Party has allied itself with some Liberals to form the Saskatchewan Party in an attempt to broaden its electoral support, following a tradition begun by Frederick Haultain and perfected by J.T.M. Anderson.

Anderson as Premier also deserves to be remembered for some of the achievements of his government. Most of these occurred early in his term before the Depression diverted attention elsewhere. First, the agreement with Ottawa to acquire the lands and resources denied since 1905 ended a long-standing and often bitter dispute, made Saskatchewan the constitutional equal of the other provinces in Confederation, and gave the province control over its own development and destiny. Second, the amendments to the School Act, though minor in themselves, mollified those in Saskatchewan's Anglo-Protestant majority who wanted the province's public school system to be free of sectarian influence and a vehicle for the dissemination of the English language. In this they found a ready champion in Dr. Anderson, who had long believed that the public school was the best means by which to integrate Saskatchewan's many immigrant groups into mainstream society. Third, Anderson's government introduced much-needed reforms in the public service of the province. The royal commissions of the early 1930s confirmed suspicions that the Liberal party had used the civil service and the provincial police force for its own political purposes, and Anderson established an independent, nonpartisan Public Service Commission to guard against this happening again. Although the Commission was abolished by Gardiner on his return to power, it was restored by the CCF and remained an important part of government in Saskatchewan until another Conservative government 50 years later reintroduced partisanship as a criterion for employment in the public service.[28] Finally, the Co-operative government's actions in some specific areas, especially education and health care, merit attention because of their long-term benefits to the province. Anderson, a former teacher and school inspector, understood the importance of access to the educational system and the need for dedicated and competent teachers. Thus, he expanded the offering of correspondence courses so that children in rural districts could complete their senior matriculation, and he also implemented a pension plan to provide good teachers with sufficient security to remain in the profession. In health care, it may be said that initiatives such as the cancer commission and the Public Health Act helped prepare the way for the hospitalization and medical care programs which followed under the CCF/NDP.

It is interesting to speculate on what J.T.M. Anderson and his government might have attempted had the Depression not intervened to divert its attention and limit its activities. This was a "progressive" conservative government by the standards of the time, and it is likely that it would have proceeded with its plans to use the powers of the state, as well as its newly acquired control over lands and natural resources, to modernize the province's infrastructure. However, the Depression made pipe dreams out of these plans as the government tried to mitigate its impact. Its actions in this context again demonstrate the progressive and compassionate nature of Anderson's conservatism. He believed that his government had a responsibility to protect the province and its people from the ravages of the Depression and he was not averse to using the resources of the state for this purpose. He regarded government as an ally of the people in this process, not an enemy, and his government did much to keep people fed, clothed, sheltered, and in possession of their farms and businesses. Most people in Saskatchewan did not live well during the Depression, but they survived, and some credit for this is due to Anderson and his colleagues. Furthermore, their willingness to use the power of the state and the resources of the province for the benefit of all the people of Saskatchewan guided every provincial Conservative leader for the next 40 years, and also had a profound influence on John Diefenbaker and Alvin Hamilton when they developed the New National Policy which inspired the federal government between 1957 and 1963. A hurried reading of Saskatchewan history might lead to the conclusion that J.T.M. Anderson was no more than a one-term Premier who left both his party and the province on the edge of bankruptcy. A closer examination of the record suggests that he deserves a kinder fate.

Notes

1. *Morning Leader*, May 28, 1925.
2. *Phoenix*, May 28 and May 30, 1925.
3. For more information on the Klan in Saskatchewan, see W. Calderwood, "The Rise and Fall of the Ku Klux Klan in Saskatchewan" (M.A. thesis, University of Saskatchewan, 1968), and Patrick Kyba, "The Saskatchewan General Election of 1929" (M.A. thesis, University of Saskatchewan, 1964).
4. Pat Emmons as quoted in the *Morning Leader*, May 23, 1927.
5. Quoted in David Smith, *Prairie Liberalism: The Liberal Party of Saskatchewan, 1905–71* (Toronto: University of Toronto Press, 1975), 139.
6. For further detail on this phenomenon, see Kyba, "Saskatchewan General Election," and A.J. Milnor, "Agrarian Protest in Saskatchewan, 1929–1948: A Study in Ethnic Politics" (Ph.D. dissertation, Duke University, 1962).
7. Norman Ward and David Smith, *Jimmy Gardiner: Relentless Liberal* (Toronto: University of Toronto Press, 1990), 99.
8. It consisted of 10 men, the largest Cabinet to date in Saskatchewan history. Of the 10, 8 were Conservatives: Anderson (Saskatoon), M.A. MacPherson (Regina), W.C. Buckle (Tisdale), Howard McConnell (Saskatoon), J.F. Bryant (Lumsden), F.D. Munroe (Moosomin), J.A. Merkley (Moose Jaw), and W.W. Smith (Swift Current); Carl Stewart (Yorkton) sat as the lone Independent and Reginald Stipe (Hanley) represented the Progressive MLAs, even though he did so without the approval of the provincial Progressive association. Anderson made Smith and Stipe ministers without portfolio and kept the ministries of Education and Natural Resources for himself. He appointed MacPherson as attorney general; McConnell as provincial treasurer and minister of Municipal Affairs; Buckle to Agriculture; Bryant to Public Works and Telephones and Telegraphs; Munroe, a physician, as minister of Public Health; Stewart to Highways; and Merkley, a CPR employee, as minister of Railways, Labour and Industries, and provincial secretary. Once in their positions, the ministers remained there for the duration, with very few exceptions. In fact, during the nearly five-year term of his government, Anderson made only two changes: he replaced McConnell with MacPherson as provincial treasurer late in 1931, and he relinquished the ministry of Natural Resources briefly in the spring of 1933 when he made the ill-fated appointment of Charles McIntosh, Liberal MLA for Kinistino, to the Cabinet. Furthermore, Anderson did not meddle with his ministers in the performance of their duties. Once appointed, they were free to conduct the business of their departments without fear of interference from the Premier as long as their actions did not violate general government policy. In fact, on occasion the Liberals and their press referred to the Cabinet as the Anderson-Stewart government because Anderson often allowed his younger colleague to introduce controversial legislation, even in areas unrelated to Highways.
9. Saskatchewan Archives Board (SAB), Gardiner Papers, S-1.137, 17839, Anderson to Gardiner, November 19, 1932.
10. *Daily Star*, February 28, 1930.
11. *Statutes of Saskatchewan, 1930*, Ch. 45, section 1(1).
12. *Saskatchewan Sessional Papers*, Speech by J.T.M. Anderson, April 2, 1930, p. 452.

13. S.J. Green, "The Origin and Operation of the Saskatchewan Farm Loan Board: 1917–1951" (M.A. thesis, University of Saskatchewan, 1951), 128. Quoted in Peter A. Russell, "The Co-operative Government in Saskatchewan: 1929–1934" (M.A. thesis, University of Saskatchewan, 1970).
14. For details, see the *Daily Star*, February 27 to March 3, 1931.
15. *Journals of the Legislative Assembly of Saskatchewan*, 4th Session, 7th Legislature, February 4, 1932, p. 12.
16. Among the best known and most quoted of these are G.E. Britnell, "Saskatchewan, 1930–1935," *CJEPS* 2, no. 2 (May 1936), and B. Neatby, "The Saskatchewan Relief Commission, 1931–34," *Saskatchewan History* 3, no. 2 (1950).
17. J. Archer, *Saskatchewan: A History* (Saskatoon: Western Producer Prairie Books, 1980), 215.
18. Speech from the Throne, Quoted in the *Daily Star*, February 6, 1930.
19. *Journals of the Legislative Assembly of the Province of Saskatchewan*, Speeches from the Throne, 1932, 1933, 1934.
20. Neatby, "Saskatchewan Relief Commission," 41.
21. Those on the commission were Henry Black (chairman), A.E. Whitmore, W.G. Yule, W.A. Munns, and Pearl Johnston.
22. Neatby, "Saskatchewan Relief Commission," 56.
23. SAB, G 11 1934.1, "Something of the Achievements of the Anderson Government."
24. Conservative Party advertisement, *Star Phoenix*, June 18, 1934.
25. Co-operative Government Election Manifesto, *Star Phoenix*, May 31, 1934.
26. *Star Phoenix*, June 18, 1934.
27. Much to Anderson's satisfaction, though not likely due to his influence, the Conservative Party adopted this all-inclusive name for the 1940 election.
28. See James M. Pitsula and Ken Rasmussen, *Privatizing a Province: The New Right in Saskatchewan* (Vancouver: New Star Books, 1990), chapter 13.

William J. Patterson

Beth Bilson

Patterson, formal portrait
(SAB RA 2670).

Lieutenant-Governor Patterson, 1954
(SAB RB 6687 (1)).

Premier Patterson campaigning, 1938
(SAB RA 10420).

Patterson, with King George VI and Queen Elizabeth, 1939
(SAB RA 23881 (1)).

Saskatchewan Premiers of the 20th Century

William J. Patterson, 1935–1944

Introduction

There are perhaps no two events which have placed as great a stamp on the province of Saskatchewan as the Depression of the 1930s and World War II. The convergence of worldwide financial crisis with disastrous agricultural conditions plunged Saskatchewan into a decade of economic and social catastrophe, and the ensuing war also presented distinctive challenges for the province. Responding to these two events fell largely to the Liberal government of William Patterson, in power from the departure of James Gardiner for federal politics in 1935 until the landslide victory of the Co-operative Commonwealth Federation (CCF) in 1944. The sixth Premier of Saskatchewan, Patterson was the first to be born in the province, the first to have seen military service, and the first to enter office as a bachelor.[1] Patterson himself was described as a popular, if unflamboyant, leader, and, in his words, never "flunked" an election.[2] His government tapped into significant amounts of federal money to support relief efforts during the Depression. The Legislature during his term passed pieces of legislation on various subjects—health care, credit unions, industrial standards, taxation—which strongly foreshadowed the legislative programs of succeeding governments, and helped to create a public policy framework which is still recognizable today.

Yet the Patterson government failed to leave any substantial footprint in the public mind, and Patterson failed to make a strong or lasting impression as a public figure. At the time, he felt compelled to respond to the characterization that his was a "do-nothing" government,[3] and to point out that in facing "the biggest job any Government in this or any province ever faced," it had managed to maintain essential government services and protect the credit of Saskatchewan.[4] The Patterson period has, however, remained in the shadow of the governments of Jimmy Gardiner and Tommy Douglas, and no catalogue of its accomplishments,[5] no protestations at the difficulties of the tasks it faced, seem to have fixed it for posterity as a memorable government.

William John Patterson was born at Grenfell, in what was then the Assiniboia District of the Northwest Territories, on May 13, 1886. His Irish father, John Patterson, a railway section foreman, began work on the Grenfell section of the CPR in 1882. His mother, Catherine Fraser, travelled out from Scotland with a sister and brother-in-law to the end of the railway line at Broadview, from whence she travelled on to Grenfell with a railway construction crew.[6] John and Catherine Patterson built a small house with lumber brought overland from Broadview,[7] and William, the first of their five children, was born there.

At the age of five, Billy Patterson was sent to school—a year early—to ensure a sufficient number of students for the community to obtain a school grant. He attended school in Grenfell until the age of 15, doing farm work during the summer vacations. After leaving school in 1902, he worked for a private bank, which was later absorbed by the Dominion Bank. In 1905, the bank transferred Patterson to Winnipeg before sending him back to Grenfell, at the age of 21, to become branch manager.

In 1910, Patterson was hired by the provincial Department of Telephones. His position as a superintendent of rural service apparently allowed him to maintain his ties with his home community. His appointment diary recorded that on February 19, 1913, he travelled by train to the Broadview Agricultural Banquet, expending a total of $3 on train fare, dinner, breakfast and a hotel room.[8]

Following the outbreak of World War I in 1914, Patterson enlisted as a cavalry officer in February 1916, arriving in England in May.[9] In a pocket diary, he described a life of training, inspections and drilling. He also did some travelling in England, and enjoyed a social life. In September 1917, he was sent to France as a lieutenant of the Canadian Light Horse Regiment, and remained at the front until September 1918, when he was wounded by a shell on the Arras-Cambrai road. In the same week, two of his brothers were also wounded in France.[10] Patterson was recuperating in England at the end of the war and was then sent back to Canada. He spent a year studying law with Grenfell lawyer G.C. Neff, and then moved to Windthorst to open an insurance and financial agency.

Patterson had always pursued a wide range of community and athletic activities, including curling, at which he was reportedly adept.[11] Perhaps his chief interest from an early age, however, had been politics. A precocious adherent of the Liberal Party, he had been a delegate, before he reached voting age, to the 1905 Liberal convention at which Walter Scott was selected as leader.

Entry to Politics

In 1921, Patterson decided to run as a Liberal candidate in the Pipestone constituency.[12] By this time, he had established a strong network of connections within the party, and allegations were later made that, following a path set by other Liberal politicians, he made improper use of public resources to pursue the nomination. A royal commission, with three senior judges as members, was established by the new government of J.T.M. Anderson in 1930 to investigate claims that the Gardiner Liberals had directed government employees to carry out Liberal campaign activities using public money, and that they had manipulated the justice system so that such measures as the Vehicles Act were enforced selectively to the benefit of Liberal supporters.[13] The allegations attracted considerable attention at the time, although the report of the commission ultimately had relatively little impact, since the principal target, Gardiner himself, was cleared of all charges.

In evidence before the commission, a former provincial police officer testified that he had been asked by Patterson to campaign on his behalf while continuing to receive his police pay. He attested that Patterson, whom he had known since 1912 or 1913, and whom he described as an "old friend," asked him to "run down" the sitting Liberal MLA, Mr. Phinn, and to make Patterson better known in the part of the constituency east of Kipling. A sample of the evidence was as follows:

> MR.COMMISSIONER MACKAY: Do you say or do you not say that there was extra expense by reason of your doing this work?
>
> A.: Yes; for instance, I might have stayed at home on that particular day because I had no complaints to attend to. I would have a patrol up to

> Kipling or Wawota.
>
> Q.: And it was...?
>
> A.: Electioneering and it would be shown on the pay sheets as local patrol.
>
> MR. DIEFENBAKER: Were those expenses that you incurred for doing this political work paid for by the Department?
>
> A.: Certainly.[14]

Though counsel for the Liberals strongly attacked the credibility of this witness on the grounds that he had subsequently fallen out with the party, the transcripts of the proceedings of the Commission raise interesting questions about political activity in Saskatchewan at the time. It is clearly no coincidence that the Conservative government commissioned a report, also presented in 1930, concerning the case for reform of the public service, which was authored by a commission of inquiry chaired by M.J. Coldwell.[15]

Having successfully obtained the nomination, Patterson won his seat in the Saskatchewan Legislature by 94 votes. The only other election in which his majority was this narrow was the sweep in 1944, when he defeated the CCF candidate, Gladys Strum, by only six votes.[16]

During his time as a backbench MLA, before 1926, and while the Liberals were in opposition after 1929, Patterson remained active on the local scene, serving as secretary, and then councillor, in the village of Windthorst, and also as secretary to three district telephone companies.

In the first Gardiner government, Patterson served as minister of Telephones, provincial treasurer and minister of Highways. When that government was re-elected in 1934, Patterson was given the portfolios of Natural Resources and Telephones.

It is difficult to imagine Patterson—or anyone else—gaining much of the limelight while Gardiner was Premier, but the situation changed suddenly. Though the partisanship of Gardiner and Prime Minister King's wariness about reinforcing the considerable clout of Saskatchewan in Ottawa may have kept him out of the federal Cabinet at an earlier point,[17] Gardiner was invited to become the federal minister of Agriculture in the fall of 1935, and stepped down as Premier in November.

Though the Liberal Council was ultimately presented with only one name—that of Patterson—to replace Gardiner as leader, there had been some division within the caucus over whether the choice should be instead the attorney general, T.C. Davis. Davis was viewed as a more vigorous and combative politician.[18] In the end, however, the more emollient Patterson was chosen.[19]

The shadow of Gardiner was a long one, and Patterson's choice—if choice it was—to retain the Gardiner Cabinet virtually intact was often held up as an illustration of his lack of imagination and personal authority. On the other hand, for a Premier of Saskatchewan coming into power in 1935, putting energy into something other than experiments with Cabinet composition made some sense.

The picture was bleak. In the year 1935–36, 50% of the total budget of the province

SAB RA 2670

Premier William J. Patterson, c. 1940.

was spent on relief for the victims of the Depression. It was by then clear that neither drought nor Depression were short-term phenomena—indeed, the low point for agricultural production did not occur until 1937. The pressures on farmers and the unemployed led to incidents of social unrest and violence, including the Regina Riot of 1935 and the relief camp "strike" at the end of 1935.[20]

In a speech given to the Liberal Council at the time of his selection as leader,[21] Patterson laid out a number of themes, to which he would return frequently during his premiership, concerning his intentions for facing the problems of the province.

As perhaps befitted someone whose background was in the financial industry, Patterson struck from the outset a note of financial prudence, emphasizing the importance of credit, of balanced budgets, and of sound fiscal management. He talked of the need for "prudence and judgement in formulating policies" and for "energy and vigour in putting them into effect."[22]

Describing the philosophy of the Liberal Party, he alluded often to the concept of balance, painting a picture of a government which valued sound administration and policies which would merit the confidence of citizens. In other early speeches,[23] he identified the appropriate role of government as one of the crucial issues in Saskatchewan politics after 1929. His own inclination was to limit the role of government in society; his concern about the threat to democratic values posed by the CCF was expressed with increasing vehemence until his departure from the political scene.

Nonetheless, he saw government as playing a significant part within its appropriate sphere, and was prepared to defend a robust definition of that role.[24] In this respect, many of his statements would not be out of place at a gathering of Canadian Liberals in the 21st century. To those who alleged that government was responsible for extravagance, inefficiency, inappropriate business activity and high taxes, he pled "guilty on all counts."

Though government expenditures seemed high, he pointed out that governments must provide services to a diverse population, and these services seemed extravagant to those not in need of them. With respect to the charge that government should not be getting into business, Patterson sketched out a rationale for government enterprise in certain fields, such as those where natural monopolies needed regulation in the public interest, or where private business could not be relied upon to give proper weight to the interests of citizens, which might detract from the bottom line.

He conceded that higher taxes would be necessary to support the government activity he regarded as necessary, though he took care to spell out the range of services which were provided to Saskatchewan families for their annual tax bill of $36.

Patterson also addressed the issue of government efficiency. Though he concluded that, all things considered, governments were not as inefficient as sometimes alleged, he acknowledged that government was driven by different concerns than those motivating private enterprise. Part of this inefficiency he attributed to the demands of individuals and groups for government attention to their particular interests—the widespread view that government should be "Santa Claus to everybody." More importantly, he stressed the need for governments to continue to take into account human as well as financial factors, in the cause of democracy, fairness and compassion.

He often sounded a communitarian note on this issue, stating that Saskatchewan had no wealthy class which could be asked to bear the tax burden, and that "all must pay their share of costs."[25]

A characteristic expression by Patterson of his personal approach to government is found in the following paragraph:

> Although many people do not seem to appreciate it, the administration of the public business of a Province is fundamentally a business proposition and the same principles which are required for the successful operation of a private business must be applied to the administration of public business. Since the present Government took office in July 1934 it has been making every effort to place the finances of the Province on a sound basis, to maintain the credit of the Province, to equalize Revenues and Expenditures, and generally to get Saskatchewan into a financial position somewhat comparable to that which it was in prior to 1929.[26]

Another Patterson theme which should be mentioned is that of modesty in the assessment of his own status as a political leader.[27] He conceded that those looking for the "spectacular"—a word he often used in this context—or the flamboyant, would not find it in his prescription of fiscal prudence, administrative conscientiousness, and political balance. He argued that more flash and dazzle would not necessarily produce better government, and observed that "sanity and practicability [are] still useful."[28]

Under Patterson, the government continued with initiatives undertaken by Gardiner. In a public speech when he became leader,[29] for example, Patterson devoted considerable attention to the amendments which had been made in 1934 to the debt adjustment legislation, expressing the view that the agencies then in place were highly successful in achieving the goal of relieving farmers from the burden of their debt to financial institutions. Though Patterson always argued that it would be counterproductive to repudiate financial obligations altogether, he did favour bringing about an amelioration of the possible implications of default for those rendered genuinely vulnerable by the current crisis.

Clearly awed by the magnitude of the problems facing Saskatchewan citizens, Patterson nonetheless expressed satisfaction with the resourcefulness of the government in addressing the crisis. Patterson referred to figures which showed that 227,000 people—nearly a quarter of the population—had received relief payments in 1935,[30] through a system which required close collaboration with municipal governments. Despite this overwhelming task, Patterson took pride in the progress which was being made towards balancing the provincial budget and in the maintenance of government programs, such as old age pensions, which were needed more than ever.[31]

Education

One of the pressing problems facing those in rural areas was the difficulty of supporting the cost of education. Local school districts had been forced to default on the payment of salaries to teachers as early as 1931. In 1935, the government devised a scheme of loans to school boards to cover the payment of promissory notes which had been issued to teachers. That these debts were significant is clear from an example, used by Patterson, of one school district where the total amount of teachers' salaries for the years 1932–38 was just over $11 million. Though the school districts had been able to pay some of this through government grants and loans, they continued to face serious difficulties in paying the cost of education.

Patterson placed a high priority on the maintenance of the educational system, ranking it second only to the provision of basic subsistence.[32] The response of his government to the problems facing the educational system was to introduce the first provincial sales tax in support of education.

Then, as now, the tax was attached to many of the purchases made by Saskatchewan citizens, and its introduction was a source of some controversy. Responding with mounting vehemence to charges that the tax revenues were being applied to purposes other than education, and that the costs of administering collection of the tax were exorbitant, Patterson laid out a careful account of the amount which had been made available in new school grants and amounts intended to pay the salary arrears for teachers.[33]

The sales tax imposed to rescue the desperate educational system in rural Saskatchewan was one illustration of the efforts being made by the Patterson government to combat the ravages of drought and depression. At the same time, Patterson was determined that the province should enjoy a balanced budget and external credit which would be as strong as possible under the circumstances.

In this context, the relationship of the province to the federal government was a critical one. With Gardiner, Dunning and other influential voices from Saskatchewan in Ottawa, the economic plight of the province was certainly placed in all its detail before the federal Cabinet. In any case, Prime Minister King was somewhat sympathetic to arguments that the fiscal arrangements between the two levels of government should be closely examined, and established a royal commission in 1937 to carry out this appraisal.

The Rowell-Sirois Commission

The Saskatchewan government put considerable effort into describing the economic situation of the province for the Rowell-Sirois Commission. Its submission, drafted in the main by F.C. Cronkite, dean of Law at the University of Saskatchewan, contained a detailed and comprehensive picture of the Saskatchewan economy of the time. The report touched on agricultural production and marketing, highways, utilities, industry, immigration, municipal affairs, and other components of the economic picture. The report devoted considerable attention to the shortcomings of the current fiscal balance of power, from the Saskatchewan point of view.[34]

While the Rowell-Sirois Commission pondered the fundamentals of Canadian federalism, the Saskatchewan government continued to press Ottawa for assistance in meeting its fiscal crisis. As Patterson served as both provincial treasurer and Premier, he was acutely aware of the scope and urgency of the difficulties the province was facing, and was directly involved in the ongoing negotiations with his federal counterparts. Some of the correspondence from Ottawa has a brusque tone, countered by descriptions of frantic financial juggling in Regina,[35] but Patterson was largely successful in obtaining timely grants and loans from the federal treasury to assist in the relief efforts in Saskatchewan. Though occasionally he was brought face to face with the dire prospect of defaulting on provincial obligations, the federal government generally came through to prevent disaster.

However absorbed he was in the struggle with the difficulties facing Saskatchewan, Patterson found time to make an important change in his personal life, a change which he made in a typically circumspect fashion. In August 1937, he announced that he would be taking a holiday in eastern Canada. His friends and associates were stunned to hear that on August 14 he had married in New York, and, further, that he had married Florence Donnelly, a woman from Saskatchewan who had been an acquaintance for many years, but who had never been identified as having any close association with Patterson.[36]

The spring of 1938 brought the first signs of possible respite from the drought. In a telegram to Ottawa, in May, an exhilarated Patterson reported that "Recent heavy rains coupled with other moisture has [sic] made seeding prospects and conditions most favourable we have experienced in years and everything indicates this province back into production."[37]

Though cheered by this climatic turn, Patterson was aware that the province still faced difficulties, and that the financial scars would remain for some time. He had, after all, reported to Dunning a few weeks earlier a staggering outlay of over $6 million for relief between September 1937 and March 1938.[38] Even as he expressed excitement about the renewed hope for the first good crop year in nearly a decade, he stressed the need to continue relief payments to allow farmers to take advantage of the promising planting season.[39]

The 1938 Election Campaign

In the campaign for the provincial election of June 8, 1938, Patterson reassured voters that relief programs would not be cancelled in the foreseeable future, pointing out that the crop year of 1937 had been the most disastrous in Saskatchewan history. He promised help to farmers in the 1938 crop year to assist with the maintenance of farm families, costs of production, seed and feed for the following year, schools and municipal government, and rehabilitation of equipment and farm homes. He described this as "protection for [an] honest man, wishing to rehabilitate his farm and re-establish himself as a producer."[40]

In a speech later in the year, Patterson reflected on the record of his government from the time he had assumed the leadership.[41] In setting out this catalogue, it was natural that he would address a lot of attention to the relief programs which had been established in collaboration with the federal government. He was clearly proud, as well, of the range of other programs which the government had managed to maintain throughout a difficult period. These included highway projects, cancer and tuberculosis treatment programs in which the province was setting an example for the nation, and youth training schemes. He also pointed to measures taken to protect workers—legislation addressing early closing, one day's rest in seven, minimum wages, and workers' compensation. Among these, he mentioned a statute which gave workers the right to form and join trade unions.[42] He further alluded to the legislation which had been passed to promote the establishment of credit unions.

Patterson concluded his speech by saying that the government had earned a vote of confidence from the electors. Although it had been accused of doing nothing, he said, "On the contrary, [it] has handled the biggest job any Government in this or any Province ever faced and done it well." With respect to this latter assessment, he used his two favourite tests—the maintenance of essential public services and of the credit of the province.

Two other things might be noted about this particular speech. The first is a reference to recent trade treaties between Canada, the United States and Britain. These signs of the friendship of the "two English-speaking peoples," he suggested, augured well for the preservation of world peace, a poignant observation at the end of 1938. The other feature of the speech was a discussion—one of many—of the threat posed by the growing support among voters for the populist policies of the Co-operative Commonwealth Federation.

Though the Liberals under Patterson's leadership secured a comfortable majority in the election of June 1938, someone of Patterson's lengthy political experience would have been acutely aware of the changes in the political landscape.[43] Though the Conservative Party, now under the leadership of John Diefenbaker, was struggling to present a clear profile, the new factor in prairie politics was the growing prominence of home-grown political parties rooted in agrarian protest and western concern about the influence of the prairie provinces in national economic policies.

It may have been fortunate for Patterson that the CCF had not yet decided whether it would be possible to reach some accommodation with the new Social Credit party which had been formed in Alberta. In the end, the two parties ran separate slates of candidates in 1938, which may have created a misleading picture of the strength both of the new parties and of the Liberals.

Though he later acknowledged that he was among those who underestimated the progress the CCF was making as a provincial force, Patterson did focus his attention on them as his main adversary. Although his critique of the CCF had taken on a shrill "Reds-under-the-beds" tone by the time he was in opposition, his comments in 1938, though obviously heartfelt, were sober and measured. In many of his speeches, he tried to articulate the nature of his concern about socialism. At the core of his anxiety was the contrast he saw between individual enterprise and action—the basis of the political philosophy he favoured—and the comprehensive state regulation (or over-regulation) of the activity of the citizens. As we have seen, Patterson was not averse to healthy levels of taxation or to some redistribution of wealth through public programs; indeed, he saw these things as hallmarks of a Liberal government. He feared that the CCF, however, would go far beyond this and introduce an unacceptable level of regimentation into government policy. His references to dictatorship, to the planned economy and to totalitarianism were indicative of the depth of his unease in the face of a political movement which he clearly saw as representing a dramatic departure from previous political tradition.

The Clouds of War

It is difficult to imagine the sentiments of Patterson and his colleagues as they realized that, as the agricultural and financial crisis of the 1930s was beginning to recede, they were being presented with new challenges by the outbreak of war in Europe. Patterson, however, had no doubt that Canada must be a vigorous participant in the war. He suggested to his own constituents that "anyone not concerned, not wondering how [we] can help, is unworthy of citizenship in a free country."[44]

Nonetheless, he recognized that the war, for a number of reasons, would pose a new set of economic problems for the province. Although Saskatchewan farmers by 1940 had enjoyed two good crop years, there was limited access to any market for the grain, as many traditional customer countries were by now occupied by German forces. In 1941, indeed, Patterson appealed for a reduction in the acreage sown to wheat, and offered government bonuses for summer fallow, coarse grains and grass.[45] In addition, a federal government now preoccupied with the war effort was asking the province to reabsorb some of the cost of relief programs.[46]

In his characteristic fashion, Patterson urged calm in a climate of hysteria about the war, and presented a typically clear-eyed and unhysterical analysis of the economic forces at work. Though there were signs of an increase in manufacturing, he cautioned that Saskatchewan was not well placed to share in any boom in this sector.[47] He expressed concern about the possible consequences if inflation were not kept in check; though there would be some appreciation of the value of land, the benefits of this would be difficult to realize, and overall, an escalation in the prices of goods would be disastrous for Saskatchewan residents. He felt there were lessons to be learned from the experience of World War I: that much apparent prosperity was illusory, that undue expansion was unwise, that quality should be maintained, and that present actions should keep in mind the retention of customers after the war.[48] In light of economic uncertainties, he offered the reassurance that "the owner of a good farm has the least to fear."[49] He also spoke often of the need to keep in view the period after the war to ensure that "the value and importance of individual effort and ability is not lost."[50]

Though the battlefields were thousands of miles away, the war was brought home to the population in a variety of ways. They were asked to support war bonds and war loans; at a concert at Darke Hall in Regina on March 1, 1942, Patterson was asked to speak, and the letter of invitation indicated that the audience would join in singing "Land of Hope and Glory."[51] And many families in Saskatchewan had more painful reasons to be aware of the war, as their children, parents and spouses joined the military. In the spring of 1942, Patterson stated that 40,000 people from Saskatchewan had joined the armed forces.[52] The tales of heroism and death at Hong Kong, Dieppe and D-Day featured young men who, like Patterson in an earlier war, had recently been working and playing in the wheatfields and the curling rinks of Saskatchewan.

Though the fate of Saskatchewan citizens on distant battlefields and the course of the war effort continued to occupy the attention of the government, matters closer to home also required consideration. One of these was the report of the Rowell-Sirois Commission, which had begun its study of the desirability of constitutional reform in 1937. The report was released in May 1940, and recommended the adoption of the principle of equalization among provinces as the basis for federal-provincial fiscal arrangements. Though Patterson and his government disagreed with some of the conclusions of the report, they approved its general direction, and were pleased when Prime Minister King convened a meeting of provincial premiers in January 1941 to consider the report.

When the conference opened on January 15, Premiers Hepburn of Ontario, Aberhart of Alberta, and Pattillo of British Columbia voiced strong criticism of the major recommendations in the report, which they saw as likely to curb the powers of the provinces in favour of more centralized fiscal authority. Premiers from the Maritimes and Manitoba joined Patterson in expressing support in principle for the proposed changes, and Premier Godbout of Quebec stated an openness to further discussion. In his speech,[53] Patterson described the changes which had taken place in Confederation since 1867, and argued that the constitutional arrangements agreed to at that time were not necessarily adequate for the nation as it had evolved—as witnessed the ineffectiveness of those arrangements in the case of the Great Depression. He also drew attention to the specific circumstances of Saskatchewan—its reliance on one industry, the dependence of that industry in turn on the vicissitudes of climate, the difficulties of transportation, and the problems of providing infrastructure and services to a small population spread over a large geographic area. "Despite that," he continued,

> the province of Saskatchewan has contributed a tremendous amount of wealth in the form of grain and agricultural products, a very large percentage of which goes to improve the financial condition of people in other parts of Canada.
>
> But we do face that particular problem [exclusive dependence on agriculture]; we do face that particular difficulty, and we do feel that in this national economy some revisions should be agreed to that would provide for greater flexibility and provide for what the commission had in mind, provide for conditions that would make it possible for the people of Canada generally, irrespective of what part of the Dominion they live in, irrespective of what particular occupations they may be engaged in, to enjoy a somewhat comparable measure of service and attention from the government under which they happen to live.

The Premiers opposing the conclusions in the report were also concerned about attempting to deal with these significant constitutional questions while the war was going on, and proposed that, at least, discussion should be deferred into the post-war period.

On the second day of the conference, during closed-door discussions, the Ontario delegation announced its intention to withdraw from the conference, and Alberta and British Columbia indicated that they would follow. Though Patterson was reluctant to lay blame, and though he had not expected thoroughgoing change of the kind envisioned in the Rowell-Sirois report to be effected at one federal-provincial meeting, he was clearly disappointed at the failure of the conference. In a radio address several weeks later, he said,

> If the Fathers of Confederation, representing independent and sovereign states were prepared to relinquish a part of their power and authority to make Confederation possible, [it] should be equally possible for the representatives of the Provinces which now constitute that Confederation, to agree to a re-arrangement of the constitution in light of present-day conditions.[54]

As the war went on, the moderate policy to which the government had always adhered came under increasing criticism. In a legislative debate on a proposed moratorium on debt, Patterson reiterated his views on the importance of trust and credit. He felt constrained to point out that not all creditors were wealthy or unscrupulous; in Saskatchewan, many of them were elderly farmers who had leased or sold their land. In any case, he clearly thought it somewhat unseemly to be worrying about financial risks when the British and Canadian sailors "protecting our products" were exposed to bombs and shells.[55]

In another, and uncharacteristically brusque speech,[56] Patterson urged his audience to include their blessings as well as their complaints in the balance sheet of assets and liabilities. "Is there somebody you want to trade places with because you cannot immediately sell your wheat?" he asked, and reminded them that 750,000 Canadians were "putting up with worse so that you may be saved from Totalitarianism."

In February 1942, the government put forward a resolution expressing support for the allied powers. Patterson said that this resolution was carefully formulated to be apolitical, and expressed disappointment that support for it was less than unanimous.[57]

Patterson was highly critical of the CCF, which he saw as acting opportunistically in the context of the war. He argued that their claims should be carefully analysed, that it was time to "call a halt to their belittling, disparaging of the country which affords them their living and their Liberty."[58]

The Extension of the Government's Term

The preoccupation with the war effort led the Patterson government to conclude that it would be an unnecessary distraction to hold an election in 1943, as required. The government thus proposed a Legislative Assembly Extension Act which would delay the election for one year. Patterson himself seems to have been somewhat ambivalent about this.[59] He marshalled the arguments in favour of the bill—that the expense would detract from the contribution to the war, and that many voters would not be able to participate fully in an election—and denied that he was fearful of facing the electorate or the opposition. On the other hand, he conceded that the extension of the life of the Legislature was inconsistent with British constitutional practice, which was why a free vote was contemplated. In defence of the bill, he said that the MLAs were representatives, not delegates, and that they were "not elected to put forward the wishes of the electorate, but to apply judgment to questions as they arise."[60]

Though the extension of the term of the Legislature arose from a desire to concentrate on the furtherance of the war, the government also began to plan for the post-war period. In October 1943, the Saskatchewan Reconstruction Council was established, with F.C. Cronkite, the principal author of the provincial submission to the Rowell-Sirois Commission, as its head.[61] A similar body was created by the federal government, and Patterson made submissions on behalf of the province to that committee.

The Saskatchewan brief was submitted in April 1944, and it must, therefore, be seen in the context of the election which had to come in the summer. Indeed, much of the brief was devoted to sketching out the plans of the Liberal government for the post-war period, stressing particularly the need for further development in health care and social services.[62]

Early in 1944, Patterson sounded an optimistic note about Liberal chances—"the tide has turned"—but urged a vigorous campaign.[63] He also asked his audiences to pay careful attention to the record of his government. He said that, though critics of the government might suggest "Saskatchewan is doing nothing," the government was spending fully one-third of its budget on health care and social programs, in addition to other spending on government services like roads and police services.[64]

In other speeches, he conceded that his party had been more involved in the war than in political activity since 1939, and, snidely, that the Liberals could not compare with their opponents in making promises.[65] He pointed to the achievements of the government, however, and carefully catalogued the measures and programs which had been introduced during his premiership. The government record of sound financial management was a source of particular pride; Patterson even quoted the leader of the opposition to this effect: "The Premier deserves credit as an orthodox financier. I do not suppose anyone could have done better under the system and circumstances of the time."[66]

He spoke of the government's general plan for health services, which would build on existing plans offering care for cancer, tuberculosis and polio. He commented on the work of the Saskatchewan Reconstruction Council on planning for post-war employment and industrial development, and returned to the theme he had pursued at the time of the Rowell-Sirois *Report* of a need for readjustment of federal-provincial fiscal power.[67]

The 1944 Provincial Election

Despite his stated determination to increase industrial diversity in the province, Patterson acknowledged that agriculture would continue to play a pre-eminent role in the Saskatchewan economy. The Liberal election manifesto outlined an agricultural program with four main features:

> (1) markets at profitable prices, (2) protection against the hazards of nature, (3) maximum utilization and conservation of soil and moisture and (4) independent ownership and operation of farms.[68]

In connection with the last of these points, Patterson warned of the threat posed to private land ownership by a "socialistic" government of the kind which would be put in place by the CCF.[69]

Such a statement was representative of a thread in the Patterson campaign which suggests that the Liberals were not facing the election with complete optimism. Though Patterson was proud of the record of his government, and although he had avoided the divisions within the party which had caused trouble a decade earlier,[70] the vigour and the strong organization of the CCF would clearly be difficult to overcome, whatever heartening statements were made in public.

It has been suggested[71] that Patterson's own fiscal conservatism played a part in his government's decline. Patterson may have been pleased with the sober and responsible approach which the government had taken to agricultural debt and provincial credit, but it is perhaps not surprising that farmers were attracted to a party which promised substantive relief from this burden through a somewhat less orthodox approach to finance. Whatever the explanation, the June 15, 1944, election produced a landslide victory for the CCF. Patterson himself was re-elected by the slimmest of margins (six votes).[72]

In speeches made after the election, Patterson continued to defend the approach his government had taken, and to try to explain the financial circumstances under which they had laboured. He conceded that the voters had found an alternative policy more appealing, but warned of the dangers of being too cavalier about debt:

> Contracts or agreements voluntarily made by the parties thereto cannot be of much value if one of the parties can repudiate it when it suits his convenience. The acceptance of this principle has been advocated by those who do not appreciate the extent to which our daily operations are facilitated by the giving and acceptance of a man's "promise," whether that promise is to do a certain thing or pay a certain amount.[73]

Speaking about the resounding defeat which his government had experienced, Patterson expressed some modest satisfaction at leaving the province in a sound financial position:

> As already pointed out, this new Government takes office under happy and fortunate circumstances and without the financial and economic problems which we had to meet ten years ago. They assume office with all immediate financial needs provided for, the credit and reputation of the Province at the highest point in its history and with more than eight million in cash to conduct socialistic experimentation and policy.[74]

This gracious statement following the victory of the CCF fails, however, to convey the disappointment which Patterson felt at losing the election. He was prepared to shoulder some of the blame for the decay of the Liberal political machine, but he was also alarmed by the advent of a new kind of government. Speaking to an audience of young Liberals, he attributed the defeat to "an organization of a nature and kind never before seen in Saskatchewan," an organization which he described as "complete, intensive, unscrupulous," in whose eyes there was "no discontent too trivial or unwarranted to be made capital of, no promise too fantastic to be promised, no criticism too unfounded to be utilized."[75]

He had often expressed concern about what he saw as the antidemocratic and "totalitarian" tendencies of socialism, but this concern had been expressed in relatively moderate terms. Once the CCF was in power, however, his rhetoric became more heated. When the new government decided that the Throne Speech should be broadcast, Patterson argued that this decision should properly have been made by the Legislature:

> This is another and a further step in the direction of centralization and control of all power and authority in the Government, a road to serfdom along which we have travelled a considerable distance in the last eighteen months.[76]

He was horrified at the suggestion that the government was using the possibility of repudiation of debt as a bargaining tactic with the federal government.[77] He also drew attention to what he described as the "invasion" of Saskatchewan by a shadowy group of experts and advisors from outside the province, who had wrested control of government from the elected representatives of the people.[78] He described this group as "the Star Chamber that is running Saskatchewan affairs."

Patterson made a sustained critique of the legislation put forward by the Douglas government, particularly those measures which he saw as infringements of property rights or restrictions on individual choice. In the Throne Speech debate of 1947, he alleged that the government was beginning, through the Department of Education, to compile dossiers on every person in the province, a charge which the government greeted with incredulity.

He was especially scathing about the Bill of Rights passed in 1947. Patterson had a strong sense of the British constitutional tradition, and it was his view that this tradition was a sufficient guarantor of the civil liberties of citizens; he characterized as absurd the idea that a government which displayed "absolute indifference to individual rights" should claim to value the protection of those rights.[79]

Out of Politics

On July 24, 1946, Patterson attended the eleventh annual picnic of his constituents at Kenosee, and announced that he would be stepping down as party leader, stating "[I] do not feel equal physically to two years of intensive work for [the] next election. [I] should step aside for some younger man."[80] Though advancing age was probably part of the explanation, Patterson was also concerned at signs of slippage in Liberal support in recent by-elections,[81] and his leadership may have been under increasingly intensive scrutiny as a result.

Patterson was reelected by the faithful electors of Cannington in the election of 1948, with a margin over the CCF candidate of more than 1,200 votes.[82] Though there was a new leader of the opposition, Walter Tucker, Patterson continued to enjoy a high profile as chief Finance critic; the Regina *Leader-Post* particularly noted his response to the budget in the 1949 session of the Legislature, in which he reiterated warnings of the dangerous implications of mounting government expenditures.[83] He resigned from the Legislature that same year when he was appointed to the federal Board of Transport Commissioners.

SAB RB 6687(4)

Lieutenant-Governor William J. Patterson reading the Speech from the Throne, February 1954.

In 1951, it was announced that Patterson was "forsaking the unmatched scenic beauties of Ottawa" to become lieutenant-governor of Saskatchewan.[84] In approving the appointment of this first Saskatchewan-born lieutenant-governor, the *Leader-Post* referred to the "herculean" efforts Patterson had made during the 1930s:

> A weaker man would have thrown up his hands in utter despair in the struggle against such overwhelming odds. But Mr. Patterson quietly carried on and he brought Saskatchewan safely through the ordeal only to have political defeat as his reward.[85]

His appointment was not uncontroversial among Saskatchewan's Liberals, as it was an instance of a decline in the previous practice of consultation of the provincial party by the federal government when making appointments of this kind.[86] His home town of Grenfell, however, saluted him enthusiastically at the celebrations of the fortieth anniversary of its incorporation. In the course of a program which included presentations on the history of Grenfell, speeches by former mayors, and entertainment by local musicians young and old, Patterson was introduced as "His honor the Lieutenant-Governor, our Billy Patterson," and spoke of the value of "a fine Christian community."[87]

Patterson settled into the ceremonial role, and lent his name to public causes, notably the Boy Scouts, with which he had had a long association. He also spoke on behalf of a "thrift campaign" sponsored by the National Council of Women, an occasion which allowed him to apply his views on sensible financial management to the Cold War context. In urging the people of Saskatchewan to adopt frugal habits, he said one of the purposes of the campaign was to ensure "that every dollar and every resource and material can become available to arm our nation to face the threat which the dictatorial states present."[88]

Retirement

When his term of office ended in 1958, Premier Douglas paid tribute to the "high dignity and devotion" which had marked Patterson's 34 years in public life. This praise was echoed in a *Leader-Post* editorial under the heading "Beloved Billy Patterson." The writer expressed the hope that he might be persuaded to return to electoral politics,[89] an invitation which Patterson, at the age of 71, did not take up.

© M. West, Regina, West's Studio Collection.
SAB RB 4533

William J. Patterson, wearing his lieutenant-governor's uniform, 1955.

Whatever the gratifications provided by a career in public office, and however much he had followed his own gospel of careful financial management, the end of Patterson's term as lieutenant-governor left him facing a straitened financial future, given that he was not entitled to any pension for his service as an MLA. In March 1958, Premier Douglas introduced a special bill which would provide a pension to his old political rival at the maximum level allowed under recent pension legislation, the cost to be borne by the treasury rather than by the superannuation fund. The bill was passed without debate or amendment.[90]

Once he had retired as lieutenant-governor, Patterson did not take any significant part in political or public affairs. He contributed a memorial piece to the newspaper on the death of Charles Dunning, lamenting that he had not been able to make his annual visit to the province.[91] However, in 1962, Patterson felt moved to break a "fifteen year silence" on political topics by cautioning the audience at a public meeting that the "financial ineptitude" of the federal Conservative government suggested that they should not be supported in the coming election.[92] His quiet retirement ended with his death on June 10, 1976, at the age of 90.

Conclusion

The Great Depression and the agricultural crisis of the 1930s altered the culture and economy of Saskatchewan in lasting ways, and this period and the ensuing wartime era continue to be touchstones for the people of this province. Yet the Premier whose government was responsible for devising a provincial response to these events is hardly remembered, and whatever legacy may be fairly attributed to him is not connected in the public mind with his name.

The election of 1944 is seen, accurately enough, as a watershed, and it is seen as having marked a turning point in the politics of Saskatchewan, and in the role played by government in the post-war economy of the province. The discontinuity from the past represented by the election of the Douglas government should not be overstated, however. In many ways, the legislative program of the Patterson government—building, in turn, on the inheritance of the Gardiner era—laid the foundation for what was to come.

When Patterson succeeded Gardiner in 1935, he faced economic conditions which were disastrous and getting worse. Though the economic power built up by the province in the 1920s, and the close relationship between the provincial and federal Liberal governments, gave Patterson a sympathetic ear in Ottawa, and access to extensive grants and loans to counter the agricultural crisis, the formal fiscal arrangements of the Canadian federation at the time contemplated that each province would cope with such adversity independently, dealing with good times or bad on the basis of its own economic strength. The recommendations of the Rowell-Sirois Commission that new constitutional arrangements based on reallocation of resources of all provinces through the federal government were, from Patterson's point of view, disappointingly slow to come into effect. There can be little doubt, however, that the acute nature of the Saskatchewan situation in the 1930s, and the force with which the implications of this situation were articulated to the commission, had a major influence on this significant reshaping of Canadian federalism.

Patterson's political philosophy was one in which a robust role for government was combined with a respect for individual rights. One of his proudest boasts was that the government of Saskatchewan had been able to maintain social programs during the darkest hours of the Depression, and that his objective of sustaining a respectable credit rating had not proved inconsistent with the provision of social services, health care and education. Notwithstanding his railing against collectivization and economic planning, he often pointed with pleasure to the catalogue of progressive legislative measures taken by his government.

If the legislation passed during the Patterson government's two terms in office did not represent a spectacular breakthrough to the post-war Canadian welfare state, it did lay the groundwork in many areas for the legislative regime with which citizens of Saskatchewan became familiar. The government proposed legislation to extend publicly funded health care, to promote the establishment of credit unions, to support education through a sales tax, to improve labour standards, to legitimize collective bargaining activity by workers, to develop northern Saskatchewan, and to continue the work of providing telephone and other services to a widely dispersed rural population.

Patterson himself characterized his work as Premier as steady, undramatic, even plodding, creating a record in which his banker's soul could take satisfaction. The steps he took were always modest ones, and his own earnest and perhaps colourless approach attracted limited attention at the time and even less after his withdrawal from politics. His government did, all the same, have a role in establishing a framework which marked the government of the province for some decades to come.

Notes

1. Regina *Leader-Post*, "Liberal Council Selects Hon. W.J. Patterson as Leader and Premier," November 1, 1935, p. 15.
2. Saskatchewan Archives Board, Patterson fonds, R-79, File 11, notes for a speech to Legislative Assembly on the Stewart Bill, March 22, 1943. Throughout these notes the abbreviation SAB denotes the Saskatchewan Archives Board, and the code R-79 denotes the collection of papers of William J. Patterson.
3. Ibid., File 14, notes for a speech in relation to a by-election, November 21, 1938.
4. Ibid.
5. A recital which Patterson made on a number of occasions. See ibid.
6. Regina *Leader-Post*, November 1, 1935, p. 15.
7. At the time of his induction as Premier, this house was in use as a shed in a lumber yard. Ibid.
8. SAB, Patterson fonds, R-79, File No. 4. The diaries also indicate an occasional struggle to stop smoking.
9. Ibid.
10. Regina *Leader-Post*, November 1, 1935, p. 18.
11. Ibid.
12. His constituency was Pipestone from 1921 to 1934, and was renamed Cannington, the constituency he served until 1949. See *Saskatchewan Executive and Legislative Directory, 1905–1970* (Regina: Saskatchewan Archives Board, 1971), 84.
13. See Garrett Wilson and Kevin Wilson, *Diefenbaker for the Defence* (Toronto: James Lorimer & Co., 1988), 127–29. John Diefenbaker was junior counsel for the Conservative Party at the hearings of what was often called the "Bryant Charges Commission" after the MLA who had levelled the accusations.
14. Royal Commission to Inquire into Statements made in Certain Statutory Declarations and Other Matters, Sittings at Regina, Monday, September 29, 1930, p. 10.
15. Public Service Inquiry Commission, *Report*, Regina, 1930.
16. Ibid.
17. David Smith, *Prairie Liberalism: The Liberal Party of Saskatchewan, 1905–71* (Toronto: University of Toronto Press, 1975), 182.
18. The Liberal Council was established in 1931 to provide a more systematic means of party governance than the ad hoc conventions which had previously been called when a question of leadership arose. Indeed, the creation of the council was an aspect of constitutional changes which took place in the wake of the 1931 convention which had given enthusiastic endorsement to Gardiner's leadership.

Membership of the council consisted of federal and provincial Liberal candidates, delegates of constituency organizations, and representatives of women's and youth groups, and the body was expected to meet annually. Like the conventions it replaced, the council had a role in considering leadership candidates put forward by the Liberal caucus in the Saskatchewan Legislature. The first test of this role, when the leadership question arose in 1935, also mirrored the role played by the conventions in that only one name was put forward, that of Patterson. See Smith, *Prairie Liberalism*, at 210 and 228.

19. Smith, *Prairie Liberalism*, 228. A veteran Liberal politician, W.F.A. Turgeon, was quoted as responding to this from his armchair in the Assiniboia Club: "You didn't choose Davis because you thought he would go off half-cocked. Now you've chosen Patterson, and you'll find he won't go off at all." This anecdote was relayed to me by Garrett Wilson, a Regina lawyer, and longtime student of Saskatchewan politics.
20. See L.A. Brown, "Unemployment Relief Camps in Saskatchewan 1933–36," *Saskatchewan History* 23: 81.
21. SAB, Patterson fonds, R-79, File 12, notes for a speech to Liberal Council, October 31, 1935. Most of Patterson's papers were never deposited in any public archive. The papers available in the SAB consist largely of notes for speeches, and these form much of the basis for the statements in this chapter.
22. Ibid.
23. Ibid., Notes for a speech during by-election, 1935.
24. Ibid., Notes for speech to Saskatoon Board of Trade, January 29, 1936.
25. See, for example, ibid., File 13, notes for a speech, "Death of J.R. Near," Moose Jaw, February 10, 1937.
26. Ibid., File 13, typed radio speech, February 2, 1937.
27. Ibid.
28. Ibid. It is hard to know, of course, the extent to which these protestations emerged from anxiety at being compared to Gardiner.
29. Ibid., File 12, undated handwritten notes. This appears to be Patterson's first public speech on becoming leader.
30. Ibid., notes for by-election speech, 1935. Though the recipients of relief were mainly rural residents, Patterson also used figures showing 47,053 urban individuals and families receiving relief in 1935–36; ibid., notes for speech in Gravelbourg by-election, Assiniboia, June 24, 1936.
31. Ibid., File 13, notes for speech, Wynyard, October 27, 1937.
32. Ibid., File 13, notes for speech on education tax (n.d.).
33. Ibid., File 14, typed speech for CJRM radio, April 28, 1938. Patterson stated that the tax had brought in $1,133,735.30 from August 1, 1937, to April 22, 1938. In the same period school grants amounting to $2,023,072.36 had been allocated, along with $123,833.36 towards teacher salary arrears.
34. The Saskatchewan submission clearly had some impact on the recommendations made in the Rowell-Sirois *Report* of 1940, though the ultimate outcome of the federal-provincial conference called in 1941 to address these recommendations did not reflect the new constitutional arrangements the Saskatchewan government had pressed for. See John H. Archer, *Saskatchewan: A History* (Saskatoon: Western Producer Prairie Books, 1980), 253.
35. SAB, Patterson fonds, R-79, File 3, correspondence between Patterson and Hon. Charles A. Dunning from September 1937 to May 1938.
36. Regina *Leader-Post*, "Premier Returns with Bride in Three Weeks," August 16, 1937, p. 1.
37. SAB. Patterson fonds, R-79, File 3, telegram from Patterson to Dunning, May 5, 1938.

38. Ibid., Patterson to Dunning, March 26, 1938.
39. Ibid., File 3, notes for speech on education tax (n.d.).
40. Ibid., File 14, notes for speech on CKCK radio, June 4, 1938.
41. Ibid., Notes for speech in by-election, November 21, 1938.
42. This statute was the forerunner of the better-known 1944 Trade Union Act which, in addition to providing workers with access to collective bargaining, imposed an obligation to bargain on employers.
43. For a discussion of this election, see Archer, *Saskatchewan*, 241.
44. SAB, Patterson fonds, R-79, File 15, notes for a speech at annual picnic at Kenosee, June, 1940.
45. Ibid., File 16, notes for a CKCK radio broadcast, April 14, 1941.
46. Ibid., File 15, notes for a speech at annual picnic at Kenosee, June, 1940.
47. Ibid., notes for a speech at Swift Current, January 12, 1940.
48. Ibid., notes for a speech at RM Convention, Saskatoon, March 7, 1940
49. Ibid., File 17, notes for a speech at North Battleford, August 11, 1943.
50. Ibid.
51. Ibid., The letter from J. Gillespie, Secretary, Regina Orchestral Society, February 24, 1942.
52. Ibid., Notes for a CKCK broadcast on the War Loan, March 6, 1942.
53. Reproduced in the *Leader-Post*, January 15, 1941, p. 14 under the headline "Able Battle by Patterson, Bracken for Sirois Report," the *Leader-Post* Ottawa correspondent stated that Patterson and Bracken had given the report its "most able and informed support."
54. SAB, Patterson fonds, R-79, File 16, typed speech for CKCK Radio broadcast, February 14, 1941.
55. Ibid., File 11, notes for legislative speech, n.d.
56. Ibid., File 18, notes for speech, Gravelbourg, November 4, 1943.
57. Ibid., File 11, notes for a speech on War Resolution, February, 1942.
58. Ibid., File 18, notes for speech to annual picnic at Kenosee, July 7, 1943.
59. Ibid., File 11, notes for a speech on the "Stewart bill," March 22, 1943.
60. Ibid.
61. Archer, *Saskatchewan*, 255.
62. Ibid., 255–57.
63. SAB, Patterson fonds, R-79, File 19, notes for a speech to Liberal Council, January 18, 1944.
64. Ibid., Notes for a speech, Saskatoon West Side, January 19, 1944.
65. Ibid., Notes for speech at Weyburn, April 6, 1944.
66. Ibid.
67. Ibid., Speech on Provincial Hook-Up, May 24, 1944.
68. Ibid.
69. Regina *Leader-Post*, "Premier warns land owners," May 18, 1944, p. 1.
70. Smith, *Prairie Liberalism*, 244.
71. Ibid.
72. *Saskatchewan Executive and Legislative Directory, 1905–1970*, 96.
73. SAB, Patterson fonds, R-79, File 19, typed speech, Radio Provincial Hook-up, August 9, 1944.
74. Ibid., Notes for speech at Young Liberal Convention, Regina, July 24, 1944.
75. Ibid.
76. Ibid., File 20, "The Speech from the Throne" speech on CKCK, February 19, 1945. In a number of his speeches during this period, Patterson referred to the work of Professor Friedrich Hayek, notably his book *The Road to Serfdom*.

77. Ibid., typed speech, provincial hookup, March 14, 1945.
78. Ibid., File 21, Typed speech, radio broadcast, CKCK, February 17, 1947.
79. Regina *Leader-Post*, "Rights bill by C.C.F. absurd says Patterson," February 5, 1947, p. 1.
80. SAB, Patterson fonds, R-79, File 21, notes for speech at Kenosee, July 24, 1946.
81. Smith, *Prairie Liberalism*, 253.
82. *Saskatchewan Executive and Legislative Directory, 1905–1970*, 97.
83. Regina *Leader-Post*, "Patterson takes oath in Regina," June 26, 1951, pp. 1 and 12.
84. Ibid., "Billy Patterson coming home," June 27, 1951, p. 15.
85. Ibid.
86. Smith, *Prairie Liberalism*, 262n; Archer, *Saskatchewan*, 283.
87. Regina *Leader-Post*, "Grenfell celebrates," November 3, 1951, p. 2.
88. Ibid., "Thrift campaign opens," November 27, 1951, p. 7.
89. Ibid., "Beloved Billy Patterson," January 30, 1958, p. 28. A letter to the editor of the paper from a friend in Vancouver, L.F. Curran, on February 21, 1958, supported this idea.
90. Ibid., "Patterson to receive pension," March 17, 1958, p. 3; "Patterson pension bill approved," March 28, 1958, p. 17. A further bill was introduced by the Thatcher government in 1967 to augment Patterson's pension, and was passed with the support of the opposition: Regina *Leader-Post*, "Bill would boost Patterson pension," March 5, 1967, p. 18.
91. Ibid., "A friend lost," October 15, 1958, p. 23.
92. Ibid., "Patterson ends 15-year silence," June 15, 1962, p. 2.; Saskatoon *Star Phoenix*, "After 15 Years—Patterson Enters Foray," June 15, 1962, p. 10.

T.C. Douglas

Thomas H. McLeod & Ian McLeod

Douglas-Thatcher debate, Mossbank, May 20, 1957
(SAB R-WS 15159 (1)).

Douglas, formal portrait
(SAB R-WS 3228.1).

Buying Red Cross Seals
(SAB RA 11,059 (2)).

Radio broadcast from the Legislative Building
(SAB 56-455-01).

T.C. Douglas, 1944–1961

Early Life

At the dawn of the 20th century, Britain reigned over the greatest empire the world had ever seen, and Scotland was one of its industrial engines. Scottish industry, centred on Glasgow and the Clyde River, produced almost half of Britain's steel, and Scottish factories produced ships, locomotives, pottery and furniture.[1]

The Douglas family lived in the city of Falkirk, northeast of Glasgow. Tom Douglas was an iron moulder at the Carron Iron Works, Scotland's oldest industrial foundry. On October 20, 1904, Tom's wife Annie gave birth to their first child, Thomas Clement. The baby was named for grandfather Tom Douglas, also an ironworker, and grandfather Andrew Clement, who ran a team of horses and a wagon in Glasgow.

Industrial Scotland was a hotbed of Labour politics. The Scottish Independent Labour Party had issued its first manifesto in 1888, railing against a state where "starvation diseases are rife among large classes, and in which one-third to one-half of the families in the country are huddled together six to a room."[2] Many older workers, like grandfather Tom, had remained with the Liberal Party; the future Premier's father had converted to Labour, and was a reader of literature on the class system, single-tax theory and politics.

Tommy Douglas was raised in an environment of political debate, and also of Scottish pride. Scotland, like Canada, depended on and profited from a powerful southern neighbour's prosperity, but the future Canadian nationalist recognized as he grew up that too strong a dependence might destroy his homeland. "It was always part of your schooling that the English are really bastards, and if they'd had their way you'd be under their thumb completely," he said in 1985. "Any accommodation with the English was for purely self-interested reasons."[3]

Grandfather Tom weaned the child on Scotland's national poet, Robert Burns. Tommy Douglas memorized much of the poet's work, and would carry a dog-eared copy of Burns in his luggage for most of his adult life, headlining at Burns Night and St. Andrew's Day dinners across Canada. As an old man, Douglas claimed that the poet's vision of perfect equality had influenced Canada through Scottish immigrants such as his father, who found themselves living and working among people from many backgrounds when they came to Canada. "My father said, this is marvelous, this is what the world should be like. Sure I can't understand the family next door, but you kids will grow up together, you'll build the same kind of world."[4]

Winnipeg and the Social Gospel

By 1910, industrial Scotland was slipping into a long decline, and Tom Douglas decided to bring his skills and his family to Canada. He came to Winnipeg with his younger brother Willie in the fall of 1910 and found a job at the Vulcan Iron Works. Annie, Tommy and his younger sister Nan followed in 1911. A second sister, Isobel, was born in the same year.

Winnipeg was the largest city in the Canadian West and the industrial and financial centre for the three prairie provinces. It was also a centre for the social gospel movement, which Douglas later defined as "the application of the gospel to social conditions."[5] This diffuse trend in the mainstream Protestant churches had put clergy, social workers and church activists on the political front lines in several countries. The Methodist and Presbyterian ministers of Winnipeg put forward regular submissions to the local and provincial governments in support of single mothers' allowances, workers' compensation, public health programs and other reforms.

Social gospel stalwarts such as Dr. Salem Bland of Wesley College helped to persuade labour and farm organizations to run their own political candidates; labour had representation on the Winnipeg City Council by 1914, and the first independent farmer candidate was elected to the Legislature in 1917. Another prominent social gospel activist and speaker was James S. Woodsworth, whose All People's Mission offered relief supplies, education and other programs for North End immigrants. As a boy, Tommy Douglas played in the gym at the Mission, and read books in the library; later in his life he adopted Woodsworth as a political mentor and role model.

The social gospel movement's direct political influence peaked and then faded before Douglas entered college, but the movement left a lifelong mark on him and many others of his generation. The movement had a euphoric quality, a tendency to see both scientific advances and political reform as evidence of God's plan to raise up humanity. There was a connection in spirit and in personnel, Douglas reflected later, between the social gospel movement and the farmer-labour political parties that emerged in the 1930s. Both underestimated the cost of progress to people and the environment; but they were tolerant and open to all, earnest in their efforts at analysis, and vitally engaged in the world.[6]

At the outbreak of World War I in 1914, Tom Douglas enlisted on the British side despite his reservations about the Empire. He joined a Scottish field ambulance unit, and the family returned to Glasgow where they shared cramped quarters with Annie's parents. Tommy grew up quickly, caring for his two sisters, learning to handle his grandfather's team of horses, and fighting his way into a local street gang to find protection from other gangs. In 1918, just before his fourteenth birthday, he left school to work in a distillery and support his family. A few months later the war ended and, with Tom still on the continent, mother and children sailed for Canada. On Tom's return to Winnipeg in 1919, he resumed his work at the foundry. He had always been a quiet man, but his experience in the trenches transformed him into a brooding presence. For the rest of his life he suffered bouts of despair, walking alone at night for miles.

Annie remained a cheerful, busy woman, who supported her son's efforts in sports and public speaking. She had attended several churches in Winnipeg and the family had attended her parents' Baptist chapel in Glasgow; after the family's return from Scotland in 1918, she settled on the Beulah Baptist congregation near their new home in the Elmwood neighbourhood. The life of the Douglas family revolved around the church. Tommy had Scouts on Tuesdays, prayer meetings on Wednesdays, the young people's meeting on Fridays, and he often went on an outing for Scouts or young people on Saturdays. On Sundays, the family attended morning and evening services, and the youngsters also went to Sunday school.[7]

Mark Talney, Tommy Douglas's scoutmaster and later his brother-in-law, remembered Beulah as "a very conservative church … within the walls of that church you readily forgot that there was a world outside."[8] However, events conspired to push Douglas past this conservatism to the political and theological left, starting with the largest general strike in Canadian history. Left-wing preachers, educators, and labour and farm leaders had worked for years to undermine the established political parties and build radical coalitions. The end of the war brought a wave of young men back to Canadian cities, strong, angry, and disciplined. The 1918 conference of the Methodist Church, Canada's largest Protestant denomination, was captured by the social gospel left and called for "A Complete Social Reconstruction" through "co-operation and public ownership."[9] By mid-May 1919, 35,000 people in a Winnipeg population of 200,000 were on strike, demanding higher wages and the right to organize.

Douglas worked as a messenger in the grain exchange, a citadel of capitalism, but on his way home he would spend time among the immense crowds that filled the public parks, listening to the strike leaders speak. On Saturday, June 23, mounted police attacked the crowd in Market Square. Douglas and his friend Mark Talney were present, and climbed to a rooftop for safety; when the police fired, the bullets whistled over their heads.[10] One citizen died, and the rest scattered. That night police arrested J.S. Woodsworth, the editor of the strike newspaper, and charged him with sedition, along with several others. A few days later the strike collapsed.

Douglas became a Labour party supporter and began to drop leaflets in political campaigns. He got a job in the printing trade, a meeting place for self-educated social critics, and he remained a printer's union member for life. He read left-wing books, including *The Farmers in Politics* by social gospel radical William Irvine of Calgary, a long-time associate of Woodsworth. Irvine argued that farmers, through their co-operative means of production, would lead Canada away from capitalism to a better life: "Co-operation is the gospel of the United Farmers, and their leaders are the apostles of it. Natural law is on their side."[11]

The wave of post-war reform sentiment had perhaps its greatest expression in the federal election of 1921. The voters elected 65 Progressive candidates from provincial farmers' movements, and two Labour candidates, Woodsworth from north Winnipeg and Irvine from Calgary, leaving the Tories in third place. The Progressive caucus was in fact a mishmash of left-wing radicals, centrists and conservatives, but for the moment it seemed that ordinary Canadians were moving in a bold new direction. Douglas and Talney decided to dedicate their lives to social reform through the Christian ministry, and began to save money for college. Douglas preached his first service as a lay minister in the fall of 1922.

Through his late teens, Douglas continued to live at home. He was short and slight, but he took up boxing at the One Big Union gym, and won enough fights to rise to the top of the Manitoba flyweight rankings in 1922 and 1923. He also acted on stage as a member of the youth wing of the Masonic Lodge. However, he later said he "never really liked the idea of being an echo of someone else's lines. I wanted to make up my own lines in life."[12]

Brandon College

In a 1964 sermon entitled "The Social Gospel and Politics," Douglas affirmed his belief that the essence of the Christian ethic is the oneness of all humanity: "In Christ there is no East or West."[13] Douglas had little or no interest in doctrinal disputes or sectarian differences, and he recognized the element of the divine in all the great religions. He had a strong sympathy for people of the Jewish faith, and often attended services and spoke at synagogues in his later years.

This religious ultra-liberalism was partly a product of his six years at Brandon College, a Baptist-run school with 200 students in a small prairie city three hours west of Winnipeg by train. The college was a stronghold of the embattled liberal wing of the Canadian Baptist church, a denomination that even in the 1920s was coming under increasing domination by theological conservatives and fundamentalists. The college had been founded around an existing Baptist institute in 1900, at the same time as the creation of the Baptist Union of Western Canada. Douglas enrolled at Brandon in the fall of 1924, and began work on his high school credits. He graduated with a degree in arts in the spring of 1930. He also collected his master's degree at Brandon in 1933, although he earned it from McMaster University, mostly by correspondence.

Brandon had ties with McMaster, a liberal Baptist school in Hamilton, Ontario, and with the University of Chicago, a great centre of learning and a liberal Baptist mecca. Scholars at all of these schools had worked for a generation to square the biblical account of Creation with the growing sciences of geology and biology. Archeologists and linguists, and then theologians, questioned the credibility of the biblical tales of Methuselah or Jonah and the Whale. Fundamentalist Baptists felt the Bible should stand above all forms of investigation and rejected this new scholarship.

In 1922 a group of fundamentalist Baptist ministers from British Columbia brought charges of heresy against Brandon's professor of New Testament studies, Harris MacNeill, who had a doctorate in divinity from Chicago. MacNeill was put before an inquisition to test his beliefs. The panel exonerated him, upholding the believer's right to freedom from church authority, and freedom to pursue the truth.[14] However, MacNeill and other liberals at Brandon remained a target in the Baptist church until 1938, when the Baptist Union, unable to carry the financial burden any longer, cut its ties to the college. MacNeill was also one of Douglas's favorite teachers, "a giant among pygmies... I would say that any intellectual curiosity I have came from MacNeill... He recognized that you have to have answers to the questions about what we are here for, and what we are supposed to be doing."[15]

Douglas proved to be a gifted student and a natural leader. He was active in debating, drama, and student government, serving both as vice-president and as president of the student body. A college friend remembered, "He had a smile and a way of dealing with people, a rare gift of language... He would get to the centre of a debate, of a musical program or a play or a lecture as if he had sort of brought it into being himself."[16]

He also devoted increasing time to working as a student supply minister, travelling on Sundays to small rural churches in the Brandon district. In February 1927 he agreed to take charge of the Knox Presbyterian church in Carberry, a conservative Anglo-Protestant village east of Brandon. Here he was responsible, while maintaining his studies at Brandon full-time, for preparing Sunday morning and evening services in Carberry, and overseeing the work of the Sunday school and the non-denominational Scout and Cub groups. Under his direction, a young people's group began to mount plays and variety nights, and a program of musical evenings featured musicians from Brandon. He opened his Sunday evening services to the community, after the fashion of Woodsworth's "People's Sunday Evenings" in pre-war Winnipeg, and regularly attracted an overflow crowd. On several occasions he preached on the history and beliefs of Judaism, and the two Jewish families in Carberry accepted invitations to attend evening services at Knox.[17]

During this period he met his future wife, Irma Dempsey of Carberry, a music student at Brandon College. Irma's father had spent his life dealing in horses, and Douglas later said jokingly that Mr. Dempsey allowed the marriage only because the younger man had learned about horses as a boy in Glasgow. They were married in the summer of 1930, and remained together for 56 years.

Douglas stayed in touch with Brandon for the rest of his life. In 1961 the college awarded him an honorary doctorate in the name of the University of Manitoba, and the new Brandon University extended its own honorary degree in 1970. In 1985, the student body dedicated its new student union building to Douglas and an old friend and fellow student, Stanley Knowles. Knowles had been a parliamentary colleague of Douglas in the 1940s, then a founding organizer of the NDP, and finally the dean of Canada's Parliament, as well as chancellor of Brandon University. The building is called the Knowles-Douglas Student Centre.

Dustbowl Preacher

Douglas won his first job out of college in a competition with his friend Stanley Knowles. In the fall and winter of 1929–30, they preached alternate Sundays at the Calvary Baptist Church in Weyburn, Saskatchewan. At that time there were regularly scheduled passenger trains to all the bigger prairie towns, and Weyburn was easily accessible from Brandon.

Weyburn was a distribution centre for implements and supplies. It had a high school, a city hospital and a large mental institution on its western fringe, with a hospital, farm and staff residences. Calvary's congregation of 140 people—merchants, teachers and railway workers—had appealed to Brandon College for a new Baptist minister. College president J.R.C. Evans assigned Douglas and Knowles to compete for the job. At a special general meeting in February 1930, the congregation chose Douglas. He moved to Weyburn in August with his new bride. The board of deacons had offered a handsome salary—$1,800 a year—at a time when elementary school principals might earn $1,200 and farm families had almost no cash income.[18] The new minister was positioned to join the local elite, and in fact he joined a Young Fellows' Club made up of young businessmen and professionals.[19] Once again, however, events pushed Douglas to the political left.

North America had suffered a financial collapse in 1929. Unemployment was high, and commodity prices were down. In 1930 began the first of a series of drought years that eventually ruined many Saskatchewan farms and villages. Douglas gravitated to the Protestant ministers—William Cameron of the Presbyterians, Herb Cobb at the United Church—

who were organizing relief, and joining local labour unions in appeals to City Hall for action. Church congregations in other provinces sent carloads of clothing and food, and Calvary became "the distributing centre for the unemployed."[20]

Douglas was spurred on by his experience in Chicago in the summer of 1931, where he was temporarily studying Sociology. His research took him to slums worse than he had seen in Glasgow, to rail yards and industrial wastelands where unemployed men wasted away their days. His stay in America's second-largest city provoked him, he said, to think more seriously about what was wrong with the economic system. It also brought him into contact with American Marxists, who in his account spent their time planning far-off revolution rather than seeking ways to make practical changes.[21]

A violent strike in the Estevan coal fields, less than two hours from Weyburn by train, showed the vulnerability of Canadian workers during the economic slump. Frustrated in their efforts to bring the mine managers to the bargaining table, the Estevan miners went on strike on September 7, 1931. The strike ended when police attacked a protest parade, injuring 23 people, including bystanders, and killing three miners. Douglas visited the strikers in the field, provoking a complaint from the mine owners to the Calvary Church board. In the midst of the strike he preached on the topic, "Jesus the Revolutionist," and asked, rhetorically, how Jesus would view the present system of "graft and exploitation."[22]

More than 60% of Saskatchewan's 920,000 people lived on farms, and the international financial collapse had created serious trouble for the farm economy. With the Saskatchewan Wheat Pool deep in debt, the United Farmers of Canada (Saskatchewan Section) (UFC(SS))[23] had chosen a radical socialist, George H. Williams, to lead them, and their convention had pledged to work for "the abolition of capitalist robbery."[24] The Progressive caucus of farm candidates elected to Parliament in 1921 had soon fragmented, and most of its Saskatchewan members had straggled into the Liberal camp. However, at its 1931 convention, the UFC(SS) agreed to create a new farmers' provincial party to fight the Liberals and Tories. The UFC also conducted an investigation of working conditions in Estevan, found them to be deplorable, and called for the right of workers to organize and bargain collectively.[25] The urban left, meanwhile, was organizing new political associations; the leading figure in this movement, Regina school principal M.J. Coldwell, was a featured speaker at meetings in the cities and the rural areas.

Douglas joined Weyburn trade unionists in mid-1931 to organize the Weyburn Independent Labour Association (WILA), "a protective association" whose aim was to "influence public opinion," and to bring in noted public speakers such as farm leader George Williams. Its program included support for an unemployment insurance program, public ownership of public utilities, and equal rights of citizenship for all regardless of sex, origin or religion.[26] However, the WILA was not initially set up to engage directly in politics. It changed this policy, significantly, over the issue of health care.

"We had about eight doctors in town," Douglas remembered later, "and a hospital: empty beds, but people stayed home sick. They couldn't pay, and you couldn't blame the hospital—the hospitals had to pay for groceries, they had to pay their staff."[27] Douglas and his fellow ministers organized an appeal to raise funds for the sick, but it became clear that voluntary action would be insufficient. He wrote for guidance to J.S. Woodsworth, the

Labour MP from North Winnipeg who now led the left-wing remnant of the Progressive forces in Parliament. Woodsworth advised Douglas to contact Coldwell in Regina, and Coldwell appeared at the young minister's door on a Saturday afternoon in January 1932. Within a few weeks, Douglas was the president of the Weyburn Independent Labour Party (ILP), affiliated with Coldwell's ILP in Regina.

Membership in Saskatchewan's ILPs peaked at about 500 in half a dozen cities. Perhaps their strongest asset was Coldwell, who reached out to most areas of the province in his weekly talks on CKRM radio: "He had a marvellous voice, that lovely English without being too English, a cultured voice."[28] Coldwell understood radio; like Aberhart in Alberta, and other politicians in the Depression era, he used the new medium to build a solid following. And with Coldwell, Labour got two organizers for the price of one; Coldwell's vice-principal at Thomson School, 25-year-old Clarence Fines, had a genius for squeezing nickels and dimes from the movement's supporters, paying for the radio broadcasts as well as some of the leader's travel expenses.

Douglas, as always, packed an enormous amount of activity into his days, "winning his way into the hearts of many people"[29] as the pastor of a growing church, tending to his pastoral visits, organizing a theatrical society and a boys' study group, and working on a master's thesis, which he completed in 1932. The thesis was based largely on his contacts with the Weyburn mental hospital, and took what now appears to be an extreme position on improving the human species by segregating and sterilizing the "mentally and morally subnormal." Such thinking was close to the mainstream at this time, and moved the government of Alberta to implement a devastating sterilization program through the 1940s and 1950s. Douglas, however, backed away from the conclusions of his thesis after 1940, and they do not appear to have influenced the programs of his government.

Pastor Douglas preached the social gospel of pre-war Winnipeg, directing his Christian family to look towards the real problems of real people. The goal was to build the Kingdom of God on Earth, an entity that early social gospel writings suggested might be a society of love and voluntary labour. This vision was trimmed considerably as the children of the social gospel gained experience in politics. Very late in his life, Douglas still described love as "the great motivating source in society," but saw the Kingdom of God as "simply an association of people who have certain ideas in common"[30]—much like a community of believers, perhaps, or even a political party.

The migration from the pulpit to politics was a relatively logical and painless one. Douglas had the support of Calvary Church members such as Ted Stinson and John E. Powers, the organizers of a local retail co-op who managed his early campaigns. Department store owner Norman McKinnon, one of the biggest merchants in the district, remained a Liberal, but his daughters became Douglas supporters and Eleanor was later his secretary for many years.

The Depression deepened, and the Weyburn ILP continued its search for solutions, inviting the public to meetings featuring Coldwell, Woodsworth, William Irvine, and others. The farm and labour parties agreed in July 1932 to merge in the Farmer Labour Group. Coldwell the orator became the leader, but George Williams chaired the party council and its agenda.

The Young Campaigner

In July 1932, delegates from the new Saskatchewan Farmer Labour Party, not including Douglas, met in Calgary with leaders from sister organizations. They agreed to found a new national political party, the Co-operative Commonwealth Federation (CCF). The term "co-operative commonwealth" had roots in both American and British radicalism; although it "had coinage on the prairies," Douglas said later, "I thought it was an awful mouthful."[31]

The initial small group engaged in intensive organizing, and in July 1933 they held the founding convention of the CCF at the Regina City Hall. The convention agreed on a structure of federated provincial sections rather than a unified national body, a pattern that is reflected in the structure of the current New Democratic Party (NDP). The convention manifesto declared its support for several social programs and initiatives that Canadian governments would adopt in the next half-century – including state health insurance, unemployment insurance, old age pensions and a Canadian constitution with an entrenched charter of rights. The manifesto also contained proposals that have been dropped from the political agenda, such as worker participation in the management of industry. Notoriously, the manifesto ended by declaring that

> No C.C.F. Government will rest content until it has eradicated capitalism and put into operation the full programme of socialized planning which will lead to the establishment in Canada of the Co-operative Commonwealth.[32]

It is sometimes implied in biographical notes about Douglas that he was a primary organizer of Canada's CCF and prominent at the Regina Convention. This is not true. His profile at the time was local. His picture is not in the convention photo and his name is not on the delegate list. The evidence suggests that he drove to Regina on the last afternoon of the three-day convention to pick up two prominent delegates from Eastern Canada. He then drove back to Weyburn for an evening meeting, where he declared the convention to have been "the finest thing I have ever seen."[33]

Douglas continued to lead the Weyburn-area Farmer Labour organization through the fall, and the local party selected him as its provincial candidate at a nomination meeting in November 1933. However, the CCF and Tommy Douglas would be denied a breakthrough in the provincial election of June 1934. Saskatchewan's Conservatives had put together their first-ever government in 1929 in a coalition with Independents and Progressives, and were now being blamed for many of the problems arising from the Depression. The voters would move decisively to the Liberals in 1934, wiping out the Tories and electing 50 Liberals and just five CCF candidates, including George Williams.

In Weyburn, Douglas faced an impossible challenge. The Liberal candidate, Hugh Eaglesham, was a pioneer physician who had brought many of the area's voters into the world. Douglas did make important contacts, though, delivering 60 speeches around the constituency. A rally with Coldwell attracted a reported 2,000 people or more, although Douglas said later that many of these were hard-core supporters from outside who travelled in groups from meeting to meeting.[34]

The provincial CCF stumbled on the central issue of the campaign, the farm crisis. The CCF put forward a convoluted proposal whereby the province would assume ownership of debt-ridden farms and lease them back to their occupants. Douglas argued that 35% of the province's farmers were close to eviction; the CCF scheme would prevent foreclosures, and leases could be traded like any other property.[35] But various CCF candidates differed on the details of the proposal, and the Liberals portrayed it as a Bolshevik threat to seize private land. In fact, the CCF's enthusiastic and somewhat vague language on nationalizing industry proved an easy target for the older parties. Douglas, for example, wrote that social institutions that serve "the best interests of all" should be preserved, but he suggested that institutions based on the profit motive should be tossed aside:

> And the profit system has touched everything. It has corrupted governments, debauched politicians, degraded morals, devitalized religion and demoralized human nature.[36]

At the same time, Douglas's 1934 campaign was strongly influenced by the theory of "social credit," which was now a rising force in neighbouring Alberta. This theory, proposed by British writer C.H. Douglas, had concluded that to offset chronic under-consumption, the state should pay a regular "social dividend" to all members of society based on the value of the nation's assets. William Irvine, the veteran Alberta Progressive MP, had adopted this idea in the 1920s and promoted it in his writings. Irvine had addressed the WILP early in 1933, leading the local party to approach City Hall a few days later and demand the issuing of local "scrip" or currency. Douglas's remarks at his nominating meeting dealt at length with banks, currency and purchasing power.[37] Monetary reform was, of course, a federal and not a provincial responsibility, but Douglas returned to it as a theme during the campaign. He proposed the creation of a provincial bank that would issue low-interest loans and redeemable tokens, with or without federal approval.[38]

Douglas's provincial election loss in June 1934 did not dampen his enthusiasm for politics. At Woodsworth's invitation he contested and won the presidency of the national CCF youth organization. He travelled widely over the fall and winter, which gave him a chance to observe the political landscape across the country.

The Depression showed no signs of lifting, and the Conservative federal government of R.B. Bennett was promising economic reform. A popular federal minister, Harry Stevens, led a commission of inquiry into the behaviour of Canada's major corporations, and reported on price-fixing and other anti-consumer behaviour as well as miserable industrial working conditions. The lone dissenting member of the commission was the Liberal MP from Weyburn, Edward Young, who defended the practices of corporate Canada. Young appeared to be ripe for defeat in Weyburn, since he was perceived as having sold out to the eastern "interests" which had long been perceived as the enemy of the prairie farmer. At a CCF meeting on Saturday afternoon, June 15, 1935, 400 people chose Tommy Douglas to contest the riding. Young's statement in Parliament that "Canadians must learn to accept a lower standard of living" became a mocking rallying cry for the Weyburn CCF.[39]

The established parties faced challenges in the West both from the CCF and from Social Credit. Social Credit support had mushroomed in Alberta, and on August 23, 1935, the new party demolished the decaying United Farmers government in a provincial election. Douglas feared that the pattern would be repeated in Saskatchewan's federal constituencies. This fear was shared by Coldwell and Williams, who on September 3 issued a joint statement apparently designed to attract Social Credit sympathizers. They stated that social credit could not be applied in a capitalist economy, but that "all credit should be social; money should be scientifically related to industrial capacity," and further that the Alberta government should be given a free hand to carry out its social credit experiment.[40]

Douglas, meanwhile, devised a strategy to attract potential Social Credit voters in Weyburn. In early September his official agent, Ted Stinson, travelled to a meeting in Moose Jaw with Social Credit's provincial organizer and won a conditional promise of support. Douglas then issued a statement that he was prepared to "initiate and support legislation in the House of Commons" that would assist the Social Credit government of Alberta to carry out its program. Stinson and other Douglas supporters helped to set up a local Social Credit committee that endorsed the Douglas campaign. The Liberals, meanwhile, set up another "dummy" Social Credit group which nominated a candidate named Morton Fletcher.

Douglas's actions caused concern among some members of the CCF central campaign in Saskatchewan, especially when posters appeared from the "Weyburn CCF-Social Credit Committee." A Social Credit official from Alberta came to Weyburn to confirm that Douglas, not Morton Fletcher, had official Social Credit support. The Regina *Leader-Post* reported that Douglas had "officially declared his willingness to support the Social Credit platform 100 per cent."[41]

Douglas and Stinson were summoned to appear before the provincial CCF executive at the Hotel Saskatchewan on October 9. They might have been ejected from the party; two weeks earlier, Jacob Benson had been stripped of his status as a candidate in Yorkton because of his declaration of support for Social Credit. However, M.J. Coldwell had sent word that the young minister should not be disciplined since he had not gone as far as Benson. Douglas was ordered, however, to issue a statement distancing himself from Social Credit.[42]

While Douglas was strategically closer to Social Credit in 1935 than he had been in the previous year, his platform was much more coherently social democratic than it had been, with statements on health care, unemployment insurance and the right to peaceful protest. He also proposed a state-run credit program for farmers, a theme he would often return to as an MP. The highlight of the campaign came at a public debate at Weyburn's Arena Rink, with 5,000 people in attendance. The incumbent, Edward Young, waved a CCF pamphlet while he denounced Douglas's proposals; Douglas waited, and then announced that the pamphlet had never been issued, but had been stolen from a print shop by Young's campaign manager. The meeting dissolved in an uproar, with Douglas shouting that Young was unfit to serve in Parliament.[43] On election day Douglas took 7,280 votes to Young's 6,979. The Liberal-sponsored "Social Credit" candidate, Fletcher, got just 362 votes.

The only other CCF winner in Saskatchewan was M.J. Coldwell in Rosetown-Biggar. Most of the rest of the province's seats went to the Liberals. Social Credit also picked up two, along with all the seats in Alberta. The official Social Credit newspaper in Edmonton expressed some confusion over the Weyburn result, reporting that Douglas "is understood to have pledged his support to social credit."[44] A few days later there was a second attempt within the Saskatchewan CCF executive to cast Douglas from the party, and again Coldwell intervened. George Williams, who became the provincial CCF leader and president with Coldwell's move to Ottawa, warned that if Douglas had double-crossed Social Credit on this occasion, he might double-cross the CCF in the future.[45]

The MP from Weyburn

Douglas accepted his last payment as the pastor of Calvary Church at the end of December 1935. He arrived in Winnipeg in time for his father's funeral, and then travelled on to Ottawa. The election had been a disappointment for the CCF, with only Woodsworth surviving from the left-wingers elected in 1921, and only four new MPs prepared to serve with Woodsworth under the CCF banner. Douglas shared an office with Coldwell on the sixth floor of the Centre Block, and sat on the Agriculture and Public Accounts committees. The hours were long and the workload heavy. Douglas and his family maintained their home in Weyburn, but during parliamentary sessions Irma and little Shirley, their daughter, came to Ottawa and stayed in a rented downtown apartment.

The CCF's declared long-range goal was to build a "co-operative commonwealth" where essential industries would be operated under public or cooperative control. In practice, however, the small group of CCF MPs worked for more short-range objectives. Douglas focused on agricultural issues, and was a strong defender of the Canadian Wheat Board created by the Bennett Conservatives in their last year in office. He agitated for the increased use of the Wheat Board to subsidize returns to farmers, and for other programs to help prairie districts manage water resources and assemble pasture lands. He scored points at home by attacking the banks and mortgage companies, insisting that Ottawa should do more to regulate collection and foreclosure practices.

Douglas also argued for "parity pricing," an idea the CCF claimed would provide a comprehensive solution to the chronic instability of the farm economy. This remained the federal NDP's position well into the 1970s. However, it was always a murky concept. Under parity pricing, the selling price for agricultural products would be set according to input costs such as seed, fuel, labour and credit. The problem was that such costs would vary from farm to farm depending on distance to market, soil conditions and other factors. Douglas admitted to Parliament in 1941 that the parity pricing idea could "start so much argument that there is not much use talking about it."[46] He also admitted that some larger farmers had continued to show a profit even through periods of low prices, but he nevertheless insisted on the need for programs for the "smaller farm of a quarter- or a half-section."[47]

Along with farm issues, Douglas took a special interest in foreign policy. He was keenly aware of the rise of fascism from the time of his election, and met with European anti-fascist activists during a parliamentary trip to Geneva in 1936. Douglas often spoke in Parliament during foreign affairs debates, and showed an impressive grasp of the facts. He was forced to contend, however, with a CCF party that was torn between two conflicting impulses—the desire to confront fascism, and the pacifism of leader J.S. Woodsworth and many of his followers. This conflict eventually led to a party split in the Commons in September 1939, with Woodsworth casting a lone vote against Canada's declaration of war on Germany.

The CCF had pledged in 1933 to oppose all capitalist wars, and Douglas spoke in Parliament as late as 1937 against any increase in military spending and the build-up of a "military clique" in Canada: "We are saying that we believe that bread is more important than bullets, that homes are more important than aeroplanes…"[48] As war drew closer he took a different tone, and after the Liberal government's approval of the 1938 Munich agreement he warned against "yielding to dictators."[49]

On September 6–7, 1939, Douglas took part in an extraordinary meeting of national and provincial CCF leaders in Ottawa. Woodsworth and Winnipeg activist Stanley Knowles expressed complete opposition to any declaration of war; George Williams of Saskatchewan urged full military participation. Douglas supported a compromise position calling for political and economic support for the Allies but no commitment of troops.[50] The 15–7 vote for the compromise marked the end of Woodsworth's leadership. Later the same day Douglas and Coldwell voted with the government and against their long-time mentor to declare war. Within a year the CCF had moved to a position of support for the use of troops, although it continued to criticize the government for allowing profiteering by munitions makers and industry. Douglas signed on as a reserve officer with the 2nd Battalion of the South Saskatchewan Regiment and took military training at Dundurn in the summer of 1941, but declined the army's offer to make him a full-time chaplain.

Douglas was re-elected to Parliament in early 1940, increasing his margin in Weyburn from 300 votes to 950. Nationally the CCF was held to eight seats, five of them from Saskatchewan. Again, the caucus was too small to have overt influence on government decisions, but Douglas was recognized as a young man of promise and talent. He was "not a great admirer" of Mackenzie King, but the Liberal Prime Minister occasionally confided in the Weyburn MP during the war years about the pressures he felt in governing the country: "He took a fancy to me for some reason. I think he saw in me what he had been like when he was a young man…"[51] When Douglas left Ottawa to enter the Saskatchewan Legislature in 1944, *Maclean's* correspondent Bruce Hutchison summed up his record: "He did not make himself popular in Parliament, but he made himself heard, and, at times, he could even penetrate the rhinoceros skin of the Government."[52]

The Approach to Power

Through the late 1930s Douglas stayed close to the provincial CCF, serving on its executive committee in 1937 and its council in 1938. The party was in a period of strategic confusion, and in several provincial and federal ridings its members were drifting into common-front campaigns with former Progressives, Communists and whoever would come along. At the official level the CCF opposed any joint campaigning, but in the lead-up to the 1938 Saskatchewan election it negotiated with Social Credit and the Conservatives over where each party should run candidates. The intention was to challenge the governing Liberals with one strong opponent per riding, an arguably cynical strategy of doubtful practical merit. Douglas later called this period "a terrible schmozzle,"[53] but he appears to have supported the strategy at the time. A month before the election, he urged party leader George Williams to pursue discussions with provincial Tory leader John Diefenbaker: "I still see nothing to prevent pulling our candidates out of such places as Turtleford, Watrous, Melfort and Torch River in return for a free field in Last Mountain, Elrose, Rosetown and Weyburn."[54] Partly as a result of this maneuvering, the CCF ran only 31 candidates to contest 52 seats.

The CCF did well in the ridings it contested, taking 10 seats. In two ridings, political fusion groups elected "Unity" candidates of doubtful allegiance. With Social Credit electing only two members and the Conservatives none, the CCF was now established as a potential government in waiting.

However, the party remained poorly organized in areas where it had not run candidates, especially in the large cities. Relations between the two senior politicians, Williams and Coldwell, had been cool or hostile since 1934; Douglas tried to build a good relationship with Williams, but was often viewed as a Coldwell agent by the Williams camp. The approach of the war brought further tension, with a pacifist group working to promote the views of Woodsworth and Williams trying to block them. Professor Carlyle King of Saskatoon, who later served as party president for many years under Douglas, led this group. King wrote in 1939 that the mood of agreement between Douglas and Williams on war issues was like the pact between Hitler and Stalin, with Douglas on the right wing of the party and Williams on the left: "My guess is that Douglas will not be with us long, for which we can be truly thankful."[55]

Williams responded to the disarray and the controversy over the war by taking sole control as supreme leader. He demanded that all inter-constituency CCF mail be routed through his hands,[56] and he rarely called council or executive meetings. In the spring of 1940, the newly expanded Saskatchewan group of CCF MPs wrote a brief proposing that the party curtail Williams' powers by splitting the two functions of party leader and party president. Williams saw this document as "the work of T.C. Douglas and an attack on my leadership."[57] When Carlyle King stepped forward at the 1940 provincial convention to contest the presidency, Williams told delegates that naming a separate president would make his job untenable, and in fact would "destroy for all time the possibilities for election of the CCF to power."[58] Finally, in January 1941, the party council agreed to consider creating a separate presidency and to hire as a full-time organizer J.T. (Jack) Douglas, a Coldwell ally. A month later Williams announced he was leaving Saskatchewan for England as a quartermaster with the 11th Hussars. At the same time, Tommy Douglas joined the provincial council and executive to serve as a liaison with the federal CCF MPs.

George Williams deserves more credit than he has received as a founder and builder of the CCF, but his last years as leader were marked by something like dementia. Before his departure for England, he wrote a rambling letter to the provincial council blaming Douglas for all the party's strategic and internal problems for at least the previous two years: "Thus it would appear that in the opinion of Rev. T.C. Douglas, the CCF is not to be a vehicle through which we may unite to build social democracy, but rather a vehicle to build M.J. Coldwell."[59] The party council, in a motion put by two Williams loyalists, found that his charges against Douglas and others were "without foundation in fact."[60]

It should be noted here that there was no immediate surge to make Douglas the party leader to replace Williams. When the Weyburn MP offered himself for the Saskatchewan CCF presidency at the 1941 convention, the absent Williams took a quarter of the votes. Douglas assumed that the jobs as leader and president came as a package, and the party newspaper, the *Commonwealth*, reported that the he had been chosen to "lead the movement." However, Carlyle King and allies such as Oak Valleau, MLA, disputed this and a party council meeting in January 1942, after "considerable discussion," declared the party leaderless until the next convention.[61]

Despite the confusion over titles, however, the mood in the party improved immediately after July 1941. A new team of Tommy Douglas, long-time party treasurer Clarence Fines, and organizer Jack Douglas set out to sell memberships and raise money. By July 1942 the party membership had gone from 4,075 to 9,482, a 133% annual increase after two years of decline. The party executive agreed to organize regional conventions in all areas of the province in fall 1941 and encourage local associations to prepare resolutions for the next year's convention. The party also set up a labour outreach committee with 14 members. This was followed in 1942 with a retail merchant's committee that included Douglas's Weyburn ally, Ted Stinson, and a young Moose Jaw alderman named Ross Thatcher. Another set of committees set out to review and expand on party policy, focusing on two issues that were expected to stand high on the priority list of any CCF government—the farm economy and health care.

The 1944 Campaign

By 1943, Canada's wartime economy was humming, and the Depression-era unemployed had found jobs and incomes. The expansion of Hitler's empire had been halted and reversed. Across the English-speaking world, the reputation of government as a social and economic manager was at an all-time high. So was support for Canada's CCF, a party that promised government action as a means to a better life. The national CCF briefly moved into first place in the opinion polls in mid-1943, and the Ontario CCF came within a few seats of taking power provincially.

In response, Prime Minister King moved his Liberal Party to a more reformist position, promising that a post-war federal government would move ahead on social issues such as health and housing. Canada's largest corporations, meanwhile, organized a scare campaign, making use of such tools as the Robert Simpson Ltd. retail catalogue operation to warn Canadians that a CCF government would confiscate land, homes, bank accounts and life insurance. By early 1944, with King moving to the left and the corporations agitating on the right, the national CCF's popularity was in decline.

Saskatchewan, however, was a different story. The big business coalition, with its banks and farm equipment companies, faced a tough audience in Saskatchewan's farmers. And the provincial Liberals, unlike their federal counterparts, claimed to lack the resources to introduce reform. Premier William Patterson was a dry, fussy man with little apparent personal following, and his government's record of achievement was slight. The rural elites—the leaders of co-ops, women's organizations, and municipal councils—were increasingly bonded to the CCF.

Douglas believed that the Liberals had maintained their grip on power through intimidation. An army of inspectors had controlled the relief system in the 1930s; Douglas claimed that they often threatened to cut off food supplies to opponents of the regime, and rewarded friends with petty jobs and contracts: "It was a terrible thing to watch ... a complete negation of democracy."[62] By the 1940s, however, many families were moving off the welfare rolls, and were ready to take political revenge.

Patterson's term should have ended in June 1943, but the Liberals passed a bill to prolong the life of the government for another year. They argued that an election campaign would distract voters from the war effort and consume strategic supplies such as motor fuel. Douglas, still sitting in the Commons, protested, but the CCF's constitutional expert Frank Scott advised him that any Legislature could "prolong its life indefinitely... The remedy is political (if that exists) and not legal."[63]

Douglas continued to attack the Liberals over their delaying tactic, but in reality the extra year gave the CCF more time to plan its victory. With Clarence Fines at head office and Jack Douglas in the field, the number of dues-paying party members continued to rise, from 9,500 in mid-1942 to more than 26,000 in June 1944. An army of volunteers brought out the CCF vote poll by poll in every riding.

Over the New Year's holiday in early 1944, 72 leading members of the national CCF gathered in Regina to review the Saskatchewan party's legislative intentions with regard to employment standards, health care, public ownership and budgeting. This helped the Douglas team to develop, test and clarify their policies.

A few weeks later Douglas hosted the provincial party's annual five-day winter school, a time for communicating campaign messages and strategies to candidates and campaign managers. Out of these meetings emerged a pocket-sized card outlining the CCF's nine-point program. This card, to be carried by every canvasser, promised farm security legislation, a new deal for labour, and the creation of a government department to support the cooperative movement. It pledged to restructure the public school system, develop industry through public ownership, and work towards a system of socialized health care. Douglas had a simple theory of campaigning. He would agree with his advisers on a clear agenda for government action, set this agenda out in plain language, campaign only on the agenda, and try to ensure that all candidates and speakers told the same story.

The political campaign of the pre-television era was vastly different from today's campaigns. It relied on face-to-face contact with voters and the small-town press as well as on radio and the city dailies. Tommy Douglas's enthusiasm for campaigning is now legendary. He had an unquenchable appetite for rallies, picnics, and kitchen-table meetings. His schedule from mid-April to June 15, 1944, took him to three public meetings a day as well as endless strategy sessions, often conducted in automobiles between engagements.

Douglas's platform performances, the cadence and timing of his rhetoric, are also legendary. But important as his speeches were in winning a following, his work really began when the speeches ended. Douglas would remain near the stage, surrounded by people anxious to shake his hand or give him advice. It was here that he established the bond between himself and his followers. He had a remarkable ability to concentrate his attention on whoever stood before him. As long as the conversation lasted, that individual was

SAB 2858(1)

One of Tommy Douglas's greatest political assets during the 1944 election campaign, and throughout his career, was his willingness to mingle with people. Here, in vintage Douglas-style, we see him at the Hudson Bay Golden Jubilee celebrations in 1955, in top hat, seated in a small cart pulled by huskies, surrounded and followed by a crowd of admirers.

the only person in his world. He had a great memory for names and family ties, and this knowledge came readily into play on a second meeting. It became commonplace in Saskatchewan for ordinary men and women to boast that they were friends of Tommy Douglas.

In the course of the 1944 campaign, Douglas returned to the themes that had dominated recent CCF conventions: patriotism, the farm economy and the improvement of health-care services. The most critical issue was security of tenure for farmers, many of whom were deeply in debt. Douglas promised to reduce the foreclosure rate, pressure the federal government to increase subsidies, and work for diversification of Saskatchewan agriculture into a wider range of products.

The Liberals, supported by the city dailies, portrayed the CCF as dangerously left wing. But to the Liberal charges that the CCF would confiscate farms, Douglas responded that the private sector had foreclosed on 6,000 Saskatchewan properties from 1935 to 1941. When they claimed the CCF would confiscate insurance policies, he replied that Canadian companies had cancelled $700 million in life insurance policies during the Depression. "The CCF does not want to own everything," he said. "In fact, we recognize that even if it were desirable ... [it] would break down under the weight of bureaucracy and red tape."[64]

With a CCF victory imminent, public expectations rose. Over the years, Douglas had often resorted to visionary terms such as "economic emancipation" and "social reconstruction" to describe the CCF's goals. Now he warned that provincial governments faced severe limits. "Don't think we can give you an entire new society," he told an audience a few days before the vote. "I don't want the CCF party to get one vote in this election by saying they are going to do things they cannot constitutionally do."[65]

On election night in June 1944, party workers from across Saskatchewan phoned the election results to Douglas's campaign office in Weyburn. The scale of the provincial victory was massive; the CCF collected almost 53% of the vote, and 47 of the 52 seats in the Legislature. In Weyburn, the CCF leader's vote share was 60%. At ten o'clock, he rode the shoulders of his supporters down Main Street. Two days later, with Clarence Fines, the Premier-elect retreated to his cottage to reflect and to ready himself for government.

The First CCF Cabinet

The CCF's first summer in government was a time of tumult. Well-wishers and cranks flooded the new Premier's office with letters of entreaty and advice, and party members angled for government positions. The departing Liberals had emptied the files of many key documents, including those pertaining to current federal-provincial relations. Douglas complained to ex-Premier Patterson, now the opposition leader, saying this act of pillage was "most improper." Patterson replied his party had followed "the rules and practices established by custom."[66]

Douglas hired three young people to manage the chaos in his office. The appointment of Eleanor McKinnon, who came from a prominent Liberal family in Weyburn, surprised party members; she would remain as Douglas's right hand for most of the next 42 years. Tommy McLeod had first met Douglas as a member of a Weyburn boys' group, had worked on Douglas's 1934 campaign, and had consulted the Weyburn MP on his academic career; he now became the Premier's policy researcher and economic adviser, and would later rise to the position of deputy provincial treasurer. Douglas selected Morris Shumiatcher of Calgary as his legal adviser. Shumiatcher later became a noted trial lawyer, stock speculator and conservative commentator.

Douglas's first major task was to select a Cabinet, knowing that many of his MLAs expected a position. In consultation with Clarence Fines and the provincial party executive, he increased the size of the Cabinet from nine members to 12, creating new departments for labour, cooperatives, social services and post-war reconstruction. Douglas used this opportunity to unite the factions in the party, and to recognize both city and country. Former adversary George Williams, returned from the war, was named to the Agriculture portfolio, although he was too ill to serve and soon resigned. Oak Valleau, prominent in the CCF pacifist faction, was chosen as Social Services minister. With regard to regional balance, half the cabinet came from the cities and half from the rural areas.

Douglas, now 39 years old, was Premier, but also took the Health portfolio. Fines, 37, the veteran party secretary and fundraiser, and Regina alderman, became the treasurer and minister responsible for the public service. When Fines took on the provincial finance job, Saskatchewan was the most deeply indebted province in Canada on a per capita basis. When he left politics in 1960, the province had no long-term debt. Fines displayed flamboyant self-confidence in his own powers, borrowing three times his annual salary in the summer of 1944 to purchase $15,000 worth of Saskatchewan bonds. He told the media about his purchase, and responded to the predictable attacks from the Liberal opposition by criticizing their failure to buy bonds and their lack of faith in the future of the province. He sold the bonds a year later at a profit of $3,000, which was more than the yearly income of most of his constituents.[67]

Cabinet's inner circle in the first term also included a veteran politician from a different generation. John Wesley Corman, at 57, had been a staunch Liberal early in his career, then a noted barrister and mayor of Moose Jaw. Like M.J. Coldwell, Corman had his own political radio broadcast, and a network of followers and contacts across the province. As attorney general, Corman managed the difficult federal-provincial issues that plagued the new government. He was also a key source of procedural and political advice for the Premier and his staff. In Cabinet, he was a sobering influence in an often tumultuous period.

SAB R-WS15159(1)

A formal portrait of Premier T.C. Douglas, 1957.

Woodrow S. Lloyd, a 31-year-old teachers' federation leader, was assigned to Education, where he took on the demanding and often unpopular job of consolidating rural schools. John Brockelbank, 40, a farmer from the northern Saskatchewan bush and an MLA since 1938, accepted the municipal affairs post. Over time, the foursome of Douglas, Fines, Lloyd and Brockelbank became the core group in Cabinet. All of them served at least four terms, and Lloyd became Premier in 1961 when Douglas returned to federal politics.

At least two others in the first CCF Cabinet deserve mention for their contribution to the province. Jack Douglas, the CCF's provincial organizer since 1941, took charge of the highways portfolio and, starting with 20 miles of paved roadway, built a modern provincial highway system. He also created an open tendering system to replace the longstanding practice of contracting highway work to friends of the government.

Natural Resources minister Joe Phelps spoke in Cabinet for the radical factions in the CCF. Phelps, a farm activist from Saltcoats, masterminded a series of industrial and commercial ventures including a woollen mill, a tannery, a shoe factory, and a brick plant. These experiments failed, but nevertheless helped educate the young government and the party's left wing about the risks of social ownership.

Douglas gave his ministers considerable latitude in their jobs, and in Cabinet meetings he sought consensus rather than imposing his own views. However, his position as leader and spokesman for government was never challenged. His colleagues recognized that for most voters, he symbolized the CCF; he had a unique ability to synthesize and clarify the government's goals and achievements, and to speak to voters in language they understood.

With the Cabinet installed, it was time to decide the fate of public servants who had been appointed by the Liberals. Judging from the mailbag, many CCF supporters expected a wholesale purge. Douglas had promised soon after the election to get rid of workers who were either "incompetent or merely political employees."[68] His assistant, Tom McLeod, advised the new ministers to rid the government of "undesirable elements."[69]

The government abolished the Saskatchewan Tax Commission and the Farm Loan Board, dismissed their chief executive officers, and transferred their functions to the Treasury Department. They cancelled the contracts of several dozen Liberal "inspectors." However, a 1945 report to the Premier shows only 18 salaried workers dismissed in the government's first year, compared with one dismissal in the previous year. Another 69 had retired, compared with 25 in 1943–44.[70] The CCF retained several deputy ministers it had denounced in the days of the Liberal regime. A number of these remained in office until their retirement and were then replaced from within the public service.

This lack of partisan ferocity frustrated some party militants. In the fall of 1944, the CCF executive resolved that only "proven socialists" should be appointed as deputy ministers and commissioners. The mover and seconder of the motion, Peter Makaroff and Carl Edy, soon got appointments to government boards, and so did a few other senior party figures. A new Public Service Act, however, soon established merit as the basis for hiring public servants. After the passage of this Act, Douglas referred letters from CCF job seekers to the Public Service Commission. He wrote to one petitioner:

> We are seeking to eliminate patronage and to have our elected members work as lawmakers and not as party bosses who hand out patronage to their friends and political supporters. I am sure, on reflection, you will agree that this will make a much better government.[71]

On September 27, 1944, the Douglas government introduced its first program of legislation. The CCF would "create a government organization sufficient in scope to meet the needs of postwar society." Over the next two months, 76 bills were passed, touching almost every area in the life of the province. These reforms reflected the combined work of the Cabinet, the legislative caucus, the CCF provincial council and executive, and several years of debate at party conventions. In the ensuing years there would be occasional tension between the party and the government's in-house advisers over questions of legislation and governance, but in Douglas's view, the party's committees remained the key source of new ideas throughout the 20 years of CCF administration. Very few of the government's actions, he said later, came as a surprise to anyone: "By the time you got it to the Legislature, there wasn't anything hidden in it. It had been beaten to death."[72]

Douglas, the Federal Government and Agriculture

When the CCF came to power, Canada was on the verge of a sustained economic boom. During the Depression there had been a cash shortage, and a goods shortage during the war years, but the end of the war brought an explosion of consumer demand and goods production. The federal government grew, too, and its program of transfer payments to the provinces became increasingly important to provincial health and education programs through the 1950s. In the long run, federal money helped to build the health-care system that led to medicare in Saskatchewan. At the beginning of the CCF period, however, relations between Saskatchewan and Ottawa were uneasy, particularly because of differences on farm issues.

In his nine years in Parliament, Douglas had often slammed the federal government for its reluctance to support prairie farmers. During and after the Depression, many farmers had surrendered their land to banks and lenders, and when the CCF took power, 40% of Saskatchewan farmers were renting their land, with many others deeply in debt. In his speeches as an MP and then as Saskatchewan CCF leader, Douglas assigned much of the blame to the federal Agriculture minister and political minister for Saskatchewan, former Premier Jimmy Gardiner. In this relationship, as in many others, Douglas was able to keep his personal and professional lives separate. For example, when the newly elected Premier visited the European battlefront in late summer 1944, he visited the grave of Gardiner's son and brought a photo home to the grieving father.

The CCF government did what it could for the rural areas. One of its first bills, the Farm Security Act, was intended to shield farmers from foreclosure. The government also moved quickly to improve rural roads and telephone systems and extend the electric power grid. The province, however, did not have the resources to implement the price supports that Douglas believed were needed to keep farmers in business. The Premier repeatedly called on Gardiner, and later his successors, to launch a "parity pricing" system "to ensure producers a fair cost-price relationship."[73] Successive federal governments, Liberal and Conservative, showed no interest. The relationship between Ottawa and the CCF government with regard to agricultural issues was often one of irritation, rather than cooperation.

One of the few documents on Douglas's desk when he became Premier was a letter from the federal minister of Finance, James Ilsley, demanding payment from Saskatchewan of $16.5 million, at that time about half the annual provincial budget. This money was to repay Ottawa for federal loans that were made to Saskatchewan farmers to buy seed grain in 1938. After a disastrous crop failure in 1937, seed had been in short supply in the spring of 1938. Ottawa had agreed to pay cash advances so that farmers could buy seed, often of poor quality, and had persuaded the province to guarantee the loans. The provincial notes given as security had been renewed from year to year, but with the CCF victory, Ottawa now demanded payment at a rate of at least $2 million per year.

Douglas's Cabinet resolved to fight what it saw as a partisan action initiated by Gardiner. Douglas told a radio audience that Saskatchewan did "not intend to pay one dollar" unless Ottawa reduced the debt by half.[74] After further dispute, the federal government began to hold back part of its statutory payments to Saskatchewan. The CCF Cabinet took the federal side to arbitration, but a three-member panel ruled in Ottawa's favour. Politics intervened; in the 1945 federal election, the CCF took 18 of 21 Saskatchewan seats despite Gardiner's efforts. In the aftermath, Ottawa proposed a compromise settlement of the seed grain debt—a $12 million repayment over 11 years. The provincial Cabinet agreed.

Just as this dispute was winding down, the King government informed Premier Douglas that it was considering the disallowance of two CCF bills, one of them the Farm Security Act. Disallowance is the sledgehammer in the federal tool kit, very rarely used, and once again Douglas smelled partisan motives. He was incensed that the federal government had given the province less than three weeks to prepare for a hearing in Ottawa before a panel of ministers, and that Justice minister Louis St. Laurent wanted to restrict Saskatchewan's intervention to one hour.[75]

The Farm Security Act provided for a mediation board to review disputes between farmers and creditors. The board was given significant powers, and could order the suspension of mortgage payments in years of crop failure. As Douglas had said in a pre-election broadcast, "If the mortgage companies want to stay in business in this province, they will have to start taking the good years with the bad, and begin shouldering their share of losses."[76] The mortgage companies disagreed, and petitioned Ottawa to strike down the Act. The other bill that was proposed for disallowance, the Mineral Taxation Act, imposed a levy on subsurface mineral rights. It was the target of a petition to Ottawa from Saskatchewan's largest private landowners, the Canadian Pacific Railway and the Hudson's Bay Company.

The Douglas government launched an information campaign on the importance of the two bills, and the Premier called on citizens to fight the federal government. The United Farmers, the trade union movement and numerous municipal councils forwarded resolutions to the federal government. Attorney general Corman, meanwhile, prepared a brief and appeared before his federal counterparts in Ottawa, arguing that only the courts should have the power to strike down provincial laws, and then only on constitutional grounds.

A panel of federal ministers heard the arguments, and, weighing the potential cost of a federal-provincial war, rejected the petitions for disallowance. The Farm Security Act remained in place, although it was weakened two years later when the Supreme Court of Canada ruled that the province could not block interest payments to lenders. Even so, the legislation continued to protect farm families in distress to the extent that they could keep their home quarter from creditors along with seed, farm equipment and household goods.

One hopeful sign emanating from Ottawa in this period was the federal government's apparent willingness to start work on a South Saskatchewan River dam. For many years, boosters of this project had seen potential for a dam to irrigate and provide electrical power to a wide area. Douglas had seconded a parliamentary motion by M.J. Coldwell in 1938 calling for water conservation measures, specifically the damming of the Saskatchewan River. Federal Agriculture minister Gardiner announced in 1944 that survey work for the project was under way. As it turned out, however, this was just the start of 15 years of planning, talk and delay.

It was not clear at first who was going to pay for the dam, the cost of which was estimated in 1947 at $66 million. After protracted study, Gardiner instructed his staff in mid-1950 to open talks with Saskatchewan on cost sharing. Saskatchewan agreed to pay the cost of secondary reservoirs, irrigation works and all power installations. The federal government then called a royal commission to study the project further. Its report, tabled in Parliament in 1953, recommended that Ottawa not fund construction on the basis that the cost would outweigh the economic benefits.

Douglas attacked the report. His office issued a press release calling the commission's cost estimates "an insult to the intelligence of any engineer familiar with the project."⁷⁷ He wrote to Prime Minister St. Laurent, demanding that the project proceed according to the earlier cost-sharing agreement. Gardiner responded for the federal side, stating that he would be pleased to look at a detailed proposal from Saskatchewan. The province made further concessions, but St. Laurent made it clear that he did not want to spend money to create "a lake in a dry area."⁷⁸ In the heat of the dispute, St. Laurent instructed Gardiner to suspend discussions with Saskatchewan, but the archives show that the federal minister and the Premier continued to exchange letters using Gardiner's farm address.

SAB RB 12762

After years of federal-provincial negotiating, the South Saskatchewan River dam project finally became a reality. Douglas is pictured here, in May 1959, riding an earth-moving machine at the official inauguration of the construction.

It took a new federal government, and a new Prime Minister from Saskatchewan, to achieve a funding formula. John Diefenbaker signed a cost-sharing agreement in 1958, less than a year after taking office. By the time the project was finished, the Liberals were back in power, and they named the new dam after James Gardiner. It is possible that Douglas had a hand in this; he had acknowledged, in a letter in 1950, that Gardiner had done what he could to create a blueprint for the dam and get the project started. In the same letter he added, "I don't need to tell you that I have disagreed with Mr. Gardiner on almost every item in domestic politics over the past twenty years."⁷⁹

Into the Modern Era

The CCF governed Saskatchewan during a time of transformation in the provincial economy. When Douglas took office, roads were unpaved and most farms operated without electrical power. Over the next two decades, Saskatchewan moved into the Canadian mainstream. The hoped-for diversification into manufacturing and services was modest; provincial license plates still billed Saskatchewan as "The Wheat Province" into the early 1960s. However, the extension of roads, power and telephones changed the nature of agriculture, and created a base for a new generation of profitable, large-scale resource industries.

At the outset, CCF partisans hoped for the creation of a socialist economy, a "planned, socialized economic order" as proposed in the "Regina Manifesto." In response to this hope, Douglas and his colleagues moved into public ownership on a scale that no other

North American government had ever tried. The Saskatchewan Power Commission, which had acted mostly as a regulatory body, was directed to buy up the small, local power companies. The rural telephone companies were likewise absorbed into Saskatchewan Government Telephones. Early in 1945, the Saskatchewan Government Insurance Office came into being, and over the years proved to be popular and profitable.

The failure of the province's one-crop economy, together with its failure to secure any meaningful portion of wartime industrial expansion, produced a growing recognition of the need for substantial economic diversification. The CCF's natural resources committee, under the chairmanship of Joe Phelps from Saltcoats, had developed a long list of ideas for meeting the province's needs when the party was in opposition. As minister of Natural Resources, Phelps was determined to follow the trail his committee had mapped out: developing Saskatchewan resources using Saskatchewan labour, and generating tax revenues that would support the province's social development. With Cabinet's agreement, Phelps acquired a northern fish-processing plant, a fur-marketing agency, a timber mill, a woollen mill, a brick plant and a shoe factory. The resource-based industries created some long-term opportunities for northern, largely Aboriginal communities. The manufacturing plants were unsuccessful, and although they represented a very small percentage of provincial investment, they became a significant political liability and were cited for many years by Liberals and Tories as evidence of CCF incompetence.

By mid-1945, it became clear to the Premier that the government needed help with economic planning, with managerial performance and management training, and with the coordination of its economic programs. An economic advisory committee, established soon after the Douglas government took office, comprised a panel of academics drawn from the University. During its brief life, it restricted itself to tax and financial issues. Douglas then decided to look beyond Saskatchewan's borders for a senior economic development professional. David Lewis, the Oxford-trained lawyer who was chief organizer for the national CCF, suggested George Cadbury, a distinguished member of the British Labour Party who had graduated from Cambridge University—where he had come under the lasting influence of John Maynard Keynes—and from the Wharton School of Finance at the University of Pennsylvania. As a working member of the Cadbury family, he had extensive experience in industry and commerce. Most recently, he had served with Britain's wartime purchasing mission in Washington. Best of all, Cadbury was available, and agreed to start work in Regina on January 1, 1946. He was appointed chair of the new Economic Advisory and Planning Board, and chief industrial executive of the Government Finance Office, positions he held until his departure in 1951. He reported directly to Douglas for the Planning Board, and to Clarence Fines for the GFO, which was formed to oversee and rationalize the management of the government's various businesses.

Douglas had often spoken of planning as an essential feature of socialism in action. He made room in the Legislative Building for a small group of experts who would have time to research new ideas about society and the economy and plan for the long term. The Economic Advisory and Planning Board went into operation the day after Cadbury arrived. Chaired by Cadbury, the board was essentially a staff agency reporting to the Premier, and through him to a special Cabinet committee comprising ministers holding portfolios related to the government's business activities.

The completion of the board's first four-year plan in early 1946 marks the end of populist economic experimentation by the Saskatchewan CCF. In opposition and in its first days in government, the party had set a high priority on social ownership and the rapid expansion of social programs and education. In this context, Douglas once recalled the words of a British Labour MP named Jimmy Thomas: "The trouble with socialists is that they let their bleeding hearts go to their bloody heads." Cadbury now argued that the government must improve the productivity of the provincial economy before it could increase its spending. The planning board proposed strict rules for the creation of new government businesses, and measures to attract private investment.

Under the new guidelines the government created a bus company, a company to mine and process sodium sulphate (potash), and a natural gas utility function as a division of the Saskatchewan Power Corporation. All proved to be durable and generally profitable. In 1947, the government created a new industrial development fund, offering low-cost loans to potential investors. In debate in the Legislature, one CCF MLA reminded Douglas that the "Regina Manifesto" had promised "the eradication of capitalism." Douglas responded that the government would encourage private enterprise "whenever it did not interfere with the welfare of the people."[80] The loan fund had modest success, supporting the creation of businesses including a dairy processing plant and a wire and cable plant. Through other incentives, the CCF helped to promote oil exploration, forest industry activity, the establishment of the IPSCO steel plant outside Regina, and eventually a wave of European investment in potash extraction and processing.

These industrial policies created new, non-farm job opportunities in Saskatchewan. The government also worked to boost the efficiency of farming, building roads and providing support for farm improvements and running water. With a single program in 1949, it extended electricity to 40,000 farms, giving farmers and their wives access to power tools and home appliances as well as radio and television. But these popular initiatives, while helping profitable farm operations to become even more so, aggravated a dilemma that the CCF never solved: should the government help competent farmers to take risks, expand their operations, prosper and buy out their neighbours? Or should it protect the smaller family farm and maintain the rural population? Douglas established the Royal Commission on Rural Life in 1952 to consider "the continued volatility of the rural economy."[81] The commission produced few answers; small farms continued to disappear, as the survivors continued to get bigger and wealthier. This contributed to the growing conservatism that gradually eroded CCF and then NDP support in rural Saskatchewan.

The modernization of the province, nevertheless, remains a key legacy of Douglas and the CCF. One aspect of this work, the application of professional standards to the public service, has had national implications. The Patterson government, like its counterparts across Canada, kept no formal agenda and no record of Cabinet proceedings. Its annual budget was essentially a compilation of one-page submissions from ministers. The CCF created specialized agencies for economic planning, budgeting, reviewing expenditure proposals and preparing Cabinet briefings. This remains the template for all of Canada's governments today.

Through his leadership qualities and the force of his personality, Tommy Douglas attracted a public service whose talents were far out of proportion to the province's size and financial resources. Douglas dealt directly, as an equal, with many of the rising planners and administrators in government. He deferred to their specialized knowledge, but he excelled at asking questions. He had a remarkable ability to relate expert advice to the real problems facing Saskatchewan communities. His government proved to be an administrative training centre of historic excellence. When the CCF government fell in 1964 and Liberal Premier Ross Thatcher smashed the public service in Regina, dozens of administrators fled to Ottawa to work for Prime Ministers Lester Pearson and then Pierre Trudeau. These refugees were referred to (with a mixture of respect and bemusement) as the "Saskatchewan Mafia." A significant number rose to the highest positions in the federal public service.

The CCF and Labour Reform

At the time the CCF took power, Saskatchewan was overwhelmingly rural. Farmers' associations had struggled to improve the economic position of farm families, but as employers, farmers resisted efforts to organize or improve conditions for farm workers. Across the Saskatchewan economy, in fact, there were no penalties for employers who refused to bargain with their workers, and there were few unionized workplaces. The strongest and best-entrenched unions were the railway unions, which worked in the federal jurisdiction.

The CCF in Saskatchewan had rural roots, but it also had ties to sister parties in Manitoba, Ontario and British Columbia, where labour played a major role. Douglas, of course, was a trade union member and the son of a trade unionist. His inner Cabinet included two teachers' union activists, Clarence Fines and Woodrow Lloyd, and Labour minister Charlie Williams came from a railway union. In its first term in office, the CCF made significant changes to provincial labour laws and policies. The Trade Union Act set out reasonable rules for union certification, prescribed penalties for employers who refused to bargain, and created a Labour Relations Board. Amendments to the Public Service Act gave public servants the right to organize and bargain collectively, the first time this had happened in Canada. The government established a minimum wage (except for farm workers), a 44-hour work week, and improved employment standards generally. It also improved the benefits available under the workers' compensation system.

In spite of these reforms, however, the relationship between the Douglas government and organized labour was uneven, and sometimes adversarial. Part of the problem stemmed from Douglas's appointment of Charles Cromwell Williams to the Labour portfolio. Canadian labour was split into two camps at the time, with the craft unions (such as carpenters, rail mechanics and printers) forming the Trades and Labour Congress (TLC) and the more militant industrial unions (autos, steel, meat-packing) the Canadian Congress of Labour (CCL). The TLC was politically neutral, sometimes leaning to the Liberals; many leaders in the CCL were prominent in the CCF, especially in Ontario. Charlie Williams was a genial, politically gifted ex-mayor of Regina, but he was a TLC man, and a weak advocate for organized labour.

When the Cabinet list was announced, the Regina Labour Council and the CCL said Williams was an unacceptable choice, and called for his immediate firing. This position was supported from Ontario by the federal CCF's chief strategist, labour lawyer David Lewis. But Douglas, habitually loyal to people he had hired or promoted, refused to fire Williams; he replied to Lewis that the CCL had become ultra left-wing, and was "on its way to committing hari kari in Saskatchewan."[82] Williams kept his job in Cabinet until 1964, with Douglas and then Woodrow Lloyd compensating for his weaknesses along the way.

The CCL lost a second round when it tried to organize the Saskatchewan government ministries. It had succeeded in signing up the Crown corporation and mental hospital workers, but organizer Alex McAuslane announced he would not work with the long-established Civil Service Association, branding it a company union and "scab" outfit. Partly as a result, the departmental civil servants chose to go with the TLC. McAuslane confronted the Premier in his office, but Douglas pointed out that the new Trade Union Act, which the CCL had sought, gave workers the freedom to join the union of their choice.

The appointment of Ontario labour economist Ken Bryden as deputy minister of Labour won support from the industrial unions. Nevertheless, the annual round of bargaining with the CCL's public-sector unions became a tough exercise. In November 1948, workers at Government Insurance went on strike to support a demand for a 49% wage increase. Inflation was running at less than 3%. Douglas wrote to Aaron Mosher, a founder of the CCF and the national president of the CCL, about the union's "fundamental lack of goodwill." Granting such a wage hike, he said, would be "tantamount to exacting a levy on the vast majority of our citizens for a mere handful of their fellows."[83] The strike was settled, but there was continuing friction, with David Lewis travelling west in 1955 to mediate a strike threat by Saskatchewan Power workers.

Union membership in Saskatchewan doubled during the Douglas period, from about 15,000 to 30,000. However, this still represented only a small minority of the working population, and there were virtually no further substantive changes to provincial labour policies in the last four terms of the CCF government. Labour's influence remained limited, even within the CCF. "We would leave the [party] convention licking our wounds," said labour activist Walter Smishek, later an NDP Cabinet minister, "saying, 'another convention, another beating'."[84] For example, the 44-hour week was still in effect when Douglas left Saskatchewan, despite labour's agitation for a 40-hour week.

Later events suggest that, in terms of practical politics, Douglas was well advised to keep Saskatchewan labour at arm's length during his tenure as Premier. When the federal CCF collapsed and David Lewis engineered a new vehicle based on a merger of the CCF membership with organized labour, many party supporters in Saskatchewan were horrified. After much reflection, Douglas agreed to lead the new labour-based party, and was trounced by Regina voters in his first outing, as was every other Saskatchewan candidate in the first election fought by the NDP.

The Minister of Public Health

On countless occasions during his long career, Tommy Douglas told audiences about his childhood introduction to the health care system. In a 1961 legislative debate on the introduction of medicare, he put it this way:

> I lay in a children's hospital in Winnipeg on and off for three years. My parents couldn't afford the services of an outstanding surgeon. I had my leg hacked and cut again and again, without any success. The only reason I can walk today, Mr. Speaker, is because a doctor doing charity work, one of the great bone surgeons of Winnipeg, who was later killed in the First World War, came into the hospital one day with a group of students, took an interest in my case, and took it over.[85]

Canada's traditional medical care system, Douglas learned, provided help mostly on either a commercial or a charitable basis. Working people often fell through the cracks. As a young preacher in the 1930s, Douglas often conducted funerals for those who had died for lack of basic medical care. The concept of state-run health care was well understood—the federal Liberals had endorsed it in principle in 1919—but governments entered the field only in preliminary ways. Saskatchewan, for example, offered free institutional care to people with tuberculosis, and would house mentally disabled people without charge if they had no property or income. Local governments struggled to fill the many remaining gaps; by 1944, one-third of Saskatchewan's municipalities had hired doctors and organized public clinics, and many had joined with neighbouring municipalities to build and manage "union hospitals" as cooperative ventures.

The CCF, including Douglas, viewed the limitations of this hodgepodge as intolerable. The need for universal health care was highlighted in the "Regina Manifesto," in campaign literature and speeches by CCF leaders during the 1930s, and in Douglas's speeches as Saskatchewan leader in the early 1940s. A 1943 statement by the Saskatchewan party executive defined medicare almost exactly as the Douglas government would introduce it in 1961: a system open to everyone, with no deterrent fees or premiums, operated from general revenues, with doctors working either for a salary or on a fee-for-service basis.[86]

Because of his special interest in health care, Douglas assumed the Health portfolio when he became Premier. The changes he introduced, given the province's financial position, were remarkable. During his tenure, Saskatchewan extended full medical coverage to seniors and to women on mothers' allowance, set up public health offices in every district, and became the first jurisdiction in North America to guarantee universal free access to hospitals.

On taking office, Douglas sought the advice of Dr. Hugh MacLean, a pioneer Saskatchewan physician and a leading member of the early CCF. Douglas and MacLean agreed that the government should move first to conduct a health services survey. MacLean proposed Dr. Henry Sigerist, Professor of the History of Medicine at Johns Hopkins University, to head the survey. Douglas telephoned Sigerist and recalled: "I think he was so astonished that anyone would have the gall to ask him, and then to tell him that we couldn't pay anything except his expenses, that he came."[87] Representatives from Saskatchewan's medical, nursing, and dental professions, as well as a health administrator, joined the international specialist in his work. The secretary to the Health Services Survey Commission was Dr. Mindel Sheps, a Winnipeg physician and a strong supporter of the CCF's health care policies.

Sigerist's report, dated October 4, 1944, confirmed that the province should work toward universal medicare, over time and as funding allowed. It recommended a decentralized system for managing health care, where regional health boards would maintain inspectors, laboratories, community clinics and travelling clinics. It also recommended free cancer treatment, in-school dental check-ups, the creation of care centres for seniors, access for on-reserve First Nations people to provincial health facilities, and the closure of the province's huge and antiquated mental hospitals. All this was to be coordinated by a Health Services Planning Commission, a body that Douglas created in November, little over a month after receiving the report.

One of the commission's first tasks was to support Douglas in negotiations with the province's physicians. The government wanted to provide medical care to 25,000 seniors, single mothers and blind people, and needed the doctors' agreement on a fee structure. During these talks Douglas made a significant compromise: where many CCF militants would have liked to see all doctors on salary, the Premier agreed to a fee-for-service plan. The new program for seniors went into operation in January 1945. However, from this point on, with the government providing an increasing number of health services, there was growing friction between the CCF and organized medicine. Medical associations across the continent viewed Saskatchewan's success as a threat; and the Saskatchewan doctors' association discouraged its members from accepting salaried positions with the province or local governments.

The Health Services Act of the fall of 1944 set out the framework for the creation of the 14 health regions and health boards. Planning commission members, including Mindel Sheps, her physician husband Dr. Cecil Sheps, and Tom McLeod, spent much of 1945 meeting with community leaders across the province to discuss regional boundaries and board responsibilities. When the regional health boards went into operation in 1946, they moved immediately into inspection programs, immunization, clinics for newborns and health education. Health Region No. 1, based in Swift Current, set up a district-wide medical insurance program, Canada's first. The program, partly financed by a regional health tax, served as a pilot project for universal medicare in Saskatchewan and across the country. However, this initiative did not spread to other health regions.

In moving forward on health care, Saskatchewan was hampered by a lack of federal funding. Prime Minister King proposed a national medicare scheme in 1945, but Ontario and several other provinces were opposed, and King refused to assist the provinces individually. Even so, Saskatchewan made great strides, especially in hospital construction. The province had the lowest number of hospital beds per capita in 1944; by 1954 it had the highest number, having doubled its total capacity. The Premier was also determined to introduce universal hospitalization insurance in the government's first term, an idea his advisers said was premature. They argued that the budget was stretched to the limit with new hospital construction, and the government lacked the technical and administrative staff to put a hospital insurance program into effect. Overriding this advice, Douglas introduced the Hospital Services Act in the spring of 1946, promising a province-wide hospitalization program by January 1, 1947.

The minister of Health's actions forced the Health Planning Commission into a period of feverish activity. Douglas persuaded the deputy surgeon-general of the United States

Army, Dr. Fred Mott, to come to Regina and provide direction, along with Dr. Len Rosenfeld, another senior public health specialist. Even with this support, the planning team pleaded for a one-year extension, to January 1948. The appeal was denied; Douglas planned to call an election in 1948, and wanted time to eliminate any bugs from the hospital insurance system.

Across the province, community- and church-run hospitals expressed concern over what they regarded as a CCF takeover of their facilities. Douglas assured them that the government only intended to pay their bills owing, and that he did not have time "to keep track of every bed-pan in Melfort."[88] As it turned out, the hospitals found relief in not having to collect fees from former patients. The hospital insurance scheme worked smoothly, although there were initial protests about the new hospitalization tax. By 1948, the hospitalization scheme was a point of pride in the CCF election platform.

Douglas left the Health portfolio in 1949, and appointed Swift Current MLA Tom Bentley to take his place. The regional health boards continued to expand their activities through the 1950s, and the standard of health among Saskatchewan's citizens continued to improve. The picture in the field of mental health, however, was more controversial. The provincial mental health budget increased fivefold under Health minister Douglas, and doubled again before 1960. The mentally disabled benefited from training and other programs. However, due partly to resistance from communities and from government unions, and to the displeasure of mental health and advocacy groups, the government did not discharge the mentally ill from the hospitals in Weyburn and North Battleford.

In 1957, a new federal government headed by Saskatchewan's John Diefenbaker announced that it would provide financial support for free hospitalization in the provinces. This created considerable space within the provincial health care budget, and within a year the Premier was considering plans for universal medicare.

Minister of Co-operation and Co-operative Development

In 1949, Premier Douglas left the health portfolio for a less demanding second job as minister of Co-operation and Co-operative Development. This change allowed Douglas to shift attention to political work. The 1948 provincial election had shocked the CCF, reducing the government caucus from 47 to 31 members in the 52-seat Legislature, and Douglas was determined to spend more time travelling the province.

As a student of politics, Douglas was well aware of the prominent role that producer and consumer cooperatives had played in Saskatchewan since early settlement. By supporting the cooperative movement, the Douglas government could further its program and make political gains at the same time. In his last year in the House of Commons, he spoke of cooperatives as "the most important form of social ownership."[89] As Premier, at a cooperative convention in 1951, he stated that, "Just as Abraham Lincoln freed the blacks, so the cooperative movement is freeing the whites from economic slavery."[90]

Douglas had set up the co-ops department in 1944 to fulfill an election promise. Lauchlan McIntosh, a farmer and an active member in the cooperative movement, was the department's first minister. Saskatchewan's cooperatives had a combined membership of more than 300,000 in 1944, with virtually every rural family belonging to one or more co-ops. These included the Wheat Pool, dairy and livestock co-ops, retail co-ops, the wholesale co-ops with their interests in food processing, lumber and petroleum refining, and the credit unions.

When the Premier took over the provincial department, one co-op official called it "a sign the movement has come of age." In fact, the movement had achieved a cautious, subdued middle age, something that became a source of disappointment to Douglas. For example, he secured financing from all three prairie governments to support a cooperative farm implement plant in Winnipeg, but other co-ops were unwilling to help with financing or distribution and the farm equipment venture failed to take root. When oil exploration started up in Saskatchewan in the early 1950s, Douglas took a political risk in reserving Crown land for the co-op oil company, but the co-ops declined to risk their capital on drilling. In a 1958 letter to a friend, Douglas lamented:

> The spirit of self-sacrifice which put up the [co-op] refinery [in the 1930s] isn't here in sufficient strength to do that kind of job today... We have acted as if all the battles have been won.[91]

Saskatchewan's experiment with co-op farming also failed during Douglas's tenure. The co-op farm, drawing half a dozen or so families into a shared operation, was seen in 1944 as an ideal way to resettle young war veterans. The planning board's first four-year plan recommended the creation of a $250,000 loan fund, and at least one co-op, at Matador, received significant financing. From 1945 to 1949, 17 co-op farms were created with 181 members.[92] However, most farmers were not interested in sharing their land, income and living space with other farmers, and most of the co-op farms broke up within a few years.

Douglas served as cooperatives minister until he left Saskatchewan in 1961. He took advantage of a late opportunity in 1959, when he turned the government's fur marketing and inland fisheries corporations—created during the rapid expansion of state ownership in the mid-1940s—over to Aboriginal-run northern cooperatives. This transition was successful.

The Provincial Opposition

Tommy Douglas had a remarkable politician's gift for making instant human contact, and for remembering faces, names, and dates: "Oh, and how is your cousin Fred doing? I haven't seen him since he had that back operation..." Tens of thousands of Saskatchewan residents regarded Douglas as a close friend on the basis of a kind word and a handshake. However, he was not universally loved; he faced opposition from two capable provincial Liberal leaders and from the big-city dailies, business groups, the professions, ranchers and conservative community leaders.

William Patterson, the scapegoat for the Liberals' massive 1944 loss, retired as party leader in 1946. His own party abandoned him, but Douglas took steps to secure a legislative pension for the former Premier. Patterson's successor was Walter Tucker, a Saskatoon lawyer and member of Parliament for Rosthern.

Tucker was never subtle in his strategies, and he soon made it clear that he planned to bring down the CCF with a campaign of red-baiting. When the two leaders engaged in an outdoor debate at the Crystal Lake golf course in the summer of 1947, Tucker charged that the Communists backed the CCF "financially and otherwise."[93] The Liberals' slogan for the 1948 election was "Tucker or Tyranny," with Tucker claiming repeatedly that the CCF followed "a direct line as laid down by Moscow."[94] The CCF's loss of 16 seats in the election may have been unrelated to Tucker's strategy, but the Liberal leader certainly succeeded in enraging the Premier and drawing him offside during the campaign. Douglas travelled to Rosthern to focus on Tucker's record as a mortgage dealer, saying Tucker had been "charged with fraud" by some unhappy customers.[95] This was not true, and Tucker sued Douglas for slander. The action died in the courts, unresolved.

After 1948, Tucker added a new strategy to his repertoire, seeking to portray the Douglas Cabinet as corrupt and unfit to hold office. His main target was the provincial treasurer, Clarence Fines, who worked diligently to reduce Saskatchewan's debt while pursuing a parallel career as a speculative investor. Fines habitually sought out stock tips during the trips he made to sell government bonds in Toronto and New York. He also dabbled in Saskatchewan resort properties and Saskatchewan mines. In 1950, he persuaded Premier Douglas to invest $500 in the "Theatre Under the Stars," a Regina drive-in movie theatre. The Liberals soon branded the drive-in "the Premier's Passion Pit." One year later, Fines, as minister responsible for government insurance, helped to approve a $75,000 mortgage loan for the drive-in's owners in connection with a separate venture. The Liberals forced the matter to a legislative committee, where the CCF majority found no evidence of corruption. The Premier defended his investment before the committee, saying, "I make no apology for investing in any local venture that can be of assistance to the community."[96]

In the 1952 election the CCF political organization delivered tens of thousands of new voters to the polls, overwhelming Tucker and the Liberals. The CCF's vote share rose to an all-time high of 54%, and the party won back more than half the seats it had lost in 1948. In the legislative session that followed, Tucker made a last sensational effort to destroy the government by targeting Clarence Fines. On March 10, 1953, he read out a statement from Joe Rawluk, a former friend of Fines and former associate of the "Theatre Under the Stars" owners. Rawluk claimed that Fines and the managing director of the Government Insurance Office were extorting money from government insurance agents. Fines, in Douglas's absence, agreed that the matter should go to a legislative committee. The hearings before the Committee on Crown Corporations began that same night, and in the ensuing days the committee heard from 26 witnesses. The *Leader-Post* and the *Star Phoenix* probably devoted more space to the affair than to any other event in Saskatchewan history, printing page after page of verbatim transcript. It came down, essentially, to two statements: Rawluk's testimony that he had put $100 in cash on a car seat next to Fines during a ride through downtown Regina, and the committee's finding that "Mr. Rawluk must be regarded as wholly unworthy of belief."[97]

As Douglas had feared, Tucker now rejected the work of the legislative committee. He called it a whitewash, and demanded a judicial inquiry. In the House, the Liberals read their own dissenting report into the record, arguing that the charges against Fines had not

SAB R-WS15172 © M. WEST, REGINA. WEST'S STUDIO COLLECTION.

The political event of the year. Crowds gather outside for the Douglas-Thatcher debate in Mossbank, on May 20, 1957. It was widely agreed afterwards that, for the first time, Douglas had met his match as a debater.

been disproved. Douglas responded for two hours and 50 minutes, and when he was finished, not a single Liberal rose to reply. The onus had been on the Liberals to prove widespread corruption, he said, and they had not come close. Did any Liberal believe Rawluk's story about the $100? "Stand up, then," he said, "come out of the bushes and let's see the colour of your liver!"[98]

Soon after this, Douglas sold his interest in the "Theatre Under the Stars," and Walter Tucker retired. The Liberals chose Hamilton McDonald as their next leader. An honest, good-natured man, he made no significant dent in the CCF's majority in the 1956 election. He went to his reward with an appointment to the Senate in 1959.

The rise of Ross Thatcher, the CCF's eventual nemesis, came about partly as a result of a Douglas miscalculation. Thatcher had been elected as a CCF MP in 1945, but was always a right-wing maverick, calling for lower corporate taxes and means tests for old-age pensioners. In 1955 he crossed the floor to the Liberals, and during the 1957 federal election contested the Assiniboia seat. As a favour to the CCF federal candidate, Hazen Argue, and perhaps because he smelled a challenge, Douglas offered to meet Thatcher in a public debate.

Nearly 1,000 people crowded into a hall in Mossbank, in the Assiniboia riding, to hear the debate. Countless thousands across the province listened in on the radio. Douglas allowed himself, unwisely, to be drawn over to Thatcher's rhetorical turf, debating the details of the government's business arrangements rather than the Douglas vision. The Premier was not a clear loser in the debate, but many observers felt he had met his political equal.

Thatcher lost to Hazen Argue in the federal election of 1957, and again in a federal election the following year. Moving to the provincial level, Thatcher succeeded McDonald as Saskatchewan Liberal leader. A hard-driven, ambitious man and a disciplined campaigner, Thatcher succeeded in scaring the CCF badly in the 1960 Saskatchewan election. The socialists, he argued, were big spenders, poor managers obsessed with state investment; prosperity would come to Saskatchewan only when the government opened the doors to private enterprise. This was not quite fair; the Vancouver *Sun* had reported, in fact, that no other province was "as eager to welcome the free-wheeling free-enterprise industrialist."[99] But Thatcher was exploiting the fact that the CCF, in its cautious fourth term, had squeezed itself into the political centre, with limited appeal on the right and little to offer the militants on the left. In Ontario, David Lewis and Stanley Knowles were preparing a merger of the party with organized labour, a dubious proposition for most Saskatchewan residents. On provincial election day in 1960, the CCF's popular vote dropped to 40%, and only a strong showing by the minor parties, the Tories and Social Credit, blocked a Thatcher victory.

It may be that the CCF was saved by a single strategic decision, signalled by Douglas during a by-election in 1959 and emphasized repeatedly during the 1960 provincial campaign. The promise: to introduce a program of public health insurance that would guarantee medical care to every resident of the province. The doctors' union fought back aggressively, the public had a clear choice, and the CCF emerged with the most seats in a multi-party race. In response to the letters of congratulations, Douglas said it had been "the hardest-fought campaign we have had to date… The result is little short of a political miracle."[100]

Medicare in Saskatchewan

Universal state-run health insurance, to be financed from general revenues, had been part of the Douglas platform from the beginning. For many years, however, Saskatchewan was not in a financial position to initiate a medicare program. Its other health programs, however, grew to be the most generous in Canada, with hospital insurance costs alone accounting for 20% of the provincial budget by 1955.

In the late 1950s, the province's fiscal position improved, due in part to increasing oil and mineral production. More importantly, the Diefenbaker government in Ottawa delivered on a deathbed promise by the St. Laurent Cabinet to create a national hospitalization insurance plan, and starting in July 1958 paid half of Saskatchewan's hospital costs. The Douglas administration now had room to move on universal health insurance and, as noted above, it also needed some dramatic action to fire up its supporters after years of caution. The Premier instructed officials to prepare legislation while he outlined his proposal to the public. In a radio address in December 1959, he predicted that the adoption of medicare in Saskatchewan would open the way for a national health insurance program within 10 years: "Once more Saskatchewan has the opportunity to lead the way. Let us therefore have the vision and courage to take this step, believing that it is another advance toward a more just and humane society."[101] In the same address, Douglas stated that the insurance plan would conform to five basic principles. First, bills would be paid directly by the insurer. Patients would never see a bill. Second, the insurance plan would operate under public control, not as a subsidy to private insurance companies. Third, the plan would cover everyone, regardless of age or disability. Fourth, the operation of medicare would not drain money from other health programs. Finally, medicare legislation must be acceptable to patients and doctors before it went into effect.

The last principle, unfortunately, proved impossible to uphold. Since the 1940s, the College of Physicians and Surgeons had made it clear that any medicare scheme must operate, to a substantial extent, under its control. The medical profession's non-profit insurance corporation served a third of the population of Saskatchewan by 1960, and doctors saw no reason to replace this service. Many physicians had come to the province from elsewhere, and had no attachment to Saskatchewan's cooperative tradition; as many as 20% had emigrated to escape from Britain's National Health plan. Woodrow Lloyd, emerging as Douglas's probable heir as Premier, warned that the doctors would go to the barricades to block the implementation of medicare. Douglas disagreed; he felt the doctors would grumble but go along, as they had with hospitalization insurance.[102] Douglas was wrong. The dispute over medicare eventually led, in the summer of 1962, to the longest doctors' strike in Canadian history.

In a March 1960 television forum, Douglas stated that if people were opposed to medicare, they should vote against the CCF in the upcoming election. Saskatchewan doctors took him at his word.[103] With the help of the Canadian Medical Association, they raised $100,000 to spend on publicity during the election campaign. However, their materials were so extreme as to be ineffective, claiming that medicare bureaucrats would control health care and might commit women with menopausal problems to insane asylums.[104] Douglas took a hard line in return, and warned the College of Physicians and Surgeons not to harass doctors who supported medicare. "What the Legislature has given," he said in reference to the College charter, "the Legislature can take away."[105]

For most of his last year as Premier, Douglas made little progress in the implementation of medicare. It can be argued that this period of delay made the government look uncertain, and set the stage for the eventual confrontation. The work of the Premier's Advisory Committee on Medical Care, appointed in April 1960, was obstructed by members who represented the medical college. The committee was to report by December, but by November it had not even started public hearings. The exasperated chair, university president W.P. Thompson, wrote to Douglas, threatening to resign.

In Cabinet, meanwhile, an incompetent minister of Health had lost the confidence of his colleagues. Douglas had appointed Walter Erb in 1956, and stood behind him as the medicare controversy worsened. In this case, his near-unconditional loyalty to political associates threatened to wreck a major initiative. As one former CCF minister put it later, "Erb was incapable of communicating a straight story to the doctors, and he was incapable of giving us a straight report on what the doctors were saying to us."[106] The spring legislative session of 1961 passed without an advisory committee report, and without a medicare

SAB RB 2871(1)

Premier T.C. Douglas as a member of a TV panel discussing the government's medicare program, March 20, 1960. Debating Douglas were Dr. E.W. Barootes (left) and Alex Jupp (centre).

bill. In June, Douglas announced that he planned to leave the province to lead the federal New Democratic Party. In September, Thompson's committee finally submitted a majority report proposing a universal health insurance program to be run by a government commission.

Douglas immediately organized a special session of the Legislature for the purposes of introducing a medicare bill. He used the Throne Speech debate to say farewell, and to predict, once again, that Saskatchewan's action would open the way for a national medicare system, to cover "not just hospitalization and medical care, but eventually dental care, optometric care, drugs and all other services which people receive."[107]

Contrary to predictions, the government's announcement did not include insurance premiums for Saskatchewan residents. All costs were to be paid from general revenues, unlike later universal plans in Ontario and British Columbia. However, the Medical Care Insurance Act disappointed some CCF supporters in that it prescribed fee-for-service payments to doctors. The government's health planners had long advised that putting doctors on salary would be a positive step, leaving them more time for counselling and health education, and removing the incentive to perform unnecessary procedures. Douglas, however, had rejected a salary system in the mid-1940s as politically unworkable, and he did so again this time.

Even so, the doctors were absolutely opposed to the CCF bill, voting 295–5 at a special meeting against cooperating with the proposed health insurance plan. They said they wanted more consultation, although it was clear that further discussions would be fruitless. The College of Physicians and Surgeons had already set out its position in the minority report of the Advisory Committee on Health Care, calling for a voluntary scheme of private insurance to be subsidized by the government.

On November 1, 1961, Tommy Douglas stepped down as Premier. A few days later, the Legislature adopted the Medical Care Insurance Act with the support of the Liberals. The new Premier, Woodrow S. Lloyd, set April 1 as the start-up day for the new health plan, and appointed William Davies to the Health portfolio to replace Walter Erb. A few months later, Erb crossed the floor.

Douglas and the Founding of the NDP

Douglas's entry into federal politics came about suddenly. It did not figure in his plans during the provincial campaign of 1960, and it happened only because the alternative, in his view, would have been the destruction of the social democratic left at the national level.

As Premier of Saskatchewan, Douglas was an ex officio figurehead in the national CCF during the 1940s and 1950s. However, his actual participation was generally limited to correspondence with his old mentor and friend, national leader M.J. Coldwell, and with other executive party members such as David Lewis and Frank Scott. After a brief heyday in the mid-1940s, the CCF had struggled and lost ground on the federal scene; the end came in March 1958 when the Progressive Conservatives under John Diefenbaker swept the nation, defeated Coldwell in Rosetown-Biggar, and reduced the CCF to a leaderless eight-member rump in the House of Commons.

Lewis, the national CCF president, immediately began a major reorganization of the party. He engineered a resolution from the Canadian Labour Congress (CLC)[108] calling for a new "broadly based people's political movement which embraces the CCF, the Labour movement, farm organizations, professional people and other liberally minded persons interested in basic social reform."[109] He then persuaded long-time MP Stanley Knowles, defeated in Winnipeg, to join the CLC staff as vice-president and help set up the new party. Premier Douglas agreed to lend his name to a national New Party Committee, designed to bring together dignitaries from the CCF and organized labour.

In Ontario, the new party effort got off to a promising start. Through 1959, numerous union locals agreed to affiliation, and dozens of "New Party Clubs" attracted voters who had never joined a party before. However, the response among CCF veterans in Saskatchewan and across the prairies was pessimistic. They saw no need to discard the CCF name and heritage, and were concerned that a formal alliance with organized labour would hurt the party in rural areas. As Woodrow Lloyd wrote to Coldwell, "The Committee to date has had an almost complete preoccupation with structure, without attempting to answer the question: structure for what?"[110]

Douglas had understood for some time that the national CCF was at a political dead end. In speeches and letters to the public, he expressed support for the new party idea, focusing especially on the Committee's (ultimately unsuccessful) efforts to bring farm organizations into the new party. Privately he worried about the loss of the CCF identity, and about the possibility that the New Party Clubs would become a haven for "communists,

Trotskyists, neo-fascists or funny-money theorists."[111] He complained to Knowles about the New Party Committee's "structure first, principles later" approach, and asked Lewis to slow down and let the movement "evolve naturally."[112] Lewis and his Ontario allies did not slow down, and set a July 1961 date for a founding convention.

Douglas proposed that Winnipeg, rather than the East, should be the site for the convention; prairie CCFers "will be hurt and offended if they get the impression that the CCF has been tricked into a founding convention at which they can be outnumbered and outvoted."[113] Lewis and Knowles chose Ottawa.

As the 1960 Saskatchewan election approached, Douglas became the focus of a rising chorus of complaint from the provincial party and Cabinet colleagues, and he moved to distance the Saskatchewan CCF from the new party. The provincial CCF, he told the Legislature, was not affected by the new party initiative, and would decide whether or not to affiliate with the new party "when and if" it was formed. Party policy, he said, would continue to be set in Saskatchewan at provincial party conventions.[114]

While Douglas was ambivalent about the formation of the new party, many others viewed him as the only logical prospect as its leadership. Douglas himself believed that David Lewis of Ontario, polished and bilingual, was the obvious choice. David Lewis, his son Stephen said later, yearned for the leader's job, but he saw Tommy Douglas as the only figure who could bridge the emerging division between the old CCF and organized labour.[115]

Through the late 1950s, Lewis lobbied continually in the CCF to promote Douglas as federal leader. As late as autumn 1960, Douglas was still resisting. He was comfortable in Saskatchewan, where he exercised real power:

> I spent nine years in Ottawa and at times I was almost overcome with the frustration and futility of being a voice crying in the wilderness... I feel that my first duty is to stay here and get this [medicare] plan operating on a strong basis.[116]

The evidence suggests that this resistance was genuine. Douglas began to waver only when it became clear that MP Hazen Argue might win the leadership of the new party by acclamation. Argue had won the interim CCF leadership at the national party's last convention in 1960 (the alternative for delegates was to leave the job vacant). He was a popular and entertaining speaker at party dinners on the prairies, but even his friends in the CCF federal caucus judged him to be indecisive as a leader and weak on the issues.

In early 1961, Lewis, Knowles and Claude Jodoin, head of the CLC, staged a news conference in Ottawa where they pledged their support to Douglas. This set off a storm of debate in Saskatchewan, with CCF caucus members and constituency associations divided on whether the Premier should stay or go. The Lewis team, meanwhile, was blocking Argue from campaigning, neglecting to inform him of new party meetings, and refusing to provide him with contact lists. In late March, the Saskatchewan Cabinet agreed that each member should write Douglas a note of advice. All but two said, reluctantly, that he should take the federal job.

Douglas, at last, signalled that he was prepared to step down as Premier. To John

Brockelbank, the senior member of Cabinet, he wrote that he would prefer to stay in Saskatchewan, but continued, "It may be that my greatest contribution to Saskatchewan would be to help win 30 or 40 seats for the New Party in 1962."[117] He informed Lewis of his decision and secured a formal release from the CCF provincial council. However, it was not until late June, just a month before the new party's founding convention, that he called reporters into his office in Regina to reveal his plans.

Douglas explained his decision by suggesting that Canadians needed a progressive alternative in politics. However, it was not clear in fact where the new party was going, since it had not yet generated a platform. It was up to Douglas to define the progressive alternative. During a brief tour of Ontario, he called for measures to create purchasing power, for national health care and improved pensions, and for a foreign policy that would promote peace. Despite the new logo and stationery, the new party message would be one of continuity with the long-time concerns of the CCF.

SAB RB 12,052

Douglas and Lloyd at the founding convention of the NDP in 1961. Lloyd succeeded Douglas as Premier of Saskatchewan.

The founding convention in Ottawa attracted about 1,800 delegates, four times as many as the largest CCF convention in history. They chose a name—the New Democratic Party—and voted on a set of policy proposals. Several of these, including protection for consumers, regional development subsidies, and foreign investment controls, would be implemented by Liberal governments over the next decade. As the last item of business, delegates chose Douglas as their leader by a 3–1 margin over Argue.

The convention generated enormous publicity for the new party and for Tommy Douglas. He became the subject of magazine articles, television feature reports and even a novelty song on the radio. The reality, however, was that the party remained underfunded and understaffed. Douglas, with his secretary Eleanor McKinnon, moved from his high-ceilinged office in the Legislature to a basement cubicle in Regina's River Heights Shopping Centre and began a life on the road. In the December 1961 by-election, the Saskatchewan CCF lost Douglas's Weyburn seat to the Liberals, bringing into doubt the "Douglas halo of invincibility."[118] Six weeks later, Hazen Argue announced that he had conferred with Ross Thatcher and agreed to join the Liberals. Argue had been stung by the Lewis machine before the founding convention and ignored in the aftermath. He now warned that the NDP was "the tool of a small labour clique ... a dark and sinister threat to democratic government in Canada."[119]

SAB RA 56-118-06

The trappings of power. In 1961, when he became federal NDP leader, Douglas traded the Premier's office in the Legislative Building, shown here in a 1956 photograph, for a basement cubicle in Regina's River Heights Shopping Centre. Note the picture of Abraham Lincoln on the mantlepiece.

Before its first convention, support for the NDP in the polls had stood at 12% nationally. Through tireless campaigning, Douglas was able to increase this to 13.5% by election day in 1962.

Minor Party Leader

Tommy Douglas led the federal New Democratic Party for 10 years. During that time the NDP fought four general elections, always winning between 17 and 22 seats in the 265-seat House of Commons. Douglas suffered two personal defeats, in Regina City in 1962 and in Burnaby-Seymour, British Columbia, in 1968, but was able to bounce back through by-election victories.

It is a tribute to Douglas's remarkable strength of character that, throughout this period and beyond, he remained a steady, good-natured leader who was unfailingly loyal to his colleagues and courteous in his public comments. He faced many disappointments and frustrations in the federal NDP, including the loss of his political base and his home in Saskatchewan, ongoing challenges to his leadership, and limited influence on national affairs.

The June 18, 1962, federal election could not have come at a worse time for Douglas as NDP candidate in Regina. The doctors' strike, which was to polarize the community, was just two weeks away. When the former Premier's campaign team organized a motorcade through the city, anti-medicare activists placed coffins on lawns along the route; they also, according to one NDP organizer, pummelled the NDP cars with two-by-fours.[120]

Douglas had chosen to run in Regina instead of Weyburn (part of the Assiniboia constituency) because it had a major airport, and he was expected to campaign nationally. He also said later that running against the now-Liberal Hazen Argue, the incumbent in Assiniboia, would have seemed "an act of vindictiveness."[121] Regina seemed a reasonable alternative; the CCF had taken the federal seat in three of the previous five elections. As it turned out, he was beaten badly.

Nationally, the public optimism generated by the formation of the new party had subsided, and the NDP was taking regular hits from the media for its financial ties to organized labour. Ironically, the CLC had backed away from the party to avoid the perception that it was in control. Other than Douglas's speaking tour there was almost no national campaign, with each constituency left to its own devices. On election day only 19 New Democrat candidates were elected, winning with vote shares as low as 32% in four-way races.

For years after this, NDP partisans claimed that the Conservatives and the Liberals had ganged up in Regina City to defeat Douglas. The fact is that Tory leader John Diefenbaker was still riding high across the prairies, and there was no room in Saskatchewan for a new, labour-based, Ontario-dominated party. Regina Tory incumbent Ken More lost votes to Social Credit while holding the seat; the Liberal vote held about steady. Douglas got only a 28% electoral share, while other New Democrats in the province did worse, with between 20% and 24% of the vote. Only Liberal Hazen Argue prevented a Conservative sweep of Saskatchewan.

Douglas's statement of concession at the CKCK television studio ("I'll lay me down and bleed awhile, and then I'll rise and fight again") ranks as a classic in the rich rhetorical tradition of NDP. However, the voters' repudiation of Douglas and other NDP candidates, some of them long-time CCF stalwarts, came as a shock to party members. It raised questions about whether Tommy Douglas had truly succeeded in changing the political culture of Saskatchewan. The wheels were now off the Douglas machine; the party was shut out again in Saskatchewan in the federal elections of 1963 and 1965, and at the provincial level Ross Thatcher and the Liberals defeated the CCF in 1964 and again, by a larger margin, in 1967.

In discussing the CCF's loss of provincial power, Douglas blamed tactical mistakes such as the handling of medicare and the decision to hold the 1964 election in March rather than June. The Toronto *Star* took a wider view:

> [The CCF] faced an accumulation of enemies: business, medicine, insurance. It faced a united political opposition, and a population less interested than formerly in the extension of the welfare system and state intervention.[122]

The Thatcher Liberals won on the slogan, "Time for a Change"; they had younger candidates and attracted a younger following than the CCF. The 1944-vintage Saskatchewan CCF leadership group had accomplished much, but its day was over. The social democrats would return to full strength only in the late 1960s with the rise of new stars such as Blakeney and Romanow, and new federal candidates such as the young Lorne Nystrom.

The 1962 federal loss in Regina set Douglas adrift, but only briefly. Just days after the general election, Burnaby-Coquitlam MP Ernie Regier informed Douglas that he would resign and force a by-election. The party executive in the suburban Vancouver riding then agreed, unanimously, to support the candidacy of the federal leader. Regier had built a strong base over a decade in the Commons, and in an October by-election Douglas took more than 50% of the vote against four other candidates.

As federal leader, Douglas found himself heading a fragmented, undisciplined caucus. In the Premier's office he had exercised the power to hire and fire, but as the leader of a small parliamentary group he had few levers to manipulate. For the first time in many years he was subject to contradiction—especially from federal NDP powerhouse David Lewis, elected from York South in 1962, and from a clutch of free-thinking MPs including Arnold Peters and Douglas Fisher. Peters would cordially invite Douglas to take a hike if he disagreed with the leader's instructions. Fisher, a journalist, nagged at Douglas to improve his television skills and image.

Already, there were fears in the federal NDP backrooms that the party had chosen the wrong man. Douglas reminded some viewers of Harry Truman, an American president from previous decades; his glasses sparkled in front of the cameras. His command of French was nonexistent, and he appeared like a relic from a former era:

> In the short bits, in the scrums and that, he was very poor. And the other thing was—and Lewis used to talk about this—there was a realization that Douglas was archaic, that his appeal was archaic... The vocabulary was of the 1930s.[123]

Politically, the 1960s might be viewed as a training period for the federal NDP. The repeated breakdown of minority governments forced frequent elections, and the party gained experience in fundraising and organizing, and in polling and advertising. The vote base crept up from 13% to over 17%. Provincial New Democratic parties flourished in Ontario and British Columbia and took power in Manitoba. However, the hoped-for breakthrough to serious status in the Commons never came. Every local victory in one part of Canada was offset by a loss somewhere else.

Early in 1968, David Lewis's son Stephen flew from Toronto to Ottawa and urged Douglas to step down. Among Douglas loyalists, this day would live in infamy, another example of the Lewises manipulating the party. Stephen Lewis said later that he acted on behalf of the NDP's Ontario legislative caucus.[124] Douglas, according to an aide, was "silent and somewhat wounded"[125] after meeting with the younger Lewis.

A few months later, the NDP took a fourth election drubbing, with the Liberals, propelled by "Trudeaumania," taking seats in British Columbia and Ontario to offset modest NDP gains on the prairies. Tommy Douglas was one of the losers; his vote share held at a healthy 45% in the new Burnaby-Seymour seat, but the collapse of the Social Credit vote allowed Liberal Ray Perrault to squeak in. Douglas flew to Ottawa and met with the federal party executive, and then announced a decision that he had actually made some weeks before, not long after meeting with Stephen Lewis. He would step down as NDP leader at a convention to be held in 1969.

Once again, however, Douglas was offered a second chance to return to Parliament, with the death of Vancouver Island MP Colin Cameron just weeks after the election. The Prime Minister set the Nanaimo by-election for February 1969. The New Democrats ran an intense campaign, with MPs and labour leaders flying in from across the country to knock on doors for Douglas. The Vancouver *Sun* had attacked the NDP leader as a "carpetbagger" for contesting the seat; when he won, with 57% of the vote, the same paper praised Douglas as "the leading debater of the Commons ... his great experience in politics, to say nothing of his practical outlook, is too valuable to be lost."[126] Douglas took his seat in the Commons; but with David Lewis already installed as parliamentary leader, Douglas did not assume control of the caucus agenda. It was agreed that the official change of leadership would now wait until the 1971 federal party convention, but the transition had begun.

For partisan purposes, New Democrats have often written that the parliamentary caucuses led by Douglas had a profound influence on the direction of the federal government.[127] The party's founding convention in 1961 called for (among other measures) national medicare, a Canada Pension Plan, consumer protection legislation and regional economic development investment. All of these were implemented by the Pearson Liberals and elaborated by the Trudeau Liberals. Not unremarkably, the NDP version of events is that the Liberals, remembering Mackenzie King's move leftward in 1943 to block the CCF, continued to steal popular NDP ideas in order to maintain power.

In Liberal accounts—notably in the memoirs of Liberal ministers—the federal NDP barely rated a mention for its work under Douglas or David Lewis. The Commons debates and newspaper reporting surrounding Liberal initiatives offer little evidence that the NDP influenced individual bills. Trudeau, commenting in the mid-1970s, compared New Democrat MPs to a flock of seagulls flying above the prow of a boat: "Because they were squawking and making a lot of noise, they thought they were actually running the ship."[128]

The record suggests that Douglas's position in Parliament remained weak because of the size of his caucus and because the NDP was reluctant to defeat governments and force costly elections. The single recorded strategy meeting between Douglas and the Liberals—a secret meeting held at the home of Finance Minister Walter Gordon in 1963—did not produce concrete results or follow-up because the NDP had no bargaining power. "We are not a major political party, and we must recognize this fact," Douglas wrote to Woodrow Lloyd.[129] He suggested that the NDP would not become "an effective political force" until such time as it won many more seats, and this time never came.

The NDP's long-term influence on public opinion is more difficult to measure. It could be argued that the federal NDP of the 1960s had its main impact outside of Parliament—in lending mainstream, adult respectability to social causes that might otherwise have been seen as juvenile and ultra-radical. Douglas was a prominent voice in the opposition to the American war in Vietnam, and also in the movement to build a more distinctive Canadian nationalism. Partly because of his personal prestige and his ability to work with other eminent Canadians, support for independent foreign and economic policies stretched across partisan lines, and created space for the federal government to act independently from the United States—for example, in the diplomatic recognition of Red China and in the regulation of foreign investment.

Through its critique of the American empire, the NDP under Douglas also attracted thousands of radical young people into its ranks. This development created tensions within the party for a few years, but its more significant long-term effect was to draw new vigour and brainpower into the NDP.

The party's appeal to radical youth was reinforced by Douglas's stand for civil liberties and against the implementation of the War Measures Act in 1970. When a British diplomat and then a Quebec provincial cabinet minister were kidnapped by members of the FLQ, the mayor of Montreal and some police warned that a revolutionary uprising was imminent. Prime Minister Trudeau responded by asking Parliament to dust off the wartime law that would allow police anywhere in Canada to search without warrant, seize property without cause and hold prisoners for 90 days without laying charges. Douglas told his NDP colleagues that they could vote as they pleased, but he would oppose Trudeau's motion. He said in Parliament that the government had no evidence of an uprising. It was "using a sledgehammer to crack a peanut."[130]

With the national mood verging on panic, Douglas and 14 other New Democrats voted against the government, and were rewarded with a torrent of criticism and abuse from the media and the public. In the ensuing weeks, the party's standing in the polls slid from 20% to 13%. Once again, Douglas's short-term degree of influence on events is debatable. However, the episode showed the NDP to be, as nothing else had done in the Douglas period, a party of principle. Besides, Douglas felt he had no choice; it was the first responsibility of the legislator, he said later, to safeguard the citizen against "the arbitrary power of the state."[131]

Elder Statesman

David Lewis had been brutally efficient in crushing any opposition to the Tommy Douglas NDP leadership bid in 1961. When it was Lewis's turn to take the leader's job, Douglas did not return the favour. Instead, he remained publicly neutral in a fractious contest between Lewis supporters and the party's radical left, many of whom had joined an organized faction called the "Waffle." Some of Douglas's young assistants campaigned openly for 26-year old Waffle leadership candidate James Laxer, who in the end took a remarkable 40% of the vote at the 1971 NDP convention.

The Waffle had appeared as a national force at the NDP's policy convention in 1969. Its manifesto, "Towards an Independent Socialist Canada," called for widespread public ownership, the withdrawal from political and economic alliances with the United States, and "the development of socialist consciousness within Canada." The Waffle's rhetoric and tactics created divisions across the party. In Saskatchewan, a fierce debate over how the party should respond triggered the resignation of provincial leader Woodrow Lloyd in March 1970. For his part, Douglas saw the Waffle's leaders, Laxer and Mel Watkins, as literate and credible. He criticized the radicals' love affair with state ownership, but a few

SOURCE: ROY AND ELEANORE ROMANOW

The elder statesman. Douglas addressing an NDP convention. Note Roy Romanow, one of Douglas's successors as Premier of Saskatchewan, seated to the left.

weeks before the 1971 convention he could still write that "the Waffle group is making a useful contribution ... provided they do not try to form a party within a party."[132]

Douglas's farewell speech as leader looked to the past and the future. He told NDP delegates that they had played a role in securing national medicare, the Canada Pension Plan, housing programs, regional investment incentives, and a new Department of the Environment. Looking forward, he predicted—incorrectly—that Canada was moving towards a fundamental shift in its economic structure:

> I look forward to the day when farmers and fishermen will own and control the processing plants that handle their commodities. I see producers and consumers as playing a vital role in a socialist society...[133]

While the leadership vote was uncomfortably close for David Lewis, his supporters were sufficiently disciplined to reject the Waffle's resolutions and shut out the radical faction from party committees. Over the next several months Waffle members became even more strident and critical of the NDP in the media, until confrontations in Saskatchewan and Ontario led to the banning of the term "Waffle" within the party. Douglas did not mourn this turn of events, but he remained interested in the development of new policy directions. Soon after retiring as leader, he became the chair of the Douglas-Coldwell Foundation, a forum for promoting discussion that would be free from threats of purges and ultimatums.

For the last eight years of his parliamentary career, Douglas served as the NDP critic on energy matters. This assignment fit well with his background in Saskatchewan as well as his interest in continental and international affairs. It has been claimed that Douglas played a major part in the creation of Petro-Canada; if this is so, it would rank as perhaps his most significant achievement as a federal legislator.

From 1972 to 1974, the NDP held the balance of power in the Commons. The rise of OPEC (Organization of Petroleum Exporting Countries) and the ballooning of oil prices had scared consumers in the industrial world. On October 25, 1973, Douglas moved a resolution in the Commons demanding "a publicly owned National Petroleum Corporation." Through channels, the NDP threatened to force an election unless the Trudeau government introduced measures to guarantee Canadian energy supplies.

Lewis, the party leader, was on a pre-election tour when Prime Minister Trudeau called Douglas to discuss the energy situation on December 5, 1973. The next day, the Prime Minister announced a plan to create a state-owned oil company to lead the way in Canada energy development. The government would also impose a ceiling on the price of oil produced and sold in Canada, and would make domestic oil available to Quebec by constructing a new pipeline. When Trudeau was speaking, Douglas said to his colleague Bill Knight, the MP for Assiniboia, "Well, how do you like that? He hardly missed a word."[134] NDP MP Terry Grier later said, "It was the cleanest and most complete capitulation to any of our demands."[135] Liberal Energy minister Donald Macdonald, on the other hand, discounted NDP influence and said the government was simply responding to public opinion.[136]

The federal decision to cap domestic oil prices, as proposed and supported by the federal NDP, did not play well in Alberta or Saskatchewan. Saskatchewan NDP Premier

Allan Blakeney confronted Douglas and Lewis at a meeting in Ottawa, stating that oil was a provincially owned resource and should not be subject to federal price controls. Lewis responded that it would be politically indefensible for the federal NDP to side with the multinational oil companies against the public, and he argued that cheap oil would provide a competitive edge for Canadian industry.[137] After more than a year of further discussion, Douglas and Blakeney agreed on the outline for a "Canadian resources security fund," where the revenue increases attributable to oil price increases would be channelled into a federal-provincial effort to find new energy reserves. Douglas put this idea to the Commons,[138] but it was never implemented in any form. Douglas also admitted, unlike most of his federal colleagues, that if a western commodity such as oil was to be subject to long-term price controls, so should other commodities and essential goods.

Over time, the Liberal government's implementation of the 1973 promises on energy fell short of NDP expectations. Petro-Canada was up and running by 1976, but the largest energy investment opportunity, in the Alberta oil sands, was left mostly to the private sector. Douglas spent much of the rest of his career explaining the dangers of multinational control of Canada's energy sector. Perhaps his last passionate cause in Parliament was to warn that if Canadians elected a Conservative government, Petro-Canada would be privatized. He felt this would rob Canadians of a national symbol and a chance for taxpayers to capture a significant rent from energy production.

Douglas retired from the Commons in 1979, at the age of 75, having served in eight Parliaments and five Legislatures. He moved to an office a few blocks from Parliament Hill, in an old house that was the federal headquarters of the NDP. He was joined there by Eleanor McKinnon, the secretary who had worked with him since 1944. He continued to chair the Douglas-Coldwell Foundation, leading a delegation to China in 1979. He was also available for speeches and interviews, and answered hundreds of letters each year from supporters and researchers. Soon after his retirement, he joined the board of directors of Calgary-based Husky Oil, a subsidiary of the Nova corporation, and became an adviser to Nova chair Robert Blair. Blair was a Scotsman and a cosmopolitan liberal, and he welcomed a diversity of views in his boardroom. He was also one of the few senior oil-patch executives who accepted federal Liberal measures to regulate oil prices and promote Canadian ownership in the industry.

Douglas was still influential in the federal NDP. In 1981 he attended the party convention, and along with Stanley Knowles spoke in favour of leader Ed Broadbent's stand on the Constitution; Broadbent was supporting Trudeau's efforts to forge a made-in-Canada Constitution. Saskatchewan Premier Allan Blakeney and many Saskatchewan delegates were opposed, at least in part because of fears that the Charter of Rights would increase the powers of the courts at the expense of the Legislatures. Some of those delegates felt that Douglas should have stayed above the fray; Yorkton-Melville MP Lorne Nystrom, for example, felt it was unfair of Broadbent to "drag" the old leaders into the debate.[139]

Douglas's great 1983 convention speech was a different story, drawing all factions in the party together. He had been informed in mid-1981 that he had an incurable cancer, and he knew that he might not have long to live. He used his time at the podium to suggest that history was instructive, but only as a key to the future. The greatest work remained yet to be done, the building of a productive, caring and peaceful world:

> In a movement like ours, as socialist movements around the world have demonstrated, we're not just interested in getting votes… We are seeking to get people who are willing to dedicate their lives to building a different kind of society … a society founded on the principles of concern for human well being and human welfare.[140]

The 1983 speech had an extraordinary effect on those who heard it, perhaps because Douglas's visionary words came at a time when the party had slipped to an all-time low in the polls. It confirmed Douglas's status as an icon, a figure whose sheer presence could fill New Democrats with pride in their history as well as a renewed belief that victory was just over the horizon. Even up to the present day, party leaders and presumptive leaders have continued to recall this speech and lay claim to the Douglas mantle—and, implicitly, his ability to ward off darkness and defeatism.

Douglas continued to draw great satisfaction from the companionship of his wife Irma, the love of his two daughters and their families and constant contact with friends and supporters. He remained active and alert almost to the day he died, on February 24, 1986. Canadians gathered in churches and assembly halls across the country to mark his passing. He was buried in Ottawa.

Conclusion

With each year that has gone by since Douglas's death, the public's level of trust in elected officials has declined as measured by opinion research. Canadians are losing interest in political parties, and even in voting. The problem, some say, is a lack of leadership, or a lack of credible leaders.

It is interesting, then, to consider the leadership qualities that Tommy Douglas brought to public life. What allowed him to form five successive majority governments in Saskatchewan? And later, what brought thousands of New Democrats out to arenas across Canada to show support for a leader who had no chance of winning?

Douglas understood the need for party organization, but he was not a great organizer or political strategist. His strength lay in his driving curiosity and his openness to new trends and challenges. And having decided what he wanted to communicate, Douglas took care to explain it in plain English and give it a personal touch.

It is difficult in a short historical account to show how Douglas used humour and anecdote to draw people to his side, in his office or at mass meetings. He expressed impeccable civility toward opponents of the day, and gracious loyalty to his supporters; he clearly viewed life as an adventure rather than a battle among interests; he spoke without pretense. These personal qualities, as they shone through from moment to moment, permitted Tommy Douglas to survive in politics against the odds and to make a significant contribution to social and economic development in Canada.

Notes

All Interviews were conducted with Ian McLeod unless otherwise noted.

1. Christopher Harvie, *No Gods and Precious Few Heroes* (Toronto: University of Toronto Press), 1981.
2. Arthur Conner, "James Keir Hardie's Life Story," pamphlet, 1917, Woodsworth collection, Thomas Fisher Library, University of Toronto.
3. T.C. Douglas interview, April 26, 1985.
4. Ibid.
5. National Archives of Canada (NA), T.C. Douglas papers, vol. 148, speech notes, March 24, 1976.
6. T.C. Douglas interview, April 23, 1984.
7. Isobel (Douglas) Crawford interview, February 8, 1976.
8. Mark Talney, taped memoir provided to the authors, 1986.
9. United Church Archives, Toronto, Methodist Acts and Proceedings, 1919.
10. Lewis H. Thomas (ed.), *The Making of a Socialist: The Recollections of T.C. Douglas* (Edmonton: University of Alberta Press), 1982.
11. William Irvine, *The Farmers in Politics* (Toronto: McClelland and Stewart, 1976), 147–48.
12. T.C. Douglas interview, April 26, 1985.
13. NA, T.C. Douglas papers, vol. 146, sermon notes, November 8, 1964.
14. See the Baptist Archives, McMaster University, Brandon College Commission files.
15. T.C. Douglas interview, April 24, 1985.
16. Edgar Bailey interview, July 24, 1985.
17. This section is drawn from the Provincial Archives of Manitoba, Carberry *News-Express*, various dates, 1927 and 1928; and also from conversations between T.H. McLeod and the late Mac Rogers, formerly of Carberry.
18. T.C. Douglas Calvary Centre, Weyburn, Minute Book, 1928–1933.
19. Junior Staveley interview, June 24, 1985.
20. T.C. Douglas interview, April 24, 1985.
21. Kenneth Falconer, "Tommy Douglas, 1930–44" (MA thesis, University of Regina, n.d.), 124–25.
22. Saskatchewan Archives Board (SAB), Weyburn *Review*, September 24, 1931; also Fred Steininger, "George H. Williams" (MA thesis, University of Regina, n.d.), 140–43.
23. In Saskatchewan, the farmers' organization was known as the United Farmers of Canada, Saskatchewan Section, although there were no other sections. Alberta had the United Farmers of Alberta, Ontario the United Farmers of Ontario, etc.
24. Steininger, "George H. Williams," 47.
25. Regina *Leader-Post*, September 24, 1931.
26. Weyburn *Review*, September 24, 1931
27. T.D. Douglas interview, April 24, 1985.
28. T.C. Douglas interview, May 14, 1985.
29. Weyburn *Review*, February 11, 1932.
30. T.D. Douglas interview, January 29, 1985.
31. NA, sound recordings, T.C. Douglas interview with Peter Stursberg, December 4, 1972.
32. The "Regina Manifesto" has been widely reprinted, for example in Kenneth McNaught, *A Prophet In Politics* (Toronto: University of Toronto Press, 1959), Appendix.

33. Weyburn *Review*, July 27, 1933.
34. T.C. Douglas interview, May 14, 1985.
35. Weyburn *Review*, May 31, 1934.
36. Ibid., June 14, 1934.
37. Ibid., November 9, 1933.
38. Ibid., June 7, 1934.
39. T.C. Douglas Calvary Centre, Weyburn, 1935 CCF campaign blotting paper.
40. SAB, Saskatoon, CCF papers, vol. II-23; also *Leader-Post*, September 5, 1935.
41. *Leader-Post*, October 1, 1935.
42. SAB, Saskatoon, CCF papers, vol. II-23, transcript of special CCF executive meeting of October 9, 1935; also *Leader-Post*, October 10, 1935.
43. Weyburn *Review*, October 3, 1935; also SAB, Saskatoon, T.D. Douglas interview with A.M. Nicholson, February 11, 1975, transcript.
44. *Social Credit Chronicle*, Edmonton, October 18, 1935.
45. SAB, Saskatoon, CCF papers, vol II-23, minutes of the executive, October 21, 1935; also Steininger, "George H. Williams," George Williams letter to Mrs. V. Kavaner.
46. Canada, House of Commons, *Debates*, November 14, 1941, p. 4434.
47. Ibid., July 25, 1940, p. 1947.
48. Ibid., February 19, 1937, p. 1059.
49. Ibid., January 24, 1939, p. 270.
50. NA, CCF papers, vol. 3, National Council minutes, September 6–7, 1939.
51. T.C. Douglas interview, November 19, 1984.
52. *Maclean's*, August 1, 1944.
53. T.C. Douglas interview, May 23, 1985.
54. SAB, Saskatoon, CCF papers, vol II-97, T.C. Douglas letter to George Williams, May 16, 1938.
55. Ibid., Carlyle King papers, vol. 20, letter to "E.B.," December 2, 1939.
56. Ibid., Carlyle King papers, vol. 150, George Williams letter to King, October 21, 1939.
57. Ibid., George Williams papers, vol. 7, text of an undelivered speech, December 26, 1940. Williams left instructions that this document, a review of his grievances against Coldwell and others, was to be read at the 1941 convention in the event of his absence, but the speech was left on the shelf.
58. *Leader-Post*, July 25, 1940.
59. SAB, George Williams papers, vol. 5, letter to CCF provincial council, March 6, 1941.
60. Ibid., minutes of the CCF provincial council, May 31, 1941.
61. *Commonwealth*, August 13, 1941; SAB, Saskatoon, CCF papers, I-2, council minutes, January 9, 1942.
62. T.C. Douglas interview, October 30, 1985.
63. NA, F.R. Scott papers, vol. 12, F.R. Scott to T.C. Douglas, January 6, 1943.
64. SAB, Saskatoon, CCF papers, transcript of a radio broadcast of May 9, 1944.
65. *Leader-Post*, June 12, 1944.
66. SAB, Regina, T.C. Douglas Premier's papers, file 815; letter to William Patterson, September 18, 1944, and reply from Patterson, October 3, 1944.
67. Clarence Fines interview, February 12, 1986.
68. SAB, Saskatoon, CCF papers, vol. VI-5, radio broadcast transcript, July 12, 1944.
69. SAB, Regina, T.C. Douglas Premier's papers, file 395, T.H. McLeod memo n.d. [1944].

70. Ibid., T.C. Douglas Premier's papers, file 400, unsigned memo, n.d. [1945].
71. Ibid., T.C. Douglas letter to Lambert Wiggins, January 22, 1946.
72. T.C. Douglas interview, October 24, 1984.
73. T.C. Douglas, Provincial Affairs broadcast, October 22, 1958.
74. SAB, Saskatoon, CCF papers, vol. VI-5, radio address transcript, September 13, 1944.
75. SAB, Regina, 33.1 XXVII, T.C. Douglas correspondence with M.J. Coldwell, autumn 1945.
76. *Commonwealth*, February 10, 1943, transcript of a January 26 radio broadcast by T.C. Douglas.
77. SAB, Regina, T.C. Douglas Premier's papers, file 19, press release, January 19, 1953.
78. Paul Martin, *A Very Public Life*, vol. 2 (Ottawa: Deneau, 1983), 20.
79. SAB, Regina, T.C. Douglas Premier's papers, file 19, letter to Alvin Hamilton, July 6, 1950.
80. National Library of Canada, Al Johnson, "Biography of a Government" (PhD dissertation, Harvard University, n.d.), 357.
81. NA, T.C. Douglas papers, vol. 142, T.C. Douglas speech, Saskatchewan Throne Speech debate, 1952.
82. SAB, Regina, T.C. Douglas Premier's papers, file 672, letter to David Lewis, August 18, 1944.
83. Ibid., file 318, letter to Aaron Mosher, December 21, 1948.
84. Walter Smishek interview, November 29, 1985.
85. Saskatchewan Legislature, *Debates and Proceedings*, 1961 Special Session, Volume 11, p. 96.
86. SAB, Saskatoon, Carlyle King papers, Saskatchewan CCF Executive, 1943 statement, n.d.
87. SAB, tape recording of a June 15, 1980, interview of T.C. Douglas by A.M Nicholson.
88. T.C. Douglas interview, October 19, 1985.
89. Canada, House of Commons, *Debates*, March 22, 1943, p. 1441.
90. SAB, Regina, Clarence Fines papers, T.C. Douglas clippings file, unidentified clipping [*Leader-Post?*], April 27, 1951.
91. Ibid., T.C. Douglas ministerial papers, file 30, letter to Bob von Pilis, April 23, 1958.
92. Ibid., T.C. Douglas executive assistant papers, file 72, report to Planning Board, November 22, 1949.
93. *Leader-Post*, July 14, 1947.
94. Ibid., April 3, 1948.
95. *Star Phoenix*, October 28, 1948.
96. Ibid., February 29, 1952; see also SAB, Regina, Clarence Fines papers, "Theatre Under the Stars" file.
97. SAB, Regina, T.C. Douglas Premier's papers, file 848, report of the Standing Committee on Crown Corporations, April 1953.
98. Saskatchewan Legislature, *Debates and Proceedings*, April 13, 1953.
99. Vancouver *Sun*, May 1960, series on Saskatchewan by Jack Scott.
100. SAB, Regina, Homer Lane papers, T.C. Douglas to Homer Lane, June 14, 1960.
101. Saskatchewan *Commonwealth*, December 23, 1959.
102. W.G. Davies interview, November 3, 1986.
103. SAB, Regina, T.C. Douglas Premier's papers, file 574, television debate with Dr. E.W. Barootes, transcript, March 1960.
104. Robin Badgeley and Samuel Wolfe, *Doctors' Strike: Medical Care and Conflict in Saskatchewan* (Toronto: Macmillan, 1967), 31–33.
105. Ken MacTaggart, *The First Decade* (Ottawa: Canadian Medical Association, 1973), 83.
106. Robert Walker interview, January 16, 1985.
107. Saskatchewan Legislature, *Debates and Proceedings*, October 13, 1961, p. 19.

108. The CLC was created through a merger of the craft union central (Trades and Labour Congress) and the industrial union central (Canadian Congress of Labour) in 1956.
109. NA, T.C. Douglas papers, volume 1, CLC news release, April 1958.
110. Ibid., volume 1, Woodrow Lloyd to M.J. Coldwell, November 19, 1959.
111. Ibid., T.C. Douglas to Carl Hamilton, August 26, 1959.
112. Ibid., T.C. Douglas letters to Knowles, April 3, 1961, and Lewis, October 7, 1959.
113. Ibid., T.C. Douglas to Hazen Argue, February 24, 1960.
114. Saskatchewan Legislature, *Debates and Proceedings*, March 9, 1960.
115. Stephen Lewis interview, September 9, 1985.
116. NA, T.C. Douglas papers, volume 1, T.C. Douglas to Andrew Brewin, November 9, 1960.
117. SAB, Regina, John Brockelbank papers, vol. IX-21, T.C. Douglas to John Brockelbank, April 2, 1961.
118. *Leader-Post*, December 10, 1961.
119. *Globe and Mail*, February 19, 1962.
120. Clifford Scotton interview, September 12, 1985.
121. NA, T.C. Douglas interview with Peter Stursberg, September 3, 1976, audio tape.
122. Toronto *Star*, editorial, April 23, 1964.
123. Douglas Fisher interview, February 26, 1985.
124. Stephen Lewis interview, September 9, 1985.
125. Jim Hayes interview, September 5, 1985.
126. University of British Columbia, Special Collections, NDP papers, vol. 20-9, Vancouver *Sun* editorial, clipping, no date [c. September 1968]; Vancouver *Sun*, editorial, February 11, 1969.
127. For example, former MP Lynn Macdonald's book, *The Party that Changed Canada: The New Democratic Party, Then and Now* (Toronto: Macmillan, 1987), is devoted to this view.
128. Canada, House of Commons, *Debates*, February 24, 1974.
129. NA, T.C. Douglas papers, vol. 130, T.C. Douglas to Woodrow Lloyd, April 12, 1963.
130. Canada, House of Commons, *Debates*, October 16, 1970, pp. 193–199.
131. NA, T.C. Douglas papers, vol. 150, T.C. Douglas speech to international parliamentarians, September 21, 1977.
132. Ibid., vol. 110, T.C. Douglas letter to Paul MacEwen, April 6, 1971.
133. Ibid., vol. 148, T.C. Douglas convention speech, April 21, 1971.
134. Bill Knight interview, June 5, 1985.
135. Terry Grier interview, July 25, 1985.
136. Donald S. Macdonald interview, February 24, 1987.
137. Allan Blakeney interview, September 18, 1985.
138. Canada, House of Commons, *Debates*, April 24, 1975, p. 5192.
139. Lorne Nystrom interview, September 10, 1985.
140. T.C. Douglas private effects, speech to federal NDP convention, July 2, 1983, tape recording.

Woodrow S. Lloyd

Dianne Llyod Norton

Lloyd, formal portrait, 1961
(M. West, Regina. West's Studio Collection. SAB R-WS 61.6272).

Lloyd and Douglas at the first NDP Convention, 1961
(SAB RB 12,052).

Woodrow Lloyd Memorial (David McLennan).

Saskatchewan Premiers of the 20th Century

Woodrow S. Lloyd, 1961–1964

A Saskatchewan Son

Born on the Canadian prairies on July 16, 1913, Woodrow Stanley Lloyd was a product of the pressures of this unique environment, and in particular of the Depression. The harshness of those early years moulded him, leaving him strengthened and determined to face the vicissitudes of life.

Of predominantly Welsh stock, his grandparents had settled first in Wisconsin, where Lloyd's father was born, and the family later emigrated and homesteaded near Antelope, Saskatchewan. Woodrow was the youngest in a family of 12 and the only one born in Canada. The family's first winter on the prairies was especially trying. There was as yet no school for the children and tedium and tension occasionally shattered the family harmony. By spring, Lloyd's father, Allen, stirred up interest in building a local school. Because of his leadership and the fact that he had the most children, the community was unanimous in naming it "Lloyd School."

Lloyd thoroughly enjoyed his early schooldays. By the end of his first year, he had worked his way through two grades, and he was to complete the elementary curriculum in five years instead of the normal eight. A fundamental part of Lloyd's early education came from his family. Especially important was his brother Lewie, 15 years his senior and passionately interested in politics. Woodrow later maintained that it was Lewie who made him a socialist and encouraged him to enter politics.

A precocious child, just after his eleventh birthday Woodrow left the protective family nest to board some 15 miles away in Webb, where he attended the high school. This early launch into independence—away from his family and considerably younger than his classmates—may go some way to explaining the solitary nature of the mature man.

Within two years, he had completed the available curriculum and made another move, this time to Regina, to complete his high school studies. At Scott Collegiate he was stimulated by a wider range of subjects than he had tackled so far. Ironically, the only class in which he fared badly was agriculture, while he completed the four-year Latin course in just one year.

In September 1929, at just 16 years of age, Lloyd enrolled at the University of Saskatchewan School of Engineering. He had shown an aptitude for mechanics around the farm so this seemed a logical choice. By the time the first year exam results showing Lloyd at the top of the class were published, he was back on the land. Still a farmer's son, there was a crop to plant. The crops were sown but so too were the seeds of depression, hunger and destitution. As the top soil blew away and the earth that remained grew hard and cracked, the family realized that there would be little enough cash for essentials let alone for university. Lloyd's academic career, like that of many other farm youngsters, was temporarily at an end. The frustration of becoming a full-time farmer was great but he knew that, for the time being, there was no alternative. That year the government was paying

$5 a month to any farmer who would employ a hired hand. Woodrow worked for his brother-in-law and the $5 became his total earnings.

The articulate teenager, having tasted the fruits of learning, was now forced to spend days collecting cow dung from the dry fields in order to have something to burn for warmth, or to struggle with stacks of green Russian thistle for cattle feed because grass and hay just could not grow. Agitation and dissension increased at almost every level. As he commented years later,

> I became very acutely aware of some of the deficiencies and denials of society. I saw at that time what was happening to my own parents and people I knew who had worked very hard and effectively all their lives and everything seemed to be destroyed for them at that moment.

Lloyd's first aim was to find some way to continue his education. He decided to train as a teacher and earn enough by teaching to finance his return to university. Despite personal appeals to a government minister and to Premier J.T.M. Anderson, it seemed there was no money available to help get an education. However, in due course, a neighbour came forward, willing to lend Woodrow's father $100, and a sympathetic clothing merchant in Webb said he would trust Woodrow with a new suit on credit. Such was his capital when, in September 1931, Lloyd set out for Moose Jaw and a career in education.

The following summer, as soon as he graduated, Lloyd was invited to take over a one-room school at Swan Lake, which the departing teacher described as having a "discipline problem." Lloyd believed that people must participate in their own destinies, and he allowed his students to make far more decisions about their activities than they were accustomed to doing. Lloyd soon found that his unruly class respected and trusted him and he was able to make great progress with the business of teaching.

The summer of 1932 was a time of intense political germination. The League for Social Reconstruction, a group of intellectuals, was developing the philosophical foundation that would pave the way for the establishment of the Co-operative Commonwealth Federation (CCF). Lloyd was among the young people who gathered in nearby Swift Current watering holes—a café that became known as "Red Square" because of the discussions that went on there, and Laycock's Drug Store, which also housed a lending library. J.G. (Bert) Laycock, an inveterate campaigner for the socialist cause, was so impressed with Lloyd that he invited him to come along on a speaking tour of southwestern Saskatchewan. To begin with, Lloyd's contribution was the demonstration of a chart produced by his brother Lewie, showing the farmer and the labourer pouring out their produce and manpower and receiving a mere dribble in return. Soon, however, Laycock, who was an apt teacher, began encouraging Lloyd to speak.

Early Political Involvement

During the school year Woodrow found satisfaction in reading and writing on political matters. Lewie kept up a lively correspondence with him in which they developed their economic and social theories. Lewie would send Woodrow clippings, with his own comments, from various progressive papers. Woodrow would then consider them, compose an article on the subject, and return it to his brother. Copies of Woodrow's articles were typed up by a friend, distributed to a small, interested group and a report of the ensuing discussion would be sent back to Woodrow.

In April 1933, Lloyd attended a meeting at which the speaker was M.J. Coldwell, leader of Farmer Labour Party and president of the Canadian Teachers' Federation, who was busily organizing for the infant CCF. Coldwell represented all the concerns with which Lloyd identified. In nature the two men were much alike. Although it would be a decade before they got to know each other, this meeting helped the younger man to see more clearly which way his future lay.

That same year, at the first CCF annual conference, the "Regina Manifesto" was enthusiastically adopted. Over the years, it would come to mean different things to different people. To some it soon became obsolete. Their analysis of the changing face of the Canadian economic structure led them to believe that the "Manifesto" had little real practical value. For others, the "Manifesto" seemed a hindrance in their attempts to appeal to a wide enough section of voters to win elections. The radical statements of the "Manifesto" were quickly diluted and the CCF's call for immediate improvements to the country's welfare programs was emphasized. There were also those for whom democratic socialism was more than just an antidote to the Depression. To them the "Manifesto" was a guide to the formation of the most just society possible. The deviation by the party from this statement of faith was painful to such people. J.S. Woodsworth, the CCF's national leader, and Woodrow Lloyd, firmly believed that the "Manifesto" should have been an enduring and constant reminder of the CCF's basic objectives, not something to be lightly cast aside because of changing circumstances and a need for electoral victories. Years later, Lloyd told a group of students about those early years of the party:

> It was strongly egalitarian in nature. It based its structure on a principle that there ought to be maximum participation by people. ... those who came together would be responsible for outlining and changing the policies and criticizing the movement by giving direction to the leaders. I can't stress too much this idea of participation, that people themselves ought to have the right to assume the responsibility to develop the disciplines that become the laws under which we live.

In June 1934, a provincial election was called. This would be the first opportunity for the CCF to test its strength at the polls. Party members in the Swift Current constituency thought they had an ideal candidate. Lloyd was young, energetic and was increasingly well known as a public speaker. He agreed to let his name stand until it was discovered that, as the election fell before his 21st birthday, he was neither eligible to vote nor to be a candidate. Allan McCallum, later to be Lloyd's deputy minister of Education, stood for the CCF but was defeated by 192 votes. The Liberals won the election, but five CCF or Farmer Labour members took their seats for the first time, and formed the official opposition.

Besides his party activities, Lloyd was becoming more involved with the teacher's "local" and it was there that he met his future wife, Victoria Leinan. Victoria co-founded the local teachers' association when she taught at Leonard School—some eight miles from

Lloyd's base at Swan Lake. The fact that Vicki possessed a car greatly simplified the progress of their romance and also gave them easier access, at least in the summer, to political meetings and social events.

Woodrow and Vicki married in July 1936 and settled in Vanguard, where Lloyd had just been appointed principal of the four-room school. The pattern of Lloyd's life changed in several ways after his marriage. For the first time, he had a home of his own after years of boarding, and at long last he was in a position to further his education. When the wedding party was over, the couple motored off towards a honeymoon in Saskatoon, where Woodrow had enrolled in Dr. Spinks' summer school course in chemistry. Every summer for the next four years he completed another course towards his BA and every winter he found the time, despite a heavy work load and his political commitments, to study another subject by correspondence. Finally, in 1940, he was awarded his Bachelor of Arts. The following year he received a permanent certificate for teaching high school.

A Vision for Education

For Lloyd it was impossible to think about education without being political. The teachers of Saskatchewan were one group that had been unified by the adversity of the Dirty Thirties. When the Saskatchewan Teachers Federation (STF) was formed in 1933, Lloyd got involved and by the following year, he was a councillor representing the Swift Current area. The education system, as it was then organized, was open to abuse. Schools and teachers were ruled by autonomous school boards composed of trustees, not always elected on the basis of their knowledge. Salaries went unpaid and personal prejudices were allowed to interfere with the selection and treatment of teachers.

The question of Larger School Units (LSUs) was hotly debated during this time, not least by Lloyd and was to become a vital issue in his career. He believed that the one- or two-room school—on its own and in the confines of a small community—was wasteful of both physical and human resources.[1]

First elected to the presidency of the STF in 1940, Lloyd held the position for the following four years. Each year, he became more frustrated by the lack of support from the Department of Education. He felt that the government had a "moral responsibility to promote the general welfare of all the people." In his mind, nothing could do this better than a sound and progressive school system. The question of the inequalities in the education of children in different parts of Canada concerned him deeply. "Money to obtain adequate education must be obtained where the wealth exists and spent where the need obtains," he said in a radio broadcast in 1942. If provincial governments could not make adequate financial provision for their schools, then there must be assistance from the federal government. Equality of opportunity must never be denied to any child, he maintained.

The shortage of teachers was another vexing issue. So many had left the profession in despair during the 1930s that some schools remained closed. The government tried to fill these vacancies with Normal School students with only a few weeks training. This policy was contrary to Lloyd's belief that deprived areas ought to be provided with teachers with the highest qualifications.

His years with the STF were crusading ones. He kept up a barrage of demands, questions and pleas, in a constant attempt to improve the system. It was not just the government he attacked—he cajoled teachers to question, discuss and above all, participate in all aspects of community life. They were to be "teacher-citizens." He saw the role of the teacher in the community as something far broader than a classroom-based pedagogue.

In the fall of 1941, Woodrow and Vicki, by then the parents of two daughters, moved to Biggar, where Lloyd became vice-principal of the high school. He soon made contact with the local CCF group and they were quick to recognize his talents.

In the same year, T.C. Douglas became leader of the Saskatchewan CCF and, stirred by rumours of an impending election, set up a series of committees to develop a program that could be enacted in the event of a CCF government being elected. Lloyd and Joe Phelps joined the group, working with the University of Saskatchewan education expert, Carlyle King, to work out the CCF blueprint for education. In the resulting document, Lloyd's hand was particularly evident in the clause which read: "Revision of curricula ... to make the material of school studies a preparation for the life of the world into which the students will go..."

The implementation of LSUs on an experimental basis was the only point on which Lloyd would have gone further. He was by no means persuaded that this basic change must come before other improvements. He found it hard to understand the timidity of some teachers advancing the argument in favour of this reform. "Such a lack of courage," he said in the STF *Bulletin*, "is neither dignified nor productive." His medicine was too strong for many teachers and while they admired his conviction they were still reluctant to place themselves in jeopardy from the recriminations of their local paymasters.

In Government: Changes and Challenges

When the 1944 provincial election approached, the search for candidates began in earnest. Although the Biggar constituency committee had a number of local farmers in mind, when they consulted Tommy Douglas he unhesitatingly suggested Lloyd. Douglas personally approached Lloyd, who needed little persuading.

From the beginning, Lloyd's shortcomings as an active politician showed themselves. These were weaknesses that were to plague him all his campaigning life. George Hindley, his campaign manager, remarked: "He had no talent for being the 'hail fellow well met.' He was always available but never took the initiative to go out and meet people. You'd never think that he was after their vote." Lloyd himself once confided to a friend that he quite liked politics, if only it were not for the elections.

Soon after the polls closed on June 15, 1944, it became obvious that Patterson was out and Douglas and the CCF were in—and with them was Woodrow Lloyd. Whatever his campaign shortcomings, as MLA for Biggar, Lloyd contested and won six subsequent elections, until he stepped down 26 years later. In the historic 1944 victory, the CCF captured 47 seats, conceding only five to the Liberals. When it came to appointing a minister of Education, no one was more qualified than the co-architect of the party's education blueprint and president of the STF. Lloyd accepted the portfolio without hesitation. Barely 31, he was the youngest member of the Cabinet, and the only one born in the province.[2] He was about to begin the most fruitful and happiest period of his life.

There were three aspects to Lloyd's new position. Within the Cabinet, he would be involved in discussions of matters affecting all departments of the government. The possibility of accommodating others' views and demands would always be present. Second, as head of the Department of Education, he would have the ruling hand over a large and complex administrative organization. He would have the opportunity to apply his belief in participatory democracy on an important body, the civil service. The team of experts he assembled placed Saskatchewan in the forefront of education in North America. Third, in the Legislature he would be on view to the public. He would have to cope with the opposition, the press and public reaction.

Lloyd knew there could be no half measures if the basic educational system in the province was to be improved. Successive governments, over the past 50 years, had tried and failed. Total revolution was called for and the plans which Lloyd and his teaching colleagues had been pressing for years could now become a reality. The battle for LSUs may today be forgotten but while it raged, and it did so over a period of several years, it was almost as fierce as the struggle which Lloyd later led to establish medicare. The qualities which he needed to win both these landmark advances were much the same. Members of school boards, often representing single schools, and other local politicians, were desperate to hang on to power, not least of which was their power to hire and fire teachers at will. Teachers could be and sometimes were dismissed for smoking, dancing, or, more sinisterly, holding political views contrary to those of some trustees.

For many people in rural communities, the fight over LSUs was more personal. They could only see that the larger units would mean the closing down of the local, often one-room, school. The issue of changes in taxation was also of keen interest. In the past, a small community would pay only enough to support its own pupils. Now an assessment of lands and resources would determine the rate of taxation, the funds being apportioned by the LSU in order to provide equal benefit for all. To counter the impression that everyone would pay more, Lloyd circulated a pamphlet throughout the province. In it he stated that all would "pay in accordance with their ability to pay. The total resources of the area would become a guarantee that no child within the boundaries of the Larger Unit of Administration shall lack for a decent education."

Even within the party and the caucus, there was unease about the LSU plan, and within weeks of being elected, Lloyd found himself engaged in a serious struggle to defend his point of view. Eventually he was forced to accept a compromise. An Act passed in the fall of 1944 provided that a petition signed by 15% of the ratepayers in any given municipality could call for a vote before the establishment of an LSU in their area. Only five communities would take advantage of this provision, and all came out in favour of the change.

The introduction of the LSUs marked a total revolution in the province's education system and was the necessary basis on which Lloyd would begin to build towards his goal of equal opportunity for every child. However, there were people who blamed Lloyd and his LSU plan for weakening the fabric of rural society. The closure of local schools left a serious void in some towns. Few people actually moved away, but over the years there was less to hold them or attract new people to small towns. But the use of buses to transport children to larger and better schools was just part of a long-term trend. With better roads and faster cars, people began to look to bigger towns for a greater selection of goods, services and entertainment. The arguments and emotions expressed then presaged in many ways the later campaigns against rail line abandonment and inland grain terminals. While LSUs did contribute to some degree of rural depopulation, they did so as part of a general pattern of life brought about by changing technology and trade patterns.

The Premiership and the Medicare Crisis

The 1960 election in Saskatchewan was a very different campaign than previous ones. The Liberal Party was now in the hands of Ross Thatcher, whose avowed aim was the destruction of socialism in Saskatchewan. The long-awaited medical care program was the key plank in the CCF platform and sparks were bound to fly. During the campaign the province's medical fraternity revealed, for the first time, a formidable organization.

The CCF won the election but this was the beginning of a period of great change and challenge for Lloyd.[3] Many, including Douglas, believed that Lloyd had the ability and the experience to take on new responsibilities, and in the Cabinet shuffle that followed the election Lloyd was appointed provincial treasurer. After 16 years he needed a new challenge and accepted the Premier's offer with little hesitation.

Lloyd thoroughly enjoyed the creative aspects of the Treasury. His approach was to question every facet, be it expenditure or taxation, in terms of the party philosophy, political practicality and human advantages. Lloyd's objective was not simply a balanced budget but ensuring that the party's program could be met within the budget available.

In February 1961, Lloyd presented his first and only budget as provincial treasurer. He was prepared to borrow and spend where he thought it necessary. He saw little chance of the current recession abating and was determined that the government should not allow a rise in unemployment or a fall in income. "We decided to borrow," he told the House, "to the extent that was reasonably possible in order to sustain public investment and economic development." But it was necessary to make cuts to some programs and he chose to apply the axe to roads and highways. Lloyd knew the necessity of good roads to rural life but felt that other aspects of the government's work had greater importance. In making this decision, he had to cope with the vexed MLAs who in turn had to confront disgruntled constituents.

Increases went to support for people with mental disabilities, hospital construction and social assistance. Education also benefited from Lloyd's budget, accounting for 28% of the total expenditure. Interest-free student loans were increased, as were grants to the university, schools, and vocational and technical training programs.

Lloyd once again demonstrated his belief that tax dollars were good dollars. In a speech broadcast the following year, as Premier, when he was preparing the electorate for the introduction of new taxes to finance medicare, he spoke about his taxation policy as a form of collective security:

> More people, sensitive to the needs of all, conscious that the only real and lasting prosperity is a shared one, have insisted on doing more things together. My claim is that the portion of our income spent through taxes for public services is the best investment we can make.

Barely four months after the budget a bigger challenge faced Lloyd. Tommy Douglas was elected to lead the newly formed New Democratic Party and, as had been widely assumed, Lloyd was chosen for the difficult task of following in his footsteps. In a sense, Lloyd felt it was his duty, and while he was certainly proud to be Premier of Saskatchewan, it was not a role he would have sought under other circumstances.

The man who had always shunned the limelight was now the centre of intense publicity. In the numerous articles that appeared after his selection, words like "charisma," "personal magnetism," and "dynamism" kept cropping up. They were used to express the qualities that Lloyd did not have and which Tommy Douglas had in abundance. But Lloyd had no intention of being a leader in the Douglas style. He was not capable of being anything other than himself and that was a basically shy man. He had not, as some journalists speculated, held himself back from the limelight so as not to detract from Douglas's colourful performance.

© M. WEST, REGINA. WEST'S STUDIO COLLECTION. SAB R-WS15163

Premier Woodrow S. Lloyd, 1961.

There were characteristics which journalists and the public alike recognized in Lloyd which were definitely assets in a party leader at this time. People had confidence in Lloyd. They trusted him, whether they agreed with his politics or not. His great organizational abilities and his complete dedication to the implementation of party programs as decided by convention were much needed by the CCF at this juncture. His courage and the firmness with which he held his beliefs were essential to the tasks he was about to assume. Without these qualities, medicare, his sternest challenge, might not have been achieved.

Medicare, the event that Canadian newspapermen voted "The News Story of the Decade," crept rather than burst upon the population of Saskatchewan. Seventeen years earlier, on May 18, 1944, Tommy Douglas, speaking at a Biggar election rally in support of Lloyd, made the promise that the CCF, if elected, would "set up medical, dental and hospital services, available to all without counting the ability of the individual to pay."

When the CCF came to power in 1944 a commission was set up to study the health services and make recommendations for improvement. Although numerous improvements were made, it was not until 15 years later that the Douglas government found itself in a financial position to advocate universal medical care. It was the federal government's announcement in 1957 that it was introducing a scheme of financial grants to provincially operated hospitalization plans that set the wheels of medicare in motion. The federal aid released a large piece of the province's capital for use in other fields. The long-promised medical coverage was the beneficiary.

Right from the beginning, there was tension and suspicion between the politicians and the doctors. Not only were the Saskatchewan doctors supported by colleagues elsewhere in Canada, the American Medical Association, fearing the socialist foot in the door, was generous with its financial and material aid in opposition to the plan. The publicity that rolled from the doctors' well-oiled machine spread through the province. Mail campaigns and doctors' spokesmen warned of the dangers of "state" medicine. Catholic women were alerted to the possibility of government control over their freedom to bear as many children as they liked, and it was suggested that women suffering from menopausal emotional disturbances might be indiscriminately confined in mental hospitals.

Douglas (who remained Premier until November 1) called a Special Session of the Saskatchewan Legislature for October 11, 1961, and tabled the Medical Care Insurance Bill. The government's decision not to show the draft of the bill to the doctors' leaders was a controversial one. The doctors held an emergency general meeting and voted 295 to 5 against cooperating with the medicare plan. Given this degree of animosity it is difficult to see what might have been gained by showing them the bill. The doctors set out preconditions before they would even discuss the plan. They proposed that tax-supported programs might be provided only for the old, infirm and those with low incomes or limited means. The doctors' desires in no way measured up to the scheme that the government was determined to introduce. To Lloyd and his colleagues, discussion with the doctors on these terms was pointless. The doctors were further enraged when the government announced the composition of the Medical Care Insurance Commission and their intention of appealing to doctors on an individual basis.

The leader of the Saskatchewan physicians, Dr. H.D. Dalgleish, finally agreed to meet with the government in April 1962. The meetings themselves were amicable. Lloyd's presence as Premier and chief negotiator, his firm belief in the efficacy of talking things through, and his skill at controlling a discussion, helped to smooth what could have been a rough encounter. No doubt he suffered from the frustration of seeming to get nowhere, but he did not show his anxiety. Even when the talks broke down after two weeks he could not bring himself to believe that the doctors would ultimately defy a plan which, as he saw it, promised so much good. He believed that the people were behind him and still believed that the majority of the doctors would cooperate.

The College of Physicians and Surgeons called a special meeting of its members for May 3, 1962. Lloyd, anxious that the plan be fully understood, asked to address the meeting.[4] Speaking with conviction, Lloyd concluded his address:

> My appeal is to what has been termed "the ancient wisdom of your profession." We seek not to change the ends of medicine. We do seek to find ways and means to adapt the financing of medical care to 20th century society and the legitimate expectations of that society. In this "the ancient mission" need not be lost. Its achievement can be advanced. I invite you to join in a bold attempt to consolidate past gains and to move toward new horizons in the field of medical care.

A polite smattering of applause followed as Lloyd stepped back from the microphone. Then, Dr. Dalgleish stepped forward and asked that all those who opposed the plan should stand. With only five exceptions the assembled body rose to their feet and commenced shouting and cheering, and Lloyd turned and walked from the hall. He was exhausted, frustrated, bitterly disappointed, but his resolve was firm. Whatever the doctors and their supporters could throw at him would be insufficient to deter him from his course. In the next few months, he would be tested time and time again. "As you've probably heard," he wrote to his daughter a few days later, "we are at war—and will be for a time."

During the next six weeks, there were many blows to the Premier's hopes for an early settlement. The doctors continued to publicize their interpretation of the plan, which implied serious control of their work by the government. Even when definite proposals were submitted to the doctors, the profession published a statement which implied their mistrust of Lloyd's ability to keep his word.

Keep Our Doctors (KOD) committees began to spring up throughout Saskatchewan, fed on the propaganda about a mass exodus of doctors and the possible importation of foreign practitioners with supposedly inferior training and standards. These coalitions of various right-wing groups and frightened individuals increased the emotionalism and fear in the province. Violence had always been anathema to Lloyd and he could see in the KODs the seeds of serious trouble. Meanwhile, the Citizens' Committee for Medical Care was publishing weekly tabloids distributed to every household in the province, producing newspaper ads and buying radio and television time to put the other side of the case.

The starting date for medicare was set for July 1, 1962. As the date approached, two-thirds of the province's doctors posted notices in their offices stating that they would not be available to their patients after that date. Both sides were making provisions for the worst. The doctors would keep open some hospitals to deal with life-and-death cases, although they let it be known that not enough doctors had volunteered to run this service.

The province's agent general in the United Kingdom, Graham Spry, was sounding out various medical organizations about the possibility of doctors going to Saskatchewan on a temporary basis should the strike take place. The response was favourable and the first British doctors actually arrived in the province prior to July 1. Some of them went to work in community clinics which were set up and run by groups of concerned patients.

In a final attempt to reach agreement and ward off an all-out doctors' strike, the two sides met for 18 heated hours in late June. For the first time since the dispute arose, the doctors presented the government with a detailed list of objections to the legislation. In these, Lloyd could find no basis for a realistic compromise.

About one-third of the province's doctors felt that the strike was unethical and refused to join the action. Members of the press, who had flocked to Regina, were rewarded on the first day of the strike with the story of a nine-month-old baby who had died in his mother's arms on the last leg of an 85-mile journey to find medical help. Some hysterical citizens were determined to lay the blame at Lloyd's feet, going so far as to call him a murderer. Even as it was revealed that medical help could not have saved the child, the tension rose. Long-standing friends and neighbours found themselves in opposing camps and it would be many years before the wounds in some towns would heal.

Lloyd suffered in silence. For the first time in his life, he was forced to protect himself from approaches by the general public. For the first few days of the strike, he tried to carry on as he always had, making himself available to anyone who wanted to talk. But as the phone rang incessantly through the night, he was often forced to listen to obscenities and vilification. Finally, his home phone was fitted with a cut-off switch and a private line installed for contact with family and close associates. Still he could not stop the letters nor would he stop answering them, no matter how harsh or rude the criticism.

It was, he admitted later, the only time in his career that he actually feared for the safety of his family. When they awoke one morning to find the word "commie" sprayed in huge red letters across the front of the house, they all began to realize the dangers. Nonetheless, Lloyd amazed people with the cheerful front he managed to present each day. In the confines of his own home, however, a degree of distress and fatigue were all too obvious.

"Rescind the Act or resign," demanded the KODs. Lloyd would do neither. Nor would he take directions from a group of people who had always opposed him. The KODs thought they offered an honourable way out by pointing out that medicare was devised and promised by Tommy Douglas, not by Lloyd: "Therefore it is in your power to repeal this Act without losing face and start anew. The choice of becoming a statesman or remaining an ambitious politician is yours for the asking." In reply, Lloyd assured the KODs that the responsibility was entirely his and he would accept no blame on Douglas's behalf.

Lloyd's constituency of Biggar was as severely hit by all the unpleasant aspects of the strike as any community in Saskatchewan. All the local doctors joined the strike and the College of Physicians and Surgeons withdrew an offer to place emergency doctors in the town. The local KOD, run by one of Lloyd's former pupils, was particularly vociferous in its objection to the plan. The Biggar newspaper ran articles against the government. When a British doctor was placed in Biggar, she became the target of scurrilous rumours concerning her qualifications and her political associations. She left after five days. However, a pro-medicare group in the town raised funds to open a clinic and an uneasy truce followed. As the situation calmed, many local businessmen dropped their KOD affiliation, leaving only a handful to carry the Biggar KOD banner to Regina in what was meant to be a vast cavalcade of cars bound for the "mass freedom rally."

The KODs predicted that the convergence of 40,000 people on the Legislative Buildings would bring the government to its knees. Dentists, druggists and many businessmen declared that they would close their offices on July 11 in order to attend the rally. At the height of the rally, however, there were scarcely more than 4,000 people, augmented by some 70 journalists and photographers and a smattering of government supporters. To add impact to their message, KOD supporters burned an effigy of Lloyd. Within the Cabinet chamber, a small delegation was received in dignified silence. Whether or not they were impressed with the Premier's cool conviction, their meeting, in that room, was the beginning of the end. Back in the light of day, the KOD supporters began to slip away through the shady park that surrounded the buildings. They were slipping away too from their support of the hard core KOD leaders.

On July 16, Lord Stephen Taylor arrived from Britain, after careful and quiet arrangements made by Lloyd and Graham Spry. Taylor, a doctor, had earned his peerage for the

SAB R-A 12109-4

The "Keep Our Doctors" rally outside the Legislative Building, July 11, 1962.

vital role he played in the design and implementation of the British National Health Service. He had agreed to come to Saskatchewan as an observer, although it was hoped he could work his way into the doctors' confidence and from there to a role as mediator.

The scene of the drama now shifted to Saskatoon, where the provincial NDP convention was being held. Lord Taylor, in reviewing the impasse, detected that Lloyd and Dalgleish, when they met, appeared to be talking about two totally different schemes. They were speaking different languages, and Taylor concluded it would be better for the time being if they did not meet at all. Taylor became a go-between, shuttling repeatedly between the Medical Arts Building and the hotel room, a few hundred yards away, occupied by Lloyd and his colleagues.

Dalgleish requested the opportunity to address the NDP convention on July 18 and for the first time, in that speech, he did not demand a complete repeal of the act. The only thing he asked for, which had not already been offered by the government, was that private insurance schemes be allowed to continue as channels for payments to those doctors who chose to work under the scheme. It was upon this request that a solution would pivot.

Lloyd's eventual accession to this demand was not taken without much soul searching. He disliked compromising his principles. In his view, the medicare plan was fine as it stood. It had been designed to give maximum benefit to the people of Saskatchewan and his stubborn determination led him to resent giving away any of the advantages. He also believed that he was right and thus he must triumph over the dissension of the doctors. On the other hand, he thought carefully about the medicare dispute and what it had done to the ordinary people of the province, of the divisions within communities and even within homes. There were those among his Cabinet and party executive who said things had gone far enough—he should concede this point. Lloyd listened to every point of view with the greatest consideration. If he had thought only of himself and his principles, he would have gone on fighting. But he knew he was not alone and in the end he yielded to the persuasion of others.

It took several days and enormous reserves of patience, tact and skill on Lord Taylor's part, before an agreement was drafted. Every word, every nuance had to be just right. At noon on July 23, government and Medical Association officials came face to face at the Bessborough Hotel. Regardless of what their inner feelings might have been, the protagonists signed the document with dignity. Lord Taylor made Premier Lloyd and Dalgleish promise to wait one week before making any statements about the agreement in order to prevent a flare-up of the old arguments. "This province has been sick," he told the waiting press, "it has had a major operation. I prescribe for it absolute rest." He went on to praise both the doctors and the politicians but the only particular compliment he made was to Lloyd: "He is one of the finest men I have ever known in my life. You should be proud to have such a premier."

The strike was over but the bitterness lingered on. Only time would mend broken friendships and some would never heal. Within a few years, however, it became difficult to find a doctor in Saskatchewan who did not think of medicare as a benefit.

Premier's Progress

When Lloyd was sworn in as Premier of Saskatchewan in November 1961 he had remarked, "I am now officially sworn in and probably, to some extent, at." Although medicare cast him as a villain in the eyes of many, and hero in others, there were other aspects of his premiership which attracted less publicity. Even while the all-consuming struggle with the doctors was going on, he continued to cope with other facets of the job.

Apart from the day-to-day business of running a government and a province, a number of other issues attracted his attention. As Premier he had the opportunity of expressing his views on matters outside the province and he made good use of the forum provided by a series of federal-provincial conferences, where his well-prepared arguments made a strong impression on his fellow Premiers. He never interjected unless necessary, nor did he let any point that he considered important for Saskatchewan pass by unnoticed.

Lloyd saw many areas where conflicting activities in various provinces, or federal restrictions, resulted in severe disadvantages to specific groups at the provincial level. One such case was that of Indian Affairs, as it was called at the time. He had long felt the frustration of trying to help Natives at a provincial level while all jurisdiction over their affairs remained in Ottawa. As Premier, he advocated transferring Indian Affairs to the provincial authorities.

In September 1963, Lloyd planned an extensive tour of northern Saskatchewan to see for himself the sort of problems faced by the region. While Lloyd and his companions progressed by plane and car among the trees and lakes of the north, he made copious notes on conditions and discussions. The welcome was friendly and many people came forward to put their cases for improvements. The travellers looked at the state of the roads, educational problems, recreational facilities, the inadequacies of housing, the progress and development of cooperative fisheries, the lack of gardens, sawmills and angling rights, and many other areas of contention. Back in his office, Lloyd sifted through his observations and prepared directives to be sent out to different departments. From these came thousands of dollars for new housing programs, road improvements, better educational facilities and a kindergarten to teach English to Native children before they entered the existing school system. Other plans were set in motion that would bring improvements to the lives of many of Saskatchewan's northern people.

Closer to home, the question of expansion for the university in Regina had been causing controversy. To Lloyd, it was not just a question of the most convenient place to erect the new buildings, it was an opportunity to examine the whole purpose of higher education and the role that a university could play within the community. To this end, he had originally supported a site near the old Regina College, in the heart of the city as an extended campus. Placing the university there, he felt, would symbolize its interdependence with the rest of the community. He wanted to make it more readily available to citizens other than full-time students, and a constant reminder of the necessity of educating individuals for a realistic role in society. However, when the ambitious, long-term plans to develop Regina's Wascana Centre were presented, Lloyd changed his mind and became an enthusiastic supporter of this visionary scheme. As it turned out, his support was essential. Many rural MLAs resented millions of dollars going to a city-based amenity, but with Lloyd's backing the opposition was overcome and the scheme swung into motion. On September 26, 1963, Lloyd laid the cornerstone of the first building on the new Regina campus.

While Lloyd was involved in the establishment of the new university in Regina, he was also fighting to save older aspects of prairie life. Throughout 1962, Lloyd bombarded Prime Minister Diefenbaker with letters and telegrams, urging him to postpone the planned abandonment of stretches of Canadian Pacific Railway lines in Saskatchewan until a new transport policy could be devised. Lloyd rallied the support of Premiers Manning and Roblin from Alberta and Manitoba and, together, they eventually got Diefenbaker to agree to a meeting. Soon afterwards the Prime Minister announced that no line would be abandoned without an examination of the effects on local farmers and businessmen. When Diefenbaker was ousted from office a few months later, Lloyd immediately asked the new Prime Minister, Lester Pearson, for his assurance that this policy would be continued. The fight went on throughout Lloyd's premiership and his time as leader of the opposition. He was ultimately unable to stop the closure of many branch lines but he managed to delay some closures, in some cases by years, and to force the federal government to examine the facts of each case.

Electoral Defeat

Traditionally, June is election month in Saskatchewan but for several reasons, when Lloyd applied himself to the question of the 1964 provincial election, he set the date for April 22. Even before the Legislative Session of that year had progressed far, he was pleased with the way the government was working. He felt that there was excellent legislation in progress and he sensed that his people were ready to go. In the two years since medicare began, the medical scene had calmed significantly. On the whole, the public and the medical profession had accepted the scheme and even the opposition Liberals pledged not to dismantle it, should they be elected. But there was no way of judging how deep the bitterness engendered by the medicare struggle had penetrated and weakened the foundations of CCF support.

It was generally felt that an uncontroversial election platform should be presented to the voters and, when it came, there was little to excite the passions of the party campaigners or the people of Saskatchewan. There were those in the Cabinet and the civil service who urged Lloyd to promise a tax cut or a supplement to family allowances—measures economically feasible at the time. The Premier, however, abhorred any sort of inducement to voters other than honest policy and record, and refused to adopt any such ideas. If there was a surplus in government funds, then he felt that they must be put aside for more beneficial developments and not squandered on buying votes.

In the 20 years since the CCF first took office in Saskatchewan, they had survived five elections. Across the country, many people looked upon this sixth trip to the polls as a mere formality. Older CCF supporters had come to believe that life without their party in power was a near impossibility. A whole new generation had grown up knowing nothing but the CCF. In February a *Financial Times* journalist wrote, "Unless the CCF cut the throats of some innocent people in broad daylight, they should win." But optimism breeds complacency, and, in retrospect, complacency was seen as one of the party's most serious enemies.

Meanwhile, Ross Thatcher, an altogether different kind of Liberal leader, was campaigning hard, offering to make Saskatchewan, "the greatest private enterprise province in Canada." He maintained that socialism had seriously inhibited economic development, claims the government countered with statistics showing how much growth had taken place. Lloyd presented his program as "honest and realistic, consistent and attainable. It contains no commitment that has not been carefully studied and analyzed—in terms of what it will cost, and how it will be done." He was aware of some complacency up and down the province but refused to resort to any flamboyant gimmicks as part of his campaign. He would, however, have been happier if his party workers had shown more enthusiasm for their program.

There was one unexpected issue that aroused strong feelings during the campaign. Olaf Turnbull, minister of Education, had introduced a bill in the previous Session which would give Catholic ratepayers, in the 16 school districts where there were separate Catholic schools, the opportunity of being excluded from taxation by the local school board. This was meant to release Catholic parents from double taxation. It did not radically alter the education given in any part of the province, but it angered many Saskatchewan Protestants. Turnbull later admitted that the timing of the legislation was wrong and suggested its introduction be postponed. Lloyd would not hear of it, feeling that the government had made a stand on an issue and must now go through with it. Although there was little public debate of the issue, many people afterwards felt that it had been a silent factor in the CCF defeat.

April 22, 1964, was possibly the most depressing day in Lloyd's political career. More than 80% of Saskatchewan voters marked a ballot that day. The sad irony of the election was that, in 1960, 40.8% of the popular vote had yielded the CCF 37 out of the 55 seats. Now, 40.3% of the popular vote gave them only 25 seats in an enlarged House of 59 seats. However, it took several weeks to reach this final result, while advanced votes were counted and a number of recounts took place.

For nearly a month, Lloyd hung in limbo. Convinced that his policies were right, it was difficult for him the grasp the fact that the CCF had lost. As well, he saw the defeat in the 1964 election as personal. As leader of the party it was his responsibility to be an acceptable figurehead and in this, he believed, he had failed.

The causes of the 1964 defeat are still debated. Medicare still rankled with some voters. As well, 20 years is a long time for any party to govern, and Thatcher's "Time for a Change" campaign clearly resonated. In a province still fundamentally an agricultural stronghold, many continued to be suspicious of labour, hence the tenacity with which the party clung to its CCF label. Nonetheless, the NDP affiliations with organized labour may have concerned some voters, while others were angered by the new legislation on Catholic schools. In Ross Thatcher, the CCF faced a dynamic leader unlike any they had previously encountered. While Lloyd's image as a solid and honest man was one that people needed time to appreciate, Thatcher's charisma made an instant impact on undecided voters. In the countryside the CCF organization had been too lax, too unwilling to consider the possibility of defeat. The Liberals, with abundant financial help and sympathetic media treatment, were well prepared for a vigorous campaign.

When the result was finally confirmed, Lloyd suggested to colleagues and supporters that he resign as leader. On every side he was met with firm resistance. Nothing would be gained, they felt, by his resignation. Once he had decided to stay on, Lloyd began to think more optimistically about the future. His job now was to get the eyes of the party off the past and on to new horizons. In opposition there would be time for him to "create some of the revolutions that need attention."

Leader of the Opposition

As leader of the opposition, Lloyd saw his role as two-fold. First, he must lead his party in constructive criticism of the new government's policies. Over the years, he successfully outmanoeuvred the Liberal government as it tried to manipulate the legislative agenda to its advantage. According to John Burton, a party researcher at the time,

> Lloyd brilliantly fended off the Liberals and staked out a solid position on the issues when, in September 1966, the Liberals thought they had the opposition on the ropes when they legislated striking SaskPower workers back to work. In my view, this was a turning point for the CCF fortunes. [And] with Woodrow's understanding of rural Saskatchewan, he exposed the shallowness of Liberal claims of accomplishments when agriculture slumped.

Second, he felt that the party must rebuild itself. It was this latter task that Lloyd pursued with the greatest amount of success. The constituency conventions held throughout the province in the summer of 1964 showed how well the party supporters had recovered, and the enthusiasm with which they were preparing for the future. At the provincial convention in July, the mood was such that a surprised CBC commentator reported, "this was no political party in defeat." In a television interview, Lloyd said, "Personally, I have never been more proud of the CCF than I am today. We launched the next election campaign three weeks ago!"

Lloyd saw that a complete overhaul of the party organization and a complete reassessment of the CCF philosophy were needed in order to successfully challenge the Liberals. To this, he devoted all of his energy, with the result that the CCF was seemingly well prepared when a provincial election was called for October 11, 1967.

In early March, Lloyd told the constituency workers to be prepared for a snap election. They thus had plenty of time to carry out a thorough campaign. Lloyd was pleased with how the campaign progressed through the late summer, and he was particularly happy with a full slate of candidates, many of whom were young and enthusiastic. The platform that the party presented to the electorate was a broad and innovative program covering every possible aspect of government activity. Compared with the 1964 platform, it was loaded with substantive proposals and well-considered new ideas.

One of the successes of the 1967 campaign was the election of what Allan Blakeney called "as impressive a freshman team as any team elected after 1944." Six young candidates, including future Premier Roy Romanow, became MLAs that year. "Woodrow did a fine job," said Blakeney, "in finding first class candidates, getting them nominated, and then getting them elected."

When the votes were counted and the CCF failed to dislodge the Liberals, Lloyd's reaction was not so much shock as devastating disappointment. Well before the election had been announced, Lloyd had again consulted some of his closest friends about resigning. In turn, he had asked them to sound out the opinions of others in key positions in the party. Although he stated on election night that he would ask the party to reassess the leadership position, the consensus was that he should stay on.

Lloyd began to talk about how much he would like to do something outside politics, particularly United Nations work or possibly an academic career, but his personal desires were subsumed by the persuasiveness of his supporters. Victoria was completely in favour of his resignation. Woodrow and Vicki had been married for over 30 years. She had always been supportive, sharing his beliefs and his desire to bring change to the province. Their friends were political colleagues. Over the past few years, however, Vicki had grown increasingly disenchanted with the life of a politician's wife. It was a role that she played gracefully and convincingly, but the years in politics had been lonely ones for her, despite being surrounded by her children, friends and by Woodrow's colleagues and supporters. She did enjoy the people with whom she came in contact, but she would have appreciated the time and the freedom to choose more of her own activities.

Moreover, Vicki was increasingly concerned about her husband's health. For decades, he had worked incredible hours. Holidays were rare oases when the family could relax together but these were too often snatched at the last minute or curtailed because of work. Lloyd's doctor shared her concern. After the defeat in 1967, he felt that Lloyd was taking less care of his health than he would have done had he still had the responsibility of being Premier.

In April 1969, Lloyd spoke to his constituents and advised them that, if chosen, he would continue as leader. "Facing these people," he wrote afterwards, "it was hard to contemplate a different decision. We'll hope it was the right one." He had made the decision without informing Vicki and his speech was a painful blow to her. He had gone against their tacit understanding that the end of his political career was in sight and, for once, she could not hide her bitter disappointment. He would not, however, contest another election. There was still much to be done to build the party in preparation for an NDP return to power.[3] This he could do, but he was convinced he was not the man to be the new Premier. He would set the stage, make everything ready, and then he would go. He was, after all, only 56 years old, with plenty of time to make a new beginning for himself.

The months left in Lloyd's political life were disappointing for him. What he saw in the world around him was cause for concern. He was horrified at Prime Minister Pearson's plans to acquire nuclear weapons for Canada. Lloyd tried to get the Legislature to express official concern at the proposed construction of anti-ballistic missiles just over the American border, which would place the missile interception area directly over Saskatchewan. Thatcher called the discussion a waste of time, but Lloyd insisted that the elected representatives of the Saskatchewan people had a duty to discuss such vital issues. For his concern about the missile sites, he received a personal commendation from American Senator George McGovern and an invitation to speak at a symposium in Montana on the matter. There he urged his audience to make people believe that peace was possible through non-aggressive means.

Bev Currie, provincial party president at the time, recalled that "when the War Measures Act was enacted during the 1970 Quebec crisis, the national NDP leader, Tommy Douglas, took the correct but unpopular stand of opposing it. The party clearly needed allies. Woodrow rose to the occasion ... making many speeches opposing it." As usual, he viewed the situation not just in terms of immediate events but also for all its long-term consequences. The War Measures Act did nothing to resolve the underlying problem and, on the other hand, had "given the government the power to smear all dissent as criminal." Once again, his views were noticed on the wider canvas and he was asked to become one of five English-speaking commissioners on The Citizens Commission of Inquiry into the War Measures Act.

Closer to home, Thatcher had buckled under pressure from the Americans, who were complaining that an oversupply of Saskatchewan potash was driving prices down. He imposed a floor price and production limits. Lloyd vehemently protested that it was not Saskatchewan's role to make the world safe for American potash.

Moving On

In early 1969, Lloyd celebrated 25 years as an MLA. Nearly a thousand people gathered to honour his contribution to the party. It was a satisfying and exciting evening for Vicki and Woodrow. Tommy Douglas made a glowing presentation speech. "Most of all there was friendship and kind words from nice people," wrote Lloyd. He went on to express a sentiment that had always been something of a personal talisman: "There are few satisfactions to compare with those of working with good people for a worthwhile purpose." But even on this happy night, cynicism crept in and he added, "even if one gets weary and impatient and frustrated and kicked around a bit at times."

Within the party itself, there was discontent. The new MLAs, whom Lloyd had done so much to elect in 1967, were increasingly open about their determination to get back into power—to pursue electoral success whatever the cost to the party political philosophy. Dr. Frank Coburn, then the Saskatchewan CCF president, believed there was a schism within the party partly based on age and experience.

On the other hand, there was a growing group which saw the only hope for the party's future in a move to the left. In many ways, what they wanted was a return to the socialism that had given birth to the "Regina Manifesto." Lloyd's view was that this group's enthusiasm for doctrinal purity was badly needed to counteract the opportunism of the right wingers in the party. It seemed to him vital that the party must contain both trends and combine them into a stronger, more effective socialist approach to government.

This concern with the party's direction was by no means limited to Saskatchewan. A new group, known as the "Waffle," presented what subsequently became known as the "Waffle Manifesto" to the federal NDP convention in 1969. Its aim was to make the NDP take a definitive stand on such issues as the control of Canada's resources.

The debate of the Waffle Manifesto polarized opinion at all levels. Waffle leaders implored Lloyd to speak on their behalf but he refused and was equally diffident about how he would vote. In the end, some 499 delegates, including present and future party leaders, voted against the Manifesto, while 284 delegates stood for it. In their midst stood Lloyd. His support provided the Waffle with respectability. It had been a difficult decision for him and, in retrospect, many people admired him for the stand he took. Even his supporters, however, admitted that his decision laid open questions about his political judgement.

Lloyd was not entirely happy with the wording of the Waffle Manifesto, nor did he agree with the implication that wholesale nationalization of key industries was the only solution to Canada's problems. However, he appreciated the group's determination to do something about what he agreed was a crisis of foreign ownership of the country's resources.

One of the outcomes of the conference which worried Lloyd was the establishment in most provinces of an organized structure to press the Waffle views—the much-criticized party-within-a-party structure. He wanted the "Wafflers" to work as a force for change within the party but he feared that they could become a divisive force.

Inside Saskatchewan, the polarization that took place was more dramatic than in other parts of the country. Many party members were angered that Bev Currie, the provincial party president, allowed his name to be associated with a number of papers circulated by the Waffle group. The caucus passed a resolution affirming their disapproval and called a joint meeting with the NDP provincial executive for March 26. Currie, while objecting to the way in which the meeting had been called, agreed to come to Regina to talk with Lloyd. During their conversation, Currie remarked that many people thought that the caucus was actually out to get Lloyd. Puffing steadily on his pipe, Lloyd replied quietly, "I know."

To avoid splitting the party, Currie agreed to advise members of the executive to attend the joint meeting, which convened in the Legislative Building. Fred Dewhurst, former speaker of the House, was in the chair and it was agreed that each person would speak only once, after Currie's initial defence and before Lloyd's summing up. A number of people had already expressed their views when Bob Walker, an ex-MLA and now party executive member, rose to his feet and launched the attack against Lloyd. He claimed that, in the country, people were asking him why they did not get a new leader. Perhaps Lloyd had been around too long. It was time for a new face. As he continued, there was a stunned silence in the room. Dewhurst did nothing to call him to order.

As Walker sat down the tension filled the room. Only those conspirators who, it later transpired, had met the day before, were ready with the right words to carry the argument forward. Lloyd's friends and supporters were staggered by Walker's attack and failed to confront him. Lloyd sat impassively. His eyes narrowed a little behind his glasses, his teeth clenched a little tighter on the stem of his pipe.

Frank Coburn, former president of the party and a long-time confidant to Lloyd, was next on the speaker's list. His immediate reaction was to ignore what Walker had stated and to try and get the meeting back on track. He later admitted that he was completely rattled by the events of the previous few minutes, and because of this, he failed to take the opportunity to defend Lloyd.

Despite others speaking out in Lloyd's defence, and various attempts to get the meeting back on course, the damage was done. Even Lloyd's composure was cracking. He could take criticism but not outright rejection. It was powerful, it was personal and it was devastating. As the meeting ended he rose to his feet, his voice strained with emotion. His resignation was on the table, he said. In a letter written the next day to his daughter, he said:

> I am disappointed in my own lack of success at convincing people that discussion of ideas and essential philosophy should get high priority over whose road to build or which tax to criticize. I'm disillusioned by those who see the party on the edge of practical power and are so frightened that they are willing to step sideways, backwards and off solid defensible positions for fear someone might be offended. I'm even a bit ashamed of myself for giving in to some of those ideas and pressures (not many) in order to keep the peace and cohesiveness of the group.

On Monday, March 30, 1970, Lloyd announced to the Legislature his intention to resign as leader of the NDP. The events of the previous week were unknown to most people so his announcement came as a shock. That he had resigned with such suddenness led to much speculation. Lloyd maintained that his decision was based on a long-considered notion that he would like to be relieved of his leadership responsibilities. "I still have a strong interest," he told the NDP provincial council, "in finding out whether I can do some other things in life which also have interest and meaning for me." He admitted that he did not fill the need for the type of "practical politician" that a significant number of people expected of their leader. Nor had he the facility, he said, "for stirring that kind of mass emotional appeal."

Although Allan Blakeney became party leader in the summer of 1970, Lloyd continued as MLA for the Biggar constituency until an election was called the following year. During that time, he accepted numerous invitations to speak, happy to have the opportunity to make contact with a variety of organizations. He was invited to join faculties of Education and Social Sciences and, although tempted, he concluded it was not the time to take up an academic appointment. He decided instead that he would like to spend some time away from Saskatchewan.

In the spring of 1970, Lloyd was approached to consider accepting a post as a Resident Representative for the United Nations Development Program (UNDP) when a suitable vacancy should arise. Over the next 20 months, he travelled back and forth between New York and Regina, sometimes spending weeks on end, camping in a hotel room, waiting for a summons from the UN which never came. Vicki was left in Regina, not knowing where they were going or when she might need to start packing. Lloyd was finally promised Guyana but waited almost a full year while the placement was sorted out, only to be rejected by that country's government because it decided it would only accept someone from another developing country.

Shortly after this blow, the UNDP announced its intention to send him to South Korea. As they had done for the last year, UNDP officials in New York continually gave Lloyd dates on which to expect definite news, only to let those days go by for weeks without a word. It took from June 24 to November 17 to confirm the appointment. He was asked to be in New York by December 1, 1971, to undergo orientation training. He and Vicki undertook a whirlwind of farewells, covering the province, saying goodbye to constituents, friends and family. Their youngest son, Evan, would go with them to their new home in Seoul.

By early February, Woodrow, Vicki and Evan were settling into a new home in Seoul. Lloyd was to coordinate the various programs that the UNDP ran across the country, and consider the best ways that international aid could be used to help the development of the country. It was a job that made full use of his skills as an administrator and it was a personal challenge for him to master the intricacies of the projects in a totally unfamiliar environment.

Having suffered from a lingering cold during his last weeks in New York, Lloyd was not in the best of health when he arrived in Seoul. Despite the exhilaration of settling into a new place and a new job, he continued to feel unwell. He felt angry with himself for not having the physical strength to get on with his work.

Shortly after Easter, his weakness and pain became more persistent, and finally, on Friday, April 7, 1972, after 48 hours in an American Army Hospital in Seoul, where an abdominal aneurysm was diagnosed, Woodrow Lloyd died.

Conclusion

Woodrow Lloyd was fortunate to have had the opportunity, over 16 years, to create an exemplary education system in Saskatchewan. He followed this by rising to the challenge thrown at him by the medicare crisis of 1962. He proved beyond doubt that he was the leader for that job. What he wrought, with his steadfast determination and adherence to

PHOTO BY DAVID McLENNAN
The Woodrow S. Lloyd Memorial, in Wascana Park, Regina

his principles, changed the course of Canadian medical history. By comparison, the experience of his later years was tinged with frustration and disappointment. Lloyd felt a sense of personal failure when electoral defeat in 1964 brought to an end 20 continuous years of CCF/NDP government. This was reinforced when, under his leadership, the party again fell short in 1967. Moreover, from his perspective, it seemed as if he had failed to inspire a new generation of socialists with his ideals. The complications which surrounded his attempts to find a new and meaningful role for his later life outside provincial politics depressed him. Nevertheless, had he lived longer, he would have realized just how significant his accomplishments were—how the solid body of change he had wrought and the political renewal he brought to his party laid the foundations for the future NDP government and a new era for Saskatchewan.

In a corner of the beautiful gardens surrounding the Saskatchewan Legislative Building a permanent memorial has been erected to Woodrow Lloyd. A path was cleared where previously there was only a gap in the hedge through which he used to slip on his countless journeys from home to work. On the plaque that contains the details of Lloyd's life there is also inscribed the poem he felt exemplified his life:

> Two roads diverged in the wood, and I,
> I took the one less travelled by,
> And that has made all the difference.
> From *The Road Not Taken*, by Robert Frost

Notes

This chapter has been significantly influenced by the knowledge and advice of my brothers, Evan and Michael Lloyd, and my sister, Maureen Neuman, for whose help and support I am very thankful. I have also been most gratified by the affectionate and generous contributions from Woodrow Lloyd's friends and colleagues, in particular, Walter Smishek, Allan Blakeney, John Burton, Les Benjamin, Frank Coburn, Bev Currie, Elwood Cowley, Dan de Vlieger, Jim Struthers, Ed and Penrose Whelan, and Wes Bolstad. Many of the quotes in this chapter are taken from letters written by Woodrow Lloyd to his family and from his diaries.

1. Despite the resistance of many parents, who did not like the idea of their children travelling extra miles to school, the 1944 Act to Establish Larger School Units was one of the first to be passed by the CCF government, of which Lloyd was the minister of Education.
2. Lloyd was also the youngest person ever appointed as a Cabinet minister in Canada up to that date.
3. Not until after the 1967 election did the CCF in Saskatchewan change its name to the New Democratic Party.

W. Ross Thatcher

DALE EISLER

Thatcher, formal portrait, 1966
(M. West, Regina. West's Studio Collection. SAB RA 8359).

Thatcher-Douglas debate, Mossbank, May 20, 1957
(SAB R-WS 15163).

As MP for Moose Jaw speaking at sod turning ceremony for new training school near Moose Jaw, 1950
(SAB RA 2937).

Examining Saskatchewan's Centennial licence plate
(SAB RA 8435).

Saskatchewan Premiers of the 20th Century

Ross Thatcher, 1964–1971

Introduction

There are two dramatically different and enduring images of Ross Thatcher that serve as bookends to the core years of his career in Saskatchewan public life. One is of a confident and determined politician who seized the moment and infused his party with hope and high expectations. The other is of a man unable to disguise his desperation, a spent political figure nearing not only the end of his time as Premier of Saskatchewan, but also of his life. Both scenes are set in Saskatchewan community halls, places that echo to this day with the voices of the province's rich political history.

First, the triumphant Thatcher. It was May 1957 in the small town of Mossbank, about 70 kilometres southwest of Moose Jaw, where Thatcher, by most accounts, had verbally outduelled Saskatchewan CCF Premier Tommy Douglas in a debate that captivated the province. It was to become a watershed event in the political life of the province.

To that point, Douglas had been in a political class by himself. He was an unparalleled orator. For many, he approached the status of a living icon, someone virtually unassailable as a politician. From that moment, Thatcher's destiny to become leader of the provincial Liberals, and ultimately end the CCF's 20-year grip on power, was sealed.

The second scene was 14 years later, in June 1971 at Temple Gardens in Thatcher's hometown of Moose Jaw. It was only days before a provincial election that Thatcher knew his ruling Liberals would lose. Before a partisan crowd the palpable sense of desperation made the atmosphere in the sweaty and muggy hall all the more stifling. Visibly tired and physically drawn, Thatcher tried to reach back and ignite the passion of years before. He failed. Even the chants of placard-waving supporters seem more superficial than spontaneous.[1]

What happened between those two events is an incredible story of how one man changed the course of Saskatchewan politics. For not only did Ross Thatcher end two decades of CCF-NDP hegemony, but he changed, in a fundamental way, how Saskatchewan people viewed themselves, their province and their aspirations as a community.

These two images of Thatcher capture an era of Saskatchewan's political economy because the story of the rise and fall of the Thatcher Liberal government is above all the story of Thatcher himself. Other than Douglas, arguably no other individual towered more over his party and provincial politics in the 20th century. He was a figure whose career spanned not only municipal, federal and provincial politics, but two parties. Rising to public prominence first as a member of city council in Moose Jaw, Thatcher became a member of Parliament (MP) for the Co-operative Commonwealth Federation (CCF), only to leave the party and become one of its harshest and most strident critics. Ultimately he led the provincial Liberals to power in 1964, ushering in a government that sought to recreate Saskatchewan's economic identity

But, curiously, the historical judgment of Thatcher has never matched the forcefulness of the man himself. The legacy of his years in politics has never been a matter of significant debate between historians and political scientists alike. For the most part, the seven years from 1964 to 1971, when Thatcher was Premier of Saskatchewan, are not viewed as particularly pivotal in terms of the province's political and economic development.

Unlike the era of Douglas, who preceded him, and that of New Democratic Party (NDP) Premier Allan Blakeney who followed, the Thatcher period traditionally has been seen as an interruption in the post-World War II era dominated by the CFF and its successor, the NDP. The consensus view is that it reflected a period in a political cycle that returned to equilibrium with the election of the NDP, rather than a turning point in the province's development.

Douglas is widely, and properly, viewed as a great visionary, particularly in terms of building a more egalitarian Saskatchewan society. His crowning achievement was the introduction of universal, publicly funded health insurance (medicare). During his 11 years as Premier throughout the 1970s and early 1980s, Blakeney is remembered as someone who built on the Douglas legacy by using government, and in particular Crown corporations, as a tool for state enterprise. Sandwiched between them, Thatcher is often considered more of a curiosity, a political aberration—a forceful personality, yes, but hardly a political and economic visionary. The treatment of Thatcher and his legacy has been, for the most part, cursory and often dismissive.

For example, Saskatchewan historian John Archer argues that Thatcher's rise to power was "not a victory of private enterprise over socialism." Rather, he says that in the election of April 1964, "the more prosperous classes in the electorate had spoken for change even though the evident prosperity in the province had come under the 'socialists'."[2] In other words, this was no seminal period, no fundamental shift of political attitudes in Saskatchewan.

Political scientist David Smith, who has studied and written extensively on the Saskatchewan Liberal Party's role in the 20th century, discerns no crucial impact by Thatcher on the political psyche of Saskatchewan. While conceding the arrival of Thatcher to power was itself significant, the outcome was not. He writes that:

> From the first the Thatcher government could lay claim to a unique place in Saskatchewan history, part of the distinctiveness arose from its commitment to private enterprise. But the tenets of that doctrine were no more a break with the tradition of Saskatchewan governments than the reluctance they inspired amongst Liberals to use their new power to develop policies. No government in Saskatchewan did so little with its mandate.[3]

Such views of Thatcher and his government tend to be the orthodoxy—an interesting period in terms of Thatcher's own personal crusade against the CCF-NDP and in support of smaller government and free enterprise, but hardly the work of a political visionary. But with the benefit of hindsight, and more than 30 years removed from the Thatcher era, such opinions need to be reconsidered.

We now live in an era of political convergence. Parties of both the so-called right and left espouse fiscal prudence, balanced budgets and a more focused role for government. Spending by provincial and federal governments in the 1970s, 1980s and first half of the 1990s spawned a political culture of entitlement and a fiscal record of mounting public sector deficits and debt. The single biggest public policy challenge of the last decade has been to reverse the fiscal trend and reduce political expectations of what government can, and should, do. Central to that challenge has been to reform Canada's publicly funded, universally accessible system of medicare that started in Saskatchewan.

These were the very issues that Thatcher spoke passionately about almost 50 years ago. He warned that without fiscal responsibility and an appreciation for limited government, politicians would plant the seeds for a fiscal crisis that would undermine the sustainability of social programs and harm most those who need support the most—the less affluent and underprivileged among us. He was someone who was moved and angered by the situation faced by Saskatchewan's Aboriginal population and predicted it would grow to become a social and economic crisis for the province. Long before it was fashionable, Thatcher sought to use government to confront the plight faced by Saskatchewan's Natives. No Premier before him, or since, was more personally committed to this social and economic challenge, which he predicted would become the most crucial issue facing the province.[4]

In a very real sense, then, the story of Ross Thatcher is the saga of a man far ahead of his time and, in many ways, out of step with his times. It is about a politician who was very much a visionary, who spoke out against the prevailing wisdom of an increasing role for government in the economy and society, whose ideas many years later have become the accepted truth. He came to power espousing free enterprise, an eagerness to accept U.S. investment, conservative fiscal policy, and a more limited role for government in a decade when those ideas were not in political fashion.

Early Years

Born on May 24, 1917, in Neville, Saskatchewan, Wilbert Ross Thatcher was the oldest of three sons of Wilbert and Marjorie Thatcher. His parents had met in Saskatchewan after moving west from Ontario, with their parents, as part of the wave of settlement drawn to Saskatchewan by the opportunity of free farmland and a new life. They had been reared by parents whose conservative values were blended with the individual resilience of pioneer life and the appreciation for community as a necessity to survive the harsh life of the prairies. In his early twenties, Wilbert Thatcher and a partner opened a small hardware and dry goods store in Neville, while Marjorie worked as a schoolteacher. Eventually, Thatcher struck out on his own and opened a similar store in Limerick and a second store in the nearby town of Valor.

No one more than his parents influenced and shaped the values that would guide Thatcher throughout his life. A man of modest tastes, a frugal lifestyle and conservative politics, Wilbert Thatcher raised his sons to appreciate the value of a dollar. He taught them that hard work was its own reward, that attention to detail and controlling costs were the necessities of a successful entrepreneur, and that devotion to one's goals was the path to success. As a schoolteacher, Marjorie Thatcher implicitly understood the value of education to achieving a secure life. She was determined her sons would succeed in school and ensured that their school work always came before helping out in the family hardware business.

By the late 1920s, the hardware business was flourishing and Wilbert Thatcher looked for expansion opportunities. With the help of the Marshall-Wells Company, a hardware wholesale supplier, Thatcher established a new store in the thriving railway town of Moose Jaw. Although the Depression struck shortly after Thatcher opened Moose Jaw Hardware, the business was not crippled by the economic downturn. Thatcher's commitment to frugality, tight inventory control, loyalty to customers and reputation as a merchant who would extend credit to those who needed it, helped his business not only to survive the Depression, but position it for greater success when good economic times returned.

Just as his parents moulded Ross Thatcher, who worked in the store after school and on weekends, the other formative influence on his life came during his first years working away from home. A strong, dedicated student, Ross was able to accelerate through high school. He graduated at age 15 and, with the help of a scholarship, had earned a Commerce degree from Queen's University in Kingston before he turned 18. After receiving his degree, he landed a job as executive assistant to N.J. McLean, vice-president of Canada Packers in Toronto. His boss was the brother of company president and wealthy industrialist J.S. McLean, who was to become a mentor to, and major influence on, the young Thatcher. Each Monday, the McLeans wanted to see a profit-and-loss statement updated from the previous week. Quickly Ross realized that his father's formula for success in a small family-owned hardware business was no different from a major national company like Canada Packers—controlling costs while delivering good service and a product people needed.

By the late 1930s, at the urging of his father, Thatcher returned to Moose Jaw to work in the family hardware business. In 1938, he married Adrah Leone (Peggie) McNaughton, the daughter of a well-known Moose Jaw businessman who owned the Western Ice Company. Ross and Peggie first met in high school, and as avid badminton players had spent their summers playing on the courts in Moose Jaw's Crescent Park. Back in Moose Jaw, Thatcher was a regular at St. Andrew's Anglican Church, and formed a church youth group that met Sunday evenings for young boys who were too old for Sunday school but still eager to be involved in the church.

Soon after returning to Moose Jaw, the young Thatcher embarked on his first personal investment venture. It provides a telling glimpse of his spirit of entrepreneurship and frugality. Within a year, Thatcher had scraped together enough money—some saved from his job at Canada Packers, some borrowed—to buy 10 houses for an average of $500 each. It was the outset of World War II and Thatcher saw the houses as an ideal investment opportunity. Quite rightly, he believed the demand for housing would grow when soldiers returned after the war and so would the value of his real estate.

Ever the bargain hunter, Thatcher bought discontinued paint for mere cents a quart from his father's store. To save on labour costs he did some of the renovations himself, or else hired painters with charge accounts at Moose Jaw Hardware. Through a combination of cash and barter—he wrote off some of the painters' charges at the store—Thatcher was able to renovate the houses. With the work done, Thatcher eventually sold some of the houses—in a few cases for more than three times his investment—and rented others.

The same kind of attention to costs, and specifically the bottom line, became Thatcher's primary motivation in business. While his father was long known as an astute buyer and manager of inventory, Ross was more fixated on costs and the bottom line. A more dominating and outgoing personality than his quieter younger brother Clarke, who also worked at the store, Ross was clearly the heir apparent in terms of taking over management of the store. And that was exactly what happened by the mid-1940s, when Wilbert Thatcher had to retire due to poor health.[5]

Interest in Politics

At the same time that Ross Thatcher was managing the growing hardware business, he also began developing an interest in politics. The hardware business helped Thatcher develop a wide network of contacts in the community, while he was building a profile as a young, up-and-coming politician. In 1942 he was elected to Moose Jaw city council, and although his background was as a young entrepreneurial businessman, on council Thatcher was known as a forceful supporter of working people. In a city like Moose Jaw, where the railway union was powerful, Thatcher was seen as a friend of labour. Although he briefly flirted with the local Liberal association before being elected to council, the older, established Liberals in town showed little interest in him. Quickly, Thatcher gravitated to the CCF, which was clearly a party on the rise across Saskatchewan in the early 1940s.

What drew Thatcher to the CCF was its activism, particularly its commitment to economic development. The promise of public investment to create jobs for young men returning from the war was the kind of action Thatcher liked. Having seen firsthand the scale of economic and industrial development in Ontario and Quebec when he worked for Canada Packers, Thatcher believed that if the private sector was not going to invest in Saskatchewan, then government should. The issue was not so much public, or private, investment, but a party that was willing to take the initiative to build the economy. Indeed, Thatcher was haunted by a particular memory from his time in Toronto during the Depression. From his office window he could see hundreds of men who would line up at the front gates of Canada Packers each morning looking for work, only to be sent away disappointed. People willing and able to work, but trapped by unemployment, was a travesty that Thatcher believed demanded a solution. The idea of public enterprise to build the economy and create opportunity in the aftermath of World War II was something Thatcher could easily embrace.

From the beginning, Thatcher was not a natural fit with the CCF. As someone steeped in business, he seemed an unlikely ally with a party that had a clear socialist perspective. Moose Jaw was a major railway centre on the prairies. In the mid-1940s, there were 5,000 employees working for the Canadian Pacific Railway and, as such, the city had a strong union presence. But any suspicion CCF members had of Thatcher were subsumed by his obvious attributes. He was young, energetic, ambitious and well known. Moreover, during his two-year term as a member of Moose Jaw city council, Thatcher spoke out forcefully for working people, supporting labour's calls for a minimum wage, hours of work legislation and the right to organize.

Member of Parliament

After a two-year term on city council, and with the support of key union activists, Thatcher won the nomination as the CCF candidate in Moose Jaw for the 1945 federal election. As a young businessman interested in public issues—particularly the need for job creation to help ease the economic transition from World War II to peacetime—Thatcher was a welcome candidate for the CCF. He was seen as someone who helped broaden the appeal of the party into the small business community. At the time the CCF was a rising force in Canadian politics, with its power base in Saskatchewan, but also with growing influence in Ontario. In the election, Thatcher easily defeated the Liberal incumbent as the CCF won 18 of 21 Saskatchewan ridings.

As a member of Parliament (MP), Thatcher was clearly on the right wing of the CCF caucus. His interest in business, economic issues and the importance of the profit motive were so clearly dominant that his relationship with the party—particularly its Ontario-based labour wing—was often uncomfortable. But Thatcher also demonstrated a strong social conscience and sense of fair play, which allowed him to be a stern critic of business if he felt the interests of ordinary people were being harmed.

For example, in 1949, as a member of a parliamentary committee investigating corporate profits after price controls were lifted following the war, Thatcher was not hesitant to criticize business profit-taking. In a series of radio broadcasts reporting on the work of the committee, Thatcher was harsh in his critique of business:

> The minutes of the committee tell an incredible story of short-sightedness, greed and selfishness on the part of many of Canada's leading industrial and commercial companies. Obviously all business must be conducted to make a profit, but surely there is a difference between profit and what might be called plunder. Very often it might be the code of plunder —buy for as little as possible and sell for all the traffic will bear, unless concessions are made to fair price or public need.
>
> The parliamentary committee found definite evidence of abnormal and excessive profits made by big Canadian firms. I say it is human nature and economic common sense for every businessman to desire a profit. In normal times competition keeps these profits at a reasonable level. But in the past two years, because of the world-wide shortage caused by the war, competition has not been a controlling factor.
>
> Business, to a considerable degree, took advantage of these shortages to force prices up. They therefore must accept some responsibility for the present high price situation.[6]

Clearly, Thatcher believed in a competitive market economy. But he believed also that in the case of market failure, when concentration of power in the hands of private business

SAB RA 2937

Ross Thatcher, as MP for Moose Jaw, speaking at a 1950 sod-turning ceremony for a nearby training school.

actually prevented the regulation and efficiency that comes with competition, then government needed to play a role. Nor did Thatcher think that the private sector always made the right market decisions. In fact, his experience working for Canada Packers in Toronto convinced him that if Saskatchewan was going to diversify its agricultural economy by building an industrial economic base, it could not necessarily depend on private investment. If the private sector was not willing to invest in the province, then government could play a role through public enterprise, which he believed would help create an economic base that would attract the necessary private investment.

But at the core of Thatcher's belief in public enterprise was pragmatism, rather than an ideological commitment that public ownership was, in itself, a virtue for society. Quite simply, Thatcher saw it is an alternative that should be used if the private sector was not willing to invest. Many in the CCF of the day opposed private capital because they saw it in Marxist terms as a dominant class controlling the means of production and the social distribution of wealth. Thatcher rejected such a perspective and eagerly embraced the profit motive that drives private capital investment. For Thatcher, the issue was to create opportunity for people and it mattered not whether the chance for employment came through the private or public sector.

Ultimately, it was government enterprise in Saskatchewan, manifest in the form of Crown corporations, coupled with the dominant role of organized labour within the CCF, that convinced Thatcher the party was misguided. He became an internal and eventually a public critic of many traditional CCF policy positions, calling for a restoration of means tests for people who received government-funded pensions, lower corporate taxes and a reduction in government spending on public works projects. While those strains became evident during his first term as an MP, they were not severe enough for Thatcher to become alienated from the party. Rather, Thatcher was tolerated as something of a maverick on the right-wing fringe of the party. But he was also seen as someone whose commitment to working people and the creation of economic opportunity was strong enough to validate his position as a CCF MP.

In fact, at times, even when Thatcher was outside the mainstream of CCF caucus positions, he found himself in good company. On at least one occasion, for example, he was at odds with the caucus but in agreement with leader M.J. Coldwell. The two found themselves offside with the majority of the CCF caucus in 1955 on the issue of German rearmament after World War II. The majority view was to oppose any sanctioning that would allow Germany to rebuild its military strength. But Coldwell and Thatcher both took the position that the rearming of Germany, under the scrutiny of NATO, was better than to risk it happening incrementally without proper multilateral supervision.

But by that point, many in the federal caucus were of the view—an opinion shared by a growing number in the party itself—that Thatcher was a member of the CCF in name only. He seldom socialized with his caucus colleagues and seemed more at ease with Liberal backbenchers, some of whom, because of the large Liberal majority, sat on the opposition side of the House.

When Thatcher broke ranks on the German question—even though Coldwell himself could not support the caucus position and had offered to resign over the issue—the opinion of many in caucus was Thatcher had to go.[7] They did not have long to wait.

In April 1955, Thatcher was ordered by Coldwell to support the CCF position on an upcoming budget vote and to remain loyal on all future caucus policy decisions. Thatcher refused to do so, and made his move.

Departure from the CCF

In the budget debate, the CCF called on federal Finance minister Douglas Abbott to raise corporate tax rates. It was a position that triggered Thatcher's decision to leave the CCF. When he rose to enter budget debate a week later as an Independent MP, Thatcher used the opportunity to flesh out the reasons for his decisions. He accused the CCF of abandoning its agrarian, populist roots and drifting to the left and into the embrace of the Ontario-dominated organized labour movement. He talked about five "fundamental differences" he had with his former party.

"For some time, I have been fearful of, and in disagreement with, what appeared to me to be the growing left-wing tendency within the party ... I feel the left-wing element has gained a dangerous and unwarranted recognition within the councils of the party," Thatcher said in his Budget debate address. More precisely, Thatcher raised the notion of communist sympathies by some in the party: "The leader of the CCF and most of his colleagues, I know, have no more use for communism and its vicious methods than I have. Nevertheless ... the CCF party has taken a line on foreign affairs that in my opinion, no matter how honestly taken, can only give comfort to communist nations."

Second, in terms of "social welfare," Thatcher opposed the CCF's position of "higher and higher benefits immediately without delay, regardless of the nation's ability to pay."

Third, he opposed the CCF's support for ever-increasing government spending, arguing that cuts to unnecessary spending were required to reduce taxes for lower-income Canadians.

Fourth, Thatcher called the CCF's position in support of increasing corporate taxation "unrealistic," and said that his view that taxes should be lowered to stimulate economic growth and jobs was often greeted with hostility by his former colleagues.

Finally, Thatcher said that he had lost faith in the notion of government ownership as a means to stimulate economic growth. "The socialized industries recently established in the province of Saskatchewan have been, to say the least, not very satisfactory," Thatcher argued.[8]

While the governing Liberals made it clear to Thatcher that they would gladly welcome him into their ranks, the MP for Moose Jaw felt uneasy about making the walk across the floor. Instead he spent a year as an Independent, before officially joining the Liberal caucus to sit as a backbencher in 1956. Before long, after the initial publicity of his decision to abandon the CCF and the brief attention that came with his move to join the Liberals, Thatcher faded from public view. He seemed destined for political anonymity, despised by his former party and, as an ex-CCFer, not fully trusted by his new Liberal colleagues.

But ironically, it was during his brief time as a Liberal backbencher that Thatcher—unwittingly perhaps—made a move that would inject him into the Saskatchewan provincial political debate and, ultimately, propel him into the position of Premier. It happened late one night in Parliament in the spring of 1956, when Thatcher rose to speak as a backbencher in a pivotal debate over legislation to establish a gas pipeline from Alberta to Ontario. The Liberal government, and more specifically Industry minister C.D. Howe, had assembled a consortium of private interests to build the pipeline. The CCF demanded the pipeline be government owned.

Here was the perfect issue for Thatcher to explain why he left the CCF and the reason he believed his former party was trapped by an ideology that was unworkable and economically destructive. Thatcher's words were delivered in the House of Commons, but they were aimed directly at the government of Saskatchewan Premier T.C. Douglas:

> I say tonight that the Saskatchewan program of socialization was born in high hopes and with laudable aspirations. But today it is apparent that the program has been bogged down in a morass of bungling, red tape, inefficiency and inexperience. I say there is not a single Saskatchewan Crown corporation that has operated in the black for a reasonable length of time without special privileges or compulsion of some kind.
>
> I say the program has been a tragedy and a very costly fiasco. I think it has been a dismal failure. At one time I believed in public ownership, but after holding office for 14 years, I am absolutely convinced that public ownership should only be used under very special circumstances. Generally speaking, people simply will not work for the government in business as efficiently as they will for private enterprise.[9]

In his speech, Thatcher reeled off the financial results of an array of government enterprises: a leather tannery, a shoe factory, a post-war housing corporation, a woollen mill and a brick plant. Each, Thatcher said, was a financial failure that cost Saskatchewan taxpayers dearly. Of the Crown corporations that had shown profits, Thatcher argued, "analysis shows that they were able to do so because they enjoyed either government compulsion or some kind of monopoly privileges."

For Douglas, the criticism struck at the core beliefs of the CCF. As a socialist party, state intervention in the economy, and in particular state enterprise in the form of Crown corporations, was a defining trait of the CCF. It was the underpinning of the Douglas government's approach to economic development, the heart of the economic engine to support equity through social programs. It was a criticism that he felt could not be left unanswered.

It led to an immense tactical and strategic blunder by Douglas, one that became a key factor in the ultimate defeat of the Saskatchewan CCF government and the election of Thatcher as Premier. Unbelievably, Douglas challenged Thatcher to a debate on the record of Crown corporations. It was a bizarre move, one that said as much about the size of Douglas's ego as it did the quality of his judgement. Thatcher quickly accepted the challenge and the stage was set for the two to meet.

The Douglas-Thatcher Debate

It happened in May 1957, in the midst of a federal election campaign, at the town of Mossbank. Thatcher was running as a Liberal candidate against CCF incumbent Hazen Argue, and leapt at the opportunity for the attention and profile he would get from debating the Premier on the hot-button issue of government enterprise. There was huge public interest across the province in the Douglas-Thatcher debate. Adherents to the CCF saw it as an opportunity for Douglas to get back at Thatcher, a political turncoat despised by many in his former party. The Liberals, both provincially and federally, felt emboldened by the brash, outspoken Thatcher, who had become one of the most vocal and strident critics of the CCF. The fact that Thatcher had gone from a supporter to an opponent of the CCF and its core beliefs added a credibility to his critique that went beyond the traditional partisan debate.

The two squared off in front of an overflow crowd of more than 1,000, who spilled outside the modest town hall, into the basement and yard outside where loudspeakers carried the exchange. The debate was also broadcast live on a network of provincial radio stations.[10]

Douglas led off the debate by attempting to deal with the criticisms Thatcher had set out of Saskatchewan Crown corporations in his speech a year earlier in Parliament. It was a tactical error. Douglas quickly became bogged down in dry statistics, when in fact this was, at its core, a debate about political beliefs, about how economies are built for the goals of the broader community, not abstract numbers from annual reports. The Premier ended his defence of public enterprise with an attack on Thatcher, who, he said, was "not fit to represent the fine people of this constituency in the Parliament of Canada."

Wisely, Thatcher picked up what he suggested was a personal attack. "I felt a moment ago that perhaps the Premier was a little bitter," Thatcher said. "I can't say I blame him for not talking about Crown corporations at all for the last 10 minutes of his speech because the record is pretty bad."

Thatcher then went through the failed enterprises launched by the Douglas government, making it sound like a litany of government ineptitude. He argued that the "impractical theories of socialist planners have discouraged private investment from coming to Saskatchewan" and, as a result, the province's economic development had lagged behind neighbouring provinces. Through it all, Thatcher showed not the slightest trace of deference to the Premier and in fact seemed wholly unimpressed with either his opponent or the policies of his former party.

SAB R-WS15159(1) © M. West, Regina. West's Studio Collection

Ross Thatcher, seated at left, listens while Premier T.C. Douglas speaks during their debate in Mossbank on May 20, 1957. His strong performance in the debate would change Thatcher's career, thrusting him into the forefront of politics in Saskatchewan.

The consensus was that at worst, the debate was a draw for Thatcher. But many, including some media reporters, suggested that Thatcher had been more impressive and confident than Douglas. Where there was no doubt was with Liberals in the crowd. They absolutely believed Thatcher performed better than Douglas and, for the first time in years, felt a surge of confidence. For years, the oratory of Tommy Douglas had been unmatched on the political scene in Saskatchewan. His stature was such that in such situations, no one was considered his equal. What Thatcher had done was demonstrate he was far from intimidated by Douglas and was a worthy opponent.

But whether he won the debate or not, what became clear a few weeks later, in no uncertain terms, was that Thatcher lost his bid to win the rural seat for the Liberals. The CCF's Hazen Argue defeated him by more than 1,500 votes and a year later in 1958, when he again ran against Argue, Thatcher finished a distant third as John Diefenbaker and the Progressive Conservatives swept to power in a national landslide. Saskatchewan, like it had been for many years, remained largely a wasteland for the federal Liberals.

Twice defeated, Thatcher retreated to running his hardware business in Moose Jaw and operating a Hereford cattle ranch he had bought just west of Moose Jaw near the town of Caron. Although disappointed by the losses, Thatcher had not lost his thirst for politics. In fact, the Mossbank debate and the clash over the provincial CCF government's approach to economic development merely whetted his appetite for provincial politics.

Thatcher did not fully retreat from sight, particularly within the Liberal Party. He helped raise funds for the party and helped organize a dinner for federal Liberal leader Lester Pearson in Regina. At the same time, there was growing unhappiness with provincial Liberal leader Hammy McDonald, a decent and likeable man, but someone who lacked the spark and charisma it would take to defeat someone of the stature of Douglas. Based on Thatcher's performance against Douglas in Mossbank and the credibility he brought to his criticisms of his former party, a movement began to unseat McDonald in favour of Thatcher. While Thatcher kept a safe distance from the behind-the-scenes effort to unseat the leader, he had little positive to say about McDonald when the subject came up with other Liberals.

The Liberal Leadership in Saskatchewan

The leadership issue came to a head in the summer of 1959. By that point, a group of influential Liberals had organized a push to force McDonald out to pave the way for Thatcher. Faced with tepid support in his own caucus and pressure from the provincial party executive to step aside, following a meeting of the executive in Regina, McDonald announced his intention to resign as leader for "health reasons." Barely two months later, Thatcher was selected provincial Liberal leader, easily defeating respected veteran MLA Alex Cameron, as well as Wilf Gardiner and Frank Foley, on the first ballot.

As leader, Thatcher brought an organizational zeal the Liberal Party had lacked. He fervently believed there were no shortcuts in building the party. It required hard work, specifically the painstaking task of selling memberships one by one. He sold his hardware business and had the party hire seven full-time organizers and a similar number to work part time. He became a true party boss, demanding dedication to the task of signing up new members. Very quickly, his right-hand man became Dave Steuart, the mayor of Prince Albert and party president who had been instrumental in deposing Hammy McDonald and organizing for Thatcher's leadership.

Thatcher's years in the CCF convinced him how important building a party organization was to success, so he applied the same formula to the Liberals that worked so well for the CCF. But to ensure he had control of the party, all money raised went to provincial Liberal headquarters, rather than some of it staying in constituency organizations, as had previously been the case. At the same time he expanded the provincial executive into a 75-member provincial council that met regularly and ensured that he could better monitor what was happening in all parts of the province.[11]

Personally, he brought a hard-edged critique of the CCF, particularly its economic development policies. Thatcher sought to change both the tone and the focus of the provincial political debate, shifting it to what he believed was the province's inability to keep pace economically with other provinces in western Canada because of the CCF's socialist principles. His message in speeches across the province never wavered:

> From hard bitter experience I am opposed to socialism. I am a Liberal by conviction, not by accident. Because of those beliefs, I crossed the floor of the House of Commons. I firmly believe the Regina CCF government

has caused economic stagnation in our province. It is our job to emerge from the dark cloud of CCF government. Canadian socialism was born here. It should be buried here.[12]

The 1960 General Election

Nine months after taking over as leader, Thatcher faced a provincial election. While progress had been made in building a stronger organization, the Liberal Party was still no match for the Douglas-led CCF juggernaut. The key plank of the CCF platform was a comprehensive, universal, government-funded medical care insurance plan. In effect, Douglas promised to extend the hospital insurance coverage already offered by government to medical care provided by doctors. On June 8, 1960, the CCF won a fifth majority government. But still, there were encouraging signs for the Thatcher Liberals even though the CCF won 38 seats and the Liberals only 16. The vote had polarized between the CCF and Liberals, with the Social Credit losing the 3 seats it held going into the election and the PCs electing no one. Moreover, the CCF popular vote fell by more than 4% (to 41%) and the Liberal vote rose by 3% (to 30%).

For Thatcher, the next four years were to be spent further polarizing the political landscape into two choices—the Liberals and the CCF. He believed that Saskatchewan provincial politics was, at its core, a left-right ideological cleavage. On one side were those who believed in free enterprise, on the other were adherents to socialism. If the choice was made clear to Saskatchewan people, Thatcher believed that power would be within his grasp.

Whether Saskatchewan people saw their provincial politics in such free enterprise-versus-socialist terms was debatable. Indeed, the politics in the province had historically divided between Liberals on one side, and some amalgamation of anti-Liberals—bearing names ranging from the Provincial Rights Party to the Conservatives, Social Credit or CCF-NDP—on the other. For example, when the CCF emerged as a force in Saskatchewan politics in the late 1930s and early 1940s, it rose at the expense of the Conservatives as the alternative to the Liberals. The one constant was the Liberal Party remaining as a source of political power.

As someone originally attracted to socialism as a tool for economic and social advancement, who evolved to the view that it was a misguided philosophy, Thatcher was determined to change the prism through which people saw their political choice in Saskatchewan. He had migrated politically to become a right-wing ideologue. As Saskatchewan Liberal leader, Thatcher embraced free enterprise, while maintaining a strong social conscience. His strategy was to frame the political debate in terms of free enterprise versus socialism, a kind of reductionism that made the choice for voters clear, unequivocal and unavoidable.

This kind of approach fit perfectly the attributes he brought to leadership. As someone who had supported CCF doctrine, seen it up close and in practice, and come to the conclusion that it was unworkable, he brought the zeal of a convert to the Liberal leadership. To achieve success, all he had to do was convince others of the same truth he had discovered.

In practical political terms for Thatcher, this meant that to succeed he had to force a clear-cut choice in provincial politics. If he was able to convince people that politics in Saskatchewan was about socialism versus free enterprise, then the only political brands that mattered were the CCF-NDP and Liberal. The simple fact would be that the CCF-NDP represented socialism and the Liberals free enterprise, and any other combatants, namely the Social Credit and Progressive Conservatives, as parties that supported free enterprise, would be rendered irrelevant because, as the dominant party on the right, the Liberals would be the vehicle to express that political sentiment. The key to success would be to convince a large majority of the more than 165,000 who had voted for the Social Credit and Progressive Conservative parties in 1960 to embrace the Liberals.

His objective, then, was to turn the Saskatchewan Liberal Party into the political vehicle of those who wanted to choose free enterprise over socialism. But Thatcher also understood that Saskatchewan provincial politics was more complex than such a black-and-white choice of left versus right. After all, although involved in small business and someone who saw the inherent logic of private enterprise and the profit motive as a positive force in economic development, Thatcher had a strong social conscience, which explains why he was originally attracted to the CCF. Much of his time as a CCF MP was spent speaking out for low-income Canadians and the unemployed. The fact that at times he questioned universal social programs was not an indictment on his commitment to the less fortunate, rather it was an expression of his view on the best means to ensure that people who needed government support received it in a way that was fiscally sustainable for government and economically sound for society.

So in framing the political debate between the Liberals and CCF, Thatcher's objective was to keep it largely confined to economic issues. He recognized, and shared, the social conscience of Saskatchewan people and sought to keep his point of differentiation with the CCF on economic, rather than social, terms.

During his time as opposition leader from 1960 to 1964, Thatcher put the organizational focus of the party on recruiting new members, particularly known PC and Socred supporters. He personally worked to build bridges with the non-CCF supporters and sought the cooperation of PC leader Martin Pederson in a plan to defeat the CCF. In a private meeting with Pederson in 1961 prior to a by-election in the Turtleford constituency, the Liberal leader spoke about the Liberals and PCs working together by engaging in strategic voting, where the object would be to support the Liberal or PC candidate who had the best chance of defeating the CCF. In the case of Turtleford, Thatcher argued the choice was the Liberal, but looking to the future, the two parties could work together in a way that would not split the anti-CCF vote. In polarized, head-to-head races, the Thatcher Liberals won Turtleford and two other by-elections—Prince Albert and Weyburn—in the 1960–64 period. Clearly, Thatcher was building political momentum, but the most compelling evidence came in December 1961 when the Liberals won with relative ease in Weyburn, which Douglas had to vacate when he took over as federal NDP leader.[13]

Aside from working to attract Tories and Socreds to the Liberal fold, Thatcher also wooed Hazen Argue, his former CCF colleague and officemate, and later his opponent in the 1957 and 1958 federal elections. In 1962, less than a year after Argue lost the federal leadership of the newly created New Democratic Party to Tommy Douglas—who had resigned as Premier to lead the party forged out of an official alliance between the CCF and organized labour—Argue deserted the NDP to sit as a Liberal.

Just as Thatcher had done when he left the CCF, Argue said his decision was based on labour's takeover of the party. "The NDP has gone beyond redemption. Because a few labour bosses have so much power, it is a hopeless situation," Argue told reporters. For Thatcher, who played a key behind-the-scenes role in recruiting Argue, the defection was a crucial part of his strategy to defeat the CCF-NDP. Argue was a strong and credible voice among farmers in Saskatchewan. Thatcher knew that Argue's declaration that the CCF-NDP was in the control of Ontario-based organized labour would weaken its appeal in rural Saskatchewan.

Beyond the political intrigue of uniting the right and working to portray the CCF-NDP as a party of labour, a far more important public policy issue worked in the Thatcher Liberals' favour during this period. The centrepiece of the CCF campaign in the 1960 provincial election was the promise of a universal, publicly funded system of medical insurance. The idea was far from radical. In fact the notion of government medical insurance predated the Douglas government in Saskatchewan politics, and during the previous decade there had been ongoing federal-provincial talks on establishing a national medical scheme. Frustrated by an inability to make progress at the national level, in 1959 Douglas said the issue was too important to wait any longer and announced Saskatchewan would take the initiative itself.

Given that Douglas won a comfortable majority campaigning openly for medicare, Thatcher realized the idea was popular. Therefore, he and the Liberals never opposed the legislation in principle when it passed through the Legislature in late 1961, but rather criticised the government for a lack of consultation and the manner of implementation.

The issue exploded into an international news story when the legislation establishing a system of medicare was implemented on July 1, 1962, and virtually all the doctors in the province announced they were withdrawing their services in protest. Quickly, panic began to set in amongst the population as the doctors' "strike" dragged on for three weeks. From the outset, the majority of public opinion was with the government and that view grew even stronger as the crisis dragged on.

What Thatcher did was not attack the government on its policy, but rather its tactics and "arrogance." At a tense meeting of doctors in May 1962 in Regina, where Premier Woodrow Lloyd received an icy reception, Thatcher criticized the government not for implementing medicare, but for how it was doing so. He called the creation of the Medical Care Insurance Commission, as the sole agent in dealing with the doctors, "vicious compulsion" and "peacetime conscription of the medical profession and the abrogation of its civil rights."

"After months … we now see the iron fist. When all else has failed to bring doctors to their knees, economic strangulation is to be tried," Thatcher said. "If the government can take away the rights of doctors today, it can take away the rights of some other minority tomorrow." Weeks later, in a theatrical gesture in front of reporters at the height of the doctors' strike in July 1962, when a mass rally by doctors and their sympathisers was held in front of the Legislature, Thatcher was photographed kicking at the locked door of the provincial legislative chamber. The move came after Thatcher had called Lloyd "a petty dictator" for not recalling the Legislature to deal with the crisis.[15]

By the time Woodrow Lloyd called a provincial election for April 1964, many key variables were in place for Thatcher and the Liberals to take the final step and end the 20-year CCF-NDP political hegemony in Saskatchewan. Ironically, at least two of the most important factors had virtually nothing to do with Thatcher.

First, Douglas himself had left for federal politics. He had reached virtually iconic status in many minds and left huge shoes that, quite frankly, no one could fill—certainly not his successor, Woodrow Lloyd, who was recognized as solid and decent, but hardly an inspiring figure like the man he replaced. Second, after 20 years, the mood for change was undeniable.

But beyond those factors, Thatcher had also been able to change the focus of the political debate in Saskatchewan and, more importantly, the perceptions Saskatchewan people had of themselves and their province. What he did was redefine the political environment in which the election would be fought. It was about Saskatchewan as an economic laggard, a province that was not reaching its potential because of a socialist government that was harming the economy with high taxes and state intervention. It was about Saskatchewan falling further and further behind its neighbours, Alberta and Manitoba, in terms of economic and population growth. It was about the need for smaller, more efficient government, lower taxes and free enterprise. It was about economic opportunity, or the framework for what he called "an opportunity state."

There was certainly evidence that Saskatchewan was not keeping pace economically with the rest of the west. The province's population was stagnant, while in Alberta and, to a lesser extent Manitoba, there was strong population growth. For example, from 1941 to 1951, Saskatchewan's population plummeted from 896,000 to less than 832,000. While it had more than recovered to 925,000 by 1961, it lagged far behind Alberta, where the population climbed from 940,000 to 1.32 million during the same period. Meanwhile, Manitoba, which since 1911 had fewer people than Saskatchewan—at one point more than 200,000 less—had pulled virtually equal to Saskatchewan in terms of population by 1961.

There was also a well-entrenched perception of greater exploration and mineral development in Manitoba, particularly near Thompson, which was attracting many young Saskatchewan men to work in the mines of northern Manitoba because no similar opportunity existed in their home province. Meanwhile, in Alberta, the oil industry was thriving and had emerged as an engine of development for the province that was reflected in the fast-growing cities of Calgary and Edmonton.

Thatcher sought to bring a new generation of Liberal candidates into politics that reflected a business attitude and approach to government. Among them were Herb Pinder, a business school graduate from Harvard University and a well-known and successful Saskatoon businessman, as well as Gordon Grant of Regina, a respected businessman and former president of the Saskatchewan Urban Municipalities Association. From Prince Albert came John Cuelenare, a highly regarded lawyer and, like Dave Steuart, a former mayor of the city.

The key to the Liberals' success in the campaign would be their ability to turn the election into an either-or choice between themselves and the CCF-NDP, between free enterprise and socialism. There was good reason for optimism. The Liberals had won all three by-elections held after the 1960 election and, in each case, the PCs and Social Credit did not run candidates. Moreover, Douglas himself had lost a bid to win a federal seat in Regina in 1962 after being selected federal NDP leader when the anti-NDP vote coalesced behind the federal PC candidate.

"I implore all of those who want to rid our province from the dark spectre of socialism to make common cause behind the Liberal candidates to ensure what happened to Tommy Douglas in Regina will happen in all seats," Thatcher said at a Liberal campaign event during the first week of the campaign.[16]

The 13-point Liberal platform called for tight control of government spending and lower taxes. Thatcher promised tax-free gas for farmers, a cut in the sales tax, the end of sales tax on children's clothing, a tax exemption for newly married couples on purchases of household essentials up to $1,000, and the elimination of the 3% minerals tax to jump-start northern mining development.

While the Liberal platform was hardly visionary, it kept the focus on the economic development theme, where Thatcher believed the CCF-NDP was most vulnerable. At the same time, there was growing distrust among rural municipal governments with the Lloyd government over plans to move towards a county system. A study done years earlier called for the amalgamation of RMs that would reduce the number of rural municipal governments from almost 300 to 65 counties.

Ultimately, all the factors converged: the mood for change, the polarization of Liberals versus CCF-NDP, and the sense Saskatchewan was not fulfilling its economic potential. Thatcher's promise of a thriving, growing economy, fuelled by private investment and 80,000 new jobs in his government's first term, was enough to turn the political tide in a new direction after 20 years. On election night, the Liberal held the winning margin in 33 seats, the CCF-NDP held 25, and leader Martin Pederson won the lone seat for the PCs.[17]

The First Thatcher Government

Consistent with determination to control the party as leader, Thatcher was equally, if not more, determined to exercise absolute control over government. In keeping with his promise of smaller government, Thatcher appointed a 13-member Cabinet, including Dave Steuart (Health), former leader Hammy McDonald (Agriculture), Herb Pinder (Industry and Information), John Cuelenare (Natural Resources), Lionel Coderre (Labour), Alex Cameron (Mineral Resources), Darrel Heald (attorney general), George Trapp (Education), Doug McFarlane (Municipal Affairs), Dave Boldt (Social Welfare and Rehabilitation), Gordon Grant (Highways and Transportation), and Wilf Gardiner (Public Works).

But the most telling choice that Thatcher made, one that demonstrated his hands-on approach and determination to control his government, was to name himself as provincial treasurer. In effect, Thatcher believed he had to apply the same cost-conscious approach to government that he did to his former hardware business. The need to control government

SAB RB 11,799(1)

In this undated photograph, Thatcher makes a point during a meeting between his Cabinet and representatives of the Saskatchewan Federation of Agriculture. Dave Steuart, Thatcher's "right-hand man," is, fittingly, seated to Thatcher's right.

spending by reducing what he saw as waste and inefficiency, while at the same time cutting taxes, were to be the central ingredients of his government's fiscal and economic strategy. Thatcher trusted no one but himself to carry out his agenda, at least in the early days, until he had put his stamp on government and set its clear direction.

Thatcher's economic development strategy was outlined clearly in his government's first budget, delivered February 19, 1965. Thatcher said four factors framed his budget planning: first, Liberal promises in the election; second, that taxes in Saskatchewan were "dangerously high" compared to the rest of Canada; third, development would occur only when a "completely new political and economic climate [was] created"; and, fourth, that much remained to be done to improve living standards of Saskatchewan people.

As Thatcher stated in the budget:

> This government believes that a greater investment of private capital in Saskatchewan is the one step that is vital in the achievement of every economic and social goal we hold dear. We passionately believe that only private enterprise methods will achieve this much needed investment. We are convinced that industrialists will establish in Saskatchewan for only one reason—because it is profitable for them to do so.
>
> This government, therefore, will endeavour to nourish our investment climate; take care of our investment worthiness; and improve our methods of attracting new capital. In every field of commercial endeavour, we propose to explore and provide sound incentives for risk-taking and development.
>
> We intend to keep the burden of taxes and regulations at their lowest possible level. By doing so, we think we can obtain new mines, new oil wells, new manufacturing plants, new businesses on a far more comprehensive scale… Moreover, with more industries and more people we shall broaden the basis of taxation, which will provide the revenues for expanding our educational, cultural, transportation, health and welfare services.[18]

Elsewhere in the budget, Thatcher set out his approach to, and expectations of, Crown corporations. He worked from the premise that government should be involved only in limited areas where it could do a better job than the private sector. He maintained that the success of some Crowns, such as Saskatchewan Government Insurance and Saskatchewan Power, was the result of their statutory monopolies rather than good business practice. He removed the requirement that public institutions, such as schools and hospitals, had to purchase their coverage from the government insurance company. He also served notice that he intended to sell, if suitable private buyers could be found, the Saskatchewan Timber Board, Saskatchewan Guarantee and Fidelity Company, the Saskatchewan sodium sulphate plant, Estevan Clay Products and Saskatchewan Government Printing.

At the same time, in his first budget—which projected a surplus of $12 million—Thatcher announced the provincial sales tax was being cut from 5% to 4% and the list of sales tax exemptions was extended to 24 farm items. As well, newly married couples would have a one-year tax-free period on the purchase of major appliances. The 3% mineral tax paid on farmland was also eliminated, as well as what Thatcher called 19 "nuisance taxes" or fees that applied mostly to farmers.

Clearly, the key message Thatcher wanted to send was to the business community outside the province. At every opportunity in his first term when he talked about the previous government, he referred to it using the collective term "socialists." By constantly framing the debate as free enterprise versus socialism, Thatcher was courting the outside business community—in particular U.S. foreign investment—by signalling that a sea change had taken place in the political and economic culture of Saskatchewan.

SAB RB 7227

As Premier, Ross Thatcher was passionately committed to improving the living conditions of Saskatchewan's Aboriginal peoples. In this 1966 photograph he appears with a group of Native children.

But the budget speech went beyond economic and fiscal issues. For example, in his address to the Legislature, Thatcher signalled his powerful personal interest in the plight of Indian and Metis people by announcing $475,000 for the creation of an Indian and Metis branch. His said the goal of his government was to assist people of "Indian ancestry to achieve higher economic standards and self-government, as well as full participation in the social and economic life of the province."

In many ways during the mid-to-late 1960s, Thatcher's rhetoric was at odds with a growing political culture of an increasing social and economic role for the state. When he talked about the "problem" of U.S. investment in Canada, which a growing chorus of voices declared was a threat to Canada, Thatcher said the only problem with American investment was that Saskatchewan didn't have enough of it. He fundamentally believed that in a small province like Saskatchewan, which lacked a significant indigenous business class, attracting outside investment was the only path to a growing economy, which could generate the tax revenue to support a social agenda. For Thatcher, the thought that government, through Crown enterprises, could be the primary engine of development was both naïve and dangerous: naïve because government enterprise lacked the entrepreneurial

SAB RA 8359 © M. West, Regina. West's Studio Collection.

Official photograph of Premier Ross Thatcher.

drive and market discipline of private enterprise; dangerous because government enterprise would distort the market due to its special status and stigmatize the province as anti-free enterprise.

In his first term, there were two sectors Thatcher believed would help rebrand the province as open for business and on the road to economic development—potash and pulp. The potash industry had been established with three mines during the final years of the CCF-NDP government, but was still far from reaching its potential. Meanwhile, the promise of a major pulp mill for northern Saskatchewan had never materialized and, in fact, efforts by the Douglas and Lloyd governments to get private investment to build a pulp mill had all failed.

By the mid-1960s, the promise of major potash development was something that Thatcher seized upon and took a personal interest in achieving. In the fall of 1965, Thatcher's government organized and help sponsored a gathering of potash industry figures in Saskatoon. It was a perfect platform for Thatcher to proclaim the potential of potash and his commitment to a business-friendly environment. He talked about how in 10 years Saskatchewan would be producing more potash than wheat, and 8,000 new direct jobs in the industry would be created. He talked about Saskatchewan as being one the last frontiers of development, a place overlooked or purposefully ignored by the private sector, in part because of "20 years of socialist government," a period in which 270,000 people left the province:

> Because we know socialism, not from text books but from hard, bitter experience, our government today is dedicated to the principles of private enterprise … we are carrying out in Saskatchewan what I like to think is an "experiment in private enterprise." It is our task to prove in the next few years that the private enterprise system can do more for our people than socialism.

The growth in the potash industry during the Thatcher government, particularly its first term, was nothing short of remarkable. Three months after taking office, Thatcher was at a news conference announcing plans by U.S. Borax to build a $60 million mine near the town of Allan that would employ 500 people. It mattered little that negotiations had been all but concluded under the previous government. Thatcher used it as evidence that his free-enterprise approach was working. Next came an announcement of a new potash mine near Lanigan by Alwinsal of Canada Ltd. In the following years there was a steady string of announcements about expansion of existing mines, or decisions to build even bigger mines than were originally planned. By 1965, potash production began expanding by 25% a year. In the 1969 budget, potash revenues to the government were estimated to be more than $3.6 million, up from less than $2 million in 1966–67.

For Thatcher, the promise of the potash industry provided him with a rhetorical flourish that allowed him to suggest that Saskatchewan potash could rival Alberta's oil as a wealth generator. "It is clear that Saskatchewan probably has the richest potash beds in the world and what oil did for Alberta in the last two decades, we believe potash will do for Saskatchewan," Thatcher said.[19]

There is no question the potash industry flourished and rapidly expanded during the Liberal government's years. But the degree to which Thatcher or his government's policies determined the pace of expansion is unknowable. The rich potash deposits in Saskatchewan, coupled with the growing demand for potash-based fertilizer to support the world's increasing agricultural production, were critical elements in the rapid development of potash mines in the second half of the 1960s. Still, Thatcher's free-enterprise rhetoric and his government's willingness to provide the necessary infrastructure for the industry—such as supply of water—were also important factors.

The other development initiative Thatcher dearly wanted as a symbol of his success in attracting private capital to broaden the province's economy was a pulp mill for the north. For years, Saskatchewan's raw timber resources of the northern forests as a supply for a value-added industry such as pulp production were a promise that governments had hoped to turn into reality. Attempts by the CCF-NDP to find investors had never materialized. In fact, prior to the 1960 election the Douglas government went so far as to announce a deal to build a pulp mill, but the project never got off the ground. Thatcher knew that if he could deliver where the CCF had failed, his political hand would be strengthened for re-election to a second term.

Typical with this hands-on approach to government, Thatcher was the driving force behind a deal between the government and Parsons and Whittemore, a New York-based pulp and paper company that operated mills around the world. With first John Cuelenare and later Dave Steuart acting as Thatcher's point men, and Toronto lawyer John Stevenson contracted to handle negotiations for the province, talks began in January 1965 and culminated 11 months later with the announcement of a $65 million pulp mill for Prince Albert.

While Thatcher wanted the project to be private-sector driven, he proved to be a tough negotiator, determined to protect the interests of Saskatchewan taxpayers. The government guaranteed a $50 million loan for Parsons and Whittemore and in return got 15% equity in the mill that produced 650 tons a day. As well, the province paid $1.5 million for an additional 15% equity, giving it a 30% interest in an enterprise with $65 million in capitalization on a cash outlay of only $1.5 million. Finally, Thatcher got the right of first refusal for the province to buy out Parsons and Whittemore should the company want to sell the mill. But there were hidden costs to taxpayers. Specifically, the agreement committed the government to build up to 1,000 miles of all-weather roads into the northern forest over a 50-year period. The public roads would help provide private loggers and Parsons and Whittemore the access they needed to harvest the trees.

There were two other aspects to the Thatcher government's first term that reinforced Thatcher's free-enterprise rhetoric. One was his relationship with the federal Liberal government of first Lester Pearson, and then Pierre Trudeau. The other was his confrontational approach to organized labour, which he saw as merely a partisan political extension of the CCF-NDP.

There were various layers to Thatcher's relationship with the federal Liberal government. At one level, the relationship was rooted in his belief that the federal Liberal government was far too empathetic to ideas often advanced by the federal NDP. Thatcher publicly was at odds with federal Finance minister Walter Gordon, a strong economic nationalist who wanted to drastically reduce the rate of U.S. investment in Canada. At one point, during a ceremony to open a new potash mine built with U.S. investment, Thatcher was quoted as calling Gordon "short-sighted and stupid." At the core of the conflict was Gordon's reluctance to offer federal tax concessions to certain kinds of potash mines. Thatcher carried his attacks on Gordon into the national media, including an appearance on CBC-TV's "Front Page Challenge." "I don't claim to be an expert on very much in politics, but I am on socialism. Mr. Gordon may have textbook experience, but politicians from Saskatchewan know from experience that socialism doesn't work," Thatcher said. "Our government is cleaning up the rubble left by 20 years of socialism and anyone from Ontario interested in socialism can visit Saskatchewan to see its effects."

A second layer of Thatcher's stormy relationship with the federal Liberal government was driven by simple political reality. The fact is, at the core of Saskatchewan federal politics was a sense of exclusion and powerlessness. Therefore, to oppose the federal government as insensitive and out-of-touch merely reflected the political psyche of the province.

Finally, the relationship was soured at a party level. As leader, Thatcher had seized complete control of the Liberal Party in the province, both the provincial and federal wings. He was the undisputed party boss in Saskatchewan and would not brook interference from anyone, particularly outsiders who wanted to exert influence over party politics within the province. As such, Thatcher demanded that he be involved and have a say in federal patronage appointments for Saskatchewan. Moreover, his constant courting of Progressive Conservative voters to find common cause with the provincial Liberals to fight the "socialists" did not sit well with the federal Liberals in Ottawa, who saw the Tories as the clear threat to the federal Liberals and people sympathetic to the NDP as potential supporters.

In terms of labour relations, Thatcher showed little tolerance for organized labour. He believed that key to attracting foreign investment was demonstrating that he would stand up to the union movement. Tactically, Thatcher believed the perfect opportunity came in the fall of 1966 when the union representing more than 1,200 employees at the Saskatchewan Power Corporation went on strike, seeking an 8% wage increase. The corporation had initially offered 3%, before raising its offer to 4%. The union did not move off its 8% demand, which was the average settlement for collective agreements that year in Canada.

At the time there was increasing labour militancy across the nation and clear signs of growing inflation. Thatcher believed the Pearson government was capitulating to labour, thereby feeding the inflation psychology. He wanted to take a hard line.

He did it by calling an emergency session of the Legislature to force through back-to-work legislation that would end the Saskatchewan Power Corporation strike by identifying essential services that would lose the right to strike. That same year, the government amended the Trade Union Act so that strikes had to be approved by a majority of all members, not just a majority of those who voted. It also included a "free speech" clause that allowed employers to talk about the union to individual members, which the Saskatchewan Federation of Labour saw as little more than a way for employers to intimidate union members.

Ultimately, the result of Thatcher's approach to labour was to create an ongoing climate of mistrust. While the NDP's direct ties were undeniable, the fact was that in the 1964 election campaign, the Thatcher Liberals had avoided acting in an overt way that would alienate labour. Thatcher realized the labour leadership, specifically the leaders of the Saskatchewan Federation of Labour, were NDP partisans. But he did not believe that rank-and-file members in unions necessarily shared that view, or could be compelled to vote against the Liberals. Therefore, in the 1964 election campaign, the Liberals promised to maintain and even improve the rights and security of trade unions, a rhetorical position that no doubt was enough for many union members to support the Liberals.

But in reality, Thatcher personally took a harsh view of the labour movement, and particularly its leaders, whom he saw as nothing more than apologists for, and advocates of, the NDP. By standing up to labour, Thatcher believed he would send a clear signal that the economic climate in Saskatchewan had changed after two decades of CCF-NDP rule. The Premier often talked about how labour relations had failed to evolve with the rest of society and the economy, and that there had to be a better way to resolve labour disputes than strikes, which were costly to all sides and damaging to the economy. He mused openly about someday eliminating strikes as a tool and replacing them with a labour court that would adjudicate and settle disputes. It was a notion that never got beyond speculation by the Premier, but one that labour saw as unconscionable.

Thatcher's tough stand with labour, and his demands on the bureaucracy to control spending, were counterbalanced by a passionate interest he had in helping to lift Saskatchewan's Indian and Metis community out of poverty. Long before sociologists raised the notion of "affirmative action" as a tool to advance the cause of disadvantaged minorities, Thatcher applied the policy of hiring quotas for Native people in the ranks of government. Restrictions imposed on bureaucracy did not apply to finding jobs for Native people. With almost 5% of Saskatchewan's population of Native ancestry, Thatcher said he expected the public service to reflect the same proportion of Indian and Metis in its ranks. He did not accept arguments that, in many cases, Native people lacked the necessary skills. Thatcher ordered they be allowed to learn on the job.

A year after taking power, the government formed an Indian and Metis Affairs branch in the Department of Natural Resources. The 10-person branch had a mandate to coordinate policies for the training and placement in jobs of Native people.

"It is a fact that in a period of unprecedented prosperity in our province, about 36,000 people of Indian and Metis background are living in conditions of deprivation and squalor that would be the shame of some of the underprivileged nations of the world," Thatcher said when he introduced the bill to establish the new branch. "We view the extension of provincial government programs to Indian people as an absolute requisite if they are to be permitted to rise from the poverty in which they now exist, and without infringement on existing treaty rights, move into the mainstream and develop."

For Thatcher, the key for rescuing Native people from poverty was the same as it was for anyone else—the chance at a job. He believed that for Native people to be brought into the economic mainstream, they had to leave their communities and reserves and find opportunities in the cities. During his years in power, there was a significant migration of Aboriginal people to urban areas, particularly Regina and Saskatoon. But the opportunities they sought were often not available. For Thatcher, conditions faced by the Native community created an issue that he believed would threaten the province socially and economically in the years to come. "I feel the people of this province will overlook these conditions at their peril," the Premier said in 1965 after visiting a reserve near North Battleford.

The other issue in which Thatcher took a strong personal interest during his first term was dental health. After years of debate, but few results, Thatcher acted. Without consulting relevant departments, Thatcher told Health minister Dave Steuart that he wanted action. In 1966, the Department of Health announced a five-point program that included a College of Dentistry at the University of Saskatchewan, bursaries for dental students and a course to train dental therapists.[20]

Thatcher's Second Term

In September 1967, less than three-and-a-half years after winning power, Thatcher called an election to seek what he termed a new mandate to convince outside private investors that Saskatchewan was firmly on the path of free enterprise. "We have reached a point where a new mandate is needed. This is required urgently to assure potential investors in Saskatchewan of a political climate which is essential to encourage continuation of our private enterprise progress," Thatcher said when he called the election for October 11, 1967. "It is also required if our people are to share in this advance to better jobs, better economic opportunities and more help for education and other government services."

Both the state of the economy and Liberal Party were solid going into the campaign and Thatcher recognized the time was right to take advantage of the situation. It was also Canada's centennial year, which had created a sense of pride and patriotism among Canadians, which clearly helped spawn a positive mood among voters.

Again Thatcher focused his attention on maintaining the coalition of voters that had originally elected his government. "I invite the Socreds and the Conservatives to tell me what this party has done that could not be supported by an orthodox conservative," Thatcher asked repeatedly throughout the campaign.[21]

The Liberal campaign was typical for an incumbent government. It did not set out a plan for new directions, but rather a continuation of the policies that Liberals said had resulted in the "new Saskatchewan." The party promised continued "sound" government, promising more tax cuts and more concerted efforts to attract even more investment and jobs to the province.

The Liberals promised to double the $50 homeowners grant it had introduced in 1965 and extend its free high school textbook program through to Grade 12. As well, Thatcher pledged to end the province's share of the federal estate tax, expand the government's policy of selling Crown land to farmers and hold plebiscites on any proposed "new costly welfare programs."

By comparison, Woodrow Lloyd and the NDP promised a much more activist and interventionist government, focussing their strategy on younger voters. The NDP campaign was weighted heavily to education, promising free university tuition, expansion of the two university campuses and technical schools, increases to student co-op housing and more financial assistance for students.

By the time of the 1967 campaign, the evidence was mixed on how well the Thatcher government's economic development strategy was working. In many ways, the results looked impressive and a credible argument could be made that Thatcher's free-enterprise gospel was good for the economy. The unemployment rate had fallen to a virtually non-existent 1.8% from 3.2% in 1963. Over the same period the labour force had grown by 12,000 to 332,000, and the province's population had grown each year the Liberals were in power, climbing from 933,000 to 957,000, and total personal income had reached $2.1 billion, up from $1.7 billion.

In terms of resource development, crude oil production was up by 31% since the last year of the Lloyd government and total capital investment had grown by almost $450 million to $1.14 billion. Moreover, in 1966, Saskatchewan qualified as a "have" province and no longer received equalization payments from the federal government, which Thatcher used as proof that Saskatchewan had entered a new era of economic development.

But at the same time, there were economic storm clouds on the horizon. Housing starts were down significantly from their levels in 1963. As well, after recovering in 1966 after two years of decline, there were troubling signs about farm income. Growing world wheat inventories were starting to put serious downward pressure on grain prices.

Still, there was a sense the Thatcher government had done a credible job and that the province had finally begun to develop an industrial base, adding breadth to what had been an economy far too dependent on agriculture. The rapid expansion of the potash industry, the development of a long-anticipated pulp mill near Prince Albert and the promise of major expansion of uranium mining in the north served as evidence that this really was the start of the "new Saskatchewan."

On election night, Thatcher received the political vindication he sought, easily being re-elected in his own riding of Morse and the Liberals winning 35 seats, 3 more than they had going into the election. The NDP won 24, a result that ultimately sealed the fate of leader Woodrow Lloyd.

While Thatcher and the Liberals campaigned on the premise that Saskatchewan's economic future had never looked more positive, from the outset of his government's second term Thatcher took a much more austere and less-than-optimistic approach. Two days after re-election, Thatcher called his Cabinet together to announce a new fiscal austerity plan for his government. It caught his cabinet and caucus completely by surprise. He told the Cabinet that he had information from the federal government that a recession was imminent and, as a result, he was imposing across-the-board cuts to government spending to avoid falling into deficit. Although he presented no hard evidence of the looming downturn, Thatcher refused to debate the fiscal approach and quickly went public by telling reporters of his austerity plans.[22]

One reason he did give was a demand by the province's doctors for an increase in the medical fees they received from government as part of publicly funded health insurance. If the fee increases went ahead, Thatcher hinted about the necessity of a "head tax" or "some sort of deterrence."

The other area of spending Thatcher wanted to rein in was education, specifically the escalating costs of university funding. The mid-to-late 1960s saw rapid growth in university enrolment as the baby boom generation moved into their post-secondary years. At the same time, the two University of Saskatchewan campuses themselves, in particular Regina campus with its emphasis on the social sciences, became a hotbed of student radicalism. The anti-Vietnam war, anti-establishment, anti-U.S. student movement deeply irked Thatcher, who saw it all as woolly-headed socialist thinking.

Shortly after the election, Thatcher gave a speech in Esterhazy where he outlined his plans to take greater control of education spending. He sought to bring university spending under his government's influence by having the Legislature approve its operating and capital budgets the same way it did government line departments. "Our government is concerned by the fact that today elected representatives of the people have virtually no control over university spending. Year after year, with few details, we in fact almost write a blank cheque," Thatcher said in October 1967 in a speech to the Potashville Education Association in Esterhazy. Instantly, the government's plan was seen as a direct attack on academic freedom, creating tense relations between the government and the university community, as well as the teaching profession in general.

Thus, an even more fiscally conservative, stern and authoritarian Ross Thatcher quickly emerged and asserted himself from the outset of his government's second term.

The framework for this conservative approach was set out in the government's budget of Friday, March 1, 1968. It soon became known widely as the "Black Friday" budget.

Although Thatcher had finally given up his dual role as Premier and provincial treasurer by appointing Dave Steuart as Treasurer, the fact was that Thatcher virtually wrote the address that Steuart delivered that day. The speech sought to mix self-congratulation for economic growth with concern about the future. But ultimately, this was a budget that sounded alarm bells about Saskatchewan's economic and fiscal outlook, particularly the growing signs of inflation that Thatcher feared would lead to ever-increasing costs, government deficits and recession:

> We in Saskatchewan now enjoy the greatest prosperity in our history ...
> however, there are weak spots in the economy—some danger signals we

cannot afford to ignore. This country faces a serious threat of inflation that must be checked. These inflationary pressures have several causes, not the least of which has been the failure of the last two federal governments to balance their budgets once in the last 10 years. Public demand on all levels of government in every part of Canada has also been a contributing factor. Wage and price increases that have had little or no relation to increased productivity have also helped force inflationary pressures to the present dangerous level.

For Thatcher, the greatest fiscal pressure was coming from education and health. Total education spending of almost $112 million—including $30.5 million to the University of Saskatchewan—represented a year-over-year increase of 17%, or 32% of total expenditures of $338.4 million.

In terms of health, the budget pointed to four areas of "grave concern": the adequacy of health services; public demand for more service; shortage of professional and technical personnel; and the fact that costs for health services were "increasing at an alarming rate." To curb these rising costs and increase revenue for government, the budget introduced health utilization fees of $1.50 for each visit to a doctor and $2.50 for each day in hospital, declining to $1.50 a day after 30 days.

The imposition of utilization fees, or "deterrent" fees as they were called by the opposition, was instantly unpopular. The NDP characterized them as an "unconscionable tax on the sick." In fact, the 1968 budget was widely recognized as a tax-increase budget, with tax hikes on tobacco, an extension of the provincial sales tax to previously exempt items and the application of a 2% tax on insurance premiums. At the same time, to contain growth in health costs, the government announced it intended to reduce the number of rural hospitals.

The sudden, dramatic shift by Thatcher to cost-cutting at the outset of his second term proved to be the undoing of his government. Fiscally responsible or not, the Black Friday budget became a focal point for an anti-Thatcher backlash. Even within the Liberal caucus there was unhappiness with Thatcher's growing dictatorial approach and his refusal to accept dissent from his backbenchers. He was not interested in debating contrary ideas, either from within his caucus or with others. In one budget, the government alienated the university community, teachers, rural areas that feared they would lose their hospitals, and the majority of the population, which saw health utilization fees as a new tax paid by the sick.

Still, in certain key respects, Thatcher was right. His concern about a coming slowdown in the Saskatchewan economy proved to be true, as growing world grain inventories and a similar glut of potash in the final years of the 1960s depressed prices for two of the province's key commodities. The federal government launched a program—Lower Inventories for Tomorrow (LIFT)—that provided incentives for Saskatchewan farmers to not grow wheat and leave their fields fallow. It was widely unpopular among farmers and made the federal Liberals a target for strident criticism in the farm community. Although Thatcher tried to distance himself from the policy by criticizing the federal government and, in particular, Otto Lang, the Saskatoon Cabinet minister who helped design the program, resentment ran deeply in rural Saskatchewan.

What particularly frustrated Thatcher about the economic slowdown in 1969–70 was his inability to exercise any influence. While he saw inflation rising nationally and took a hard line in Saskatchewan on government spending and labour settlements, ultimately he knew a provincial government could have little impact on inflation.

One reality he refused to accept was overproduction in the potash sector. The rapid expansion of the industry after the Liberals took office led to a collapse in price and massive layoffs in the province's mines. By 1969, the industry was in a mess. It was operating at 50% capacity and U.S. potash prices were at record lows. Yet the inelasticity of potash demand meant that production was falling, even with low prices. Moreover, two new mines were scheduled to come into production in 1970–71, with several others due to reach full capacity at the same time. As a result, some mines faced bankruptcy and could close, throwing people out of work and further reducing already declining government potash revenue.

Rather than sit idly by, Thatcher decided to take control of the situation. Ignoring the fact that international trade in potash was a federal responsibility, Thatcher met with New Mexico Governor David Cargo in a bid to impose discipline in the market. Fearing U.S. legislation against the flood of Canadian potash into the U.S. market, Thatcher made common cause with Cargo, who governed the state that produced the vast majority of the U.S. potash. All of the eight U.S. producers in Saskatchewan also operated in New Mexico.

Together, Thatcher and Cargo introduced a system of pro-rationing that regulated production at a minimum price, which was enough to ensure that the higher-cost mines in New Mexico would remain profitable. The system took effect January 1, 1970. The floor price was set at $18.75 U.S. a ton and each producer had to take out disposal and production licences from the province, that ensured the government could control the market. Production levels were set by the government's Potash Conservation Board.[23]

For his part, Thatcher never disguised his anger with the potash companies and what he saw as their lack of market foresight and planning. "Seldom in the economic annals of Canada have we seen such responsible corporations get into such an economic mess. Lack of co-operation and lack of planning have brought major companies to the brink of disaster," Thatcher said when he and Cargo announced the system of pro-rationing. Ultimately, Thatcher was named as an unindicted co-conspirator in a U.S. anti-trust case against the Saskatchewan pro-rationing scheme, an accusation Thatcher dismissed as frivolous and irrelevant.

The way Thatcher handled the potash overproduction issue provides a fascinating glimpse into his economic beliefs. Committed as he was to free enterprise, the free market and foreign investment, Thatcher believed corporations had a moral obligation to act responsibly in terms of the market and the broader public good. As Premier, his first obligation was to protect the public interest and if that meant massive intervention in the economy to rescue the industry from itself, then he had no second thoughts about doing so. But at the same time, the near collapse of the potash industry was itself a criticism of the Thatcher government's eagerness to develop the industry while failing to fully appreciate the implications such rapid expansion would ultimately create.

There is no question that Thatcher's pro-rationing system helped to stabilize the industry and probably prevented widespread layoffs and mine closures. Indeed, it was a policy embraced by the NDP government that followed him.

But by the time the Premier called a provincial election for June 1971, the forces lined up against Thatcher and the Liberals were simply too great. As a leader who ruled the party like a boss, the enthusiasm that existed at the party grassroots for the leader in 1964 and, to a lesser degree in 1967, had dissipated.

The convergence of a troubled farm economy, a wounded potash sector and a lengthy construction trades strike in the final years of the Thatcher government had sapped the economy. The optimism of a greater, more economically mature and diverse Saskatchewan that Thatcher had promised in his march to power had taken on a hollow ring by the spring campaign of 1971. As Dave Steuart, in retrospect, was fond of saying: "If there was someone or some group in the province we hadn't alienated by the election of 1971, it was because we hadn't met them yet."

That kind of grim reality engulfed the Liberal campaign and Thatcher himself, as he used a small airplane to get around the province, while the new, more youthful NDP leader, Allan Blakeney, travelled by bus, portraying himself as a man of the people.

A sense of the inevitable hung heavy in the air near the end of the campaign at Thatcher's rally that night at Temple Gardens in Moose Jaw. Reaching deep, Thatcher tried to summon some of the biting passion that had brought him to power as he warned those in the hall about the "threat of the socialists." But he seemed a shadow of his former self, looking tired and drawn, his voice weak.

Defeat and Death

The result on election night, June 23, 1971, was a crushing blow for Thatcher. The NDP swept to power, winning 45 seats and reducing the Liberals to 15. The result was clearly a rebuke of Thatcher. After towering over the party and his government, the election was in many ways a referendum on Thatcher himself. Still, on election night, Thatcher accepted the will of the electorate gracefully. When the result was official, Thatcher made his way to the NDP campaign headquarters in downtown Regina, surprising the hall packed with celebrating New Democrats. Amid boos and catcalls, Thatcher made his way to the stage, congratulated Blakeney and the NDP for running such a successful campaign and wished Blakeney well as Premier. As he left the stage, some in the crowd broke into a chorus of "He's a Jolly Good Fellow."

For Thatcher, the result was so decisive and so clearly a rejection of his leadership, that within days he told a meeting of his caucus that he would be stepping down as leader. Preliminary plans began for a leadership convention later in the fall.

Then, three weeks later, the Liberal Party and the Saskatchewan political scene were shocked with word that Thatcher, who suffered from diabetes, had died in the night at his Regina home of an apparent heart attack at age 54. Instantly, the curtain came down on an era in Saskatchewan politics.

There is little doubt that Thatcher's sudden death left a void on the political scene. He left a party not only reeling from defeat, but without the leader who had ruled it with a firm hand for more than a decade. His death also meant that his place in the province's history was to fade with his memory, his legacy often overlooked and overtaken by events as the 1970s unfolded with the NDP government of Allan Blakeney.

There can be little question that Ross Thatcher failed to deliver the promise of a "new Saskatchewan," one that would emerge from agricultural dependence by developing an industrial and stronger natural resource-based economy. By the time he left office, the Saskatchewan economy was struggling. In the 1971 budget, resource revenues were projected to total less than 10% of total provincial revenues, compared to almost 16% in 1964. While potash revenues to government grew from approximately $370,000 in 1963 to $1.9 million in 1967, before falling to $1.5 million in 1969 as world oversupply began to depress prices, it was clear that potash was not going to mean the riches for Saskatchewan that oil was for Alberta, as Thatcher had predicted.[24]

There can be legitimate criticism of Thatcher's approach to foreign investment and his willingness to allow outsiders to profit from Saskatchewan's natural resources without getting a fair return for the people of the province in the form of royalties and taxation. Indeed, while resource development grew dramatically during Thatcher's time as Premier, at the same time, federal transfer payments had climbed to 20.6% of the provincial budget, compared to less than 12.5% in 1964. It was the growing perception that Thatcher's government was not getting a fair share from resources for the public purse that became a crucial political vulnerability, leading to the Liberals' defeat. But that is also too narrow a view of Thatcher's legacy, one distorted by the timing of an economic slowdown that hit the province in the final years of his time in power.

The fact is, his government presided over a period when Saskatchewan's potash industry took root, when uranium development began in the far north and the pulp industry was finally established in Saskatchewan. From that foundation, the NDP government of the 1970s was able to use the Crown corporation sector as a means to try and take greater control of the economy.

It was Thatcher who transformed the political debate in Saskatchewan by focussing on the fact that the province was not keeping economic pace with other western provinces. In that sense, he advanced the public discourse by pushing the province to change its own identity. It was Thatcher who strove to modernize the Saskatchewan economy.

More significantly, Thatcher was a visionary in three other crucial areas. First, he recognized the limits of government and realized if the role of government was not constrained, it would lead to fiscal crises in the form of deficits and mounting debts. Ultimately, governments would be forced to cut spending and the most vulnerable in society would pay the heaviest price.

Second, he understood that the publicly funded health care system was headed to unsustainability. Long before anyone else, Thatcher talked about how a universal, publicly funded system brought together two irreconcilable forces—unconstrained demand for what was perceived as a "free" service, and finite public resources.

Third, Thatcher was far ahead of his time in terms of the most pressing and daunting economic and social issue facing the province—the integration of Aboriginal people into the economic mainstream of life. Thatcher was moved by the plight of Native people and

PHOTO BY DAVID MCLENNAN
The Thatcher Memorial in Wascana Park, Regina.

took a passionate interest in using government as a tool to alleviate the problems they faced. His formula was assimilation, and while it too failed, at least he had the fortitude to act where other Premiers before him and since have done little more than preside over the growth of a social and economic issue that now far overshadows any other facing the province.

So, while Ross Thatcher in many ways failed to transform the province the way he promised, he did point the way to our future. The Saskatchewan of today, a province struggling with economic uncertainty and fiscal constraints, is one he predicted decades ago. It is also a future he sought to avoid by changing our expectations of government and its relationship with the economy and society.

Notes

This chapter was inspired by the book *Rumours of Glory, Saskatchewan and the Thatcher Years*, by Dale Eisler (Edmonton: Hurtig Publishers, 1987). The book relies heavily on interviews with people who were part of the era.
1. Event attended by author, then reporter with the Moose Jaw *Times Herald*.

2. John H. Archer, *Saskatchewan: A History* (Saskatoon: Western Producer Prairie Books, 1980), 316.
3. David E. Smith, *Prairie Liberalism: The Liberal Party in Saskatchewan 1905–71* (Toronto: University of Toronto Press, 1975), 303.
4. Associates, such as then Deputy Premier Dave Steuart, talk of Thatcher's passion about dealing with Indian and Metis issues and his frustration at the level of poverty on reserves in the province.
5. Early years in business based on various interview sources for *Rumours of Glory*. The key was Jack Weymark, who worked in the hardware business with Thatcher and eventually bought the Moose Jaw business from him.
6. Audio transcripts of Thatcher radio addresses available at the Saskatchewan Archives Board.
7. Walter D. Young, *Anatomy of a Party* (Toronto: University of Toronto Press, 1969), 227.
8. House of Commons, *Debates and Proceedings*, May 2, 1955, pps. 3346–48.
9. Thatcher's critique can be found in House of Commons, *Debates*, May 22, 1956, pps. 4193–96.
10. The author has audio and written transcript of Mossbank debate.
11. Thatcher's commitment to building the Liberal Party organization and fundraising was an attribute consistently referenced by his contemporaries in interviews.
12. The *Saskatchewan Liberal*, the monthly newspaper of the Liberal Party during the Thatcher period, is a primary source of Thatcher's partisan rhetoric.
13. All provincial election results from *Provincial Elections in Saskatchewan 1905–1983*, published by the Chief Electoral Office, province of Saskatchewan
14. The Regina *Leader-Post*, Saskatoon *Star Phoenix* and Moose Jaw *Times Herald* carried extensive coverage of Argue's defection.
15. The medicare crisis and doctors' strike received international media coverage, as did the photo of Thatcher kicking the locked opposition door into the legislative chamber.
16. Details of the election campaign were drawn from newspaper coverage at the time, party publications and interviews with participants.
17. The Liberals lost their brief, tenuous hold on Hanley when the election result was overturned and the NDP won a subsequent by-election in December 1964.
18. Thatcher's first budget speech is an excellent manifesto of his economic, fiscal and social beliefs. Other fiscal and economic data were obtained from subsequent budgets (1965–71).
19. For a good overview of Thatcher's approach to the potash industry as a source of job growth and economic development for the province, see his remarks in a keynote speech entitled "Saskatchewan and World Hunger," at the October 25, 1965, potash conference in Saskatoon.
20. For reference to some of Thatcher's policies, see Eleanor Glor, *Policy Innovation in the Saskatchewan Public Sector, 1971–82* (North York, ON: Captus Press, 1997).
21. The call for solidarity of conservative, free enterprise-minded people behind the Liberal banner was the key message Thatcher delivered when he announced the election at an event in Saskatoon.
22. Many of his former colleagues say that Thatcher changed after he won re-election, becoming more authoritarian and obsessed with the idea of fiscal conservatism.
23. For a good overview of the potash industry and the pro-rationing issue see Nancy Olewiler's Economic Council of Canada 1986 report, "An Assessment of the Creation and Performance of a Crown Corporation."
24. See Government of Saskatchewan, Department of Mineral Resources, *Annual Reports*.

Allan E. Blakeney
Dennis Gruending

At the flame-lighting ceremony for the Saskatchewan Summer Games, 1972 (SAB RA 26,549).

Blakeney, c. 1972 (SAB RA 23,088).

At the First Ministers' Conference in Ottawa, November 1981 (SAB RA 22,495 (1)).

Saskatchewan Premiers of the 20th Century

Allan E. Blakeney, 1971–1982

Early Years

Allan Blakeney's ancestors were English on his father's side and Welsh on his mother's. Bertha May Davies was born in the mountain valleys of Wales where her people were miners. She trained as a nurse and moved to London, and there she met John Cline Blakeney, a young Canadian soldier who had been wounded during action in World War I. When they were married in 1919, Bertha's family gave her a Bible and wished her well in Canada.

Following their return to Nova Scotia, John set up a wholesaling business in Bridgewater, just inland from Lunenburg, supplying fresh fruit by truck to small stores in the area. Allan Emrys Blakeney was born in Bridgewater on September 7, 1925, one of three children in a comfortable but modest household. John's business took off quickly in the 1920s, but barely survived the 1930s.

Although the family's fortunes later improved, the Depression left its mark on his son. "I always grew up thinking that money didn't come easily," Blakeney said, "and we shouldn't spend it unless there was a reason." His personal life has always been characterized by thrift and a lack of ostentation, and as Premier he insisted that those habits guide both elected members and civil servants. His aversion to government deficits probably owed much to his youthful experience with shaky family ledgers.

He was a bright student, curious, nervously energetic and socially awkward. He graduated from Bridgewater High School with top marks in 1942 at the age of 16. He also had the best marks in his law class at Dalhousie University in Halifax, and in his graduating year he won the university gold medal.

He tried to join the air force in 1944, but they were no longer taking recruits. However, the war did have an important impact on him, turning him toward the CCF in a province that was barren ground for social democracy. In Canada, the later years of the war were a time of intellectual ferment, with both civilians and soldiers determined that a new society should emerge from the ashes of war.

People feared a return to the Depression and mass unemployment when tens of thousands of soldiers became civilians again. The CCF captured the popular imagination with their demand to have the country put all Canadians to work during peacetime, just as had been done in war. Social democrats believed this could only be done through centralized social planning. They called for government to cushion the shock of the expected post-war slump through a series of social programs, including unemployment insurance and public health care. The CCF slogan of the day was "left turn, Canada," and voters appeared to be paying attention.

John Blakeney was a Tory and had been his son's political mentor before he went off to university. He was surprised and disappointed when Allan joined the CCF, and the news created a mild sensation in conservative Bridgewater, where the people clucked their tongues and said that it was too bad about the Blakeney boy.

At Dalhousie, Blakeney met Molly Schwartz, who was studying zoology. Her mother had been a nurse and her father was a doctor. She had been born with a congenital heart defect, but while her family considered her somewhat frail she lived a normal student's life. During Blakeney's final year at Dalhousie in 1947, he and Molly were close. They went to movies and on Sundays for walks in the park. He had Sunday supper at her house and afterward they would sit in the family living room. Their courtship was proper but unmistakable.

Meanwhile his professors encouraged him to apply for scholarships at an American university, perhaps Harvard. He had planned quietly all along to apply at Oxford, and he was awarded the Rhodes scholarship for Nova Scotia in 1947. That summer he boarded ship for England. He and Molly had a private understanding that when he returned they would get married.

At Oxford, he registered in a two-year course called "Modern Greats," which emphasized economics and modern history, as well as some philosophy. His mandatory reading list included David Hume, Descartes, John Stuart Mill and Bertrand Russell. In economics, he was especially interested in the work of one of the Oxford dons, Sir William Beveridge, whose books included *Full Employment in a Free Society*. "That was the great blueprint for democratic socialism," Blakeney recalled. "It's a book that I studied with some care." He was determined to use the Oxford experience to expand his horizons: "I was not going to take an advanced degree in law. I was going to take philosophy, politics and economics. It gave me confidence that I understood something in economics."

Blakeney's membership in the CCF had come to the attention of the party prior to his leaving Canada in 1947, and he received a letter from David Lewis, the CCF national secretary, who had also been a Rhodes Scholar. Lewis encouraged him to become familiar with the British Labour movement, and offered to arrange meetings with party officials. Blakeney followed that advice and came to several conclusions that were vital to his political development.

"These were highly skilled people," he remembered, "yet they had all manner of problems in transforming Britain. That told me government and political ideology was something that did not consist of a checklist, but of a direction and an approach. That makes me much more of a pragmatic socialist than some I've run into, and it also makes me exceedingly sceptical of campaigns for privatization, and that type of thing. I'm not just sceptical of the nostrums of the right. I'm sceptical of nostrums of the left as well."

When his Oxford classes were completed in 1949, Blakeney and four friends packed into a 1931 Austin and headed for a trip to Europe, which was still digging itself out from under the rubble of war. When he returned to Canada, he did his articles with a firm in Lunenburg, close enough to live at home and commute.

During his final year at Oxford, he had been looking for jobs with the federal government and at several law schools. He sought advice from a former professor at Dalhousie, and was referred to George Tamaki, a Dalhousie graduate working as legal secretary to the Government Finance Office (GFO) in Saskatchewan.

He wrote to Tamaki, who replied that there was no position at the time, but there might be one in the future. Blakeney moved to Edmonton and was working there when Tamaki wrote again to say that he was leaving and his job was open. Blakeney promptly accepted the Saskatchewan position. He returned to Nova Scotia to marry Molly, and following their honeymoon, they headed off by car for Regina. "It wasn't Paris," he said, recalling that they were homesick and had no intention of staying for long.

His job initially was to serve as an understudy to Tamaki in his capacity as secretary and legal advisor to the GFO, which acted as a holding company for Crown corporations. Blakeney had walked into what was likely the best civil service in Canada, in the most unlikely of provinces. A mere six years earlier, Saskatchewan had the highest per capita debt in Canada, a province just emerging from a battering during the Great Depression, nearly bankrupt and with a poor credit rating.

The CCF had arrived in government with an ambitious set of policies, and succeeded with many of them. They included a health planning commission, progressive trade union legislation, cooperatives, and expanded rural and social services. Crown corporations were the favoured instrument for providing important services.

The GFO was a central agency for the Crowns, providing them with accounting, financial, legal, and industrial relations services. Each Crown had a manager, but it also had a minister in charge. Blakeney played a pivotal role, acting as secretary, directing the flow of information, and also providing legal advice to the province's Industrial Development Fund (later called SEDCO).

Blakeney is not a sentimental man, but he talks of that period in the 1950s with a special fondness. Everything was new, and he was working hard and learning all the time. He even remembers once attending a budget meeting on Christmas Day. He was able to apply his academic knowledge in law and economics, and found his early experience in his father's wholesale business was valuable when applied to public corporations.

The government placed its public sector emphasis on utility and service corporations, where it had a monopoly—power, telephones, a northern airline, and auto insurance. Blakeney became convinced that public ownership could work as efficiently as private enterprise, and often with desirable social goals attached. "In 1955 SaskPower took natural gas quickly and cheaply to all sorts of people, to small places in Saskatchewan which were not getting gas at that time," he said. "It made me believe that a great deal was possible and that there was no mystique in private management."

Blakeney's work and his friendships with the bureaucratic elite placed him in an enviable position to see government at work. His was also in frequent contact with the Premier and Cabinet ministers. The Premier was "Mr. Douglas" to him, and that formal relationship continued until Blakeney entered politics himself. He had been raised in a solid Baptist household, and found it easy to work for a Premier who was as comfortable on the pulpit as on a campaign platform. Protestant ministers, including Woodsworth, Knowles and Douglas, were stalwarts in the CCF.

But if Blakeney had a political mentor, it was not the irrepressible Douglas but rather Clarence Fines. A Regina teacher, Fines became involved in the Saskatchewan CCF in its earliest days and he is generally credited with putting the province back onto its financial feet. He was a shrewd and capable Treasurer who produced a string of balanced budgets. "He spent a lot of time getting quality people," Blakeney recalled. "He insisted on performance. He attempted to define the job he wanted you to do, then he told you to go and do it, not to come back and ask him about it."

Allan and Molly lived for several years in a modest rented suite before joining a co-operative where families built their own homes. Despite her heart condition, Molly lived a normal life and gave birth to two children, Hugh and Barbara.

Blakeney left the GFO in 1955 to become the chief officer of the Saskatchewan Securities Commission, a position that provided him with an insider's view on how companies are financed, and the confidence that he knew how business worked. But he had always planned to get into politics and found that his job, which limited any partisan activity, placed too many constraints upon him. He decided to go into a private law practice, and began to watch for an opportunity.

During the night of December 27, 1957, Molly awakened her husband to tell him that she was desperately ill. Before the doctor arrived she had died from a Stokes-Adams attack, a condition characterized by extreme slowness of pulse. What happened in the following days remains a blur in Blakeney's usually commanding memory. He had two young children, but no family in Saskatchewan, so he had to depend for help on friends and people from his congregation at church. Later he hired a housekeeper to be with the children six days a week, while he was there for the seventh.

His plan to move into private law practice was delayed but not abandoned. In April 1958, he became a partner in a small firm, practicing mainly corporate law on behalf of small companies.

Anne Gorham was learning to ski at Mount Baker in Washington during the Christmas holidays in 1957 when she was informed that her friend Molly Blakeney had died. They had known each other since childhood in Nova Scotia, and Anne, a botanist teaching in Victoria, had spent holidays with Molly and Allan on different occasions. In April 1958, Allan wrote to say that he would be visiting Victoria and would like to see her. "He was still in a state of bereaved shock," Anne recalled.

With that visit began a courtship that culminated in their engagement, announced at a December 1958 house party attended by civil service and political friends in Regina. They were married in Victoria in May 1959, and Anne moved to Regina to become a mother, and soon, a political wife.

Political Involvement

The Trianon Ballroom was an elegant landmark in downtown Regina, a building with hardwood floors, balustrades and balconies. It was there on April 19, 1960, that Allan Blakeney, with the blessing of party stalwarts Tommy Douglas and Clarence Fines, was nominated as a candidate in the pending election.

The government planned to run on its record and the charisma of Douglas, but a proposal by the government to create North America's first public, tax-financed health care system turned the campaign into a single-issue contest with organized medicine bitterly opposed to the idea.

Douglas was re-elected and within two months Blakeney was named minister of Education and appointed to the Treasury Board committee of Cabinet. He established himself quickly as a capable and valuable minister, with an encyclopedic knowledge of the government and its bureaucracy.

By 1960 there was mounting pressure on Douglas to contest the leadership of a new national party in which the CCF would join with organized labour. He acceded to those pleas in the summer of 1961 and was succeeded as Premier by Woodrow S. Lloyd. Lloyd moved quickly to juggle his Cabinet, and named Blakeney as provincial treasurer. Blakeney delivered the numbers in his first budget speech, but he also outlined his political philosophy. "There are those in politics who see the government's role as minimal," he said, "maintaining law and order while protecting the role of the private sector. A second group, which includes social democrats, sees government as an instrument for creating growth, to be sure, but also providing important public services and pursuing greater equality for citizens."

Douglas had already left for Ottawa when the Saskatchewan Medical Care Insurance Act was introduced into the Legislature on October 13, 1961, and it fell to Lloyd to proceed with the plan. The legislation provided for medical care to be supported by taxes and administered by a public commission, but it did not say how doctors would be paid, and that became a point of further conflict.

Lloyd named Blakeney to an inner committee of Cabinet responsible for negotiating with doctors, drafting legislation and establishing machinery to administer medicare. The committee also moved to make contingency plans, as a threatened doctors' strike loomed.

Blakeney prepared legislation whereby doctors, after seeing patients, would send their bills to the insurance commission, which in turn would pay them. Throughout the winter and spring of 1962, the doctors refused to negotiate with the government, which delayed introducing its legislation once but was determined to do so on July 1. As the countdown approached, the doctors and their supporters created "Keep Our Doctors" (KOD) committees to mount a public relations campaign.

Blakeney was constantly at Lloyd's side, as his key negotiator with the doctors. As the situation became more tense, and verbal attacks on the government more extreme, there was talk in Cabinet of capitulating, but Blakeney let it be known quietly that he would resign if that were to occur.

On July 1, Saskatchewan was plunged into a frightening 22-day doctors' strike. There were emotional KOD rallies, and harsh attacks on the government by the provincial media. The American Medical Association, fearing that medicare in a small Canadian province could become contagious, helped to finance a public relations campaign. There were threats of violence, and someone in the night used red paint to daub the word "commie" on the stucco wall of Woodrow Lloyd's house.

At one point during the tense weeks, Lloyd slipped away from Regina to get advice from Frank Scott, the Montreal poet and constitutional lawyer. Scott urged him to remain firm. While Lloyd was away, Blakeney and others covered for him, "running a scam," in Blakeney's words. "We parked his car in front of the building, and moved it and put his office lights on and off." Anyone calling his office was told that the Premier was busy. Amazingly, his absence of several days was not discovered.

Lloyd returned fortified and announced that Lord Malcolm Taylor, from Great Britain, would be invited to assist the government in negotiating an end to the strike. By this time, an airlift of doctors from Britain and other parts of Canada had attracted about 100 sympathetic physicians, and many Saskatchewan doctors were quietly slipping back to work.

Lord Taylor shuttled between two buildings on Saskatoon's riverbank, using a combination of patrician charm and arrogance to broker an agreement. The strike ended with the signing of the Saskatoon Agreement on July 23, 1962. Within weeks, Lloyd had shifted Blakeney to the sensitive Health portfolio, with instructions to get the Medical Care Insurance Commission working according to the terms negotiated.

The medicare dispute focussed the energies of Lloyd's government, but it also created a sense of fatigue at its centre. It was the last great hurrah for the CCF, which had held power for an uninterrupted 20 years. When Lloyd called an election in 1964, he was defeated by Ross Thatcher and the Liberals. Thatcher, who had earlier described the health plan as the "civil conscription" of doctors, had decided by 1964 that it was too popular to be undone.

Blakeney won easy personal victory in 1964, but the immediate result of the government's defeat meant that he had to look for work. Lloyd appointed him as Finance critic, and he played a role in rebuilding a party whose political arteries had hardened over the years. However, the salary of an opposition politician would not support a family. The transition was not an easy one because few firms wanted him on their name plate in a province now ruled by the Liberals. Eventually he began a small legal practice focussing on real estate, wills and estates, and commercial work for small companies.

Ross Thatcher moved quickly to take control of the government, firing senior civil servants, many of them Blakeney's friends and long-time colleagues. Thatcher's industrial strategy was to announce that Saskatchewan was open for enterprise, and his major initial move was to declare a royalty holiday for oil companies, which had been large donors to his campaigns.

Thatcher called a snap election in 1967, campaigning on the promise of prosperity under free enterprise, and he won again. Blakeney opposed Thatcher politically, but liked him personally and also respected him. "He was a good politician, a hard-nosed guy, he had a direct, sometimes even abrupt way about him," Blakeney said. "No nonsense Ross, mind the store, but by my standards he delegated far too little of his decision making."

Thatcher's 1967 campaign had focused on the brave new world open to Saskatchewan under his leadership. But at the first Cabinet meeting following the election he stunned his ministers by announcing that he intended to embark on a harsh austerity program.

There was a glut of grain on the world market, which meant bulging bins and thin wallets for Saskatchewan farmers. Surplus wheat glut and low prices meant that farmers everywhere were cutting back on fertilzer use, and that hit Saskatchewan's potash industry, which had been chaotically overbuilt.

Thatcher feared a recession and his instinctive reaction was to cut government spending. He set wage ceilings not only for the civil service, but also for the employees of companies with government contracts. He also passed legislation that threatened to legislate teachers back to work if they went on strike. Blakeney's mantra as Finance critic was that Liberal times were hard times.

The CCF, however, was having problems of its own. The defeat in 1964 had been terribly dispiriting. Many believed they would not have lost if Douglas had remained in Saskatchewan. Lloyd was much admired, and had earned his spurs on the CCF's "long march," but he was a plodding man without Douglas's spark, and he lived in mute contrast to Ross Thatcher's take-charge manner and brash eloquence. Lloyd recognized his lack of charisma and considered stepping down, but was apparently urged by friends and advisers to stay on.

After 1964, he set about refocussing the caucus in its opposition role, and he recruited a number of new candidates, including Roy Romanow, Jack Messer, Gordon Snyder and Ted Bowerman, all of whom won in 1967. The NDP (as the provincial CCF was now called) improved its performance over 1964, but there was muted discussion about someone running against Lloyd as leader at the 1968 convention. Blakeney had been approached by dissident MLAs prior to an earlier convention, but he curtly refused their overtures.

Lloyd was a philosophical man with a strong interest in policy, and after the defeat in 1967, he decided to open the windows to new ideas in a party whose intellectual force had peaked 15 years earlier. He appealed to constituencies to engage in serious policy debate, and he encouraged the formation of study groups to talk about issues. There were also task forces on agriculture, housing and education that reported to the provincial convention. He organized special seminars for his caucus on issues in education, agriculture, and the environment. He established a committee to work toward a long-term program for the next NDP government. He had not been successful electorally, but Lloyd did rebuild the party in both policy and organization.

Blakeney was Lloyd's political confidant and his trusted lieutenant. As Finance critic, he shared much of the burden in the Legislature. His skills at analysis and problem solving were invaluable. However, while he always made himself available to speak at conventions and constituency events, he saw his role as one of supporting the leader.

The Blakeney family continued for years to live in a modest bungalow and he drove a Volkswagen, but they did buy a cottage at Last Mountain Lake near Regina. He and Anne had two more children, David and Margaret, and decided to move their young family into a home that they had built in a poor neighbourhood within his Regina Centre constituency. "If I was going to represent that area," he said, "we were going to live there, and my children were to go to school there."

The home on King Street was a clear indication that Blakeney intended to continue in politics. He had toyed with the idea of running federally in the 1968 election, but Lloyd talked him out of it. Blakeney had his own provincial leadership ambitions, and approached Lloyd, but the leader gave him no clear signal about his own intentions. He merely told Blakeney that he was a valued member of the team, and Lloyd would be sorry to see him leave. Blakeney stayed.

The federal NDP convention in 1969 debated the "Waffle Manifesto" on the cavernous floor of the Winnipeg Auditorium. The leadership called on its heavyweights to speak and they included Blakeney, then a federal party vice-president. The Waffle resolution referred to Canada's subservience to the "American empire," described as a militarist and racist power conducting a "barbarous" war in Vietnam. Among the speakers calling for an explicitly socialist program for Canada were Mel Watkins and Laurier Lapierre, as well as Saskatchewan MLA Walter Smishek and Carol Gudmundson, a Saskatchewan party vice-president.

For more than an hour the convention was consumed by passionate debate, with competing choruses of shouts, boos, catcalls and applause. Douglas, who had been attempting to avoid any painful splits, eventually spoke against the manifesto, calling it "ambiguous and ambivalent." Among the Saskatchewan delegation, Woodrow Lloyd remained stubbornly silent, but when a standing vote was called he pushed himself heavily to his feet in support of the Waffle motion, which lost by a vote of 499 to 284.

The federal party executive responded to the manifesto with a long counter-resolution that had been drafted by the NDP national council. It pledged action to achieve Canadian economic independence, and for a program of selective nationalization to curb foreign investment. The convention passed it on the following day, and undoubtedly it did move the NDP in a leftist, nationalist direction.

The convention elected Blakeney to be party president. He was studiously low key at the news conference that followed, describing himself to reporters as a "slightly left-of-centre moderate," although some of his colleagues in Saskatchewan would have described him as a right-of-centre moderate. He said that he favoured some of the manifesto's principles, but not its stridency. He said that the party owed a debt to the manifesto's authors.

Blakeney had opposed the Waffle manifesto on the convention floor, and so had opposed his leader, but maintained there was no serious breach:

> This was just a 60–40 judgement call. I didn't have any quarrel with our considering new ideas, but no socialist party is going to get anywhere unless we organize elections, and that involved organizational loyalty. I think there was a feeling that the people who were pressing for the Waffle clause were people who were unwilling to go out there and do the slugging.

Blakeney always regarded himself as a Canadian nationalist, but disliked what he considered to be the imported, extremist rhetoric of the new left. He thought it unsuitable to political debate in Canada, where he believed the system still provided an opportunity for democratic change.

He had been a member of the Lakeview CCF Club a decade earlier and involved at the local level in the national effort to replace the party's 1932 "Regina Manifesto" with something more contemporary and moderate. The review resulted in the Winnipeg Declaration of 1956, which avoided the clarion call to socialism and the nationalization of industry. It talked instead about a positive role for private industry in Canadian society. Much of the new thinking flowed from the experience of the Douglas government in Saskatchewan, which, confronted by the day-to-day challenges of governing, had softened the party line. Blakeney was there when it happened, and he approved.

The aftermath of the 1969 Winnipeg convention debate spilled over like molten lava into Saskatchewan, where Lloyd's judgement and eventually his leadership were called into question. The Wafflers began to meet as a caucus, and ran candidates for party office at the 1969 provincial convention. Tensions were exacerbated when the Waffle decided to put candidates forward in selected provincial nominations. They were charged with trying to create a party within the party, something that they denied.

Allan Blakeney

Matters came to a head at an emergency caucus meeting in March 1970 and a second meeting, of the party's executive, a few days later. No one kept notes and the recollections of participants vary greatly, but Lloyd was attacked and at the end of the second meeting he resigned as leader.

Blakeney had always planned to run for the leadership after Lloyd departed, but now he was unsure. The manner of Lloyd's leaving was unsettling and Blakeney may have believed that he had not supported his friend and colleague in his hour of need. MLA Walter Smishek encouraged Blakeney to run, but recalled that he was dispirited and reluctant.

By mid-April, however, when the party began to plan for a July convention, Blakeney was in the race. Roy Romanow's entry was announced on May 15, followed by Waffler Don Mitchell and labour lawyer George Taylor, who was seen as a candidate of the party's old left.

The centrepiece of the leadership campaign was a series of town hall meetings. Blakeney touted his experience, Romanow the need for a new style, and Mitchell concentrated on a socialist platform. The last of the meetings occurred before 500 people in Saskatoon's Centennial Auditorium, and the convention was held in the Armouries in Regina on July 4.

Blakeney had expected to lead throughout, and was shocked when Romanow defeated him on the first ballot. Taylor finished last and dropped off. Romanow won the second ballot too, but gained only 20 votes. Much of Taylor's support went to Don Mitchell, who finished third on the ballot and then huddled with his supporters. They decided to abstain on the third ballot, although not all of them did. Blakeney gained almost 100 votes, and that gave him the victory. In the end it was a combination of the NDP old guard and the new left that saw Blakeney as preferable to Romanow.

Blakeney's victory was less convincing than he would have liked, but it was a victory nonetheless. He had proven his mettle in Cabinet and caucus, but he had not attracted a popular following. He had not yet arrived as an effective campaigner, and his leadership effort had been efficient without being very exciting. In his victory speech, he promised unity and a team effort. He would attract people who would compensate for whatever shortcomings he might have as leader. He built an immediate bridge to Romanow, saying that there would likely be a Cabinet position for him in an NDP government.

Blakeney had arrived in Saskatchewan 20 years earlier, and had bided his time, moving deliberately toward a goal that he must have always carried within him. Now it remained to been seen whether he could muster the political mettle to deal with Ross Thatcher.

The 1971 Election

Ross Thatcher was expected to call an election in the spring of 1971. Reporters dogged his every step, and at a Liberal coffee party in Saskatoon in May, the podium bristled with microphones and television lights bathed the room. To the disappointment of journalists, Thatcher finished his speech and sat down, but just as the camera lights were to be shut down he bounced back to his feet and said that he had something to add—there would be an election on June 23.

The NDP leadership transition had been smooth, with Lloyd clearly pleased with Blakeney as his replacement. The Liberals were pleased too, because it was Romanow, the smooth young campaigner, whom they feared more than Blakeney.

In the NDP offices, there was a frank assessment of the new leader's strengths and weaknesses. He was perceived as competent but rather square. Thatcher was fiery, a bombastic, one-man band with a compelling platform style honed in the days of the town hall debate. As Blakeney later recalled,

> I think someone made the judgement that you could never make me into a competitor with Ross Thatcher. Nor was I going to be a tribune of the people like Tommy Douglas, who could encapsulate their hopes and fears in a phrase. I was always going to be the quasi-scholar or the retread public servant who would analyze the problems and say, this is what we ought to do.

Blakeney has a surprising lack of ego for someone with his skills and energy. He was content to promote the NDP as a team with new ideas and the competence to put them into effect. Policy was their great strength, and the task was to distill dozens of resolutions emanating from the earlier wide-ranging seminars and conventions into a coherent platform.

The result was an exceptionally detailed program. Early in 1971, the policies were reworked into a concise program called *New Deal for People*. It was 21 pages long and divided into sections. Each offered a brief statement on an issue or problem, invariably blaming the Liberals for waste, mismanagement, and sell-outs, then provided a numbered list of NDP policies to remedy the situation. The booklet contained approximately 140 promises and the NDP called it their "blueprint for the 70s."

The party did not wait for the election call but published tens of thousands of the slim, blue-on-white booklets, and released them in February just as the Liberals were tabling their Speech from the Throne. "We wanted to have it contrasted with the Liberal program in the Throne Speech," Blakeney said. "We wanted them to ridicule our program in the Legislature, which was successful. When you get the government talking about the opposition's program, you're moving right along."

The NDP electoral machine had been idling, but was now set into high gear. The orange signs went up overnight; pamphlets and literature were already with the printers awaiting only the election date. By the morning following the election call, they were printed and ready to distribute.

Blakeney's routine was to start the day early, hitting as many towns as possible before an evening rally that might not end until midnight. Blakeney had worked hard in the year since the leadership to improve his speaking style and his platform performance was markedly better. At each evening rally, he attacked the Liberals, but he also outlined the NDP promises—abolishing Liberal deterrent fees, which charged people for visits to the doctor; abolishing Bill 2, which forbade public sector strikes; promoting a two-price system for wheat; paving the streets in small towns.

Thatcher ran on his record of responsible, tight-fisted government, and cast this as another round in the unending battle of free enterprise against socialism, a theme the

SAB RA 21,674(1)

Allan Blakeney addresses an NDP rally on June 19, 1971. Four days later, his party swept Ross Thatcher's Liberals from power, winning 45 of 60 seats. Blakeney's wife, Anne, is seated to his left.

Liberals had pursued in every election since the 1930s. He ran a personalist campaign, travelling in an airplane to rallies featuring the leader. Blakeney, in deliberate contrast, travelled in a bus rented from the Crown-owned Saskatchewan Transportation Company, saying that he wanted to be on the ground "where the voters are," an obvious reference to Thatcher's mode of transportation.

The NDP had decided that every attempt should be made to link Thatcher to unpopular federal Liberal policies, especially those in agriculture. Saskatchewan was mired in a farm crisis brought on by soft markets for wheat and a price lower than any since the Depression. The federal Liberals responded with their 1969 Task Force on Agriculture. The report predicted that by 1990, two-thirds of Canadian farmers would be out of the business, and the Liberals appeared quite prepared to let the market take its toll. In rural Saskatchewan, the reality was as harsh as the prediction. In the 10 years ending in 1971, the province had lost 17,000 farm families.

The television and radio ads, the door-to-door canvassing and the policy booklet all reinforced the theme that Thatcher was in collusion with Ottawa to drive small farmers out of business. One effective television commercial showed a hand descending on a toy farmyard and wiping the buildings and fences off of the table. A voice then said that the Liberals would do away with two of every three Saskatchewan farms.

The NDP promised to promote a maximum number of family farms; to restrict foreign ownership of farmland; to set up a Land Bank to assist with the transfer of land between generations; to provide low-interest loans to young farmers and to support marketing boards. They promised to keep local hospitals and schools open; to develop a public housing corporation; to build more rinks and ball diamonds; to decentralize government services and to help small business.

Blakeney promised a publicly financed prescription drug program; a dental program for children; support for community clinics; more day care centres and a higher minimum wage. There was to be a human rights code and a commission to enforce it, and a provincial Ombudsman. In response to blatant Liberal gerrymanders in the 1960s, he promised an independent electoral boundaries commission. He promised to control pollution, and to establish a separate department for the environment. He promised to set up a separate government department for northern Saskatchewan.

The NDP message was complemented by a door-to-door canvass and a literature drop, techniques successfully tested in an earlier by-election. Don Faris, NDP provincial secretary in 1971, stated: "We took the intensive urban organizing style of eastern Canada and applied it as best we could to Saskatchewan, with intensive sign campaigns, two or three canvasses of every home and good election-day organization."

By the end of the campaign, Blakeney was confident that the election was won, just as surely as Thatcher and his lieutenant Dave Steuart knew that it was lost. On June 23, the NDP won 45 of 60 seats and took 55% of the popular vote. Ross Thatcher, subdued and dignified on election night, walked into the sweltering NDP headquarters to concede defeat and congratulate the victors. Unknown to almost everyone, Thatcher had suffered a slight stroke prior to the campaign, and his diabetes had flared up again. Woodrow Lloyd was there too, wearing a new beard and looking relaxed. The reins of government, he said, would be back in the hands of the people. Both men were to die within months.

The Blakeney home later on the night of June 23 received a steady stream of NDP activists and well-wishers. Blakeney had prepared for a victory party by having some friends buy a case of whiskey on his behalf. When his wife Anne discovered their purchase, she chafed at the extravagance and sent it back. Hearing about that, Blakeney wrote a new cheque and sent his friends back to the store, and given the expectant crowds on election night, it was fortunate that he did.

Premier of Saskatchewan

Allan Blakeney was sworn in as Saskatchewan's tenth Premier on June 30, 1971, in the red-carpeted legislative chamber. He opted for a small, eight-member Cabinet, keeping the Treasury and Industry portfolios for himself. Roy Romanow was sworn in first among ministers and named Deputy Premier, a position he would retain throughout the Blakeney years. The two men never became close friends, but they had an exemplary working relationship.

The other appointments included Jack Messer, Walter Smishek, Everett Wood, Gordon Snyder, Ted Bowerman, Neil Byers and Gordon MacMurchy. Six of the eight would remain in Cabinet throughout Blakeney's premiership. The average age of the ministers was 42 years. Of these men, besides Blakeney himself, only Everett Wood had previous Cabinet experience. Gordon MacMurchy had not sat in the Legislature at all, although he had a long experience in public affairs and in the party.

Within days of the first round of Cabinet appointments, Eiling Kramer, a veteran politician and North Battleford auctioneer, was added as a result of his own fierce lobby. Six months later, Blakeney added two more ministers—Kim Thorson, an Estevan lawyer, and John Brockelbank, the son of party pioneer J.H. Brockelbank. Blakeney was to add five more ministers during his first administration. Three were young men: Ed Tchzorewski, Don Cody, and Elwood Cowley, who took over Finance from Blakeney in May 1972. The others were veteran MLAs Wes Robbins and John Kowalchuk.

In his Cabinet appointments, Blakeney was sending a message about party unity. He was reaching out to his own supporters, but also to Romanow and those who supported him. His appointment of Walter Smishek, who had supported George Taylor, was a message of inclusion to the party's old left, albeit a weaker one. The younger Waffle members were largely shut out.

Blakeney sent another signal by initially keeping Industry and Finance for himself. His would be a government interested in economic development and diversification. "We wanted to put an economic underpinning under what we hoped would be a broad social service safety net," he said, "and you can't do that in Saskatchewan unless you have a more diversified economy."

In 1971, there were several big jobs to tackle immediately, and a trust to maintain. Blakeney had defined agriculture as a major issue in the campaign, and the NDP had promised a Land Bank to make it easier for land to be transferred from one generation to the next. The NDP had also promised a separate new department for northern Saskatchewan. Finally, there was Ross Thatcher's area bargaining plan for teachers' salaries. Negotiations occurred locally but in reality salary levels were dictated from Regina. It was a recipe for frustration among trustees and teachers, an important NDP support group. Blakeney instructed Gordon MacMurchy, a former school trustee, to work something out that would satisfy both teachers and trustees. MacMurchy set up a system whereby salary negotiations occurred provincially, with local bargaining for conditions of work.

By the time the Cabinet was sworn in, Blakeney was ensconced in his office, with its silver-and-blue tapestried walls, and its fireplace with an oak-trimmed mantle. He had photographs of CCF-NDP icons on his walls—Woodsworth, Coldwell, Douglas, Lloyd and David Lewis.

Blakeney's personal secretary, Florence Wilke, made the move with him to the Premier's office. She had a history in government going back to 1944, and she had also worked with Woodrow Lloyd in the opposition leader's office. She lived in Blakeney's Regina constituency and was on his executive. She was in charge of his schedule and met with him daily. Given her history in the party and her sensitive jobs in the legislative offices, she was also a good source of intelligence for Blakeney, who was often oblivious to gossip and the details of people's personal lives.

Jack Kinzel, another trusted Lloyd operative, also moved along with Blakeney to the inner sanctum. Kinzel was a consummate communications professional. Blakeney wanted him as his major speechwriter, and as an advisor on communication and potential trouble spots. No matter what his changes of title, Kinzel always remained nearby in the early years of Blakeney's tenure.

Beyond the Premier's office, there was the imposing task of rebuilding the machinery of government, which Blakeney believed Ross Thatcher had allowed fall into disuse. Blakeney needed civil servants who could do the more ambitious work that he had in mind, but first he had to make decisions about the people he already had in place. He turned to an old-time friend and civil servant Grant Mitchell, who had survived the Thatcher years and knew pretty well everyone in government.

Mitchell's immediate task was to compile a list of all the deputy ministers and senior civil servants. He made a chart, and then he and Blakeney pored over its names. Blakeney did not want a purge, so only a few people were fired. Most everyone else retained a job, although many people were shuffled. There was room to move people, and often with salary increases, because Blakeney thought Thatcher's civil service had been underpaid.

SAB RA 23,088
Premier Allan Blakeney, c. 1972.

Mitchell's second major task was to recruit new people and he quickly compiled a short list for the senior jobs. He looked immediately to the Faculty of Administration at the University of Saskatchewan's Regina campus. The dean, Wes Bolstad, had worked in the Budget Bureau in the 1950s, and in turn ran Woodrow Lloyd's office after 1962. In the summer of 1971, he was camping in the Cypress Hills when the call came from Blakeney for him to become Cabinet secretary.

Blakeney set up a small task force in August 1971 to provide recommendations for re-establishing a central planning unit attached to executive council (essentially those offices around the Premier). By 1972, he had hired a planning officer, and that summer Blakeney appointed a Cabinet planning committee.

Blakeney placed great emphasis on the Finance department. He wanted budgets to be prepared well, then scrutinized regularly as the year progressed. He also wanted to take the best possible advantage of Ottawa's cost-shared programs, which had become a burgeoning source of income in the 1970s. Many of the brightest people were recruited to Finance, which became a training ground for those who would later become deputy ministers and senior civil servants.

Allan Blakeney carried with him, in 1971, a detailed model of the governing structures that he intended to put into place. Many of them hearkened back to his experience as a civil servant, and later a Cabinet minister. Cabinet was central. Blakeney did not, in his words, "want to be minister of everything" as he thought Ross Thatcher had been. He was a delegator, and he placed a great emphasis on process.

The ministers met regularly on Tuesdays in the large Cabinet room off Blakeney's offices. They gathered at 9:30 a.m. with Romanow always seated to Blakeney's right at the large oval table. The meetings continued through a sandwich lunch into at least mid-afternoon. Wes Bolstad, the Cabinet secretary, sat in a corner taking notes and recalled that Blakeney expected his ministers to attend.

Blakeney also wanted Cabinet to deal with policy and not administrative detail, with recommendations and not with problems. The procedures became increasingly refined: "The Cabinet agenda had to be on paper," he said. "I wanted an outline of the problems, but with some recommendations. If it wasn't worth someone's time to figure out what the answer was, or at least recommend an answer, then why was it worth ours?"

Roy Romanow recalled that Blakeney was a stickler for process, rules, procedure and thoroughness: "Bring in the Kentucky Fried Chicken, and we would sit there until one or two in the morning, with ministers half asleep, and Al stuck on the Stray Animal Act amendments. But these were occasions that held us in good stead."

The Premier gave short shrift to any civil servant who came with problems rather than recommendations. Stories are legion about devastating Blakeney cross-examinations delivered in an icy and impersonal manner, which would bring an unstructured presentation tumbling down on its unfortunate presenter. If Blakeney was at times curt with his staff, he was gentler, although no less effective, with his ministers. If any among them carried a proposal prepared by a deputy but was not knowledgeable about it, a few penetrating questions by Blakeney could prove embarrassing. "He could cut your idea up quickly," Elwood Cowley said. "Three sentences, then he quit and so did you."

Blakeney insisted that ministers leave their departmental hats at the door. They were expected to consider the needs of the whole government. If departments were having turf wars, he wanted them worked out in advance. He wanted everyone to participate in Cabinet discussions, and did not want ministers lying in the reeds. Several former ministers describe him as "schoolmasterish," always wanting to be sure that everyone understood the issues. He worked on the basis on consensus. "If there was something he was uneasy about or that Cabinet was divided about," said Cowley, "he'd worry the damned thing to death."

Blakeney had his own categories for ministers and tended to look to them for help in those areas. In the House, he relied particularly on Romanow, Messer and Cowley. He wanted Kramer and MacMurchy to tell him what people were thinking in the country. Cowely provided political, and Romanow, tactical, advice. Ed Tchzorewski gave guidance on how the party might react to certain issues. Once in Cabinet, the political categories of left and right became less important as Blakeney looked to ministers for the specific skills they brought to the table to advance the government's program.

He had a clear idea of the administrative relationship that ministers should maintain with senior civil servants. He gave a lecture around the oval table every time a new minister was added, and it came complete with a chart. "It would have the Cabinet and ministers on top," said Wes Bolstad. "Then there would be a line drawn with deputy ministers below it. He was telling ministers that they were not to get involved in the administration of their departments. And he would tell deputies not to delegate problems up to ministers, but to look at policy options, weigh them, and make a recommendation."

Ministers knew it as "the speech," and it was transformed into literature when Blakeney presented it as an address to the Institute of Public Administration of Canada. It was central to his view of how to govern. The emphasis was on public servants to create policy options. The role of Cabinet ministers was political, testing those ideas on the public and also informing the planners how supportive people were likely to be toward a new policy. The politician had the added responsibility of explaining the policy in a way that built public support. In Blakeney's view, any policy that fell outside of the range of public acceptability could not be pursued no matter how appealing to the planners.

Every Wednesday morning Blakeney held a news conference in a small studio in the basement of the Legislative Building. He might have an announcement or simply respond to questions, providing answers in detail that sometimes left reporters with glazed eyes. All the while, he sipped tea brewed in a small, stainless steel pot, and usually whizzed through these encounters without anyone laying a glove on him.

He met with his speechwriters following the news conference, and together they reviewed upcoming engagements. While the writers made notes he would pace the floor, throwing out themes that he wanted to communicate, providing a framework and a background. "That outline off the top of his head," said Garry Aldridge, who wrote for Blakeney, "would have more detail than most people get by sitting down to write a first draft."

Ted Bowen, a speechwriter in the later Blakeney years, said: "He understood rhetoric and literature and history. I would throw Northrop Frye into his speeches from time to time." Blakeney had a caustic sense of humour in informal situations, but was cautious about using it in public. He liked one-liners, which he could use and then move on. A certain understatement came naturally to him, and he rarely departed from his prepared texts. He did not want to say anything that would come back to haunt him. He knew that everything he said was on the record and he was uncommonly cautious about what he said.

Excellence in public administration was a legacy of the Douglas and Lloyd governments, and Blakeney expected it too. He believed that social democrats offer a "high service" government, and to do so, they need a sterling civil service. Doug McArthur, who served both as a senior deputy minister and a Cabinet minister, said, "We felt as civil servants that we worked for a Premier who wanted us to be the best. He had very high standards, but he recognized and appreciated the civil service."

Blakeney liked policy and he liked administration, taking ideas and putting them into action in an organized form. It was politics that he found less pleasant and more demanding. Basically a shy man, Blakeney had to force himself to press the flesh on main street and maintain personal links to the party. His self-analysis was revealing:

> I've never found it easy to go out and glad-hand. I always think I should have a purpose. I have a certain fondness for precision, and that is really a disability, because an awful lot of human discourse depends on the exuding of warmth or sympathy. I'm a literalist. Frequently, I'm listening to what people are saying rather than what they are conveying. But that's always been true and I'm not sure you can change that.

SAB RB 12,553

Premier Allan Blakeney in a crowd of children and adults, during his bus tour of the province, June 1973.

His favourite meet-the-people exercise was his annual summer bus tour, when for a week or two the Blakeney bus would roll into the main streets of Saskatchewan towns, stopping so that he and Anne could visit with men at the grain elevator office or have tea with citizens at the nursing home. He appeared happiest as the bus rolled past the golden fields, and he could stand at the front step treating reporters and aides to a running commentary about the ethnic mix in the town ahead, or long-term crop yields in the municipality just past. He had a special fondness for rural people and an admiration for their ability to quickly organize themselves around any issue or disaster.

He was attentive to his Regina Elphinstone constituency, doing the obligatory door knocking (which he disliked) and taking his turn along with other MLAs at an urban office on weekday evenings to meet anyone who arrived. Constituency meetings were often held in the Blakeney living room and bake sales in their garage.

His wife Anne was involved in the constituency and the neighbourhood, volunteering at the school, attending the nearby United Church, and participating in a latchkey program for children. She hosted constituency teas and at party events she was admired for her willingness to roll up her sleeves and plunge her hands into the dishwater. But the Blakeneys had an agreement about her political involvement. She did not want a high profile as the Premier's wife, and she carefully chose the events that she wished to attend. She worked in election campaigns and accompanied him on the summer bus tour, but she did not speak out on public issues or make pronouncements.

The Premier's work was constant and demanding. During the week it was the office or the Legislative session, night events and frequent travel. On weekends, there were often party meetings. He wanted one Sunday free at least every two weeks when he would nap, watch sports on television and perhaps go to church. On the Friday afternoons preceding such weekends, he might be found in the stacks of the legislative library, searching for a mystery novel. His idea of relaxing was to be cocooned at home with a book.

Close social contacts for the Blakeneys waned in direct proportion to his succession through the political ranks. Many of their closest friends in the bureaucracy left after the Thatcher purge in 1964. The Blakeneys maintained an easy and open contact with them, but did not often see them. In Regina, Walter and Ruth Smishek remained close friends throughout and had a cottage next to the Blakeneys on Last Mountain Lake. The list of close Cabinet and caucus friendships ended there, although there were Christmas parties and the odd singsong. Blakeney believed that for a Premier, isolation was part of the job: "The more senior you are in your political office, the fewer friends you have," he said. Like Tommy Douglas before him, he chose to isolate himself, because at that level, friendships cannot always survive politics.

Blakeney regularly attended meetings of the NDP provincial council. He didn't leave the meetings after his reports, but stayed to listen and make notes. The council met four times a year and, like the fowl suppers in his constituency, he wanted them on his calendar.

He tended to delegate party and political tasks to ministers who would play that role for him—MacMurchy, Cowley, Tchzorewksi, or to Bill Knight, who became NDP party secretary and a close advisor. He appointed these same men and others to a Cabinet political committee with special responsibilities for party organization and election planning. "I'm not as skilled at party organization as I am in party policy or government organization," Blakeney said.

But there are those who challenge the assertion that while Blakeney was a good administrator, he was not a good politician. His advisor Bill Knight said that a politician has to be judged not only on the ability to make rousing speeches and to remember people's names, but also on the ability to get elected and to govern:

> Allan Blakeney had the brains and the discipline. He combined them with an incredible knowledge of a whole range of issues. He could fight a battle with the federal government on health care like nobody else. He could handle the constitution. He could switch back to economic fights over the ownership of industries and the like. He had the agility to move philosophically within the party to handle its changing moods and positions.

Blakeney was not a populist as Douglas had been, but rather a playing coach, a good judge of talent who used his team to its best advantage. He was a process man who surrounded himself with competent people. He had been scrupulous in handling potential caucus divisions that had arisen near the end of Woodrow Lloyd's tenure. He had defeated Ross Thatcher convincingly in the 1971 election, and once in the Premier's office, it became obvious that behind Blakeney's rather bland appearance there lurked an exceptional competence and determination. He was in a commanding position after the 1971 victory to embark on his "new deal."

Agricultural Policy and the Land Bank

Allan Blakeney won the election in 1971, not because he looked at home on a tractor, but in large part because the NDP had mounted a slash-and-burn attack on federal agricultural policy, linking it to Ross Thatcher. Blakeney was fond of saying that Liberal times were hard times, and people in 1971 agreed.

The NDP rural recovery plan included grants and loans to farmers to diversify into livestock production and new crops, and a package of tax relief grants and programs to brighten up small-town Saskatchewan, but its centerpiece was the proposed Land Bank.

Aging farmers wanting out had a difficult time finding buyers. Younger people, family members in many cases, wanted to get into the business but often could not find the money to buy. The Land Bank proposed having the government purchase land and lease it back, with a preference shown toward family members. After five years the leasing farmer had the option to repurchase the land.

The debate about land tenure was not new. In 1931, the Saskatchewan section of the United Farmers of Canada had called flatly for the nationalization of all farmland, which would then be leased back to farmers. The CCF backed away from that proposal, but did propose a use-lease program in 1934. In the context of Depression foreclosures, the proposal was concerned more with guaranteeing permanent tenure than with an ideological commitment to public ownership. The use-lease proposal had become a political liability by 1944 and was dropped from the CCF program.

The succeeding Douglas and Lloyd governments made no attempt to deal with land tenure, but the issue surfaced again during the farm crisis of the late 1960s. The NDP's search for new answers led them back to old ones. The left, particularly those in the Waffle, pushed the issue, and the Land Bank was accepted in principle at the 1970 provincial convention that elected Blakeney as leader.

He had not emphasized a Land Bank in his leadership campaign, and was not as enthusiastic about the idea as others in the party. He was fond of quoting former Agriculture minister Toby Nollet who had said that problems in agriculture could not be solved by "tinkering with tenure." But at its 1970 convention, the party accepted the Land Bank in principle, and Blakeney took the party seriously.

The left wanted a Land Bank as an alternative to private ownership, providing long-term leases on publicly owned land. After the convention there was intense internal debate around the option to purchase. "I took an active part in some of these battles, saying we really have to have the right to repurchase," Blakeney recalled. "It was not our purpose to have a vast store of land owned by the government of Saskatchewan." He perceived the Land Bank as a method of transfer from one generation to another, and not as a fundamental change in the system of tenure. There would be no dusting off of the use-lease program under his tenure.

Blakeney's view prevailed and after the 1971 election, he appointed Jack Messer as minister of Agriculture with the task of getting the program up and running. Messer was an entrepreneur but he thought it made good sense for young farmers to lease from the Land Bank, putting their own money into farm diversification or into off-farm investments. That would provide some security for the times when farming was in a down cycle.

SAB RA 26,551

Premier Allan Blakeney, discussing agricultural issues with an unidentified farmer.

The program immediately created a buzz in the countryside, and in the first year, applications poured in from 2,200 farmers who wanted to sell. The Land Bank Commission made offers on 600 parcels and had 1,500 people apply to lease. The applicants were judged on a point system, with preference given to younger farmers whose holdings were not too large. In cases where a farmer wanted to lease to a younger family member, the transaction was made without reference to the point system.

With time, the Land Bank Commission purchased 600,000 acres of land and had 1,300 lessees. Their average age was 32, and one lessee in six was a direct descendant of the person who had sold to the Land Bank. The program received press attention, most of it favourable, from all over North America. But it was a difficult program to administer and fraught with political controversy. Virtually all farmers wanted more land, so there was an intense competition for its purchase or rental. For every farmer who received land from the Land Bank, there might be as many as 20 applicants who did not, and that led to many unhappy farmers and inevitable suspicion about the choice of lessees. The sellers complained about the purchase prices, which were quite low given the depressed farm economy. On the other hand, those who wished to buy land on the market complained that the Land Bank's very existence as a potential purchaser was inflating land prices.

Ironically, the program was to be undermined by the return of farm prosperity. Canada made large wheat sales to the Soviet Union and China in the early 1970s, and prices rose three- and fourfold. Farmers who had been fearful that every car coming down the road was the sheriff or a banker were now making money and felt less need for a government Land Bank, and many resented its very existence.

The Liberals, led by Dave Steuart following the death of Ross Thatcher in 1971, sensed the potential for a political issue. Farmers had the option to purchase land that they leased, but that did not prevent the Liberals from charging that the program was a plot by Big Brother to turn farmers into serfs. That touched a raw nerve among Saskatchewan's rural population, many thousands of them descended from immigrants in countries where it was difficult or impossible for farmers to own land. The Liberals used the theme in the 1975 election, where the NDP lost seats and votes.

The Land Bank was an attempt to slow rural depopulation and to get land into the hands of younger people, but it went beyond the realm of the acceptable for Saskatchewan farmers. The government never did purchase more than a small percentage of Saskatchewan's farmland, and all of it was available for repurchase. Yet the program became an easy political target, and some MLAs chose not to defend it. The Land Bank remained on the NDP books throughout the Blakeney years, but was quickly dropped after the government was defeated in 1982.

The CCF began as a farmers' movement and became a farmers' government in 1944. The force of change bearing down on the rural community, however, was inexorable. Blakeney's years as Premier coincided with a period of farm prosperity, and for a few good years, the historical tide of people leaving the countryside slowed to some extent, but ultimately those international trends were beyond the control of a provincial government. Blakeney's programs aimed at agricultural diversification were stymied by the facts of geography and international economy. The government spent millions of dollars lending farmers money to feed hogs rather than exporting their grain. When international grain prices rose, many of the hog barns sat empty as farmers went back to wheat.

By the end of the government's first term in 1975, most of the farm programs were in place and would remain so. By then Blakeney concluded that the key to the province's diversification and its prosperity lay in Saskatchewan's burgeoning mineral sector, and that came to occupy much of his attention and that of his government.

The North

Saskatchewan is known for its grain elevators and golden fields of wheat, but fully half of the province is comprised of forests and lakes, a vast hinterland inhabited mainly by Dene in the far north, and Woodland Cree and the Metis farther south. Their lives differ in most respects from those in the south, but their needs were, if anything, even more pressing in 1971.

When Tommy Douglas was elected in 1944, most northern Native people lived a largely self-sufficient existence in their villages and on their traplines. Their life expectancy increased in the 1950s and 1960s and accordingly their numbers increased too. A burgeoning Native population accompanied by an increasing number of white lumberjacks, miners, and tourists placed a strain on the hunting and gathering economy. Within a generation, many people moved from self-sufficiency to an equally meagre, but much less dignified, existence.

Ross Thatcher had established an Indian and Metis department, and set minimum hiring quotas for Natives, both in the public sector and with firms wanting to do business with the government. The NDP said the approach failed because it was rooted in the paternalistic perceptions of the white middle class. Thatcher's approach actually was basically similar to that of Woodrow Lloyd and Tommy Douglas before him. They all believed that the best option for Native people lay in integration into non-Aboriginal society.

Those ideas were being seriously challenged by 1971. Indian bands in Saskatchewan had joined others across the country, responding in shock and anger when Jean Chretien's 1969 White Paper suggested broadly based assimilation of Indian people. There was growing talk by 1970 of Indian self-government, and a militant Metis nationalism was emerging as well.

Blakeney's response for northern Saskatchewan was to promise a special government department. He was not much taken with the rhetoric of colonization and oppression that flowed freely in that day, but he did believe that a single department could improve government services and help to nurture local government structures more effectively than the existing model of having numerous line departments at work.

After the 1971 election, Blakeney's first obstacle was not in the north, but in Regina, where personnel from the Department of Natural Resources (DNR), long the pervasive government force in the north, resisted any change. The northern file was an important one to Blakeney and the resistance irked him. "The DNR just wouldn't let go," he recalled. "They thought we were crazy with DNS. I had to make a ministerial change." He replaced Eiling Kramer with Ted Bowerman, and within months he also replaced the deputy minister as well. Doug McArthur, who had been hired as the deputy in Agriculture to create the administrative structures for the Land Bank, was sent north to La Ronge as the deputy minister in the Department of Northern Saskatchewan (DNS).

McArthur said that upon his arrival he found the DNS experiment had blown up. "Everything was in a mess. The place was in turmoil. There were all these factions, and there was a tremendous distrust of the department in the communities." He moved to streamline government structures and build trust. His major accomplishment was to open and maintain a dialogue with town councils, school boards and with major political leaders. Blakeney, and not the minister, had appointed McArthur and now the Premier established a Regina-based management committee to back him up. Blakeney also chose to remain in close personal contact, an indication of the importance he attached to the northern file.

The *New Deal for People* had promised northern self-government and full consultation with Native people. To people like Jim Sinclair, leader of the Metis Society of Saskatchewan, that meant a northern government controlled by Natives. Northern treaty Indians had their reserve governments, but Sinclair believed that elsewhere the Metis should be in control.

Blakeney's government did provide some money to Native political organizations, and promised to consult with them when creating new programs. But the Premier had never intended to provide more than limited municipal-government responsibility to northerners. He rejected Sinclair's ideas about Native self-government, saying that would divide people in the north along racial lines.

He also became increasingly frustrated by the Metis Society's poor administration and its shoe-box accounting for money provided by the provincial government. He tightened the strings, and the Metis responded with numerous demonstrations, including setting up a tent city on the grounds of the Legislature.

The relationship with the Federation of Saskatchewan Indians was much smoother. The responsibility for most services for treaty Indians rested with Ottawa, and the federal government was the focus of most of their discontent. The province did provide some limited assistance, and significantly the Blakeney government agreed to become a party to negotiations for Indian land entitlements—providing land to compensate for that which had been promised to Indian bands at the time of treaty, but which either had not been provided or had been taken away from them.

Despite the setbacks and the controversy, the government's DNS strategy changed the face of northern Saskatchewan. Those changes were obvious upon driving into any of the northern towns, which received new water and sewer works, halls, community centres, arenas, and especially new housing. There were new schools with newly elected boards, and there were a good number of Native teachers, in most cases graduates from a new Northern Teacher Education Program.

What DNS did not do was provide a new economic base. The traditional industries, hunting and fishing, were in decline. Forest leases were held by big companies who hired only a few Native northerners, and the NDP government did not significantly change that relationship. When new uranium mines began to come onstream, however, Blakeney seized the opportunity to negotiate surface leases that guaranteed Native northerners a percentage of the jobs.

By the mid-1970s Blakeney had come to realize that the most serious problems for Native people were not in the north, but in the cities. Natives were increasingly moving to urban areas where they encountered poverty and discrimination. The tried and trusted NDP approach of creating universal programs to meet broad social priorities was not suited to meeting those specialized needs.

Following the election victory in 1978, Blakeney responded by creating special urban-based programs aimed at Native people. There was an affirmative action plan for hiring in government, and an economic development corporation, providing investment money to Native entrepreneurs and cooperatives.

The thrust in education was to provide Native teachers and aides, to develop a curriculum more suitable to native students, and to create community schools, which fostered a closer relationship between parents and schools.

The employment programs were only modestly successful, but there were more promising results in education, featuring the community schools and new, Native-controlled post-secondary institutions. The Saskatchewan Indian Federated College became a leader in Indian education, and the Metis operated the Gabriel Dumont Institute.

Programs aimed specifically at Natives were often not popular with other people in society, among them some members of the NDP caucus. Blakeney took a political risk with his affirmative action programs, and for his willingness to negotiate with Indian people for unfilled land entitlements. If he was not resoundingly successful in his politics and programs regarding Native people, he was, in any event, years ahead of his time.

The 1975 Election

As he surveyed the political landscape in 1974, Allan Blakeney might have been excused for a lightness in his step. "Next Year Country" had seemingly finally arrived in Saskatchewan. The province had wheat, oil and potash, all in great demand. The Soviets and the Chinese were buying grain. Farmers everywhere were buying fertilizer again, and Saskatchewan's mountains of stockpiled potash began to move, at much-enhanced prices. In October 1973, the Yom Kippur War in the Middle East precipitated an oil boycott by producing countries, most of them Arab, and prices rose from $3 to $10 a barrel, immediately increasing Saskatchewan government oil royalties by 50%.

The first term of the Blakeney government qualified as a reform period by any standard. Blakeney had made good on his promise of new health and social programs, an ombudsman, a Human Rights Commission and an Independent Boundaries Commission. In the countryside, there were the Land Bank and Farm Start programs, and a Hog Marketing Commission. New community colleges were popular, especially in rural Saskatchewan. The government had instituted a Property Improvement Grant, a rebate on home and land taxes. Cities and towns were getting more money with fewer strings attached, and a Community Capital Fund was allowing them to do some badly needed rebuilding.

But there were some troubling indicators too. Prosperity had returned to rural Saskatchewan, but if many individual farmers were better off, their well-being masked weaknesses in rural communities and the small business sector. Blakeney's planners told him bluntly that the improved farm economy might be slowing rural depopulation, but not halting it. The NDP had high hopes for secondary industry but the gains were modest, and by 1974 they did not appear to hold great promise.

The new frontier was to be in natural resources. Blakeney had come to office suspicious of resource megaprojects. Pulp mills and potash mines in Saskatchewan had usually involved the government providing cash or guaranteeing loans, in return for ridiculously low royalties. It was expensive and did not provide many jobs. Yet it was resource development, albeit with a new and decidedly NDP twist, that became the centrepiece of Blakeney's economic development strategy.

The government was shaken by the shutdown in the early 1970s of most of the province's oil refineries. By 1974, the government had still not decided how to proceed on its resource policy, but it had begun to develop principles. Blakeney had his planners at work, and after much discussion, the conclusion was that government should take an active role in economic development, but one that was selective in its approach.

His ideas about a mixed economy were grounded in his experience as a senior civil servant in the Douglas and Lloyd governments. Where there was stiff competition and marketing made the difference, he did not believe the government would do well. In resource industries, with fewer buyers and sellers, and where marketing was a simpler matter, he held quite a different view. His approach was summed up in a comment to Saskatchewan Wheat Pool president Ted Turner during a Cabinet consultation: "The greater the extent to which a project moves away from resource development and toward secondary industry, the less the government wishes to become involved."

Blakeney had a long and profound experience with the province's Crown corporations, and they would become his chosen instruments. The government had created SaskOil, and early in 1975, the Potash Corporation of Saskatchewan.

The province's attempts to tax windfall oil profits after 1973, and its emerging commitment to public ventures, put it on a collision course with both the industries and with Ottawa, since the federal government also wanted a greater share of the increased resource revenues too. Prime Minister Trudeau concluded that the pendulum had swung too far in the direction of provincial rights, and he intended to pull it back.

During the potash glut of the 1960s, Premier Thatcher, under pressure from American companies, had agreed to ration production from Saskatchewan mines. The NDP had criticized his action, but once in power, Blakeney thought it the lesser of the evils. With prices rising, one of the same companies, believing it was losing market share through the rationing arrangement, took the government to court. It argued that Saskatchewan's rationing was unconstitutional because provinces had no jurisdiction over international trade. The federal government took the unusual step of intervening before the courts on behalf of the company.

On May 7, Mr. Justice D.C. Disberry ruled against the province. Blakeney's emerging economic development policy intersected with his political needs. The NDP had been searching for a big issue as an election approached in 1975. After four years in power, the party had nothing as exciting as the 1971 *New Deal for People* to offer its citizens. Disberry's ruling provided the issue.

Blakeney called a June election, with the twin themes of improving life in rural Saskatchewan and diversifying the economy through resource development. The court ruling allowed him to run against Ottawa as well. He asked voters for a "mandate to protect our resources," and suggested that a vote for the Liberals would be a vote for Ottawa in the resource dispute.

The NDP won a comfortable majority, but lost six seats and dropped 15% in the popular vote. The Liberals retained their 15 seats, but dropped to 32% of the vote. However, the big winners were the Conservatives, who under new leader Dick Collver, rose from 2% to 28% in the popular vote, winning 7 seats. Both the Liberals and the NDP began to hear the tread of heavy footsteps behind them.

Blakeney took two lessons from what was for him a disappointing electoral result. He should slow the pace of introducing government programs, and secondly he should never refuse an excuse to run against Ottawa and Pierre Trudeau. The growing rifts over resources made that an easy decision.

Nationalization of the Potash Industry

There was feverish movement in and out of a suite of rooms in the Legislative Building throughout the days of early autumn in 1975. There were no nameplates posted on the doors to the suite of basement offices, whose telephones were not listed in the government directory. Each member of the group had a key to the building, the better to avoid commissionaires in the coming and going. The individuals chose not to arrive or leave in groups, and did not sit together in the legislative cafeteria.

Now and then the Premier would arrive with studied casualness, then dart through an unmarked door into the "Bunker," where the mystery team was working on what they called the "hot option"—a plan to take over some or all of Saskatchewan's potash industry.

It was a long and winding road that led Allan Blakeney, normally a cautious man, to play riverboat gambler with the potash industry, although he insisted that it was not a gamble so much as a decision taken for pragmatic reasons. Rather, it was a series of bruising experiences with the potash industry that solidified his opinion and moved him to dramatic action.

The development of potash policy following 1971 illustrates how Allan Blakeney ran a government. Initially he was cautious and there was little change because he needed time. His manner of arriving at policy was complex and bureaucratic, and placed a great emphasis on Cabinet considering a range of options. He always built in escape routes in case one of the choices backfired.

Potassium chloride (potash) was first discovered in Saskatchewan in 1942. As exploratory work continued over the years, the province was found to have the largest reserves in the world. The Douglas government considered developing the industry publicly, but decided against it, believing that it would be both expensive and risky. The reserves were rich and plentiful but they were deep in the earth, and early private attempts to mine them were unsuccessful. The CCF could not take the political gamble of having so large a public enterprise end in failure.

The Potash Company of America went into production near Saskatoon in 1958, and the province agreed to take only low royalties through 1977 because of flooding problems that the company encountered. The government was negotiating for more mines in the 1960s, but they did not arrive until Ross Thatcher was in power. Soon there were 10 mineshafts rising above the prairies and Thatcher extended the low royalty rates to all of them through 1981. However, Saskatchewan's rash expansion of the industry helped to drive potash prices down during the farm recession of the late 1960s, and Thatcher agreed to have the government administer a plan rationing production.

Within weeks of the 1971 provincial election, potash industry executives came calling and requested that the rationing program remain in place. Blakeney was reluctant because he had criticized Thatcher for participating in the scheme, but more importantly because it meant production quotas, layoffs at Saskatchewan mines, and a floor price of a mere $34 a ton for potash. Having no alternative policy in place, he began to weave a spider's web of options. He instructed his minister, Ted Bowerman, to make an offer to the potash executives. The government would continue with the rationing system, but would charge a fee for administering it, and would also raise the royalties.

In 1972, Central Canada Potash broke ranks with the other companies. It was an American-based cooperative and its farmer members had begun to buy fertilizer as grain prices rose. Central Canada came to believe that it was losing market share through the rationing system, and decided to take Saskatchewan to court, arguing that the province was exceeding its constitutional authority by administering the regime.

Blakeney was annoyed because it was the companies which had insisted on the rationing program in the first place. To make matters worse, Ottawa joined in the suit against Saskatchewan. "It signaled that the federal government was going to battle the western provinces for control of our resources," Blakeney said, "and that we had better sharpen our swords."

Blakeney asked the Department of Mineral Resources for options, but he also put his central planning group to work. In fact, he created a special potash task force led by John Burton, a former Saskatchewan NDP MP. By 1973 the planners were working on the assumption that government would take some degree of public ownership in the industry. No policy decision had been taken, but Blakeney's growing preference was to become involved in joint ventures with the industry for new mines.

His new Natural Resources minister, Kim Thorson, was not interested in public ownership options, and he brusquely asked the Cabinet planners why they were meddling in his affairs. Blakeney replaced him with Elwood Cowley, a tough negotiator who informed the industry in 1974 that there would be a new potash reserves tax, and that the government intended to become involved as a joint venture partner in any new mines. The companies reacted angrily, saying they would not pay the new tax.

The situation became even more strained after the federal budget in 1974. Finance minister John Turner announced that provincial royalties, including the new reserves tax, would not be allowed as a deduction for purposes of federal taxation. It was another move in the constitutional chess game between governments regarding who controlled the resource, and who should benefit from rising prices.

Blakeney considered Turner's budget a second shot across the bow (the first had been Ottawa's siding with Central Canada Potash in the legal case on rationing). The budget also had an effect on Blakeney's strategic thinking. Saskatchewan was in court over a tax and might lose, but were the province to own the mines, the tax issue would disappear because Crown corporations did not pay federal taxes. Blakeney, who maintained a keen interest in constitutional questions, had received a legal opinion in 1972 suggesting just such a possibility. Early in 1975, the government established the Potash Corporation of Saskatchewan but the industry made it clear it was solidly opposed to any joint ventures with the government.

The Disberry ruling against Saskatchewan in the rationing case arrived in May 1975, just prior to the June election. During the campaign, the industry made its political statement in a campaign of television, radio and newspaper advertising. The companies announced that they were canceling $200 million in planned expansions because of the government's new reserve tax.

In the month following the NDP victory, industry-government relations reached a new low. The companies did not pay approximately $30 million in provincial taxes on their due date, and jointly they took the government to court, saying the reserve tax was unconstitutional.

Blakeney considered this a declaration of all-out war. He wanted the money the taxes would deliver, but Saskatchewan contained the world's richest potash reserves and he wanted the industry to expand. The stakes were high. Prices had risen from a low of $20 a ton in 1969 to $80 a ton in 1975.

In August 1975, Blakeney asked Cabinet to consider nationalization as a serious option. The team in the "Bunker" went to work. They had to predict the legal and constitutional implications of such a move, the likely reaction by financiers, not to mention preparing a new Crown corporation to own and operate mines and to market their product.

Discussions in Cabinet carried on interminably throughout the fall. The air of excitement was cut by an edge of uncertainty. "We had a lot of people in Cabinet who weren't sure where we should be going," said Elwood Cowley. "Blakeney was uncertain too."

Cabinet's resolve was strengthened by news that the entire industry was joining in the lawsuit to challenge the province's rationing legislation. The courts had ordered Saskatchewan to refund the company's rationing fees in the Central Canada Potash case. Now the rest of the industry wanted its money back too. "That just hit me the wrong way," Blakeney recalled. The companies that had begged him to keep the rationing system were now suing him for having done it. "This was really double-dealing," he added.

Cabinet made its decision in October, and that same month Blakeney informed the party's executive and council. Despite all of those people knowing, word never leaked to the press or the opposition. On November 13, Lieutenant-Governor George Porteous read the Speech from the Throne, which announced that the government would "acquire the assets of some or all of the producing mines in the province."

The opposition and the industry were stunned, and the public nervously astonished. A fierce public relations battle erupted in the following months. The Canadian Potash Producers' Association financed a media blitz and the Saskatoon Board of Trade mounted a campaign to attack the government's action.

When the legislation reached the floor of the House, the Liberals opposed and filibustered while the industry continued its campaign of negative advertising. The companies published results of an opinion poll that indicated 52% of Saskatchewan respondents were opposed to the prospect of a potash takeover while only 22% were in favour. The government's own polling in January 1976 showed an even greater opposition to its action. The mood in Cabinet became one of near panic.

Blakeney had assembled a special Cabinet potash committee and a team of civil servants to provide support. The strategy was twofold. Elwood Cowley, the minister in charge, would lead negotiations on purchases and build the company. Secondly, Roy Romanow would guide the legislation through the House, and he, along with other key Cabinet ministers, would fan out, explaining and promoting the government's move to people in the province.

Cabinet followed the advice of Blakeney's media guru Jack Kinzel, deciding that the response to attacks would be cool and rational, arguing that the takeover was a good business move rather than ideologically driven. Blakeney went to New York to speak to investment bankers, and turned a frigid crowd into a supportive audience with his history lesson about Saskatchewan, its history of hardships and its tradition of activist but responsible government. He made other forays to New York and Chicago, and his reassuring message was that the compensation paid for mines would be fair, and there would be an assured supply of Saskatchewan potash at reasonable prices.

The province by now had an excellent credit rating, and was able to borrow money to buy the Duval potash mine near Saskatoon in October 1976. After that purchase, criticism began to fade, and within the next two years PCS purchased three more mines and a share in a fourth. The government paid $520 million to buy 40% of the provincial industry.

Dave Steuart, the Liberal leader, remained critical of the move but he said company presidents went missing in their haste to sell once they heard what Blakeney had offered for Duval: "I remember every day the gallery was full of potash people, then one day it was empty."

Companies began to make their peace with the government, and the U.S. administration concluded that the industry was being fairly compensated. By the time of the 1978 election, Blakeney's potash gamble appeared to have paid off. PCS was turning a profit, and the government's polls indicated that 60% of those asked now approved the public ownership of potash.

There are those who say that Blakeney wanted to leave a publicly owned potash industry as his legacy, but he scoffed at that claim:

> I have read some of these analyses of how we had a great master plan that took five years to unroll. I don't know whether those are flattering or not, but they are inaccurate. The actions of the potash industry forced us to make some decisions.

But Blakeney did see in the revenues accruing from potash, uranium and other resources the foundation for his social democratic dream. The government would play a major role in creating wealth to be redistributed in better health care, education, and social programs, and keeping people home and employed in Saskatchewan. To pay for all of that, he would use Crown corporations to thrust the public sector into the economy to an extent that earlier governments had never attempted.

Uranium and the Anti-nuclear Debate

When he came to power in 1971, Blakeney had no idea that within a few short years, Saskatchewan would be described as the Saudi Arabia of uranium producers. It was a development that held great promise for the future, but which erupted into a battle for the very heart and soul of social democracy in Saskatchewan.

In Saskatchewan, uranium had first been discovered in 1935 by prospectors looking for gold on the shores of Lake Athabasca. But it was only after the war that large sales to the U.S. set off an exploration boom in the province, and a significant post-war discovery led to development of Eldorado Nuclear's Beaverlodge mine at Uranium City. Eldorado was owned by the Canadian government and throughout the 1950s sold Canadian uranium to the United States, where it was used in the nuclear weapons program. However, the Americans had developed a sufficient stockpile by late in the decade and Saskatchewan's industry went bust.

There was a second boom in the 1970s. By then, uranium ore was used to create fuel in civilian nuclear reactors, and predictions were that they would represent a vast new market. Canadian companies and others had created a price-fixing cartel which increased fourfold in the early 1970s. Prospectors once again prowled the scrub forests of the Athabasca Sandstone Basin in northern Saskatchewan, where they made a string of incredibly rich discoveries. Soon it was estimated that 10–13% of the richest uranium reserves in the non-Communist world were to be found in Saskatchewan.

Blakeney viewed the uranium boom as good fortune in the same way that he welcomed improved markets and rising prices for oil and potash. Managed prudently, they would support long-term prosperity in Saskatchewan.

After he won office in 1971, Blakeney initiated a review of the province's uranium policy, and it led to conclusions similar to those in the oil and potash sectors. The government wanted to become involved in the action to help control the pace of development, and to capture a greater share of the rent from these resources.

In 1974, the province created the Saskatchewan Mining Development Corporation (SMDC) as a joint-venture vehicle that was to be offered a 50% equity stake in any significant new uranium operations. Cabinet decided in the same year that Saskatchewan should pursue a uranium refinery. That decision, too, was consistent with Blakeney's intention to add value to raw resources before they left Saskatchewan. But by the 1970s, others in the province had come to see uranium as a death-dealing substance. They said it should be left in the ground, and questioned the morality of a government that was promoting its development and sale.

Blakeney could not understand the fuss. Uranium had been mined in Saskatchewan since the 1950s, and there was no civilian use for it at that time. Anyone in the know realized that Saskatchewan uranium fed the American nuclear weapons program. Many activists in the peace movement of the day were also members of the CCF, yet Saskatchewan's uranium industry did not become a topic of debate. Blakeney's view was that the way to achieve disarmament was to negotiate it internationally, and not to make a symbolic gesture by leaving the product in the ground.

A number of key events occurred in 1976. A French-owned company, Amok, announced that it wanted to proceed with a new mine at Cluff Lake. As well, the provincial government purchased a stake in German-owned Uranerz, using SMDC as a vehicle for participation. An unbelievably rich strike was made at Key Lake. Finally, the government and Eldorado Nuclear were moving ahead with their plans to build a uranium refinery near Warman, just north of Saskatoon.

Internationally, the nuclear power industry was poised for unprecedented expansion, but in Sweden, Britain, France, Germany, the United States and Canada there was growing disagreement about the wisdom of such development. Nuclear development became a heated topic of discussion at the United Nations Habitat Conference in Vancouver in May 1976, and a number of Saskatchewan people who attended that conference were later instrumental in the debate at home.

As late as 1975, the most contentious environmental issue debated at the NDP convention concerned returnable bottles. By 1976 a fierce opposition was growing to uranium development, based on both environmental and ethical grounds, and much of that opposition emanated from within the ranks of the NDP itself.

Debate began to rage within the party and a committee was set up to report to the convention in November 1976. Ten constituencies sent in moratorium resolutions. There was a heated, if unsatisfactory, debate at the convention, which asked the government to call an inquiry into uranium development. Blakeney's ministers worked the crowd and the microphones to ward off calls for the moratorium, but Blakeney promised in his leader's address that he would appoint a board of inquiry with broad terms of reference.

When Gulf Minerals had decided to build a uranium mine at Rabbit Lake in 1968, there was not a whisper about an independent environmental assessment. The Thatcher government did not have an environment minister, but in the 1971 election campaign Blakeney promised just such a department. It was created in 1972, and established the machinery for environmental reviews, assessments and public hearings.

In December 1976, the government appointed a three-member board of inquiry led by Mr. Justice E.D. Bayda, a member of the Saskatchewan Court of Appeal. It was to investigate the Cluff Lake mining proposal, with power to say if it should proceed, not proceed, or proceed with conditions. The signals, however, were mixed. The company was given permission to continue site development, and other uranium companies, including the SMDC, were allowed to continue prospecting for uranium.

When it reported in 1978, the Commission gave the green light for development, with conditions. Blakeney insisted that while he expected Bayda to recommend in favour of development, the government was prepared to back off if the recommendations had been contrary.

Amok went ahead with its mine, and in 1978 the government negotiated surface leases with the company. The contract included a promise by Amok that northerners would perform half of the work at Cluff Lake during its operations phase. The government did not follow a recommendation from Bayda that it share uranium revenues directly with northern communities.

Opposition to uranium development continued, much of it housed within the NDP. But when Blakeney called an election for October 1978, he predicted that uranium development would not be an issue, and he was right. He won the election, but the issue smouldered within his party.

The government pressed ahead with its planned joint venture for a refinery at Warman. Eldorado Nuclear, as a Crown corporation, was subject to federal environmental assessment hearings. Throughout the bitterly cold days of January 1980, the towns halls of Warman and nearby Martensville were the scenes of hearings in which the company took a public relations drubbing. One after another, ruddy-faced Mennonite farmers, sincere Catholic nuns, and tweedy university professors took their turns at the microphone pleading with the panel to recommend against development.

The panel's chair warned them that his was an environmental assessment, and the number of participants or their emotion would not sway him. But when the panel reported in 1980, it was obvious that numbers and the sensitivities of the local, largely Mennonite community did have an impact. The panel accepted the refinery on environmental grounds, but said that Eldorado's studies on social impact were deficient. The company should either come back with better information, or look at other locations. Eldorado chose to abandon the project entirely, and the foes of uranium development claimed victory.

The anti-nuclear coalition included a good number of people from Saskatchewan churches. Some of them accused Blakeney of lacking moral conviction, an assertion that stung and angered him. He countered their arguments against the development of nuclear power by asking how moral it would be to deprive the world of energy, or people in northern Saskatchewan of jobs. He promised stringent environmental oversight and close attention to international treaties regarding nuclear proliferation.

Blakeney continues to believe that his critics were not taking account of his moral arguments in favour of uranium development: "I think that there were some very real questions to be debated and that no one could assume that their side of the argument was necessarily right in moral terms, and the other side was necessarily wrong."

The issue continued to bedevil the party. After its defeat in 1982, the NDP shifted its position and called for a moratorium, a policy that was soon reversed after it regained power in 1991. The uranium debate was difficult and acrimonious because it was a contest for the high ground in a party that had always traded on its morality.

The 1978 Election

By 1978, Saskatchewan had escaped the mentality of the dust bowl, and was tentatively beginning to believe its press clippings. After decades of deprivation, it was officially a "have" province, along with Ontario, British Columbia and Alberta.

Blakeney was receiving his share of press clippings too —"Blakeney's New Deal," read one, and "Blakeney's Vision," said another. Journalist Paul Grescoe, writing in *Canadian Magazine*, quoted an unnamed Conservative source as saying that Blakeney was "the best Premier in the country." Another writer said that among the Premiers, "only Saskatchewan's Allan Blakeney can match wits with Pierre Trudeau."

Blakeney had been underestimated as a politician, someone who suffered in public comparison to his predecessor, Tommy Douglas, mainly because he could not deliver similar eloquent and visionary speeches, and because he was a shy man who did not easily press the flesh and make small talk. But he was a very good Premier, and now he was finally getting his due. His way of dealing with his lack of popular appeal was to accept that it was more important to be respected than liked. He was exceptionally competent and voters recognized it.

But there were some long shadows on the horizon, which Blakeney believed could prevent Saskatchewan from taking its rightful place in Confederation. There was the struggle over the control and prices of gas, oil and potash. Trudeau acted unilaterally to peg domestic oil at a level well below world prices. Alberta Premier Peter Lougheed retaliated by tightening the taps and reducing production. Blakeney's oft-repeated quotation was that Moose Jaw should not be expected to subsidize London, Ontario. Trudeau's made-in-Canada oil prices, he said, were costing Saskatchewan citizens $575 million a year. Blakeney actually supported a national energy policy, but he insisted that Saskatchewan and the producing provinces should not have to pay the entire price of providing cheaper oil and gas to other Canadians.

Then there were the court cases launched by the Saskatchewan potash and oil companies that had been winding their way through the courts for years. The Saskatchewan appeal court had ruled in favour of Central Canada Potash in the rationing case in 1975. Canadian Industrial Oil and Gas also went to court, arguing that Saskatchewan's oil taxes were unconstitutional. In November 1977 the Supreme Court ruled in the company's favour, declaring that the province had no jurisdiction over the prices of resources entering interprovincial trade.

The NDP began in 1977 to think seriously about the next election, and there was a good deal of nervousness in the ranks. The party, which had always relied on MLA reports from coffee row for its political intelligence, had now begun to poll and the news was not good. The upstart Tories had replaced the Liberals as the main opposition, and the NDP political brain trust was shocked to find that respondents in the polls preferred the Tories to the NDP. Many people disliked the Land Bank, some opposed the potash nationalization, and a surprising number resented compulsory seat belt legislation. The Tories were scoring with their criticism of big government.

Their leader was Dick Collver, an Alberta management consultant who had arrived early in the 1970s to become the property and business manager for the Baltzans, a family of medical doctors and investors in Saskatoon. Collver, unlike the veterans Blakeney and Liberal leader David Steuart, was new to politics but in the 1975 election the Conservatives won seven seats. A combination of Liberal defections and by-election victories soon gave them 11 seats and the political momentum.

Blakeney spent the hazy days of August 1978 in Nova Scotia visiting old friends and the haunts of his childhood. His vacation ended abruptly when Pierre Trudeau, who had read his own polls and found them Tory blue, announced that there would be no fall election. That upset Blakeney's own timetable. He had planned a spring election in 1979, but did not want to risk the confusion of concurrent campaigns. His planners were predicting a softening of the economy and he had already begun to tighten up on government programs and civil service hiring. He did, however, have the option of breaking with his preference of elections spaced regularly every four years.

It was not a decision he would make alone, so when he got home he called a quick Cabinet meeting and asked for advice. The review of polls was intriguing. They showed a dislike for Trudeau bordering on rage. The numbers also showed Blakeney running well ahead of his own party, while Dick Collver was beginning to lag behind the Conservative Party in popularity.

Collver's feet of clay had started to show. First, there was a nasty lawsuit between him and his former partners the Baltzans, involving a dispute over property that Collver said that they had turned over to him. Then in the spring of 1978, the Regina *Leader-Post* printed a series of stories about Collver's bad debts with the Saskatchewan Government Insurance Office (SGIO). He had signed loan guarantees for a construction company that had failed before completing the projects it had undertaken. SGIO wanted its money, could not get it, and a top official discreetly leaked the story to the press.

Collver was suddenly vulnerable and the NDP was prepared to exploit that weakness. Blakeney called the election for October 18. The NDP began the campaign with a series of negative ads threatening that the Conservatives would "tax the sick" by bringing back Ross Thatcher's disliked deterrent fees on health care.

The Tories had not expected a fall election and were caught off guard. They spent precious time and resources preparing advertisements to prove that Conservatives had always been in favour of medicare. By that time, the NDP was into stage two, attacking federal resource policies and saying that only Blakeney could stand up to Trudeau. The *New Deal* campaigns of 1971 and 1975 had emphasized the NDP policy, but this time the campaign was built around Blakeney as the leader.

Early in October, the Supreme Court handed him the election. It released a judgement saying that Saskatchewan's potash reserves tax was unconstitutional, and another ordering the province to repay $500 million collected under its oil tax, which had earlier been declared unconstitutional. Blakeney, who was usually respectful toward the judiciary, went on a minor rampage, saying that the judgement once again showed a bias in favour of eastern Canada. He called on Saskatchewan people to support him in seeking constitutional changes to allow the province greater control over its resources.

He won 48% of the popular vote and 44 seats. The Conservatives won 17 seats, while the Liberals were wiped out. But they had expected to win, and were bitter. The Liberals and the NDP were long-time rivals, but they understood one another and an unspoken legislative protocol existed between them. No such decorum existed between the NDP and the Conservatives, who felt they had been sucker-punched, and the mood once the new legislative session convened was not a pleasant one.

After the 1978 election and his third successive victory, Blakeney appeared as invincible as anyone can be in politics. Bill Knight, a key advisor, said that while many people in the party did not give him the political credit for the 1971 and 1975 victories, "in 1978 nobody could argue that it wasn't his election."

Blakeney viewed the election results as an endorsement of his economic policies. The government pushed ahead with expansions at Crown-owned potash mines, and maintained a vigorous exploration and development program for uranium. During the campaign, Blakeney had talked about a new heavy oil upgrader at Lloydminster.

As a young civil servant in the 1950s, he had cut his teeth in the Government Finance Office. Now, almost 30 years later, he set up sophisticated machinery to coordinate the government's presence in the resource sector. He created the Crown Investments Corporation (CIC), which became the holding company for 17 Crown corporations, traditional utility companies like SaskTel and SaskPower, but also the newer resource companies, including the Potash Corporation of Saskatchewan, the Saskatchewan Mining Development Corporation and SaskOil. The stakes were exponentially higher than they had been in the 1950s. By 1979, the CIC was the holding company for corporations with revenues of over $1 billion and assets of $3.5 billion.

The government used the public corporations as profit-makers, returning millions to a Heritage Fund that had assets of $900 million by 1980–81. About half of that was returned as a dividend to be used for annual expenditures on roads, parks and social programs. The stern international schoolmasters who provide report cards called credit ratings gave Saskatchewan a glowing "AA" in 1979.

Blakeney's preference for a mixed economy, including an aggressive role for the public sector, was an approach that made good sense for a hinterland province far from most markets and financial centres of power. The threats to his approach were strained relations with certain sectors of business, the fight with Ottawa over who owned and could tax resource revenues, and a Saskatchewan public that was less accepting of big government than appeared to be the case.

The Canadian Constitutional Debate

Ross Thatcher, the former Liberal Premier, often said that on a list of 100 priorities for Saskatchewan, constitutional change was number 101. Thatcher believed that Saskatchewan citizens wanted him to spend his time on concerns closer to home, and in any event, he suspected that in Pierre Trudeau's case, constitutional approaches were framed with Quebec uppermost in mind.

Allan Blakeney was aware of the political risks, but despite them, he played a significant role in the constitutional debates of the 1980s. He was a staunch federalist, and believed that he and his province should play a role in national affairs. He also believed that Saskatchewan had a stake in the division of powers. The 1970s had seen a constant tug of war between Trudeau, who wanted more power for the federal government, and the provinces that wanted to see a devolution of power.

Trudeau's unilateral move to impose a domestic price for Alberta and Saskatchewan oil had caused bitterness in the West. Blakeney saw the disputes over taxation and court battles over the province's control of its resources as a threat to Saskatchewan's well-being, just at a time when the province was emerging from its traditional status as a poor cousin in Confederation.

The Canadian Constitution, the musty old British North America Act, existed as an Act of the British Parliament. Any changes to it had to be made in London, a symbol of lingering political immaturity in Canada. Politicians in Canada had been squabbling for years about how to bring the Constitution home, but they had never been able to agree on the terms.

The patriation of the Constitution had long been Pierre Trudeau's dream, and in the same package he wanted to embed language rights and education for both French and English minorities. He tried in 1971, and again in 1976, but he could not get agreement. His government was defeated in 1979 by Joe Clark and the Conservatives, and Trudeau's constitutional aspirations appeared destined to fade with his resignation and departure from politics. But Clark's minority government fumbled the parliamentary ball after nine months, and Trudeau made a comeback in 1980. His determination to do something about the Constitution was reinforced when Quebec's René Levesque held a referendum in May 1980 to ascertain if Quebec's citizens wanted to leave Canada. Trudeau promised Quebec that a vote for Canada would also be a vote for constitutional change.

Blakeney played a federalist role in the lead-up to the referendum, making a speaking tour of Ontario and Quebec in April. Saskatchewan was not interested in negotiating sovereignty-association with Quebec, he said, but was interested in strengthening the federation. He supported Trudeau's proposal to entrench language rights, but he also demanded constitutional changes regarding resources and equalization payments.

The day following the federalist win in the Quebec referendum, Trudeau announced that the constitutional process was on again, proposing to include a "people's package" of individual rights—the freedom of religion, speech, association and due process of law—in the Constitution. He also planned to extend the concept to collective rights, embedding the protection of language rights and education for both English- and French-speaking minorities within Canada.

Blakeney also argued that for Saskatchewan, control over resources was a "people's" issue every bit as important as other rights. The courts had deemed certain of Saskatchewan's resource taxes to be unconstitutional, and ordered the province to repay $500 million to oil and potash companies. That money might have allowed Saskatchewan to extend its dental program to older children, or to put more housing and skating rinks into Saskatchewan towns.

Beyond those arguments, however, there existed a fundamental difference in the philosophies of the two men. Trudeau was a liberal individualist, and his Charter proposals reflected that philosophy. Blakeney was a democrat in the British tradition, and believed that individual rights were better protected by Parliament. He believed the Charter would remove power from elected legislators and hand it to judges: "The charters have been so misused in American history that I just don't believe they add much to the total rights and freedoms of the people."

Blakeney knew as well that there would be great political risks in entering Trudeau's wind tunnel of constitutional change. If he were seen to be cooperating with the Prime Minister, Blakeney knew that he would risk neutralizing the potent political weapon of Ottawa-bashing. His senior ministers advised him strongly not to make any deals with Trudeau. Blakeney understood all of this, but believed that he had to take the risk: "One has to remember the mood of the hour. As the Parti Québecois made clear that they were going for separation or sovereignty-association, the possibility of a break-up of Canada as we knew it was a clear and present danger."

Trudeau could not achieve agreement from the Premiers in September 1980, so in October he announced that he would move unilaterally to present Ottawa's amendments to the British Parliament for approval. His package would include a Charter of Rights, and possibly the option to hold a national referendum on it.

There were those who were overtly hostile to Trudeau and his plan, among them René Levesque (Quebec), Sterling Lyon (Manitoba), Brian Peckford (Newfoundland), Bill Bennett (British Columbia), Angus MacLean (Prince Edward Island), and Peter Lougheed (Alberta). To oppose the plan, they formed an alliance, which Blakeney, along with John Buchanan of Nova Scotia, chose not to join. Blakeney thought it wise to remain on good terms with them, particularly with Lougheed whom he liked and admired, while keeping a door open to Trudeau's supporters, including Premiers William Davis of Ontario and Richard Hatfield of New Brunswick.

Initially, Blakeney had another reason for caution. Much to Blakeney's chagrin, NDP leader Ed Broadbent was publicly supporting Trudeau's proposals. Blakeney felt that "it was outrageous for Trudeau to say that he was going to amend the Constitution without provincial consent, and outrageous for the federal NDP to agree," but he did not want a divisive public airing of their disagreement.

Beyond the question of Trudeau's process, Broadbent and Blakeney disagreed on the Charter of Rights, which Broadbent supported, and on the degree of centralization that should exist in Confederation. Broadbent's views were consistent with the federal party's historical position. The party had been calling for a Charter of Rights since 1940, and also took a centralist view on the division of powers.

The NDP placed great stock in national planning and public ownership, and believed that to accomplish those ends, Canada needed a strong central government. But the dream of national power had eluded the social democrats. The party's greater success came at the provincial level, particularly in Saskatchewan. Blakeney had also begun his political life as a centralist, but years of political experience led him to modify his beliefs: "I once believed that we could develop in Canada a sufficient consensus to proceed with a fair number of things nationally. I later saw that people like to deal on many issues with organizations which are a little closer to them. It was easier to do social experiments on a provincial level."

Trudeau thought that Saskatchewan might be persuaded to join Ontario and New Brunswick in supporting his proposals, and he met Blakeney privately in Regina. Blakeney did support him on language rights, but sharply disagreed with him on process. He insisted that, at the very least, Trudeau should refer his plan for unilateral action to the Supreme Court for a legal opinion. The Premier later repeated that advice to a parliamentary committee in December 1980.

In January, Blakeney and Trudeau came close to agreement when the Prime Minister made a final offer. But Trudeau was carrying on multiple negotiations and at the eleventh hour it became clear that he had agreed that the Senate would receive a veto over future constitutional change. Blakeney thought the Senate should be abolished, not given new and unprecedented powers, and the deal fell apart. Trudeau believed that Blakeney was simply looking for a pretext to say no, and he was angry. Blakeney insisted that he was bargaining in good faith and that his concerns were real.

By April 1981, Saskatchewan and Nova Scotia had joined the dissident group of six Premiers, making it a "gang of eight," which included Quebec's René Levesque. Blakeney made it clear, however, that his participation was provisional. If they were able to stop Trudeau from acting unilaterally, then each province must once again be free to deal on its own.

Trudeau was persuaded, reluctantly, to refer the question to the Supreme Court. Blakeney had a close hand in preparing Saskatchewan's brief, arguing that it was illegal for Ottawa to amend the Constitution unilaterally. As a backup argument, the province held that such action offended the existing political conventions, because federal governments had always obtained provincial consent for constitutional changes. Saskatchewan conceded that not all provinces had to agree, but that a "sufficient measure of provincial consent" was needed for change to occur.

When the judgement arrived in September 1981, it was clear that Saskatchewan's argument had been influential. The court ruled that Trudeau's action was not illegal, but that it did offend Canadian political conventions. The court was, in effect, telling Trudeau and the Premiers to go back to the negotiating table, and that set the stage for a dramatic week in November.

Following the judgement, Saskatchewan made it clear to its partners in the "gang of eight" that it would seek a deal to conclude the issue. Shortly after the judgement, Blakeney's constitutional point man, Roy Romanow, had talked with Ontario's attorney general, Roy McMurtry, and with Jean Chretien, who was acting on Trudeau's behalf.

SAB RA 22,496(2)

Premier Allan Blakeney and Roy Romanow at the First Ministers' Conference, November 1981. Behind and between Blakeney and Romanow is Dr. Howard Leeson, one of the Saskatchewan government's key constitutional advisers, and later editor of Saskatchewan Politics: Into the Twenty-first Century.

On Monday, November 2, the Prime Minister and the Premiers met in the Ottawa Conference Centre, a renovated old railway station, for a last try at breaking the constitutional impasse. All of the leaders made statements carried live on television and radio, then they moved to closed-door meetings, which were inconclusive. Tuesday, too, came and went without agreement.

Jean Chrétien called Romanow on Wednesday morning, and they decided to invite Roy McMurtry to join them. They sat with their feet up and talked about the elements of a possible agreement while Romanow scribbled notes on a pad. That discussion, in turn, led to an afternoon huddle among Trudeau, Davis and Blakeney. Trudeau's proposal now was for an agreement that discarded the possibility for any one province to veto constitutional change. The document would contain a limited Charter of Rights, subject to legislative override, which had been Blakeney's earlier position. He later recalled thinking that the new proposal was a "tremendous breakthrough," but he played it cool, saying that he wanted time to think about it. He asked Romanow to do some further checking with his contacts. Romanow sought out Chrétien and returned to say, "This is for real."

Romanow and Chrétien headed off in search of a private place to talk. They found a pantry and began where they had left off that morning, but decided to search out Roy McMurtry once again. In that small pantry the so-called "kitchen accord" entered Canadian political folklore, with Romanow again scratching out elements of the deal on his notepad.

Meanwhile, Blakeney contacted other provinces that he believed were open to an agreement. Their officials met in his suite early in the evening and began an all-night drafting session. Saskatchewan kept Ontario informed, and Premier Davis stayed in telephone contact with Trudeau. Two provinces not included in the nocturnal negotiations were Manitoba and Quebec. "We didn't get in touch with them," Blakeney said, "because we didn't think they would be contributing to coming up with this compromise."

Manitoba's Sterling Lyon was fighting an election and had already left for home. He was informed of the deal on Thursday morning. Other Premiers were briefed early Thursday as well, but René Levesque found out only when he arrived for breakfast with them. While other provinces had worked through the night, Levesque and his party remained unaware in their hotel rooms across the river in Hull. Now, at the breakfast table, Levesque accused the others of treachery.

Chrétien's officials had been kept abreast of negotiations throughout the night. On Thursday morning, he and Trudeau negotiated some slight changes and it was all over by lunch. Levesque refused to sign and accused the other Premiers of "the most despicable betrayal."

Quebec's exclusion from those deliberations remains a bitter memory in that province, and some hold that Quebec's isolation then has helped drive separatist aspirations ever since. Blakeney continues to believe that Levesque would not have signed any deal that was acceptable to Trudeau—that Quebec's goal was to prevent any constitutional reform that would undercut the ultimate goal of sovereignty.

Levesque was not alone in feeling betrayed. Most of the constitutional drafts had contained a guarantee that Aboriginal rights would be protected, but that clause had been dropped during hard bargaining in the final 24 hours.

Native groups were angry when they found out, and some of them contacted Blakeney. He told them that Saskatchewan had favoured including those protections, but that provinces such as British Columbia had balked. He promised that if the accord were reopened he would push for reinstatement of Aboriginal rights.

Women's groups were also angry. They wanted a separate clause guaranteeing equality of the sexes, and the Charter's Section 28 did so. Blakeney had been a strong proponent of the right of Legislatures to override provisions of the Charter of Rights, and now it appeared to women that their enshrined rights could be undone by any Legislature. They were outraged and began to lobby to have Section 28 stand free and clear of any override. They were intense and effective in their action. Blakeney was a reluctant convert and when he did agree to Ottawa's urgent invitation that Section 28 should stand free and clear, he said he would agree only if the Aboriginal rights clause were reinstated. It was, with slightly altered wording.

Then it was over. Blakeney regretted that Quebec had been isolated, but he was pleased that he had helped to prevent Trudeau's acting unilaterally, and that he had been instrumental in maintaining the primacy of elected officials over appointed judges. He thought Saskatchewan had also made some important gains in its jurisdiction over resources.

Asked about the effects of the Charter 20 years later, Blakeney said it had negative effects, but fewer than he had feared:

Many people now look to the courts and not to the Legislatures for solutions to their problems and people have become much less interested in governments, to the great detriment of the public welfare. On the other hand, the courts have broken new ground, and that would have been done only much more slowly by the Legislatures. Many people, including Aboriginals and women, have felt empowered by using the courts.

By Christmas of 1981 all but the formalities of the constitutional accord had been completed, and Blakeney began to turn his attention to provincial affairs, and the election that he planned to call in 1982. He was to pay a price for his preoccupation with constitutional affairs.

The 1982 Election

The NDP appeared all but certain to win a fourth term of government in 1982. The province could boast of 10 successive balanced budgets, and its Heritage Fund, a repository of surpluses from the sale of natural resources, had assets of $1 billion. The campaign slogan would be "Tested and Trusted," the same theme used by the CCF in 1960 when Allan Blakeney was first a candidate and T.C. Douglas was Premier.

The Conservatives had replaced the Liberals as the major opposition, but Grant Devine, a 37-year-old agricultural economist who had replaced Dick Collver as Conservative leader, had never been elected to anything and was politically unknown. The government could run on its record of economic management, and if needed, had Blakeney's leadership as the arrow in its campaign quiver, comparing him to the inexperienced Devine.

The NDP needed a rural issue to neutralize the Conservatives in the countryside. They thought they had one in the Trudeau government's plans to kill the Crow rate, a subsidized price that western farmers paid the railroads to move their grain to eastern and foreign markets. The Crow was also a ready-made, anti-Ottawa issue, one that was intended to offset any political damage from Blakeney's having, reluctantly, cooperated with Trudeau on the Constitution.

The party's polls showed the NDP with support of almost 50% of decided voters, although the Conservatives insisted that their numbers showed them trailing by only a few percentage points.

Despite their seeming invincibility, Blakeney and some party insiders were growing uneasy as early as 1980. The CCF-NDP tradition was one of faith in government as an instrument of the people's will. But elsewhere neo-conservatives Margaret Thatcher and Ronald Reagan ran, ironically, against government and were elected in Great Britain and the United States. Both appealed explicitly to individual self-interest rather than to collective well-being.

Trudeau was defeated by Joe Clark in 1979, although the Conservative minority government was to fall within nine months. Clark was not a neo-conservative, but his victory signaled a citizen fatigue with federal-provincial conflict, inflation, growing public debt and high interest rates.

The NDP ran a high-service administration, and Blakeney had taken it to a new level of complexity and organization. The government was managing the province well, but at a retreat in 1980, caucus members were unsure about what to do next. They were searching for new meaning, or at least some significant new social programs, but there was a determination among the more powerful ministers and deputies to keep the focus on economic management.

The major social initiatives in the 1978–82 period were affirmative action programs aimed at Native people, women and the handicapped. Those plans had achieved only limited impact by 1982, and in fact they had a political downside. They were more narrowly cast than the universal social programs that had always characterized the CCF-NDP. Some people came to resent them, particularly the programs aimed at Native people, and the Conservatives were fanning those flames.

By the early 1980s, inflation in Canada was running in the double digits. In an attempt to control it, the Bank of Canada raised prime interest rates to a ruinous 22.75%. Farmers were losing their land and consumers their homes. Blakeney criticized the bank and the federal government, but he did not offer any promises of direct help to people in Saskatchewan.

There was pressure from within Cabinet to do something, but Blakeney's advisors told him that a recession already extant in Ontario would soon hit the west as well. He believed that government would need all of its resources simply to meet the needs of existing programs. He resisted any direct transfers to individuals as perhaps politically popular, but financially irresponsible. Finance Minister Ed Tchorzewski tabled a budget in March 1982 that ran a small surplus and contained no new tax increases, but there were no new bonanzas for anyone.

The NDP talked up its good management, and its budget surpluses, based in large part on the earnings generated by what the government called the "family" of Crown corporations. Those were not the family values that interested Grant Devine. He said that while the government and its Crowns were doing just fine, people in Saskatchewan were enduring hard times.

Blakeney called an election on March 29 and the omens were immediately bad. Unions were enraged when, on the day prior to the call, the government legislated striking CUPE hospital workers back to their posts. At his own nominating meeting, Blakeney had to push past angry and noisy demonstrators to get into the hall. CUPE decided not to support the NDP in the election with money or workers, a signal of the general disaffection that labour felt towards the government. The party's passionate internal debate over uranium development had also taken its toll. Rather than knocking on doors, many discouraged party activists simply sat on their hands in 1982.

The Conservatives had been caught off guard in 1978, but this time Devine was ready with two major promises. The Tories would remove the provincial tax from gasoline, and they would provide mortgage protection to both farmers and homeowners. These promises would cost $250 million in the first year, and that did not include promised reductions to income tax. Where, asked Blakeney, would the Tories get the money? The questions were the right ones, but without major programs of their own to promote, the NDP was on the defensive, falling into precisely the same trap that they had set for Ross Thatcher in 1971.

On April 26, the outcome was devastating for the NDP. Devine and the Conservatives won 54% of the vote and the NDP was left with only nine seats, including Blakeney's in Regina Elphinstone. In Saskatoon, Roy Romanow lost by 13 votes to a university student. The next day, a subdued and ashen Allan Blakeney met reporters. He admitted that the NDP had clearly misread the polls, and that he had not received the right information "either from my people or from my pores."

Blakeney told the NDP convention later in the year that the success of NDP resource programs led to "a perception that our government was well off, but people were not." He also said that the NDP had done a poor job of communicating its message, that resource policies and Crown corporations "were the means to provide society with the general wealth to help the less fortunate among us."

Doug McArthur, a member of Blakeney's Cabinet, came to a somewhat different conclusion. Cabinet, he said in an interview, had come to exist at an "immense distance" from the people: "They were hurting from high interest rates and the government was obsessed with competence and balanced budgets. No one should ever make the mistake of thinking that we didn't fail the political challenge of that time. We did, badly."

The weight of defeat falls ultimately on the leader, and Blakeney bore it stoically, bottling up his feelings, as was his habit in times of crisis. He missed being Premier, but not being the centre of attention at the many social occasions that accompanied the job. Now at a public event he might be seen picking gingerly at the food while the other guests lavished their attention on the newly elected Conservatives. He had always been able to disappear into a crowd, even as Premier. Now it became even easier to do.

The Tories kept their promises on the gasoline tax, and the farm and home mortgage programs. The result was a $227 million deficit in 1982–83, a year in which the provincial economy was growing. The Devine string of deficits continued unbroken throughout his nine years in office, saddling Saskatchewan with the highest per capita debt in the country and almost bankrupting the province. Grant Devine once said that Saskatchewan was so well endowed that the province could be mismanaged and still break even. Unfortunately, only the first half of his prediction came true.

Blakeney's leadership was never openly challenged. He had planned to step down a year or two after the anticipated victory in 1982, but now he felt he had to stay. All of the potential leadership candidates, with the possible exception of Dwayne Lingenfelter, had been defeated.

Blakeney believed there was no hope for an NDP victory in 1986. He thought that he should stay to rebuild the party, then give way to a new leader after another election. But by 1985, the Tories were stumbling badly, and Blakeney began to believe that they were vulnerable. He had to make an important decision about whether to stay or go. Roy Romanow was not in the Legislature, although Ed Tchorzewski, another potential candidate, had been returned in a by-election. Blakeney decided to stay, and in the 1986 election the NDP actually received more votes than the Tories, but lost by 38 seats to 25.

He wanted to leave soon after the election and he told the party so. He had been in the Legislature for 26 years, and had been Premier for 11 of them. The NDP had a strong caucus with a handful of people who might seek the leadership. He wanted to get on with a life outside of politics.

Blakeney stepped down as leader on November 6, 1987, and was saluted by all sides in the usually raucous legislative chamber. He joked that he had just taken his pulse to convince himself that he had not died and then stumbled into his own political wake. He spent his last day in the House in March 1988, and then made a clean break. He and Anne traveled in Egypt, Greece and continental Europe between April and June. They spent much of the summer at home sifting through papers and possessions, shedding much of both. They sold their home and cottage and moved into a Regina condominium.

He accepted the Bora Laskin Chair in Public Law at Osgoode Hall in Toronto for that fall. He fit well into the academic environment and enjoyed it so much that he stayed for a second year, but turned down the offer of a permanent position.

The Blakeneys had toyed with retiring to their native Nova Scotia, but decided that they were too attached to Saskatchewan. When they left Toronto, they settled in Saskatoon, where he first occupied the Law Foundation Chair, and later remained as a visiting scholar at the law college, where he maintains a modest office.

During his long career in politics, Blakeney had tasted both sweet victory and bitter defeat. His advice to anyone who wanted to become a politician was to work hard to win while being prepared to lose. Almost everyone, he reasoned, loses at one time or another.

On that bittersweet election evening in 1986, Blakeney brought the NDP back from near annihilation to competitive respectability. When he spoke to reporters amid the din of election night festivities, he described the results not as a defeat, but as a disappointment. "I would say you have to meet triumph and disaster and treat those two imposters just the same," he said, paraphrasing Rudyard Kipling.

He had fought the good fight, and now he would lay down his shield.

Life After Politics

Allan Blakeney is a much more relaxed man in retirement than he was in politics. He once said that as Premier he kept in mind the symbol of a reel-to-reel tape turning slowly and recording his every word. That image spoke to his innate caution and to the seriousness with which he accepted his role.

He and Anne live in a modest home near the riverbank in Saskatoon, and he spends a part of most days at his small office at the university's law college. They are comfortable financially, but not wealthy. Thomas McLeod, a long-time friend, says that Blakeney could have been a rich lawyer had he made that choice, "But you just wouldn't think of Al doing that. It isn't his way of life."

The Blakeneys continue to spend their summers in Nova Scotia, and have good friends there half a century after having left. They make occasional visits to Ottawa, to visit the three of their four adult children who live there, along with several grandchildren. They have friends in Ottawa, too, most of them civil servants, retired now, who had served in the Douglas, Lloyd and Blakeney governments in Saskatchewan, then went on to work with the federal government.

Blakeney has remained a useful citizen in his retirement, serving on boards and volunteer associations. Bob Rae, when he was Ontario's Premier, asked Blakeney to sit on the board of Algoma Steel when the NDP government restructured it to stave off bankruptcy.

Blakeney has also sat on the boards of Cameco, the Saskatchewan uranium company, and of Regina-based Crown Life as well. He has been on the executive of the Canadian Civil Liberties Association, and served as president of the World Federalists of Canada.

He has lectured extensively and done some writing, mostly about Canadian federalism and the structures of government. He admits that he is more interested in how governments work than he is in political organization. His fondest and most intense engagements have been projects to build democratic structures in Russia, and in South Africa following the dismantling of apartheid. He has made five visits to South Africa, working through the International Development Research Centre, and has met the South Africans on several of their trips to Canada.

He has been consciously cutting back on his commitments in recent years and now considers himself to be retired. He remains intellectually current, as any conversation with him or a quick perusal of the bookshelves in his Saskatoon home indicate. The authors range from John Kenneth Galbraith, through American novelist Tony Morrison to a biography of the life of Christ, and his periodical subscriptions include *Harper's*, *Maclean's*, and the Canadian Centre for Policy Alternatives newsletter. He does not seek the political or any other limelight, and particularly tries to avoid being conscripted during election campaigns. He remains a keen observer of public debate and policy, and will comment in detail, but only if he is asked.

He watched with growing dismay in the late 1980s as the Devine Conservatives accumulated a provincial debt of almost $16 billion. "This created extreme financial pressures on government," he says, "and since the Conservative defeat in 1991 ensuing governments have had to deal with heavy debt payments, and that continues until today."

Blakeney says that Conservative mismanagement made it next to impossible for Saskatchewan to have a high-service social democratic government. "The NDP government in 1991 inherited public expectations that it would pursue social programs as vigorously as we did in the 1971–82 years," he says, "but without the public realization that the government no longer had the resources to do so. The government was seen as failing by many people, especially its own supporters, who blame the failure on ideology, or lack of commitment to principles, when really the failure is one of resources."

He has mostly avoided comment regarding the Conservative MLAs, ministers and staff who have been convicted on various criminal charges of defrauding the Saskatchewan public. It is inconceivable that such activity would have occurred when Blakeney was firmly at the helm as Premier. His great concern is that those activities have brought disrepute to public life and to government in general.

Blakeney has always been a Canadian nationalist, an inheritance perhaps from his Loyalist roots and reinforced by his many years as a social democrat. He believes that our free trade agreements, particularly NAFTA, have removed from government the power to maintain sovereignty, and to attempt to use government to reduce the inequality in society.

"Canada's adherence to NAFTA," he says, "has not delivered its chief promised benefit, which was supposed to be ready access to the U.S. market, and with a smoothly functioning dispute resolution mechanism. On the other hand, NAFTA clearly means heavy

U.S. influence on how Canada operates internally." He has concluded that Canada should press for changes to NAFTA, and failing this, Canada should abrogate:

> This would not mean Canada's withdrawal from the World Trade Organization, which deals primarily with trade in goods," he says. "The WTO does not attempt to say, for example, that member countries must have competitive health care systems, or must not use Crown corporations. Nor does the WTO permit foreign companies to sue national governments, as does NAFTA. We can have most of the benefits in the WTO without the limitations flowing from NAFTA, and we can also achieve a more equitable distribution of wealth and power.

Blakeney remains staunchly convinced that government has a role to play in achieving greater equality among citizens, but he knows that any successful political party has to have a convincing plan to get there. He wishes that the federal NDP had a more coherent economic policy:

> We have to do a balancing act to create conditions that allow the production of wealth, then the distributing of that wealth to create a maximum amount of well-being. The task for social democrats is to strike a new balance leaving us with the benefits of free and international trade, while restoring the ability of governments to redistribute wealth and power.

Tommy Douglas once summarized the contributions of his successor, saying that Allan Blakeney "proved social democracy is not just an impossible dream." Blakeney brought to his task as Premier an extraordinary mix of intellect, stamina and experience. He was a principled pragmatist, a decent, extremely capable man who provided honest, good, and compassionate government, an accomplishment not nearly as easy as it might sound, and a most valuable contribution in any age.

Notes

This chapter has been adapted from a book that I wrote, entitled *Promises to Keep: A Political Biography of Allan Blakeney* (Saskatoon: Western Producer Prairie Books, 1990). All quotations used in this chapter are drawn from interviews that I conducted for the book. It was thoroughly researched, making good use of Mr. Blakeney's papers at the Saskatchewan Archives Board and much other material. *Promises to Keep* contains detailed endnotes, and readers wishing to check sources found in this chapter will find them there.

Grant Devine
JAMES M. PITSULA

Devine discussing rural issues (SAB 84-1494-R16-30A).

Devine, formal portrait, 1982 (SAB 82-773-754A).

Devine addressing the "Open for Business" conference, November 1982 (SAB 82-2101-R405).

SASKATCHEWAN PREMIERS OF THE 20TH CENTURY
Grant Devine, 1982–1991

Introduction

Margaret Thatcher, Great Britain's Iron Lady, once said, "I am not a consensus politician … I'm a conviction politician."[1] Consensus politicians "go with the flow"; they constantly consult, pacify, conciliate, compromise and generally blur the issues. They move to the implementation of their policy goals, if they have any, by slow degrees, being careful not to move too far in advance of public opinion. Their strategy is to figure out which way the parade is heading and then jump to the front and say, "Follow me." In Canadian political history, the classic model of the consensus politician was William Lyon Mackenzie King, who "never did anything by halves that he could do by quarters." The "conviction politician," by contrast, has a vision, or a mission that he or she intends to fulfill. Holding on to power is secondary to holding fast to principles. Such politicians do what they think is right in the sure knowledge that history is on their side. Pierre Trudeau was such a leader, especially on the subject of patriating the Constitution and introducing the Charter of Rights and Freedoms. Although he infuriated many people, he accomplished what he set out to do.

Of the two types (and admittedly there are many between the two extremes), Grant Devine, Premier of Saskatchewan from 1982 to 1991, was more a "conviction" than a "consensus" politician. His mission was to undo what he considered to be the baneful effects of "socialist" policies in Saskatchewan and to unleash the forces of free enterprise. The CCF-NDP, which had been in power for all but seven of the 38 years preceding Devine's taking office, had built a regime based on Crown corporations, medicare, social welfare, and support for labour unions. Devine believed that high taxes and too much public ownership had smothered private initiative and stifled economic growth. Government was too big and too intrusive; it needed to be cut back so that individuals and communities could achieve their full potential. "There is so much more we can be" was the slogan in the 1982 campaign that lifted him to power.

Devine's mission was not a modest, trifling one. His was not a government content to follow the well-worn traces of its predecessors, but one that sought to steer Saskatchewan in a new direction. He wanted to break the social democratic mould that had been established since World War II and to build a pro-business, entrepreneurial culture. He was of the school of thought that Saskatchewan, if liberated from socialism, could be as prosperous as Alberta. A terrible mistake had been made in choosing the socialist path, but it could be undone. In the first session of the Legislature after the sweeping victory of 1982, Devine said, "The people of Saskatchewan freely chose to march to the beat of a different drummer. The journey began on April 26 and will continue for generations to come."[2]

Nine years later, the Devine government was soundly defeated, reduced to 10 seats and 25% of the vote, and the NDP were back in power with 55 seats and a majority of the popular vote. The economy was in bad shape, and the province laboured under a record debt load. A cloud of scandal was soon to descend, as 12 Conservative MLAs (but not Devine himself) were convicted on fraud charges arising from the misuse of their communications or constituency allowances. But despite what seemed like nearly total defeat, Devine had been successful in implementing at least part of his agenda. He carried out a massive privatization of Crown corporations, cut back the welfare state and curbed the power of labour unions. He did not take the government out of business, but instead offered incentives, subsidies, loan guarantees, and other financial inducements to stimulate and support private enterprise. It was not free enterprise in the pure sense, but rather government-assisted free enterprise. By these devices, the government helped establish such industries as heavy-oil upgraders, a bacon-processing plant, a paper mill, a pulp mill and a fertilizer plant.

Devine was an inveterate optimist, who was always upbeat about the future of Saskatchewan. He was famous for his folksy sayings such as "Give 'er snoose Bruce," "Don't say whoa in a mud-hole," and "Saskatchewan is the best kept secret in the world." As a "conviction" politician, he was apt to polarize the electorate rather than bringing people together. His attacks on the NDP were stinging and categorical: "This beautiful country of Canada was not founded by Marx, not founded by Lenin and it wasn't founded by Chairman Mao. And today, these great people are not going to bend, or bow or be broken by new Marxist zealots."[3] Since 30% to 40% of the Saskatchewan electorate usually voted NDP (even in 1982 the NDP obtained 37.6% of the vote), Devine's fervid rhetoric, as well as his policies, could not help but antagonize a large section of the population. But it is the nature of the "conviction" politician to say exactly what he thinks.

The government's greatest failure was the massive debt it incurred. Extravagant tax cuts and spending promises in the first term, both of which the public eagerly accepted, led to financial crisis in the second term. Severe cutbacks in programs, the reintroduction of taxes previously abolished, and the imposition of brand new taxes alienated and angered the electorate. Privatization was linked in the public mind to the debt problem. It seemed that the government had first run up the bills and then started to sell the province's assets in order to pay them. The government acquired a reputation for financial mismanagement and ideological extremism, squandering the good will it had been accorded in 1982. The judgement of the voters in 1991 was unequivocal.

Rise to Power

Donald Grant Devine was born July 5, 1944, in Regina and raised on a farm that his grandfather had homesteaded near Lake Valley, not far from Moose Jaw. After high school, he enrolled at the University of Saskatchewan where he earned a Bachelor of Science degree in Agriculture. He pursued post-graduate studies at the University of Alberta, obtaining two Masters degrees, one in Agricultural Economics and the other in Business Administration. Upon graduating in 1970, he took a job as a marketing specialist with the Department of Agriculture in Ottawa. His duties included assisting with agricultural commodity legislation and acting as an advisor to the Food Prices Review Board. Following his stint in Ottawa, he left Canada in 1972 to pursue a PhD in Agricultural Economics at Ohio State University.

For his doctoral thesis he studied price levels and customer satisfaction in the retail food industry. He examined the impact of making comparative price information available to consumers in a test market. For a five-week period, information was published in the newspaper about what various supermarkets were charging for groceries. It was found that prices declined by 7%, and then, two weeks after the termination of the public information program, prices began to rise and increased 8.8% by the end of the study period. Consumers who received the additional information reported higher levels of satisfaction, and 43% of them said they changed stores as a result of the information program. The thesis concluded that public price monitoring programs should be put in place as a means of improving market performance:

> The fact that society is unhappy with market performance has been demonstrated throughout the developed world by such actions as wage and price controls and increased government involvement, not only in the regulation of the market but in the actual public provision of goods and services. The question is, has society adequately addressed the problem particularly at the consumer level of market transaction? To do so we may have to consider market information as a public good.[4]

Although the study was specialized and limited in scope, it gave insight into Devine's economic philosophy. While admitting the existence of flaws in the operation of the market system, he attributed them to imperfect consumer knowledge rather than defects in the system itself.

Devine received his PhD in 1976 and joined the faculty of the University of Saskatchewan, where he taught Agricultural Marketing and Consumer Economics. He was drawn to politics at a time when the fortunes of the Progressive Conservative Party were rising. The Conservatives had not been in power or even a serious contender in Saskatchewan elections since 1934. Although John Diefenbaker had dominated in federal elections, his influence had not transferred to the provincial level. Instead, there had been a pattern of voting CCF/NDP provincially and Tory federally. The man who began to change all that was Dick Collver, elected leader of the PC party of Saskatchewan in 1973. His message was that, with the defeat of the Liberal government of Ross Thatcher in 1971, the province had entered a new political cycle. He argued that the Liberals would be unelectable for many years to come, and the only way to dislodge the NDP was to build an anti-socialist coalition around the Conservatives. The provincial Liberals carried the albatross of the unpopular, Trudeau-led federal Liberals. In addition, Dave Steuart, Thatcher's successor as Liberal leader, made the mistake of moving the Liberal Party to the left, on the false assumption that the Liberals had the right-of-centre vote sewn up. The Conservatives occupied the vacuum that had been created. Collver also went after a portion of the NDP vote, targeting the working man with wife, children and mortgage, who paid his bills and taxes and was looking for a fair break. As the Conservative leader put it, there were more Archie Bunkers than bleeding hearts in Saskatchewan.[5]

Collver's brand of right-wing populism had appeal. The NDP won the 1975 election handily, taking 39 seats to the Liberals' 15 and the Conservatives' 7, but the popular vote revealed that the Conservatives now rivaled the Liberals as the alternative to the governing party. The PCs had 28% of the vote, compared to the Liberals' 32% and the NDP's 40%. The trend was confirmed in the 1978 election when the NDP won 44 seats and the Conservatives 17, while the Liberals were wiped out. The election marked Grant Devine's entry into electoral politics. He contested the constituency of Saskatoon Nutana and was soundly defeated. Undeterred, he put his name forward for the leadership of the Progressive Conservative Party of Saskatchewan and cruised to victory at the November 1979 convention. In the fall of 1980, the sitting Conservative MLA for Estevan resigned his seat, opening a by-election for Devine to enter the Legislature. His loss to the NDP candidate was a serious blow—his second failure in three years to win a seat—but Devine kept his composure and promised to return to Estevan in the next general election.

The summer of 1981 was the low ebb for Devine. The Conservative caucus meeting at Kenosee Lake delivered a strong critique of his leadership, and some even wanted his resignation. Devine weathered the attacks, and, as it became evident that the NDP was vulnerable, the party rallied around him. Interest rates were at record high levels, and there was a feeling that Allan Blakeney's 11-year-old government was out of touch with the people. The government was deeply involved in federal-provincial discussions concerning the patriation and amendment of the Canadian Constitution. As important as this was, it was far removed from the bread-and-butter issues of the average person. Devine played effectively on the NDP's perceived "big-government," bureaucratic style. He mocked government advertising in praise of the "family of Crown corporations," saying that the Conservatives cared about "real" families. Even Blakeney's prudent management of the province's finances was transformed into a liability. He always balanced the budget and the province enjoyed a premium credit rating, but people were led to ask, "If the province is so well-off, why don't we have more money in our pockets?"

The NDP government's 1982 pre-election budget increased spending on health, education, social services, senior citizens, and low-income housing, but it did not offer tax relief. When the election was called for April 26, Devine announced on the first day of the campaign that he would eliminate the provincial tax on gasoline. The Conservatives appeared confused as to the savings to the consumer. They put out the figure 40¢ per gallon, when the correct figure was 26¢, but nobody seemed to care.[6] Devine grabbed the headlines, and he never looked back for the rest of the campaign. Later he would have to reimpose the gas tax, as the province fell deeper into debt, but in the heady days of the spring of 1982, such thoughts were far away. The Devine Conservatives were rolling to victory.

In addition to repealing the gas tax, Devine promised relief on home mortgages. The Bank of Canada was trying to squeeze inflation out of the economy, and interest rates had soared to 18% and higher. The Conservatives guaranteed a ceiling of 13.25% on home mortgages up to a value of $50,000 for a three-year period. They further pledged to phase out the 5% provincial sales tax and to reduce provincial income tax by 10%. Farmers were promised loans at guaranteed rates of 8% in the first five years and 12% in the second five years.

Just before the election call, the NDP managed to alienate one of its principal allies. Nearly 5,000 hospital staff workers went on strike, compromising health services at a politically inopportune moment. The government responded by legislating the strikers back to work and prohibiting all strikes in essential services for the duration of the election campaign. Unionists cried foul, and many refrained from working for NDP candidates. The NDP's efforts to woo the farm vote were equally futile. Blakeney tried to make an issue out of the fight with the federal government for the retention of the Crow rate (the subsidized freight rates for grain that farmers had enjoyed since the turn of the century). The Trudeau government was intent on terminating the subsidy, and the NDP attempted to mount a crusade to protect the rate. The campaign fell flat, despite the province-wide distribution of "Save the Crow" pamphlets and much heated rhetoric on the subject. Farmers seemed resigned to the change, sensing that there was little the province could do to force Ottawa to change its mind.

Devine proved a gifted campaigner. His down-home, populist style contrasted with Blakeney's more formal, reserved manner. Devine was especially effective in rural areas, where he related well to the people. He was never shy to point out that he was the only political leader in the country to hold a Wheat Board permit book. His theme was that Saskatchewan was like a sleeping beauty waiting to be reawakened from the socialist spell. "Profit has become a dirty word in Saskatchewan," he said, "We have to become proud of profit." The NDP "wants to own more of the farms and more of the businesses and more of our life." He promised to overthrow "socialist tyranny" and restore "personal ambition, aspiration, and competition that the NDP has replaced with mediocrity."[7]

At the same time, Devine said that his was a compassionate conservatism in the tradition of John Diefenbaker. He maintained that the NDP had tried to impose compassion, which could not be done, and it had tried to stamp out competition, which equally could not be done. Devine claimed that he stood for a balance of compassion and competition:

> Be progressive on the one hand, and be conservative on the other. Make sure that you provide those kinds of programs that are needed by seniors, by young people, by handicapped, or by those that are less fortunate. Look after health, look after education, look after social programs, but make sure that you do it right. And at the same time, be very conservative when it comes to providing economic incentives to people who go to work, and particularly with tax cuts and incentives.[8]

In the 1982 election campaign, Devine did not speak of dismantling social programs or the welfare state. On the contrary, he chastised the Blakeney government for its inadequate funding of medicare. The Conservatives presented themselves as better friends of socialized medicine than were the NDP.

Devine summed up his personal and political philosophy as "God first, family second, the Conservative Party third, and the NDP under my thumb." Though raised in the United Church, Devine converted to Roman Catholicism at the age of 22 when he married Chantal Guillaume. He made no apologies for his plain-spokenness on matters of religion and morality. "I think one of the biggest challenges we face in this country and North America is one of morals," he said on one occasion. His views on the subject were highlighted in a 1988 interview with journalist Peter Gzowski, who chided him for his public pronouncements on issues such as gay rights and abortion: "That's a handy little sermon you gave me about how to live my life inside the home, but you're a politician!" Devine answered that many politicians, including Tommy Douglas, had once been preachers. Religion, values and beliefs were not just for Sunday.[9]

The 1982 election was a personal triumph for Devine. Momentum grew as the campaign progressed, and the Conservatives sensed the tide turning in their favor. Devine predicted they would win 50 seats, but he underestimated the size of the victory. On April 26, the Tories received 54.1% of the popular vote and 55 out of 64 seats in the Legislature, the largest majority in Saskatchewan political history. The NDP were humiliated with only 9 seats.

The First Term

Devine's first task after the election was to assemble a Cabinet. The clear choice for Deputy Premier was Eric Berntson, a farmer from southeastern Saskatchewan. First elected in 1975, he emerged as a dominant figure in the party and Devine's right-hand man. In addition to the deputy premiership, he was appointed minister of Agriculture and Government House Leader. Other Cabinet heavyweights included Bob Andrew (Finance), Gary Lane (Justice, and minister responsible for SaskTel), Colin Thatcher (Energy and Mines, with responsibility for SaskOil and the Saskatchewan Mining Development Corporation), Paul Rousseau (Industry, and minister for Saskatchewan Government Insurance, the Saskatchewan Economic Development Corporation, and the Crown Investments Corporation), Graham Taylor (Health), and Patricia Smith (Social Services). Twelve of 17 Cabinet ministers represented rural areas; by occupation, there were six farmers, four business operators, four teachers, two lawyers and a public relations manager. The missing ingredient was experience. The Conservatives had been out of power for so long that none of the ministers had served in Cabinet before. Many were new to the Legislative Assembly as well.

The government was convinced that international investors shunned Saskatchewan because of its socialist reputation. A new image was needed. This was the main idea behind the "Open for Business" conference co-hosted by the Saskatchewan government and the *Financial Post* on October 19–20, 1982. The event was part of a public relations effort to communicate the message that private business was welcome in the province, and, as a corollary, restraints would be placed on the growth of Crown corporations. Devine in his speech to the conference promised to rescind a large number of regulations that inhibited business (including relaxation of the environmental regulation review process) and cancelled the back-in rights of the Saskatchewan Mining Development Corporation (the latter had given the Crown corporation the automatic option of participating in new mineral exploration or development projects in northern Saskatchewan). But the main purpose of the "Open for Business" conference was to change attitudes and perceptions. The goal was to stimulate entrepreneurial thinking and investor confidence—to jolt Saskatchewan out of the habit of relying upon the government to lead the economy.

Privatization was not a major thrust of the Devine government in its first term. Devine

SAB 82-2101-R4-5
Premier Grant Devine addressing the "Open for Business" conference, November 1982.

signaled in 1983 that Crown corporations were a valuable part of the Saskatchewan economy, particularly those Crowns that sold natural resource products in the international market:

> There's a strong and vital role for Crown corporations in this activity [international trade]. The Crown corporations in the resource sector couldn't help but succeed with growing world demand. The test now is to be competitive and capture a market share through inventiveness and flexibility when the world market demand is not as strong.

He said he was less enthusiastic about certain other publicly owned corporations:

> For those Crowns that operate primarily within our borders, we believe there needs to be a better balance between the public sector and the private sector. And balance we will have. We are responding to the imbalance in directing the Crowns so they complement rather than compete with our citizens.[10]

The CCF-NDP attitude to the Crowns had been quite different. Social democratic governments had been determined to use public enterprise as a means to achieve economic diversification. The hinterland status of the province had predisposed even non-socialist governments to adopt some forms of public ownership. Liberal governments from 1905 to 1929 had initiated telephone service and the distribution of electric power. The Tommy Douglas government elected in 1944 consolidated and greatly expanded these efforts to create Saskatchewan Government Telephones (later SaskTel) and the Saskatchewan Power Corporation (later SaskPower). But there had never been full consensus in the province on the subject of public ownership. On May 20, 1957, Tommy Douglas engaged in a famous debate on Crown corporations with Ross Thatcher at Mossbank. Thatcher decried what he regarded as the dismal financial performance of the Crowns, while Douglas said they served the province well. Later, when Thatcher was Premier in the 1960s, he kept a tight rein on the Crowns, but did not sell them. He supported the idea of public ownership of utilities and said that government ownership in other areas was tolerable as a last resort.[11]

SAB 82-773-0024

Grant Devine, shortly after being elected as Premier of Saskatchewan, 1982.

The Blakeney government in the 1970s aggressively promoted Crown corporations, especially in the natural resource sector, the "family of Crown corporations" that the PCs mocked in the 1982 election campaign. Although Devine did not at first advocate privatization, he made it clear that the Crowns would not be allowed to grow, and expansions that had been contemplated by the NDP were cancelled. SGI's [Saskatchewan Government Insurance] tentative plans to enter the life insurance business, to set up auto-body repair shops and to get into the hotel business were permanently scrapped. PCS International, a new offshore marketing subsidiary of the Potash Corporation, was disbanded a month before it was scheduled to start operation. SaskPower sold its Poplar River mine at Coronach to Manalta Coal of Calgary and contracted out much of its maintenance work. The Saskatchewan Fur Marketing Corporation was abolished in October 1982, and SaskMedia, which produced films and other educational media, was dissolved in March 1983. All of this added up to something less than a no-holds-barred, all-out attack on public ownership. The *Financial Post* commented in January 1983 that, "In spite of restraints placed on the Crowns, so far what is emerging in Saskatchewan is not preparation for a massive assault on public enterprise, but rather an atmosphere of détente between the free-enterprise government and the Crowns it inherited."[12]

On one point, however, Devine was adamant. The government should not be in the business of owning farm land. The Farm Purchase Program (government guaranteed loans to farmers at 8%) was the Conservatives' answer to the Land Bank, which had been introduced by the NDP in 1972 as a means of facilitating intergenerational land transfer. The problem the Land Bank sought to address was that older farmers, who needed a retirement income, wanted to sell their land, but young people, who wished to establish themselves in farming, could not afford to buy. Land that was put on the market was often sold to well-off farmers who already owned large acreages, thus reinforcing the trend towards the concentration of land in fewer hands and the decline of the family farm. The NDP solution was to allow retiring farmers the option of selling their land to the government, which in turn leased it to young farmers. After a five-year period, Land Bank tenants had the opportunity to buy the land they rented from the government. This program was extremely unpopular with the Conservatives. Minister of Agriculture Eric Berntson likened it to Stalin's collective farms and said the NDP was out to make "sharecroppers" out of the farmers of Saskatchewan.[13] Abolition of the Land Bank was one of the first items of business of the new government.

Some 5,905 farmers took advantage of the Farm Purchase Program during the first five years of its operation, and by 1987 a total of $617 million in loans had been subsidized. Unfortunately, the program did not do much to advance its stated objective of increasing the level of farm ownership. The great objection to the Land Bank was that the government, not the individual farmer, ended up with title to the land. Between 1981 and 1986, following the dismantling of the Land Bank, approximately 2.5 million acres of land in Saskatchewan changed from "ownership" to "rented" status. This was 2.5 times the holdings of the Land Bank prior to 1982. A report by the federal Farm Debt Review Board in 1989 gave the bleak news that 5,968 foreclosure notices came before the FDRB and the Farm Land Security Board.[14] A poor farm economy and heavy debt loads threatened farmers with bankruptcy and loss of their land.

With respect to the fiscal management of the province, the government ran a series of deficits that grew larger year by year. The deficit for 1982–83 was $227 million, caused in large part by the elimination of the gasoline tax and other expensive campaign promises. Finance minister Bob Andrew said the financial shortfall was no cause for alarm: "This is a minimized and manageable deficit, which has been directly translated into assistance for the people of this province."[15] The deficit for 1983–84 was $331 million; for 1984–85, $380 million; and for 1985–86, $579 million, leaving an accumulated debt after four years of Tory rule of more than $1.5 billion. In 1985 the shortage of money forced the government to introduce tax increases, contradictory as they were to the Conservative theme in the 1982 election campaign. The 1985 budget imposed a 1% flat tax on all personal income and an unprecedented tax on the sale of used vehicles (repealed the following year because of the public outcry), and abolished property improvement grants and renters' rebates. New York lowered the province's credit rating from "AA1" to "AA."

One of the controversial features of the Devine government's fiscal regime was the change in oil royalty rates. The Blakeney government in 1981 had received 64.9% of the value of oil production in taxes and royalties. The Conservatives took it as a given that excessively high royalties depressed the oil industry. Devine avowed in Lloyminster that nobody makes any money if you stop working, if the oil isn't flowing and people aren't working... The government doesn't make any money, the people don't make any money and you close down and leave. The potential here in this part of the province is fantastic and we're fools if we don't take advantage of it.[16]

During the summer of 1982, the government worked out a new royalty structure. Implemented in July, it reduced royalty rates for existing production and provided for a three-year royalty-free period for new wells. In 1981, the province obtained $532 million in royalties on production valued at $821 million. In 1985, royalties were $674 million on total production worth $2,253 million. Thus the province received a much smaller share of the value of production, but a modest increase in absolute terms. The precise relationship between royalty structure and oil production was difficult to establish because so many variables entered the picture—federal government policies, international prices, oil shortages, the overall state of the economy, wars in the Middle East, the weather, and so on. However, it seemed safe to assume that the royalty holiday boosted production. The province benefited from the sale of exploration rights and from the spin-off activities arising from increased investment and employment in the oil patch, but royalty revenue share declined drastically.

The 1986 Election

Devine waited until four-and-a-half years into his first term to call an election. When voters went to the polls on October 20, 1986, the Conservatives knew that their best hope for re-election was in the rural areas. Since 1982, the government had catered to the needs of farmers. The Land Bank had been abolished and replaced with low-interest loans for young farmers trying to get established. Natural gas lines were being extended to rural homes at a cost to SaskPower of $484 million. Benefits in the form of rebates on farm fuel, livestock cash advances, and loans for livestock facilities poured out of the treasury. The Farmland Security Act was passed to restrict farm foreclosures, and financial aid was given to farmers hit by drought.

For urban voters, Devine unveiled his housing policy in the summer of 1986. It provided home mortgage interest rates subsidized at 9.75% for 10 years, matching grants of $1,500 for home improvements, $10,000 home improvement loans at 6%, and $3,000 grants for first-time home buyers. The PC election theme was "Keep on Building Saskatchewan"—building not just houses, decks, swimming pools and other home improvements, but also industrial projects such as a paper mill in Prince Albert, a bacon processing plant in North Battleford, and a heavy oil upgrader in Regina. Despite this activity, unemployment in Saskatchewan in April 1986 stood at 40,000 compared to 28,000 when the Conservatives took office in April 1982. In 1985, 6,040 more people left the province than arrived. From a surplus of more than $140 million in May 1982, the treasury had been depleted to a debt approaching $2 billion.

The NDP, led by Allan Blakeney, unveiled what it called a "7-7-7" housing program. It was intended to create 18,000 jobs by providing $7,000 grants to first-time buyers of new

SAB 84-1494-R16-30A

Grant Devine's close ties to the farm community were instrumental in allowing him to hold on to power in the 1986 provincial election, where he lost the popular vote to the NDP, but won more seats, mainly those in rural areas.

homes, renovation grants of up to $7,000 for existing homes, and a guaranteed 7% interest rate on the first $70,000 of house mortgages for seven years. The NDP also pledged to give loans to small businesses at 7% for seven years. The fixation with the number "7" had an air of mumbo-jumbo about it. In their desperation not to be outbid and outmanoeuvred as in 1982, the NDP imitated the PC tactic of expensive promises. The 1986 election turned out to be one of sorriest episodes in Saskatchewan political history. The NDP made extravagant promises in a futile effort to get elected, and the PCs bought rumpus room carpets, hot tubs, and wet bars for people who did not need them with money the government did not have. Only the Liberals preached fiscal responsibility.

During the campaign, interest focussed on whether farmers would receive a special deficiency payment from the federal government to compensate for low grain prices. It was argued that since both the United States and the European Community were subsidizing grain growers, Ottawa had an obligation to do the same. At 5:30 a.m. on October 3, 1986, less than three weeks before voting day, a reporter was awakened in a Kelvington motel by the sound of an intense telephone conversation in the adjoining room. He heard Devine plead for a farm bail-out: "If I lose this, it's going to be damned tough for Mulroney next time around."[17] The message got through, and a few hours later the Prime Minister publicly declared that he was working closely with Devine to devise an effective financial program for farmers. The initial estimate was $1 billion, $457 million of which went to Saskatchewan.

The perfectly timed announcement gave the Conservatives a vital boost. Although more people voted for the NDP (45.06%) than for the PCs (44.8%), the Conservatives captured 38 seats and the NDP only 25. The Liberals secured 9.93% of the vote, up from 4.5% in 1982, and elected one member. Devine's coalition, though weakened, still held. The election exposed a wide gulf between the urban and rural parts of the province, with the NDP winning 20 of the 24 seats in the larger urban centres and the Tories sweeping the rural seats. Among the latter, only Humboldt and the Quill Lakes voted NDP, and Assiniboia-Gravelbourg elected Liberal leader Ralph Goodale.

Fiscal Crisis and Post-election Cutbacks

After the election, the Conservatives admitted that the deficit for 1986–87 was $1.2 billion, much more than the fictitious $389 million presented in the pre-election budget and larger than any deficit previously recorded in Saskatchewan. Devine now said that some very serious measures would have to be taken to bring the province's finances under control. Day after day in the spring of 1987 came a steady stream of gloomy edicts. The compassionate conservatism of the first term was not much in evidence as services were reduced, programs cancelled, and employees fired.

Transition houses for battered women and children had their budgets trimmed between 1.5% and 14.5%; the Legal Aid Commission was cut 8%; the Mental Health Association, 30%; the Voice of the Handicapped, 37%; the Saskatchewan Human Rights Association, 16%; the Saskatoon Crisis Intervention Service, 10%; and the Planned Parenthood Association and Saskatchewan Pro-Life Association, 100%. Operating grants to schools, hospitals, municipalities and universities were frozen for two years at a time when inflation was running at 4%. Wages for government workers were not allowed to rise, even though wage increases on the average had not kept up with inflation since 1982. The government set a goal of cutting 2,000 jobs from the civil service. At the end of the exercise, 561 vacant jobs had been eliminated, 1,200 people had taken early retirement, and 407 people had been fired. On the revenue side, the flat tax was increased from 1% to 1.5% and the provincial sales tax rose two points to 7%. The gasoline tax, which had been removed with such fanfare in 1982, was reintroduced with the provision that Saskatchewan residents could save their receipts and apply for a rebate at the end of the year.

The government announced most of the bad news in small doses prior to the formal presentation of the budget. The latter is normally brought down in March or April, but in 1987–88 it did not appear until June. The strategy was to dissipate discontent by dragging out the process as long as possible, but when the budget was finally introduced, it provoked an explosion of angry protest. The resentment over the firings, cutbacks, and tax increases was compounded by a general belief that the public had been misled during the election campaign regarding the true state of the province's finances. More than 7,000 people, one of the largest demonstration in the history of the province, marched on the Legislature. As the marchers made their way through the streets of downtown Regina, car horns sounded and bystanders clapped and waved. Even a wedding party pulled over to the side of the street, opened the car windows and cheered the protesters. Polls showed a decline in support for the Conservatives from 44.8% in October 1986 to 27.7% in June 1987.

The issue of deficits loomed ever larger in Devine's second term of office. The budgets were never balanced, the debt burden increased and interest charges mounted. The deficits were as follows: 1987–88, $542 million; 1988–89, $324 million; 1989–90, $378 million; 1990–91, $360 million and 1991–92, $842 million. In the last year of Devine's premiership, interest payments on the accumulated debt reached $502 million. This was the largest line item in the budget except for health and education. Social services came fourth at $390 million.

Analysis reveals that during Devine's first term in office, total annual revenue to the province increased by 5.15%, while expenditures increased by 67.5%. In the second term, the pattern was reversed. Revenues increased by 59%, and expenditures by 15%. Half of the second-term expenditure increase was consumed by debt-service charges. Indeed, in 1989–90 and 1990–91 the government actually achieved substantial surpluses on operating expenditures excluding interest payments. The problem was that the province had to go deeper into debt in order to pay the interest on previously accumulated debt, which made the interest charges the next year even higher, and so the vicious circle went. Basically what happened was that the Devine government in its first term created a monster that it could not control.[18]

The elimination of the gasoline tax in 1982 resulted in a drop in revenue from $120,686,000 in 1981–82 to $15,046,007 in 1982–83. The small amount that was collected came from taxes on aviation fuel and on diesel fuel used by railway locomotives. When the gasoline tax was reimposed, albeit with a rebate provision, the revenue from this source increased to $161,168,000 in 1987–88. In 1989, the rebatable fuel tax was increased from 7¢ per litre to 10¢. Then, two weeks before the Legislature was to open for the 1990 spring session, Devine made a special television appearance to abolish the rebate and to reintroduce the fuel tax as it had been in 1982 (except that it was now 10¢ rather than 6.6¢ per litre). If the fuel tax had stayed at 6.6¢ throughout the decade, the Saskatchewan government would have received an extra $735 million in revenue. Since the foregone revenue resulted in debt charges, interest payments have to be factored in to arrive at the true cost of the cheap gasoline policy. When this is done, it becomes apparent that the 1982 cancellation of the fuel tax resulted in over $1 billion of government debt.[19]

The cost to the treasury, if any, of the reduction in royalty rates on oil production is more difficult to calculate. If 1981 royalty rates had remained in place, and if oil production had stayed at the levels actually achieved during the Devine years, the province would have received an additional $3,897,610,000 from 1982 to 1989. This is close to the size of the entire provincial deficit for this period.[20] The flaw in the argument is that lower royalty rates likely increased production, and, therefore, it is misleading to combine the old royalty rate with the new production levels. The impact on provincial revenue of the tax holiday given to oil companies must remain in the realm of speculation.

The population of Saskatchewan through the 1980s was fairly stable. It was 989,900 in 1982 and 1,006,300 in 1991.[21] The economy, though sluggish, was not uniformly so. The provincial Gross Domestic Product declined 0.6% in 1987 and 3.2% in 1988 (in constant 1986 dollars), but the annual average increase in GDP from 1982 to 1991 was 2.94% (again, in constant 1986 dollars).[22] The debt cannot be laid at the door of a poor economy.

It was a result of deliberate choices, specifically the campaign promises of 1982 and the undisciplined spending of the 1986 election year.

Privatization and Economic Development

In its first term the Conservative government was low-key on privatization, and its moves in this area were hesitant and tentative. Colin Thatcher, the minister responsible for SaskOil, said that he assumed his "mandate was to whip it into shape and sell it."[23] The government announced in October 1985 that one-third of the company was to be offered to private buyers. The share offering sold out, raising $110 million, 54% of which came from Saskatchewan investors and 46% from out-of-province purchasers.

In 1986, the government sold Papco (Prince Albert Pulp Company) to Weyerhaeuser Corporation of Tacoma, Washington. Weyerhaeuser, one of the largest forest products companies in the United States, obtained the Prince Albert pulp mill, a chemical plant in Saskatoon, and a sawmill in Big River for no cash down. The purchase price of $236 million was paid with money the company borrowed from the government of Saskatchewan in the form of a 30-year debenture at 8.5%. Weyerhaeuser did not have to make any loan payments except in years when it made profits on the mill exceeding 12%. Any losses on the project from 1986 to 1989 up to the amount of $73 million could be deducted from the purchase price. Weyerhaeuser also obtained exclusive control over an estimated seven million acres of northern forest and a government promise to build 32 kilometres of forest roads per year for the company's use. In exchange, Weyerhaeuser promised to upgrade the pulp mill and build a $250 million paper mill in Prince Albert, which would provide 215 new full-time jobs.

Neither the SaskOil share offering nor the Papco sale was a true test of the government's commitment to privatization. In the former case, the government retained a controlling interest, and in the latter, even the NDP had tried to find a Canadian buyer for the struggling pulp mill. Finance minister Bob Andrew declared in 1985 that "privatization is yesterday's theory … it doesn't make sense for one government to build these things and for the next one to come and sell it off."[24] In the second term there was a major shift, and privatization moved to the top of the government's agenda.

The PCs drew inspiration and borrowed expertise from Margaret Thatcher's Conservative government, which was engaged in dismantling the legacy of socialism in Great Britain. By 1989, Thatcher had sold off public assets worth $44 billion, including such companies as British Telecom, British Gas, and British Airways. In carrying out these sales, British Conservatives developed a philosophy and methodology of privatization. Books were written discussing the basic principles, and techniques were devised to implement the policy with a minimum of fuss and resistance. Articulate British experts like Madsen Pirie, the head of the Adam Smith Institute in London, and Oliver Letwin, director of the International Privatization Unit for N.M. Rothschild and Sons Ltd., began showing up in Saskatchewan. Early in 1987, dozens of photocopies of an essay by Pirie entitled "The Buying out of Socialism" circulated through the provincial civil service, and there was a special screening of a three-hour British television documentary, *The Death of Socialism*, for the PC caucus.

Devine publicly embraced privatization at the Saskatchewan PC convention in November 1987, when he announced that all Crown corporations except the utilities were for sale. An important step in carrying out the program was the establishment of the Department of Public Participation. The choice of name signified the government's view that selling Crown corporations to private shareholders gave the "public" the opportunity to assume ownership. By this logic, when the government owned a company, it was not publicly owned.

The Devine government presented privatization as a kind of crusade. What was at stake was nothing less than a social revolution and the creation of an "entrepreneurial culture." According to the British privatizers, Britons had to be weaned off socialism if they were to be competitive in the global economy. The privatization project in Saskatchewan aimed at a cultural revolution of similar scope and nature. The concept of Crown corporations taking a leading role in the economic development of the province was to be replaced by a vision of progress based on individual initiative and private enterprise. It was the death of socialism and Grant Devine was the dragon slayer. At the heart of privatization, said Graham Taylor, the minister of Public Participation, was the need "to change the thinking of Saskatchewan people."[25] Business columnist Paul Martin promoted Devine as "the new Tommy Douglas."[26] Just as Douglas steered the province in a new direction with the adoption of public enterprise, Devine was changing course 180° in a move of equal historic significance.

The Crown corporations up for sale included SaskMinerals, the Saskatchewan Mining Development Corporation (SMDC), the remainder of SaskOil, the general insurance side of SGI, the Saskatchewan Computer Utility Corporation, parts of SaskTel, the natural gas division of SaskPower, Saskatchewan Government Printing, Saskatchewan Forest Products, and the Potash Corporation of Saskatchewan. They varied widely in size and significance, the printing company selling for $1.5 million and SMDC for close to $1 billion. There was also some privatization of government services such as highway construction and provincial parks development.

As privatization proceeded apace through 1988 and early 1989, the NDP and the labour unions put up stiff opposition, but the public at large seemed to adopt a "wait and see" attitude. At a Conservative fundraising dinner in April 1988, Oliver Letwin, a British privatization expert in the employ of the Devine government, praised the Saskatchewan privatization program as one of the best-planned schemes he had seen. Letwin said there were two mistakes that could be made in the "privatization game." One was to go too quickly; the other was to suppose that, because things were going slowly, nothing was being done. He thought the pace of privatization in Saskatchewan was "about right."[27]

The largest privatization was that of the Potash Corporation of Saskatchewan. Valued at up to $2 billion, it was a symbol of the NDP's efforts to assert provincial control over basic resource industries and to obtain a larger share of resource revenue. The Devine government in its first term hobbled the corporation to the benefit of the private sector. As Energy and Mines minister Colin Thatcher explained, "We intend to give private potash companies a larger share of the action along with the burden of risk and potential profits from expansion."[28] The most blatant example of this policy was the decision to force PCS to stay in Canpotex, the marketing organization through which Saskatchewan companies sold their potash overseas. Each member of Canpotex had one vote and an equal say in running the organization. The drawback for PCS was that, even though it supplied 60% of the product sold by Canpotex, it was consistently outvoted by a combination of foreign-owned companies. By 1985, the Crown corporation was reduced to working at 50% capacity, while the rest of the industry worked at 70% capacity or more. Its sales relative to capacity were lower than the industry average, and PCS's share of Canpotex volume dropped from 60% to 45%.[29] The Crown corporation sustained a loss of $18 million in 1983 and even more staggering losses in subsequent years. The NDP charged that the government was running PCS into the ground so that the public would not object if it was sold.

Soon after the 1986 election, a new president of PCS was appointed. Chuck Childers was an American and a former vice-president of the International Minerals and Chemical Corporation (IMC), the chief competitor of PCS. The next step was the transfer of $662 million of PCS debt to the Crown Management Board, the holding company for the Crowns. This made the corporation more attractive to potential buyers, who would be able to assume the assets without the liabilities. In April 1989, the government introduced the bill to privatize the corporation. Bill 20 stipulated that a maximum of 45% would be sold to foreign investors, and that foreigners would not be allowed to cast more than 25% of the votes at annual meetings. After 120 hours of debate, the government used closure on August 7, 1989, to force the bill through the House. It was the first time in the history of the province that closure had been invoked.[30] After the bill passed, government members rose and cheered the passing of a major symbol of state ownership.

The action that turned public opinion against privatization was the attempt to sell SaskEnergy, the natural gas division of SaskPower. When Devine initially announced the privatization program, he had specifically exempted utilities. Now the government went back on its word. Roy Romanow, who succeeded Allan Blakeney as NDP leader in November 1987, decided to make a battleground of the SaskEnergy sale. When the bells rang to summon the members for the vote on the first reading of the bill, the NDP MLAs walked out in protest. Saskatchewan was one of only two provinces, the other being Ontario, where the government was not able to force a vote with the opposition absent. The bells kept ringing, and legislative proceedings ground to a halt. It was a calculated gamble for the NDP to dramatize its opposition in this way, because there was a chance that the public might see their boycott as irresponsible and undemocratic. The Conservatives declared that they had been elected to govern and that the NDP had no right to shut down the Legislature.

The public sided with the NDP. Within a matter of weeks 100,000 people had signed a petition demanding that the government back off from the sale of the gas utility. Romanow addressed huge, emotional rallies in Prince Albert, Yorkton, Saskatoon and Regina. The anger in the crowds was palpable, and the NDP leader was interrupted repeatedly by ovations and shouts of "Ring those bells," and "Let's fight back." An Angus Reid poll showed that 67% of the people were opposed to the privatization of SaskEnergy by means of a public share offering, 22% approved, and 10% had no opinion. What is more, 58% said they were generally opposed to the Devine government's privatization measures. Devine shrugged off the poll: "I'm not going to be intimidated by somebody running around and asking the wrong questions."[31] The NDP boycott of the Legislature stretched to 17 calendar days, setting a new parliamentary record in Canada. Finally, the opposition returned to the Legislature with the understanding that the privatization bill would die on the order paper. The government had blinked; it now said that the sale of SaskEnergy would not occur until the people were ready for it.

The privatization revolution was supposed to mean the triumph of the free market and the birth of entrepreneurial culture, but the revolution was not complete. It was easier to declare the province open for business than to conjure businesses into existence. As it turned out, privatization did not mean the end of government intervention and participation in the economy. The Devine government found it expedient to give grants, loans, subsidies, and guarantees to private business. In Saskatchewan, it seemed it was necessary for the state to prop up free enterprise.

A case in point was Char Inc., which was set up to manufacture barbecue briquettes in Estevan. The entrepreneur received a $220,000 loan from the Saskatchewan Economic Development Corporation (SEDCO), $145,000 from the provincial government and $182,413 from the federal Department of Regional Economic Expansion. The business closed after three weeks and laid off all but three employees, who remained to make kitty litter. Supercart International, a Regina manufacturer of shopping carts, received $366,000 from the federal government, $250,000 from the provincial government, $400,000 from SEDCO, $65,000 from the city of Regina, and $1 million through the provincial Venture Capital Corporation (VCC) scheme. The latter was created by the government in March 1984 as a vehicle for funneling risk capital to businesses. Individuals could claim a 30% provincial tax credit on investments of up to $10,000 in an approved VCC. Despite generous government assistance, Supercart folded without having produced any shopping carts, other than a few prototypes.

GigaText was the most notorious of the entrepreneurial misadventures supported by the Devine government. Businessman Guy Monpetit claimed that his company had the computer technology to translate English text into French. For the Saskatchewan government, his appearance on the scene must have seemed providential since the province, prompted by a Supreme Court ruling, had undertaken to translate some of its laws into the second official language. The government invested $4 million in GigaText for 25% of the shares. GigaText used the money to purchase 20 computers from another Montpetit-owned company, Lisp, which in turn had obtained the computers from GigaMos Systems Inc., yet another Montpetit company. GigaMos had obtained the computers from a bankrupt U.S. computer company a few months earlier. They were part of the U.S. company's inventory, and, according to an independent court-appointed auditor, had a value of $39,000.[32] However, GigaMoss billed Lisp $1.5 million for the computers, which GigaText then bought for $2.9 million.

The government noticed in the fall of 1988 that not all was well with its GigaText investment. Five months had passed since the start-up of the company, $4 million had been spent, but no laws had been translated. The government loaned another $1.25 million to keep the company afloat while it struggled to make the technology work. The media was called in to observe the GigaText computer translate a 21-word sentence, but, when the reporters asked to submit a sentence of their own, they were refused. Finally, in mid-November 1989, the government, having invested another $75,000 in addition to the $5.25 million it had previously doled out, closed down the company.

Other projects were more successful. The government went out of its way to subsidize the construction of heavy oil upgraders. Prior to the Conservatives' taking power, SaskOil had joined an upgrader consortium consisting of Husky Oil, Gulf Resources Canada, Shell and Petro-Canada, but the consortium disintegrated in September 1982. After being frustrated by the unwillingness of the multinationals to negotiate seriously about the project, the Devine government began to look for another partner. It found one in Federated Co-operatives Ltd., owner of Consumers' Co-operative Refinery Limited in Regina. The talks involving Federated Co-op, the federal government, and the provincial government were prolonged and difficult. In the end, it was decided to proceed with an upgrader attached to the Co-op refinery at an estimated construction cost of $700 million. The Saskatchewan government agreed to put up 15% of the equity, while CCRL contributed 5%. The remaining 80% of the financing was raised through loans that were guaranteed by the provincial and federal governments. CCRL's equity payment was subsequently deferred until the money could be obtained from future earnings. The upgrader, formally known as NewGrade Energy Inc., but colloquially as the Co-op Upgrader, was 50% owned by the Government of Saskatchewan and 50% owned by Federated Co-op, even though the development money came directly from the provincial government or in the form of government-guaranteed loans.[33] The NDP government elected in 1991 renegotiated the deal, and the upgrader became a going concern. Just weeks before the 1988 federal election, Ottawa and the provincial government reached an agreement with Husky Oil to secure the construction of a second upgrader. Located near Lloydminster, it struggled in the early years, but eventually turned a profit.

The Devine government offered Edmonton businessman Peter Pocklington $22 million in loans and grants on the condition that he invest $15 million of his own money to build three pork-processing plants. Gainers, the meat-packing company that Pocklington controlled, built the first stage, a $7 million bacon-processing plant in North Battleford, using government grants and low-cost loans. The city of North Battleford also paid a $3,500 subsidy for every job created provided the job lasted at least three years. The second and third plants, which were to have involved investment by Pocklington, were later cancelled because of "adverse market conditions." Blakeney taunted Devine for giving grants to a self-proclaimed free enterpriser. "How did you manage to get him to take all those tax dollars?" he asked. Devine replied, "I couldn't find a socialist to invest in Saskatchewan."[34]

The megaproject of the 1980s was the construction by SaskPower of the Shand generating station and the Rafferty-Alameda dams, located in Devine's Estevan constituency and the adjoining Souris-Cannington constituency of Deputy Premier Eric Berntson. The Rafferty Dam was built across the Souris River and the Alameda across Moose Mountain Creek, a tributary of the Souris. Their purpose was to provide flood control, water for irrigation, recreation, and cooling the turbines of the power plant. Environmentalists argued that the project would do serious harm to the wildlife habitat of the region and that the reservoir could be filled only by diverting water from the South Saskatchewan River. Opponents organized under the acronym SCRAP (Stop Construction of the Rafferty-Alameda Project), while supporters rallied behind the Souris Basin Support Association.

In June 1988, the federal Department of the Environment issued a license for the dams, but in November, the Canadian Wildlife Federation took legal action against Ottawa for failing to conduct a proper environmental assessment in accordance with the terms of the Canadian Environment Protection Act. The Federal Court of Canada in April 1989 suspended the federal license for the project. Berntson told an angry crowd in Estevan that the province was appealing the ruling and that the federal review was a waste of money.[35] The federal government tried to stop construction by securing an injunction, but was denied by the courts, because Crown corporations, in this case SaskPower, were not subject to injunctions. The legal battle was somewhat farcical and the environmental review process in disarray, since the dams were completed while the arguments dragged on. The dams eventually held two narrow lakes, stretching over 80 kilometres and reaching a maximum depth of 35 metres. Golf courses and resort areas sprang up along the reservoir banks, and the Souris River, which had been notorious for its erratic floods, became a steady stream, averaging a few metres wide and one or two metres deep.[36]

The Conservatives' economic development strategy was hampered by a generally poor economic environment. In spite of Devine's statement in 1982 that Saskatchewan had "decided not to participate in the recession," the reality was different.[37] Saskatchewan has an open, vulnerable economy. Exports to the rest of Canada and other countries accounted in the 1980s for approximately 40% of Saskatchewan's Gross Domestic Product.[38] When the prices of potash, uranium or oil slumped, there was little the province could do about it. Devine admitted as much when he said in March 1983: "We do not set the economic rules in isolation. We cannot legislate prosperity. We, as traders, must respond to economic times, and respond we will."[39] Part of the response was to sell Crown corporations to private shareholders and to assist private companies with government funds. The result was something less than the booming, free-enterprise economy to which the Devine government aspired.

Agriculture

Agriculture was a major problem area, particularly the grains and oilseeds sector. The difficulties were deep-rooted and the result of long-term trends. Huge farm subsidies by the European Economic Community and the United States created a major oversupply of grains, which depressed real prices for grain below the levels received by farmers in the 1930s. Low prices, increasing debt loads, high interest rates, escalating input costs, and poor weather conditions combined to force farmers off the land. The crisis in agriculture went beyond immediate market conditions. It reflected the fact that for several decades, farms in Saskatchewan had been increasing in size and becoming more capital intensive due to changes in technology. From 1931 to 1981 the number of Saskatchewan farms declined from 136,472 to 67,318, and the average farm size increased from 408 acres to 943 acres. This trend continued in the 1980s when the number of farms fell to 63,431 in 1986 and about 60,000 in 1990.

The decrease in the number of farms had spin-off effects for the entire infrastructure of rural life. A study prepared by the Christian Farm Crisis Action Committee in 1988 described the social and economic impact that the loss of 15 farm families had on a small town. It was estimated that there was a reduction of expenditure dollars to local businesses of $770,000. Assuming the 15 families were made up of 62 people, 32 of whom were school-age children, two teaching positions were phased out, with a resulting payroll reduction of $60,000. The combined drop in sales from the displaced farmers and teachers led to the closing down of at least one retail store, causing yet another two families to leave. The tax base of the community shrank by about $20,000, and the demand for health, social, recreational and other services declined. The people who remained found it increasingly difficult to maintain the community-oriented volunteer organizations that were so much a part of the quality of life in rural towns.[40] It was a bleak scenario, one that was confirmed by a University of Saskatchewan study in 1991, which predicted a "rural 7-Eleven" future for 90% of the province's 598 towns and villages.[41]

The Devine government made a strong commitment to the family farm and to rural Saskatchewan. He himself operated a farm and seemed thoroughly supportive of the values and culture of rural life. Moreover, a focus on the farm made good political sense. The outcome of the 1986 election showed that the NDP owned the cities, and the Tories ruled the country. The basic strategy of the Devine government in the face of the agricultural crisis was to give financial assistance, mostly in the form of low-interest loans, and to pry out of the federal government as much as possible in deficiency and drought-relief payments.

The 1982 election had prompted the 8% farm purchase loan program. It was followed in the 1986 election by the offer to all farmers of a $25 per acre production loan at 6% on a no-questions-asked basis. Neither financial need nor the ability to repay had to be demonstrated, and no collateral or security was required. Wealthy farmers could take the loan and simply deposit the money in a bank account bearing a higher interest rate, making a tidy profit at the government's expense. In addition, hog producers received a cash advance of $25 per hog, and those in the livestock business obtained livestock facilities tax credits worth a total of $1.75 million per year. In the 1990 provincial budget, in the run up to yet another election, farmers were offered operating loans of up to $12.50 per acre at a subsidized interest rate of 10.75%.

The 1990 loan program was not as generous as its 1986 counterpart, reflecting the weakened financial condition of the province by that time. Spending on agricultural and rural programs increased from $120 million in 1981–82 to a peak of $398 million in 1986–87, or in proportional terms from 4.97% of the total provincial budget in 1981–82 to 9.88% in 1986–87. After the 1986 election, spending on agriculture fell in both dollars and budget share. It was $320 million in 1990–91, which represented 6.89% of the budget. Even farmers had to bear some of the cost of restraining the deficit.[42] Meanwhile, the total debt carried by farmers increased from $4.435 billion in 1983 to $5.78 billion in 1987.[43]

The Saskatchewan government did not deal with root causes of the agricultural crisis, which were beyond its legislative and fiscal capacity. It could not compete with the treasuries of the United States and the EEC in the subsidy wars. It gave farmers as much short-term financial assistance as it could afford, possibly more than it could afford. Some of the programs, especially the 6% production loans of 1986, were poorly designed and ill-focussed, but the government was able to convey to farmers that it cared about their plight and was doing its best to come to their aid. The solutions were band-aid, but they were better than no solutions at all. In 1990, the federal government outlined two new support packages, the Gross Revenue Insurance Plan (GRIP), which guaranteed a minimum income to farmers, and the Net Income Stabilization Account (NISA), which assisted farmers if their incomes fell below a certain amount. The plans, though better than pure ad hockery, were not enough to stabilize prairie agriculture.

Social Policy

In the realm of social policy, the Devine government introduced welfare reform to encourage welfare recipients to move off social assistance rolls and into the workforce. The goals were to reduce welfare expenditures, eliminate fraud and abuse, and promote self-sufficiency. Single, employable people were required to participate in short-term, low-wage jobs offered through the Saskatchewan Employment Development Program (SEDP) or New Careers Corporation (NCC), and in upgrading and skills courses through the Saskatchewan Skills Development Program (SSDP). Their social assistance benefits were cut by 35% to induce them to accept workfare employment. The $9 million saved thereby was used to pay for short-term job programs and wage subsidies to business.[44] The majority of the jobs subsidized through welfare reform lasted only 20 to 26 weeks, just long enough for social assistance recipients to qualify for unemployment insurance. In this way, financial responsibility was shifted to the federal government, which bore 90% of the cost of unemployment insurance and only 50% of the cost of social assistance.

Five years after welfare reform was introduced in 1984, the social assistance case load remained 27% higher than when the Devine government came into office in 1982. This reflected the poor state of the economy and suggested that it was not easy to move social assistance recipients off welfare when permanent jobs were not available. Nevertheless, there was a decrease of 1,678 social assistance cases between 1985 and 1988. The decline was in all probability the result of more stringent eligibility requirements. The government sought to reintroduce the distinction between the deserving and undeserving poor and to use the welfare system as an instrument of moral reformation and character development.[45] The fully employable were denied benefits if they failed to conduct an "adequate" job search, if they dropped out of an approved training course, or if they quit or were fired from a job. The Department of Social Services sought to ensure that any money received by an applicant in the two-year period prior to an application for social assistance had been disposed of in an approved manner. If it had not, assistance could be withheld. The Department also took pains to establish whether or not a recipient was living in a common-law relationship. If so, it was expected that the alleged common-law spouse would help support the family.[46]

The Devine government operated on the assumption that welfare abuse was rampant. Welfare recipients classified as employable were obliged to pick up their cheques in person at designated times, rather than having the cheques mailed to them. Being late for the appointment, failing to pick up the cheque, or having identification with a different address from that in the case file could lead to loss of eligibility for assistance. By August 1989, 2,910 people were cut off for failing to collect their cheques at the proper time. Of these, 1,160 were reinstated after explaining why they had missed the appointment. The remaining 1,750 were permanently struck from the rolls. To weed out cases of fraud, the Department of Social Services established a new unit called the Special Investigations Branch (nicknamed the "Fraud Squad"). It was composed of former RCMP officers who brought their investigative techniques to bear on suspected welfare cheaters.

Welfare reform was implemented in the context of a general reduction in social assistance benefits. By 1988, the real purchasing power of the entitlement for a single fully employable person had fallen to $207 in constant 1981 dollars, or by 64.4%. For a single mother and her two children, it had dropped by 28.8% and for the husband/wife family by 27.7% (both in constant 1981 dollars).[47] In 1984, the maximum rental allowance for single, fully employable persons was cut from $300 to $200 per month. Since actual costs were invariably higher, the difference had to be taken out of the allowance for food and other necessities. The first food bank in the province appeared in Regina in 1983, with others being established in Saskatoon and Prince Albert the following year. Between 1983 and 1988, food bank usage increased by 70% in Regina, 165% in Saskatoon, and 89% in Prince Albert.[48] Food banks were not confined to the larger cities; they sprang up also in small towns and rural communities. Most of the clientele were social assistance recipients who ran out of money before the end of the month, and children formed the largest group of beneficiaries.

In many of his speeches, Devine said that his brand of Conservatism was a blend of "compassion" and "competition." He invoked John Diefenbaker as the embodiment of "progressive" Conservatism, and at times suggested that Tommy Douglas was a kindred spirit. The welfare policies of the government bore a closer resemblance to the ideas of the neo-conservative movement and the American new right. Neo-conservatives rejected collectivism, and had little use for the social programs of the welfare state, trade unions, or government-owned companies. They minimized the role of government as an instrument of collective responsibility, cooperation, community interest, or social solidarity.[49] This was the ideological spirit of the Devine government's welfare reforms.

The same can be said of the government's labour policy. The minister of Labour, Lorne McLaren, was not enamoured of unions. As general manager of Morris Rod Weeder Ltd., a farm implement manufacturing company in Yorkton, he had been party to numerous and prolonged labour disputes. The certification of the union was hotly contested, and six unfair labour practice decisions were issued against the company by the Labour Relations Board. The Devine government wasted no time amending the Trade Union Act. Bill 104, introduced in June 1983, contained 17 amendments to the existing legislation, none of them favorable to labour. The Labour Relations Board was given discretionary authority to exclude employees from the bargaining unit, making it easier for management to increase the number of out-of-scope workers.[50] Another amendment took away the power of a union to discipline members for crossing a picket line during a strike, as long as the member paid dues.

The core of Bill 104 was a series of measures to make union organizing and certification more difficult. A clause specified that where an application for certification had been dismissed, another application could not be made for six months. The bill also featured a "freedom of speech" amendment which gave employers the right to communicate with their employees during a union organizing drive, provided their anti-union message was presented in a manner that did not involve intimidation, threat, or coercion. The unions' biggest concerns centred around the "30-day rule," which had been introduced by the Ross Thatcher government in the 1960s and repealed by the NDP in 1971. Reinstituted by Bill 104, it empowered the Labour Relations Board to order a vote on the employer's last offer once a strike had gone on for 30 days. Many felt this would encourage employers to refuse negotiations in an attempt to force a vote, while they tried in the interim to convince part of the work force to accept the deal. The clause was seen as interfering with the practice of good-faith bargaining.

The changes in labour relations pertained not only to the contents of the Trade Union Act, but also to administrative practices. The Labour Relations Board made a number of innovative rulings that had the effect of weakening the rights of unions. A clause in the Trade Union Act specified that where a collective agreement had expired, it was illegal for an employer unilaterally to change rates of pay, hours of work, or other conditions of employment "without bargaining collectively respecting the changes with the trade union representing the majority of employees in the appropriate unit."[51] For 20 years this had been taken to mean that these conditions could not be changed by the employer unless the union agreed. The new interpretation advanced by the Board was that employers could unilaterally change the conditions of employment and rates of pay so long as they had bargained collectively in good faith.

The net outcome of the Devine government's labour policy was a decline in the union movement. Whereas in 1981, 32.9% of the nonagricultural labour force was unionized, only 29.2% was unionized in 1989. The number of applications for certification dropped from 183 in 1982–83 to 78 in 1987–88. The construction workers' unions were hit particularly hard. The Devine government repealed the Construction Labour Relations Act (CLRA), which had allowed for industry-wide collective bargaining. Section 17 of the CLRA had prevented unionized contractors and firms from setting up non-union subsidiaries. With its removal, contractors established "spin-off" or "double-breasted" companies, forcing unionized employees either to accept lower wages or face the prospect of being laid off. Before long, virtually every major construction job went to non-union firms, whose bids were as much as a third lower than those of union firms. Union workers stood around in union hiring halls without work or hid their union membership so that they could work on non-union jobs. In 1982, an estimated 70% of the building trades were unionized; by 1989 only 5% were. Tradesmen accepted wages with non-union contractors that were between 20% and 40% less than union rates.

Unorganized workers were also adversely affected. When the Conservatives took office, the minimum wage stood at $4.25 per hour, the highest in Canada. A series of 25¢ per hour increases had been scheduled for six-month intervals. The new government cancelled the planned increases and kept the minimum wage constant except for increases of 25¢ per hour every four years. Between 1982 and 1990, the purchasing power of a worker on minimum wage declined by 28%. The Labour Standards Branch under the Conservatives was far less zealous than it had been under the NDP in following up complaints and resolving them in favour of the workers. In the five-year period from 1983–84 to 1987–88, the number of complaints increased by 37%, while the number of prosecutions decreased by 87%. In 1986, the Branch ceased making routine inspections, and acted only on the basis of complaints. This made it impossible for an investigation to occur without alerting the employer to the fact that an employee had reported the matter, thereby increasing the likelihood of reprisals.

The Devine government inherited a system for enforcing occupational health and safety (OHS) that was widely recognized as offering good protection to workers.[52] The core of the system was the mandatory provision for a joint labour-management OHS committee in every workplace with more than 10 employees. Workers had the right to refuse any job that presented an unusual risk to health or safety and the right to information about potential hazards. The Occupational Health and Safety Branch of the Department of Labour provided educational and technical services to the OHS committees. It conducted inspections, adjudicated cases where the worker had refused to perform a job thought to be unsafe, and prosecuted employers who violated OHS legislation or regulations. Although the Devine government did not change the legislation, it weakened its impact through less diligent administration and enforcement. Two years after the Conservatives took office, the number of inspections by the Health and Safety Standards Unit of the OHS Branch declined from 2,629 to 1,864. The number of contacts with workplace committees fell from 1,519 to 847. The government imposed a temporary moratorium on prosecutions that lasted for close to two years. Workplace committees knew that the threat of "calling in an inspector" was a hollow one, and thus the effectiveness of the committees, from the workers' perspective, was greatly diminished.

The Devine Conservatives were hostile to labour unions and sought to curb their power. Union briefs were inevitably labeled "fanciful" or "politically motivated." Upon reading one such brief, Grant Schmidt, who succeeded McLaren as Labour minister, summed up the government's attitude with the comment, "You would think it was written by the opposition."[53] The PCs were of the view that high wages and restrictions on the way employers managed the workplace spoiled the "open for business" atmosphere the government was trying to create. As a result, the government and organized labour were constantly at loggerheads, a situation, ironically, not conducive to attracting new investment to the province.

Health is a highly politicized issue in Saskatchewan, given the province's history as the birthplace of hospital insurance and medicare. The NDP defeated the PCs in 1978 partly by raising the fear that the Conservatives had a secret agenda to undermine the health care system. The Devine government was intent upon demonstrating that such insinuations were totally unfounded. In 1983 it introduced a health budget of close to $1 billion, which represented a $250 million increase from the previous year. Transfers of programs to the Department of Health that had previously been housed in other government departments accounted for 70% of the increase. Grants for special care facilities (approximately $148 million) and home care services ($18 million) were taken from Department of Social Services budget and moved to Health. Another $3.5 million was transferred from the Department of Northern Saskatchewan. As for real increases in spending, much of it was dedicated to hospital construction and upgrading, which consumed 25% of the overall growth in the budget. Expenditures for staff and equipment lagged behind, leading to a deterioration of health services, including bed closures and long waiting lists for surgery. For example, the waiting list at St. Paul's Hospital in Saskatoon grew from 1,200 in 1982 to 2,000 in 1986.[54]

After the 1986 election and the ensuing budget crisis, the government abolished or severely curtailed a number of programs. The Saskatchewan Dental Plan, which had been established in 1974, provided free dental health education, preventive services, and treatment to 144,000 Saskatchewan children aged 4 to 16 in 578 school dental clinics scattered across the province. The program ensured that all children had their teeth looked after, regardless of socio-economic status or the level of supervision given by parents. The Devine government did away with the plan, firing 111 dental therapists, 148 dental assistants, 7 equipment technicians, and 16 clerical and administrative staff. Children between the ages of 5 and 13 could still receive free dental care, if their parents took them to a dentist, but adolescents aged 14 to 16 were no longer covered.

Under the Prescription Drug Plan introduced by the Blakeney government in 1975, Saskatchewan residents received prescribed drugs at no cost except for a $3.95 processing fee paid to the pharmacist for each prescription. In 1987, the government imposed a deductible of $125 per year for single people and families, $75 per year for families with one senior citizen, and $50 per year for single seniors. After the patient had paid the full cost of drugs up to the level of the deductible in a given year, he or she could apply to the government for reimbursement of 80% of the cost of any additional prescriptions. Although the changes to the drug and dental plans attracted the most publicity, there were other cutbacks, too. In 1987, $1 million was removed from the mental health services budget, over $550,000 from the Saskatchewan Hearing Aid Plan, and close to $200,000 from the community services budget. There was also a 66% increase in user fees for home care services and a freeze in hospital operating budgets for two years.

Relative to other departments, however, the health budget continued to receive high priority. In 1989 it reached a record high $1.37 billion with money targeted for 370 new nursing positions, hospital renovations, increased surgical capacities, a breast cancer screening project and a program to fight drug and alcohol abuse. The construction of hospitals, especially in rural areas where the PCs had their core political support, took precedence over allocations for operating expenses. The average annual increase for hospital capital costs from 1982 to 1988 was 37%; for operating costs, only 5%. In one year alone (it happened to be an election year), the capital budget for hospitals increased over 100%.[55] The imbalance between capital and operating funds led to chronic understaffing, increased workloads and a greater reliance on part-time staff. Under Devine, the health budget soared, but the allocation of spending was not guided by a well thought-out plan to make the system more efficient.

The National Scene

As a provincial Premier participating in discussions at the national level, Devine was well known as a staunch supporter of Brian Mulroney. This perception was shared by the other Premiers. At one First Ministers' meeting, Devine was so frustrated that he threw up his arms and said, "Look, you guys, you think I'm calling the PM and reporting to him and

SAB 84-3656-R5-13

Premier Grant Devine and wife Chantal, with Prime Minister Brian Mulroney (left). Devine and Mulroney forged a strong political alliance that proved to be mutually beneficial.

everything. It's not true."⁵⁶ Devine's loyalty to Mulroney was nowhere more evident than in the debate centred on the Meech Lake Accord. The Constitution Act, 1982, patriated the fundamental law of the land, entrenched an amending formula and enshrined the Canadian Charter of Rights and Freedoms, but it had the defect of not having been approved by the National Assembly of Quebec. Although the document was legally binding on all provinces, Quebec's isolation was a source of bitterness and discontent. Whether these feelings would have gradually faded away, we will never know, since Prime Minister Mulroney took it upon himself to reopen the constitutional negotiations. His goal was to secure amendments to the Constitution enabling Quebec to sign it "with honour and enthusiasm."

Quebec presented five minimal conditions: recognition as a "distinct society," more power in the field of immigration, a role in the selection of the three Quebec judges on the Supreme Court of Canada, the right to opt out of federal spending programs in areas of exclusive provincial jurisdiction without suffering fiscal penalty, and a constitutional veto on all matters affecting the province's interests. The conditions were agreed to in the Meech Lake Accord, which was signed by the Prime Minister and all 10 premiers including Grant Devine on June 3, 1987. The Accord extended the powers being granted to Quebec to all the provinces except for the "distinct society" clause, which applied to Quebec alone. From the beginning, no one really understood what the clause meant or how the judges would deal with it.⁵⁷ It was not to be included in the preamble where its weight would be slight, but as the first substantive section, which meant that it would serve as guide for the legal interpretation of the entire Constitution.

According to the amending formula in the Constitution Act, 1982, all 10 provincial Legislatures had to pass the resolution supporting the Meech Lake Accord before it could go into effect. Once it had been passed by one Legislature, the others had to pass it within three years or it would expire. Quebec's National Assembly approved the Accord on June 23, 1987, which started the clock ticking. Saskatchewan was second, passing the resolution on September 23, 1987, by a vote of 43–3. In the three years that followed, the Accord began to unravel. Pierre Trudeau came out of retirement to denounce it as a sellout to Quebec nationalists that would render the federal government "totally impotent" and governed by "political eunuchs."[58] There were fears that the distinct society clause would undermine the Charter of Rights, fears that were fed by Premier Robert Bourassa's use of the override clause in the 1982 Constitution to enforce French-only commercial signs in Quebec. He said that if the Meech Lake Accord had been in force, it would not have been necessary to use the override clause.

Matters came to a head on June 3, 1990, just days before the deadline for all 10 provinces to pass the Accord. The First Ministers gathered in Ottawa for seven days of gruelling negotiations. They stayed behind closed doors, emerging from time to time to give vague pronouncements on how the talks were going. The main gain for Saskatchewan that Devine saw in the Meech Lake Accord was veto power over future constitutional amendments. This would place Saskatchewan on an equal basis with the other provinces. Apart from this item, he was not greatly concerned about the contents of the agreement. His main priority was to get the thing settled, one way or another, so that the country could move on to more important matters. He said that Canadians wanted "to stop bickering and start building."[59]

The hold-out provinces were Manitoba and Newfoundland. Devine traveled to St. John's to make a last-ditch appeal to the members of the Assembly. He frankly admitted that "the constitutional accord and its discussion are not popular in rural Saskatchewan where I get my support," but he said he believed in the measure for the good of the country.[60] In the end, Meech Lake could not be saved. MLA Elijah Harper blocked the Accord in the Manitoba Legislature because it left out Aboriginal rights, and the Newfoundland House of Assembly adjourned without voting on it. Perhaps it was just as well. A poll conducted in April 1990 reported that 59% of Canadians were against the Accord, and 71% wanted a national referendum on it.

The other national issue of great consequence in the 1980s was the Free Trade Agreement (FTA) with the United States. Once again, Devine was firmly in Mulroney's camp and in support of the FTA. The Premier made a series of speeches across the province claiming that free trade would improve access for western Canadian producers to the American market and stimulate the diversification of the western economy. He sent a letter to 60,000 Saskatchewan farmers praising the benefits of the FTA and assuring them that the status of the Canadian Wheat Board would not be affected. The provincial government sponsored a "fact-finding" mission to investigate the "effects of American investment and free trade in Ontario." In a visit to the General Motors plant in Oshawa, Devine stated that GM had invested billions of dollars in Ontario and that "Saskatchewan would like to share in those opportunities."[61]

It was natural for Devine to support the Free Trade Agreement because the whole point of it was to strengthen the role of the market and weaken the role of government in the economy. The FTA restricted the ability of governments to make rules about trade and investment. It stated that American companies operating in Canada had to be given "national treatment," meaning they had to be treated the same way as Canadian companies. Canadian businesses were in a position to demand a "level playing field," that is, similar tax rates, labour laws and social programs to those in the United States or else they would not be able to compete. The underlying ideology of the Free Trade Agreement was pro-market and neo-conservative and, therefore, completely in line with Devine's economic and political philosophy.

At the same time, the fight for the FTA confirmed and strengthened the Devine/Mulroney alliance. Devine departed from the old rule of Saskatchewan politics, as expressed by former Premier Jimmy Gardiner: "Have a fight with Ottawa at election time."[62] Saskatchewan's economic vulnerability in the 1980s and its need for federal aid changed the rules of the game. Mulroney gave major pay-outs to hard-pressed farmers during the 1986 provincial election and the 1988 federal election, and Devine gave loyal support to the Meech Lake Accord and the FTA. It was not exactly a *quid pro quo*, because the two leaders shared the same ideological outlook and agreed on most major issues anyway. The happy coincidence of interest worked out well for both parties, but especially for Devine and Saskatchewan farmers.

Aboriginal Policy

Another major issue of federal-provincial negotiations was Aboriginal policy. The Constitution Act recognized existing Aboriginal and treaty rights, but it did not define what those rights were. In particular, it offered no definition of the Aboriginal right to self-government. The Act stipulated that within a year of the new Constitution coming into effect the Prime Minister was to convene a First Ministers conference to discuss the matter. Besides the provincial Premiers, the representatives of Aboriginal peoples were to be invited. The conference took place in March 1983. Although progress was made in some areas, notably the guarantee of equality of Aboriginal and treaty rights to male and female persons, agreement was not achieved on self-government. More conferences were held in 1984, 1985 and 1987, but there was still no settlement. The federal government and many of the provinces, Saskatchewan included, were fearful of placing such an abstract right in the Constitution subject to the "vagaries of judicial interpretation."[63] Aboriginal leaders asserted that they had the right to self-government before Europeans arrived and had never relinquished it. Devine staked out the position that preoccupation with the Constitution resulted in failure to address what he considered more pressing issues: "economic development, education and training, federal fiscal responsibility for treaty Indians, to name a few."[64]

Although self-government stalled, progress was made in the area of treaty land entitlements. This was an old issue stemming from the late 19th and early 20th century treaties that provided for the surrender of Aboriginal title in Saskatchewan in return for reserves, guaranteed hunting and fishing rights, annual payments, education, health care, and certain other programs.[65] The treaties stated that one square mile would be set aside for each family of five, that is, 128 acres per capita. Some of the land was duly provided, but not enough to satisfy the total entitlement. The federal government retained control of public lands in Saskatchewan until 1930, at which time the province assumed jurisdiction. A clause in the transfer agreement protected Indian rights with respect to treaty land entitlements. This is how the provincial government became involved in what was essentially a federal matter, since the treaties were signed with the federal government in the name of the Crown. The Blakeney government arrived at a formula for the settlement of the outstanding entitlements (the "Saskatchewan formula"), but regrettably agreement was not formally sealed with the federal government.

It remained unfinished business when Devine took over. His government became embroiled in differences of opinion with the federal government as to the formula to be applied. The federal government wanted to calculate the size of the entitlement on the basis of the Indian population at the time of the first survey of the reserve. The Saskatchewan formula proposed the 1976 population as the base line for quantifying the entitlement. The Devine government initiated a "freeze" in order to review its policy. Finally, in September 1991, shortly before the provincial election, a framework agreement was reached involving the government of Canada, the government of Saskatchewan and the Federation of Saskatchewan Indian Nations. The federal and provincial governments promised to pay $431 million to 27 bands over 15 years for the purchase of 1.5 million acres of land.[66] Progress had been made to settle a long-lasting dispute.

Decline and Fall

The year 1989 was a turning point for the Devine Conservatives. The bell-ringing episode related to the attempted privatization of SaskEnergy set the government back on its heels. The NDP jumped to a 20-point lead in the polls, and Devine admitted that he was "a Premier in some trouble." He said that he intended to "get back to the kitchen tables of the province."[67] Political scientist David E. Smith observed, "After the legislative fireworks of 1989, the Devine government adopted a policy of legislative avoidance in 1990." The session lasted 67 days compared with 105 days the previous year, one-half the number of government bills were introduced, and more business was transacted by orders-in-council.[68]

Announcing that the "world ha[d] declared economic war on Saskatchewan," Devine cancelled the gas tax rebate and scaled down the mortgage protection plan. The measures had been key to his election victory in 1982, and now they had to be withdrawn. Soon after, "Consensus Saskatchewan" was launched as an exercise in going back to the people at the grassroots to see what they wanted the government to do. A committee of 100 government-appointed members held 108 meetings in communities across the province. The final report offered 112 recommendations, many of them fairly general and bland, such as: "Every Saskatchewan person must become a salesperson for the province" and "Legislation must be passed which severely restricts the possibility of a deficit."[69]

Eric Berntson, a pillar of the government, resigned in 1990 to accept a position as one of the "GST Senators," appointed by Brian Mulroney when extra votes were needed to push the tax through the Senate. An Angus Reid poll taken in the spring placed the Conservatives in third place at 11%. By September 1990, Devine had ruled out a fall election, warning vaguely that tough decisions lay ahead: "It's almost at the point in public life where you have to do the kinds of things that are right but unpopular and might even get you unelected."[70] Three seats fell vacant, but no by-elections were called.

In February 1991, the Devine government announced its intention to harmonize the provincial sales tax (PST) with the federal GST, thereby extending the coverage of the provincial tax to services as well as goods. Of the projected $161 million in additional revenue from this source, $125 million was to be used to pay for the province's share of farm safety-net programs. It was a move that drove a wedge between urban and rural Saskatchewan. The government also announced "Fair Share Saskatchewan," a plan to transfer 1,500 public service jobs out of Regina to small towns around the province. The Liquor Board employees were to go to Hudson Bay, six minority language officers to Gravelbourg, the Department of Agriculture to Humboldt, and so on. The political strategy behind the plan seemed obvious. Regina was solid NDP territory, the public sector unions were unfriendly to the PCs, and rural Saskatchewan was their main hope. But the political motivation was a little too obvious. The Saskatchewan Wheat Pool president protested that "people [were] being used as pawns," and even the Association of Saskatchewan Taxpayers, a low-tax, pro-business organization, could find no financial justification for the large-scale relocation of civil servants. The Conservative House Leader, Grant Hodgins, resigned from Cabinet on June 17, 1991, saying that Fair Share Saskatchewan represented "politics to a degree … that I find personally unacceptable."[71]

The next day, to everyone's complete surprise, Devine asked Lieutenant-Governor Sylvia Fedoruk to prorogue the Legislature. The Premier defended the decision saying that it gave people an opportunity "to … take a bit of a break, let people relax."[72] The 1991–92 budget had not been passed, and the government had to operate on special warrants requested on a monthly basis from the lieutenant-governor. Although the NDP called the use of warrants under these circumstances "illegal and unconstitutional," the case was not tested in court. An Angus Reid poll in June gave the NDP a 44% lead over the Conservatives and named Devine the least-favoured candidate for Premier, trailing both Roy Romanow and Lynda Haverstock, the new Liberal leader.

The voters went to the polls on October 21, 1991, five years and one day after the last provincial election. The government was so unpopular that the NDP did not have to offer much by way of a platform. Romanow promised to repeal the PST, abolish the flat tax, halt Fair Share, restore social programs and review all privatizations. The PCs lured Crown Life Insurance Company (and up to 1,200 jobs) from Toronto to Regina with a $250 million loan guarantee, but it was too late. The voters had made up their minds. The NDP won a majority of the popular vote and 55 seats; the Conservatives had 25% and 10 seats, the Liberals, 24% and 1 seat.

After the election, Grant Devine continued to sit as the MLA for Estevan. He stepped down as leader of the Conservative Party in 1992, and did not run in the 1995 provincial election. In 1997, four Liberal MLAs and four Conservative MLAs came together to form the Saskatchewan Party, led by former Reform Party member of Parliament, Elwin Hermanson. Later that year, the Saskatchewan Conservative Party was "put to sleep" for 10 years, after which time a decision was to be taken whether to revive it or not.

On June 9, 1992, an official with the Canadian Imperial Bank of Commerce in Regina reported to the police that a pile of $1,000 bills had been discovered in a safety deposit box. The bank was in the process of closing its Cornwall Centre branch and had mailed letters to its customers informing them of the fact. A series of letters was sent to Fred

Peters, the holder of a safety deposit box, who had given his address as room 201 at the Legislative Building, where the office of the Conservative caucus was located. When the sealed letters were returned, the safety deposit box was opened, revealing $150,000 in $1,000 bills. Another safety deposit box rented by Peters at the bank's main branch was found to contain $90,000 in $1,000 bills—a total of $240,000. The RCMP was eventually able to establish that Fred Peters was a pseudonym for John Scraba, the PC caucus communications director.

Through diligent police work, the story was slowly pieced together. Irregularities had occurred in the use of Conservative MLAs' communication allowances. Each MLA was entitled to an allowance to pay for expenses related to keeping in touch with constituents. On average it was about $13,000 a year. If the MLA did not spend the entire allowance, unspent funds could not be carried over from one year to the next. The MLA's handbook specified that acceptable expenditures included postage, greeting cards, newsletters, and items such as pens inscribed with the MLA's name. Material of an overtly partisan nature, such as appeals for donations to a political party, was not allowed. To obtain the money, MLAs filled out Request for Payment forms, accompanied by appropriate receipts, and submitted them to the Legislative Assembly Office (LAO). Alternatively, the MLA could submit a Request for Payment form with an invoice for an eligible expenditure, and the LAO would pay the specified amount to the company named on the invoice.[73]

A number of Conservative MLAs decided in the spring of 1987 to designate a portion of their individual communications allowances to a central fund to be used for government advertising of a generic nature. Communications director John Scraba was placed in charge of the operation. The individual MLAs signed Request for Payment forms and Scraba supplied the accompanying invoice for the work that was supposedly being done. The invoices were for communications services, such as newsletters and video presentations, supplied by three companies: Airwaves Advertising, Images Consulting, and Communications Group Advertising. These were numbered companies (582806, 582807, and 582808 respectively) that Scraba had set up.[74] All had the same mailing address, and none of them was listed in the telephone directory.

Although the invoices were bogus, the money was paid by the LAO to the numbered companies, a total of $837,000 from 1987 to 1991. Scraba transferred funds from the numbered companies' accounts to the PC caucus account. Cash was then paid out from the caucus account for various and sundry purposes, including the placing of $240,000 in safety deposit boxes. Money was also paid out in cash to Conservative MLAs or used for expenditures, such as the purchase of computers, that were not allowed under communications allowance regulations.[75]

Devine said the police investigation was a witch hunt driven by politics and that bookkeeping errors were being criminalized. In some instances, judges showed leniency when it appeared that those charged were innocent victims of an invoicing system that they had not fully understood. Lorne Kopelchuk, MLA from Canora, was charged with using a false expense claim to draw $1,568 from his communications allowance to purchase a portable, electronic public address system. The actual cost of the system, taxes included, was $1,005.80, the balance being paid to Scraba. The expenditure was allowable under the constituency office and services allowance, but not the communications allowance. The judge acquitted Kopelchuk, saying that it was reasonable for him to have trusted Scraba and that there was no evidence that Kopelchuk knew about the misleading invoice.[76]

In other cases, the courts were more severe. Caucus chairman Lorne McLaren pleaded guilty to diverting $125,000 from the PC caucus account to the PC Party of Saskatchewan and appropriating $114,200 for his own use. Senator Eric Berntson was found guilty of making false claims on his constituency office and secretarial allowances, but was acquitted on a charge of breach of trust in the diversion of $125,000 to the PC Party.[77] The Supreme Court of Canada upheld the conviction, with the result that Berntson had to resign his Senate seat. Altogether, 12 Conservative MLAs and two caucus employees (including Scraba) were found guilty on various fraud charges.

The scandal tarnished the reputation of the PC government and has tinged assessments of the Devine years. At a more fundamental and ideological level, Devine will be remembered for his attempt to steer Saskatchewan away from CCF-NDP "socialism." Since World War II, with the possible exception of the Ross Thatcher premiership from 1964 to 1971, social democratic ideas and approaches ruled the province. It was taken for granted that government had a large role to play in the economy as "capitalist of last resort." Crown corporations were accepted as normal instruments of economic diversification and a means for Saskatchewan people to achieve a degree of control over an economy that was mainly dominated by outside forces. Along with Crown corporations, the CCF-NDP built the welfare state comprising medicare, social welfare programs and recognition of collective bargaining rights for labour unions. All of this implied a balancing of collective rights and responsibilities with individual rights and responsibilities.

When Devine was elected, he promised "there is so much more we can be." He believed that excessive collectivism and too large a role for government were holding Saskatchewan back, preventing the province from realizing its true potential. He wanted to roll back government and let private enterprise flourish. To some extent, he succeeded. Over the course of his nine-year premiership, billions of dollars of public assets were privatized, including such major Crown corporations as the Potash Corporation of Saskatchewan and the Saskatchewan Mining Development Corporation. Social welfare spending was cut and labour union rights pulled back. Nonetheless, private enterprise continued to rely heavily on government support. The major projects of the Devine years— the oil upgraders, fertilizer plant, paper mill, meat-processing plant—all required substantial government financing. The real debate between Devine and the NDP was not over *whether* government should be involved in the economy but *how and on what terms.*

The greatest failure of the Devine years was the accumulation of an unprecedented and burdensome debt. Ironically, the problem began on the day the Devine government was sworn into office when the gasoline tax was eliminated. The error was compounded in excessive spending during the 1986 election. The government created a debt monster in its first term and spent the entire second term struggling unsuccessfully to come to terms with it. Although the government cut programs and spending, the debt kept getting larger because of the need to borrow more to pay the interest on the previously incurred debt. It was almost as though the Devine Conservatives made a Faustian bargain. To win power, they made what proved to be financially unsustainable promises, and, in the end, those promises came back to haunt them.

At the same time, Devine deserves credit for never failing to project optimism and faith in the future of Saskatchewan, maintaining that

> The people of Saskatchewan dream of the future. They know that this is a very powerful province. They believe, as we do, that this province can not only be a Canadian leader, but a world leader. We have been blessed with natural resources unmatched anywhere in this planet, and with a very strong-willed people. We now have over one million citizens that are capable of reaching for the stars, of making Saskatchewan a magical place to be envied world-wide. They just require the tools, and the opportunities to succeed.[78]

A story is told of a servant who fell out of favour with the king and was sentenced to death. He pleaded for his life, promising that if he were given one more year to live, he would teach the king's horse how to talk. The king relented and gave the servant a year's reprieve. A friend of the servant admonished him, "How can you promise that? You know you can't teach a horse to talk." The servant replied, "In a year, the king may be dead, or I may be dead, or the horse may be dead, or maybe the horse will talk." Saskatchewan's predicament is much like that of the servant in the story. Subject to the vagaries of a harsh climate and at the mercy of the whims of the international market place, it needs to have a certain amount of exuberant optimism. You never know—maybe the horse will talk, but if it does, the consequences are onerous for all concerned.

Notes

1. Peter Jenkins, *Mrs. Thatcher's Revolution: The Ending of the Socialist Era* (Cambridge, MA: Harvard University Press, 1988), 3.
2. Legislative Assembly of Saskatchewan, *Debates*, Grant Devine, June 23, 1982, 201.
3. Dale Eisler, Regina *Leader-Post*, November 16, 1987.
4. Donald Grant Devine, "An Examination of the Effects of Publishing Comparative Price Information on Price Dispersion and Consumer Satisfaction" (PhD dissertation, Ohio State University, 1976), 143–44.
5. Colin Thatcher, *Backrooms: A Story of Politics* (Saskatoon: Western Producer Prairie Books, 1985), 91.
6. James Pitsula and Ken Rasmussen, *Privatizing a Province: The New Right in Saskatchewan* (Vancouver: New Star Books, 1990), 31.
7. *Leader-Post*, April 24, 1982, April 20, 1982, cited in Pitsula and Rasmussen, *Privatizing a Province*.
8. Legislative Assembly of Saskatchewan, *Debates*, Grant Devine, March 27, 1984, 918.
9. Dale Eisler, *Leader-Post*, March 3, 1988; Susan Swedburg-Kohli, "Devine Shows Tougher Side," *Saskatchewan Report* (May 1988).
10. Legislative Assembly of Saskatchewan, *Debates*, Grant Devine, March 28, 1983, 343.
11. James M. Pitsula, "The Social and Economic Impact of Crown Corporations," in John R. Allan (ed.), *Public Enterprise in an Era of Change* (Regina: Canadian Plains Research Center, 1998), 146.

12. *Financial Post*, January 1, 1983.
13. *Leader-Post*, December 7, 1982.
14. Terry Pugh, "Cultivating the Corporate Agenda," in Lesley Biggs and Mark Stobbe (eds.), *Devine Rule in Saskatchewan: A Decade of Hope and Hardship* (Saskatoon: Fifth House, 1991), 72, 78.
15. Mark Stobbe, "Political Conservatism and Fiscal Irresponsibility," in Biggs and Stobbe, *Devine Rule*, 16.
16. Ibid., 18.
17. J.R. Miller, "Saskatchewan," *Canadian Annual Review of Politics and Public Affairs* (1986), 323.
18. Mark Stobbe, "Political Conservatism and Fiscal Irresponsibility," in Biggs and Stobbe, *Devine Rule*, 31.
19. Ibid., 20.
20. Ibid., 21-22.
21. Statistics Canada, *Canada Year Book, 1999*, 85.
22. Saskatchewan Bureau of Statistics, *Economic Review* 51 (1997), 35.
23. Thatcher, *Backrooms*, 193.
24. Moose Jaw *Times Herald*, January 29, 1985, quoted in Maureen Appel Malot, "The Provinces and Privatization: Are the Provinces Really Getting Out of Business?" in Allan Tupper and G. Bruce Doern (eds.), *Privatization, Public Policy and Public Corporations in Canada* (Montreal: Institute for Research on Public Policy, 1988), 412.
25. *Globe and Mail*, March 20, 1989.
26. *Star Phoenix*, April 15, 1989.
27. Dale Eisler, *Leader-Post*, July 8, 1988.
28. *Leader-Post*, October 20, 1982.
29. *Star Phoenix*, November 26, 1985.
30. W.A Waiser, "Saskatchewan," *Canadian Annual Review of Politics and Public Affairs* (1989), 209.
31. *Leader-Post*, May 4, 1989.
32. *Globe and Mail*, June 22, 1989.
33. Details of the NewGrade Upgrader deal can be found in C.W. Boyd, "The NewGrade Energy Co-op Upgrader," in H. Schroeder, *Cases in Business Policy* (Toronto: Nelson, 1996). This case study can also be obtained directly from C. Boyd at the College of Commerce, University of Saskatchewan.
34. J.R. Miller, "Saskatchewan," *Canadian Annual Review of Politics and Public Affairs* (1985), 363–64.
35. Waiser, "Saskatchewan," 205.
36. Les Perreaux, "Devine Achievement," *National Post*, June 15, 2001.
37. J.R. Miller, "Saskatchewan," 295.
38. Timothy Bruce Krywulak, "The Free Trade Debate in Saskatchewan, 1985–88" (MA thesis, University of Regina, 2000), 97.
39. Legislative Assembly of Saskatchewan, *Debates*, Grant Devine, March 28, 1983, 343.
40. Pugh, "Cultivating the Corporate Agenda," 74–75.
41. David Smith, "Saskatchewan," *Canadian Annual Review of Politics and Public* Affairs (1991), 237.
42. Stobbe, "Political Conservatism and Fiscal Irresponsibility," 28.
43. Pugh, "Cultivating the Corporate Agenda," 76.
44. Graham Riches and Loralee Manning, "The Breakdown of Public Welfare in Saskatchewan," in Biggs and Stobbe, *Devine Rule*, 255.
45. This was a not uncommon approach prior to the advent of the welfare state. For a positive view of charitable giving on the basis of the deserving/undeserving classification of the poor see Gertrude

Himmelfarb, *Poverty and Compassion: The Moral Imagination of the Late Victorians* (New York: Alfred A. Knopf, 1991, especially 185–206). For a negative view, see Michael B. Katz, *In the Shadow of the Poorhouse: A Social History of Welfare in America* (New York: Basic Books, 1986).

46. Diana Ralph and Mark Stobbe, "Welfare as Moral Reform in Saskatchewan," in Biggs and Stobbe, *Devine Rule*, 272.
47. Riches and Manning, "The Breakdown of Public Welfare in Saskatchewan," 257.
48. Graham Riches and Lorelee Manning, *Welfare Reform and the Canada Assistance Plan: The Breakdown of Public Welfare in Saskatchewan, 1981–89* (Regina: Social Administration Research Unit, 1989), 5.
49. Pitsula and Rasmussen, *Privatizing a Province*, 8.
50. Ian McCuaig, Bob Sass, and Mark Stobbe, "Labour Pains: The Birth of New Industrial Relations Order in Saskatchewan," in Biggs and Stobbe, *Devine Rule*, 151.
51. Ibid., 153.
52. Ibid., 167.
53. *Star Phoenix*, April 1, 1986.
54. Lesley Biggs, "Building Binges and Budget Cuts: Health Care in Saskatchewan, 1982–1989," in Biggs and Stobbe, *Devine Rule*, 181.
55. Ibid., 191, 308.
56. Andrew Cohen, *A Deal Undone: The Making and Breaking of the Meech Lake Accord* (Vancouver: Douglas & McIntyre, 1990), 36.
57. Peter H. Russell, *Constitutional Odyssey: Can Canadians Become a Sovereign People?* (Toronto: University of Toronto Press, 1993), 140.
58. Ibid., 139.
59. Cohen, *A Deal Undone*, 233.
60. David Smith, "Saskatchewan," *Canadian Annual Review of Politics and Public Affairs* (1990), 219.
61. Krywulak, "The Free Trade Debate in Saskatchewan," 165.
62. Thatcher, *Backrooms*, 5.
63. Russell, *Constitutional Odyssey*, 132.
64. Legislative Assembly of Saskatchewan, *Debates*, Grant Devine, November 30, 1983, 384.
65. Richard Bartlett, "Native Land Claims: Outstanding Treaty Land Entitlements in Saskatchewan, 1982–1989," in Biggs and Stobbe, *Devine Rule*, 138.
66. Smith, "Saskatchewan" (1991), 239.
67. Waiser, "Saskatchewan," 212.
68. Smith, "Saskatchewan" (1990), 212.
69. Ibid., 214.
70. Ibid., 217.
71. Smith, "Saskatchewan" (1991), 231.
71. Ibid., 230.
73. Gerry Jones, *SaskScandal: The Death of Political Idealism in Saskatchewan* (Calgary: Fifth House, 2000), 13–14.
74. Ibid., 22.
75. Ibid., 31–32.
76. Ibid., 76–79.
77. Luiza Chwialkowska, "Conviction Upheld," *National Post*, February 24, 2001.
78. Legislative Assembly of Saskatchewan, *Debates*, Grant Devine. March 27, 1984, 910.

Roy Romanow

Gregory P. Marchildon

Romanow, formal portrait
(Oktober Revolution Photography).

On the air, 1978
(SAB 78-906-112).

At the First Ministers'
Conference,
Ottawa, November 1981
(SAB RA 22,516 (2)).

Saskatchewan Premiers of the 20th Century

Roy Romanow, 1991–2001

Life Before Politics, 1939–1966

Roy Romanow's parents, Michael and Tekla, were Ukrainian immigrants from the village of Ordiv, about 45 kilometres northeast of the city of Lviv in western Ukraine. They settled on the west side of Saskatoon, along with hundreds of other poor immigrants, many from the same region of eastern Europe including two of Michael Romanow's uncles. Arriving first in 1927, Michael was not joined by his wife and daughter, Ann, until April 1938—once he was well established as a section man for the Canadian Pacific Railway and had bought a small house. On August 12, 1939, Roy John Romanow was born in St. Paul's Hospital, the final member of the family, and the only one unaffected by the pain of long separation and the extreme poverty of eastern Europe.

Aside from their modest home, the centre of the Romanow universe was the Ukrainian National Federation's (UNF) community centre on the west side, which Michael Romanow helped build and supported to the day he died. This was where Roy would learn Ukrainian music, dance and poetry, receive instruction in language and boxing, celebrate his sister's marriage, and join in the singing of *Shane Merla Ukrainia* ("Ukraine has not yet died") at the end of all formal functions. When Romanow started school, his first language was Ukrainian—the language of home, church, the UNF centre and friends. He had picked up some English on the street but in school he was required to speak it all the time.

Roy first attended Westmount School where he had his first experience with broadcasting. A Ukrainian friend wired a microphone from the school to a sound box outside, and Romanow would stand inside the school overlooking the rink giving his "NHL-style" running commentary during the games. Eventually, a complaint was made to the police about the noise but not before someone alerted a Saskatoon radio station called CKOM about the talented kid who was calling the games. Twelve years old at the time, Romanow was put on "Waterman Waterbury Roving Microphone," a radio show searching out oddities. Impressed, CKOM hired him to announce city-wide pee-wee hockey games for their community broadcasts at $5 a week. Told that his heavy Ukrainian accent would prevent him from a career in mainstream broadcasting, however, Romanow studied his taped broadcasts and spent countless hours trying to change his pronunciation. By the end of high school and the beginning of university, he had broken through the "language" barrier and was doing mainstream baseball, hockey and disk jockey work.[1]

Romanow attended Bedford Road Collegiate where he found himself living in two worlds. While some of his old Ukrainian pals were with him, the majority of the students were not Ukrainians and some were not even "immigrant kids." While his broadcasting work added to his popularity, he became more conscious of his Ukrainian background and the common prejudices held by some of the other students. He was never really sure about being accepted outside his own community. He recalled one particularly painful situation in which he had been invited by a grade 12 cheerleader from Nutana Collegiate to dinner

SOURCE: ROY AND ELEANORE ROMANOW
Romanow with father Michael and mother Tekla.

with her parents. Crossing the railway bridge to get to her home on the "WASP" and wealthier side of Saskatoon, he felt as if he were walking into a new world. Excitement gave way to shame, however, as he faced the girl's physician father and mother, and realized that he had no idea of what to do with the three forks and the three knives sitting on either side of his plate. Their dispassionate conversation and quietly polite manners made him feel like a complete outsider and he slinked away as soon as possible.[2]

Despite his insecurities, Romanow refused to fade into the background. He was ambitious for a larger and more exciting life, one in which he could stand out. He also craved approval and acceptance. With the support of some of his old Ukrainian friends as well as some new acquaintances, he launched a campaign to become president of the students' council at Bedford Road. Unfortunately, his chief opponent was the popular quarterback of the high school football team—a non-immigrant golden boy—and Romanow lost. While he loathed defeat and the feelings it unleashed, he enjoyed the campaign immensely and found that he had some skill at oratory, no doubt helped by his broadcasting experience. This duality—the insecurity of an outsider struggling with the ambition to make it as an insider—would accompany Romanow for all of his political career.

Entering the University of Saskatchewan in the fall of 1957, Romanow found himself drawn to campus politics. He was so absorbed in publicly debating the issues of the day as well as student politics that his grades suffered. Unlike high school, where he was in the "eight A club" because of his superior achievements, his marks in university drifted downwards. He majored in politics, studying under such luminaries as George Britnell, Vernon Fowke and Norman Ward in the university's renowned Department of Political Economy.[3] He became president of the Men's Arts and Sciences Association and a member of the University of Saskatchewan's debating team. Although he graduated with a B.A. in 1960, Romanow did an extra year of study in the Department, hoping to do post-graduate work in Political Studies. Given his marks, however, it would have been difficult to find a graduate spot, and Norman Ward gently steered Romanow towards law school. He and a close friend, Harold MacKay, hoped for a scholarship to attend Dalhousie Law School, while applying for entry to law school in Saskatoon. Having better marks, MacKay ultimately received the Dalhousie scholarship, leaving Romanow at the University of Saskatchewan.[4]

SOURCE: ROY AND ELEANORE ROMANOW
Radio announcer at CKOM.

At this time, Romanow still had high hopes for a professional career in radio broadcasting, in the meantime using his earnings from part-time radio work to pay for his university tuition. He saw being a lawyer as a backup in case his first choice did not turn out. At the same time, he was just beginning to think in terms of a career in politics, largely because of his exposure to Tommy Douglas. Romanow had first met Douglas in the 1960 provincial election campaign. A short time later, just after Douglas had assumed the leadership of the fledgling federal New Democratic Party (NDP), Romanow introduced Douglas on a radio broadcast from the Bessborough Hotel. Lavishly praising Romanow's communication abilities, Douglas encouraged Romanow to become more politically active. Naturally, Romanow was flattered by Douglas's attention—a man who had been a legend to him since he was a young boy sitting beside his father listening to Douglas's provincial radio broadcasts. Romanow continued to introduce Douglas on radio and through these broadcasts he became known to many of the most senior CCF politicians and party activists. He also started to become known as a "CCFer" on campus, supporting Douglas's position on almost everything, particularly medicare, which Douglas and his party had been touting for 15 years. It was around this time that Romanow actually joined the CCF.[5]

In law school, Romanow again became embroiled in student politics, and the experience became an important apprenticeship for the future. In second year, he was acclaimed president of the Students' Representative Council for the university. By this time, he was recognized as the "Big Man on Campus," a student activist who also enjoyed a good time with his wide circle of friends. These friends included Bill Deverell, later the author of numerous thriller novels but then an outspoken leftist and editor of the student newspaper, who helped Romanow's campaign by writing a series of favourable articles. Towards the end of his first year of law school, Romanow became very well known to the entire student body as the medicare controversy heated up in spring 1962. He was seen as one of the more articulate student voices in the debate that was forcing everyone to take sides. To Romanow, it seemed that most students, repeating the view of their middle-class parents, were against medicare, while he was drawn to that vocal minority of left-wing students supporting the CCF's move to publicly insured physician services.

SOURCE: ROY AND ELEANORE ROMANOW

Romanow and Douglas maintained a warm relationship over the years. They appear together here during a trip to China.

Frequently arguing the virtues and advantages of public health care, Romanow debated on and off campus. At CKOM, where he still worked part-time, he would argue his case during the breaks between the news and current affairs programming that focussed on the conflict. He also found it the talk of the studio at CFQC-TV, the Saskatoon television station where Romanow landed a part-time job in 1962. When he wasn't announcing, Romanow found himself the butt of every jab on medicare from studio staff. He soon retaliated in kind. After about one week on the job, Romanow and the rest of the staff were trading insults during the intermission when the general manager walked in and overheard the exchange. Unfortunately, CFQC-TV's general manager just happened to be Walter (Spike) Romanow, Roy Romanow's older cousin and a rabid anti-CCFer. Infuriated and embarrassed over Roy's behaviour, Spike Romanow marched up to his young cousin to fire him. Knowing full well what was coming, Roy announced that he was quitting at the same time that Spike opened his mouth, and Roy's career in television was over.[6]

By the end of his first year in law school, Romanow could see that the government was struggling against the tide of anti-medicare rallies and negative media. When the doctors' strike began, he and some of his fellow students went to Regina to volunteer their help. They walked directly into the Legislative Building and asked what they could do. Romanow was temporarily assigned to assist Allan Blakeney, the minister of Health, and his staff. His main job was to follow Blakeney around carrying his bags, but he also observed the occasional anti-medicare meeting. Then he received an offer to work in the

Department of Health for the summer but, afraid to lose his radio job at CKOM, he returned to Saskatoon. Once back, he worked with the CCF as a volunteer, defending medicare for the rest of the summer. Through this, he met George Taylor, a lawyer who, as a young man, had fought in the Spanish Civil War as a committed socialist. Taylor was legal counsel for the provincial government and, later, the local community clinic doctors who, in part because of their support for medicare, were being denied hospital privileges by the physicians' regulatory body.[7]

Even after a solution was mediated that ended the doctors' strike and allowed for the implementation of medicare, the hostilities continued. Hospital privileges for community clinic doctors continued to be such an issue that Premier Woodrow Lloyd initiated a Royal Commission, chaired by Justice Mervyn Woods of the Saskatchewan Court of Appeal, to examine the complaints of five community clinic doctors working in Estevan, Regina and Saskatoon. The tiny Commission staff included Romanow as assistant secretary, a remarkable appointment for a young law student, and one made in part on the recommendation of George Taylor. The Commission delivered a 100-page report in December 1963. Concluding that it "was easy to see that community clinic doctors would have reason to doubt the good faith of those physicians" evaluating their applications for hospital privileges, the Commission recommended the establishment of a hospital privileges appeal board independent of the provincial College of Physicians and Surgeons.[8]

The Lloyd government accepted the Commission's recommendations, and Romanow was finishing his final term of law school when the members of the new hospital privileges board were appointed by the Lloyd government. Then, on April 22, just after his final examinations, the Lloyd government was narrowly defeated by Ross Thatcher and the Liberals, bringing to a close two decades of successive CCF governments. Although unwilling to dismantle medicare because of its popularity since implementation, Thatcher did reverse the Lloyd government's decision to create an independent hospital privileges board, much to Romanow's consternation.[9]

A New Breed of Politician

As the new Liberal administration took over the reins of power, Romanow began articling for George Taylor. Still living with his mother on the west side of Saskatoon (his father having died quite suddenly years before), Romanow also began to work diligently for the CCF in his Riversdale constituency. Because of his radio experience, he was asked by the provincial CCF party organization in Regina to work on public outreach and soon found himself the party chair responsible for publicity. While he was deeply interested in national issues and the federal NDP, he was encouraged to seek the nomination of Riversdale constituency by prominent members of the provincial party. His popularity with local residents—including some Ukrainian-Canadians who had previously been wary of the "socialists"—clinched the deal, and his nomination went uncontested in October 1966.[10] From that moment forward, his life would revolve around politics.

In mid-August of 1967, Romanow married Eleanore Boykowich. Eleanore's father was a dentist, a first-generation Ukrainian-Canadian, who lived on the more prosperous east side of Saskatoon, and generally supported the Conservative Party. Eleanore was a successful

SOURCE: ROY AND ELEANORE ROMANOW
With Eleanore, at home in Saskatoon.

writer and producer of radio advertising and had worked for years in major commercial radio studios in Edmonton, Vancouver, Toronto and Montreal. They first met when she paid a visit to CKOM while Roy was working there part time to put himself through law school. They carried on a long-distance romance until deciding to get married in 1967. During his first term of government, Eleanore lived with Roy in Regina, but remained in Saskatoon, separating her husband's political life in the capital from their personal life in Saskatoon, although she made a point of attending every major governmental and political event.[11]

Almost immediately after the wedding, Romanow began campaigning in the 1967 provincial election. Still not completely accepting the formal linkages with organized labour that had produced the federal NDP, the provincial CCF was trying to put a new face on its party and policies during the campaign, and Romanow was sent all over the province as the poster boy of change. He soon became one of the most visible figures in the election. His personal popularity was so great that he won the second biggest majority in the province. Overall, however, the CCF did not do well enough to prevent the Thatcher Liberals from eking out a slim victory.[12] Moreover, when he joined his new opposition caucus members in Regina, Romanow discovered that his vote-grabbing election style, his effective use of the media, and his telegenic, almost Kennedy-like style, had upset some of the CCF's old guard. Some accused him of being more flash than substance, and of being too obviously ambitious. Romanow's election success and the internal controversy this sparked meant that he was the new man—some said "boy wonder"—to be watched in the Legislature. He made some mistakes at first but, according to Dave Steuart, then Thatcher's Deputy Premier, Romanow soon established himself as a "dynamic orator" in the Legislature and, whatever the grumbling by some of the old stalwarts, one of the opposition party's most important new assets.[13]

In 1969, Woodrow Lloyd recognized Romanow's abilities by moving him, along with two others of the recently elected "young Turks," to the front row, upsetting decades of tradition based upon seniority.[14] That same year, however, Romanow found himself in deep opposition to the growing Waffle movement which he felt was polarizing and dividing the party. Highly influenced by the student anti-war movement, the Waffle had sprung up as a left-wing faction within the NDP. In Saskatchewan, Waffle members operated like a party within a party, inviting select members of the provincial caucus of the NDP (the CCF label had finally been cast off) who shared their ideological outlook to Waffle meetings.[15] Like many others in the caucus, Romanow felt that these tactics were destructive of the party's cohesiveness and sense of common mission. When Woodrow Lloyd supported a Waffle resolution at a national NDP convention, Romanow may not have been alone in his criticism of Lloyd and the Waffle, but Romanow's high profile guaranteed the enmity of the Waffle when Lloyd resigned suddenly, after a late-night caucus session questioning his leadership in March 1970.[16] Perceived by many as the leading member of the pragmatic "young Turks" within the party who had grown restless with Lloyd's leadership, Romanow was automatically fingered by Lloyd's supporters as part of the cabal that had lobbied for a new leader to replace Lloyd.[17]

In the leadership campaign that followed Lloyd's resignation, four candidates came forward. Each was seen to represent a faction within the provincial NDP. Allan Blakeney was the first to declare his intention to run for party leader. With many years of experience as a senior civil servant in the Douglas administration and a minister in the Lloyd government, Blakeney was perceived as the party establishment's favoured candidate.[18] Roy Romanow was next. He represented the pragramtic "young Turks" within the caucus and party who wanted to revamp the party and its policy platform to make it more relevant for the 1970s.[19] The Waffle had Don Mitchell, a candidate who favoured government ownership of resources, food processing and agricultural inputs, and urged a "land bank" in which the province would purchase land from farmers and then lease it back to them on generous terms. Mitchell argued that he represented the "principled position of [the] CCF's original Regina Manifesto" in contrast to what he described as the "bankruptcy of image politics" represented by Blakeney and Romanow.[20] George Taylor, the fourth and last candidate to declare, represented the Old Left within the party, a group that always believed both Douglas and Lloyd had deviated too much from the 1933 CCF Manifesto during their many years of government, and wanted a return to a purer form of socialism.[21]

At least initially, Romanow did not expect to win. He hid his actual age of 29, worried that party members would think him too young and inexperienced to run a party. He did, however, want a highly public forum for his message on the importance of modernizing the party's platform and policies even while remaining true to what he felt were the fundamental principles that created the movement.[22] With his populist speeches and his fellow

SOURCE: ROY AND ELEANORE ROMANOW

Four generations of Premiers. This historic photograph, taken at the 1970 Saskatchewan NDP leadership convention, brings together the four men who were the province's CCF-NDP Premiers in the twentieth century. From left to right: Woodrow S. Lloyd (1961–1964), Allan Blakeney (1971–1982), Tommy Douglas (1944–1961), and Roy Romanow (1991–2001).

"young Turks" driving all over the province on his behalf, Romanow saw his campaign begin to overshadow Blakeney's, and to almost everyone's surprise, Romanow won the first ballot against Blakeney. Then, even more shocking, Romanow won the second ballot. But just when Romanow began to believe that victory was within his grasp, George Taylor worked hard to get the left wing to support Blakeney. Although many Waffle members abstained rather than vote for a candidate they felt represented the right almost as much as Romanow, enough of the left in the party did vote for Blakeney to give the more experienced candidate a victory on the third ballot. Some had never forgotten the fact that Romanow had struck out much harder against the Waffle's policy and its methods than Blakeney.[23] Given their close relationship in the past, Romanow found Taylor's decision painful to accept. Just before Romanow mounted the podium with the other candidates, he was taken aside by Tommy Douglas, who explained that a government can only have one conductor at a time. Blakeney was now that conductor—that the party had made the right decision in choosing experience and proven ability over youthful exuberance—but Romanow's time would eventually come.[24] Taking the stage, Romanow seized the moment by grabbing the microphone and hailing Blakeney as "the next Premier of Saskatchewan," imploring all the delegates to make Blakeney's nomination as party leader unanimous. A huge cheer went up, breaking the tension of what had been one of the most bruising and divisive leadership campaigns in the NDP's history.[25]

Deputy Premier and Attorney General Under Blakeney

In the election campaign of 1971, Romanow again travelled across the province as one of the most visible spokespersons for the NDP. The party's platform for the election, the *New Deal for People*, was built in part on the Waffle positions during the leadership campaign, including the notion of a land bank commission.[26] On election day, the NDP soundly defeated the Thatcher Liberals, and Romanow became part of a government for the first time. Now a force to be reckoned with inside the party as well as outside, Romanow became Blakeney's chief political minister, simultaneously holding the positions of Deputy Premier, House leader and attorney general. The two perfectly complemented each other in terms of their very different strengths. While Blakeney understood the mechanics of how a government should run, and was masterful in directing its complex bureaucratic machinery, Romanow stayed in close touch with all caucus members, thereby making his job as government house leader that much smoother.[27] He also communicated the government's direction and messages to the media and the general public, and was the best debater in the Legislature.[28] One political staffer described Blakeney as the government's Clydesdale—"tough, hard-nosed, straightforward, plodding, never veering off the path"— and Romanow as its thoroughbred—"finicky, hard to get into the gate, always kicking up a storm"—but once out of the gate, "running in front, always performing 110 per cent."[29] Together, Blakeney and Romanow were the most potent political combination of the day.

The 1970s were a time of innovation and expansion for governments generally. As attorney general, Romanow pioneered more than his share of new initiatives. These included one of the first provincial human rights codes and accompanying human rights commission, a new ombudsman office to act as a public watchdog, an Indian constables' program with the RCMP, and the Meewasin Valley Authority to provide a long-term development plan that would protect and enhance the riverbank in Saskatoon. Following a study of the provincial court system by Supreme Court Justice Emmett Hall, Romanow rationalized and simplified the existing multilayered system.[30] As well, he introduced the first provincial legal aid plan with full-time, salaried lawyers to provide the poor with access to criminal defence services throughout the province, including the north, a reform he had been calling since his 1966 nomination as the CCF candidate for Riversdale.[31]

The 1970s were also turbulent times for the Canadian federation, and as attorney general responsible for provincial and constitutional law, Romanow emerged by the end of the period as one of the country's most influential ministers. In the province's resource battle with the federal government, Romanow was instrumental in the potash nationalization, drafting much of the specific legislation and then piloting the bills through the Legislature.[32] Although not hostile to private ownership of natural resources, Romanow concluded that the federal position on royalty taxation combined with the potash industry's behaviour warranted direct ownership by the provincial government through a Crown corporation.[33] Romanow felt that the Trudeau government had not respected the delicate balance between a strong, central government with sufficient capacity to act on behalf of all Canadians and the legitimate, regional aspirations of a province to diversify and stabilize its economy on behalf of its residents.[34]

In his view, the national interest was always best served by carefully balancing these two tendencies within the federation, through the process of constant negotiation and compromise. Indeed, he saw the national interest as the meeting point of these two tendencies. The nature of the Canadian constitution itself required this. Contesting the "watertight compartment" view of the constitution, Romanow pointed to the numerous areas of shared and overlapping jurisdiction. This, in his view, created the need for positive entanglement between both orders of government, and he was fond of repeating the words of legal scholar William Lederman: "Divided jurisdiction, where there is a need for co-operation across the jurisdictional lines, has to be seen as an invitation to practice co-operative federalism— to agree on a complementary use of federation and provincial powers and resources."[35] In such "divided" areas of jurisdiction, it was contrary to the national interest for either federal or provincial governments to act unilaterally. Romanow felt that the Trudeau government alternated between cooperative federalism and unilateralism, albeit occasionally in response to a Quebec government that increasingly behaved in a unilateral manner following the election of the Parti Québecois in 1976.

The Making of the Constitution, 1978–1982

It was only natural for Premier Blakeney to appoint Roy Romanow to the "Continuing Committee of Ministers on the Constitution," first established at the First Ministers' Conference on October 30, 1978. As attorney general, Romanow was responsible for all matters pertaining to the Constitution, and as Deputy Premier, he was the government's lead political minister, and constitutional matters were by definition high politics. Neither could foresee the four-year constitutional odyssey that lay ahead, nor the consequences from the patriation of the constitution to the loss of the 1982 provincial election. For the first two years of this long journey, the federal government stayed on the cooperative federalism path. After the federal election of 1980, however, the Trudeau government moved on to a more unilateral path, with enormous consequences for both Saskatchewan and Canada.[36]

From November 1978 until February 1979, Romanow and his fellow committee members met throughout Canada in an effort to find a compromise that would allow the constitution to be amended and moved from Britain to Canada with a federal-provincial consensus. During these months, the ministers produced several "best effort" draft texts on a broad range of constitutional issues. To support Romanow in the negotiations, a new Department of Intergovernmental Affairs was created to provide a systematic stream of constitutional and federal-provincial advice, as well as prepare proactive Saskatchewan proposals on all of the key constitutional issues.[37]

When the Trudeau government was elected in February 1980, however, it dropped the federal-provincial ministerial process in favour of a more unilateral approach, and according to Romanow it did so for three reasons. First, it was intent on defeating the first Quebec referendum on separation later that year. Second, it wanted to shift the balance of power from the provinces to Ottawa. Third, it wanted to freeze this shift in the balance of power through a more centralizing Constitution. In Romanow's view, the first objective was eminently justifiable, but the second and third were overreactions by Trudeau to the province-building and rather limited decentralization that had occurred in the 1970s.[38]

While the Trudeau government succeeded on the first count, its efforts on the second and third were so strongly opposed by a majority of eight provinces, including Saskatchewan, that Ottawa ultimately failed to achieve these objectives. In September 1981, after the Supreme Court of Canada handed down a decision that endorsed, in part, the provincial position, the federal government was forced to negotiate with the provinces.[39] During the difficult negotiations that lay ahead, Romanow managed to strike up a warm working relationship with Jean Chrétien, Trudeau's point person, and the two so dominated the constitutional negotiations that the media would often refer to the sessions as the "Toque and the Uke" show.[40] In early November, the First Ministers met, and Romanow, in conjunction with Chrétien, joined by Roy McMurtry, Ontario's attorney general, played a pivotal role in negotiating a solution. The "Kitchen Accord," as it came to be called, was a short, two-page document hand-written by Romanow, that set out a compromise package on patriation, including key provisions concerning the federal spending power and the new Charter of Rights and Freedoms.[41]

However, the new constitutional agreement suffered one major shortcoming. It did not include Quebec as a signatory, and the Premier of Quebec, René Levesque, blamed Blakeney and Romanow for putting together a proposal that was acceptable to every jurisdiction except Quebec, and then "purposely" shutting out his negotiators.[42] From Romanow's perspective, Levesque had broken faith with the group of eight dissident provinces by agreeing to Trudeau's proposal for a constitutional referendum the day before, and never had the intention of reaching a compromise. Given their lead role in the negotiations, Romanow and Chrétien were personally blamed for the "night of the long knives," a graphic allusion to Quebec's alleged betrayal and one that remains deeply entrenched in the Quebec mentality.

Mired in controversy as it was, the negotiations finally allowed Canada to have its own Constitution with amendments that embraced a workable compromise between the provinces and Ottawa. Reflecting on the change decades later, Romanow concluded that the "patriation of Canada's Constitution, and the creation of the Charter of Rights and Freedoms" would "be judged by historians as the final step in the achievement of full Canadian sovereignty and a confirmation" of the country's "national maturity."[43] Although at the time Romanow publicly supported his Premier's strong opposition to the Charter, privately he was conflicted.[44] He always believed that governments were better able than the courts to construct the proactive policies and institutions necessary to improve society, and the two orders of government constantly working at accommodation are a more flexible instrument than the courts in achieving the national interest. However, he could see the advantage of placing the most basic human rights—both individual and collective—above the regular laws of the land, thereby providing a valuable "weapon against discrimination."[45] In Romanow's view, the Charter soon proved its worth as this most valuable weapon, changing the basic ethos of the country in the process.

Political Death and Resurrection, 1982–1991

When election time arrived in the spring of 1982, Romanow realized that he had devoted almost four years to building a new Constitution. For him, it was the highest form of politics—nation-building in the deepest sense. It was about finding accommodation

SAB RA 22,517(2)
Left to right: Roy McMurtry, Jean Chrétien and Roy Romanow, the authors of the "Kitchen Accord."

among the various values and visions that make up this complex country—discovering the common thread that held it all together, however tenuously. In this task, he felt he had achieved much, but when he began campaigning, he quickly discovered that his preoccupation was perceived as a lack of concern about domestic issues in Saskatchewan. Although the economy was doing very well, high interest rates had put the squeeze on farmers and business owners as well as ordinary home owners with mortgages. Many residents concluded that it was time for a change, and the NDP government went down to a crushing defeat. Most surprising of all was Romanow's own defeat—by a mere 19 votes—at the hands of Jo-Ann Zazelenchuk, a 23-year-old Progressive-Conservative university student who worked part-time as a gas station attendant. Romanow came to agree with the conventional wisdom that he and his party had lost touch with the people. In this sense, he felt a defeat was perhaps deserved, but not the drubbing he and his party actually received.[46]

Not knowing what to do in the aftermath of defeat, Romanow quickly accepted an offer to become a visiting scholar at the University of Saskatchewan. Using the College of Law as his base, Romanow also spent blocks of time at Queen's University and the University of Alberta, where he worked with advisors and acquaintances from his government days who had returned to academic life. He used his time to reflect and write articles concerning the various issues he had grappled with in government.[47] Working with Howard Leeson and John Whyte, his two leading bureaucratic advisors on the Constitution and federal-provincial relations, he co-authored a book entitled *Canada Notwithstanding* on the long and tortuous negotiations that led to the new Constitution, published in 1984.[48]

SOURCE: ROY AND ELEANORE ROMANOW

Back in the ring: Romanow on the campaign trail in the 1991 provincial election.

Romanow then attempted to practice law for a short time, but found the work lacked the stimulation of politics and public policy, and he concentrated on rebuilding support among voters in his old constituency. Few were surprised when he entered the political fray again and defeated Zazelenchuk in the 1986 election. Although the Devine Conservatives squeaked by with a narrow victory, the NDP now had a sizeable opposition. Less than a year after appointing Romanow as House leader, however, Blakeney announced his own resignation. Others considered taking on the job of leader—including Ed Tchorzewski (a former finance minister under Blakeney), Lorne Nystrom (a long-serving member of Parliament), Bob Lyons (a left-leaning member of caucus supported by organized labour) and Dwain Lingenfelter (a right-leaning member of caucus who had served as a minister under Blakeney)—but all knew that Romanow would be virtually unbeatable if he decided to run for leadership. What followed was an awkward month in which Romanow considered his options, but when he finally announced his decision, all the others dropped their intentions to run for leadership. Despite this, Romanow conducted himself as if he were running a campaign, visiting all the constituencies in the province in a hectic, four-week provincial tour in a bid to drum up some excitement for the coming annual convention and the prospect of defeating the Devine government.[49]

Romanow returned to a Legislature that had changed dramatically during his absence. Proceedings were now televised and effective debate in question period now meant short and simple sound bites rather than the lengthier and more complicated responses of the past. Not used to being bested in the nightly news clips, Romanow initially found it difficult to adjust. He worked assiduously at mastering the short clip both in and outside the House. Relearning his debating skills, Romanow would spend the next four years leading his forces in an increasingly biting critique of the Devine government even while preparing for government.

During the late 1990s, the major *cause célèbre* for the Romanow opposition was the Conservative's privatization initiatives. Having hived off the natural gas assets of SaskPower into a separate Crown corporation called SaskEnergy, the Devine government then tried to sell the company. When the legislation to do so came before the Legislature, Romanow was urged by party members and caucus to boycott the Legislature itself. Personally, he was opposed to such tactics as they offended his sense of parliamentary propriety, but he also knew that if he opposed his own caucus, he would end up following, rather than leading, the parade, as well as making him look indecisive. He opted to lead the boycott, letting the division bells ring in the House for 17 days. During this period, popular opposition to the privatization built up to the point that Devine abandoned his bill when the Legislature resumed. It was a great victory both in terms of preventing what he considered a great mistake and in solidifying his leadership, but one that Romanow couldn't help but feel had been purchased at a high price.[50] When the legislation to privatize the Potash Corporation of Saskatchewan came up, Romanow and his caucus fought the bill inside the house but did not walk out a second time fearing a negative public reaction for resorting to such extra-parliamentary means. Romanow also found that he was more personally vulnerable during the debate, with the Conservatives branding him a "man of the 70s," an old-style potash nationalizer out of touch with the realities of the 1980s. Despite the furious fight in the house and through the media, Romanow and his opposition caucus were unable to block the ultimate privatization of the Potash Corporation, something which most in the caucus, including Romanow, would come to regret in the 1990s.

Victory and the Premiership

While Romanow was confident of victory, he could hardly have predicted the enormous sweep in the election of October 21, 1991. When the dust had cleared, the NDP found itself with 55 elected members compared to 11 opposition MLAs. The victory did much to ease the pain of the Devine sweep nine years before. That night, Romanow jubilantly declared to his supporters: "Let the word go forth from every corner of our province tonight that Saskatchewan is back."[51] Almost immediately, he made two decisions. The first was to appoint an extremely small Cabinet of 11 (including himself), leaving a huge backbench of 44 members. Romanow wanted a small "War Cabinet" that would be capable of making a host of decisions and moving quickly on key priorities in the first months of government.[52]

The second immediate decision by Romanow was to avoid triggering a purge of the civil service of the scale and type conducted by the Devine Conservatives in 1982.[53] Romanow had always had great respect for civil servants in general, and for the competence of the Saskatchewan public service in particular. While the quality and morale of the civil service had plummeted during the previous decade due to political appointments, Romanow knew that removing all those who were hired on questionable grounds during that time would simply have perpetuated the blood feud for another generation. While appointing some of the key people he trusted into more senior and politically sensitive order-in-council positions, he refused to countenance a wholesale review. He was also prepared to take criticism directly for some difficult personnel decisions. After much soul-searching, for example, he decided to keep John Wright, the deputy minister of Finance, in the same position he had served the Devine administration. Although attacked by many within the party, Romanow was convinced that Wright was not partisan, and would do everything possible to reverse the financial legacy left by the previous government.

Unlike the *New Deal for People* in 1971, the Romanow government had been elected without a detailed policy platform. This was partly a consequence of the desire to

SOURCE: CABINET SECRETARY'S OFFICE, GOVERNMENT OF SASKATCHEWAN

Romanow's first Cabinet, 1991. Seated, from left: Dwain Lingenfelter, Roy Romanow, Lieutenant-Governor Sylvia Fedoruk, Ed Tchorzewski. Standing, from left: Carol Teichrob, Louise Simard, Darrel Cunningham, Bob Mitchell, John Penner, Berny Wiens, Carol Carson, Janice MacKinnon. The greatest challenge facing the incoming administration was Saskatchewan's desperate financial situation.

capitalize on the mistakes of the Devine government, but it was primarily due to Romanow's cautiousness. In his view, it was too easy for an opposition party to make mistakes in designing detailed policy alternatives that an existing government, enjoying the benefit of expert civil service advice, could expose and destroy. Almost as important, he knew that his new government would be facing a large deficit that made expensive campaign promises a very dangerous proposition. As a consequence, however, there was no precise, detailed plan of action for the government, perhaps an advantage given what Romanow would soon discover about the state of the province's finances.

The Debt Crisis

Romanow inherited a decade of successive deficit budgets that had produced a mountain of debt and an accompanying annual interest repayment that was unsustainable. Moving the province from chronic deficit budgeting to annual surpluses was the Romanow legacy to future governments. This may have seemed unusual for a social democratic government, particularly in light of the experience of NDP governments in Ontario and British Columbia in the 1990s, but in reality it was simply a return to the values of past social democratic governments in Saskatchewan. Despite the legacy left by the Great Depression, Tommy Douglas insisted on balanced budgets from 1944 until his departure in 1961.

SOURCE: ROY AND ELEANORE ROMANOW

Romanow being sworn in as Premier of Saskatchewan.

Keynesian deficit financing was rejected as an option given the province's open economy and Douglas's fear of being controlled by the banks. The price paid for the approach was the fact that social policies and programs were not initiated before the means to pay for them in full were found. The most obvious example of this was medicare, which took almost 18 years to implement.[54]

Nonetheless, reversing a decade of deficit budgeting was a dramatic policy change in an environment of growing cynicism towards government.[55] The Romanow government's ultimate success depended on a number of factors, including: the coherence and comprehensiveness of a four-year plan to achieve a balanced budget; the demonstrable commitment to the plan by government itself, including salary cuts for all members of Cabinet and more senior members of the civil service; the speed of the change, involving an aggressive four-year plan that involved sharp expenditure cuts and revenue increases in the first two years of the four-year plan; and the leadership provided by the Premier and key members of his Cabinet in convincing the public, including those most directly affected by the expenditure cuts, of the need for the plan and its inherent fairness.[56] On all counts, Romanow's government largely succeeded, and in the process, led the way in the struggle for Canadian governments to regain control over their fiscal futures, with Romanow communicating the reasons to the public while sustaining support within his own government for the unpleasant mission.[57]

Within days of the election, Romanow set up an independent commission under accountant Don Gass to review the "books" and provide a report to the government and the general public. In the meantime, he took some immediate cost-saving steps to prepare the public for what was coming. Romanow and his Cabinet closed Saskatchewan trade offices in Minneapolis and Hong Kong, cut their own salaries by 10% and required that all ministers and senior civil servants travel economy class.[58] Although the savings generated by these measures were minimal, they were important symbolic gestures that the government would be first to step up to the plate for its dose of the deficit medicine.

In February 1992, the Gass Commission report dropped like a bomb on the Saskatchewan public. It revealed that the province's debt as of March 31, 1991, was $7.5 billion, more than double the amount estimated by the Devine government shortly before leaving office. In addition, the deficit for 1990–91 was revised upwards from $360 million to $975 million.[59] With these more realistic revisions, it now became obvious that Saskatchewan faced the largest per capita debt and deficit problem in the country. The debt itself amounted to 180% of the province's annual revenue.[60] Indeed, Saskatchewan's tax-supported debt as a percentage of provincial GDP was the highest of any province in Canada—55% in the 1991–92 fiscal year.[61] Within a few weeks of the Gass Commission report, the New York debt rating agency, Moody's, again downgraded the province's credit rating.[62]

With the threat of further credit downgrades hanging over Saskatchewan, Romanow initiated a thorough review of all government spending and his Finance minister, Ed Tchorzewski, presented a "tough-love" budget to Cabinet. The struggle inside Cabinet and the caucus was fierce as dreams and hopes were sacrificed. While many in the province quietly agreed with the Premier that there was no viable alternative, and grimly accepted their share of the medicine, others remained opposed. Indeed, some of the most vocal critics of the decision in general were on the left, both inside and outside the NDP. They believed that Romanow was fixated with the debt and all too willing to sacrifice progressive social programs on the altar of fiscal prudence. Arguing that the debt crisis was exaggerated, or even fabricated, by the right wing, they concluded that Romanow had become captive to the "neo-liberal" agenda to shrink the role of government.[63] The Saskatchewan Federation of Labour did its own review of the budget and, contrary to Romanow's assessment, argued that Saskatchewan's deficit was "not that out of line with other provinces."[64] They urged Romanow to consider the alternative of continuing to run deficits and hiking taxes, particularly against resource corporations, and let the province eventually grow its way out of the problem. If the international banks and credit rating agencies negatively assessed the province as a consequence, then default on the debt was always an option. After all, why should his government pay the price for a previous government's maladministration?

Romanow rejected this advice for a number of reasons. To continue running deficits meant that the debt would grow, and with it, the percentage of revenue earmarked for interest repayment. Because of compounding interest, this amounted to an ever-growing tax on future generations and could only further limit the ability of government to invest in physical and social infrastructure for years to come. From what he had experienced, history also worked against the alternative. Despite high economic growth for extensive periods within the last three decades, no Canadian government—provincial or federal—had used its growth to pay down accumulated debt in a systematic way. In fact, the opposite had occurred. Moreover, to recover most of the cost of debt repayment through resource taxation would, he judged, damage the healthiest sector of the economy and might actually produce a fall in revenue rather than an increase. As for defaulting, it would trigger a host of consequences, many of which, he believed, would be far more negative for the province's future than the simple inability to borrow money in the short run.[65]

Most of all, Romanow wanted to restore the general public's confidence in government. Despite what his critics on the left argued, he believed passionately in the positive role of government, and concluded that bankruptcy would forever tarnish the public's faith in the competence of the provincial government to be an active and constructive participant in their lives. The dilemma was that he was forced to reduce the role of government in certain sectors in the short run in order to achieve his longer-term objectives.

At the same time, he fully realized the tension between the inherent desire of a social democratic government to expand social programs and the immediate need to reduce spending in order to restore confidence in the province. As he admitted the day his first Cabinet was announced: "In ideological terms we are left-of-centre and social democrats," but after a decade of fiscal mismanagement, what the Saskatchewan public wanted more than anything was "lean and efficient government."[66] At the same time, Romanow believed that lean and efficient government was only a means to an end, with the end being the ability of government, as an extension of the community, to improve the quality of life for all.

Dealing every day with the implications of the fiscal crisis, every member of the War Cabinet accepted the responsibility for cleaning up the fiscal mess left by the Devine government more easily than the backbench members of the NDP caucus, and it was not long before a gulf opened up between the two. Usually politically attuned to the sentiment within caucus, Romanow himself did not realize the extent of the problem until a loyal member of the backbench gave him a caucus health committee's report critical of rumoured cuts to health care and warned him about a potential caucus revolt. He immediately brought the Cabinet together and explained that henceforth they would all talk to their backbench colleagues on a regular basis, and that any member of Cabinet losing support of caucus was also in danger of being eliminated from Cabinet. He also explained that, contrary to past practice, the entire caucus would be given advanced briefings despite the danger of budget leaks.[67]

In the end, while a minority of backbenchers continued to challenge the War Cabinet's debt crisis perspective, the dissident members of caucus did not publicly break with the government on the 1992 budget. Indeed, many backbenchers worked as hard as Cabinet ministers in convincing those most negatively affected by the cuts of the need for them. This should have given Romanow considerable comfort but he soon found that his government would have to go even further than expected to turn the fiscal corner. The 1992 budget had estimated a deficit of $517 million, a significant improvement over the previous year, but as the months rolled on, this estimate had to be revised upwards to above $600 million, the threshold level set by the credit rating agencies. Through the fall of 1992, a new budget was formulated that cut even deeper. By the end of the year, it was obvious that putting together a second tough budget while facing enormous pressures from within the NDP had taken an tremendous toll on the health of Romanow's Deputy Premier, Ed Tchorzewski. Suffering from shingles, Tchorzewski resigned as finance minister immediately following the Christmas break. He was replaced by Janice MacKinnon, a less-experienced minister but whose toughness would soon earn her the nickname "Combat Barbie" in the civil service.

When the 1993 budget was presented to caucus, some backbenchers suggested defaulting on the debt as an alternative. Romanow intervened, saying that default would simply result in control by Ottawa, with the federal minister of Finance and the governor of the Bank of Canada making decisions instead of the provincial Cabinet.

He became emotive, telling all the members of his government that they were elected in order to clean up the mess and that they all had an obligation to do so. If they were unwilling or incapable of fulfilling their obligation, then his government was finished. "If this caucus," he declared, "will not support the wishes of the people of Saskatchewan, then I will see to it that people of Saskatchewan have a chance to choose a government that will." On this startling conclusion, he walked out of the room. He then met with the lieutenant-governor, Sylvia Fedoruk, explaining that he would be asking her to dissolve the Legislature and call an election if the government members could not support the budget. Naturally, news of Romanow's meeting with the lieutenant-governor spread like wildfire among the caucus members, causing much discussion in the absence of the Premier. Returning to caucus over an hour later, Romanow discovered that previously dissident voices had fallen silent.[68]

While some private griping continued, this ended any further discussion about the province defaulting on its debt, and ensured full government support when the budget was presented in the Legislature in March. Moreover, despite the pain caused by the spending cuts, the government again received broad public support. This support held as the fiscal picture finally began to improve, allowing Saskatchewan to present its first balanced budget the following year. With an improving economy and upgrades in its credit rating, the province was finally struggling to its feet after years of mismanagement followed by belt-tightening. Despite facing the worst debt crisis in Canada, Saskatchewan moved faster and more extensively than any province in the country towards a balanced budget.[69] There were, however, some unintended policy consequences, the most significant of which affected health care.

Wellness and Health Reform

Although the 1991 NDP election platform avoided many specific policy promises, Romanow had been clear on the need for major health reform. He appointed Louise Simard as his first Health minister because of her work as opposition Health critic. She had heard the public's views while traveling the province for two years as the opposition "watchdog" on the Devine government's Commission on New Directions for Health Care.[70] Romanow was excited by the potential of the changes she proposed, including a "determinants of health" approach that would emphasize upstream investments in illness prevention that he was calling the "wellness" model as early as 1987.[71] In this, he felt that he was embarking on the second of the two essential stages in fundamental health reform highlighted by Tommy Douglas in one of his last speeches. As Douglas described it, the first stage was to "remove the financial barrier between those giving the service and those receiving it." This had been largely achieved through hospitalization and medicare, with all of Romanow's predecessors—Douglas, Lloyd and Blakeney—playing major roles in their design and implementation. The second stage, not yet achieved, was to "reorganize and revamp the delivery system," the objective of the wellness reforms and, he hoped, his own contribution to this proud legacy.[72]

In policy terms, this meant improving the coordination of care through an administrative structure capable of integrating health services in a region, introducing more local and democratic control through a regional health authority structure, and improving the continuity of care through primary care reform.[73] Simard and her department recommended implementing change in two phases. In the first phase, there would be a "complete reorganization of the governance machinery," including transforming small, rural-based hospitals into wellness centres. This was to be "followed by a reorganization and renewal" of "primary care health services which would be offered through these new delivery structures."[74]

In January 1992, Romanow met with Simard and Duane Adams, the experienced deputy minister the government had hired in large part because of his commitment to reform. To jumpstart the radical changes, Romanow supported their proposal to consolidate the various hospital boards in Saskatoon, excluding the one Catholic hospital board—St. Paul's Hospital—for the time being, to be followed by a similar consolidation in Regina. Then, based upon the intensive work of a hand-picked group of seven experts, a public discussion document was released inviting all Saskatchewanians "to participate in a community-based process to introduce wellness and health reform."[75] By August 1992, when this document first circulated throughout Saskatchewan, Romanow was aware of the full magnitude of the fiscal crisis and the fact that money for the health service alternatives his government was proposing would have to come out of the existing health budget including hospital, drug plan, primary care physician and nursing home expenditures. This created a dilemma that his government never fully escaped.

On the one hand, the fiscal crisis created the political willingness to embark upon difficult, radical change that had been too easy to avoid in easier times. After all, a reoriented health system offered the promise of better value for money spent. On the other hand, however, one-third of provincial government expenditures went into health, too large a sum to avoid being part of the solution to the deficit problem. The closure and conversion of rural hospitals was one of the most visible, and negatively received, reflections of this change. In addition, the government's fiscal inability to build and provide alternative institutions and services in advance of removing the old institutions and services meant that many Saskatchewan residents keenly felt the loss of a local hospital or health professional.[76] The drug plan was pared down to a needs-based program, a far cry from the universal plan first initiated during the 1970s. In addition, the school-based children's dental plan that had been introduced by Blakeney and then eliminated by Devine, was not re-established despite promises to do so by both Romanow and Simard while in opposition. Romanow hoped that his government could eventually reinvest in these areas, but only if the debt crisis was effectively defeated in the immediate term.[77]

The end result was that the innovative health reforms were tarnished from the beginning by the government's fiscal crisis and overall cost containment strategy. Using Duane Adams' imagery, there was a race between the white horse of progressive health reform and the black horse of reducing public health care expenditures.[78] The minister of Health's department rode the white horse of health reform, while the minister of Finance's department rode the black horse of cost containment, with no one knowing who would win the race until the very end.[79] Romanow was personally pulled in two directions, but since he principally spoke to the fiscal crisis in his first two years of office, he was largely perceived as supporting the black horse of cost containment.

As a consequence of the difficulties associated with the first, structural phase of health reform, combined with a government tiring of public criticism for its health reform changes, the second phase of service delivery changes began to stall by 1998. After much debate, Romanow decided to kickstart the second phase of reform by initiating a Commission on Medicare. Led by health consultanat Kenneth Fyke, a former provincial deputy minister of Health and health region manager, the Commission was to recommend changes needed to improve delivery, as well as provide a judgment as to whether some organizational fine tuning was required concerning the first phase of the reforms. At the time, Romanow realized the possibility that the Fyke Commission would report after he left office—and this indeed turned out to be the case—but he felt strongly that the government needed a plan of action so that the earlier wellness reform efforts could mature into a recognizably better health system.[80]

Economic Development and the Role of Government

While Romanow's views on health care had been set during the crucible of the medicare struggle of the early 1960s, his views on the role of government in economic development were forged during the Waffle debate of the late 1960s. Though he belonged to the same generation of individuals who provided the impetus behind the movement, Romanow was fundamentally opposed to the Waffle's insistence that the state be directly involved in numerous sectors of the economy, particularly in finance and the resource industries.[81] He personally believed that private enterprise—especially locally controlled small business—should play a significant role in the provincial economy. While in opposition, he argued that "small business people are the pillars of mainstreet Saskatchewan," generating "most of the jobs that are created in the province."[82] In fact, Romanow was quite satisfied with how the province had evolved with a combination of private, cooperative and government ownership, and would always return to the notion of this balance in political life. This view fit with what Romanow always believed to be Tommy Douglas's own sense of balance and the appropriate role of the state.[83] Similar to Douglas, he faced those within his own party who consistently urged more state involvement in the business of the province.

Almost all farmers in the province were, in effect, private businesses. Cooperative enterprises were initiated when the pooling of resources became necessary in the face of an unforgiving climate and land, as well as the inadequacies of private enterprises. Government ownership evolved in areas where the private sector found it unprofitable to engage. Ultimately, the coexistence of the three types of ownership, properly regulated in the public interest, was, after an early and brief struggle over the issue, what Douglas left as his party's legacy to Blakeney and Romanow.[84] In contrast, members of the Saskatchewan Waffle and their ideological successors were dissatisfied with the status quo, and pushed hard for greater public ownership at the expense of private-sector ownership.[85] While Romanow supported the creation of the Potash Corporation of Saskatchewan, he had to be driven there by what he considered the unreasonable actions of potash companies acting contrary to the public interest, and the aggressive positioning of a federal government that had checkmated the province on a resource taxation policy that could have served as an alternative to ownership.[86] In other words, public ownership was not a matter of dogma to Romanow but a pragmatic response to circumstances that would vary depending on the time, the nature and behaviour of the industry involved, and even the intergovernmental environment.[87]

Whatever Romanow's views on the matter, Blakeney had gone further on public ownership than Tommy Douglas.[88] When he took over as leader of the NDP, Romanow tried to downplay somewhat this legacy, stating that Crown corporations were only one part of an "overall economic strategy for the development of a vibrant mixed economy."[89] In opposition, while he fought against the privatization of the Potash Corporation of Saskatchewan as a "theft" of private assets, and successfully blocked the sale of SaskEnergy, he had no intention of initiating an aggressive new program of public ownership upon becoming Premier.[90] At the same time, he did not sell any Crown corporations in a bid to raise revenue for his cash-starved government.

When he turned his mind to the future of Crown corporations, Romanow discovered that his views concerning the Crowns had hardly budged since the 1960s, except for two new factors, both of which operated at cross-purposes. On the one hand, he felt that "province-building" through the Crowns was now a more limited option because of new constraints imposed by trade agreements such as NAFTA and the Internal Trade Agreement within Canada, deregulation of utilities, as well as the global impact of information and communication technologies. On the other hand, however, the years since the Blakeney administration had witnessed the loss of a number of private-sector head offices in Saskatchewan to Alberta and the United States, accompanied by a permanent loss of high-level expertise and senior personnel. This put more emphasis on the head offices that remained in the province, including Crown corporations. Since selling a Crown corporation almost invariably meant losing one more head office, Romanow and his Cabinet were reluctant to do so, irrespective of their diverse views and philosophies concerning public ownership.

In 1996, Romanow ordered the Saskatchewan Crown Corporations Review in the hope that it would shed new light on public ownership and the path his government should take.[91] The review focussed on the five largest Crowns plus six major investments held by the Crown Investments Corporation (CIC), the Crown holding company and investment bank.[92] As far as the Crown utilities (in electricity, gas, telecommunications, insurance and transportation) were concerned, Romanow was looking for a viable third option to the status quo on the one hand and privatization on the other. In his own words, the review was "designed to make sure" that Saskatchewan had "the most modern, efficient, strongest Crown Corporations into the twenty-first century, owned by the people of Saskatchewan, [and] working for the people of Saskatchewan."[93]

The final report recommended allowing the Crowns greater freedom to compete outside the province as deregulation injected new competition within the province.[94] While Romanow and his Cabinet ultimately approved of the change, the reaction by the media and the public was mixed to negative, particularly concerning some of the less successful overseas investments by the Crowns. Despite these criticisms, including the concerns raised regarding SaskPower's efforts to purchase the main power company in Guyana, South America, as well as the losses suffered in the natural gas market by one of its subsidiaries, the Romanow government continued to permit the Crowns to operate beyond the borders of the province.⁹⁵ This created a political dilemma. The government found it difficult to defend growing Crown investments outside Saskatchewan at the very time that public investment in essential social and physical infrastructure—from health care to highways—was being constrained. The political pressure could only intensify when the Crowns suffered the occasional loss on a foreign investment, a normal event in business perhaps, but one which was easily used by the opposition to criticize the government for not investing adequately in the province.

Indeed, while in opposition, Romanow had been highly critical of the Devine government's economic development mega-projects during the 1980s, most of which were financed through the investment arm of the CIC. During the 1991 election campaign, he promised to review all such deals, including a large oil upgrader project in Regina known as NewGrade. Federated Co-operatives Limited (FCL) had negotiated an arrangement with the CIC that left the provincial government with the lion's share of risk. The Romanow government asked FCL to negotiate major changes to the arrangement. When the FCL refused, Romanow then brought in former Supreme Court of Canada Justice Willard Estey to mediate the dispute. Initially, FCL was enthusiastic about Estey's selection. In April 1993, Estey's final report said that NewGrade posed a serious financial risk for the province and that it was unreasonable to expect Saskatchewan taxpayers to permanently subsidize the project. After a year of what the government considered fruitless negotiations, the deal was changed through legislation.⁹⁶ The whole affair created a major political problem for the government and jeopardized its historically tight relationship with the cooperative movement. John Penner, the minister then responsible for CIC, had to travel throughout the province explaining the government's actions to local NDP constituency presidents, a number of whom were also presidents of local cooperatives. The strain within the party was palpable and Penner suffered from serious health problems that prevented him from running in the 1995 election campaign. Fortunately for the government, the disposition of most of the other mega-projects reduced the province's financial risk without creating similar political problems.⁹⁷

Given the experience with mega-projects in 1980s, it is hardly surprising that Romanow was much more comfortable with a provincial economic development strategy that emphasized small business and employment creation on a modest scale. Consistent with administrations since Douglas, Romanow's key objective was to encourage more diversification in the provincial economy, a natural consequence of having one of the most volatile economies in the country. In some respects, the province had made progress since the 1970s. In agriculture, farmers had moved even further from wheat, and cultivated a broad array of crops, with more livestock being introduced. Oil and natural gas contributed more to the province's gross domestic product than agriculture itself. Forestry, potash and uranium were now mature resource industries. A biotechnology sector was growing around the research infrastructure connected to the University of Saskatchewan. A small but vibrant farm implement manufacturing industry had taken hold. The province's only steel company, IPSCO, was now a major player in the North American industry with numerous plants in the United States and Canada. For most of the 1990s, this combination produced the highest per capita economic growth in Canada.

Beneath the surface, however, not all was well. In agriculture, commodity prices began to drift downwards in part because of highly subsidized exports from the European Union and the United States to the same third-world markets that Saskatchewan producers were selling into. By the late 1990s, prices had dropped so precipitously that it created an agricultural crisis for western producers, and brought implement manufacturers and dealers, as well as the once-mighty Saskatchewan Wheat Pool, to their respective knees. The head offices of almost all the originally Saskatchewan-based oil companies migrated to Alberta, including Wascana Energy, the privatized successor to the Crown-held SaskOil first created in the 1970s. By the time that Wascana Energy was sold to Canadian Occidental, it had already moved most of its head-office functions to Calgary. In the late 1990s, IPSCO formally moved its head office to Chicago, and there were fears that the Potash Corporation of Saskatchewan might eventually do the same.

In this environment, keeping head offices, and the highly skilled employment that supported them, should have been a priority. But with little other than moral suasion at its disposal, the Romanow government fought a rear-guard action that was ultimately unsuccessful at keeping head offices in the province. Given this, Romanow found it increasingly difficult to transmit a sense of confidence in the economic future of the province. While the Saskatchewan economy was growing faster than the Canadian average on a per capita basis (what economists call *intensive* growth), it was generating few jobs overall (and therefore slower *extensive* growth) due to the growing capital-intensity of the resource industries and ever-expanding farm size. The contrast was Alberta, where the economy was creating new jobs as well as wealth, acting as a magnet for young people from Saskatchewan, the parents of whom found it difficult to remain optimistic about the province's future.

Aboriginal Development and Self-Government

Aside from the debt crisis, one of the first issues Romanow had to contend with upon becoming Premier was the demand by Saskatchewan First Nations to create casinos in a province that had always prohibited organized gambling beyond charity bingos. The matter was brought to a head by the threatened construction of a casino on the White Bear reserve in southeastern Saskatchewan. Following the pattern set by some American Indian bands that had set up similar enterprises on their territories, a number of Saskatchewan First Nations' governments firmly believed that casinos would provide the most effective and immediate strategy to generate economic development within their rural reserves. These band governments, with the support of the Federation of Saskatchewan Indian Nations (FSIN), argued that the province could not, on constitutional grounds, either bar or regulate gambling activities on reserves.

On a very fundamental level, Romanow objected to the business of organized gambling. He abhorred its social impact, which he felt was a "tax on the poor," but he also concluded that it would be difficult, and perhaps impossible, to stop the First Nations from proceeding. As a result, he pragmatically entered into negotiations that ultimately produced a compromise revenue-sharing agreement that allowed the province to regulate the new industry. On the positive side, the new industry created employment for a growing number of Aboriginal people. But on the negative side, the incidence of gambling addiction rose, and programs had to be put in place to deal with this growing social problem. Addiction was not limited to individuals, however, as both First Nations and the provincial government soon became dependent on the substantial revenue flows generated by gaming.

Romanow preferred to see job creation for Aboriginal people through other forms of economic development. The need was obvious. The rapid growth of the Aboriginal population, the impact of poverty, the high rates of alcohol and substance addiction and incarceration, the low rate of educational attainment, the poor state of Aboriginal-white relations in the province's major cities, also spoke to the importance of focussing on incorporating Aboriginal peoples into the economic mainstream of the province even while encouraging a certain degree of social, cultural and even political autonomy. The First Nations' population—not including Métis and non-status Aboriginal residents—was expected to grow from 7.8% of the provincial population in 1990 to 10.3% a decade later. This was, and remains, the largest proportion of any province.[98] This translated into a young and growing Aboriginal population that required education and training to participate fully in the province's future. To prepare for this, Romanow encouraged a more innovative labour market training strategy in the mid-1990s, as well as provincial funding for the Saskatchewan Indian Federated College (renamed the First Nations University of Canada in 2003).

Since most of the province's Aboriginal population live in northern Saskatchewan, Romanow initiated the Office of Northern Affairs, a small central agency run from La Ronge, to coordinate the province's northern economic development, and to foster new partnership initiatives with northern peoples.[99] He also insisted that future forest-cutting permits be tied to the ability of existing companies forming partnerships with Aboriginal enterprises. Within his Cabinet and caucus, he had two powerful champions of Aboriginal economic development. First entering the Cabinet as provincial secretary in 1992, Keith Goulet was the minister of Northern Affairs from 1995 until 2001 and the first person of Aboriginal ancestry in the Saskatchewan Cabinet.[100] Former mayor of the northern Métis community of Ile à la Crosse, Buckley Belanger was minister of Environment and Resource Management from 1999.[101]

These initiatives were part of the larger objective of ensuring that Aboriginal communities throughout the province could achieve greater independence and control over their destinies, even while remaining part of the Saskatchewan polity and participating fully in the provincial economy. In Romanow's view, self-government did not mean sovereignty-association of First Nations with the provincial government but the working out of practical, day-to-day arrangements in which greater political, cultural and linguistic independence lived side-by-side with greater economic integration, and with it, the incentive to participate more fully in the political life of the province. In this, he would apply his federal-provincial philosophy of constructive negotiation to Aboriginal self-government within Saskatchewan. Romanow also recognized that some historic promises concerning the transfer of lands under the various treaties that covered the First Nations in Saskatchewan had never been kept. These lands were subject to protracted negotiations through the 1970s and the 1980s. By the time Romanow became Premier, he found that the Devine government had done most of the work in completing the transfer of lands that became known as Treaty Land Entitlement (TLE). The main spur for the original TLE process had been basic justice but Romanow hoped that economic development might be a by-product from this transfer of wealth to Saskatchewan First Nations.

A Provincial Premier Acting in the National Interest

From his days working on the Constitution during the Blakeney administration, Romanow had always felt that national unity was a first-order priority, irrespective of how unpopular this view was at home. In his view, cooperative federalism represented the difficult business of federal and provincial governments negotiating inherently difficult compromises based on their differing but legitimate histories, perspectives and long-term interests. He believed that for some particularly important provincial or regional issues, the national interest was best served by recognizing the paramount nature of the key provincial interest in these cases. In the case of Quebec, the issue was language, and Romanow supported strong (some would argue, exceptional) protection of the French language in Quebec. At home, he had established a French-language school board to better protect the French language in Saskatchewan, and for Québec, he permitted one of his officials to send up a trial balloon on a constitutional amendment that would ensure the powers necessary for the Québec government to protect the French language within its province in the aftermath of the referendum.[102] In the case of the prairies, the most important issues were control over resource development and the support of western agriculture and the transportation of agricultural commodities from this land-locked part of the country to far-flung markets. He argued that a new national policy was needed, one that would allow the prairie economy to diversify and stabilize by having its own industries.[103] In this view of the world, the Quebec government was acting in the national interest by protecting and nurturing the French language, while the Saskatchewan government was doing the same by making Ottawa and the provinces aware of the unique economic needs of the prairies.[104] In the case of western agriculture, Romanow found himself at odds with the federal government through almost all of the 1990s.

Almost immediately after becoming Premier, Romanow terminated an agricultural safety net agreement reached by Devine and the federal government, and replaced it with a safety net that was less expensive and more market sensitive as part of his government's deficit reduction efforts. In his view, the safety net program then in place encouraged farmers to farm the program more than the land, and when he concluded that Otttawa had no intention of making changes, he moved unilaterally. Two years later, the federal government finally terminated its subsidy for the transportation of western agricultural exports, also part of its overall plan to reach a balanced budget. This change most negatively affected Saskatchewan farmers because of their greater distance from eastern and western ports. A final payout plus higher commodity prices saved farmers for the first couple of years, but drought combined with lower commodity prices plus much higher shipping costs transpired to push net farm income to negative levels by 1999.[105]

This precipitated a year-long negotiation between Romanow and Prime Minister Jean

Chrétien. Romanow's objective was to obtain some temporary assistance to provincial farmers in order to avoid a massive number of bankruptcies. However, Chrétien feared that, with the United States and the Europeans showing no sign of reducing export subsidies, the downturn might be long-term, and was opposed to setting a permanent precedent. The struggle tested the limits of the relationship between the two old friends. The low point was reached when Romanow accompanied by Gary Doer, the newly elected Premier of Manitoba, traveled to Ottawa to meet with Chrétien in a bid to get temporary federal support for prairie agriculture. The meeting degenerated into a fruitless debate over the statistical evidence for the decline in the real income of western farmers. Chrétien refused to budge and the two Premiers came home empty-handed. Romanow in particular was humiliated by the manner in which the Prime Minister had dismissed his arguments. Despite this, the difficult negotiations were continued by officials behind the scenes, and months later, a compromise was finally reached in which the federal government shared with the provinces of Saskatchewan and Manitoba the cost of a relief package on a 60:40 basis.[106]

Federal cost-sharing of provincial social programs had always provided fertile ground for intergovernmental conflict. In 1995, when the federal government announced its cuts to social program transfers, and the creation of an omnibus block transfer to the provinces that would eventually become known as the Canada Health and Social Transfer (CHST), it was perhaps the most radical shift in federal government policy since the creation of shared-cost financing for hospitalization in the 1950s. Romanow was appalled. He believed that the transfers from Ottawa underpinned the national dimensions of medicare, social assistance and post-secondary education. By reducing its contribution, Ottawa was reducing its ability to protect and promote the common, Canada-wide features of programs, policies and institutions administered by the provinces. He viewed the country as a string of pearls—each pearl representing a unique region whether it be Quebec, Ontario, British Columbia, the Atlantic provinces or the prairie provinces. The country could not survive without the consent of each region, but at the same time each was tied to the other by a common Canadian strand. Federal transfer funding for social programs added important strength to that common strand which he now saw as unravelling.[107] In the media, Romanow criticized the CHST cuts as "un-Canadian," a comment that so angered Chrétien, he refused to speak to Romanow for weeks afterwards.[108]

Instead of continuing to criticize Chrétien, however, Romanow fought back with an alternative that came to be known as the social union. In his view, the time had come for the provinces to exercise some leadership to help repair and rebuild the national web of health care, post-secondary education, social services and assistance that made up the social union.[109] In Romanow's view, however, the social union was "not merely the sum of the social programs in the country," it was an expression of Canadians' deepest values, including a collective sense of responsibility as citizens within a federation. He argued that provinces acting in isolation from each other would inevitably erode the national dimensions of these values. It was time, he argued, for provincial governments to "accept their national responsibilities for social programs and work with Ottawa to renew, reinforce and, in some cases, strengthen national standards." In his view, enforceable national standards, in which the provinces played a "major policy and coordinating role," would keep the balance between innovative change at the provincial level and common national linkages.[110] In his words, keeping Canada together was "like gluing together two pieces of wood; the trick is to put just the right amount of glue on the joint. Too much glue, and you have a stifling uniformity imposed on the provinces by the federal government. Too little glue, and you end up eliminating the standards and linkages that protect the national aspects of the social union."[111]

Romanow's national initiatives were based upon his own domestic welfare reforms, entitled "Building Independence," that were unveiled immediately following the 1995 election, and eventually led by his minister of Social Services, Lorne Calvert. Originally implemented in the 1960s, traditional social assistance programs had worked well in providing passive support to the poorest in society but they had, in Romanow's view, actually impeded entry to the labour market. By removing these barriers, the best aspects of income support could be kept while breaking the cycle of welfare dependency. Income supplements replaced penalties for taking on part-time or other work. Family health benefits were made available to the working poor as well as welfare recipients. New provincial training allowances provided parents with the opportunity to gain new job skills. A Children's Action Plan provided some of the community supports necessary to improving the social, health and educational environment of poorer children. A Saskatchewan Child Benefit was created that targeted children in poverty, and erased some of the line previously drawn between the working poor and the welfare poor.[112]

These changes were expensive, however, and national action involving the federal spending power would allow the Saskatchewan reforms to go further than if done in isolation. The social union discussion offered the opportunity to obtain this coordinated action. The work eventually produced the National Child Benefit, the first pan-Canadian social program in three decades, as well as a pan-Canadian Children's Action Plan. It also prompted a major re-examination of roles and responsibilities in social policy that culminated in the Social Union Framework Agreement (SUFA) in 1999, by which time Ottawa was beginning to reinvest in social policy transfers to the provinces through cash increases to the CHST.[113] As was the case with the patriation of the Constitution, however, the Parti Québecois government in the end accepted the increase in federal transfers but refused to sign SUFA. To avoid this outcome, Romanow spent hours trying to convince the Premier of Quebec, Lucien Bouchard, of the extent to which SUFA had the potential to better balance the roles and responsibilities of the two orders of government as well as put reasonable limits on the spending power of the federal government.[114] However, the PQ's continuing secessionist agenda worked against Bouchard accepting the concept of the social union which, according to Romanow, was an effort to strengthen the federation through administrative reform. Without doubt, the PQ agenda of secession, even on Bouchard's more gradualist approach, was in direct conflict with Romanow's agenda of strengthening national unity.

Indeed, in terms of the threat to the federation, no period could compare to the 1990s. It began with the collapse in 1990 of the Meech Lake Accord, a constitutional amendment aimed at bringing Quebec back into the constitutional fold. This was followed by an even larger constitutional negotiation that culminated in the Charlottetown Accord, a major rewriting of the Constitution that was defeated in a national referendum in 1992. Despite his preoccupation with the debt crisis, Romanow nonetheless felt that his government had an obligation to devote considerable time to the negotiations. At one point, he interrupted his hectic domestic schedule to meet with Premier Robert Bourassa to try and find a constitutional compromise suitable to Quebec.[115] Responding to the demands of numerous interest groups and organizations, however, Romanow also felt that the resulting Charlottetown Accord was both unwieldy and disturbing in some of it details. Nonetheless, he gave it his government's full support, believing that the alternative might be secession, and travelled the province to sell the accord.[116] Despite his government's best efforts, however, 55% voted against the Accord in Saskatchewan, 1% above the national average.[117]

The Meech Lake and Charlottetown failures contributed to the Parti Québécois victory in Quebec in 1994, and a resurgence in support for a secessionist option. Romanow first clashed with the new PQ Premier, Jacques Parizeau, at the Annual Premiers Conference in the summer of 1995. By this time, Parizeau had begun his campaign for a referendum on sovereignty, and refused to meet with his fellow Premiers unless he could introduce his own agenda item on internal trade. Suspicious of the Quebec Premier's intentions from the beginning, Romanow directly contested Parizeau in the private meeting when it became clear that his communiqué proposal was a ploy to get a resolution through the Premiers that could then be used to convince Quebecers that economic union with the English-speaking provinces would be easy to achieve following Quebec's separation from Canada. Parizeau then left the meeting early, walked out to the media, and provided precisely the interpretation that Romanow predicted to the francophone media. Parizeau also took the time to describe the generally amiable character of most of the Premiers, the one notable exception being Romanow, who was portayed once again as trying to isolate Quebec, as had happened in the "night of the long knives" in November 1981. When Romanow discovered what was transpiring, he left the private meeting of Premiers to give his differing view to the media. After debating Parizeau in the meeting, Romanow then met with the media to rebut Parizeau's interpretation, and to argue against the separatist position, including the contention that the provinces would treat Quebec in the same way on matters of trade and investment after departing the federalist family.

As the Quebec referendum campaign heated up in September, Romanow became uneasy with what he viewed as the federal government's complacent attitude. He also chafed at the hints being dropped by Chrétien that he preferred the Premiers to stay out of the referendum debate. Romanow refused, and presented his more aggressive case against secession in Washington, DC, where he gave a highly publicized speech at Johns Hopkins University's School of Advanced International Studies.[118] In the week immediately preceding the referendum, private polling revealed the high risk of a sovereigntist victory. While preparing for the worst, Romanow hoped for the best, his spirits picked up by the spontaneous rally in favour of federalism in Montreal, and he went to Montreal himself on the night of the vote to act as a television commentator. When the results came in, he realized that the country had come within a whisker of breaking up, and that more would have to be done to make it clear that federalism could work for Quebecers, virtually half of whom had voted in favour of sovereignty.

While Romanow felt that 80% of the changes needed to fix the federation could come through administrative action such as that represented in the social union negotiations, 20% of the changes—particularly the reforms needed to address Quebec's traditional demands—would have to be constitutional.[119] Calling this the 80:20 formulation, Romanow closely worked with Frank McKenna, the Premier of New Brunswick, to convince the other Premiers to at least consider constitutional change down the road. By doing this, the Premiers of Canada could speak beyond the PQ government directly to Quebecers, recognizing the "unique character of Quebec" and the Quebec government's historic role in protecting and promoting the province's language and culture. Two essential assumptions underpinned Romanow's argument. First, Canadians outside Quebec could support such a recognition of Quebec as long as their own rights and identity were not thereby reduced. Second, francophone Quebecers would reject secession in any future referendum only if there was a viable way to guarantee their linguistic and cultural security through the federation.[120] These issues were debated during a Premier's meeting (minus the government of Quebec) on the social union and national unity in Calgary.[121]

The Calgary Declaration was then used as the starting point for consultations in every province followed by, in many cases, all-party resolutions in provincial Legislatures supporting the direction and principles contained in the Calgary Declaration. When trying to convince his own party members to participate in the public consultation, Romanow repeated Canadian historian Jacques Monet's definition of Canada as an "experiment that bursts through the limits of nationalism to embrace men and women of diverse ways and diverse tongues in what it means to be a Canadian. You see, it is not [just] a question of economics or common sense. It is a question of the heart."[122] The Calgary Declaration was part of Plan A, the constructive efforts to keep Quebec in the federation.

Plan B on the other hand involved preparing for secession and the potential fracturing of the rest of Canada, and considerably occupied the time and energy of the federal government. Romanow felt that he must also prepare the province for a potential split and, in the months leading up to the Quebec referendum, he had actually allowed a tiny group of senior civil servants to work out the scenarios facing the province, thereby better preparing the government to protect provincial interests in the event of Quebec's secession.[123] Similarly, he supported the Prime Minister's desire to have the rules of any future referendum spelled out in advance to ensure the integrity of the referendum question and process, and to mitigate to the degree possible the political and legal disruption caused by the outcome.

When the federal government announced that it would be placing a reference on the legal issue of secession to the Supreme Court of Canada, Romanow had Saskatchewan apply for intervener status in the case, one of only two provinces to do so.[124] In the province's oral argument, the possibility, even the potential legitimacy, of secession was admitted, but only after it was negotiated with all the partners in the federation, and within the framework of the existing constitution. As full partners in the federation, the provinces must be involved in any negotiation involving the departure of a partner. In the memorable words of the oral argument presented by John Whyte, Saskatchewan's deputy minister of Justice:

> A nation is built when the communities that comprise it make commitments to it, when they forego choices and opportunities on behalf of a nation, when they discover within the nation new opportunities, when the communities that comprise it make compromises, when they offer each other guarantees, when they make transfers and, perhaps most pointedly, when they receive from others the benefits of national solidarity. The threads of a thousand acts of accommodation are the fabric of a nation.[125]

The Supreme Court accepted the essence of the argument, rejecting the notion of any unilateral declaration of secession in favour of a negotiated process involving the provinces as well as the federal government.[126]

Likewise, Romanow vocally supported the federal government's Clarity Bill.[127] A federal piece of legislation setting out the ground rules for a negotiated secession built upon the Supreme Court's decision in the Secession Reference, this law required that a simple and direct question be used in any future referendum on sovereignty. Again, Romanow took his arguments beyond Saskatchewan, explaining the need for a Clarity Bill to an audience at Harvard University. While Chrétien was pleased to receive Romanow's support on this issue, at the same time he was disconcerted to find the Premier of Saskatchewan also arguing that the federal government was not living up to its national responsibilities in other areas, particularly public health care.

Romanow had become increasingly concerned about the reaction of some provinces to the CHST cuts. Their view, simply put, was that Ottawa's funding contribution had deteriorated to the point that it no longer should have a voice in setting national standards and principles in health care. While federal transfers to health were finally increased in 1999, some provinces argued that it was too little, too late, and began to consider reforms that appeared to threaten the universal and public character of the core system. Some had ordered task forces and were in the process of making fundamental decisions of the direction of their provincial plans. Romanow, too, had ordered a provincial commission, but he made it clear in the terms of reference that the five principles of the Canada Health Act—public administration, universality, accessibility, comprehensiveness and portability—would remain the bedrock for any future system.[128] In a presentation to the Public Policy Forum in Ottawa in March 2000, Romanow urged the federal government to establish a federal royal commission on the future of medicare in order to trigger a national discussion, and one in which the national feature of medicare would not be ignored, as they were within the isolated provincial task forces.[129] In his view, Alberta was already beginning to go down a separate track in its health care reforms with little regard for the national dimensions of the system and he found himself locked in a bitter argument with Alberta Premier Ralph Klein at the Western Premiers Conference later that summer. The debate carried over into the Annual Premiers Conference in Winnipeg where he found that Klein was aided in his arguments by Premier Mike Harris of Ontario. This rancorous meeting was followed by a First Ministers' Conference that ostensibly produced an agreement on both money and principles in September 2000 but did little to lessen federal-provincial tensions or reduce public anxiety about the direction of medicare in Canada. Romanow believed more than ever that a high-profile royal commission would be essential to provide public input and direction on the issue but little did he realize at the time that he would eventually be called upon to lead such a commission.[130]

Coalition Government, Partisan Politics and Departure

Roy Romanow had experienced much more of victory than defeat in his long political career. Some of his victories were by acclamation, from the presidency of the student's council to the leadership of the New Democratic Party in Saskatchewan. His electoral victories were often won by enormous margins. At the same time, he had experienced defeats in his life. The first, for party leadership in 1970, he hardly regarded as a defeat given the initial odds he faced. The second—the 1982 election—was different. Although the margin of his personal loss was minute, it was humiliating for someone who had become one of the best-known politicians in the country. While this election defeat "gave him iron in his soul," which he used to his advantage in making tough decisions in the 1990s, this strength was already beginning to wear thin when the NDP snatched a razor-thin victory from the jaws of defeat in the election of 1999.[131]

Although officially a victory in terms of the number of seats, the newly formed Saskatchewan Party had gained slightly more votes than the NDP. As a consequence, Romanow felt that his leadership had been rejected by a sizeable number of voters, a consequence of growing anger and resentment in rural Saskatchewan, due in large part to tumbling world crop prices but also to the perception that his government was complicit in the decline of services and infrastructure in rural communities. In addition, he knew that some of his decline at the polls was related to his direct involvement in the negotiations that led to a protracted and bitter nurses' strike in the months preceding the election.[132]

The result put his government in such a dangerous position, however, that Romanow could not afford to spend much time examing the entrails of the 1999 election. Although reluctant at first, Romanow realized the advantage of forging a coalition with the three Liberal members who had been elected. This alliance would bring stability to a government that would otherwise be subject to potential defeat in a vote in the Legislature. Such arrangements are rare in parliamentary governments, but after examining a few potential models, Romanow offered a full coalition government to the Liberal members. After some discussion, a formal coalition agreement was concluded, and then disseminated publicly. Two Liberal MLAs became Cabinet ministers in the Romanow government, and the third was elected speaker of the House.

The coalition continued through the life of the Romanow government. Since negotiation and compromise across strongly competing views had always been Romanow's *modus operandi* in federal-provincial relations, he had little difficulty working in the same manner within his own government. The exercise proved more difficult for some of his old colleagues who now sat side-by-side with individuals they once considered the enemy. Romanow's willingness to work so closely with the elected Liberal members likely confirmed the view of some that he had always been a closet Liberal himself, tacking to the left or to the right whenever convenient. It was true that throughout his career, Romanow had always sought the electoral support of those outside the core NDP base. In his view, elections could never be won on the party vote alone. He felt compelled to reach beyond the party's ideology and gain the support of the majority in order to form a government capable of making changes. His choice of close friends and advisors over his lifetime, many of whom were not party members and some of whom were members of other parties, emphasized this non-partisan part of his character.[133]

However comfortable he was with the political arrangement after September 1999, the coalition government made life increasingly difficult for Romanow. In addition to the normal, but difficult, business of managing Cabinet and caucus, he now had to manage relations between the Liberal members of caucus and Cabinet and those of his own party. And as relations began to sour between elected and non-elected wings of the Liberal Party, he found himself trying to influence relations within the Liberal caucus itself. Through it all, the balance between government and opposition members was so delicate, he could not afford to remove or demote Cabinet members for fear that they would resign. Cabinet discipline, a difficult business for all First Ministers in the best of times, became even more of a headache during this period.

As a consequence of all these pressures, Romanow found that each day became more burdensome. For the first time in his life, he felt the joy of public life was fading and he began to look forward to a time when he could shed the responsibilities of office. Once he realized this, it was only a matter of time to his resignation. In September 2000, one year following the election, he informed his Cabinet colleagues followed by the public and media that he was leaving government.[134] He then acted as caretaker until a new leader, Lorne Calvert, became Premier in February 2001. Roy Romanow's departure marked the end of an era that had its roots in the provincial NDP leadership convention of 1970. Blakeney and Romanow, along with the people that supported their respective leadership bids, became the dominant figures within the party, government and opposition for three decades. Of his government generation, Romanow was the last to depart.

Conclusion

Roy Romanow's career as a politician spanned almost four decades of Saskatchewan history. Almost from the beginning, he set his sights on becoming Premier of the province, despite the fact that he was a first generation Canadian from the poor west side of Saskatoon. He would eventually succeed, but only after a long and productive apprenticeship under Allan Blakeney who himself had apprenticed under Premiers Douglas and Lloyd. During these years, he also came to know the rest of Canada almost as intimately as his home province and, after he finally achieved his ultimate goal of becoming Premier, he used this knowledge and maturation to try and act in the national interest. Always a proud Canadian, he worked assiduously to improve public policy within the country and the federation upon which it was based.

Roy Romanow's career as Premier was marked by his determination to restore fiscal health to the province after years of mismanagement and put it back on a trajectory of growth and prosperity. Without doubt he succeeded in making Saskatchewan the first province to get its fiscal house in order, leading the trend followed by almost every jurisdiction in the country. For a province that was teetering on the edge of bankruptcy, such a

SOURCE: ROY AND ELEANORE ROMANOW

Romanow at the end of the press conference, announcing he would step down as Premier of Saskatchewan.

reversal of fortune could only have been possible with determined leadership of the most remarkable character. As for growth and prosperity, the results remain a debating point. While the province enjoyed the highest per capita growth rate in the country during the 1990s, population growth remained sluggish due in large part to growing farm size and low employment within the province's sizeable resource sector. While Romanow wanted to balance public ownership with private and cooperative ownership, he found that the head offices of large private companies migrated to other parts of Canada and the United States, shrinking the size of the private sector. He encouraged the commercial Crown corporations to invest abroad to improve their viability but this precipitated yet another debate concerning the continued role of public ownership.

Good fiscal management and economic growth, however, are only a means to an end. Most of all, Romanow wanted the quality of life improved for all, particularly those who were most impoverished or marginalized, and he was prepared to use the instrument of government as a force for positive change. In social policy, this meant rejecting workfare in favour of reforms that would break the welfare cycle through investing in their employment, training and education rather than more social assistance. It also meant revamping the health care system in terms of governance, administrative and service delivery, and improving the state of Canada's public health care system would remain a theme in his life even after leaving provincial politics.

The irony is that the debt pressures of the early 1990s forced Romanow to become a "bean counter," a role he never desired. He waited patiently, for almost two decades, to become Premier, only to find that he had to put aside his original objectives and interests to deal with a fiscal crisis. No doubt the desire to move on to a more proactive agenda played some role in his decision to restore the government's finances within as short a time frame as possible. His most satisfying moments came when he could push elements of his social policy agenda onto the national agenda, as he did with the National Child Benefit, the Children's Action Plan and health care reform within the principles of universality and public administration. On this national stage, he was perceived as the most experienced and statesmanlike of Premiers, always prepared to act in the national interest. But while he may even have seemed the consummate political insider given his close relationship with the Prime Minister, and his ability to work with Premiers of varying ideological stripes, he always saw himself as the outsider, the poor Ukrainian kid from the west-side of Saskatoon, lucky to be among those in a position to improve upon an already great country.

Notes

The author would like to thank his research assistants, Jennifer Neiszner and Kevin Schwab, for their work in transcribing interviews and researching newspaper and periodical material. He is particularly grateful to David E. Smith for reviewing this chapter at an early stage.

1. The facts concerning Romanow's early life were drawn from a lengthy interview conducted with him on March 19, 2003 (hereafter Romanow interview), and an article in *The Commonwealth* (January 1991), 5–12.
2. Romanow interview.
3. This environment was captured in Shirley Spafford, *No Ordinary Academics: Economics and Political Science at the University of Saskatchewan, 1910–1960* (Toronto: University of Toronto Press, 2000).
4. Romanow interview.
5. Ibid. Committing himself to the CCF at this early date somewhat contradicts the impression Romanow left with Dennis Gruending in a later interview: see "The Man who would be Premier," *Saskatchewan Business* (October 1990), 10.
6. Romanow interview.
7. Ibid.
8. Saskatchewan Archives Board, Regina (SABR), Blakeney Papers, R353, 138, Woods Royal Commission on Hospital Privileges.
9. Edwin A. Tollefson, "The Aftermath of the Medicare Dispute in Saskatchewan," *Queen's Quarterly* 72, no. 3 (1965): 452–65.
10. Saskatoon *Star Phoenix*, October 29, 1966, 14.
11. Romanow interview; *The Commonwealth* (January 1991), 9–10.
12. Although the CCF won 44.4% of the popular vote, compared to the Liberal's 45.6%, only 25 CCF members were elected relative to 32 Liberal members. See Appendix A in Howard Leeson (ed.), *Saskatchewan Politics: Into the Twenty-first Century* (Regina: Canadian Plains Research Center, 2001), 407–10.
13. Dave Steuart quoted in the Regina *Leader-Post*, November 7, 1987, A10.
14. Aside from Romanow, the "young Turks" included John (Jack) Messer, Ted Bowerman, John Kowalchuk, Miro Kwasnica and Adolph Matsalla. Lloyd selected Romanow, Messer and Bowerman to sit in the front row. Romanow interview; Dennis Gruending, *Promises to Keep: A Political Biography of Allan Blakeney* (Saskatoon: Prairie Books, 1990), 60.
15. See chapter 7 on the Saskatchewan Waffle in Gruending, *Promises to Keep*.
16. Romanow interview; Diane Lloyd, *Woodrow: A Biography of W.S. Lloyd* (Regina: Woodrow Lloyd Memorial Fund, 1979), 170–75.
17. This perception was fueled in part by the fact that Bob Walker, the individual who was most responsible for the attack on Lloyd that evening, was Romanow's law partner: Gruending, *Promises to Keep*, 70. This perception continues: see Lorne Brown, Joseph Roberts and John Warnock, *Saskatchewan Politics from Left to Right, '44 to '99* (Regina: Heartland Publications, 1999), 23.
18. *The Commonwealth* (May 17, 1970), 3, ibid. (June 24, 1970), 3.
19. According to John A. Archer, *Saskatchewan: A History* (Saskatoon: Prairie Books, 1980), 334, Romanow was seen as "somewhat right of the party's centre."

20. *The Commonwealth* (June 10, 1970), 2.
21. Ibid. (June 24, 1970), 6, ibid. (July 8, 1970). The most complete account of the 1970 leadership campaign is in Gruending, *Promises to Keep*, chapter 8. For a "Waffle" view of Blakeney and Romanow's role in the leadership convention, see *Briarpatch*, December 1987/January 1988, 22–24.
22. *The Commonwealth* (March 18, 1970), ibid. (May 27, 1970), 3.
23. Ibid. (June 10, 1970), 8; Gruending, *Promises to Keep*, 75.
24. Romanow interview.
25. *The Commonwealth* (July 8, 1970), 1.
26. Archer, *Saskatchewan*, 338.
27. On Romanow's role as House Leader, see Allan Blakeney and Sandford Borins, *Political Management in Canada*, 2nd ed. (Toronto: University of Toronto Press, 1998), 78.
28. In Blakeney's view, he was the "bean counter" and Romanow the "mouthpiece" for the government. Blakeney and Borins, *Political Management in Canada*, 13–15. Even before assuming government in 1971, Blakeney described Romanow as "one of the best, if not the best, debators in the Saskatchewan Legislature": *The Commonwealth* (December 9, 1970), 1.
29. Quoted in Dennis Gruending, "The Man who would be Premier," 20.
30. Emmett M. Hall, *Report of the Survey of the Court Structure in Saskatchewan and its Utilization done pursuant to order-in-council 474-43 dated April 6, 1973* (Regina: Department of the Attorney-General, 1974).
31. Saskatoon *Star Phoenix*, October 29, 1966, 14. The idea was then fleshed out by Roger Carter, a professor at the College of Law, University of Saskatchewan, and the new plan implemented on the basis of Carter's report. While Saskatchewan had the first provincial plan, the Northwest Territories had the first government-run plan with these features. Jennie Abell, "Ideology and the Emergence of Legal Aid in Saskatchewan," *Dalhousie Law Journal* 16 (Spring 1993), 159.
32. *The Commonwealth* (December 10, 1975), 6, ibid. (February 11, 1976), 4, ibid. (February 25, 1976), 5; Gruending, *Promises to Keep*, 42–44; Blakeney and Borins, *Political Management in Canada*, 25.
33. On the potash fight, see John Richards and Larry Pratt, *Prairie Capitalism: Power and Influence in the New West* (Toronto: McClelland and Stewart, 1979), 250–78, and John S. Burton, "Resource Rent and Taxation: Application of New Principles and Approaches in Saskatchewan" in Eleanor D. Glor (ed.), *Policy Innovation in the Saskatchewan Public Sector, 1971–82* (Toronto: Captus Press, 1997), 59–77.
34. Romanow described this as the "perennial dilemma of Canadian federalism." See Roy Romanow, "Provincial Crown Resource Corporations: Some Constitutional Issues," in Nigel Bankes and J. Owen Saunders (eds.), *Public Disposition of Natural Resources* (Calgary: Institute of Natural Resources Law, 1983), 308.
35. W.R. Lederman, "The Constitution: A Basis for Bargaining," in Anthony Scott (ed.), *Natural Resources Revenues: A Test of Federalism* (Vancouver: University of British Columbia Press, 1976), 58. Quoted in Romanow, "Provincial Crown Resource Corporations," 336.
36. This was the way that Romanow described it in "Reworking the Miracle: The Constitutional Accord 1981," *Queen's Law Journal* 8 (1982/1983): 74–98.
37. Howard Leeson, "The Intergovernmental Affairs Function in Saskatchewan, 1960–83," *Canadian Public Administration* 30, no. 3 (Fall 1987): 399–420.
38. Roy Romanow, "Fiscal Arrangements: A Western Perspective," in Roy Romanow, Claude Ryan and Robert L. Stanfield (eds.), *Ottawa and the Provinces: Regional Perspectives* (Toronto: Ontario Research Council, 1984), 3.

39. *Reference Re Amendment of the Constitution of Canada* (1981), 125 D.L.R. (3rd) 1.
40. *Ottawa Citizen*, October 22, 1997, A1.
41. Romanow, "Reworking the Miracle."
42. Letter, René Levesque, Premier of Quebec, to Peter Lougheed, Premier of Alberta, May 5, 1982. In particular, Levesque referred to the amending formula that "gave Quebec neither a veto nor the right of opting out."
43. Roy Romanow, "Stepping Down: Choices for the Future," *The Commonwealth* (November-December 2000), 1.
44. Gruending, *Promises to Keep*, 198.
45. See Roy Romanow, "Courts and Legislatures in the Age of the Charter," *Canadian Parliamentary Review* 9 (Spring 1986): 2–3. Allan Blakeney remains more negative about the impact of the Charter than Romanow. Blakeney interview by Dennis Gruending, *The Commonwealth* (July-August 2003), 33.
46. Romanow quoted in the Regina *Leader-Post*, November 7, 1987, A10.
47. Roy J. Romanow, Peter J. Meekinson and William D. Moull, *Origins and Meanings of Section 92A: The 1982 Constitutional Amendment on Resources* (Montreal: Institute for Research on Public Policy, 1985).
48. Roy Romanow, John Whyte and Howard Leeson, *Canada Notwithstanding: The Making of the Constitution, 1976–1982* (Toronto: Methuen, 1984).
49. *The Commonwealth* (August 2, 1987), 2, ibid. (October 14, 1987), 1, ibid. (November 18, 1987), 1.
50. Interview, Roy Romanow, July 19, 2003; *Maclean's*, May 13, 1991, 16.
51. Romanow quoted in Janice MacKinnon, *Minding the Public Purse: The Fiscal Crisis, Political Trade-offs, and Canada's Future* (Montreal and Kingston: McGill-Queen's University Press, 2003), 61.
52. *Ottawa Citizen*, October 22, 1991, A1.
53. Hans J. Michelmann and Jeffrey S. Steeves, "The 1982 Transition in Power in Saskatchewan: The Progressive Conservatives and the Public Service," *Canadian Public Administration* 28, no. 1 (Spring 1985).
54. On this legacy, see A.W. Johnson, *Biography of a Government* (Toronto: University of Toronto Press, forthcoming 2004). For a contrary view, see Jocelyn Praud and Sarah McQuarrie, "The Saskatchewan CCF-NDP from the Regina Manifesto to the Romanow Years," in Leeson (ed.), *Saskatchewan Politics*, 143–67.
55. This was, in part, due to the revelation of political fraud that was becoming public in the early part of the Romanow administration. See Gerry Jones, *SaskScandal: The Death of Political Idealism in Saskatchewan* (Calgary: Fifth House, 2000).
56. This draws loosely on Cristine de Clercy's four general propositions in "Policy Innovation and Deficit Reduction: Saskatchewan, Alberta and British Columbia," in Paul Boothe and Bradford Reid (eds.), *Deficit Reduction in the Far West: The Great Experiment* (Edmonton: University of Alberta Press, 2001), 208–9.
57. On the precise expenditure and revenue measures, and their timing, relative to Alberta and British Columbia, see the summary in de Clercy, "Policy Innovation and Deficit Reduction," 218–19.
58. MacKinnon, *Minding the Public Purse*, 100.
59. Don Gass, *Report of the Saskatchewan Final Management Review Commission* [the Gass Commission] (Regina: Saskatchewan Finance, February 1992).
60. MacKinnon, *Minding the Public Purse*, 102.
61. John Richards, *Now that the Coat Fits the Cloth: Spending Wisely in a Trimmed-Down Age* (Toronto: C.D. Howe Institute Commentary no. 143, 2000), table 5, 31.

62. MacKinnon, *Minding the Public Purse*, 107.
63. Various issues of *Briarpatch* in 1992 and 1993. Linda McQuaig's *Shooting the Hippo: Death by Deficit and other Canadian Myths* (Toronto: Penguin, 1996) would become the most popular, national expression of these sentiments.
64. Brown et al., *Saskatchewan Politics from Left to Right*, 55.
65. Within the NDP, Romanow's position continues to be criticized, and arguments favouring a higher tax/royalty regime continue to be advocated. See Erin Weir, "Sinews of Social Democracy: Saskatchewan Taxes, Royalties and Expenditures," *The Commonwealth* (September/October 2003), 32–35.
66. Romanow quoted in Patricia Elliott, "Who's New in Cabinet," *Briarpatch* (February 1992), 8.
67. MacKinnon, *Minding the Public Purse*, 104–5.
68. This account is drawn from an interview with Roy Romanow, April 29, 2003.
69. For a comparison of Saskatchewan's deficit efforts with those in Alberta and British Columbia, see Paul Boothe, "Slaying the Deficit Dragon? Anti-Deficit Policies in the West," in Boothe and Reid, *Deficit Reduction in the Far West*, 135–64.
70. *The Commonwealth* (June 1988), 1, 20.
71. Interview with Roy Romanow, *Briarpatch* (December 1987/January 1988), 21.
72. Quotes from T.C. Douglas's speech in Roy Romanow, "Setting the Direction for our Second Term," *The Commonwealth* (December 1996), 7–9.
73. The health districts were initially responsible for acute care, long-term care, home care and ambulance services. In April 1995, they became responsible for mental health, public health and addiction services, involving a transfer of more than 1,400 of the 2,200 staff from the provincial Department of Health to the districts. Kathy Langlois, "A Saskatchewan Vision for Health: Who Really Makes the Decisions?," in Robin Ford and David Zussman (eds.), *Alternative Service Delivery: Sharing Governance in Canada* (Toronto: KPMG/IPAC, 1997), 177.
74. Duane Adams, "The White and the Black Horse Race: Saskatchewan Health Reform in the 1990s," in Leeson (ed.), *Saskatchewan Politics*, 267.
75. Louise Simard, minister of Health, *A Saskatchewan Vision for Health: A Framework for Change* (Regina: Saskatchewan Health, 1992), 5.
76. Amanda M. Jones, "Closing Rural Hospitals in Saskatchewan: On the Road to Wellness?," *Social Science & Medicine* 49 (1999): 1021–34.
77. *The Commonwealth* (October 5, 1988), 4; interview, Roy Romanow, July 19, 2003.
78. Adams, "The White and the Black Horse Race," 267–93.
79. Kevin O'Fee, "Critical Mass: Health Care Reform and 'the Wellness Model'" (MA thesis, University of Regina, 2001).
80. Interview, Roy Romanow, April 29, 2003.
81. Desmond Morton, *The New Democrats, 1961–1986: The Politics of Change* (Toronto: Copp Clark Pittman, 1986).
82. Romanow quoted in *The Commonwealth* (November/December 1988), 11.
83. This view of Douglas is supported in A.W. Johnson's *Biography of a Government* (Toronto: University of Toronto Press, forthcoming 2004).
84. On the debate within the CCF, see Richards and Pratt, *Prairie Capitalism*.
85. In *Saskatchewan Politics: From Left to Right*, Brown et al. refer sympathetically to the state-ownership

side of the debate (versus the alternative of regulation and taxation) in the Douglas government, never once mentioning Tommy Douglas's own position.

86. Romanow, "Provincial Crown Resource Corporations," 307–33.
87. As Romanow stated quite clearly in an interview for *Briarpatch* (December 1987/January 1988), 21.
88. This is also Gruending's conclusion in *Promises to Keep*. In *The Commonwealth* (December 10, 1975), 6, T.C. Douglas states that his administration lacked the capital for more public investment.
89. Romanow quoted in the Regina *Leader-Post*, November 7, 1987, A10.
90. Dennis Gruending, "The Man who would be Premier," 19. In 1992, however, Romanow approved a strategy that would have seen the provincial government's shares used to regain some control over the board of the Potash Corporation of Saskatchewan. The attempt failed. Interview, Roy Romanow, April 29, 2003. On Romanow's opposition to privatization during the Devine era, see James M. Pitsula and Kenneth A. Rasmussen, *Privatizing a Province: The New Right in Saskatchewan* (Vancouver: New Star Books, 1990).
91. Crown Investments Corporation (CIC), *Saskatchewan Crown Corporations Review 1996* (Regina: CIC, 1996); Roy Romanow, "Crown Corporations in an Era of Change," *The Commonwealth* (April 1996), 3.
92. John R. Allan, "Introduction and Overview," in John R. Allan (ed.), *Public Enterprise in an Era of Change* (Regina: Canadian Plains Research Center, 1998), vii.
93. Romanow quoted in his speech to the Saskatchewan NDP annual convention, *The Commonwealth* (December 1996), 5.
94. *Saskatchewan Crown Corporations Review 1996* (Regina: Crown Investments Corporation, 1996).
95. J.F. Conway, "Portents for the Future," *Briarpatch* (September 1998), 33.
96. Roy Romanow, "A Mega-Project on the Edge," *The Commonwealth* (June 1993), 3.
97. Interview, Roy Romanow, July 19, 2003.
98. Federation of Saskatchewan Indian Nations, *Saskatchewan and Aboriginal Peoples in the 21st Century: Social, Economic and Political Changes and Challenges* (Regina: PrintWest Publishing, 1997), 19.
99. *Northern Saskatchewan—A Transformation* (Regina: Saskatchewan Northern Affairs, 2002).
100. Keith Goulet, "NDP Record on Aboriginal and Northern Issues," *The Commonwealth* (Summer 1999), 10.
101. SABR, list of members of provincial ministries.
102. Gregory P. Marchildon, "An Attempt to Reconcile the Irreconcilable," *Inroads* 5 (1996).
103. *The Commonwealth* (January 2, 1974), 3.
104. In 1980, Romanow drew the parallel between the economic discrimination of the West and the cultural and linguistic discrimination felt in Quebec: *The Commonwealth* (February 27, 1980), 3.
105. Gregory P. Marchildon (ed.), *Agriculture at the Border: Canada-U.S. Trade Relations in the Global Food Regime* (Regina: Canadian Plains Research Center, 2000), vii.
106. Gregory P. Marchildon, "Chronology of Events Leading Up to the Federal-Provincial Agreement on Agricultural Relief, 1999–2000" (unpublished typescript, February 2000).
107. The "string of pearls" analogy was used by Romanow as early as 1980: *The Commonwealth* (May 7, 1980), 3.
108. Roy Romanow, "Setting the Direction for our Second Term," *The Commonwealth* (December 1996), 33.
109. Roy Romanow, "Social Policy Reform must recognize core Canadian values," *The Commonwealth* (September 1995), 3.

110. Roy Romanow, "Renewing Federalism: Why Social Reform is Necessary," speech to the Canadian Council on Social Development, Ottawa, May 24, 1996.
111. Roy Romanow, "Reinforcing 'the Ties that Bind'," *Policy Options* (November 1998): 11.
112. "Building Independence-Investing in Families," special supplement to *The Commonwealth* (June 1998), 1–4; Roy Romanow, "Child Poverty: A Damning Indictment," *The Commonwealth* (January 1997), 4–5; Roy Romanow, notes for remarks to Canada's Children Future Conference, November 27, 1996.
113. On the Saskatchewan origins of the social union, see Gregory P. Marchildon and Brent Cotter, "Saskatchewan and the Social Union," in Leeson (ed.), *Saskatchewan Politics*, 367–80.
114. For some of the differences between Saskatchewan and Quebec, see Gregory P. Marchildon, "A Step in the Right Direction," *Inroads* 9 (2000): 124–33.
115. *Maclean's*, June 22, 1992, 16–17.
116. *The Commonwealth* (October 1992), 3, 6–7.
117. The result in Saskatchewan was 55.5% against, and 45.5% in favour, of the Charlottetown Accord. This was very close to the national average of 54.2% against, and 44.8% in favour, of Charlottetown. Peter H. Russell, *Constitutional Odyssey: Can Canadians Become a Sovereign People?*, 2nd ed. (Toronto: University of Toronto Press, 1993), 227.
118. Roy Romanow, notes for remarks, Paul H. Nitze School of Advanced International Studies, Johns Hopkins University, Washington, DC, September 15, 1995.
119. Roy Romanow, notes for remarks, Empire Club, Toronto, April 2, 1997.
120. Roy Romanow, "The Road from Calgary to Quebec City," speech at Université Laval, February 26, 1998.
121. Canadian Integovernmental Conference Secretariat, news release (ref: 850-065/045), "Premiers Agree to Consult Canadians on Unity" plus "Framework for Discussion on National Unity," Premiers' Meeting, Calgary, Alberta, September 14, 1997.
122. Roy Romanow, "Canada's Agenda is Saskatchewan's Agenda," *The Commonwealth* (October 1997), 31.
123. Known as the "constitutional contingencies" exercise, the steering committee was led by the deputy provincial secretary (responsible for intergovernmental affairs), and included the deputy ministers of Justice and Finance as well as the Premier's chief of staff.
124. The notice of intervention was filed on November 29, 1996, and recognized by the Supreme Court on January 17, 1997. Factum of the attorney general for Saskatchewan, Intervener, Court File no. 25506.
125. Typescript, presentation of John D. Whyte, deputy minister of Justice on behalf of the attorney general of Saskatchewan to the Supreme Court of Canada: Quebec Secession Reference, February 17, 1998.
126. *Reference re Secession of Quebec* [1998] 2 S.C.R. 217.
127. Clarity Act (2000, c. 26), Parliament of Canada.
128. Commission on Medicare [Fyke Commission], *Caring for Medicare: Sustaining a Quality System* (Regina: Saskatchewan Health, 1991), appendix A, terms of reference, 86–87.
129. Romanow's speech was presented on March 31, 2000, and reprinted in *The Commonwealth* (May-June 2000), 1–4.
130. Roy Romanow was appointed sole chair of the Royal Commission on the Future of Health Care in Canada in April 2001, just two months after leaving the office of premier. His final report, *Building on*

Values: The Future of Health Care in Canada (Ottawa: Commission on the Future of Health Care in Canada), was released on November 28, 2002.

131. Quotation from Aydon Charlton, Romanow's executive assistant from 1979 to 1982, in Mary Nemeth, "The Middle Way," *Maclean's*, June 12, 1995, 13.

132. Brian Bergman, "A Shock for Romanow," *Maclean's*, September 27, 1999, 32–33. On the rapid rise of the Saskatchewan Party and the decline of the provincial Liberal Party see Kevin Wishlow, "Rethinking the Polarization Thesis: The Formation and Growth of the Saskatchewan Party," in Leeson (ed.), *Saskatchewan Politics*, 169–97; and Lynda Haverstock, "The Saskatchewan Liberal Party," also in Leeson (ed.), *Saskatchewan Politics*, 199–250.

133. Interview, Roy Romanow, July 19, 2003.

134. Robert Sheppard, "Quitting the Club," *Maclean's*, October 9, 2000, 6. Romanow's news conference statement announcing his resignation, dated September 25, 2000, was reproduced in *The Commonwealth* (November-December 2000), 1–3.

Index

A
Abbott, Douglas, 245
Abel, Jennie, 389
Aberhart, William (Alberta), 92, 149, 168
Aboriginal people, 240, 257
    alcohol and substance abuse, 378
    communities of, 184, 378
    economic development, 378-9
    education of, 345
    entrepreneurs and cooperatives, 294
    health care of, 345
    hiring quotas for, 293
    integration of, 268
    job creation for, 261-2, 378
    land entitlement, 294
    migration of to cities, 262
    northern cooperatives, 191
    rights of, 310, 344-6
    self-government of, 293, 345, 378
    treaty rights, 345
    see also treaty land entitlements
Act to Establish Larger School Units (1944), 236
Act to Facilitate the Adjustment of Agricultural Debts, 130
Adam Smith Institute, 331
Adams, Duane, 373, 391
addiction services, 391
Advisory Committee on Medical Care, 195, 197
affirmative action programs, 261, 294, 312
agrarian movement, 55
Agrarian Socialism: The Cooperative Commonwealth Federation in Saskatchewan. A Study in Political Sociology, 68
agricultural
    college, 18
    crisis, 156, 336-7
    dependence, 268
    diversification, 292
    economy, 20
    issues, 172, 181, 229, 291
    organizations, 47
    production, 259
    reform movement, 19
agriculture, 5, 61, 71, 121, 146, 149, 177, 263, 278, 282, 284, 290, 336, 376-7
Agriculture at the Border: Canada-U.S. Trade Relations in the Global Food Regime, 392
airline corporation, 274
Airwaves Advertising, 348
Alberta Co-operative Wheat Producers' Limited, 76

Alberta, University of, 319, 365
alcohol, sale of, *see* liquor
alcohol and substance addiction, 378
Aldridge, Garry, 287
Algoma Steel, 314
All People's Mission, 163
Allan, John R.
    Public Enterprise in an Era of Change, 350, 392
Alternative Service Delivery: Sharing Governance in Canada, 391
Alwinsal of Canada Ltd., 259
American Medical Association, 222, 276
Amok, 301
Anatomy of a Party, 270
Anderson, Arthur, 110
Anderson, Edith (née Redgewick), 110, 134
Anderson, James Thomas Milton, 54-5, 90, 100, 103, 110–16, 119–28, 130, 132-5, 137, 141, 215
    The Education of the New Canadian: A Treatise on Canada's Greatest Educational Problem, 54, 68, 99, 110
    government of, 101-2, 121, 123–9, 131, 136
Andrew, Bob, 323, 326, 331
Anglican Church, 99, 110
Annual Premiers Conference, 382, 384
anti-war movement, 360
Archer, John H, 239
    Saskatchewan: A History, 138, 158-60, 270, 388
Archer, S., 86
Argue, Hazen, 193-4, 198, 201, 212, 247-8, 251-2, 270
Association of Saskatchewan Taxpayers, 347
Atkinson, C.J., 3-4
auto insurance, 274
Autonomy Bills (Acts), 5-6, 9, 26-7, 46-7, 53, 118
autonomy debate (western Canada), xiii, 5

B
Backrooms: A Story of Politics, 350-2
bacon-processing plant, 319, 327, 335
Badgeley, Robin
    Doctors' Strike: Medical Care and Conflict in Saskatchewan, 211
Bailey, Edgar, 209
Balfour, James, 40
Bank of Canada, 312, 321, 371
bank, provincial, 170
Bankes, Nigel
    Public Disposition of Natural Resources, 389
Baptist Union of Western Canada, 165
Baptists, Fundamentalist, 165

Barnhart, Gordon L.
  "Peace, Progress and Prosperity": A Biography of Saskatchewan's First Premier, T. Walter Scott, 36, 67, 85
Barootes, Dr. E.W., 196, 211
Bartlett, Richard, 352
Bayda, Justice E.D., 302
Bedford Road Collegiate, 354-5
Belanger, Buckley, 378
Bell Telephones, 20
Benjamin, Les, 236
Bennett, Bill (British Columbia), 307
Bennett, R.B., 101, 103, 116, 129, 133-4, 170, 172
Benson, Jacob, 122, 124, 171
Bentley, Tom, 190
Bergman, Brian, 394
Berntson, Eric, 323, 326, 335-6, 346, 349
Beulah Baptist church, 163
Beveridge, Sir William
  Full Employment in a Free Society, 273
Biggs, Lesley, 352
  Devine Rule in Saskatchewan: A Decade of Hope and Hardship, 351-2
Bill 20, 333
Bill of Rights (1947), 153
Biography of a Government, 390-1
Black Friday budget, 264-5
Black, Henry, 138
Blair, Robert, 207
Blakeney, Allan Emrys, 7, 90, 202, 207, 212, 230, 234, 236, 267, 276, 360-1, 363
  in cabinet, 277, 280
  early years, 272, 274-5
  government of, 268, 294-5, 298, 314, 316, 321-2, 325-7, 342, 346, 372-5, 379, 386
  as NDP leader, 281-3
  Political Management in Canada, 388
  as premier, 239, 284-5, 287-92, 295-7, 299-315, 333, 335, 357, 389-90
  resignation of, 366
Blakeney, Anne (née Gorham), 275, 278, 283, 288, 314
Blakeney, Barbara, 275
Blakeney, Bertha May (nee Davies), 272
Blakeney, David, 278
Blakeney, Hugh, 275
Blakeney, John Cline, 272
Blakeney, Margaret, 278
Blakeney, Molly (née Schwartz), 273, 275
Bland, Dr. Salem, 163
Board of Grain Commissioners, 57
Board of Railway Commissioners, 43-4
Board of Transport Commissioners, 153
Boldt, Dave, 254
Bolstad, Wes, 236, 285-6

Boothe, Paul
  Deficit Reduction in the Far West: The Great Experiment, 390-1
Borden, Robert (Prime Minister), 51, 97
Bouchard, Lucien, 381
Bourassa, Robert, 344, 382
Bowen, Ted, 287
Bowerman, Ted, 278, 283, 293, 297, 388
Boy Scouts, 154, 163, 166
boycott of legislature, by NDP, 333-4, 366-7
Boyd, C.W., 351
Bracken, John (Manitoba), 75, 85, 123
Bradshaw affair, 26
Bradshaw, J.E., 24-5, 46
Brandon College (University), 165-6
breast cancer screening project, 342
Bredt, P.M., 6
Brennan, J. William, 38, 85, 87
Brewin, Andrew, 212
brick plant, 179, 184, 246
Briers, Bill, 80
British Airways, 331
British Gas, 331
British Labour Party, 184, 273
British National Health Service, 225
British North America Act, 306
British Telecom, 331
Britnell, George E., 107, 138, 355
Brown, J.P., 38
Brown, Lorne, 158
  Saskatchewan Politics from Left to Right, '44 to '99, 388, 391
Broadbent, Ed, 307
Broadview Agricultural Banquet, 141
Brockelbank, J.H., 284
Brockelbank, John, 179, 199, 212, 284
Brown Elwood commission, 26, 29
Brown, George W., 6-7
Bryan, William Jennings, 76
Bryant, J.F., 54, 110, 115, 120-1, 132, 137
Bryden, Ken, 187
Buchanan, John, 307
Buckle, W.C., 113, 121, 137
Building on Values: The Future of Health Care in Canada, 394
Bulyea, G.H.V., 7, 37
Burns, Robert, 162
Burton, John S., 229, 236, 298, 389
Byers, Neil, 283

C
Cadbury, George, 184-5
Calder, James, 7, 9-10, 13-4, 16, 25-6, 29-30, 33, 46-7, 51
Calderwood, W., 137

Calgary Declaration, 383
Calvary Baptist Church, 166-8, 172
Calvert, Lorne, 381, 386
Cambridge University, 184
Cameco, 315
Cameron, Alex, 249, 254
Cameron, Colin, 202
Cameron, William, 166
Canada Health Act, 384
Canada Health and Social Transfer (CHST), 380, 384
Canada Notwithstanding: The Making of the Constitution, 1976-1982, 365, 390
Canada Packers (Toronto), 241-2, 244
Canada Pension Plan, 203, 206
Canadian Annual Review, 1908, The, 19, 67
Canadian Annual Review of Public Affairs, 1916, The, 67
Canadian Annual Review of Public Affairs, 1918, The, 53, 68
Canadian Annual Review of Public Affairs, 1921, The, 68
Canadian Armed forces, 50-1
Canadian Baptist church, 165
Canadian Centre for Policy Alternatives, 315
Canadian Charter of Rights and Freedoms, *see* Charter of Rights and Freedoms
Canadian Civil Liberties Association, 315
Canadian Congress of Labour (CCL), 186
Canadian Constitution, *see* Constitution, Canadian
Canadian Council of Agriculture, 47, 63
Canadian Environment Protection Act, 336
Canadian Expeditionary Force, 51
Canadian Federation of Agriculture, 60
Canadian Imperial Bank of Commerce, 347
Canadian Industrial Oil and Gas, 303
Canadian Labour Congress (CLC), 197
Canadian Light Horse Regiment, 141
Canadian Manufacturers' Association, 44
Canadian Medical Association, 195
Canadian Northern Railway, 11, 44
Canadian Occidental, 377
Canadian Pacific Railway (CPR), 5-6, 11, 34, 120, 140, 182, 227, 354
Canadian Potash Producers' Association, 299
Canadian Public Railway, 242
Canadian Teachers' Federation, 216
Canadian Wheat Board, 58, 72, 84-5, 172, 344
Canadian Wheat Board Act, 73
Canadian Wildlife Federation, 336
Canpotex, 333
capitalism, 164, 167, 169, 185, 171, 173
Cargo, David, 266
Carson, Carol, 368
Carter, Roger, 389
casinos, 377
Castellain, Marian St. Clair, xiv
Catholics, *see* Roman Catholic
Cawthorpe, C.H., 38

CBC-TV, 260
CCF, federal, 174-6, 187, 197-8, 201
CCF, provincial, 90, 101, 106, 124, 133-6, 212, 272, 278, 284, 290, 297, 301, 311, 318, 320, 324, 349, 356-9, 361, 388
  during Douglas, 169, 170, 172–4, 177-8, 180-1, 183-4, 215-6, 218, 221, 228-30, 232, 235-6185-6, 188, 190, 192, 194-6, 199
  during Patterson, 140, 142-3, 147-8, 150, 153
  during Thatcher, 238, 242-6, 248-54, 258-60
  see also NDP, provincial
Central Canada Potash, 297-9, 303
Century of Canadian Grain: Government Policy to 1951, A, 85
CFQC-TV, 357
Char Inc, 334
Charlottetown Accord, 382, 393
Charlton, Aydon, 394
Charter of Rights and Freedoms, 169, 207, 210, 307, 309, 318, 343-4, 364
Chicago, University of, 165
Childers, Chuck, 333
Children's Action Plan, 381, 387
children's dental plan, 373
  see also dental health
Chretien, Jean, 308-10, 364-5, 379-80, 382, 384
Christian Farm Crisis Action Committee, 337
Churchill, Winston, 100
Chwialkowksa, Luiza, 352
Citizens Commission of Inquiry into the War Measures Act, The, 231
Citizens' Committee for Medical Care, 223
civil liberties, 153, 204
civil rights, 252
civil service, 35, 131, 219, 228, 274, 277, 285, 287, 304, 329, 367-9, 371, 383
Civil Service Association, 187
CKOM (radio), 354, 356-9
Clarity Act, 393
Clarity Bill, 384
Clark, Joe, 306, 311
Clement, Andrew, 162
Cleverdon, Catherine L.
  The Woman Suffrage Movement in Canada, 38
Climenhaga, D.B., 87
closure, legislative, 333
coal strike (Estevan), 167
coalition government (federal), 51
Cobb, Herb, 166
Coburn, Dr. Frank, 232-3, 236
Cochran, L.B., 4
Coderre, Lionel, 254
Cody, Don, 284
Cohen, Andrew
  A Deal Undone: The Making and Breaking of the Meech Lake Accord, 352

Coldwell, M.J., 124, 127, 133-4, 142, 167-9, 171-4, 179, 182, 197, 210-2, 216, 244-5, 284
collective agreement, 261, 340, 349
  see also unions
College of Physicians and Surgeons, 195, 197, 222, 224, 358
Colligan-Yano, F.
  The Urban Age: Building a Place for Urban Government in Saskatchewan, 87
Collver, Dick, 296, 304, 311, 320
commercial ventures, social ownership of, 179
Commission on Medicare, 374
Commission on New Directions for Health Care, 372
Committee on Crown Corporations, 192
Commonwealth, The, 175, 211, 388-91, 393
communication allowances, for MLAs, 348
Communications Group Advertising, 348
communism, 173, 192, 245
Community Capital Fund, 295
community colleges, 295
community schools, 294
companies, government-owned, 339
  see also industries
compassionate conservatism, 322, 329
Conner, Arthur, 209
conscientious objectors (war), 51
conscription, compulsory, 51, 59
consensus politicians, 318
Consensus Saskatchewan, 346
Conservatism, 110, 136, 164, 339
Conservative Party, federal, 3, 25, 43-4, 51, 58, 110, 129, 133-4, 170, 172-3, 181, 207
Conservative Party, provincial, 8, 11, 24-5, 27, 66, 71, 82, 138, 142, 147, 155, 157, 134-8, 169, 201, 250, 262, 296, 303-5, 311-3, 358, 366-7
  during Anderson, 110–124, 126, 130-1, 133
  during Devine, 319, 321-3, 326-7, 329, 331, 335, 340-1, 346-9
  during Gardiner, 99-102, 106
  during Martin, 43, 46, 51, 53-4, 59, 61, 63-4
Constitution Act (1982), 343, 345
Constitution, Canadian, 363-4
  patriation of, 318, 321, 363-4, 381
constitutional
  accord, 311
  amendments, 308-9, 344, 379
  debates, 306
  reform, 149, 310, 383
Constitutional Odyssey: Can Canadians Become a Sovereign People?, 352, 393
Construction Labour Relations Act (CLRA), 340
consumer protection legislation, 203
Consumers' Co-operative Refinery Limited, 335
Conway, J.F., 392
Cotter, Brent, 393
co-op farming, *see* cooperatives

co-op oil company, *see* cooperatives
Co-op Upgrader, 335
co-operative commonwealth, 169, 172
Co-operative Commonwealth Federation, *see* CCF
Cooperative Elevator Company, *see* Saskatchewan Cooperative Elevator Company
cooperatives, 99, 176, 178, 190, 274, 376
  dairy, 191
  farm implement plant, 191
  farming, 191
  federalism, 363, 379
  fisheries, 227
  government, 101, 103, 123, 131, 135-6
  livestock, 191
  oil company, 191
  retail, 191
  wholesale, 191
Corman, John Wesley, 179, 182
corporations, public ownership of, 274
correspondence schools, 128
Courville, L.D., 87
Cowley, Elwood, 236, 284, 286, 289, 298-9
Crawford, Isobel (née Douglas), 209
creameries, 99
Crear, T.A., 63
credit unions, 140, 147, 156
Cronkite, F.C., 145, 151
crop prices, 385
Cross of Gold speech, 76
Cross, J.A., 72, 79, 96
Crow rate, 311, 322
Crown corporations, 187, 239, 244, 246-7, 256-7, 268, 274, 295, 298-300, 302, 305, 312-3, 316, 318, 321, 324-5, 332-3, 336, 349, 362, 387
  privatization of, 319, 325
  sale of, 336, 366, 375
Crown Investments Corporation (CIC), 305, 323, 375-6, 392
Crown lands, control over, 34, 44, 58, 61, 64
Crown Life Insurance Company, 134, 315, 347
Crown Management Board, 333
Crown utilities, *see* public utilities
Cuelenare, John, 253-4, 259
Cunningham, Darrel, 368
Curran, L.F., 160
Currie, Bev, 231-3, 236

D
Dafoe, J.W., 27, 30, 106
Daily Standard, 27
Daily Star, 127, 137-8
dairy co-ops, *see* cooperatives
dairy processing plant, 185
Dalgleish, Dr. H.D., 222, 225-6
Dalhousie Law School, 355
Dalhousie University, 17, 21, 272-3

Darling and Pearson (architectural firm), 14
Davies, William G., 197, 211
Davin, Nicholas Flood, 3-5
Davis, T.C., 96, 127, 142
Davis, William, 307, 309-10
Dawson, Reverend Leonard, 3
de Clercy, Cristine, 390
de Vlieger, Dan, 236
Deal Undone: The Making and Breaking of the Meech Lake Accord, A, 352
Death of Socialism, The, 331
Debt Adjustment Act, 131
Debt Adjustment Board, 131
Debt Adjustment Commission, 132
debt adjustment legislation, 144
Deficit Reduction in the Far West: The Great Experiment, 390-1
democracy, participatory, 219
democratic socialism, 216, 273
  see also socialism
dental health, 221, 262, 283, 307, 342
Department of Agriculture, 319, 347
Department of Education, 9, 11, 27, 34, 217, 219
Department of the Environment, 336
Department of Health, 262, 341, 358, 391
Department of Intergovernmental Affairs, 363
Department of Labour, 341
Department of Mineral Resources, 298
Department of Natural Resources (DNR), 262, 293
Department of Northern Saskatchewan (DNS), 293-4, 341
Department of Public Participation, 332
Department of Regional Economic Expansion, 334
Department of Social Services, 338-9, 341
Department of Telephones, 26, 46, 141
Depression, 95, 122–6, 128-31, 133, 135-6, 140, 143, 149, 156, 168-70, 175, 177, 180-1, 214, 216, 241-2, 274, 282, 290, 368
Descartes, Rene, 273
Developing West: Essays on Canadian History in Honour of Lewis H. Thomas, The, 67
Deverell, William, 356
Devine, Donald Grant, 90, 311-3, 319, 321-3, 350
  economic philosophy of, 320, 345-6
  fraud charges of government officials, 349
  government of, 315, 318, 326, 330, 332-5, 337-43, 347, 349, 366-9, 371-3, 376, 379
  as premier, 318, 324-9, 332
Devine Rule in Sask.: A Decade of Hope and Hardship, 351-2
Devline, E.H., 38
Dewhurst, Fred, 233
Diefenbaker for the Defence, 157
Diefenbaker, John G., 96, 105-6, 134-6, 142, 147, 157, 174, 183, 190, 194, 197, 201, 227, 248, 320, 322, 339

One Canada: Memoirs of the Right Honourable John G. Diefenbaker, The Crusading Years, 107
direct democracy, 59, 62, 66
Disberry, Justice D.C., 296, 298
dispute resolution mechanism, 315
distinct society clause, 343-4
  see Constitution, Canadian
Dixon, R.M.H., 85, 87
doctors' strike, 200, 223-4, 252, 270, 276, 357-8
Doctors' Strike: Medical Care and Conflict in Saskatchewan, 211
Doer, Gary, 380
Doern, G. Bruce
  Privatization, Public Policy and Public Corporations in Canada, 351
Dominion Bank, 140
"Dominion Lands" Policy, 107
Donnelly, Florence, 146
Douglas, Annie, 162-3
Douglas, Irma (née Dempsey), 166, 172, 208
Douglas, Isobel, 162
Douglas, J.T. (Jack), 174, 176, 179
Douglas, Nan, 162
Douglas, Thomas Clement, 35, 67, 90, 140, 155, 165-6, 218, 220, 222, 224, 250, 275-8, 281, 284, 287, 289, 292, 316, 323, 332, 339, 356-7, 361, 386, 391
  as campaigner, 169–80
  early years, 162-4
  in federal politics, 197-205, 207-8, 251-4
  government of, 153, 156, 180-4, 186, 188, 190, 194, 221, 247, 252, 258-9, 279, 290, 293, 295, 297, 325, 360, 368-9, 372, 374-6, 392
  interviews with, 209-12
  as preacher, 166-8
  as premier, 185-7, 189, 192-3, 195-6, 238-9, 246, 248-9, 303, 311, 314
  resignation of, 197
  as visionary, 239
Douglas, Willie, 162
Douglas-Coldwell Foundation, 206-7
Douglas-Thatcher debate, 247-8
Doukhobors, 50-2
drug and alcohol abuse, 342
drug plan budget, 373
Dunkards, 92, 106-7
Dunlop, William, 110
Dunn, C.M., 107
Dunning, Ada (née Rowlatt), 70
Dunning, Avery Charles, 70
Dunning, Charles Avery, 22, 47, 60-1, 64, 70, 72, 80, 82-5, 90-1, 93-4, 110, 112, 145-6, 155, 158-9
  death of, 84
  government of, 74, 79
  and prohibition, 77-8, 81
  and Wheat Board, 73, 75-7, 86
Dunning, Katherine (née Hall), 70

Dunning, Katherine Ada, 70
Dunning, Samuel, 70

E
Eager, Evelyn, 19
    Saskatchewan Government: Politics and Pragmatism, 37, 85
Eaglesham, Hugh, 169
Economic Advisory and Planning Board, 184
economic development, 140, 178, 220, 228, 239, 247, 249, 251, 254-5, 258, 263, 284, 294-6, 332, 336, 374, 376, 378
economic diversification, 284, 296, 324, 349, 362, 376
Education Act, 28
Education of the New Canadian: A Treatise on Canada's Greatest Educational Problem, The, 54, 68, 99, 110
educational system, xiii, 111-3, 124, 131, 136, 156, 163, 181, 185, 217-9, 227, 234, 256, 263, 265, 278, 321-2
    budget, 330
    compulsory for children, 49-50, 52-4
    immigrants in, 28, 48-9, 55
    language issue in, 28, 52-5
    reforms, 54-5, 64
    religious, 27, 54
    rights of minorities in, 26-29, 34-5, 54
    rural, 48, 145
    taxes for, 27, 46
    see also separate school system
Edward and W.S. Maxwell (architectural firm), 15
Edwards, George F., 82
Edy, Carl, 180
80:20 formulation, 383
Eisler, Dale, 350-1
    Rumours of Glory, Saskatchewan and the Thatcher Years, 269-70
Eldorado Nuclear mine, 300-2
electoral reforms, 64
electricity, 181-3, 325, 375
    see also power
Elliott, Patricia, 391
Elwood, Brown, 46
Embury, J.F., 127
Emmons, Patrick, 114, 116, 137
employment programs, 294
employment standards, 176, 186
Endicott, Rev. Charles, 79, 86
Ens, Aldoft
    Subjects or Citizens? The Mennonite Experience in Canada, 1870-1925, 68
Ens, Gerhard, 38
entitlement, culture of, 240
entrepreneurial culture, 334
environmental assessment, 336
environmental issues, 301
equal rights for citizens, 167

Equal Suffrage Association, 24
Erb, Walter, 195-6
Estevan Clay Products, 256
Estey, Justice Willard, 376
European Economic Community (EEC), 336-7, 377
Evans, J.R.C., 166
Evans, John, 82
Evans, Una Maclean, 107
Evening Province, 25

F
Fair Share Saskatchewan, 347
Fairbairn, G.
    From Prairie Roots: The Remarkable Story of Saskatchewan Wheat Pool, 86
Falconer, Kenneth, 209
family farms, 282, 337
    decline of, 326
    ownership of, 326
    land transfer, intergenerational, 326
    see also farms
Faris, Don, 283
Farm Debt Review Board, 326
farm families, 20, 146, 166, 182, 186, 282, 337
    see also farmers
farm fuel, rebates on, 327
farm implement manufacturing industry, 376
Farm Land Security Board, 326
Farm Loan Board, 127, 180
farm organizations, 114, 163, 197
Farm Purchase Program, 326, 337
farm safety-net programs, 347
Farm Security Act, 176, 181-2
Farm Start Program, 295
Farmer Labour Party, 101-2, 122, 124, 133-4, 167-9, 216
farmer-labour political parties, 163, 168
farmers, 148, 150, 152
    cooperative organizations, 57-8, 61, 64, 164
    credit program for, 49, 61, 171, 290
    organized, 70, 101, 124, 292
Farmers in Politics, The, 164, 209
Farmers' Union of Canada, 76, 83
Farmland Security Act, 327
farms
    crisis in, 282
    debt-ridden, 170
    decrease in number, 337
    diversification of, 290
    improvements to, 185
    issues in, 172, 181
    nationalization of, 290
    operations, profitable, 185
    subsidies to, 336
    see also family farms
federal transfer payments, 181, 268, 380

federalism, 146, 156, 382
Federated Co-operatives Limited (FCL), 335, 376
Federation of Saskatchewan Indian Nations (FSIN),
    294, 346, 377
    Saskatchewan and Aboriginal Peoples in the 21st
    Century: Social, Economic and Political Changes and
    Challenges, 392
Fedoruk, Sylvia, 347, 368, 372
fertilizer plant, 319, 349
Fielding, William S., 29, 45
Financial Post, 323, 325, 351
Financial Times, 228
Fines, Clarence, 168, 175-6, 178-9, 184, 186, 192,
    210-1, 274-5
First Decade, The, 211
First Ministers' Conference, 363, 384
First Nations, health care for, 189
    see also Aboriginal people
First Nations University of Canada, 378
Fisher, Douglas, 202, 212
fish-processing plant, 184
Fleming, H.C., 82
Fletcher, Morton, 171
FLQ, 204
Foght, Harold W., 48, 54
    A Survey of Education in the Province of Saskatchewan,
    Canada, 68
Foley, Frank, 249
food bank, 339
Food Prices Review Board, 319
Ford, Robin
    Alternative Service Delivery: Sharing Governance in
    Canada, 391
foreign policy, 199
forest industry, 185, 376
Forget, A.E., xiii-xiv, 8-9, 67
Foster, John E.
    The Developing West: Essays on Canadian History in
    Honour of Lewis H. Thomas, 67, 85
Fowke, Vernon, 355
free enterprise, 250, 253-4, 259-60, 262-3, 266, 277,
    281, 318-9, 334, 336
Free Trade Agreement (FTA), 344-5
freedom of speech amendment, 340
freight rates, 322
French language, protection of, 379
French-Canadians, xiii, 28, 51, 53
French-speaking minorities, 306
Friendly Dictatorship, The, ix
Friesen, P.M., 54
    From Prairie Roots: The Remarkable Story of
    Saskatchewan Wheat Pool, 86
Front Page Challenge (TV), 260
Frontier Statesman of the Canadian Northwest, Frederick
    Haultain, xiv

Frost, Robert
    The Road Not Taken, 235
Frye, Northrop, 287
    Full Employment in a Free Society, 273
fur-marketing agency, 184
Fyke Commission, 393
Fyke, Kenneth, 374

G
Gabriel Dumont Institute, 294
Galbraith, John Kenneth, 315
gambling, organized, 377-8
    see also casinos
Gardiner, Beth, 106
Gardiner Dam, 106
Gardiner, Edwin, 106
Gardiner, Florence, 106
Gardiner, James G., 72, 90-1, 93, 95-6, 98, 100-7, 114,
    116, 123, 127, 129, 133, 136-7, 140-1, 144-5,
    156-7, 181-3, 345
    government of, 99, 101-2, 116-21, 132, 135, 142
    and natural resources, 97
    in opposition, 93
    resignation of, 121
Gardiner Machine, 90, 95-6, 106
Gardiner, Violet, 106
Gardiner, Wilfrid, 106, 249, 254
gas utility
    pipeline, 246
    prices, 303
    sale of, 333
    see also natural resources
gasoline tax, 321, 326, 329
    elimination of, 330, 349
Gass Commission, 369-70
Gass, Don, 369
    Report of the Saskatchewan Final Management Review
    Commission, 390
gay rights, 323
Giga Text, 334-5
GigaMos Systems, 334
Gilmour, Mrs. W.B., xiv
Ginger Group, 83
Globe and Mail, 26, 45, 67, 212, 351
Glor, Eleanor D.
    Policy Innovation in the Saskatchewan Public Sector,
    1971-82, 270, 389
Goodale, Ralph, 87, 329
Goodhue, Bertram (NY), 14
Gordon, Walter, 203, 260
Goulet, Keith, 378, 392
Government Finance Office, *see* Saskatchewan
    Government Finance Office
Government Insurance Office, *see* Saskatchewan
    Government Insurance Office

government unions, 190
graft, allegations of, 70
Grain Growers Grain Company, 43
Grain Growers' Guide, 75, 85-6
grain industry, 20, 58
  elevators, 21, 99
  growers, 43, 60-2, 328
  handling, 43, 59
  marketing, 59
  trade, 72
  transportation, 20, 43
Grainers, 335
Grand Trunk Pacific Railway, 11, 42
Grant, Gordon, 253-4
Great Depression, *see* Depression
Great War Veterans' Association, 78
Green, F.W., 21
Green, S.J., 138
Greenfield, Herbert, 74-5, 85
Greenfield, Samuel, 55
Grescoe, Paul, 303
Grey, Earl, 8, 15
Grier, Terry, 206, 212
Gross Domestic Product, 330, 336, 370
Gross Revenue Insurance Plan (GRIP), 338
Gruending, Dennis, 388-90
  Promises to Keep: A Political Biography of Allan Blakeney, 316, 388-90, 392
GST, harmonized with PST, 347
Gudmundson, Carol, 278
Guillaume, Chantal, 322
Gulf Minerals, 302
Gulf Resources Canada, 335
Gzowski, Peter, 322

H
hail insurance, 99
Hall, Justice Emmett, 45, 362
  Report of the Survey of the Court Structure in Saskatchewan and its Utilization, 389
Hamilton, Alvin, 135-6, 211
Hamilton, C.M., 60, 72, 94, 212
Harper, Elijah, 344
Harper's, 315
Harris, Mike, 384
Harrison High School, 40
Harvard University, 253, 273, 384
Harvie, Christopher
  No Gods and Precious Few Heroes, 209
Hatfield, Richard, 307
Haultain, Frederick William Alpin George, xii-xiv, 5, 7-11, 26, 31, 35, 46, 66, 135
Haverstock, Lynda, 347
Hawkes, A.G., 82
Hawkins, J.H., 116

Hayden, Michael, 17
  Seeking a Balance: The University of Saskatchewan, 1907-1982, 37, 68
Hayes, Jim, 212
Heald, Darrel, 254
health care system, 124, 127, 131, 136, 140, 151, 156, 167, 171, 175, 187, 289, 300, 316, 371, 376, 384, 387
  boards, regional, 189-90, 372
  budget, 330, 341, 373
  fees, 304
  programs, 181, 221, 295, 341
  publicly funded, 268, 272, 275
  reform, 372-4, 384, 387
  for seniors, 189
  services, 177, 189, 256, 265, 321, 337, 342
  socialized, 176, 188
  universal, 188
health insurance program
  national, 133, 169, 194, 196, 199, 239-40
  publicy funded, 194, 239-40, 264
  universal, 194, 196
  see also hospitalization insurance plan; medical care insurance plan; medicare
Health and Safety Standards Unit (of OHS branch), 341
Health Services Act (1944), 189
Health Services Planning Commission, 189, 274
Health Services Survey Commission, 188
heavy-oil upgraders, 319, 327, 335, 349, 376
Henderson, Andrew, 68
Heritage Fund, 305, 311
Hermanson, Elwin, 347
high school textbook program, 263
higher education, 227
highways, 70, 124, 128, 146, 179, 332, 376
  see also roads
Himmelfarb, Gertrude
  Poverty and Compassion: The Moral Imagination of the Late Victorians, 352
Hindley, George, 218
Historical Directory of Saskatchewan Newspapers, 1878-1983, 37
Hitchcock, A., 4
Hodgins, Grant, 347
Hog Marketing Commission, 295
homeowners grant, 263
homes, *see* housing
homesteading, 5, 24, 40-1, 58, 97, 319
Homewood centre, 33
Hopkins, J. Castell
  The Canadian Annual Review, 1908, 67
  The Canadian Annual Review of Public Affairs, 1916, 67
  The Canadian Annual Review of Public Affairs, 1918, 68

The Canadian Annual Review of Public Affairs, 1921, 68
hospital privileges board, independent, 358
Hospital Services Act (1946), 189
hospitalization insurance plan, 189-90, 194-5, 250, 341, 372
 see also medical care insurance plan; medicare
hospitals
 budgets for, 373
 construction of, 189, 220, 341-2
 mental, 222
 rural, 265
 services in, 221
 universal free access to, 188
housing, 175, 278
 corporation, 246, 283
 improvement loans, 327
 low-income, 321
 mortgage interest rates, 327-8
 programs, 206, 226-7
Hudson's Bay Company, 97, 118, 182
Hudson's Bay Railway, 44, 112
Huel, Raymond, 38
human rights codes, provincial, 283, 362, 364
Human Rights Commission, 295, 362
Hume, David, 273
Husky Oil, 207, 335
Hutchison, Bruce, 103, 173
 The Incredible Canadian: A Candid Portrait of Mackenzie King, His Works, His Times, and His Nation, 108

I
Ilsley, James, 181
Images Consulting, 348
immigration, 112-20, 124, 126, 131-2, 136, 146, 162-3, 292, 343, 354
 communities of, 35, 48, 50-2, 54-5, 58
In the Shadow of the Poorhouse: A Social History of Welfare in America, 352
Incredible Canadian: A Candid Portrait of Mackenzie King, His Works, His Times, and His Nation, The, 108
Independent Boundaries Commission, 295
Independent Labour Association, 168
Independent Labour Party, 124
Indian Affairs, 226, 293
Indian and Metis people, 257, 261-2, 270
 see also Aboriginal people
 see also Metis
Industrial Development Fund, 274
industries
 cooperative ownership, 374, 387
 government ownership, 374
 nationalization of, 232, 279
 private ownership, 244, 374, 387

public ownership of, 185, 298, 318, 325, 387
resource-based, 184
Institute of Public Administration of Canada, 287
insurance companies, private, 195, 197, 225, 375
Internal Trade Agreement, 375
International Development Research Centre, 315
International Minerals and Chemical Corporation (IMC), 333
International Order of the Daughters of the Empire (IODE), 49
International Privatization Unit for N.M. Rothschild and Sons Ltd., 331
international trade, 324
investor confidence, 323
IPSCO steel plant, 185, 376-7
irrigation projects, 133, 182, 335
Irvine, William, 168, 170
 The Farmers in Politics, 164, 209

J
Janzen, William
 Limits on Liberty: The Experience of Mennonite, Hutterite, and Doukhobor Communities in Canada, 67-8
Jenkins, Peter
 Mrs. Thatcher's Revolution: The Ending of the Socialist Era, 350
Jimmy Gardiner: Relentless Liberal, 106, 137
Jodoin, Claude, 198
Johns Hopkins University, 188, 382
Johnson, A.W.
 Biography of a Government, 390-1
Johnson, Al, 211
Johnson, Pearl, 138
Johnstone, Dr. David, 124, 133
Jones, Amanda M., 391
Jones, Gerry
 SaskScandal: The Death of Political Idealism in Saskatchewan, 352, 390
Judaism, 166
Jupp, Alex, 196

K
Katz, Michael B.
 In the Shadow of the Poorhouse: A Social History of Welfare in America, 352
Keep Our Doctors (KOD) committees, 223-5, 276
Keynes, John Maynard, 184
King, Carlyle, 174-5, 218
King, William Lyon Mackenzie, 45, 60-1, 63, 73-4, 83-5, 92, 94, 98, 103, 107, 125, 142, 145, 149, 173, 175, 182, 189, 203, 318
Kinzel, Jack, 284, 299
Kitchen Accord, 364-5
Klein, Ralph, 384
Knight, Bill, 206, 212, 289, 305

Knowles, Stanley, 166, 173, 194, 197-8, 207, 212, 274
Knox Presbyterian church (Carberry), 165-6
Kopelchuk, Lorne, 348-9
Kowalchuk, John, 284, 388
Kramer, Eiling, 284, 286, 293
Krywulak, Timothy Bruce, 351-2
Ku Klux Klan, 99, 114-6, 118-20, 127, 135, 137
Kwasnica, Miro, 388
Kyba, Patrick, 137

L

labour, organized, 186, 194, 198, 201, 229, 244, 252, 260, 339, 341, 359, 366
 movement, 115, 197, 245, 261
 settlements, 266
 unions, 163, 167, 318-9, 332, 349
Labour party, 164
Labour Party, Scottish, 162
Labour Relations Board, 186, 339-40
Lake, Richard S., 25, 47
Lamont, John H., 10, 26, 30
Land Bank Commission, 282, 284, 290-3, 295, 304, 326-7, 360, 362
Lane, Gary, 323
Lane, Homer, 211
Lang, Otto, 265
Langley, George, 19, 21, 47, 60, 62, 70
Langlois, Kathy, 391
language rights, 55, 306, 308
Lapierre, Laurier, 278
Lapointe, Ernest, 96, 107
Larger School Units (LSUs), 217-20
Latta, S.J., 60, 72, 94, 110
Laurier, Sir Wilfrid, xii-xiii, 6-9, 31, 45, 51
Laxer, James, 204
Laycock, J.G. (Bert), 215
League for Social Reconstruction, 215
leather tannery, 246
Lederman, William, 363, 389
Leeson, Howard, 309, 365, 389
 Canada Notwithstanding: The Making of the Constitution, 1976-1982, 390
 Saskatchewan Politics: Into the Twenty-first Century, ix, 388, 393-4
Legal Aid Commission, 329
legal aid plan, 362
Legislative Assembly Extension Act, 150
Letwin, Oliver, 331-2
Levesque, Rene, 306-8, 310, 364, 390
Lewis, David, 184, 187, 194, 197-9, 202-4, 206-7, 273, 284
Lewis, Stephen, 198, 202-3, 212
Liberal Party, federal, xii-xiii, 3-6, 29, 41-3, 45, 50-1, 60-3, 72-3, 82, 91, 156, 168, 170, 173, 175, 181, 183, 199, 203, 248-9, 260, 265, 282

Liberal Party, provincial
 during Anderson, 110-6, 118-27, 129-30, 132-6
 during Blakeney, 277, 281-2, 290, 296, 304-6, 311
 during Devine, 320-1, 329, 347
 during Douglas, 167, 170-1, 175-7, 179-80, 184, 186, 191-3, 197, 201
 during Dunning, 70-1, 81, 83-4
 during Gardiner, 90-1, 94, 96, 98-103, 106
 during Lloyd, 218, 220, 228-9
 during Martin, 40, 43, 46-51, 53, 57, 59-64
 during Patterson, 141-3, 147-8, 151-4, 158
 during Romanow, 358-9, 362, 385-6, 388
 during Scott, 6-11, 13-4, 17, 19, 21, 26, 28, 30-1, 33, 36
 during Thatcher, 238-9, 242-3, 245-51, 253-4, 260, 262-3, 270
Liberal Party, Scottish, 162
Liberalism, 90-1, 94, 102
Life and Letters of Sir Wilfrid Laurier, Vol. II, 37
Limitation of Civil Rights Act, 131
Limits on Liberty: The Experience of Mennonite, Hutterite, and Doukhobor Communities in Canada, 67-8
Lincoln, Abraham, 200
Lingard, C. Cecil
 Territorial Government in Canada: The Autonomy Question in the Old North-West Territories, 37, 67
Lingenfelter, Dwain, 313, 366, 368
Lipset, Seymour Martin
 Agrarian Socialism: The Cooperative Commonwealth Federation in Saskatchewan. A Study in Political Sociology, 68
liquor, 119
 legislation, 26, 46
 policy, 78-9, 84
 sale of, 2203, 49, 77-81
 stores, 23, 35, 77, 80-1
Liquor Act, The, 80, 96, 127
Liquor Board, 347
Lisp, 334
livestock co-ops, *see* cooperatives
Lloyd, Allen, 214
Lloyd, Diane
 Woodrow: A Biography of W.S. Lloyd, 388
Lloyd, Evan, 234, 236
Lloyd, Lewie, 214-5
Lloyd, Michael, 236
Lloyd, Victoria (née Leinan), 216-8, 230-1, 234
Lloyd, Woodrow Stanley, 90, 179, 186-7, 195, 197, 199, 203-4, 212, 214-9, 235-6, 276, 283-5, 287, 289
 government of, 277-81, 290, 293, 295, 314, 358, 360, 372, 386
 and medicare crisis, 223-6, 234
 as premier, 221, 227, 229-33, 252-4, 258, 263, 358, 360-1
 resignation of, 233-4, 360
Lougheed, Peter, 303, 307, 390

Lower Inventories for Tomorrow (LIFT), 265
Lyon, Sterling, 307, 310
Lyon, Steward, 26
Lyons, Bob, 366

M
MacDonald, Christine, 37-8
Macdonald, Donald S., 206, 212
Macdonald, John A., 106
MacEwan, Grant
   Frontier Statesman of the Canadian Northwest, Frederick Haultain, xiv
MacEwen, Paul, 212
MacKay, Harold, 355
MacKenzie, D.S., 37
Mackenzie King, *see* King, William Lyon Mackenzie
Mackenzie King and the Prairie West, 87
MacKinnon, Janice, 368, 371
   Minding the Public Purse: The Fiscal Crisis, Political Trade-offs and Canada's Future, 390-1
MacKinnon, Reverend Murdock, 27-9, 38, 46, 48
MacLean, Angus, 307
MacLean, Dr. Hugh, 188
Maclean's, 173, 210, 315, 390, 393-4
MacMurchy, Gordon, 283-4, 286, 289
MacNeill, Harris, 165
MacPherson, M.A., 113, 120, 137
MacTaggart, Ken
   The First Decade, 211
Magill commission, 21
Magill, Professor Robert, 21
Maharg, John A., 61-4, 71-2, 76, 82-3
Makaroff, Peter, 180
   Making of a Socialist: The Recollections of T.C. Douglas, The, 209
Malot, Maureen Appel, 351
Manalta Coal (Calgary), 325
Manitoba College, 92
Manitoba Free Press, 30, 106
Manitoba Liberal, 3
Manitoba, University of, 110, 166
Manning, Ernest (Alberta), 227
Manning, Loralee, 351-2
   Welfare Reform and the Canada Assistance Plan: The Breakdown of Public Welfare in Saskatchewan, 1981-89, 352
Maple Leaf Milling Company, 74
Marchildon, Gregory P., 393
   Agriculture at the Border: Canada-U.S. Trade Relations in the Global Food Regime, 392
marketing and inland fisheries corporations, 191
Marshall-Wells Company, 241
Martin, Chester, 97
   "Dominion Lands" Policy, 107
Martin, Christina (née Jamieson), 40

Martin, Douglas Thompson, 40
Martin, Paul, 108, 332
   A Very Public Life, 211
Martin, William (father), 40
Martin, William Kenneth, 40
Martin, William Melville, 40-1, 45, 52-4, 55-60, 63, 67-8, 71, 83, 90-2
   government of, 72, 78, 84, 110
   leadership of, 64-6
   natural resources, control of, 44, 49, 58, 61
   as premier, 42-3, 47-8, 53, 64
   resignation of, 62, 64
Martin, Violette Florence (née Thompson), 40
Marxism, 244
Marxists, American, 167
Matsalla, Adolph, 388
McArthur, Doug, 287, 293, 313
McAuslane, Alex, 187
McCallum, Allan, 216
McCallum Hill and Company, 13
McColl, D.P., 16
McConnell, Howard, 114, 132, 137
McConnell, W.H.
   Prairie Justice, 67
McCuaig, Ian, 352
McCulloch, Arthur T., 111
McDonald, Hamilton, 193-4, 249, 254
Mcdonald, Lynn
   The Party that Changed Canada: The New Democratic Party, Then and Now, 212
McFarlane, Doug, 254
McGill University, 14
McGovern, George, 231
McInnis, J.K., 4
McIntosh, Charles, 123-4, 137
McIntosh, Lauchlan, 190
McKay, J., 127
McKenna, Frank, 383
McKenzie, P.E., 127
McKinnon, Eleanor, 168, 178, 199, 207
McKinnon, Norman, 168
McLaren, Lorne, 339, 341, 349
McLean, J.S., 241
McLean, Donald, 61
McLean, N.J., 241
McLeod, Ian, 208
McLeod, Thomas, 178, 180, 189, 210, 314
McLorg, Judge, 27, 29
McMaster University, 165
McMurtry, Roy, 308, 364-5
McNab, Archibald P., 17, 72, 94
McNaught, Kenneth
   A Prophet in Politics, 209
McNaughton, Violet, 82
McPhail, A.J., 82

McQuaig, Linda
  Shooting the Hippo: Death by Deficit and other Canadian Myths, 391
McQuarrie, Sarah, 390
meat-processing plant, 349
Medical Association, 226
Medical Care Insurance Act, 196, 197
Medical Care Insurance Bill, 222
Medical Care Insurance Commission, 222, 252, 277
medical care insurance plan, 118, 221, 189, 250, 252
  see also medicare
medical services, *see* health care system
medicare, 181, 187-8, 219, 221, 223-7, 229, 239-40, 252, 276, 304, 318, 341, 349, 356-8, 369, 372, 374, 380
  crisis in, 223-6, 228, 270, 234
  funding of, 196, 201, 322
  future of, 384
  implementation of, 195
  program, 194, 195, 198
  system, national, 189, 196, 203, 206
  universal, 189-90
  see also health insurance program; hospitalization insurance plan; medical care insurance plan
Meech Lake Accord, 343-5, 381-2
Meekinson, Peter J.
  Origins and Meaning of Section 92A: The 1982 Constitutional Amendment on Resources, 390
Meewasin Valley Authority, 362
Meighen, Arthur, 92, 111
Mennonites, 50-4
mental health, 190, 391
  services budget, 342
Mental Health Association, 329
mental hospitals, 70, 189
  see also hospitals
Menzies, June, 37-8
Merkley, John, 128, 137
Messer, John (Jack), 278, 283, 286, 290, 388
Metheral, S., 86
Methodist Church, 164
Metis, 292, 378
  see also Indian and Metis people
Metis nationalism, 293
Metis Society of Saskatchewan, 293-4
Michelmann, Hans J., 390
Miles, Frank, 14
Mill, John Stuart, 273
Miller, J.R., 351
Milnor, A.J., 137
Minding the Public Purse: The Fiscal Crisis, Political Trade-offs, and Canada's Future, 390-1
mine and process sodium sulphate (potash), 185
mineral exploration and development, 253-4, 323
mineral production, 194

Mineral Taxation Act, 182
Mines Act (1932), 128
Minimum Wage Act, 128
Mitchell, Bob, 368
Mitchell, Don, 279, 360
Mitchell, Grant, 285
Mitchell, Dr. Silas Weir, 30-2
Moderation League of Saskatchewan, 78-9, 86
Monet, Jacques, 383
monetary reform, 170
Monpetit, Guy, 334
Moose Jaw Hardware, 241
Moose Jaw Times, 4, 32
Moose Jaw Times Herald, 269-70, 351
More, Ken, 201
Morning Leader, 112, 122, 137
Morris Rod Weeder Ltd., 339
Morrison, Tony, 315
mortgage legislation, 48
Morton, Desmond
  The New Democrats, 1961-1986: The Politics of Change, 391
Morton, W.L., 19
  The Progressive Party in Canada, 37, 68
Mosher, Aaron, 187, 211
Motherwell, W.R., 9-10, 19, 21, 28, 32-3, 47, 55, 60-3, 70-1, 73, 85, 93-4, 96, 103, 107
Mott, Dr. Fred, 190
Moull, William D.
  Origins and Meaning of Section 92A: The 1982 Constitutional Amendment on Resources, 390
  Mrs. Thatcher's Revolution: The Ending of the Socialist Era, 350
Mulroney, Brian, 328, 342-3, 345-6
multiculturalism, 99
Munich agreement (1938), 173
Munns, W.A., 138
Munroe, F.D., 127, 137
Murray, David R.
  The Prairie Builder: Walter Murray of Saskatchewan, 37
Murray, J.E., 37
Murray, Jean, 13
Murray, Robert A.
  The Prairie Builder: Walter Murray of Saskatchewan, 37
Murray, Thomas, 62
Murray, Walter, 17-8, 20-1, 55-6
Musselman, J.B., 82

N
NAFTA, 315-6, 375
Nasserden, Ed, 135
National Child Benefit, 381
National Council of Women, 154
national energy policy, 303
National Health Plan (Britain), 195

National Petroleum Corporation, 206
National Progressive Party, 60-4, 66
    see also Progressive Party
nationalism, Canadian, 203
nation-building, 364
Native people, see Aboriginal people
Native entrepreneurs and cooperatives, 294
Native people, jobs for, 261-2
Natives, hiring quotas for, 293
NATO, 245
natural gas utility, 185, 327, 366, 376
natural resources, 95, 97, 113, 116-7, 124-6, 131-2, 136, 142, 156, 184, 295, 311, 324, 350, 377
    control over, xii, xiii, 44, 58, 64
    development of, 296
    private ownership of, 362
    see also gas utility
natural resource-based economy, 268
Natural Resources in Revenues: A Test of Federalism, 389
NDP, federal, 200-8, 232, 279, 298, 307-8, 359
NDP, provincial, 90, 136, 166, 391
    and Blakeney, 278, 280-4, 289-90, 292-6, 302-5, 311-4
    and Devine, 318-24, 328-9, 331, 333, 337, 340, 346-7, 349
    and Douglas, 169, 172, 185, 187, 196, 199-200
    and Lloyd, 221, 225, 231, 233, 235-6
    and Romanow, 356, 358, 360-2, 365-7, 370-2, 375, 385
    and Thatcher, 238-9, 251-4, 258-61, 263, 267
    see also CCF, provincial
Neatby, H. Blair, 107, 138
Neiszner, Jennifer, 388
neo-conservatism movement, 339
Nesbitt, L.D.
    Tides in the West, 86
Net Income Stabilization Account (NISA), 338
Neuman, Maureen (née Lloyd), 236
New Careers Corporation (NCC), 338
New Deal for People, 281, 293, 296, 362, 367
New Democratic Party, see NDP
New Democrats, 1961-1986: The Politics of Change, The, 391
New National Policy, 136
New Party Clubs, 197
New Party Committee, 197-8
NewGrade Energy Inc., 335, 376
Newlands, H.W., 121
Nicholson, A.M., 210-1
Nicol, Rev. John, 86
No Gods and Precious Few Heroes, 209
No Ordinary Academics: Economics and Political Science at U S, 1910-1960, 388
Nobbs, Professor Percy, 14
Nollet, Toby, 290
Norris, T.C., 73

Northern Teacher Education Program, 294
North-West Mounted Police (NWMP), 9, 13, 43
North-West Resistance, 3
North-West Territories Act (1897), xii
Norton, M.
    The Urban Age: Building a Place for Urban Government in Saskatchewan, 87
Nova corporation, 207
Now that the Coat Fits the Cloth: Spending Wisely in a Trimmed-Down Age, 390
nuclear power industry, 301
nuclear weapons program, 300-1
nurses' strike, 385
Nutana Collegiate, 354
Nystrom, Lorne, 202, 207, 212, 366

O
occupational health and safety (OHS), 341
O'Fee, Kevin, 391
Office of the Lieutenant-Governor, The, 67
Ohio State University, 319
oil industry, 253, 295, 326, 376
    boycott, 295
    companies, 207, 303, 307, 330, 377
    exploration, 185, 191, 327
    prices, 301, 303, 336
    production, 194, 326-7, 330
    public ownership of, 207
    refineries, 295
    shortages, 327
    tax, 305
Old Age Pension Bill, 83
old-age pensioners, 145, 169, 193, 199
Olewiler, Nancy, 270
Oliver, E.H., 6, 54
One Canada: Memoirs of the Right Honourable John G. Diefenbaker., The Crusading Years, 107
One Days Rest in Seven Act (1930), 128
Ontario School of Pedagogy, 40
Orange Lodge, 99
Orange Order, The, 27
Organization of Petroleum Exporting Countries, 206
organized labour, see labour, organized
Origins and Meaning of Section 92A: The 1982 Constitutional Amendment on Resources, 390
Osgoode Hall, 10, 40, 314
Ottawa Citizen, 390
Ottawa and the Provinces: Regional Perspectives, 389
Oxford University, 273

P
P. Lyall and Sons (Montreal), 15-6
pacifism, 172, 174, 178
Palliser Triangle, 104
paper mill, 319, 327, 349
Parizeau, Jacques, 382

Parsons and Whittemore, 259-60
Parti Quebecois, 363, 381-2
Party that Changed Canada: The New Democratic Party, Then and Now, The, 212
patriotism, 177, 262
patronage appointments, 17, 43
Patterson, Catherine (nee Fraser), 140
Patterson, William John, 90, 93, 127, 141–6, 148–55, 157-9, 175-6, 178, 191, 210, 218
  government of, 140, 150, 156, 185
Paulson, W.H., 127
peace movement, 301
Peace, Progress and Prosperity: A Biography of Saskatchewan's First Premier, T. Walter Scott, 36, 67
Pearson, Lester, 186, 203, 227, 231, 249, 260-1
PCS International, 325
Peckford, Brian, 307
Pederson, Martin, 135, 251, 254
Penner, John (Jack), 368, 376
Pennington, A.S., 31
Pennsylvania, University of, 184
pensions, government-funded, 244
people with mental disabilities, 220
  see also sterilization program
Perrault, Ray, 202
Perreaux, Les, 351
personal income tax, 326
Peters, Arnold, 202
Peters, Fred (John Scraba), 347-8
Petro-Canada, 206-7
Phelps, Joe, 179, 184, 218
Phinn, Mr., 141
Phoenix, 137
  see also Saskatoon *Star Phoenix*
Pierce, H.C., 38
Pinder, Herb, 253, 254
pioneer life, 70, 240
Pirie, Madsen, 331
Pistula, James M.
  Privatizing a Province: The New Right in Saskatchewan, 138, 350, 352, 392
Planned Parenthood Association, 329
Pocklington, Peter, 335
Policy Innovation in the Saskatchewan Public Sector, 1971-82, 270, 389
Political Management in Canada, 388
Politics in Saskatchewan, 37
populism, 185, 320, 360
pork-processing plants, 335
Porteous, George, 299
post-secondary education, 380
post-war reconstruction, 178
Potash Company of America, 297
Potash Conservation Board, 266
Potash Corporation of Saskatchewan (PCS), 296, 298-300, 305, 325, 332-3, 349, 367, 375, 377, 392

potash industry, 258, 263, 270, 277, 297, 307, 362, 376
  extracton and processing, 185
  mines, 259-60, 266-7, 295, 299-300, 305
  nationalization of, 296, 362
  overproduction, 266
  prices, 266, 297, 301, 303, 336
  production, 231, 258-9
  reserves, 298, 305
  revenues, 268, 300
Potashville Education Association (Esterhazy), 264
Poverty and Compassion: The Moral Imagination of the Late Victorians, 352
power
  corporation, 274
  generation, 124
  system, 128, 131
  see also electricity
Powers, John E., 168
pragmatism, 244
Prairie Builder: Walter Murray of Saskatchewan, The, 37
Prairie Capitalism: Power and Influence in the New West, 389, 391
Prairie Farm Assistance Act (PFAA), 104-5
Prairie Justice, 67
Prairie Liberalism: The Liberal Party in Saskatchewan, 1905-1971, 37, 67-8, 107, 137, 157-60, 270
Pratt, Larry
  Prairie Capitalism: Power and Influence in the New West, 389, 391
Praud, Jocelyn, 390
Presbyterian Church, 2, 27, 29, 34, 40, 47-8, 166
Presbyterian Theological College, 54
Prescription Drug Plan, 342
prescription drug program, 283
primary health care reform, 372-3 (health care)?)
Prince Albert Pulp Company (Papco), 331
private enterprise, 239, 251, 256, 258, 274, 319, 323, 332, 349, 374
  capital investment, 185, 244, 247, 254
  land ownership, 152
private sector, balance with public sector, 324
privatization, 323, 331, 332, 333, 334, 347, 366-7, 375
Privatization, Public Policy and Public Corporations in Canada, 351
Privatizing a Province: The New Right in Saskatchewan, 138, 350, 352, 392
Progressive Party, 71, 73, 82-4, 94, 98, 100, 102, 111–16, 119-23, 127, 135, 137, 164, 167-70, 173
Progressive Party in Canada, The, 37, 68
Progressive Conservative Party, 197, 248, 251, 254, 260, 320-1, 325, 327-8, 332, 341-2, 348-9, 365
prohibition, 22-3, 77-80, 96
Prohibition League of Saskatchewan, The, 79
Promises to Keep: A Political Biography of Allan Blakeney, 316, 388-90, 392
Property Improvement Grant, 295

property rights, 153
Prophet in Politics, A, 209
protest, peaceful, right to, 171
Provincial Elections in Saskatchewan 1905-1983, 270
provincial parks development, 332
Provincial Police Act, 96
Provincial Rights Party, xiv, 10-1, 19, 66, 250
Public Disposition of Natural Resources, 389
public enterprise, 325, 332
Public Enterprise in an Era of Change, 350, 392
Public Health Act, 136
public health care, 128, 163, 357, 373, 384, 387, 391
public ownership, *see* industries
public school system, 114-5, 117, 120, 125, 132, 135, 176
   sectarianism in, 116-7, 119, 124-5, 132, 135
public sector
   balance with private sector, 324
   deficits in, 240
public service, 9, 44, 124, 142, 147, 367
Public Service Act, 180, 186
Public Service Commission, 136, 180
Public Service Enquiry Commission, 127
public utilities, public ownership of, 167, 375
   see also utilities
public works projects, 244
Pugh, Terry, 351
pulp industry, 259, 268
   mills, 258-9, 263, 319

Q
Quebec
   referendum, 363, 379, 382
   separatism, 310, 382-4
Queen's University, 84, 241, 365

R
racial hatred, 99
racial tolerance, 114
radicalism, 169
Rae, Bob, 314
Rafferty-Alameda dams, 335
railways, 20, 42-3
   companies, 97
   construction, 5
   freight rates of, 43-4, 49, 58, 61, 64
   line abandonment, 220
   tax exemption, 6
   unions, 186, 242
Ralph, Diana, 352
Ramsay, Rupert, 135
Rasmussen, Kenneth A.
   Privatizing a Province: The New Right in Saskatchewan, 138, 350, 352, 392
Rattenbury, F.M., 14
Rawluk, Joe, 192, 193

RCMP, 95-6, 102, 339, 348, 362
Read, E.B., 3
Reagan, Ronald, 311
recall, of elected officials, 59, 62
recession, 264, 277, 336
recreational services, 337
Reform Party, 347
Regehr, T.D., 67
Regier, Ernie, 202
Regina College, 227
Regina *Daily Post*, 65
Regina *Daily Star*, 116
Regina *Journal*, 3-4
Regina *Leader*, 3-4, 8, 29, 58, 64, 66, 107
Regina *Leader-Post*, 48, 66-8, 153-5, 157-60, 171, 192, 209-12, 270, 304, 350-1, 388, 390, 392
Regina Manifesto, 183, 185, 188, 209, 216, 232, 279, 360
Regina *Morning Leader*, 18, 79, 85
Regina *Post*, 48
Regina Riot (1935), 102-3, 143
Regina, university in, 227
regional economic development investment, 203
   see also economic development
Regional Labour Council, 186
Reid, Bradford
   Deficit Reduction in the Far West: The Great Experiment, 390-1
Reid, Escott, 107
relief payments, 145-8, 176
relief supplies, 163
religious tolerance, 114
religious ultra-liberalism, 165
Report of the Saskatchewan Final Management Review Commission, 390
Report of the Survey of the Court Structure in Saskatchewan and its Utilization, 389
resources, government ownership of, 360
   revenue from, 332
   taxation policy, 374
retail co-ops, *see* cooperatives
Retail Merchants' Association, 78
Richards, John
   Now that the Coat Fits the Cloth: Spending Wisely in a Trimmed-Down Age, 390
   Prairie Capitalism: Power and Influence in the New West, 389, 391
Riches, Graham, 351-2
   Welfare Reform and the Canada Assistance Plan: The Breakdown of Public Welfare in Saskatchewan, 352
Riddell, F.W., 74
Riel, Louis, 3
Road Not Taken, The, 235
roads, 181, 183, 220, 305
   construction of, 26, 42, 185
   see also highways

Robbins, Wes, 284
Robert Simpson Ltd., 175
Roberts, Joseph
    Saskatchewan Politics from Left to Right, '44 to '99, 388, 391
Robinette, T.C., 40
Robinson, F.J., 14, 15
Roblin, Duff (Manitoba), 227
Rogers, Robert, 25
Roman Catholic Church, 5, 27-8, 34, 99, 113-5, 117, 119-20, 125, 322
Roman Catholics, 46, 47, 48
    religious instruction, 34
    separate schools, 47, 53, 228-9
    see also separate school system
Romanow, Ann, 354
Romanow, Eleanore (née Boykowich), 358-9
Romanow, Michael, 354-5
Romanow, Roy John, 90, 202, 205, 230, 278, 280-1, 283, 286, 299, 308-9, 313, 333, 347, 360, 380, 392-3
    Building on Values: The Future of Health Care in Canada, 394
    Canada Notwithstanding: The Making of the Constitution, 1976-1982, 365, 390
    coalition government of, 385-6
    and constitution, 363-5
    early years, 354-9, 388
    government of, 367, 369-77, 381-2, 384, 390
    leadership race of, 361-2
    opposition to privatization, 367
    Origins and Meaning of Section 92A: The 1982 Constitutional Amendment on Resources, 390
    Ottawa and the Provinces: Regional Perspectives, 389
    as premier, 361, 366-8, 379, 383, 385, 387, 389
    resignation of, 386-7
Romanow, Tekla, 354-5
Romanow, Walter (Spike), 357
Rosenfeld, Dr. Len, 190
Ross, J.H. (Jim), 3-5, 21, 25, 29, 33
Rousseau, Paul, 323
Rowell-Sirois Commission, 145-6, 149-51, 156, 158-9
Royal Commission on Administrative Scandals, 127
Royal Commission on the Future of Health Care in Canada, 393
Royal Commission on Rural Life (1952), 185
royalty rates, 326-7, 330, 362
Rumours of Glory, Saskatchewan and the Thatcher Years, 269-70
rural municipalities, 35, 42, 337
    depopulation in, 220, 292, 295
    services in, 274
    telephone companies in, 184
Russell, Bertrand, 273
Russell, Peter A., 138

Russell, Peter H., 107
    Constitutional Odyssey: Can Canadians Become a Sovereign People?, 352, 393
Ryan, Claude
    Ottawa and the Provinces: Regional Perspectives, 389

S
safety net program, 379
Sales, Thomas, 82
Sapiro, Aaron, 75, 76
Saskatchewan, 13-6, 30, 34-5, 45, 64
    agricultural industry in, 19, 22, 42, 175, 177, 244, 267, 291, 295
    cooperative tradition in, 195
    debt crisis in, 319, 326, 330, 349, 368-72, 377, 379, 382, 387
    economic development in, 140, 332, 336
    recession in, 264 277, 336
    religious tolerance in, 53
    unemployment in, 327
    union membership in, 187
    see also rural municipalities
Saskatchewan and Aboriginal Peoples in the 21st Century: Social, Economic and Political Changes and Challenges, 392
Saskatchewan Act, The, 6, 9, 11
Saskatchewan Association of Rural Municipalities (SARM), 78
Saskatchewan Bar Review, 66
Saskatchewan Child Benefit, 381
Saskatchewan Computer Utility Corporation, 332
Saskatchewan Co-operative Elevator Company, 47, 58, 60, 70-1, 74, 76-7, 82
Saskatchewan Cooperative Grain Elevator Company, 20-1
Saskatchewan Co-operative Wheat Producers Limited, 77
Saskatchewan Crown Corporation Review, 375
Saskatchewan Dental Plan, 342
Saskatchewan Economic Development Corporation (SEDCO), 323, 334
Saskatchewan Employment Development Program (SEDP), 338
Saskatchewan Farmer Labour Party, 169
Saskatchewan Federation of Agriculture, 255
Saskatchewan Federation of Labour, 261, 370
Saskatchewan First Nations, 377, 379
Saskatchewan Forest Products, 332
Saskatchewan Fur Marketing Corporation, 325
Saskatchewan Government Finance Office, 184, 273-5, 305
Saskatchewan Government Insurance Office (SGIO), 184, 187, 192, 256, 304, 323, 325, 332
Saskatchewan Government: Politics and Pragmatism, 37
Saskatchewan Government Printing, 256, 332

Saskatchewan Government Telephones, 184, 325
Saskatchewan Grain Growers' Association (SGGA), 19-23, 47, 49, 54, 59-64, 70-2, 76, 78-9, 81-3, 86, 93
Saskatchewan Guarantee and Fidelity Company, 256
Saskatchewan Hearing Aid Plan, 342
Saskatchewan: A History, 138, 158-60, 270, 388
Saskatchewan Human Rights Association, 329
Saskatchewan Indian Federated College, 294, 378
Saskatchewan Liberal, 270
Saskatchewan Liberal Party, *see* Liberal Party, provincial
Saskatchewan Mafia, 186
Saskatchewan Medical Care Insurance Act, 276
Saskatchewan Mining Development Corporation (SMDC), 301-2, 305, 323, 332, 349
Saskatchewan Party, 347, 385, 394
Saskatchewan Politics from Left to Right, '44 to '99, 388, 391
Saskatchewan Politics: Into the Twenty-first Century, ix, 388, 393-4
Saskatchewan Power Commission, 99, 184-5, 187, 256, 260-1, 325
  see also SaskPower
Saskatchewan Pro-Life Association, 329
Saskatchewan Provincial Police, 95-6
Saskatchewan Public Education League, 54
Saskatchewan Reconstruction Council, 151
Saskatchewan Relief Commission, 130, 132
Saskatchewan School Act, 46, 49, 55
Saskatchewan Securities Commission, 275
Saskatchewan Skills Development Program (SSDP), 338
Saskatchewan sodium sulphate plant, 256
Saskatchewan Synod of the Presbyterian Church, 53
Saskatchewan Tax Commission, 180
Saskatchewan Teachers Federation (STF), 217-8
Saskatchewan Temperance Act (STA), 49, 72, 77-9, 86
Saskatchewan Timber Board, 256
Saskatchewan Trades and Labour Council, 78, 128
Saskatchewan Transportation Company, 282
Saskatchewan Urban Municipalities Association, 253
Saskatchewan Wheat Board, 57-8, 73-5, 75-7, 86, 322
Saskatchewan Wheat Pool, 58, 77, 79, 83, 129, 167, 191, 295, 347, 377
Saskatchewan, University of, xiii-xiv, 16-8, 20, 36, 55-6, 76, 106, 145, 184, 214, 218, 262, 264-5, 285, 319-20, 337, 355, 365, 376, 389
Saskatchewan Vision for Health: A Framework for Change, A, 391
Saskatoon Agreement, 277
Saskatoon Board of Trade, 299
Saskatoon Crisis Intervention Service, 329
Saskatoon *Star Phoenix*, 138, 160, 192, 211, 270, 351-2, 388-9
Saskatoon Trades and Labour Council, 56

SaskEnergy, 333, 346, 366, 375
  privatization of, 333
SaskMedia, 325
SaskMinerals, 332
SaskOil, 296, 305, 323, 331-2, 335
SaskPower, 229, 274, 305, 325, 327, 332-3, 335-6, 366, 375
SaskScandal: The Death of Political Idealism in Saskatchewan, 352, 390
SaskTel, 305, 323, 325, 332
Sass, Bob, 352
Saunders, J. Owen
  Public Disposition of Natural Resources, 389
Sawatzky, Harold Leonard
  They Sought a Country: Mennonite Colonization in Mexico, 68
Saywell, John T.
  The Office of the Lieutenant-Governor, 67
scandals, 71
Schmidt, Grant, 341
School Act, 27, 28, 29, 114, 128, 135
School Attendance Act, 53
School Lands Fund, 125
School Trustees Association, 110
school system, *see* educational system
Schwab, Kevin, 388
Scott, Adam, 2
Scott, Anthony
  Natural Resources in Revenues: A Test of Federalism, 389
Scott, Dorothy, 33
Scott, Frank, 176, 197, 276
Scott, George, 2
Scott, Jessie Florence (née Read), 3, 32, 35
Scott, Lewis A., 114
Scott, Thomas Walter, xii, xvi, 4-7, 20-1, 14-8, 22-3, 26-31, 35, 38, 41-5, 53, 55, 60, 64, 71, 90-2
  and agriculture, 5, 10, 18-9, 22, 34, 36
  allegations of bribes, 25-6, 46-8, 64
  cooperative principle of, 34,-5
  early years, 2-3, 37
  government of, 9-11, 13
  health of, 29-30, 32-3, 46-7
  as Liberal leader, 7-8, 10
  as Premier, 9-10, 33-4, 36
  resignation of, 29, 33, 47, 70
  and women suffrage, 24-5, 34
Scottish Independent Labour Party, 162
Scotton, Clifford, 212
Scraba, John (aka Fred Peters), 347-9
scrip (currency), 170
Seaborn, W.E., 7
Secession Reference, 384
Seeking a Balance: The University of Saskatchewan, 1907-1982, 37, 68

senior citizens' services, 321
separate school system, 5, 26-8, 46-8, 53, 93
separatism, *see* Quebec
settlement programs, federal, xiii
7-7-7 housing program, 327
Shell and Petro-Canada, 335
Sheppard, Robert, 394
Sheps, Dr. Cecil, 189
Sheps, Dr. Mindel, 188-9
shoe factory, 179, 184, 246
Shoefelt, Edward, 41
Shoefelt case, 67
Shooting the Hippo: Death by Deficit and other Canadian Myths, 391
Shumiatcher, Morris, 178
Sifton, Clifford, 5-6, 30, 106
Sigerist, Dr. Henry, 188
Simard, Louise, 368, 372-3
A Saskatchewan Vision for Health: A Framework for Change, 391
Simington, E., 108
Simpson, Jeffrey
   The Friendly Dictatorship, ix
Sinclair, Jim, 293
single mothers' allowances, 163
   see also welfare system
Skelton, O.D., 6
   Life and Letters of Sir Wilfrid Laurier, Vol. II, 37
Smishek, Ruth, 289
Smishek, Walter, 187, 211, 236, 278, 280, 283-4, 289
Smith, David E., 63, 239, 346, 351-2, 388
   Jimmy Gardiner: Relentless Liberal, 137
   Prairie Liberalism: The Liberal Party in Saskatchewan, 1905-1971, 37, 67, 85, 107, 137, 157–60, 270
Smith, Patricia, 323
Smith, W.W., 137
Snyder, Gordon, 278, 283
social assistance, 220, 338-9, 380-1, 387
   see also welfare system
social credit experiment, 171
Social Credit party, 92, 135, 147, 170, 172-4, 194, 201-2, 250-1, 254, 262
social credit, theory of, 170
social democracy, 171, 174, 197, 272, 276, 287, 300, 308, 315-6, 324, 268, 371
social gospel movement, 163, 168
social planning, 272
social programs, provincial, 245, 318, 349
   federal cost-share of, 380
social problems, 156, 169, 185, 240, 247, 251, 272, 295, 300, 305, 312, 315, 322, 339, 345, 347, 369-71, 380, 384
social reconstruction, 178
social services, 151, 156, 178, 274, 321, 330, 337
social union, 380, 381, 383
Social Union Framework Agreement (SUFA), 381

socialism, 147, 152-3, 184, 194, 214, 208, 216, 220, 222, 228, 232, 235, 239, 249, 251, 253-4, 256, 258, 260, 273, 279-81, 318, 332, 335, 349, 358, 360
Souris Basin Support Association, 336
South Saskatchewan River dam, 106, 182
sovereignty of Canada, 382, 384
Spafford, D.S., 37, 87
   Politics in Saskatchewan, 37
Spafford, Shirley
   No Ordinary Academics: Economics and Political Science at University of Saskatchewan, 1910-1960, 388
Spry, Graham, 223-4
St. Andrew's Anglican Church, 241
St. Laurent, Louis, 106, 182-3, 194
St. Paul's Hospital, 342, 354, 373
Stanfield, Robert L.
   Ottawa and the Provinces: Regional Perspectives, 389
Star Phoenix, *see* Saskatoon *Star Phoenix*
Steeves, Jeffrey S., 390
Steuart, Dave, 249, 253-5, 259, 262, 264, 267, 270, 283, 292, 300, 304, 360, 388
Stevens, Harry, 170
Stevenson, John, 259
Stewart, Carl, 137
Stewart, James, 74
Steininger, Fred, 209, 210
sterilization program, for mentally disabled, 168
   see also people with mental disabilities
STF Bulletin, 218
Stinson, Ted, 168, 171, 175
Stipe, Reginald, 137
Stobbe, Mark, 351-2
   Devine Rule in Saskatchewan: A Decade of Hope and Hardship, 351-2
Stocks, John, 37
Stop Construction of the Rafferty-Alameda Project (SCRAP), 336
Stray Animal Act, 286
strikes, 261, 321-2
   see also coal strike; doctors' strike; nurses' strike
Strome Henderson General Store, 3
Struggle for Responsible Government in the North-West Territories, 1870-1897, The, 67
Strum, Gladys, 142
Struthers, Jim, 236
student loans, 220
Subjects or Citizens? The Mennonite Experience in Canada, 1870-1925, 68
Sulaty, William, 62
Supercart International, 334
Survey of Education in the Province of Saskatchewan, Canada, A, 68
Sutherland, W.C., 13
Swedburg-Kohli, Susan, 350

T

Talney, Mark, 164, 209
Tamaki, George, 273-4
tannery, 179
tariff commission, 44
tariff rates, 43, 58, 63-4
Task Force on Agriculture (1969), 282
Taylor, George, 279, 284, 358, 360-1
Taylor, Graham, 323, 332
Taylor, Lord Malcolm, 276-7, 280
Taylor, Lord Stephen, 224-6
Tchzorewski, Ed, 284, 286, 289, 312-3, 366, 368, 370-1
Teichrob, Carol, 368
telecommunications, 375
telephone system, 98-9, 128, 142, 156, 181, 183, 184, 274
   public ownership of, 20
   service, 42, 325
Telfer, Isabella, 2
Telfer, James, 3
Temperance Reform League, 78
Territorial Government in Canada: The Autonomy Question in the Old North-West Territories, 37, 67
Territorial Grain Growers Association, 9, 60
Thatcher, Adrah Leone (née McNaughton), 241
Thatcher, Clarke, 242
Thatcher, Colin, 323, 331-2
   Backrooms: A Story of Politics, 350-2
Thatcher, Margaret, 311, 318, 331
Thatcher, Marjorie, 240
Thatcher, Wilbert, 240-2
Thatcher, Wilbert Ross, 90, 106, 175, 186, 193, 194, 199, 201, 220, 228, 229, 231, 245, 277-8, 280, 282-6, 289-90, 292-3
   death of, 267-9
   early years, 240-2
   government of, 254-5, 258-61, 263-7, 270, 302, 304, 320, 340, 362
   as M.P., 243-6, 248-9
   as premier, 238-9, 250-1, 253, 256-8, 296-7, 306, 312, 325, 349, 358-60
   as visionary, 268
Theatre Under the Stars, 192-3
They Sought a Country: Mennonite Colonization in Mexico, 68
Third Avenue Methodist Church, 76
30-day rule (union organizing), 340
Thomas, Jimmy, 185
Thomas, Lewis H.
   The Making of a Socialist: The Recollections of T.C. Douglas, 209
   The Struggle for Responsible Gov in the North-West Territories, 1870-1897, 67
Thompson, Bram, 107, 118
Thompson, W.P., 195-6
Thomson School, 168
Thorson, Kim, 284, 298
Tides in the West, 86
timber mill, 184
timber resources, 259
Todd, Frederick, 14
Tollefson, Edwin A., 388
Toronto Star, 201, 212
Toronto, University of, xii, 40, 110
totalitarianism, 148, 150, 153
Trade Union Act, 159, 186-7, 261, 340
trade unions, 147, 182, 186, 339
   see also unions
Trades and Labour Congress (TLC), 186, 212
Trades and Labour Council, *see* Saskatchewan Trades and Labour Council
training allowances, for welfare recipients, 381
Tran, Dr. Charles, 114
transfer payments to provinces, *see* federal transfer payments
transportation, 42, 375
Trapp, George, 254
Treaty Land Entitlement (TLE), 379
treaty land entitlements, 345-6
   see also Aboriginal people
Trudeau, Pierre Elliott, 186, 203-4, 206-7, 296, 303-4, 306-9, 311, 318, 320, 322, 344, 362-4
Trudeaumania, 202
Truman, Harry, 202
Tucker, Walter, 153, 191-3
Tupper, Allan
   Privatization, Public Policy and Public Corporations in Canada, 351
Turgeon, W.F.A., 47, 98, 158
Turnbull, Olaf, 228
Turner, Harris, 111
Turner, John, 298
Turner, Ted, 295
Turriff, J.G., 6, 60

U

Uhrich, J.M., 72, 85, 113
Ukrainian National Federation (UNF), 354
Underhill, Frank, 76
unemployment, 175, 220, 242, 272
   insurance program, 167, 169, 171, 272, 338
unilaterism, 363
Union coalition government, 51, 59-61, 93
Union of Saskatchewan Municipalities (USM), 81
unions
   certification of, 339-40
   industrial, 186-7
   legislation, 274
   movement, decline of, 340
   public-sector, 187, 347
   rights of, 340
United Church of Canada, 93, 166, 288, 322

United Farmers of Canada, 115, 124, 164, 167, 171, 209, 290
United Farmers of Manitoba, 75
United Grain Growers Limited, 74, 77
United Nations Development Program (UNDP), 234
United Nations Habitat Conference (1976), 301
United States
  reciprocity treaty with, 43
university funding, 264
University of Saskatchewan Act, 16, 17, 56
university tuition, 263
Uranerz, 301
uranium industry, 301, 376
  development of, 268, 301-3, 305, 312
  mines, 263, 294, 301-2
  prices, 336
  reserves, 300
  revenues, 300, 302
Urban Age: Building a Place for Urban Government in Saskatchewan, The, 87
U.S. Borax, 258
utilities, 146, 375
  deregulation of, 375
  public control of, 11, 98
  see also public utilities
utilities commission, 114

V
Valleau, Oak, 175, 178
Vancouver *Sun*, 194, 203, 211-2
Vehicles Act, 141
Venture Capital Corporation (VCC), 334
Vietnam War, 203, 278
vocational schools, 128
  see also educational system
Voice of the Handicapped, 329
Volstead Act, 77
Voluntary Relief Committee, 130
volunteer organizations, 337
Vonda school district (decision), 27-8
Vulcan Iron Works, 162
Very Public Life, A, 211

W
Waffle group, 204, 206, 232, 279-80, 284, 290, 360-2, 374, 389
Waffle Manifesto, 232, 278-9
wage, minimum, 186, 243, 340
wage and price controls, 320
Waiser, W.A., 351
Walker, Bob, 211, 233, 388
war, controversy over, 174
war effort, 150
War Measures Act (1970), 204, 231
Ward, Norman, 106, 355
  Jimmy Gardiner: Relentless Liberal, 106, 137

Politics in Saskatchewan, 37
Wardhaugh, R.A.
  Mackenzie King and the Prairie West, 87
Warnock, John
  Saskatchewan Politics from Left to Right, '44 to '99, 388, 391
Wartime Elections Act, 51
Wascana Centre (Regina), 227
Wascana Energy, 377
Wascana Park, 269
water conservation, 133, 182
Waterman Waterbury Roving Microphone, 354
Watkins, Mel, 204, 278
wealth, social distribution of, 244
Weekly Half-Day Holiday Act (1931), 128
Weir, Erin, 391
Welfare Reform and the Canada Assistance Plan: The Breakdown of Public Welfare in Saskatchewan, 81-89, 352
welfare state, 322, 349, 351
welfare system, 201, 240
  abuse, 338
  programs, 216
  reform, 338-9, 381
  services, 256
Wellington County Reform, 40
wellness model, 372-4
Wesley College, 163
western economy, diversification of, 344
Western Ice Company, 241
Western Premiers Conference, 384
Westmount School, 354
Weston, Walter, 127
Wetmore, Edward L., 17, 26, 46
Weyburn Independent Labour Association (WILA), 167-8, 170
Weyburn *Review*, 209, 210
Weyerhaeuser Corporation, 331
Weymark, Jack, 270
Wharton School of Finance, 184
Whatley, Samuel, 122, 124
wheat, 295, 376
  handling, 61
  marketing, 57
  prices, 43, 57, 72, 77, 81, 101, 282
  production, 19
Wheat Board, *see* Saskatchewan Wheat Board
Wheat Pool, *see* Saskatchewan Wheat Pool
Whelan, Ed & Penrose, 236
White Bear reserve, 377
White, Clinton O., 107
Whitmore, A.E., 138
wholesale co-ops, *see* cooperatives
Whyte, John, 365, 383, 393
  Canada Notwithstanding: The Making of the Constitution, 1976-1982, 390

Wiens, Berny, 368
Wiggins, Lambert, 211
Wilke, Florence, 284
Williams, Charles Cromwell, 186
Williams, George H., 167-9, 171-5, 210
Wilson, C.F.
　A Century of Canadian Grain: Government Policy to 1951, 85
Wilson, Garrett, 158
　Diefenbaker for the Defence, 157
Wilson, Kevin
　Diefenbaker for the Defence, 157
Winnipeg Declaration (1956), 279
Winnipeg Grain Exchange, 57, 75
wire and cable plant, 185
Wishlow, Kevin, 394
Wolfe, Samuel
　Doctors' Strike: Medical Care and Conflict in Saskatchewan, 211
Woman Suffrage Movement in Canada, The, 38
women
　equality, 310
　organizations, 175
　voting by (suffrage), 24-5, 34, 48, 50
Women's Christian Temperance Movement, 49
Women's Christian Temperance Union, 78
Women's Grain Growers' of Saskatchewan, 24
Wood, Everett, 283
Woodland Cree, 292
Woodrow: A Biography of W.S. Lloyd, 388
Woods, Justice Mervyn, 358
Woodsworth, James S., 163-4, 167-8, 170, 172-3, 216, 274, 284
woollen mill, 179, 184, 246
workers compensation system, 147, 163, 186
workers legislation, 147
workfare, 387
Workmen's Compensation Act, 128
World Federalists of Canada, 315
World Trade Organization, 316
World War I, 22, 24, 44, 71, 86, 92, 96, 141, 148, 163, 188, 272
World War II, 140, 239, 241-3, 245, 318, 349
Wright and Havelock Foundry, 80
Wright, John, 367

Y
Yom Kippur War, 295
Young, Edward, 170-1
Young, Walter D.
　Anatomy of a Party, 270
Yule, W.G., 138

Z
Zazelenchuk, Jo-Ann, 365-6
Zussman, David
　Alternative Service Delivery: Sharing Governance in Canada, 391

Contributors

GORDON L. BARNHART was born and raised in Saltcoats, Saskatchewan, and received his BA (Hons) from the University of Saskatchewan, MA in history from the University of Regina and a PhD in History from the University of Saskatchewan. He is presently the University Secretary with the University of Saskatchewan. Gordon served as Clerk of the Legislative Assembly from 1969 to 1989 and as Clerk of the Senate of Canada from 1989 to 1994. Currently Acdemic Director of the Internship Program with the Legislative Assembly of Saskatchewan, Gordon has two grown children and two grandchildren. Amongst his numerous articles and books, Gordon is the author of *"Peace, Progress and Prosperity": A Biography of Saskatchewan's First Premier, T. Walter Scott* and *Building for the Future: A Photo Journal of Saskatchewan's Legislative Building*.

BETH BILSON has degrees in law and history from the University of Saskatchewan, and a doctoral degree in law from the University of London. She has been a member of the faculty of the College of Law at the University of Saskatchewan since 1979, teaching and writing in the areas of torts, labour and administrative law, and legal history; she became Dean of the College in July 1999, and served in that capacity until 2002. She was admitted to the Bar in Saskatchewan in 1984. She served as Senior Grievance Officer of the University of Saskatchewan Faculty Association from 1982 to 1985, and as Assistant Vice-President (Administration) for the University from 1986 to 1988, with special responsibility for faculty collective bargaining. From 1992 to 1997 she chaired the Saskatchewan Labour Relations Board. In addition to acting as a labour arbitrator in Saskatchewan, she has acted as a part-time member of the federal Public Service Staff Relations Board, and as a Deputy Chair of the Discipline Committee of the College of Physicians and Surgeons of Saskatchewan. She was recently appointed as chair of a federal task force on pay equity. She was awarded the designation of Queen's Counsel for Saskatchewan in January of 2000.

J. WILLIAM BRENNAN has taught western Canadian and Saskatchewan history at the University of Regina since 1974. He has written several articles on Saskatchewan politics (including two on Charles Dunning) and edited *"Building the Co-operative Commonwealth": Essays on the Democratic Socialist Tradition in Canada*.

DALE EISLER is a former journalist who has written extensively on Saskatchewan politics, public policy and government. Among his work is *Rumours of Glory: Saskatchewan and the Thatcher Years*, a book that chronicled the political life and times of former Liberal Premier Ross Thatcher. Mr. Eisler is currently an Assistant Deputy Minister with the federal Department of Finance in Ottawa. He has studied political economy at the University of Saskatchewan, Regina Campus, University of Toronto and Vermont College of the Union Institute and University.

DENNIS GRUENDING is the former Member of Parliament for Saskatoon-Rosetown-Biggar. He is a writer and journalist who was born and raised in Saskatchewan. He has worked as a reporter for three Canadian newspapers, and as a CBC producer, reporter and radio host.

He has written four books, including biographies of Allan Blakeney and Emmett Hall. He is married to Martha Wiebe and they have two daughters, Maria and Anna.

PATRICK KYBA is Professor Emeritus in the Department of Political Science at the University of Guelph. He was born in Canora and educated at Neilburg, Melfort, the University of Saskatchewan and the London School of Economics and Political Science. He has written on Saskatchewan and Canadian political history as well as environmental politics. Among his books are *Alvin: A Biography of the Hon. Alvin Hamilton* and *Sustainable Development and Canada: National and International Perspectives*.

GREGORY P. MARCHILDON currently holds a Canada Research Chair in Public Policy and Economic History at the University of Regina. He is also a visiting fellow at the School of Policy Studies at Queen's University. He was most recently the Executive Director of the Commission on the Future of Health Care in Canada. Launched on May 1, 2001, the Commission was chaired by the Honourable Roy Romanow, Q.C, who was given a mandate by the Prime Minister to provide recommendations concerning the future of Canada's publicly funded health care system. The Commission's final report *Building on Values* was tabled in the Canadian Parliament on November 27, 2002. His book, *Profits and Politics: Beaverbrook and the Gilded Age of Canadian Finance*, was published by the University of Toronto Press in 1996. He has since co-authored *Canoeing the Churchill: A Practical Guide to the Historic Voyageur Highway* which won the 2002 Saskatchewan Book Award for scholarly writing for its historical research. He has also edited or co-edited a number of books, including: *Canadian Agriculture at the Border* (2000); *The NAFTA Puzzle* (1994); *Canadian Multinationals and International Finance* (1992); and *Mergers and Acquisitions* (1991).

IAN MCLEOD was born in Saskatoon on 1953. A former journalist and public servant, he now works as a consultant to municipal and provincial government agencies in British Columbia.

THOMAS H. MCLEOD was born in Weyburn in 1918, and was a friend and political supporter of T.C. Douglas during the Depression. He joined Douglas's office in 1944 as a legislative and economic advisor, worked with the Health Planning Commission and the Economic Advisory and Planning Board, and became director of the budget bureau and then Deputy Provincial Treasurer. From 1952 to 1971 he worked in senior administrative positions for the University of Saskatchewan and launched a parallel career as a planner and consultant in the field of international development. He retired from the federal public service in 1983 after working in several senior executive positions. McLeod was awarded the Order of Canada in January 2002. He lives in Victoria. Ian and Thomas McLeod co-authored a biography of Douglas, entitled *Tommy Douglas: The Road to Jerusalem*, which was published in 1987 by Hurtig Publishers, Edmonton.

DIANNE LLOYD NORTON, despite having lived in England for more than 40 years, still thinks of herself as thoroughly Canadian. Attending University in Saskatchewan, she gained further qualifications at the London School of Economics and, inspired by writing about Woodrow Lloyd, the Institute of Education. After raising three children, she began a career in educational gerontology, as a writer and editor, and was instrumental in the development of several important national initiatives. She continues this work alongside managing her own publishing company, Third Age Press, focusing on positive aspects of later life.

JAMES M. PITSULA is a professor at the Department of History, University of Regina. He has written books and articles dealing with the history of social services, privatization, higher education, and Saskatchewan Government/First Nations policy. His most recent book is *Helping Families Through Life: A History of Family Service Regina* (2001), and he is currently at work on *As One Who Serves: The Making of the University of Regina*.

T.D. REGEHR is Professor Emeritus of History, University of Saskatchewan, and Adjunct Professor of History, University of Calgary. He specializes in the history of the prairies, Canadian business history, and Canadian Mennonite history. He is the author of several books including a history the Canadian Northern Railway and a volume in the three-volume history of Mennonites in Canada. He and his wife Sylvia live in Calgary. They are the parents to two married children and have three grandchildren.

DAVID E. SMITH is a Professor of Political Studies at the University of Saskatchewan. He holds degrees from the University of Western Ontario (BA), Duke University (MA and PhD), and the University of Saskatchewan (D.Litt.). He is the author of *Prairie Liberalism: The Liberal Party in Saskatchewan, 1905–71*; *Regional Decline of a National Party: Liberals on the Prairies*; (with Norman Ward) *James G. Gardiner: Relentless Liberal*; *The Invisible Crown: The First Principle of Canadian Government*; and editor of *Building a Province: A History of Saskatchewan in Documents*, as well as co-editor of *After Meech Lake: Lessons for the Future*; *Drawing Boundaries: Courts, Legislatures and Electoral Values*, and *Citizenship, Diversity and Pluralism*. A faculty member of the University of Saskatchewan since 1964, he was elected Fellow of the Royal Society of Canada in 1981. In 1994–95 he was President of the Canadian Political Science Association. Professor Smith received the Léger Fellowship in 1992 and a Killam Fellowship in 1995–97. His book *The Republican Option in Canada, Past and Present*, which appeared in 1999, received the Smiley Prize from the Canadian Political Science Association as the best book in Canadian politics and government for 1998 and 1999. His most recent book is *The Canadian Senate in Bicameral Perspective*.